Linux: The Complete Reference

Richard Petersen

Osborne **McGraw-Hill**

Berkeley New York St. Louis San Francisco
Auckland Bogotá Hamburg London Madrid
Mexico City Milan Montreal New Delhi Panama City
Paris São Paulo Singapore Sydney
Tokyo Toronto

Osborne **McGraw-Hill**
2600 Tenth Street
Berkeley, California 94710
U.S.A.

For information on translations or book distributors outside the U.S.A., or to arrange bulk purchase discounts for sales promotions, premiums, or fundraisers, please contact Osborne **McGraw-Hill** at the above address.

Linux: The Complete Reference

1234567890 DOC 99876

ISBN 0-07-882189-4

Executive Editor
Scott Rogers

Project Editor
Mark Karmendy

Copy Editor
Judith Brown

Proofreader
Stefany Otis

Indexer
Valerie Robbins

Computer Designer
Jani Beckwith

Illustrator
Lance Ravella

Cover Design
emdesign, cary mc.

Quality Control Specialist
Joe Scuderi

To my brothers,
George, Robert, and Mark

About the Author

Richard Petersen holds a Ph.D in Library
and Information Studies. He currently
teaches Unix and C/C++ courses at the
University of California, Berkeley.

Contents

Part I

Introduction to Linux

Part II

Linux Operations

Part III

Networking

Part IV

Shells

14 Filters 469

Part V

Editors and Utilities

Part VI

System Administration

Acknowledgments

I would like to thank all those at Osborne McGraw-Hill who made this book a reality, particularly Scott Rogers, acquisitions editor, for his continued encouragement and analysis as well as management of such a complex project; Heidi Poulin, editorial assistant, who provided needed resources and helpful advice; Judith Brown, copy editor, for her excellent job editing as well as insightful comments; and project editor Mark Karmendy who incorporated the large number of features found in this book as well as coordinating the intricate task of generating the final version. Thanks also to Brad Shimmin who initiated the project.

I would also like to thank Caldera for their advice and support, and for the Caldera Lite Linux system that they provided for this book. Thanks to Ransome Love who directed development of Caldera Lite Linux, as well as to Nick Wells and Greg Page for their technical advice and support.

Special thanks to Linus Torvalds, the creator of Linux, and to those who continue to develop Linux as an open, professional, and effective operating system accessible to anyone. Thanks also to the academic community whose special dedication has developed Unix as a flexible and versatile operating system. I would also like to thank professors and students at the University of California, Berkeley, for their experience and support in developing new and different ways of understanding operating system technologies.

I would also like to thank my parents, George and Cecelia, and my brothers, George, Robert, and Mark, for their support and encouragement with such a difficult project. Also Valerie and Marylou and my nieces and nephews, Aleina, Larisa, Justin, Christopher, and Dylan, for their support and deadline reminders.

Introduction

The Linux operating system has become a viable alternative for anyone with a PC. It brings all the power and flexibility of a Unix workstation as well as a complete set of Internet applications and a fully functional desktop interface. All of this can easily be installed on any 486 or Pentium PC. This book is designed not only to be a complete reference on Linux, but also to provide clear and detailed explanations of Linux features. No prior knowledge of Unix is assumed; Linux is an operating system anyone can use.

This book identifies three major Linux topics; the Internet, Unix, and System Administration. For the Internet, Linux has become a platform for very powerful Internet applications. You can not only use the Internet, but, with Linux, become a part of it, creating your own Web, ftp, Gopher, and WAIS sites. Other users can access your Linux systems, several at the same time, using different services. You can also use very powerful Unix-based applications for mail and news.

But Linux systems are not limited to the Internet. You can use it on any local Intranet, setting up an ftp or Web site for your network. The Caldera Lite Linux system provided with this book comes equipped with fully functional ftp and Web servers already installed and ready to use. All you need to do is add the files you want onto your site.

Linux is also a fully functional Unix operating system. It has all the standard features of a powerful Unix system. There are shells for managing your commands.

Linux uses two of the more advanced Unix shells, the Bourne Again Shell and the TCSH shell. Each supports a complete shell programming language that you can use to create your own shell scripts. A wide array of Unix applications operates on Linux. The GNU public licensed software provides professional level applications such as programming development tools, editors and word processors, as well as numerous specialized applications such as those for graphics and sound. A massive amount of software is available at online Linux sites where you can download applications and then easily install them onto your system.

Linux has the same level of system administration features that you find on standard Unix systems. It has the same multiuser and multitasking capabilities. You can set up accounts for different users and each can access your system at the same time. Each user can have several programs running concurrently. With Linux you can control access, set up network connections, and install new devices. Your Caldera Lite Linux system includes several easy-to-use, window-based configuration utilities that you can use to perform system administration tasks such as installing printers, adding users, and establishing new network connections.

Since this book is really three books in one—an Internet book, a Unix book, and a System Administration book—how you choose to use it depends upon how you want to use your Linux system. If you only want to use Linux for its Internet services, then you only have to learn a simple set of Unix operations and concentrate on the Internet applications, most of which are already installed for you. If you want to use Linux as a Unix workstation, the book provides a detailed presentation of Unix features such as shell programming, file management, filters and editors, as well as Unix mailers and newsreaders. If you want to use Linux as a multiuser system servicing many users or integrate it into a local network, you can use the detailed system, file, and network administration information provided in the administration chapters. None of these tasks are in any way exclusive. If you are working in a business environment, you will probably make use of all three aspects. Single users may concentrate more on the Internet features, whereas programmers may make more use of the Unix features.

The book is designed to help you start using Linux quickly. After a streamlined installation procedure taking about 40 minutes in Part I, you are introduced to the Caldera Desktop that provides an easy-to-use window-based interface. You can run all your applications from here using icons, menus, and windows. The Caldera Desktop is a fully configurable interface with an icon bar and desktop layouts, as well as a window-based text editor, CRiSPlite. At any time, you can open up a terminal window through which you can enter standard Unix commands on a command line.

You are then introduced to a set of basic Unix operations in Part II that you will need in order to work on your Linux system. Many of these can also be performed using the Caldera Desktop, but others require that you know how the Unix command line interface works. In particular, you will need Unix commands for accessing your CD-ROM or floppy drive, downloading software from Internet sites, and creating shell scripts for customized operations.

The book then discusses in detail the many Internet applications you can use on your Linux system. The Caldera Lite Linux automatically installs mail, ftp, and Web browser applications, as well as ftp and Web servers. On your Caldera Lite CD-ROM there are also other mail applications, newsreaders, and Internet tools such as Gopher clients that you can easily install from your desktop. In addition, the book describes how to download and install Internet applications such as the Netscape and Mosaic Web browsers, Gopher and Archie clients, and Gopher and WAIS servers. Chapter 11 is devoted entirely to the Web, discussing the major Web browsers and how to create your own Web pages. Chapter 12 discusses the four different types of Internet servers; ftp, Web, Gopher, and WAIS. Although ftp and Web servers are already installed for you, this chapter describes how they are set up. A discussion follows on how to download and install Gopher and WAIS servers, in order to set up your own Gopher and WAIS Internet sites.

Part IV of the book discusses the more complex features of Linux as a Unix system. The very powerful set of Unix filters is described in Chapter 14. Shell programming for both Bourne and C-shells are presented with examples of the different programming commands in Chapters 15 and 16. Chapters 17 and 18 cover the standard editors, Vi and Emacs, and include techniques designed to start you using these editors quickly and easily.

Chapters 19 and 20 discuss system and network administration, respectively. These chapters emphasize the use of special system management utilities that you can operate from the desktop and use to set up your network easily, add users, and configure devices such as printers. There is also a detailed description of the configuration files used in management and how to make entries in them. Various aspects of network administration are discussed such as network connections and routes, Domain Name services, Network File Servers, and Hostname designations. For those using modems to connect to networks such as the Internet, the SLIP and PPP protocols are discussed in detail, including how to use the **dip** and **pppd** program to make SLIP and PPP connections. Numerous scripts and examples are provided.

Finally, there are four appendixes covering hardware boot parameters, how to configure the X-Windows system, the software packages included on the Caldera CD-ROM, and how to create nonstandard install diskettes, all for your reference.

 NOTE: The book includes numerous tables that list different commands and their options. In most cases, you will find the tables placed at the end of the chapters where you can easily locate and refer to them. For example, the end of Chapter 1 holds tables listing Internet sites where you can obtain information about Linux, and sites that hold Linux software that you can download and install.

PART ONE

Introduction to Linux

Chapter One

The Linux Operating System

Linux is an operating system for PC computers that use 386, 486, or Pentium processors, such as IBM compatibles. It was developed in the early 1990s by Linus Torvald along with other programmers around the world. As an operating system it performs many of the same functions as DOS or Windows. However, Linux is distinguished by its power and flexibility. Most PC operating systems, such as DOS, began their development within the confines of small restricted personal computers that have only recently become more versatile machines. Such operating systems are constantly being upgraded to keep up with the ever changing capabilities of PC hardware. Linux, on the other hand, was developed in a very different context. Linux is a PC version of the Unix operating system that has been used for decades on mainframes and minicomputers and is currently the system of choice for workstations. Linux brings the speed, efficiency, and flexibility of Unix to your PC, taking advantage of all the capabilities that personal computers can now provide.

Linux does all this at a great price. It is free. Unlike the official Unix operating system, Linux is distributed freely under a GNU general public license as specified by the Free Software Foundation, making it available to anyone who wants to use it. Linux is copyrighted and is not public domain. However, a GNU public license has much the same effect as being in the public domain. The license is designed to ensure that Linux remains free, and, at the same time, standardized. There is only one official Linux.

The fact that Linux is free sometimes gives people the mistaken impression that it is somehow less than a professional operating system. Linux is, in fact, a PC version of Unix. To truly appreciate Linux, you need to understand the special context in which the Unix operating system was developed. Unix, unlike most other operating systems, was developed in a research and academic environment. In universities and research laboratories, Unix is the system of choice. Its development paralleled the entire computer and communications revolution over the past several decades. Computer professionals often developed new computer technologies on Unix, such as those developed for the Internet. Though a very sophisticated system, Unix was designed from the beginning to be flexible. The Unix system itself can be easily modified to create different versions. In fact, many different vendors maintain different official versions of Unix. IBM, Sun, and Hewlett-Packard all sell and maintain their own versions of Unix. People involved in research programs will often create their own versions of Unix, tailored to their own special needs. This inherent flexibility in the Unix design in no way detracts from its quality. In fact, it attests to its ruggedness, allowing it to adapt to practically any environment. It is in this context that Linux was developed. Linux is, in this sense, one other version of Unix—a version for the PC. Its development by computer professionals working in a research-like environment reflects the way Unix versions have usually been developed. The fact that Linux is publicly licensed and free reflects the deep roots that Unix has in academic institutions, with their sense of public service and support. Linux is a top rate operating system accessible to everyone, free of charge.

As a way of introducing Linux, this chapter discusses Linux as an operating system, the history of Linux and Unix, and the overall design of Linux. The chapter also discusses how best to use this book. People often come to Linux with very different backgrounds. Some features may appear familiar, while others may seem completely alien. This book presents different features of Linux within an organized context that will provide you with a clear understanding of the Linux operating system, no matter what your background.

Operating Systems and Linux

An *operating system* is a program that manages computer hardware and software for the user. Operating systems were originally designed to perform repetitive hardware tasks. These tasks centered around managing files, running programs, and receiving commands from the user. You interact with an operating system through a user interface. This user interface allows the operating system to receive and interpret instructions sent by the user. You only need to send an instruction to the operating system to perform a task, such as reading a file or printing a document. An operating system's user interface can be as simple as entering commands on a line, or as complex as selecting menus and icons.

An operating system also manages software applications. To perform different tasks, such as editing documents or performing calculations, you need specific software applications. An editor is an example of a software application. An editor allows you to edit a document, making changes and adding new text. The editor itself is a program consisting of instructions to be executed by the computer. To use the program it must first be loaded into computer memory, and then its instructions executed. The operating system controls the loading and execution of all programs, including any software applications. When you want to use an editor, you simply instruct the operating system to load the editor application and execute it.

File management, program management, and user interaction are traditional features common to all operating systems. Linux, like all versions of Unix, adds two more features. Linux is a multiuser and multitasking system. As a multitasking system, you can ask the system to perform several tasks at the same time. While one task is being done, you can work on another. For example, you can edit a file while another file is being printed. You do not have to wait for the other file to finish printing before you edit. As a multiuser system, several users can log into the system at the same time, each interacting with the system through his or her own terminal.

Operating systems were originally designed to support hardware efficiency. When computers were first developed, their capabilities were limited and the operating system had to make the most of them. In this respect, operating systems were designed with the hardware in mind, not the user. Operating systems tended to be rigid and inflexible, forcing the user to conform to the demands of hardware efficiency.

Linux, on the other hand, is designed to be flexible, reflecting its Unix roots. As a version of Unix, Linux shares the same flexibility designed for Unix, a flexibility stemming from Unix's research origins. The Unix operating system was developed by Ken Thompson at AT&T Bell Laboratories in the late 1960s and early 1970s. It incorporated many new developments in operating system design. Originally, Unix was designed as an operating system for researchers. One major goal was to create a system that could support the researcher's changing demands. To do this, Thompson had to design a system that could deal with many different kinds of tasks. Flexibility became more important than hardware efficiency. Like Unix, Linux has the advantage of being able to deal with the variety of tasks any user may face.

This flexibility allows Linux to be an operating system that is accessible to the user. The user is not confined to limited and rigid interactions with the operating system. Instead, the operating system is thought of as providing a set of highly effective tools that the user can make use of. This user-oriented philosophy means that you can configure and program the system to meet your specific needs. With Linux, the operating system becomes an *operating environment*.

History of Linux and Unix

As a version of Unix, the history of Linux naturally begins with Unix. The story begins in the late 1960s when there was a concerted effort to develop new operating system techniques. In 1968, a consortium of researchers from General Electric, AT&T Bell Laboratories, and the Massachusetts Institute of Technology carried out a special operating system research project called Multics. Multics incorporated many new concepts in multitasking, file management, and user interaction. In 1969, Ken Thompson of AT&T Bell Laboratories developed the Unix operating system, incorporating many of the features of the Multics research project. He tailored the system for the needs of a research environment, designing it to run on minicomputers. From its inception, Unix was an affordable and efficient multiuser and multitasking operating system.

The Unix system became popular at Bell Labs as more and more researchers started using the system. In 1970, Dennis Ritchie collaborated with Ken Thompson to rewrite the programming code for the Unix system in the C programming language. Dennis Ritchie, a fellow researcher at Bell Labs, developed the C programming language as a flexible tool for program development. One of the advantages of C is that it can directly access the hardware architecture of a computer with a generalized set of programming commands. Up until this time, an operating system had to be specially rewritten in a hardware-specific assembly language for each type of computer. The C programming language allowed Dennis Ritchie and Ken Thompson to write only one version of the Unix operating system that could then be compiled by C compilers on different computers. In effect, the Unix operating system became transportable—able to run on a variety of different computers with little or no reprogramming.

Unix gradually grew from one person's tailored design to a standard software product distributed by many different vendors such as Novell and IBM. Initially, Unix was treated as a research product. The first versions of Unix were distributed free to the computer science departments of many noted universities. In 1972 Bell Labs began issuing official versions of Unix and licensing the system to different users. One of these users was the computer science department of the University of California, Berkeley. Berkeley added many new features to the system that later became standard. In 1975 Berkeley released its own version of Unix known by its distribution arm, Berkeley Software Distribution (BSD). This BSD version of Unix became a major contender to the AT&T Bell Labs version. Other independently developed versions of Unix sprouted up. In 1980 Microsoft developed a PC version of Unix called Xenix. AT&T developed several research versions of Unix, and in 1982 they released the first commercial version, called System 3. This was later followed by System V, which became a seriously supported commercial software product.

At the same time, the BSD version of Unix was developing through several releases. In the late 1970s, BSD Unix became the basis of a research project by the Department of Defense's Advanced Research Projects Agency (DARPA). As a result, in 1983, Berkeley released a powerful version of Unix called BSD release 4.2. It included sophisticated file management as well as networking features based on TCP/IP network protocols—the same protocols now used for the Internet. BSD release 4.2 was widely distributed and adopted by many vendors such as Sun Microsystems.

The proliferation of different versions of Unix led to a need for a Unix standard. Software developers had no way of knowing what versions of Unix their programs would actually run on. In the mid-1980s, two competing standards emerged, one based on the AT&T version of Unix, and the other on the BSD version. In bookstores today you will see many different books on Unix for one or the other version. Some specify System V Unix, others focus on BSD Unix.

AT&T moved Unix to a new organization called Unix System Laboratories that could focus on developing a standard system, integrating the different major versions of Unix. In 1991 Unix System Laboratories developed System V release 4, which incorporated almost all the features found in System V release 3, BSD release 4.3, SunOS, and Xenix. In response to System V release 4, several other companies, such as IBM and Hewlett-Packard, established the Open Software Foundation (OSF) to create their own standard version of Unix. There were then two commercial standard versions of Unix—the OSF version and System V release 4. In 1993 AT&T sold off its interest in Unix to Novell. Unix Systems Laboratories are now part of Novell's UNIX System's Group. Novell has since issued its own versions of Unix based on System V release 4, called UnixWare. UnixWare is designed to interact with Novell's NetWare system.

Throughout much of its development, Unix remained a large and demanding operating system requiring a workstation or minicomputer to be effective. Several versions of Unix were designed primarily for the workstation environment. SunOS was developed for Sun workstations, and AIX was designed for IBM workstations. However, as personal computers became more powerful, efforts were made to develop a PC version of Unix. Xenix and System V/386 are commercial versions of Unix designed for IBM-compatible PCs. AUX is a Unix version that runs on the Macintosh. It is a testament to Unix's inherent portability that it can be found on almost any type of computer: workstations, minicomputers, and even supercomputers. This inherent portability made possible an effective PC version of Unix.

Linux is designed specifically for Intel-based personal computers. It started out as a personal project of a computer science student named Linus Torvald at the University of Helsinki. At that time, students were making use of a program called Minix that highlighted different Unix features. Minix was created by Professor Andrew Tannebaum and widely distributed over the Internet to students around the world. Linus's intention was to create an effective PC version of Unix for Minix users. He called it Linux and in 1991 released version 0.11. Linux was widely distributed over the Internet, and in the following years other programmers refined and added to it, incorporating most of the applications and features now found in standard Unix systems. All the major window managers have been ported to Linux. Linux has all the Internet utilities, such as ftp, telnet, and slip. It also has a full set of program development utilities, such as C++ compilers and debuggers. Given all its features, the Linux operating system remains small, stable, and fast. In its simplest format it can run effectively on just 4MB of memory.

Though Linux has developed in the free and open environment of the Internet, it adheres to official Unix standards. Due to the proliferation of Unix versions in the previous decades, the Institute of Electrical and Electronics Engineers (IEEE) developed an independent Unix standard for the American National Standards Institute (ANSI). This new ANSI-standard Unix is called the Portable Operating System Interface for Computer Environments (POSIX). The standard defines how a Unix-like system needs to operate, specifying details such as system calls and interfaces. POSIX defines a universal standard that all Unix versions must adhere to. Most popular versions of Unix are now POSIX compliant. Linux was developed from the beginning according to the POSIX standard.

Linux Overview

Like Unix, Linux can be generally divided into four major components: the kernel, the shell, the file structure, and the utilities. The *kernel* is the core program that runs programs and manages hardware devices such as disks and printers. The *shell* provides an interface for the user. It receives commands from the user and sends those commands to the kernel for execution. The *file structure* organizes the way files are stored on a storage device such as a disk. Files are organized into directories. Each directory may contain any number of subdirectories, each holding files.

Together, the kernel, the shell, and the file structure form the basic operating system structure. With these three you can run programs, manage files, and interact with the system. In addition, Linux has software programs called utilities that have come to be considered standard features of the system. The *utilities* are specialized programs, such as editors, compilers, and communications programs, that perform standard computing operations. You can even create your own utilities.

Shell: Bourne, Korn, and C-Shell

The shell provides an interface between the kernel and the user. It can be described as an interpreter. It interprets commands entered by the user and sends them to the kernel. The shell interface is very simple. It usually consists of a prompt at which you type a command and then press ENTER. In a sense, you are typing the command on a line; this line is often referred to as the *command line*. You will find that the commands entered on the command line can become very complex.

As an alternative to a command line interface, Linux provides a graphical user interface (GUI) called X-Windows that has several window managers for you to use. A window manager operates much like the Windows and Mac GUIs. You have windows, icons, and menus, all managed through mouse controls. Two of the more popular window managers are the Free Virtual Window Manager (fvwm) and the Open-Look window manager (olwm). The Motif window manager is also available, but Motif is a proprietary program that you have to purchase separately. In addition to window managers, you will also need to use file and program managers. There are several different file and program managers available, and many Linux vendors supply their own. For example, the Caldera Network Desktop included with this text provides a sophisticated file manager and program manager, making use of icon bars and directory folders.

Though a window manager makes for a flexible and engaging interface, keep in mind that it is really just a front for the shell. The window manager simply passes off the commands it receives to the shell. It is the shell that actually interprets the command and sends it to the kernel. Figure 1-1 shows the relationship of the shell to the kernel and other system components.

The shell does more than just interpret commands, it provides an environment that you can configure and program. The shell also has its own programming language that allows you to write programs that execute Linux commands in complex ways. The shell programming language has many of the features of normal programming languages, such as loop and branch control structures. You can even create complex shell programs that are as powerful as many applications programs.

Each user on a Linux system has his or her own user interface, or shell. Users can tailor their shells to their own special needs. In this sense, a user's shell functions more as an operating environment, which the user can control.

Over the years, several different kinds of shells have been developed. Currently there are three major shells: Bourne, Korn, and C-shell. The Bourne shell was developed at Bell Labs for System V. The C-shell was developed for the BSD version of Unix. The Korn shell is a further enhancement of the Bourne shell. Current versions of Unix, including Linux, incorporate all three shells, allowing you to choose the one you prefer. However, Linux uses enhanced or public domain versions of these shells: the Bourne Again shell, the TC-shell, and the Public Domain Korn shell. When you start

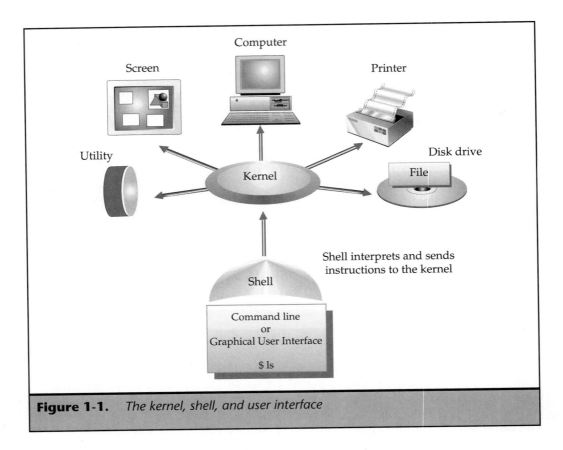

Figure 1-1.   *The kernel, shell, and user interface*

your Linux system, you will be placed in the Bourne Again shell, an updated version of the Bourne shell. From there you can switch to other shells as you wish.

File Structure: Directories and Files

In Linux, files are organized into directories, much as they are in DOS. However, unlike DOS, you have much more flexibility and control over your files. The entire Linux file system is one large interconnected set of directories, each containing files. Some directories are standard directories reserved for system use. You can create your own directories for your own files, as well as easily move files from one directory to another. You can even move entire directories and share directories and files with other users on your system. With Linux, you can also set permissions on directories and files, allowing others to access them or restricting access to you alone.

The directories of each user are in fact ultimately connected to the directories of other users. Directories are organized into a hierarchical tree structure, beginning with an initial root directory. All other directories are ultimately derived from this first root

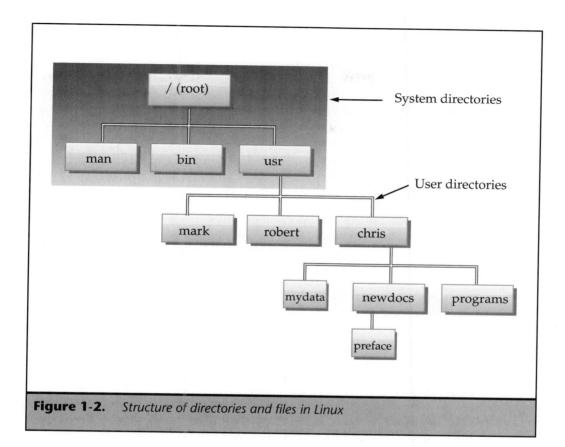

Figure 1-2. *Structure of directories and files in Linux*

directory. Figure 1-2 shows an example of this tree-like, hierarchical file structure. You can actually travel throughout the system, entering any directory that may be open to you. This interconnectivity of the file structure makes it easy to share data. Several users could access the same files.

The root directory is a special directory that you will need to make use of when you first set up your Linux system. Linux is a multiuser system. You could have several users sharing the same operating system. However, the operating system itself resides in programs placed in special directories beginning with the root directory. These are sometimes referred to as *system directories*. In Figure 1-2, the system directories are those just below the root: man, bin, and usr. There are many others. System directories are described in Chapter 5.

Utilities: Editors, Filters, and Communications

Linux contains a great number of utilities. Some utilities perform simple operations; others are complex programs with their own sets of commands. To begin with, many utilities can be classified into three general categories: editors, filters, and communications programs. Of course, not all utilities fit these categories. There are also utilities that perform file operations and program management.

There are several standard editors available on all Unix versions, including Linux: Ed, Ex, Vi, and Emacs. Ed and Ex are line editors, whereas Vi and Emacs are full-screen editors. All the standard editors were developed for early, less powerful machines that could not handle full-screen cursor movement like today's PC word processors can. Even though Vi and Emacs have full-screen capability, they are not as fluid and easy to use as many mouse-driven word processors. Ed and Ex are line editors that display and edit only one line at a time. Even with these limitations, however, the editors are highly effective. They have a large set of commands that can be combined into complex operations.

Another set of utilities can best be described as filters. A *filter* reads input from either the user, a file, or some other source, examines and processes the data, and outputs the result. In this sense, they filter data that is passed through them. There are many different types of filters. Some use line editing commands to output edited versions of a file. Others search files for a pattern and output only that part of the data with the pattern. Still others perform word processing operations, detecting format commands in a file and outputting a formatted version of the file. The input for a filter does not have to be a file. It can be data input by the user from the keyboard. It can also be the output of another filter. Filters can be connected together, whereby the output of one filter can become the input of another filter, and so on. It is even possible to program your own filters. A filter programming language called Awk enables you to write your own filters.

Linux also has a set of utilities that allow you to communicate with other users on your own system or other systems. As a multiuser system, Linux must maintain contact with and keep track of all users. The basic need for monitoring and the basic interconnectivity of the file structure make an electronic mail system easy to implement. Messages can be sent to and received from other users on the system. You can even broadcast a message to several users at once, or directly connect to another user and carry on a real-time conversation.

One of the most important features of Linux, as well as all Unix systems, is its set of Internet tools. The Internet was designed and developed on Unix systems. Internet tools such as ftp and telnet were first implemented on BSD versions of Unix. Darpanet, the precursor to the Internet, was set up to link Unix systems at different universities across the nation. Linux contains a full set of Internet tools as well as those providing direct Internet connections, such as slip. WEB browsers, such as Mosaic, that were originally designed for use on Unix, are also available for Linux. Some Linux vendors, including Caldera, provide their own WEB browsers.

In recent years, efforts have been made to enhance Unix's network capabilities. Novell has worked to interface UnixWare (its version of Unix) with its networking software, NetWare. In accordance with this approach, the Linux vendor Caldera has extended Linux to interface more easily with networking protocols. The Caldera

Network Desktop Linux can easily interface with Novell and other network servers, allowing you to link Linux systems into networks.

Linux Software and Information Sources on the Internet

Linux was developed as a cooperative effort over the Internet. No company or institution controls Linux. Development often takes place when Linux users decide to work on a project together. When completed, the software is posted at an ftp site on the Internet. Any Linux user can then access the site and download the software. One of the major ftp sites for both Linux software and documentation is sunsite.unc.edu in the directory /pub/linux. You can find other sites through your archie or gopher Internet utilities. Most of the Linux software and documentation currently available is already included on your Caldera Network CD-ROM. However, in the future, you may need to directly access Linux Internet sites for up-to-date information and software.

Table 1-1 lists different ftp sites. Homesites are where Linux software is originally posted. Mirror sites are copies of these homesites.

Most Linux software is copyrighted under a GNU public license provided by the Free Software Foundation, and is often referred to as GNU software. GNU software is distributed free, provided that it will be freely distributed to others. Proven to be very reliable and effective, GNU software applications include many of the popular Linux utilities such as C compilers, shells, and editors. Installed with your Caldera Network Desktop are the GNU C++ and Lisp compilers, Vi and Emacs editors, BASH and TCSH shells, as well as Tex and Ghostscript document formatters. Furthermore, many other GNU software applications are available at different ftp sites on the Internet such as sunsite.unc.edu. Chapter 7 of this book describes in detail the process of downloading software applications from Internet sites and installing them on your system.

Lately, major software companies are also developing a Linux version of their most popular applications. For example, Netscape provides a Linux version of their popular Web browser that you can download from their ftp site: ftp2.netscape.com. There is also a Linux version of Sun's Java available at ftp.blackdown.org. There is even a Linux version of Wordperfect available, and Caldera provides a Linux version of Novell's NetWare.

Linux documentation has also been developed over the Internet. Much of the documentation currently available for Linux can be downloaded from Internet ftp sites. A special Linux project called the Linux Documentation Project, headed by Matt Welsh, is currently developing a complete set of Linux manuals. The documentation, at its current level, is available at tsx-11.mit.edu in the directory /pub/linux/ALPHA/LDP. The documentation includes a user's guide, an introduction, and administration guides, and is available in text, PostScript, or Web page format. Table 1-2 lists these guides. You can find briefer explanations in what are referred to as HOW-TO documents. HOW-TO documents are available for different subjects such as installation, printing, and email. The documents are available at the ftp site sunsite.unc.edu in the directory /pub/linux/doc/HOW-TO.

You can find a listing of different Linux information sites in the file META-FAQ located at the ftp site sunsite.unc.edu in the directory /pub/linux/doc. On the same site and directory you can also download the Linux Software Map, LSM. This is a listing of most of the software currently available for Linux. Also, many companies have Web sites that provide information about their Linux applications. Some of these are listed in Table 1-3.

In addition to ftp sites, there are also Linux Usenet newsgroups. Through your Internet connection you can access Linux newsgroups to read the comments of other Linux users and post messages of your own. There are several Linux newsgroups, each beginning with comp.os.linux. One of particular interest to the beginner is comp.os.linux help, where you can post questions.

Table 1-4 lists the different Linux newsgroups available on Usenet. Currently, the only publication dealing with Linux is the *Linux Journal*. You can obtain information about it from:

Linux Journal
P.O. Box 85867
Seattle, WA 98145
206-527-3385

Linux Releases

Although there is only one standard version of Linux, there are actually several different releases. Different companies and groups have packaged Linux and Linux software in slightly different ways. Each company or group then releases the Linux package, usually on a CD-ROM. Later releases may include updated versions of programs or new software. Some of the more popular releases are Slackware, Red Hat, TAMU, Yggdrasil, and Infomagic. The Caldera Network Desktop included in this text contains the Red Hat release of Linux.

Caldera Network Desktop

The Caldera Network Desktop included with this book contains the complete Linux system and software packages. It includes the Redhat distribution of Linux with all the

GNU software packages, as well as the X-Windows window managers and Internet tools. It is POSIX compliant, adhering to Unix standards. In addition, Caldera has several proprietary, licensed software packages that are not freely distributable: a desktop metaphor, a font server, and a network client. The desktop metaphor provides an icon-based program and file manager. The font installer and font server software supports TrueType, Type 1, and Speedo fonts. The network client allows connection to NetWare 3 and NetWare 4 servers.

Summary: The Linux Operating System

Linux is a version of the Unix operating system that was developed by Linus Torvald for PCs with 386, 486, or Pentium processors. Linux is distinguished by its power and flexibility, bringing all the features of Unix, including multitasking and multiuser capabilities, to your PC. Linux is available free under a GNU public license. It is a carefully maintained operating system adhering to POSIX standards.

Your Linux software package includes not only the Linux operating system but also a series of software applications such as compilers and editors. It also includes the X-Windows GUI with several window managers, allowing you to use windows, icons, and menus to interact with the system.

The Linux system is made up of a kernel, the shell, a file structure, and utilities. The kernel is the heart of the system. It contains the control programs that directly manage the computer hardware. The shell is the user interface. The shell receives commands from the user and sends them to the kernel for execution. The shell can be tailored to an individual user's needs. The shell even has a programming language that can be used to program commands. The file structure consists of directories within which files are placed. Directories provide you with a convenient way to organize your files. You can move from one directory to another and set permissions on directories, opening up and sharing the files in them with other users.

A set of programs that is standard for the Linux system are commonly called utilities. Utilities can be generally categorized as editors, filters, or communications programs. Some of the editors, though powerful, are not as easy to use as many current PC editors. Filters are specialized utilities that receive data and generate a modified form of that data. Communications utilities allow you to send messages to and receive messages from other users. Internet tools allow you easy access to information services such as Usenet and the WEB. Table 1-5 lists the various Internet servers.

Linux Homesite		Directory	
sunsite.unc.edu	(152.2.22.81)	/pub/linux	
tsx-11.mit.edu	(18.172.1.2)	/pub/linux	
nic.funet.fi	(128.214.6.100)	/pub/os/linux	
Mirror site			
ftp.mcc.ac.uk	(130.88.200.7)	/pub/linux	Britain
ftp.ibp.fr	(132.227.60.2)	/pub/linux	France
ftp.dfv.rwth-aachen.de	(137.226.4.105)	/pub/linux	Germany
kirk.bu.oz.au	(131.244.1.1)	/pub/linux	Australia
ftp.caldera.com		/pub/linux	
Linux Application		**Description**	
ftp.ncsa.uiuc.edu		Mosaic Web Browser and Web Server software for Linux	
ftp2.netscape.com		Netscape Web Browser for Linux	
ftp.blackdown.org		Sun's Java Development Kit for Linux	

Table 1-1. *ftp Sites*

Guides	Internet Sites
Linux Installation and Getting Started	www.caldera.com/
Linux User's Guide	tsx-11.mit.edu /pub/linux/ALPHA/LDP
Linux System Administrator's Guide	sunsite.unc.edu /mdw
Linux Network Adiminstrator's Guide	
Linux Kenel Hacker's Guide	

Table 1-2. *Linux Documentation Project*

Web Site	Description
www.caldera.com	Caldera Web site
www.blackdown.org	Web site for Linux Java
www.netscape.com	Netscape Web site
sunsite.unc.com/mdw/linux.html	Linux Documentation Project Web page

Table 1-3. *Web Sites*

Usenet Newsgroup	Description
comp.os.linux.announce	Announcements of Linux developments
comp.os.linux.devlopment.apps	For programmers developing Linux applications
comp.os.linux.devlopment.system	For programmers working on the Linux operating system
comp.os.linux.hardware	Linux hardware specifications
comp.os.linux.admin	System adiministration questions
comp.os.linux.misc	Special questions and issues
comp.os.linux.setup	Installation problems
comp.os.linux.answers	Answers to command problems
comp.os.linux.help	Questions and answers for particular problems
comp.os.linux.networking	Linux network questions and issues

Table 1-4. *Usenet Newsgroups*

Server	Site
ftp	**sunsite.unc.edu** and its mirror sites **/pub/Linux/systems/Network/info-systems/**
Web	**sunsite.unc.edu** and its mirror sites **/pub/Linux/systems/Network/info-systems/www/servers**
NCSA	**ftp.ncsa.edu** **http://boohoo.ncsa.uiuc.edu**
CERN	**info.cern.ch.pub/www.bin**
Plexus	**austin.bsdi.com/lexus/2.2.1/dist/Plexus.html**
Gopher	**sunsite.unc.edu** and its mirror sites **/pub/Linux/system/Network/info-systems/gopher** **/pub/packages/infosystems/gophers**
University of Minnesota	**boombox.micro.umn.edu/pub.gopher**
GN gopher, a GNU Public Licensed Gopher	**sunsite.unc.edu/pub/packages/infosystems/gopher** **/servers/gn**
WAIS	**sunsite.unc.edu** and its mirror sites **/pub/packages/systems/Network/info-systems** **/wais/linux**
CNIDR	**ftp.cnidr.org /pub/CNIDR.tools/freewais/**

Table 1-5. *Internet Servers*

Chapter Two

Installing Linux

This chapter describes the installation procedure for the Caldera Network Desktop provided on the enclosed CD-ROM. The procedure includes the Redhat distribution of Linux as well as several other applications, such as the Netscape Web Browser, the Caldera Netware client, and Internet server support. Different Linux distributions usually have their own installation programs. For example, the Slackware distribution of Linux uses a very different installation program from that of Redhat. The Caldera installation program is designed to be efficient and brief while installing as many features as possible. Certain features, such as Web server support, would ordinarily require specialized and often complex configuration operations. The Caldera Network Desktop automatically installs and configures many of these features.

Installing Linux involves several steps. First you need to determine whether your computer meets the basic hardware requirements. These days, most Intel-based PCs do. Then you will have to look up certain technical specifications about the hardware you use, such as your monitor type and the type of chips used in your video card. This kind of information is available in the manuals that came with the hardware.

If you want to have your Linux system share a hard drive with another operating system, you may need to repartition your hard disk. There are several different options for partitioning your hard drive, depending on whether or not it already contains data you need to preserve.

You then need to prepare several boot disks with which you will start the installation program. Once the installation program begins, you simply follow the instructions, screen by screen. Most of the time you will only need to make simple selections or provide yes and no answers. The installation program progresses through several phases. First you create Linux partitions on your hard drive. Then you install the software packages. After that you need to configure X-Windows, the graphical user interface, for your computer. And finally, if you have a network connection, you can configure your network clients. Both the X-Windows and network configuration can be performed independently at a later time.

Once your system is installed, you are ready to start it and log in. You will be logging into a simple command line interface. From the command line, you can then invoke X-Windows, which will provide you with a full graphical user interface called the Caldera Network Desktop.

The installation program installs a basic set of Linux software packages. However, there are many more packages available on your Caldera CD-ROM. Chapter 3 describes how you can use the glint utility or the Redhat Package Manager to install, or even uninstall, these software packages.

Hardware, Software, Information Requirements

Before installing Linux, you need to be sure that your computer meets certain minimum hardware requirements. You will also need certain software, namely hard disk preparation programs such as fdisk. These are standard on all DOS systems and are also provided on your Caldera CD-ROM. There is also certain specific information that you will need to have ready concerning your monitor, video card, mouse, and CD-ROM drive. All the requirements are presented in detail in the following sections. Be sure to read them carefully before you begin installation. During the installation program, you will need to provide responses based on the configuration of your computer.

Hardware Requirements

Listed here are the minimum hardware requirements for installing a Linux system.

- A 32-bit Intel-based personal computer. An Intel or compatible 80386, 80486, or Pentium microprocessor is required. Both SX and DX CPUs are acceptable.
- A 3 1/2-inch floppy disk drive.
- At least 8MB RAM, though 16MB are recommended.
- At least 200MB free hard disk space; 200 to 300MB are recommended. You will need at least 370MB to load and make use of all the software packages on your Caldera CD-ROM. The Express installation of basic software packages takes 140MB, plus 16MB required for swap space. If you have less than 200MB, you can elect to perform a minimum install, installing only the Linux kernel without most of the applications. You could later install the applications you want one at a time.
- A 3 1/2-inch, DOS-formatted, high-density (HD) floppy disk, to be used to create a boot disk.
- A CD-ROM drive.
- Four empty DOS-formatted, 3 1/2-inch, high-density (HD) floppy disks. You will use these as boot disks in the installation process.

If you plan to use the X-Windows graphical user interface, you will also need:

- A video graphics card
- A mouse or other pointing device

Software Requirements

There are only a few software requirements. Basically, you need an operating system from which you can create your Linux boot disk, and if you plan to have both DOS and Linux on the same hard drive, you will need DOS partition software. Accordingly, if you have OS/2, you will need OS/2 partition software.

The operating system is required to allow you to prepare your installation disks. Using a DOS system, you can access the Caldera CD-ROM and issue DOS-like commands to create your installation disks. Any type of DOS will do, and you can even use the same commands on OS/2. However, you do not need DOS to run Linux. Linux is a separate operating system in its own right.

If you want to have Linux share your hard disk with another operating system, say DOS, you will need certain utilities to prepare the hard disk for sharing. For DOS you need either the defrag and fips utilities, or the fdisk utility. The fips utility is provided on your Caldera CD-ROM. It will perform a nondestructive partition of your hard disk, freeing up space for your Linux system. Defrag and fdisk are standard DOS utilities, usually located in your **dos** directory. Defrag is used with fips to defragment your hard disk before fips partitions it. There are, of course, other commercial utilities that can also perform the required defragmentation. Fdisk is an alternative to fips that performs a destructive partition, erasing everything on your hard disk and requiring a complete reformat and DOS installation.

Information Requirements

Part of adapting a powerful operating system like Linux to the PC entails making the most efficient use of the computer hardware at hand. To do so, Linux requires specific information about the computer components that it is dealing with. For example, special Linux configuration files are tailored to work with special makes and models of video cards and monitors. Before installing Linux, you will need to have such information on hand. The information is usually available in the manual that came with your hardware peripherals or computer.

CD-ROM, Hard Disk, and Mouse Information

If you have a SCSI CD-ROM drive, you will need the manufacturer's name and model. If you have an IDE CD-ROM drive, just make note of that fact.

Decide how much of your hard drive (in megabytes) you want to dedicate to your Linux system. You need to make this decision before you install. You cannot change the size later. If you are sharing with DOS, decide how much you want for DOS and how much for Linux.

Decide how much space you want for your swap partition. Your swap partition must be at least 16MB. It is used by Linux as an extension of your computer's RAM. If you have 16MB RAM or more, your swap space should be 32MB.

Find the make and model of the mouse you are using. Linux supports both serial and bus mice. The following mice are supported:

- Serial mice for Microsoft (and compatible), Mouse Systems, Logitech, mmseries, and Hitachi
- Bus mice for Logitech, Microsoft, and ATI XL
- C&T 82C710 or PS/2 style, and Logitech MouseMan

Know which serial port your mouse is using: COM1, COM2, or none if you use the PS/2 mouse port.

Video and Monitor Information

You will need to know the following information about your video card and monitor.

- What is the make and mode of your video card?
- What chipset does your video card use?
- How much memory is on your video card?
- What is the manufacturer and model of your monitor? Linux supports several monitors. If yours is not one of them, you can choose a generic profile, or you can enter information for a custom profile. To do that you will need the following information:
  - The horizontal refresh rate in kHz
  - Vertical refresh rate in Hz
  - Scan rate in MHz
- What time zone you are in. If your computer is directly connected to the Internet, you may want to use Greenwich mean time (GMT) as your time zone. If, however, you are using a stand-alone computer that also runs DOS, you may want to use a local time zone.
- Decide the names of any user accounts you want to create at the time of installation. You should create at least one for yourself. You can, however, always set up user accounts at any time.

Network Configuration Information

Except for deciding your hostname, you do not have to configure your network during installation. You can put it off to a later time and use the netcfg utility to perform network configuration. However, if the information is readily available, the installation procedure will automatically configure your network, placing needed entries in the appropriate configuration files. If you are on a network, you will have to obtain most of this information from your network administrator. If you are using an Internet Service Provider, they should provide you with much of this information. If you are setting up a network yourself, you will have to determine each piece of information. The installation program will prompt you to enter in these values.

- Decide on a name for your computer (this is called a hostname). Your computer will be identified by this name on the Internet.
- Your domain name.
- The IP (Internet Protocol) address assigned to your machine. Every host on the Internet is assigned an IP address. This address is a set of four numbers, separated by periods, that uniquely identifies a single location on the Internet, allowing information from other locations to reach that computer.

- Your network address. This address is usually the same as the IP address, but with an added 0.

- The netmask. This is usually 255.255.255.0 for class C IP addresses. If, however, you are part of a large network, check with your network administrator.

- The broadcast address for your network. Usually your broadcast address is the same as your IP address with the number 255 added at the end.

- If you have a gateway, you will need the gateway (router) address for your network.

- The address of any nameservers that your network uses.

Opening Disk Space for Linux Partitions

If you are using an entire hard drive for your Linux system, you can skip this section and go on to installing Linux. If, however, your Linux system is going to share a hard drive with your DOS system, you will need to partition and format your hard drive so that part of it is used for DOS and the remaining part is free for Linux installation. How you go about this process depends on the current state of your hard disk. If you have a new hard disk and you are going to install both DOS and Linux on it, you need to be sure to install DOS on only part of the hard drive, leaving the rest free for Linux. However, if you are already using this hard disk, you must either delete partitions you already have or repartition your entire hard disk, leaving part of it free for Linux. The objective in each situation is to free up space for Linux. When you install Linux, you will then partition and format that free space for use by Linux.

A hard disk is organized into partitions. The partitions are further formatted to the specification of a given operating system. When you installed DOS, you first needed to divide your hard disk into different partitions. You then used the DOS format operation to format each partition into a DOS disk, each identified by a letter. For example, you may have divided your disk into two partitions, one formatted as the C disk and the other as the D disk. Alternatively, you may have divided your hard disk into just one partition and formatted it as the C disk. In order to share your hard drive with Linux, you will need to free up some space by either reducing their size or deleting some of those partitions.

First decide how much space you will need for your Linux system. You will probably need a minimum of 200MB, though more is recommended. As stated earlier, the basic set of Linux software packages takes up 140MB, whereas the entire set of software packages, including all their source code files, takes 340MB. In addition, you will need space for a Linux swap partition used to implement virtual memory. This takes between 16 and 32MB. At 200MB you could install the basic package and have about 40MB for your own use, though you will quickly find this too limited if you need to install any other software packages. A more practical minimum would be 250 to 300MB.

Once you have determined the space you need for your Linux system, you can then set about freeing up that space on your hard drive. Depending on how your hard disk is partitioned, you will have to take slightly different steps to free up this space. If you have several partitions already, you will probably only need to delete a few of them.

To see what options are best for you, you should first determine what your partitions are and their sizes. You can do this with the fdisk utility. To start this utility, enter **fdisk** at the DOS prompt, and press ENTER.

```
C:\> fdisk
```

This brings up the menu of fdisk options, as shown in Figure 2-1. Choose option 4 to display a list of all your current partitions and the size of each. You can determine whether you need either to reduce or repartition your disk, or whether you can get away with just deleting some unused partitions.

If you have only a couple or just one large partition covering the entire disk, you have two options. You can use the DOS defrag and Linux fips utilities to nondestructively create free space from unused space on your hard drive. You should still make a backup of your important data for safety's sake. But you would not have to reinstall

```
                        MS-DOS Version 6
                     Fixed Disk Setup Program
              (C)Copyright Microsoft Corp. 1983 - 1993

                          FDISK Options

      Current fixed disk drive: 1

      Choose one of the following:

      1. Create DOS partition or Logical DOS Drive
      2. Set active partition
      3. Delete partition or Logical DOS Drive
      4. Display partition information




      Enter choice: [1]




      Press Esc to exit FDISK
```

Figure 2-1.   *The fdisk menu*

DOS and restore your backups. Everything would be preserved. Alternatively, you can repartition your entire disk, erasing all your data. You will then have to reinstall DOS and restore your data from backups, as well as reformat your hard drive. If you are installing a new hard drive on which you want to have both DOS and Linux, you would follow the same steps for repartitioning your disk, though you will not need to delete any partitions, since you would have none to begin with.

Deleting Partitions

In most cases a user will have several partitions on the hard drive. If you have DOS partitions that are rarely used or have very little data on them, you may consider deleting them to free up space for your Linux system. In this case, simply determine how many and which ones you want to delete. Deleting a partition will erase all the data on it, so be sure to back up any data first. Partitions are of fixed size, so you could end up with more space than you need. If this happens you could just add a new DOS partition of a smaller size.

Bear in mind that there is a critical difference between a DOS partition and a Linux partition. If you already have a Linux system on your disk and you want to remove those Linux partitions to install a new system, you must use the Linux fdisk utility, *not* DOS's fdisk. A Linux partition can only be safely removed by the Linux fdisk utility located on your Linux CD-ROM.

To delete partitions, first start the fdisk utility.

```
C:\> fdisk
```

From the fdisk menu, select option 3, Delete partition or Logical DOS Drive. This will bring up a list of the current drives and prompt you to enter the number of the partition. Each partition entry will list the type, volume label, and the number of megabytes it uses. Do *not* delete a partition whose type is PRI DOS. This is usually the first partition. A safe bet is to start with the last partition.

After entering a partition's number, you will be prompted for the volume label. (The volume label is listed in the partition entry on the fdisk menu.) When you are asked to confirm, type **y** to delete the partition. If you then go back and select option 4, Display partition information, you will see that the partition is gone and in its place is an entry specifying free space. This tells you how much free space is open for Linux to use.

If you need more space, you can delete another partition by repeating the previous steps. With each partition you delete, you will increase your free space. If deleting a partition has freed up too much space, you can use the Add option in the fdisk menu to add a new smaller DOS partition.

To add a partition, select the Partition Creation option in the fdisk menu. This displays the Partition Creation menu, from which you then select the Create Extended DOS Partition option, option 2. You will be prompted to set the size of the partition.

After adding the partition, check the listing of partitions by selecting the fourth item in the fdisk options menu. The last entry will specify the amount of free space. Be sure you leave enough for your Linux system.

Nondestructive Repartition

If you already have a large amount of data and programs on your PC that you don't want to have to reinstall, you can attempt a nondestructive repartition using the defrag and fips utilities. You should, however, back up your data just as a precaution. To perform a nondestructive partition, you first need to know if you already have enough unused space on your hard drive that can be used for Linux. If you do not, you will have to delete some files. You can use CHKDSK on each of the drives on your hard drive to see how much space is available. See if they add up to as much or more free space needed for Linux. If not, delete some unwanted files and check again, until you have enough space.

When DOS creates and saves files, it places them in different sectors on your hard disk. Your files are spread out across your hard disk with a lot of empty space in between. This has the effect of fragmenting the remaining unused space into smaller sections separated by files. The defrag utility performs a defragmentation process that moves all the files into adjoining space on the hard disk, thereby leaving all the unused space as one large continuous segment. Once you have defragmented your disk, you can use the fips utility to create free space using part or all of the unused space. Fips is a version of fdisk designed to detect continuous unused space and delete it from its current DOS partition, opening unpartitioned free space that can then be used by Linux. All your DOS partitions and drives remain intact with all their data and programs. They are just smaller.

To run the defrag utility, enter the command **defrag**. This is a DOS command found in the **dos** directory.

```
C:\>  dos\defrag
```

Defrag will display a screen with colored blocks representing the different sectors on your hard disk. It will carry out an optimization of your hard disk, moving all your used sectors, your data and programs, together on the hard disk. This may take a few minutes. When complete, you will see the used sectors arranged together on the screen. You can then exit the defrag utility.

Now you are ready to run the fips utility to actually free up space. Fips is located on your Linux CD-ROM, also in a directory named **dos**. Change to your CD-ROM drive, and run the fips utility. In the following example, the CD-ROM drive is drive E.

```
C:\>  e:
E:\>  \dos\fips
```

Fips will display a screen showing the amount of free space. Use your arrow keys to make the space smaller if you do not need all your free space for Linux. You should leave some free space for your DOS programs. Then press ENTER to free the space.

Destructive Repartitioning of Your Entire Hard Drive

Instead of reducing your current DOS partitions, you could just eliminate them and start over from scratch. This process destructively partitions your hard disk, erasing all data on your hard drive. There are several situations in which you may want to do this.

The fips utility simply reduces the size of the partitions that you have, it does not eliminate any. If you have several partitions, you could end up with a lot of small partitions, whereas you may prefer a few larger partitions. If you want larger partitions, you must destructively repartition your disk, creating all new ones. You could then restore your DOS system and data from backups.

If you have a new hard drive that you just bought and are now installing, you will need to perform the same steps for destructively partitioning the hard drive (of course, without any backup or restoration of data, since with a new hard drive, there is no data yet).

If you are using most of your hard drive already and there would be a great many files to erase to open up space for fips to work, you could just back up your files, and then destructively repartition your hard disk. You could then later restore only those files you want.

Before you partition your entire disk, you need to back up any data to floppies or tape. Having done that, you are ready to destructively partition your disk. Again, be warned that partitioning your hard drive will erase all data on that hard drive.

The next steps describe how you create a DOS boot disk with the format and fdisk utilities. First insert a blank floppy disk into your floppy disk drive. Use the **format** command and the option **/s** to format the disk and copy the system files to it at the same time. Be sure to specify the letter of the floppy drive. In the next example it is the A drive. Copy the **command.com**, **format.com**, and **fdisk.exe** files to the A drive. Both format and fdisk are in the **dos** directory.

```
C:\> format a: /s
C:\> copy command.com  a:
C:\> copy dos/format.com  a:
C:\> copy dos/fdisk.exe  a:
```

You now have a DOS boot disk. Restart your computer with the DOS boot disk in your floppy drive. The system will boot from that disk instead of your hard disk. You will see the A:\> prompt. Now you are ready to repartition your hard disk using fdisk. Enter the command:

```
A:\> fdisk
```

This will bring up the fdisk menu with its list of partition options. You can create, delete, or simply list your partitions.

If you are not installing a new hard disk, your hard disk will already contain partitions that you will first have to delete. In this case, select option 3 from the fdisk options menu to delete a partition. Your current partitions will be displayed, and you will be prompted to enter the number of the partition to be deleted. Then you will be prompted for the volume name. Next you will be asked if you really want to delete it. Press **y**. You are then returned to the fdisk options menu. Select option 3 and repeat the previous steps to delete another partition. Continue this process until all your partitions are deleted. Each time you delete a partition, you will notice the list of partitions become smaller and a new entry specifying free space become larger.

Once you have deleted all the partitions, you are ready to partition your hard disk with new DOS partitions, leaving enough free space for your Linux partitions. Select option 1 from the fdisk options menu to add a partition. This will give a menu specifying three different types of partitions: a primary DOS partition, an extended DOS partition, and a logical DOS partition. Your first partition has to be a primary DOS partition, so enter 1 as your choice.

You will then have to set this DOS partition as an active partition so it can be used to boot DOS. You select the second option from the fdisk menu, and then select partition 1 as an active partition.

Now you can add another partition. For added partitions you should select the Create Extended DOS Partition option in the Partition Creation menu, option 2. After adding partitions, check the listing of partitions by selecting option 4 in the fdisk options menu. The last entry will specify the amount of free space. Be sure you leave enough for your Linux system.

Once you have finished partitioning the DOS part of your hard drive, you need to format those partitions. Use the **format** command with **/s** when formatting your primary partition so the system files will be copied to it and it can boot. The primary partition is usually labeled C.

```
A:\>   format c: /s
```

The remaining partitions can be formatted with a simple **format** command. The next example formats the partition labeled D.

```
A:\>   format d:
```

Once you have finished formatting the partitions, you can remove your boot disk and restart your computer. The computer will boot from your hard drive. You can now reinstall DOS and Windows, as well as any other data you backed up and any programs you have.

Creating the Caldera Install Disks

You will install your Caldera Network Desktop using an Install disk whose image is currently located on your Caldera CD-ROM. You first have to create the Install disk, using that disk image, on a computer that runs DOS. Begin by starting your computer and entering **DOS**. Then perform the following steps:

1. Insert the Caldera Network Desktop CD-ROM into your CD-ROM drive.

2. At your DOS prompt, change to your CD-ROM drive, using whatever the letter for that drive may be. For example, if your CD-ROM drive is the E: drive, just enter **e:** and press ENTER.

   ```
   C:\> e:
   E:\>
   ```

3. Once you have changed to the CD-ROM drive you then need to change to the **IMAGES.CND** directory. The Install disk images are there. There are two install disks, one for PC computers called **GENERIC.IMG**, and one for laptops called **PCMCIA.IMG**. First change to that directory.

   ```
   E:\> cd IMAGES.CND
   E:\IMAGES.CND>
   ```

4. Then insert your blank DOS-formatted 3 1/2-inch floppy diskette into your floppy drive.

5. Now start the **rawrite** command. The **rawrite** command will actually write the disk image to your floppy disk. **rawrite** is a DOS command located in the DOS directory on the CD-ROM (it is also a standard command found in the DOS directory of your hard drive). The **rawrite** command will first prompt you for the name of the disk image file you want to copy. Enter in the full name of the **GENERIC.IMG** file. It will then ask you to enter the letter of the floppy drive where you put your floppy disk. On many systems this will be the **A** drive.

   ```
   E:\IMAGES.CND > \dos\rawrite
   Enter disk image source file name: GENERIC.IMG
   Enter target diskette drive: A
   ```

6. Press ENTER to confirm that you have a blank diskette in the drive. **rawrite** will then copy the image file to your diskette, creating your install disk. When it finishes, remove your diskette from the floppy drive. This is the diskette that

the Installation procedure described later refers to as the Install diskette. If you have a laptop that you want to install the Caldera Network Desktop on, you have to create the PCMCIA Install disk, using the **PCMCIA.IMG** disk image.

Installing Linux

Installing Linux involves several processes, beginning with creating Linux partitions, then loading the Linux software, configuring your X-Windows interface, installing Linux Loader (LILO) that will boot your system, and creating new user accounts. The installation program is a screen-based program that takes you through all these processes, step by step, as one continuous procedure. You will be able to use your mouse, as well as the arrow keys, SPACEBAR, and ENTER. There is very little you have to do other than make selections and choose options. Some screens, such as the monitor screen, will provide a list of options from which you make a selection. Others will just ask you to choose YES or NO. In a few cases you will be asked for information you should already have if you followed the steps earlier in this chapter. For example, the video card screen in the X-Windows installation will present you with a list of graphics chips and ask you to select the chips used in your video card. The information you should have before you start is listed in the previous section on required information.

You are now ready to begin installation. The steps for each part of the procedure are delineated in the following sections. It should take you no more than an hour.

Booting the Computer and Creating Linux Partitions

If you followed the instructions in the first part of the chapter, you have freed up space on your hard drive and created your boot and root disks, and you are now ready to create your Linux partitions. To do this, you will need to boot your computer using the boot and root disks that you made earlier. When you start your computer, the installation program will begin, and through that you can access the Linux fdisk utility with which you will create your Linux partitions.

1. Insert the Linux boot disk into your floppy drive and reboot your computer.
   The installation program will start, presenting you with an Introduction screen. After a moment, the following prompt will appear at the bottom of your screen.

   ```
   boot:
   ```

2. Press ENTER.
   Configuration information will fill your screen as the installation program attempts to detect your hardware components automatically. Should Linux have a problem identifying one of your components, that fact will be listed

here. The auto-detection messages will fill up several screens. This information is, at this point, held by the installation program for you to examine. Check it to make sure the auto-detection procedure has correctly identified your hardware components. You can move back to a previous screen by holding down the left SHIFT key and pressing PAGE UP. Holding down the left SHIFT key and pressing PAGE DOWN moves you forward to the next page. If your hardware was not correctly detected, you may have to start over and reenter the appropriate hardware specifications at the boot prompt. For example, for an Ethernet card, you would enter the IRQ, port, starting address, ending address, and device. Appendix A lists the syntax for entering information for different devices.

3. Press ENTER to continue.

   A screen is displayed that shows a list of keyboards.

4. Choose your keyboard from the list and press ENTER.

   More information about the installation is displayed, and you are prompted for the next step to continue with the installation.

5. Type **install** and press ENTER.

   After a moment, the System Analysis screen appears. This screen provides a detailed description of all the hardware that the auto-detection process identified. The information takes up several screens, and you can use your arrow keys to examine all the entries. If everything checks out, you can continue.

6. Press ENTER at the System Analysis screen to continue installation.

   In the next screen, you are given three choices—cdrom, hard disk, or network—from which to install Linux.

7. Choose cdrom to install the Caldera Network Desktop included with this text.

   Upon choosing cdrom, a list of CD-ROM drives, with yours highlighted, will be displayed. You have to confirm that this is your CD-ROM drive. If not, look through the list to find yours and click on it.

8. Press ENTER to confirm your CD-ROM drive. (If it is not listed, you will have to start over and enter the hardware specification for it when the boot prompt appears.)

   Alternatively, you can use the hard disk option if you should have difficulty accessing your CD-ROM. You could copy the CD-ROM to a DOS partition and then install from there. The network install allows you to access the Caldera CD-ROM remotely, across a network such as an NFS network. You could also have the CD-ROM copied to a hard drive partition and then load it from there across a network. If you choose a hard drive install, you have to specify the hard disk partition and the directory where the copy of the CD-ROM was placed. **/dev/hda1** indicates the first partition. If you choose a network install, you have to specify the server address and the directory path where the Linux CD-ROM is located.

Next you are asked to choose the partition where your Caldera Network Desktop is to be installed. The first time you install, you will not have any Linux partitions, so you only have one choice.

9. Choose Change Hard Disk Partition Table, the last option.

You are now in the Linux fdisk program. You will be taking the free space that you created earlier and partitioning and formatting it for your Linux operating system. Or, if you are using your entire hard disk for Linux, you will be creating all the partitions for that hard disk.

You need to create two Linux partitions, the main partition and the swap partition. The partitions have different types that you need to specify. Linux fdisk is a line-oriented program. It has a set of one-character commands that you simply press. Then you may be prompted to type in certain information and press ENTER. If you run into trouble during the fdisk procedure, you can press **q** at any time, and you will return to the previous screen without any changes having been made. No changes are actually made to your hard disk until you press **w**. This would be your very last command. It makes the actual changes to your hard disk and then quits fdisk, returning you to the installation program.

Perform the following steps to create your Linux partitions. You will first be creating the swap partition.

a. Press **p** to display your current partitions.

b. Press **n** to define a new partition.
   You will be asked if it is a primary partition.

c. Press **p** to indicate that it is a primary partition.
   You are then prompted to enter the size of the partition. You can enter the size in megabytes by entering a + before the number and an M after it; **+32M** specifies a partition of 32MB.

d. Enter a size for the swap partition, between 16 and 32MB.

e. Press **t** to indicate that you want to set the type for the Linux partition. At the prompt enter **82**. This is the type for the Linux swap partition.

f. Press **n** to define another new partition and **p** to mark it as a primary partition.

g. Enter a size for your Linux main partition. Remember that a standard install uses at least 200MB. Anywhere from 200 to 300MB would be appropriate, though if you have the space, you can make it larger. Bear in mind that the size cannot be larger than your free space. Also, recall that the full package with all source code files will take 350MB, though you may not need all of this.

h. Press **a** to set the BOOT flag for this main Linux partition. When you display the partitions again, you will see an asterisk under the boot field.

i. Press **t** to indicate that you want to set the type for the Linux partition. At the prompt enter **83**. This is the type for a standard Linux partition.

j. Press **w** to write out the changes to the hard disk.

You have now returned to the screen displaying your Linux partitions. You will see your new Linux partitions listed—both your swap and main partitions. Note that if you have another version of Linux installed and you want to replace it with the Caldera Network Desktop, you can use Linux fdisk to delete those old Linux partitions. Remember, only a Linux fdisk can safely delete a Linux partition. First press **p** to display the partitions so that you can determine the partition number of the old Linux partition you want to remove. Then enter **d**, and you will be prompted for the partition number to delete. Be very careful to give the correct number. If you accidentally enter the one for your DOS partition, fdisk will delete it and you will lose everything on it. If this should happen, you can always press **q** to abandon the fdisk sessions. No changes will be made and nothing will be deleted. You can then start over.

The next screen prompts you to reboot your computer. Recall that your Linux boot disk is still in your floppy disk drive. If it is not, insert it now.

10. Press ENTER to reboot. You will begin installation all over again, but your hard disk partitions will now be ready. Continue with the next section to perform installation.

Installing Your Linux System: the Caldera Network Desktop

Now that you have created your Linux partitions, you are ready to install your Linux system. In step 10, your computer rebooted. As before, introductory information is displayed, and a boot prompt appears at the bottom of the screen. You will be repeating steps 2 through 8 to again start up the installation program. But this time you will skip partitioning since it is already done, and you will continue with the actual installation of the Linux system.

11. Repeat steps 2 through 8 in the previous section.

The list of partitions on your hard disk is again displayed. The partition you created for your Linux main partition should be highlighted. At this point you are selecting the main Linux partition for formatting.

12. Select the Linux main partition and press ENTER to format it.

Wait a moment for the partition to be formatted. You are then asked if you have additional partitions in the root partition. This question allows you to mount other partitions automatically, such as your DOS partition. For beginners, it is best to skip this option for now. Chapter 7 provides a detailed explanation of how to automatically mount a partition.

13. Answer NO to having additional partitions in the root partition.
    Next you are asked to choose an install option. There are three choices, dependent largely on the amount of space you have.

    ■ Basic Caldera Network Desktop: standard default installation; takes 180MB.

    ■ Minimal system: a complete Linux system without window support or many of the standard applications; takes only 62MB.

    ■ Complete system: includes the entire set of packages on the Caldera CD-ROM, including tools for developers; takes about 365MB.

14. Choose the installation you want and press ENTER.

15. Read the notice that appears and press ENTER.
    It takes approximately 30 to 45 minutes for the system to be installed. During this time, a screen will first appear indicating that the Linux partitions are being formatted. Then a screen will appear showing the progress of the installation, indicating the percentage completed. The Linux screen saver will be active, so, after a while your monitor will go dark. To reactivate the screen, just press either the SHIFT, CTRL, or ALT key.
    When the installation process is finished, a screen will prompt you for a hostname for your computer. If your computer does not already have a hostname, you can decide on one now yourself—they are usually from 4 to 20 characters long—and enter it. (If your computer is already connected to a network, it will probably have a hostname. In that case check with your network administrator for the hostname, if you do not know it.)

16. Type in the hostname for your system and press ENTER.
    The next screen will list a series of mouse types.

17. Choose the type for your mouse and press ENTER.
    The next screen prompts you to choose the serial port you are using for your mouse.

18. Select the port and press ENTER.
    The next two screens ask you to choose local time or Greenwich mean time for your system and the proper time zone. Local time would be the more common choice for PC users. DOS systems usually operate according to local time. However, Greenwich mean time (GMT) is the standard for Unix computers and will provide better interoperability with other Unix computers on the Internet, worldwide.

19. Choose the type of time and press ENTER. At the next screen, select a time zone and press ENTER.
    The next screen displays the partition you created for your Linux swap space. By selecting it you will format it. Be sure you select the Linux swap partition. It will have a type of 82. Be careful not to select the larger Linux standard partition.

20. Choose the partition for your Linux swap space and press ENTER.

Network Configuration

You will now be asked to configure your networking.

21. If you are not connected to a network, choose NO and continue with the steps under "Installing and Configuring X-Windows." (If you have a stand-alone PC, you are probably not connected to a network.)

   ■ If you are connected to a network, you will need the information listed in the earlier section, "Network Configuration Information," to configure Linux to interface with that network

   ■ The hostname for your computer

   ■ Your domain name

   ■ The IP address assigned to your computer

   ■ Your network address

   ■ The netmask

   ■ The broadcast address for your network

   ■ The gateway router address (if your network has a gateway)

   ■ The address of any nameservers your network uses

   It is best not to perform network configuration until you have this information. You can easily use your Caldera Desktop tools to enter the configuration information later. However, if you do have the information, you can continue with the network configuration steps that follow.

22. Choose YES to configure your Linux network connection.
   You are asked to confirm that your network device is eth0. This is the default device for an Ethernet setting.

23. Choose the default, or if your network is not Ethernet, choose NO. You are then prompted for your network information.

   a. Enter your four-part IP address.

   b. Enter your netmask. A default is shown that works for most configurations.

   c. Enter the broadcast address for your network.

   d. If you have a router or gateway system on your network, enter the IP address of that router or gateway.

   e. Indicate whether you have a DNS nameserver. If so, enter the IP address of that nameserver.

Your network configuration is now complete. You will create a backup boot disk to start your system in case, for any reason, you cannot boot from your hard disk.

24. Remove the Caldera Install disk from your 3 1/2-inch floppy disk drive and insert a blank PC-formatted floppy disk.

25. At the prompt, press ENTER to create your boot disk. Note that if you had to specify any special hardware configuration information when you first started the installation, you should enter that here also.

Installing and Configuring X-Windows

You now have to configure both your graphics card and monitor to support your X-Windows interface. First you will have to choose the correct X-Windows driver for your graphics card. Linux has many drivers available that are designed to take full advantage of most of the different PC graphics cards. The installation program uses a special program called **Xconfigurator** that allows easy configuration of your entire X-Windows interface. **Xconfigurator** takes you step by step through the configuration process.

26. The first screen lists the different chipsets for various video cards. Choose the one for your card. The next screen will list a series of mouse types. Most standard mice are Microsoft serial. Choose the type for your mouse and press ENTER. If you choose a serial mouse, choose the serial port that your mouse is using. If you indicated a nonserial mouse, then you will not be asked for a serial port. You are then presented with a notice about X-Windows configuration. Press ENTER.

27. You will then be asked if your video card has a programmable chip. Choose NO if you do not know the answer. (If it does have a programmable chip, choose YES.) If you choose YES, you will be shown a list of clock chips from which you will select the one for your video card.

    Now the installation program will attempt to automatically detect the type of video card you have, making use of the information you have supplied so far. There will be a warning saying that the autodetection is not always successful. Be sure that the correct card is specified. Choose OK.

    The autodetection is performed and the chipset detected on your video card is displayed. Choose YES to confirm that the chipset displayed is correct. On the next screen, choose YES to confirm the amount of memory on your card, and on the following screen, choose YES to confirm the clocks on your card.

28. The next screen lists monitors currently supported by X-Windows. If your monitor is not listed, you can choose generic multi-sync or generic-plain and specify any parameters of your monitor that are requested (see your monitor manual). Choose your monitor from the list of monitors, and press ENTER.

A list of possible video modes for that monitor is then displayed. Use the SPACEBAR to mark the ones you want to use by moving to the mode you want and pressing the SPACEBAR. An "x" will appear before the entry. Having selected your video modes, choose OK to continue.

Now the list of video modes that you selected in the previous screen is displayed. Move to the one that you want to use as your default mode, the one automatically used when you start X-Windows. In X-Windows you can change from one mode to the next with the CTRL+ALT++ key combination. Upon selecting your default video mode, choose OK to continue. The next screen asks a question about Sync Green. Answer by selecting NO.

29. The next screen lists special configuration options. In most cases, you will not select any entries on this screen. Choose OK to continue. You are then asked how many buttons your mouse has. Select the number of buttons on your mouse.

On the next screen, choose OK to confirm that X-Windows configuration is complete. Should you have any problems, you can run **Xconfigurator** again from Linux, or use the **xf86Config** configuration program.

Installing LILO

The next screen asks if you want to install LILO, the Linux Loader. LILO will start your Linux system when you boot up. However, if you have more than one operating system on your hard disk, LILO will allow you to choose the one you want to start. LILO will designate one of the operating systems as the default to start if one is not specified. So if you have both DOS and Linux on your hard disk, LILO will let you choose the one you want to use.

30. Choose YES to install LILO.

31. Choose where to install the LILO boot manager.
    If you are unsure where to install LILO, choose the selected default. This will be the entry already highlighted. The default is chosen based on the system's analysis.

32. Choose the image you want to have booted. This is usually vmlinuz.
    You are then asked to enter a label for the Caldera system you just installed. This is the term you use to instruct LILO to start Linux.

33. Enter **linux** or any other label you wish.

34. If you had to specify any special hardware specifications when you started up, you will have to confirm them now.
    You can now make additional entries for other operating systems, such as DOS. You can enter a label for DOS and use it to have LILO start DOS instead of Linux. When making an additional entry, the screen will list all the partitions on your hard drive, DOS as well as Linux.

35. Choose the partition for the other operating system. For example, if you have DOS installed on one of the partitions, choose that partition.

    You are then asked to choose the partition of the operating system that you want to be the default and enter a name for it.

36. Choose Linux or DOS for your default partition and enter a name, such as **dos** for DOS.

    Now you are asked if there are any other operating systems on your hard drive. Most people would have no more than two, DOS and Linux.

37. Choose NO to leave the LILO installation and continue. If you should have a third operating system on your hard disk, choose YES and repeat the previous steps to identify it.

    Once you have finished making entries, your **lilo.conf** file will be displayed. This is the file that actually configures LILO. You will see the entries for Linux and other operating systems, such as DOS.

38. Press ENTER to confirm installation of LILO.

39. When LILO finishes its installation, press ENTER again to continue.

    You have now completed your installation. A notice to that effect will be displayed.

40. Remove the boot floppy in your disk drive and press ENTER to restart your system.

Root Access and a New User

When your system restarts, the login prompt will appear. Here, you will have to enter a password for your root user and create a new account for yourself. First you log in as the root user. This will allow you to create a new user.

41. Type in **root** at the login prompt and press ENTER.

    You will be immediately prompted to enter a password for the root user. Make it simple and easy to remember. You will have to log in as the root user many times to configure your system. System configuration can only be performed by the root user.

42. At the password prompt enter the root user password you decide on.

43. You will be prompted to enter it again. Do so.

    You are then asked to create a new user. Recall that Unix is a multiuser system. You can create as many users as you wish. At this point, you are being asked to create one user, yourself, and provide a user name. Though all systems automatically create a root user through which you perform administrative operations, you should have a personal user account of your own. Your user name must be eight characters or less. It is usually something simple and identifiable, such as your initials or your first name, though it can be any name you choose.

44. Enter in your user name.

45. Enter a password for the user. You will be prompted to enter it again. Do so. You are then logged out of the system. You can now log back in to start using your Linux system. See Chapter 3 about how to log in and out of your system.

When you are ready to shut down the system, hold down the CTRL and ALT keys and press DEL, (CTRL+ALT+DEL). It is very important that you always use CTRL+ALT+DEL to shut down the system; never just turn it off as you do with DOS.

Summary: Installing Linux

Initial installation of your Linux system is performed by an installation manager that takes you step by step through the process. Installation will include X-Windows and network configuration. You can repeat both of these later should you need to. To configure X-Windows again, you first log into Linux as the root user and then issue the command **Xsetup**. You can perform network configuration using tools provided on the Caldera Desktop.

If you want to have Linux share a hard disk with another operating system, such as DOS, you need to designate space for each. This requires partitioning the hard disk, and there are several ways to do that depending on the circumstances.

Chapter Three

Getting Started with Linux

To start using Linux, you will need to know how to access your Linux system and, once you are on the system, how to execute commands and run applications. Accessing Linux involves more than just turning on your computer. Once Linux is running, you have to log into the system using a predetermined login name and password. Once on the system, you can start executing commands and running applications. You can then interact with your Linux system using either a command line interface or a graphical user interface (GUI). The Caldera distribution of Linux provides a GUI called the Caldera Network Desktop, which lets you use windows, menus, and icons to interact with your system.

It is very easy to obtain information quickly about Linux commands and utilities while logged into the system. Linux has several online utilities that provide information and help. You can access an online manual that describes each command, or obtain help that provides more detailed explanations of different Unix features. A complete set of manuals provided by the Linux Documentation Project is on your system and available for you to print or browse through.

This chapter will discuss how to access your Linux system, including logging in and out of user accounts as well as starting the system and shutting it down. Linux commands and utilities are also covered, along with basic operations of the Caldera Desktop. The chapter ends with an explanation of basic system administration operations, such as creating new user accounts and installing software packages.

User Accounts

You never directly access a Linux system. Instead, Linux sets up an interface through which you can interact with it. A Linux system can actually set up and operate several such user interfaces at once, accommodating several users at the same time. In fact, you can have several users working off the same computer running a Linux system. To a particular user, it appears as if he or she is the only one working on the system. It is as if Linux can set up several virtual computers, and each user can then work on his or her own virtual computer. Such virtual computers are really individually managed interfaces whereby each user interacts with the Linux system.

These user interfaces are commonly referred to as accounts. Unix was first used on large minicomputers and mainframes that could accommodate hundreds of users at the same time. Using one of many terminals connected to the computer, users could log into the Unix system using their login names and passwords. All of this activity was managed by system administrators. To gain access to the system, you needed to have a user interface set up for you. This was commonly known as "opening an account." A system administrator would create the account on the Unix system, assigning a login name and password for it. You then used your account to log in and use the system.

Each account is identified by a login name with access protected by a password. Of course, you can access any account if you know its login name and password. On your Linux system you can create several accounts, logging into different ones as you wish.

Other people can access your Linux system, making use of login names and passwords you provide for them. In effect, they will have their own accounts on your system.

Recall that in the previous chapter on installing Linux, you created a login name and password for yourself. These are what you will use to access Linux regularly. When you created the login name and password, you were actually creating a new user account for yourself.

You can, in fact, create other new user accounts using special system administration tools. These tools become available to you when you log in as the root user. The root user is a special user account reserved for system administration tasks such as creating users and installing new software. Basic system administration operations are discussed briefly in this chapter, and in detail in Chapters 7, 19, and 20. For now, you will only need your regular login name and password.

Accessing Your Linux System

To access and make use of your Linux system, you must carefully follow required startup and shutdown procedures. You do not simply turn off and turn on your computer as you do with DOS. You can think of your Linux operating system as operating on three different levels, one running on top of the other. When you start your Linux system, the system loads and runs. It has control of your computer and all its peripherals. However, you still are not able to interact with it. After Linux starts, it will display a login prompt, waiting for a user to come along and log into the system to start using it. To gain access to Linux, you first have to log in.

You can think of logging in and using Linux as the next level. Now you can issue commands instructing Linux to perform tasks. You can use utilities and programs such as editors or compilers, even games. However, after you initially log in, you will be interacting with the system using a simple command line interface. You type in a command and press ENTER to have the system perform actions. As an alternative to the command line interface, you can use an X-Windows graphical user interface. The Caldera distribution of Linux combines X-Windows with its own desktop metaphor to provide a very powerful GUI. In Linux, the command **startx** will start the X-Windows GUI that will then allow you to interact with the system using windows, menus, and icons. You can think of the window manager as the third level. The X-Windows window manager runs on top of your command line interface.

The three levels become important in your shutdown procedure. If you are running the X-Windows GUI and you want to shut down, you first need to exit the X-Windows GUI, returning to the command line interface. Then you log out of your shell and return to the system's login prompt. Logging out does *not* shut down the system. It is still running and has control of your machine. You then need to tell the system to shut itself down by issuing a shutdown command: hold down the CTRL and ALT keys and press the DEL key. The system shuts itself down and reboots. When rebooting starts, only then can you turn off your computer.

You can use some shortcuts to move from one level to another. If you are logged in as a root user, you can have Linux both log out and shut down by issuing a shutdown command (see Chapter 19 for a detailed discussion of the shutdown process). There is also a way to have Linux automatically start your X-Windows window manager when you log in (see Appendix B).

First, here is a review of the basic operations for starting and shutting down Linux, logging in and out, and starting and exiting from your window manager.

Starting and Shutting Down Linux

When you turn on or reset your computer, the Linux Loader, LILO, will first decide what operating system to load and run. You will see the following prompt:

```
LILO:
```

If you wait a moment or press the ENTER key, LILO will load the default operating system, in this case, Linux. Recall that earlier you designated Linux as the default operating system. If you want to run DOS instead, LILO will give you a moment at the prompt to type in the name you gave for DOS, such as **dos**.

As Linux loads, you will see several messages displayed. Then you will be given a login prompt. The system is now running and waiting for a user to log in and use it. You can enter your user name and password to use the system. The login prompt will be preceded by the hostname you gave your system. In this example, the hostname is **pluto**:

```
Caldera Network Desktop - version 1.0
Redhat Linux - release 2.1
Kernel 1.2.13 on a I486
After X11 is configured, login and run 'startx' to start the Desktop
pluto login:
```

When you are finished using Linux, you first log out. Linux will then display the exact same login prompt, waiting for you or another user to log in again.

Should you want to turn off your computer, you must first shut down Linux. If you don't, you could, at best (the usual case), require Linux to perform a lengthy systems check when it starts up again or, at worst (though rarely) corrupt some of your system files, requiring you to reinstall the system.

You shut down your system by holding down both the CTRL and ALT keys and pressing the DEL key, CTRL-ALT-DEL. You will see several messages as Linux shuts itself down. Linux will then reboot your computer. During the reboot process, you can turn off your computer. The following describes all the startup and shutdown procedures. Try them to see how they work.

1. Boot your computer.

2. At the LILO prompt do nothing or press ENTER.

3. After a few messages, the login prompt appears, and you can log into the system and use it.

4. At the login prompt you can also shut down the system. The login prompt will reappear after you log out. To shut down the system press CTRL-ALT-DEL. Shutdown messages appear and the system reboots.

5. You can now turn off your computer.

Logging into and out of Linux: The Command Line

Once you log in, you can enter and execute commands. After you have finished, you need to log out of the system before you shut it down. You do not have to shut down the system if you don't want to. You will be presented with a login prompt, and you could then log in using a different user name, or log in as the root user.

Logging into Linux

Logging into your Linux account involves two steps: entering your user name and then your password. You already know what the login prompt looks like. Type in the login name for your user account. If you make a mistake, you can erase characters with the BACKSPACE key. In the next example, the user enters the user name **richlp**, and is then prompted to enter the password.

```
Caldera Network Desktop - version 1.0
Redhat Linux - release 2.1
Kernel 1.2.13 on a I486
Run 'startx' to start the Desktop
Kernel 1.2.13 on a I486
pluto login: richlp
Password:
```

When you type in your password, it will not appear on the screen. This is to protect your password from being seen by others. If you enter either the login or password incorrectly, the system will respond with the error message "Login incorrect" and will ask for your login name again, starting the login process over. You can then reenter your login name and password.

Once you have entered your user name and password correctly, you are logged into the system. Your command line prompt will be displayed, waiting for you to enter a command. Notice that the command line prompt is a dollar sign, **$**, not a sharp sign, **#**. The **$** is the prompt for regular users, whereas the **#** sign is the prompt solely for the root user. In this version of Linux, your prompt will be preceded by the hostname and the directory you are in. Both will be bounded by a set of brackets.

```
[pluto /home/richlp]$
```

Changing Your Password

Recall that when you first logged in as the root user in the previous chapter, you created a password for your personal user account. Once created, you can change your password for your personal account anytime you wish. You can do this while logged into your personal account. You do not have to be logged in as the root user. This is true of any user on the system. Each user can change his or her own password at any time.

Once logged in, you can change your password with the **passwd** command. First decide what your new password should be. It should be easy to remember and at least seven to eight characters. If you are concerned with security, the password should include upper- and lowercase characters as well as some numbers.

When you have chosen your new password, you are ready to change it. Type in the command **passwd** on the command line and press ENTER. The command prompts you for your current password. After entering that and pressing ENTER, you are then prompted for your new password. After entering the new password, you are asked to reenter it. This is to make sure that you actually entered the password that you intended to enter. Because password characters are not displayed when you type them in, it is easy to make a mistake and press a wrong key.

```
$ passwd
Old password:
New password:
Retype new password:
$
```

If you make a mistake entering the new password, the system displays an error message, and the password will not be changed. The system detects mistakes by matching the two new password entries. If they do not match, an error is detected. If they do match, the entries are considered correct.

The **passwd** command registers your new password with the system immediately. When you log in again you use the new password.

Logging Out

To end your session, you issue the **logout** command. This returns you to the login prompt, and Linux waits for another user to log in.

$ **logout**

Starting and Exiting the Caldera Desktop: X-Windows

Once logged into the system, you have the option of starting the X-Windows GUI and using it to interact with your Linux system. You start the X-Windows GUI by entering **startx** on the command line. X-Windows then loads along with the designated window manager. Your Caldera distribution of Linux will also load a desktop metaphor, providing a file and program manager. The X-Windows GUI used with your Caldera distribution of Linux is referred to as the Caldera Desktop. Once it is loaded, you can use your mouse to access menus, open windows, and start programs. Figure 3-1 shows you what the Caldera desktop looks like.

The features of the Caldera Desktop are just like those in any window environment. You point and click with a mouse to select different icons, menus, and windows. The windows display information, list files, or open applications. As with all window systems, you can have several windows open at the same time. However,

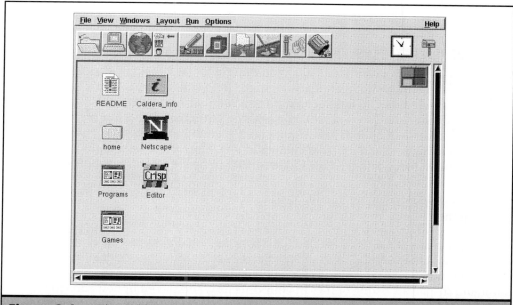

Figure 3-1.   *The Caldera Desktop*

only one of those windows will be active. The active window will have purple-colored borders, while all the other inactive windows will have pale gray borders. Moving your mouse pointer to a particular window makes it the active window, rendering all others inactive. The movement of the mouse pointer alone from one window to another will change the active window. There is no need to click the mouse as in other GUIs, such as Microsoft Windows or Mac OS.

One of the more confusing aspects of this design occurs with the overlapping windows. Making a window the active window does not automatically bring it to the front. An active window could still be partially hidden by other overlapping windows. To bring a window to the front, you need to click on that window's title bar, the bar across the top of the window containing the window's name. Clicking anywhere else on the window would only make it the active window, not bring it to the front.

You exit the Caldera Desktop by choosing the Exit Desktop option in the File menu. Across the top of the screen, there is a menu part with several menu entries, one of which is the File menu. Just click on File at the top of the screen to pull down the File menu. Exit Desktop is the last entry. Once you choose Exit Desktop, Linux will shut down X-Windows and return to the command line interface, presenting you with the **$** prompt. You can restart X-Windows anytime by entering **startx** on the command line.

Keep in mind that if you are using the X-Windows GUI (in this case the Caldera Desktop), and you want to log out, you first need to exit the GUI. Then, once you have returned to the command line, you can log out by entering **logout** or **exit**.

Linux Commands

Linux has a large set of commands that you can use for such tasks as managing and editing files or communicating with other users. Reflecting its Unix roots, Linux commands are designed to be executed using a command line interface. Even with a GUI you will often need to execute commands on a command line. Linux commands make extensive use of options and arguments. Be careful to place your arguments and options in their correct order on the command line. The format for a Linux command is the command name followed by options and then by arguments, as shown here:

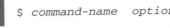

```
$ command-name   options   arguments
```

An option is a one-letter code preceded by a dash that modifies the type of action the command takes. Options and arguments may or may not be optional, depending on the command. For example, the **ls** command can take an option **-s**. The **ls** command displays a listing of files in your directory, and the **-s** option adds the size of each file in blocks. You would enter the command and its option on the command line as:

```
$ ls -s
```

An argument is data that the command may need to execute its task. In many cases it will be a file name. An argument is entered as a word on the command line after any options. For example, to get information about a particular command, you can use the **man** command with the command's name as its argument. The **man** command used with the command name **ls** would be entered on the command line as:

```
$ man ls
```

Online Manual

Your Linux system also has utilities such as editors, mailers, and manuals. Such utilities are separate programs that have their own interfaces with their own sets of commands. One example is the man online manual that allows you to display information about any Linux command or program. To use the online manual, you just type in the command **man** followed by the name of the command you want information on.

man documents on a command may be organized into different levels starting from one. The first level may give basic information about a command, while another level may provide more detailed information. You display a document for a specfic level by including the level number as an argument before the command name. For example, to display the man document for crontab at the eighth level, you enter

```
$ man 8 crontab
```

These other level documents will be listed at the end of whatever level document your man operation brings up. Most commands have just one level that is brought up with just the **man** command without a level argument.

Upon pressing ENTER, you are placed in the man utility, displaying the first page of the **ls** document. man has its own set of commands, usually consisting of single keys. Pressing either the SPACEBAR or the **f** key will advance you to the next page. Pressing the **b** key will move you back a page. When you are finished, you press the **q** key to quit the man utility and return to the command line.

A manual entry is organized into several segments. Five of the more common segments are the synopsis, description, options, files, and cross-references for the command. The synopsis presents the command's syntax, listing its possible options and arguments. The description of the command tells you exactly what it does on the system. Next, the options are listed and explained. The files segment lists the system files used by the command, and the cross-references list other related commands and manual entries. A shortened version of the manual entry for the **ls** command follows.

```
LS(1L)                                                          LS(1L)


NAME
     ls, dir, vdir - list contents of directories

SYNOPSIS
     ls  [-abcdfgiklmnpqrstuxABCFGLNQRSUX1] [-w cols] [-T cols]
     [-I pattern] [--all] [--directory]  [--inode][--kilobytes]
     [--no-group]  [--hide-control-chars] [--reverse] [--size]
     [--width=cols][--sort={none,time,size,extension}]
DESCRIPTION
     This manual page documents the GNU version of ls.  dir and
     vdir are versions of ls with different default output for-
     mats.   These  programs  list each given file or directory
     name.  Directory contents are sorted alphabetically.   For
     ls,  files are by default listed in columns, sorted verti-
     cally, if the standard output  is  a  terminal;  otherwise
     they  are  listed  one  per  line.   For dir, files are by
     default listed in columns, sorted vertically.   For  vdir,
     files are by default listed in long format.
OPTIONS
     -a, --all
            List  all files in directories, including all files
            that start with '.'.
     -b, --escape
            Quote nongraphic characters  in  file  names  using
            alphabetic and octal backslash sequences like those
            used in C.
     -c, --time=ctime, --time=status
            Sort directory contents  according  to  the  files'
            status  change  time  instead  of  the modification
            time.  If the long listing format  is  being  used,
            print the status change time instead of the modifi-
            cation time.
     -d, --directory
            List directories  like  other  files,  rather  than
```

```
            listing their contents.
    -f      Do  not sort directory contents; list them in what-
            ever order they are stored on the disk.   The  same
            as enabling -a and -U and disabling -l, -s, and -t.
    --full-time
            List times in full, rather than using the  standard
FSF                      GNU File Utilities                      1
```

The man utility has several other helpful features, such as a search capability. You activate a search by pressing either the slash, **/**, or question mark, **?**. A **/** will search forward and the **?** backward. Upon pressing the **/**, a line will open at the bottom of your screen, and you then enter a word to search for. Press ENTER to activate the search. The search is actually a pattern search, so you can enter part of a word, or almost any set of characters for that matter. You can repeat the same search by pressing the **n** key. You don't have to reenter the pattern.

The **whatis** and **apropos** commands will search a database of man titles and display any titles they find along with a short description of each. **whatis** will search man titles by whole words. For example, if you wanted to see all the manual entries with the letter *x* in them, you would use the following command (this will give you manual entries dealing with X-Windows topics).

```
$ whatis x
X (3)                  - a portable, network-transparent window system
X Consortium (3)       - X Consortium information
X Standards (3)        - X Consortium Standards
X security (3)         - X display access control
X (3)                  - a portable, network-transparent window system
X Consortium (3)       - X Consortium information
X Standards (3)        - X Consortium Standards
X security (3)         - X display access control
(END)
$
```

Both the **whatis** and **apropos** commands place you in a man type of interface. If the results take up more than one page, you can use the **f** and **b** keys to move forward or backward. You can also perform pattern searches with the **/** and **?** keys. To quit, you press the **q** key. Only then will you return to the command line.

The **apropos** command performs the same task as the **whatis** command, but it searches by pattern instead of whole words. For example, the command **apropos x** will produce a lengthy result of several pages, listing all the man entries beginning with *x*, such as **xwpe** and **xloadimage**. In the next example, the user lists all the manual entries beginning with the pattern **ls**. This will include the **ls** command as well as many others, such as **lseek** or **lsearch**.

```
$ apropos ls
ls, dir, vdir (1)      - list contents of directories
lsattr (1)             - list file attributes on a Linux second
extended file system
lsearch (n)            - See if a list contains a particular element
lseek (2)              - reposition read/write file offset
lsort (n)              - Sort the elements of a list
lsattr (1)             - list file attributes on a Linux second
extended file system
lsearch (n)            - See if a list contains a particular element
lseek (2)              - reposition read/write file offset
lsort (n)              - Sort the elements of a list
(END)
$
```

You can also use the Helptool utility to search for keywords in Linux manual documents. Helptool can search any information page or text file. Just enter **helptool**, and then choose from the list of topics displayed.

Online Documentation

The Caldera information icon on your desktop opens a Web page with Netscape that allows you to access extensive documentation on both your own system and on the Caldera and Redhat Web sites. To use the Caldera and Redhat Web sites, you first have to be connected to the Internet. However, your CD-ROM and your system contain extensive documentation showing you how to use the desktop and taking you through a detailed explanation of Linux applications, including the Vi editor and shell operations.

You can also access HOW-TO text files in the **/usr/doc/HOWTO** directory. The **/user/doc** directory contains the online documentation for many Linux applications. The **/doc** directory on your Caldera CD-ROM also contains extensive documentation. In addition, **/doc/HOWTO/HTML** holds documentation such as information about JAVA, where to find it, and how to install it.

Installing Software Packages

You are your own system administrator for your Linux system. There are certain administrative tasks you may have to perform, such as creating new users or installing new software. You perform these within a special system administration account called the root. To gain access to this account, you log in as the root user. As the root user you will have complete control over your system; you can change it in almost any way you want. You can install software packages, create new accounts, add new devices or disks to your system, or configure X-Windows or your network interfaces. Many standard operations are very easy to perform in the Caldera Desktop, though all can be done on the standard command line. These tasks are discussed in detail in Chapters 7, 19, and 20. Here you will learn how to install software packages. The root user is sometimes called the *superuser*. If you are not careful, you could easily corrupt your system, requiring a reinstallation. If you use the available administrative utilities to make changes, however, you will be all right.

Recall that during installation you specified a password for the root user. It is this password that you will use to log in as the root user. If other people are using your Linux system, be careful to keep your root password secret. Anyone logging in as the root user has superuser capabilities and has the power to destroy any or all of your Linux system.

To log in as the root user, type in **root** at the login prompt. (If you are already logged into your regular user account, you need to log out first.) Then you enter your password for the root user.

```
Caldera Network Desktop - version 1.0
Redhat Linux - release 2.1
Kernel 1.2.13 on a I486
After X11 is configured, login and run 'startx' to start the
Desktop
richlp login: root
Password:
```

Once logged in, you will be given the root user prompt, the **#** symbol. Note how this differs from the user prompt, **$**. At the root user prompt, enter the **startx** command to start the Caldera Desktop.

```
# startx
```

On the desktop for the root user you will have a different set of icons than those displayed for a regular user. Several utilities, such as glint and usercfg, are special system administration utilities used to perform tasks such as creating new users and installing software.

Now that you know how to start Linux and access the root user, you can install any other software packages you may want. Installing software is an administrative function performed by the root user. Unless you chose the Complete Install option during your installation, only a few of the many applications and utilities available for users on Linux were installed on your system. Appendix C contains a full listing of all the software packages available on your Caldera CD-ROM.

There are several methods of installing software. You can use the graphical interface called glint from your desktop. This is the easiest and most effective way to install several packages. You can also use the Redhat Package Manager (RPM), which is invoked by the **rpm** command from your command line. (See Table 3-1 at the end of the chapter.) However, this is a more complex operation. Finally, you can download software from online sources and then use **rpm** to install them. This operation is described briefly here, and a detailed explanation is provided in Chapter 7.

Unlike other distributions of Linux, the Redhat distribution, used by the Caldera Network Desktop, organizes Linux software into different software packages. A software package operates like its own installation program for a software application. A Linux software application will often consist of several files that need to be installed in different directories. The program itself will most likely be placed in a directory called **/usr/bin**, online manual files will go in another directory, and source code files in yet another. In addition, the installation may require modification of certain configuration files on your system. The software packages on your Caldera CD-ROM will perform all these tasks for you. Also, if you should later decide that you don't want a specific application, you can uninstall packages to remove all the files and configuration information from your system for you.

Linux Installation Manager: glint

The glint utility's user-friendly interface makes installing software easy: simply point and click with your mouse. glint automatically copies the software to its appropriate directory, including any other special configuration files there may be. Uninstalling is just as simple. glint can locate all the files that make up a software package and remove them. The glint icon is only displayed on the root user desktop.

To use glint, first log in as the root user, not as your personal user name. For the password, be sure to use the root password that you created when you first logged in as the root user.

Once logged in, you will see the **#** symbol. At the root user prompt, enter **startx** to start the Caldera Desktop.

The Caldera Desktop will appear, and several icons will be displayed within the main window. One of the icons, labeled "glint," will appear as shown here:

With your mouse, double-click on that icon to start the glint utility. The glint window will be displayed, as shown in Figure 3-2. glint works like a file manager window. It displays application and folder icons. Applications of the same category will be located within the same folder. For example, the Emacs editor will be placed in a folder called Editors, which will in turn be placed in a folder called Applications.

The folders and icons of software packages that you see are the ones already installed on your system (see Figure 3-2). You can use this window to see which software packages you already have and to remove an installed package. Just locate its icon within the appropriate folder, click on it to select it, and then click on the Uninstall button to the right. When you select a package, its icon will have a red border. You can select several icons by clicking on them, and then uninstall them all at once. To deselect an icon you have already selected, just click on it again. You will see the red border disappear.

When you open and display the contents of a folder, you will notice that one of the icons has the name "Back" with a large black arrow. This is the icon you click on to return to the upper folder that you just came from. For example, if you open the Applications folder by double-clicking on it, the icons for that folder, such as the Games folder, will be displayed along with the Back icon. Clicking on the Games folder opens and displays the icons for the games packages along with a Back icon. To return to the Applications folder, click on the Back icon. Once in the Applications

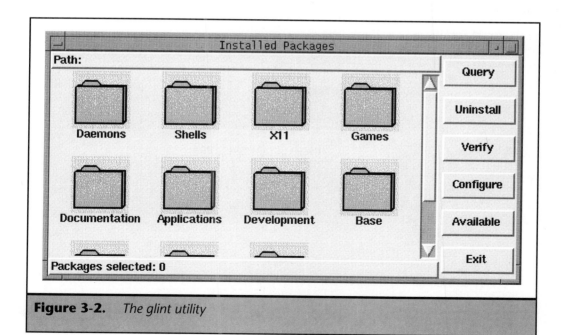

Figure 3-2.   *The glint utility*

folder, you can click on its Back icon to return to the main folder. By clicking on folders and their Back icons, you can move back and forth through the different collections of software packages.

To install a new software package, first click on the Available button on the right-hand side of the glint window. This opens up a new glint window labeled "Available," which displays folders and icons of uninstalled packages available on your Caldera CD-ROM (see Figure 3-3). The packages are collected within their appropriate folders. Just click on their folders to display them. To install a package, select it by clicking on its icon, and then click on the Install button on the right side of glint's Available window. You can select several packages by clicking on them, and then install them all at once by clicking on the Install button. If you select a package and decide not to install it, you can deselect it by again clicking on its icon. Selected packages will show a red border around their icons. Once you have installed a package, its icon will disappear from the Available window, and it will show up in the Installed window.

To obtain a brief description of any package, select its icon and then click on the Info button in the glint window.

If you try to open the Available window and receive an error message to the effect that there are no RPMS packages to install (and you did not choose the Complete Install option), most likely your Caldera CD-ROM is not accessible. The simplest way to make it accessible is to shut down your system completely, put your Caldera

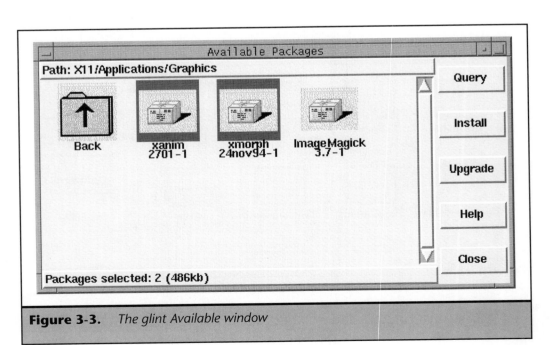

Figure 3-3. *The glint Available window*

Network Desktop CD-ROM in your CD-ROM drive, and then restart Linux. Alternatively, you can issue the following commands that performs an operation called mounting a file system, which makes a disc in your CD-ROM drive accessible to the Linux system.

```
$ cd /mnt
$ mount cdrom
$ cd
```

The **cd /mnt** command moves you to a special directory called **/mnt**. The **mount cdrom** command attaches your CD-ROM to the Linux file system. The last command, **cd**, returns you to what is called your home directory, which for the root is the **root** directory. Mounting file systems is discussed in detail in Chapter 7.

Command Line Installation: Redhat Package Manager

If you do not have access to the Caldera Desktop, or would prefer to work from the command line interface, you can use the **rpm** command to manage and install software packages. **rpm** stands for the Redhat Package Manager. It manages the installation, removal, and verification of software packages. In fact, glint is a front end to the **rpm** operation. However, glint performs certain safety and consistency checks that **rpm** does not.

Your Caldera Network Desktop maintains a package-based software installation system. Special files provide records detailing what packages have been installed, allowing them to be uninstalled or verified. Each software package is actually an RPM package, consisting of an archive of software files and information about how to install those files. Each archive resides as a single file with a name that ends with **-rpm**, indicating that it is a software package that can be installed by the **rpm** command.

You can use **rpm** to install or uninstall different packages. **rpm** uses a set of options to determine what action to take. The **-i** option will install the specified software package. With a **-u** option, **rpm** will uninstall the package. A **q** placed before an **i** (**-qi**) will query the system to see if a software package is already installed. The **--h** option provides a complete list of **rpm** options. The syntax for the **rpm** command is as follows (*rpm-package-name* is the name of the software package that you want to install).

```
rpm options rpm-package-name
```

The software package name is usually very lengthy, including information about version and release date in its name. All end with **-rpm**. To install a software package from your Caldera CD-ROM, it is easier to move first to the **RPMS** directory and then install the package you want. If you cannot change to that directory, your CD-ROM may not be mounted on your file system. If so, refer to the previous section on how to mount your CD-ROM. To change to the **RPMS** directory, enter the command:

```
$ cd /mnt/cdrom/Packages/RPMS
```

An **ls** command will list all the software packages. If you know how the name of a package begins, you should include that with the **ls** command and an attached *. The list of packages is extensive and will not all fit on one screen. The following command lists all the X-Windows packages.

```
$ ls x*
```

In the next example, the user installs the Emacs editor using the **rpm** command. Notice that the full file name is entered.

```
$ rpm  -i emacs-19.29-5.i386.rpm
```

The **RPMS** directory holds all the packages that you can use for your Linux system. No distinction is made between installed and uninstalled packages. You have to know the one you want to install and whether or not it is already installed. To find out if a package is already installed, use the **-qi** option with **rpm**. The **-q** stands for query. In the next example, the user checks to see if the Emacs editor is already installed on the system. Notice that the full file name of the **rpm** archive is not needed. If installed, your system has already registered the name of the package and where it is located.

```
$ rpm -qi emacs
```

To remove a software package from your system, first use **rpm -qi** to make sure it is actually installed. Then use the **-u** option to uninstall it. As with the **-qi** option, you do not have to use the full name of the installed file. You only need the name of the application. In the next example, the user removes the game Doom from the system.

```
$ rpm  -u  doom
```

A complete description of **rpm** and its capabilities is provided in the online manual.

```
$ man rpm
```

Installing Software from Online Sources

Installing software from online sources is complicated by the fact that you first have to access remote sites. To do this, you need to know where the software is located and then use either Netscape or the ftp utility to download the package. The software is usually compressed, so, once downloaded, you use the **gunzip** command to decompress it. Some packages may not use an RPM format. Instead, they may be archived. Others may be both archived and have the RPM format. To open archived files, you use the **tar** command. If you download a package that has an **rpm** at the end of its name, you must use the **rpm** command to install it.

The next example uses ftp to connect to the **sunsite.unc.edu** Linux ftp site. The user enters **anonymous** for the login ID and an Internet address for the password. The download mode is set to binary by entering the keyword **binary**. With the **cd** command, the user changes to the **/pub/Linux** directory where Linux software is located, then changes to the **/Packages** directory to get the Emacs software package. The **get** command then downloads the packages. The **close** command cuts the connection, and **quit** leaves the ftp utility. If the ftp site is too busy, it will usually display a list of other sites from which you can access the same software.

```
$ ftp sunsite.unc.edu
login: anonymous
password:
ftp> binary
ftp> cd  /pub/Linux
ftp> cd  /Packages
ftp> get emacs-19.29-5.i386.rpm
ftp> close
ftp> quit
$
```

Alternatively, you could use Netscape to access, browse through, and download software without having to bother with all the ftp commands. Be sure to precede an ftp site name with the term **ftp://** instead of the usual **http://**. For **sunsite** you would enter **ftp://sunsite.unc.edu**. Once you have selected the software you want, you double-click on it to download it.

Once downloaded, any file that ends with a **.Z** or **.gz** is a compressed file that has to be decompressed. You would use the **gunzip** command followed by the name of the file.

```
$ gunzip emacs-19.29-5.i386.rpm.tar.gz
```

If the file then ends with **.tar**, it is an archived file that has to be opened. You use the **tar** command with the **xvf** option and the file name (no dash before the **xvf**).

```
$ tar xvf emacs-19.29-5.i386.rpm.tar
```

If the file ends with **rpm**, you have to use the **rpm -i** command to install it.

```
$ rpm   -i emacs-19.29-5.i386.rpm
```

Downloaded software will usually include readme files or other documentation. Be sure to consult them.

Monitor and Network Configuration

With the Network Configuration utility you can change and add to your network configuration. If you are connected to a network and did not configure it during installation, you can use this utility to perform that configuration. The Network Configuration utility is represented by the netcfg icon located on the root user desktop. To start the utility, double-click the icon; a small window opens in which you can perform your network configuration. See Chapter 20 for a detailed discussion of the netcfg utility.

If you were not able to start your Caldera Network Desktop, you may not have been able to install the correct graphics driver for your system. Though the Accelerated X program provides drivers for most graphics cards, there are some that it cannot support. See Appendix B for a detailed listing.

As an alternative to Accelerated X, you can use the Xfree86 graphics drivers. These are available on your Caldera CD-ROM. You will have to first install the software package for the Xfree86 graphics driver for your system. Then you have to use a configuration program such as Xconfigurator or xf86config to configure the graphics driver. Appendix B provides a listing of the Xfree86 graphics driver with instructions on how to install them. You can also obtain further information about them form the Caldera Web page.

Summary: Getting Started with Linux

To use your Linux system you enter your login name at the login prompt and then your password at the password prompt. Once logged in, you are presented with a command line interface on which you can type commands. Commands can take options and arguments. To execute a command, you type the command with any options and arguments on the command line and then press ENTER. When you are finished using the system, you log out with the **logout** command. The login prompt reappears. If you want to turn off your computer, you first have to shut down the Linux system. You do this by pressing CTRL-ALT-DEL.

Be sure to keep all the necessary startup and shutdown steps in mind when accessing your Linux system. To access the desktop you need to perform three tasks. First you start your Linux system. Once running, you log into the system. You then issue the command **startx** to start the Caldera Network Desktop. To shut down the system, you exit the desktop, then log out, and then shut down the system with CTRL-ALT-DEL.

You can also use a window manager to interact with your system using menus, windows, and icons. In the Caldera distribution of Linux, the **startx** command starts the Caldera Desktop, which uses the fvwm window manager and its own file and program managers. You exit the desktop by selecting Exit Desktop from the File menu.

All the steps you need to perform for accessing Linux are listed here. Keep in mind the login and GUI startup procedures as well as the GUI exit, logout, and shutdown procedures.

1. Boot the computer.

2. At the LILO prompt press ENTER.

   ```
   LILO:
   ```

3. At the login prompt enter your user name, and then at the password prompt enter your password.

   ```
   login: richlp
   Password:
   ```

4. Once logged in, you are presented with the command line prompt, **$**.

   ```
   $
   ```

5. To start the X-Windows GUI you enter the command **startx** at the shell prompt:

   ```
   $ startx
   ```

This loads the X-Windows GUI that includes X-Windows, the manager, and the Caldera Desktop metaphor. They are collectively referred to as the Caldera Desktop.

6. To exit the X-Windows GUI, select Exit Desktop from the File menu. This returns you to the command line prompt.

```
$
```

7. To log out enter either **exit** or **logout** on the command line and press ENTER.

```
$ logout
```

8. This returns you to the login prompt. You can then log in again, log into another account with another user name, or log in as the root.

```
login:
```

9. Now you can shut down Linux by holding down the CTRL and ALT keys and pressing the DEL key: CTRL-ALT-DEL.

10. When the screen goes blank, your computer will start to reboot. At this point you can turn off your computer.

You may need to perform certain system administration tasks, such as creating new user accounts and installing software. You perform such tasks as the root user. You log in as the root user, using the root password. You can then start the desktop and use system administration utilities to perform these tasks. For example, usercfg will allow you to create and remove users; netcfg will allow you to configure your network connections.

The Caldera distribution of Linux organizes software into packages that you can easily install or uninstall using the glint utility or the **rpm** command. The glint utility is located on the desktop, and you can use **rpm** tools to perform the same actions on the command line.

Mode of Operation	Effect
rpm **–i***options package-file*	Installs a package; the complete name of the package file is required
rpm **–u***options package-name*	Uninstalls a package; you only need the name of the package, often one word
rpm **–q***options*	Queries a package; an option can be a package name or a further option and package name, or an option applied to all packages
rpm **–bO***options package-specifications*	Builds your own **rpm** package
rpm **–verify***options*	Verifies that a package is correctly installed; uses same options as query; you can use **–V** or **–y** in place of **–verify**
Install Options (to be used with –i)	
–U	Upgrade; same as install, but any previous version is removed
–p	Displays percentage of package during installation
–t	Tests installation; does not install, just checks for conflicts
–f	Forces installation despite conflicts
–root*directory-path*	Installs at *directory*
Uninstall Options (to be used with –u)	
–t	Tests uninstall; does not remove, just checks for what will be removed; use with **–v**

Table 3-1. *Redhat Package Manager (RPM)*

Mode of Operation	Effect
Query Options (to be used with -q)	
package-name	Queries package
-a	Queries all packages
-f *filename*	Queries package that owns *filename*
-F	Queries package that owns *filename*; *filename* is read from standard input
-p *package-name*	Queries an uninstalled package
-i	Displays all package information
-l	Lists files in package
-d	Lists only documentation files in package
-c	Lists only configuration files in package
-t	Tests uninstall; does not remove, just checks for what will be removed; use with **-v**
General Options (to be used with any option)	
-v	Verbose; displays descriptions of all actions taken
-quit	Displays only error messages
-version	Displays **rpm** version number
-root*directory*	Uses directory as top-level directory for all operations (instead of root)
Other Sources of Information	
RPM-HOWTO on **www.redhat.com**	More detailed information, particularly on how to build your own **rpm** packages
`man rpm`	Detailed list of options

Table 3-1. *Redhat Package Manager (RPM) (continued)*

Chapter Four

The Caldera Desktop

The Caldera Network Desktop is a complete user interface, providing you with windows, menus, and icons with which you can manage your files, run programs, and configure your system. The Caldera Desktop provides easy access to Internet tools as well as the many Linux software programs available. You are granted one free year of use of the Caldera Network Desktop included on the CD-ROM with this book. You will be able to take full advantage of all Caldera Network Desktop features, such as toolbars, configuration utilities, file management windows, and automatic history lists. When you start the Caldera Desktop, you will notice an icon bar displayed across the top. It initially contains icons that represent common Linux operations such as opening a terminal window or locating files. This is a configurable icon bar. You can add your own icons for specific operations. The desktop also has a versatile file manager. For each directory, you can open a window that shows all the files in that directory displayed as icons. You can then run applications by double-clicking on their icons, or you can move the icons out of the file manager window and onto the desktop for easier access. This chapter examines all of these features in more detail.

Starting and Exiting the Caldera Desktop

As noted in the previous chapter, you start the Caldera Desktop by entering **startx** on the command line. The Caldera Desktop then loads, providing a window, file, and program managers. You can use your mouse to access menus, open windows, and start programs.

You exit the desktop by choosing the Exit Desktop option in the File menu. Like most windows applications, the desktop has a list of menus across the top of the screen. Just click on File to pull down the menu. Exit Desktop is the last entry.

Once you choose Exit Desktop, Linux will shut down the Caldera Desktop and return to the command line interface, presenting you with the **$** prompt. You can restart the Caldera Desktop anytime you want by entering **startx** on the command line.

The Desktop

The desktop is a window on which you can place icons. Scroll bars on the right side and bottom let you move across those icons should there be too many to fit on your screen (see Figure 4-1). You will notice that several icons are already on your desktop window. These are for some commonly used Linux programs and utilities. For example, one icon represents the CRiSPlite editor and another the mail utility. You can remove any of these icons and add others as you wish.

The icon bar across the top of the desktop contains frequently used Linux operations, such as the file manager or terminal window. You can add icons of your own to the icon bar, or remove any of the ones already there. To the right of the icon bar are your clock and an icon for obtaining help. The desktop help feature will display balloon help text for any part of the desktop you point to.

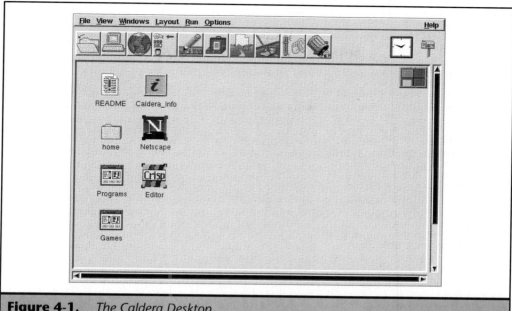

Figure 4-1. *The Caldera Desktop*

Above the icon bar is a standard menu bar. The different entries cover operations to configure the desktop or issue Linux commands. You have already seen the Exit Desktop entry in the File menu. Notice the underlined letter in each menu name. This represents a keyboard shortcut that you can use to execute a command. To open the File menu, for example, you can press **f** instead of moving your mouse up to the menu bar to click on the File entry.

You select different windows, menus, and icons on your screen using a mouse. When you move the mouse, a corresponding arrow moves on your screen. The buttons on top of the mouse are used to select objects displayed on the screen. If you move the arrow to an icon and then click your left mouse button, the icon becomes highlighted. The icon is now selected and you can perform operations on it. Double-clicking on the left mouse button will run the application associated with the icon, opening a new window for it.

The right mouse button opens a File drop-down menu. Instead of moving the mouse up to the menu bar, you can click on the right mouse button to open the File menu on your screen at that position. You can then select an option, such as Exit Desktop.

You will notice a small square in the upper-right corner of your Caldera Desktop. The square is further divided into four smaller squares. You can think of each square as a separate extension of your desktop. It's as if you have a very large desk, only part of which is shown on the screen. The active part of the desk is highlighted, usually in pink. By moving this highlighted portion you can move to different parts of the desk. You can also click on one of the four squares to move to that part of your desk. You could place different windows in different parts of your desk and then move to that part when you want to use them. This way, everything you want on your desktop does not have to be displayed on your screen at once, cluttering it up. If you are working on the desktop and everything suddenly disappears, it may be that you accidentally clicked on one of the other squares. Just click on the upper-left square again to return to your original display. You should see your original windows reappear. Icons that you have placed on your desktop will appear in the same position in every section. That way you always have access to an icon on the desktop.

Depending upon how you installed your graphics driver, you may find that the area displayed on your screen may be only part of the desktop. Moving your mouse pointer to the edge of your screen moves the screen over the hidden portions of the desktop.

Windows and Icons

You run applications, display information, or list files in windows. A window is made up of several basic components. The outer border contains resize controls. There are also several buttons with which you can control the size of a window or close the window. Inside the outer border are the main components of the window: the title bar, which displays the name of the window, the menu, through which you can issue commands, and the window pane, which displays the contents of a window.

The Caldera Desktop window allows you to change its shape and size using buttons and resize areas. The resize areas are the corner borders of the window. Click and hold on a resize area and move the mouse to make the window larger or smaller in both height and width.

You can also make the window fill the whole screen by clicking on the maximize button—the small square within a square—in the upper-right corner of the window. To reduce the window to its original size, just click on the maximize button again.

If you want to reduce the window to an icon, click on the minimize button. It's the small square with a dot in the center next to the maximize button. Once you have reduced the window to an icon, you can reopen it later by double-clicking on that icon.

You can move any window around the desktop by selecting either its title bar or border (not a corner). Move your mouse pointer to the window's title bar; then click and hold on it while you move your mouse pointer. You will see the window move. When you have reached the position you want, release the mouse button. Just clicking on the title bar will move the window to the front of any overlapping windows. The same process holds true for borders. Move the mouse pointer to the edge of the window until you see the pointer transform into a small straight line. Then click and hold on that edge, and move the mouse pointer. You will see the entire window move.

You execute commands in a window using menus and icons. If you are running an application such as an editor, the contents of the window will be data that the menus operate on. If you are using the file manager, then the contents will be icons representing files and directories. Some windows, such as terminal windows, will not have menus.

You can have several windows open at the same time. However, only one of those windows will be active. The active window will have purple borders, and the inactive windows will have pale gray borders. Moving your mouse pointer to a particular window makes it the active window, rendering all others inactive. You don't need to click the mouse, as you do in other GUIs such as Microsoft Windows or Mac OS.

The overlapping windows sometimes cause confusion. Making a window the active window does not automatically bring it to the front. An active window could still be partially hidden by other overlapping windows. To bring a window to the front, you need to click on that window's title bar. Clicking anywhere else on the window would only make it the active window, not bring it to the front.

Icons represent either applications you can run or data files for those applications. They appear on your desktop window and within file manager windows, with the name of the file or application below them. To run an application, you just double-click on its icon.

The Terminal Window: The Unix Command Line

In the Caldera Desktop, you can open the terminal window, which will provide you with a standard command line interface. To open a terminal window, double-click on the Terminal icon located on the icon bar at the top left of your desktop. It looks like this:

Once opened, the window will display a shell prompt, usually the **$**, and you can enter Linux commands just as you would on the command line. You will see any results of your commands displayed within the terminal window, followed by a shell prompt indicating the beginning of the command line. Keep in mind that your terminal window needs to be your active window for you to use its command line. If it is not the active window, you will need to move the mouse pointer to it to make it active.

When you are finished using the terminal window, you can close it by typing the command **exit** on the command line. Each terminal window is its own shell, and **exit** is the command to end a shell. Shells are discussed in detail in Chapter 5.

Figure 4-2 shows the terminal window. The user has entered several commands, and the output is displayed in the window. As you reach the bottom of the window, the text displayed will scroll up, line by line, just as a normal terminal screen would.

You can, of course, use the window controls to make the terminal window larger or smaller. You can even minimize it to an icon and later reopen it.

Desktop Multitasking

One of the most useful features of your Caldera Network Desktop is its ability to open several operations at the same time, each with its own window. Notice that in the command line interface you can only work on one task at a time (there is an exception discussed later in the book dealing with what are called background processes). You issue a command and after it executes, you can execute another. On the desktop you can have several different applications running at once. Moving your mouse pointer from one window to another effectively moves you from one application to another. This feature of your desktop illustrates one of the most useful capabilities of Linux, concurrency. You can have several processes operating at the same time. In your desktop, you can have several applications running at the same time, each with its own window.

This feature can be easily illustrated using terminal windows. You can have several terminal windows open at the same time, each with its own command line. Recall that to open a terminal window you double-click on the Terminal icon in the icon bar. To open a second terminal window, you double-click on the Terminal icon again. To open yet another terminal window, just double-click on the icon yet again, and so on. Each

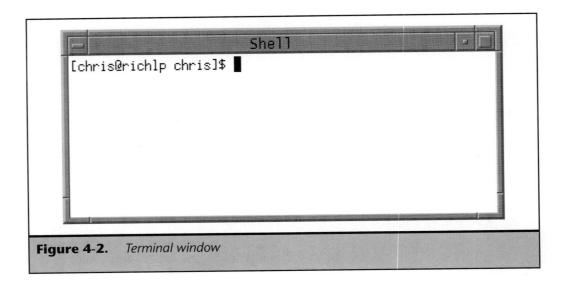

Figure 4-2. *Terminal window*

terminal window will have its own command line, and moving your mouse pointer from one window to another moves you from one command line to another. You can type in a command in the active window and execute it. You can then move to another terminal window and type in another command. Each terminal window operates independently of the other. If you issue a command that takes a while to execute, and you move to another window, you will notice that the command in the window you just left is still executing.

Directory Windows

Instead of a command line on which you enter commands and file name arguments, the directory windows on the Caldera Network Desktop allow you to use menus, icons, and windows to manage files and directories. In the desktop, a directory is displayed as a window. Instead of using an **ls** command to display the files in your directory, the files are already displayed for you as icons. The directories are represented by icons that look like folders. The idea is that directories operate like folders that hold documents—that is to say, files. You open a directory and examine the files in it, just as you would open a folder and examine its contents.

Through the directory window you interact with the system, performing operations on the files in the window, such as copying, moving, and deleting. Operations you perform through the window are interpreted and sent to your Linux system for execution. You can also create new directories and move from one directory to another by opening other directory windows.

All directory windows have the same set of menus for performing file and directory operations: File, View, Create, Sort, Select, Run, and Color. The File menu allows you to perform basic file operations. The View menu allows you to display your files in different ways, either as icons, names, or names with their full set of file information. The Create menu allows you to create new directories. The Sort menu lets you sort your files either by name, size, type, or any other file feature. With the Select menu, you can select a set of files by pattern matches on file names, or just select all the files in the directory. The Run menu lets you open a command line for entering commands, and the Color menu lets you color code your file names. The commands provided in these menus are listed in Table 4-1.

To open a directory window you move your mouse pointer to the folder icon located on the icon bar, as shown here:

When you double-click on this icon, the Open Directory window appears, in which you can specify the name of the directory you want to open. A box labeled "Directory:" is at the top of the window. In the box the last directory that you accessed will be highlighted. To access your home directory, leave this box empty. Press the DEL or BACKSPACE key to erase the highlighted path name already there. Then just click on the OK button at the bottom of the window. A file manager window will then open for your home directory, displaying all the files and directories in it (see Figure 4-3).

You can use the Open Directory window to access any directory you wish. All you need to do is enter the path name of that directory in the Directory box. As an aid to entering path names, the Open Directory window includes a History box that lists the path names of all the previous directories you have accessed. If you see one listed that you want to access, just click on it and its path name appears in the "Directory:" box.

There are several different ways that you can view the icons in the directory window. By default, the directory window is divided into a top and bottom pane. The folder icons for the directories appear in the top pane, and in the bottom the file icons show different pictures depending on the application they are used for. To the right of each pane is a scroll bar that you can use to scroll through the display of either your directories or the files in a particular directory. You can also change the size of each pane. Between the two panes, next to their scroll bars, is a small bar that you can use to make one pane larger and the other smaller. Moving the bar up makes the directory pane smaller while increasing the size of the file pane. Moving down does the opposite.

This two-pane organization is only one way of viewing a directory window. In the View menu you can select other alternatives, such as the Positionable option that uses

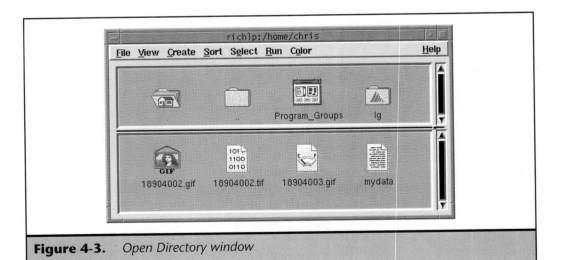

Figure 4-3.   *Open Directory window*

only one pane to mix both directories and files, much like the Macintosh or Windows operating system. The Name option will simply display your files and directories as a list of names with miniature icons to the left of each. The Icon option returns you to the icon display, and deselecting the Positionable option will return you to the default two-pane organization for directories and files. The Wide option will display your files and directories as a list of names with file information for each, such as its size, file type, owner, and the time of the last update (see Figure 4-4). You can sort the list by any field, listing them in order by size or date, or even file type.

You perform an operation on a file by first selecting its icon in the directory window and then choosing an option from the directory window menus. If you need to perform an operation on several files at once, you can select them all by moving the icon to a corner of the grouped icons and, while holding down your mouse button, moving your mouse pointer diagonally across them.

Once selected, you can perform an operation on the icon or icons. For example, to copy a file, select the file's icon and then choose the Copy option in the File menu. A special window will open, prompting you for the name of the copy. To erase a file, select the file's icon and then choose the Remove option in the File menu. The file will be deleted and its icon removed from the directory window. Figure 4-5 shows the File menu.

One of the basic operations on an icon is the Open operation. You can open an icon either by moving the mouse to it and double-clicking, or by clicking on the icon and then selecting the Open option in the File menu. Depending on whether the icon is a file, directory, or application, different actions take place. If you open an application, the application's window opens and the application begins execution. On the other hand, if you open a directory, another directory window opens up, displaying the

Figure 4-4.   *The Wide view of the file manager window and the View menu*

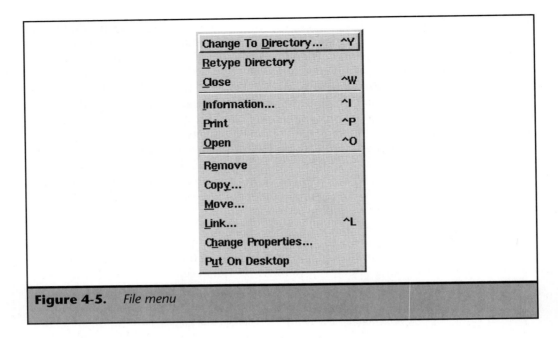

Figure 4-5. *File menu*

icons in that directory. If, however, you open a file icon, the application associated with that file is executed using that file. For example, if the **mydata** file is a CRiSPlite editor data file, then when you double-click on the file's icon, the CRiSPlite editor application window opens with the **mydata** file as the text to be edited.

Creating and Opening Directories

You can create your own directories in a directory window just as, in the command line interface, you can use **mkdir** to create directories. To create a directory you first choose the Directory option in the Create menu. This creates a new directory icon with the default name Dir1 highlighted below it, as shown here:

Simply type in the name you want for the new directory. The new name will replace Dir1. Once you have finished typing the new name, you can deselect it by clicking anywhere else on the window.

A directory will reside as an icon in a window until you open its own window. There are two ways of opening a directory window. You can either open a separate window for the directory, or you can change the current window to that directory. To change the window to display a new directory, you simply double-click on the icon for that directory. The current window display will be replaced by the directories and files of the selected directory. The directory's name will appear on the window's title bar. To achieve the same effect, you can choose the Change to Directory option in the File menu. This opens an Open Directory window. You enter the name of the directory you want in the box labeled "Open". Upon clicking the OK button, the new directory is displayed in the window. In effect, opening a directory is the same as changing your working directory with the **cd** command. Your menu options will then operate on the files and icons in this newly displayed directory.

Alternatively, you can open a new window for a directory. You could have a separate window open for each directory, if you wish. To open a separate window, first select the directory icon by clicking on it, and then choose the Open option in the File menu. A new window displaying that directory's icons will open. This window will have its own menus through which you can issue commands for files in that directory. This differs from your command line interface which limits you to working from one directory at a time. With directory windows you can have several directories open at the same time, moving from one to the other as you work.

You will notice that among the directory icons displayed in your file manager window is a directory with a name consisting of two periods, **. .** The two periods represent the parent directory. If you want to move to the parent directory for the current directory, you simply double-click on this directory icon. Doing so is equivalent to the **cd . .** command.

Moving Files

You use the Move option in the File menu either to rename or move a file. To rename a file you select the file's icon and choose the Move option. This opens a dialog window with a box at the top labeled "Move to:". You just enter the new name for the file.

To move files from one directory to another, you can use the same Move option or you can click and drag with the mouse. Using the File menu, first select the file's icon and then choose the Move option in the File menu. This opens the Move Items to Directory dialog window. In the box labeled "Move to:" you enter the name of the directory you want to move the file to. If the directory is not a child directory of the current window, you can enter a full path name for the directory. You can either type in the path name yourself, or, if you see it listed in the History box, you can click on it there and the path name will appear in the "Move to:" box. By adding a new file name at the end of the directory's path, you can also change the name of the file. To then move the file, click on the OK button at the bottom of the dialog window. The file is moved to the directory that you specified.

With the mouse alone, you can use the click-and-drag method to move a file from one directory to another. First open a separate window for the directory that you want to move the file to. Then move the mouse to the icon of the file you want to move. Press and hold down your left mouse button while you drag the icon over to the window of the directory you want to move the file to. Then lift up on the mouse button. The file's icon will appear in the new directory.

Copying Files

As with the Move operation, there are two ways to copy a file: either click and drag with the mouse, or use the Copy option in the File menu. Using the File menu, you first select the file's icon and then choose the Copy option. This opens the Copy Items to Directory dialog window. Type the name of the copy in the box toward the top of the window labeled "Copy to:". Then click on the OK button at the bottom of the dialog window.

If you want to copy a file to another directory, you need to specify that directory in the "Copy to:" box in the dialog window. To give the copy a new name, just specify the name after the directory name, separated by a slash. For example, **reports/newdoc** entered into the "Copy to:" box would copy a selected file to the **reports** directory and give the copy the name **newdoc**. The History box, just below the "Copy to:" box, will list the path names of previous directories you have accessed. If you see the directory you want listed there, you can just click on it and its path name will appear in the "Copy to:" box. You can then simply add the new file name to the end of this path name.

Alternatively, with the mouse and the CTRL key, you can use the click-and-drag method to copy a file from one directory to another. The click-and-drag method for copying differs from the one for moving in that you must hold down the CTRL key during the whole operation. As in moving a file, you first open the window of the directory that you want to copy the file to. Then move the mouse to the icon of the file you want to copy and select it. Holding down the CTRL key, press and hold down your left mouse button as you drag the icon over to the new window. Lift up on the mouse button and the CTRL key, and the file's icon will appear in the other directory.

Removing Files

You can erase files either by dragging the file's icon to the trash can icon, or by choosing the Remove entry in the File menu. If you drag a file to the trash can, it remains there until you empty the trash. You can also remove whole directories, if you wish, by dragging their directory icons to the trash can.

Command Line Window

Within each directory window or from the desktop, you can choose the command line entry in the Run menu to open a command line window. This window has a box for entering commands as if you were entering them on the command line. Click on the box and type in the command. At the bottom of the window are several buttons.

To execute the command, click on the Run button. Do not press ENTER. A terminal window will open and execute your command.

Below the command line box is a larger box that lists previous commands you have entered. This is a history list. To reexecute a command in the history list, just click on it. It will appear in the command line box, and you can then click on the Run button to execute it. You can also click on the command line box and edit the command before running it. This is particularly helpful for complex commands with several options and arguments. If you need to run the same command on different files, you can simply replace the file name for the command and click Run.

The history list applies to the directory window from which the command line window was opened. Different directory windows will have different history lists. The desktop will have its own history list for its command line window.

Directory and File Permissions

You can set any of the permissions for a file or directory by selecting the Information item in the File menu. This opens a window with three selections: Access, Ownership, and Dates. Click on the button for Access to open a window listing the Access permissions. Here, you can click on buttons to specify read, write, and execute permissions for owner, group, or other. Permissions are explained in detail in Chapter 7. The Ownership selection allows you to change a file's owner.

The CRiSPlite Editor

A very easy-to-use and full-featured text editor called CRiSPlite is provided for you by the Caldera Network Desktop. The CRiSPlite editor incorporates many of the features found in the Vi and Emacs editors (see Chapters 17 and 18). At the same time, you have the ease of use provided by a Windows-based editor. You can select commands using menus and toolbars, scroll through text with scrollbars, resize your window, and use your mouse to select text and easily move, copy, or delete it. Through the Help menu on the CRiSPlite window, you can open the CRiSPlite manual which provides a detailed explanation of all CRiSPlite features.

The CRiSPlite editor is already installed on your Caldera Network Desktop. On the Desktop you will see an icon for the CRiSPlite editor as shown here. Just double-click on it to start it up.

The CRiSPlite editor opens a window with menus and a toolbar, as shown in Figure 4-6. Within the window you can enter text, and with your mouse you can click and drag to select text. The toolbar buttons provide easy access to standard editing functions such as opening and saving files, and copying and pasting text. CRiSPlite is designed to let you work on many different files at the same time. You can have several windows open, each operating on a separate file, and you can use your mouse to click from one to the other. You can also open up buffers to compose text that you can later move into a file.

You can also use a simple screen-based version of CRiSPlite with your command line interface. You do not have to start up X-windows and the Desktop. This command line version of CRiSPlite uses only arrow keys to move the cursor, and control and function keys to issue commands. But it does provide a full-screen view, allowing you to work on your text screen by screen. You start up the command line version of CRiSPlite with the **cr** command, usually followed by the name of the file you want to edit.

```
$ cr myfile
```

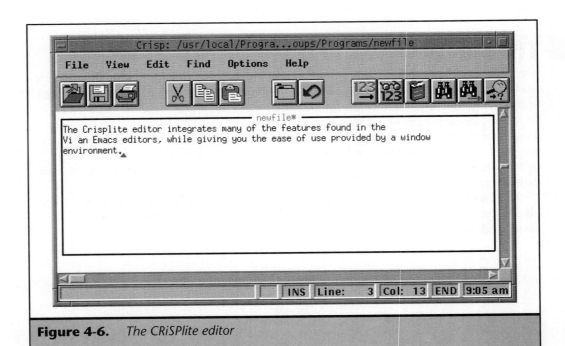

Figure 4-6. *The CRiSPlite editor*

The file you are editing will be displayed on the screen. You can then type in new text or use the arrow keys to move to different parts of the text. The CTRL-**w** key saves your file and the CTRL-**e** command allows you to open another file or start a new one. The CTRL-**x** command quits the editor. See the CRiSPlite manual for a listing of editing commands. For those who want to use CRiSPlite with the Vi command set, you can invoke the editor with the **-mvi** option, **cr -mvi**.

The CRiSPlite editor is provided on your Caldera Lite CD-ROM with a 90-day trial. When you upgrade to the full Caldera Network Desktop you will receive the CRiSPlite editor with no restriction.

Managing Your Desktop

The desktop is an interface that you can customize for your own needs. You can place file, program, and directory icons on your desktop for easy access. You can create layouts of your desktop, saving snapshots of a certain set of open windows and icons on your desktop. You can then select a layout that automatically opens those windows and displays those icons. You can also configure your desktop by specifying items for your icon bar or setting preferences for how files are created, displayed, or removed.

Icons

You can place any icons displayed in your directory windows on your desktop. This provides you with easy access to a program, directory, or file. You first have to use your directory window to find the icon you want to place on your desktop. Then click and drag it to the desktop. A copy of the icon will appear where you dragged it. You can also just select it and then choose the Put On Desktop item from the File menu. For example, to place the Netscape icon on your desktop, first use a directory window to display the directory the Netscape icon is in, usually **/bin**. Then drag the icon to your desktop. Now to run Netscape, you just double-click on the Netscape icon on your desktop. You don't have to go searching through directory windows to find it first. You can think of the desktop copy of the icon as an alias—another way to access the file or program. You can still open the directory for an icon and access it that way.

To remove an icon from the desktop, first select it and then choose Take Off Desktop from the File menu. This, of course, only removes the copy of the icon displayed on the desktop. It does not affect the original file in your directory.

Layouts

As you work on your desktop you may need to have different icons, windows, or programs open for different tasks. For example, if you are working with a database, you might have a database program window open and the directory window for the database files open. For graphics work you might have icons for graphics programs on your desktop and directory windows for graphics files. Instead of opening and closing windows when you move from one task to another, you can save your entire desktop as a layout. Then, to work on a particular task, just open that layout. For the database work, a user could create a layout for it called something like "datawork" and then open that layout whenever he or she needed to work on the database.

To create a layout, set your desktop the way you want the layout to look, opening the windows you want and placing icons you want on the desktop. Then select the Layouts item in the Layout menu. This opens a Layout window. In the box labeled "Layouts", click on the Currents entry (the first entry). Below the Layouts box is a Name field. Click on it and type in the name you want to give the layout. Then, from among the buttons at the bottom of this window, click on the Save button. Click on the Close button to close the Layout window. The new layout will be listed in the Layout menu. To restore it, just select its entry in the menu.

Configuring Your Desktop

You can configure your Caldera Network Desktop by selecting items from the Options menu. Selecting the IconBar item in the Options menu opens a window listing different icons and their functions. You can then add or remove icons from the icon bar.

Choosing the Environment item in the Options menu opens a window that lists your environment variables. You can then modify your environment variables or add new ones. Chapter 15 discusses environment variables.

The Preferences item in the Options menu is a submenu listing different types of preferences you can set. Your desktop has certain defaults for executing programs, for creating, removing, and displaying files, and for using color and sound. There is an item for each of these preferences and you can change any of them.

Caldera NetWare Client

Caldera has developed a NetWare Client that interfaces with Novell NetWare networks. The software was developed in close cooperation with Novell. It uses both the NetWare Core Protocol (NCP) and the IPX protocols. With the NetWare client, you can directly access directories and files on a NetWare network. You can log into the NetWare network and display files using directory windows. It allows you to manage both Bindery objects and NetWare Directory Services on a NetWare 4 server. You can also print files and access printer queues. The NetWare client is not on the CD-ROM enclosed with this book. To obtain the NetWare client you will have to purchase the complete Caldera Network Desktop from Caldera.

X-Windows and Window Managers

All Linux and Unix systems, including the Caldera Network Desktop, use the same standard underlying graphics interface called X-Windows. This means that any X-Window-based program can run on the Caldera Network Desktop. X-Window-based software is often found at ftp sites in directories labeled X11. You can download any of these packages and run them on your Caldera Desktop.

X-Windows is an underlying graphics utility that various user interfaces, organized into different tasks using separate programs, can make use of. For example, a window manager handles windowing operatons such as resizing and moving windows, a file manager handles file operations such as copying and erasing files, and a program manager runs programs. Normally you would have to install separately each of these components. Indeed, there are several window management programs available such as fvwm and xview; however, the Caldera Network Desktop integrates all these tasks into one cohesive interface. All you have to do is start up the desktop.

A more detailed discussion of X-Windows and other window managers is provided in Appendix B.

Summary: The Caldera Desktop

With the Caldera Network Desktop, you can interact with your system using menus, windows, and icons as well as set up efficient and easy access to Linux programs and Internet tools. To start the Caldera Network Desktop, you enter the command **startx** on the command line.

With directory windows you can use icons and menus to manage files and directories. The menus of a directory window contain commands that you can use to copy, move, print, erase, or perform other operations on files. You can move from one directory window to another by opening the window for a particular directory.

With the Caldera Network Desktop, you can easily configure your interface, creating layouts and customizing the toolbar. You can also configure your Linux system, making use of the desktop interface instead of tracking down obscure configuration files.

The Caldera Network Desktop includes a NetWare client and a Font Server. The NetWare client allows you to easily connect to any Novell NetWare server. Both are available along with the full Caldera Network Desktop package from Caldera at a discount to the buyers of this book. The version of the Caldera Network Desktop included on this book's CD-ROM is free for use for one year.

Menu and Menu Item	Effect
File	
Change To Directory	Changes the current directory window to display a new directory
Retype Directory	Determines the file types in a directory; this is done automatically when a directory window is first opened
Close	Closes the directory window
Information	Displays information and sets preferences for selected files and directories
Print	Prints selected files
Open	Opens a directory window or file of the selected icon; if the icon is a directory, a new directory window is opened; if the icon is a file, the associated application for that file is run
Remove	Deletes selected files or directories
Copy	Copies selected files to a directory; alternatively you can use the mouse to copy a file; while holding down the CTRL key, use your mouse to click and drag the file icon to the window of the directory where you want to copy the file
Move	Moves or renames a file or directory; alternatively you can use the mouse to move a file; use your mouse to click and drag the file icon to the window of the directory where you want to copy the file
Link	Creates links (other names) for a file; links can be placed in other directories
Change Properties	Changes properties of selected files or directories
Put On Desktop	Displays the selected icon on the desktop from which you can then directly access it

Table 4-1. *Directory Window Menus*

Menu and Menu Item	Effect
View	
Name	Displays small icons and names of files and directories
Icons	Displays files and directories as icons
Wide	Displays small icons and full file and directory information such as size and time
Positionable	Displays both files and directories in one window pane and allows users to move the icons
Show Hidden Files	Shows dot files such as those used for system configuration
Size	Shows the size of the file in bytes
Create	
Directory	Creates a new directory; displays new icon with highlighted default name in which you type the directory's name
File	Creates a new empty file
Device	Creates a new device file
Fifo	Creates a new pipe file
Sort	
Name	Sorts files and directories by name alphabetically
Color	Sorts by color of file names
Size	Sorts by size
Type	Sorts by file type
Ascending	Sorts by ascending order
Descending	Sorts by reverse order

Table 4-1. *Directory Window Menus* (continued)

Menu and Menu Item	Effect
Select	
Select By Pattern	Selects files whose names match the pattern you enter; you can enter a partial pattern
Select All Directories	Selects all directory icons in the window
Select All Files	Selects all file icons in the window
Find	Searches for files or directories
Run	
Terminal Emulator	Opens a terminal window in which you can enter Linux commands on a command line using the directory for the open window as the current working directory
Command Line	Opens a command line window in which you can enter Linux commands; the window holds a history of previously executed commands
Color	Lists colors that you can use to color the name of files and directories; you can even sort files and directories by these colors

Table 4-1. *Directory Window Menus* (continued)

PART TWO

Linux Operations

Chapter Five

Shell Operations

The shell is a command interpreter that provides a line-oriented interactive interface between the user and the operating system. You enter commands on a command line, and they are then interpreted by the shell and sent as instructions to the operating system. This interpretive capability of the shell provides for many sophisticated features. For example, the shell has a set of special characters that can generate file names. It can redirect input and output. It can also run operations in the background, freeing you to perform other tasks.

Three different types of shells have been developed for Linux: the Bourne Again shell (BASH), the Public Domain Korn shell (PDKSH), and the TCSH shell. All three shells are available for your use, although the BASH shell is the default. All examples so far in this book have used the BASH shell. You only need one type of shell to do your work. This chapter discusses features common to all shells, whereas Chapters 15 and 16 cover distinguishing features of the BASH, PDKSH, and TCSH shells. You will see how you can configure shells using aliases, history events, and system variables. The shells even have their own programming languages. This chapter focuses on common features of command execution; specifically, command line editing, special characters, redirection, pipes, variables, scripts, and job control.

The Command Line

When you log into Linux, you are presented with a command line interface. This consists of a single line into which you enter commands with any of their options and arguments. A shell *prompt*, such as the one shown here, marks the beginning of the command line:

```
$
```

Linux installs with the Bourne Again Shell, commonly referred to as the BASH shell. The BASH shell has a dollar sign prompt; but Linux has several other types of shells, each with its own prompt. The different types of shells are discussed at length beginning with Chapter 15.

When the system prompt appears, you are logged into the system. The prompt designates the beginning of the command line. You are now ready to enter a command and its arguments at the prompt. In the next example, the user enters the **date** command, which displays the date. The user types the command on the first line and then presses ENTER to execute the command.

```
$ date
Sun July 7 10:30:21 PST 1996
```

When you log in, you are actually placed into the shell, which interprets the commands you enter and sends them to the system. The shell follows a special *syntax* for interpreting the command line. The first word entered on a command line must be the name of a command. The next words are options and arguments for the command. Each word on the command line must be separated by one or more spaces or tabs.

```
$ Command     Options     Arguments
```

When you enter a Linux command, the shell first reads the command name and then checks to see if there is an actual command by that name. If there is no such command, the shell issues an error message.

Options and Arguments

An *option* is a one-letter code preceded by a dash that modifies the type of action that the command takes. One example of a command that has options is the **ls** command. The **ls** command, with no options, displays a list of all the files in your current directory. It merely lists the name of each file with no other information.

With a **-l** option, the **ls** command will modify its task by displaying a line of information about each file, listing such data as its size and the date and time it was last modified. In the next example, the user enters the **ls** command followed by a **-l** option. The dash before the **-l** option is required. Linux uses it to distinguish an option from an argument.

```
$ ls -l
```

Another option, **-a**, lists all the files in your directory, including what are known as hidden files. *Hidden files* are often configuration files and always have names beginning with a period. For this reason they are often referred to as *dot files*. In most cases, you can also combine options. You do so by preceding the options with an initial dash and then listing the options you want. The options **-al**, for example, will list information about all the files in your directory, including any hidden files.

```
$ ls -al
```

Another option for the **ls** command is **-F**. With this option, the **ls** command displays directory names with a preceding slash so that you can easily identify them.

Most commands are designed to take arguments. An *argument* is a word that you type in on the command line after any options. Many file management commands take file names as their arguments. For example, if you only wanted the information displayed for a particular file, you could add that file's name after the **-l** option:

```
$ ls -l mydata
```

Depending on the command, you may or may not have to enter arguments. Some commands, such as **ls**, do not require any arguments. Other commands may require a minimum number of arguments. For example, the **cp** command requires at least two arguments. If the number of arguments does not match the number required by the command, then the shell issues an error message.

Remember that options are entered on the command line before the arguments. In the case of the **cp** command, the **-i** option for checking the overwrite condition is entered before the file name arguments. Here are some examples of entering commands:

```
$ ls                          Command without options
$ ls -F                       Command with option
$ cp -i mydata newdata        Command with option and arguments
```

Command Line Features

The command line is actually a buffer of text that you can edit. Before you press ENTER, you can perform editing commands on the text you have entered. The editing capabilities are limited, but they do provide a way for correcting mistakes. The BACKSPACE and DEL keys allow you to erase the character just typed in. With this character-erasing capability, you can backspace over the entire line if you wish, erasing what you have entered. The CTRL-U key combination erases the whole line and lets you start over again at the prompt. In the next example, the user types **datl** instead of **date**. Using BACKSPACE, the user erases the **l** and then enters an **e**.

```
$ datl
$ dat
$ date
```

The shell you will start working in is the BASH shell, your default shell. This shell has special command line editing capabilities that you may find very helpful as you learn Linux. You can easily modify commands you have entered before executing them, moving anywhere on the command line and inserting or deleting characters. This is particularly helpful for very complex commands. You can use CTRL-F or RIGHT ARROW key to move forward a character, the CTRL-B or the LEFT ARROW key to move back a character. CTRL-D or DEL deletes the character the cursor is on, and CTRL-H or BACKSPACE deletes the character before the cursor. To add text, you just use the arrow keys to move the cursor to where you want to insert text and type in the new characters. At any time, you can press ENTER to execute the command. For example, if you make a spelling mistake when entering a command, rather than re-entering the entire command, you can use the editing operations to correct the mistake.

You can also use the UP ARROW key to redisplay your previously executed command. You can then re-execute that command or edit it and execute the modified command. You can then re-execute that command or edit it and execute the modified version. You'll find this very helpful when you have to repeat certain operations over and over, such as editing the same file. It is also helpful when you've already executed a command that you had entered incorrectly. In this case you would be presented with an error message and a new, empty command line. By pressing the UP ARROW key you can redisplay your previous command, make corrections to it, and then execute it again. This way, you would not have to enter the whole command over again.

The BASH shell keeps a list, called a *history list*, of your previously entered commands. You can display each command in turn on your command line by pressing the UP ARROW key. The DOWN ARROW key will move you down the list. You can modify and execute any of these previous commands when you display them on your command line. This history feature is discussed in more detail in Chapter 15.

Some commands can be very complex and take some time to execute. When you mistakenly execute the wrong command, you can interrupt and stop such commands with the interrupt keys—CTRL-C or DEL.

You can place more than one command on the same line, or you can use several lines to enter a single command. To enter more than one command on the same line, separate the commands with a semicolon. The next example shows the **ls** command and the **cp** command entered on the same line.

```
$ ls -F ; cp -i mydata newdata
```

You can enter a command on several lines by typing a backslash just before you press ENTER. The backslash "escapes" the ENTER key, effectively continuing the same command line to the next line. In the next example, the **cp** command is entered on three lines. The first two lines end in a backslash, effectively making all three lines one command line.

```
$ cp -i \
mydata \
newdata
```

Special Characters and File Name Arguments: *, ?, [ ]

File names are the most common arguments used in a command. Often you may know only part of the file name, or you may want to reference several file names that have the same extension or begin with the same characters. The shell provides a set of special characters that search out, match, and generate a list of file names. These special characters are the asterisk, question mark, and brackets (*****, **?**, **[ ]**). Given a partial file name, the shell uses these matching operators to search for files and generate a list of file names found. The shell replaces the partial file name argument with the list of matched file names. This list of file names can then become the arguments for commands such as **ls** that can operate on many files. Table 5-1 (found at the end of this chapter) lists the shell's special characters.

You can use the asterisk, *****, to reference files beginning or ending with a specific set of characters. You place the asterisk before or after a set of characters that form a pattern to be searched for in file names. If the asterisk is placed before the pattern, file names that end in that pattern are searched for. If the asterisk is placed after the pattern, file names that begin with that pattern are searched for. Any matching file name is copied into a list of file names generated by this operation. In the next example, all file names beginning with the pattern "doc" are searched for and a list generated. Then all file names ending with the pattern "day" are searched for and a list generated.

```
$ ls
doc1 doc2 document docs mydoc monday tuesday
$ ls doc*
doc1 doc2 document docs
$ ls *day
monday tuesday
$
```

File names often include an extension specified with a period and followed by a single character. The extension has no special status. It is only part of the characters making up the file name. Using the asterisk makes it easy to select files with a given extension. In the next example, the asterisk is used to list only those files with a **.c** extension. The asterisk placed before the **.c** constitutes the argument for **ls**.

```
$ ls *.c
calc.c main.c
```

You can use the special character, *****, with the **rm** command to erase several files at once. The asterisk first selects a list of files with a given extension, or beginning or ending with a given set of characters, and then presents this list of files to the **rm** command to be erased. In the next example, the **rm** command erases all files beginning with the pattern "doc".

```
$ rm doc*
```

The asterisk by itself matches all files. If you use a single asterisk as the argument for an **rm** command, all your files will be erased. In the next example, the **ls *** command lists all files, and the **rm *** command erases all files.

```
$ ls *
doc1 doc2 document docs mydoc myletter yourletter
$ rm *
$ ls
$
```

Use the ***** special character carefully and sparingly with the **rm** command. The combination can be very dangerous. A misplaced ***** in an **rm** command without the **-i** option could easily erase all your files. The first command in the next example erases only those files with a **.c** extension. The second command, however, erases all files. Notice the space between the asterisk and the period in the second command. A space in a command line functions as a *delimiter*, separating arguments. The asterisk is considered one argument and the **.c** another. The asterisk by itself matches all files and, when used as an argument with the **rm** command, instructs **rm** to erase all your files.

```
$ rm *.c
$ rm * .c
```

The question mark, **?**, matches only a single incomplete character in file names. Suppose you want to match the files **doc1** and **docA**, but not document. Whereas the asterisk will match file names of any length, the question mark limits the match to just one extra character. The next example matches files that begin with the word "doc" followed by a single differing letter.

```
$ ls
doc1 docA document
$ ls doc?
doc1 docA
```

You can use more than one question mark in a pattern if you wish, and you can place the question marks anywhere in the pattern. The next example searches for a pattern with three possible differing characters.

```
$ ls ?y?oc?
mydocs mylock Sydoc1
```

You can combine the **?** with other special characters to construct very powerful matching operations. Suppose you want to find all files that have a single character extension. You could use the asterisk to match the file name proper, and the **?** to match the single character extension: ***.?**. In the next example, the user displays all files that have a single character extension.

```
$ ls *.?
calc.c   lib.a
```

Whereas the ***** and **?** special characters specify incomplete portions of a file name, the brackets, **[]**, allow you to specify a set of valid characters to search for. Any character placed within the brackets will be matched in the file name. Suppose you want to list files beginning with "doc" but only ending in 1 or A. You are not interested in file names ending in 2, or B, or any other character. Here is how it's done:

```
$ ls
doc1 doc2 doc3 docA docB docD document
$ ls doc[1A]
doc1 docA
```

You can also specify a set of characters as a range, rather than listing them one by one. A dash placed between the upper and lower bound of a set of characters selects all characters within that range. The range is usually determined by the character set in use. In an ASCII character set, the range a-g will select all lowercase alphabetic characters from *a* through *g* inclusive. In the next example, files beginning with the pattern "doc" and ending in characters 1 through 3 are selected. Then those ending in characters B through E are matched.

```
$ ls doc[1-3]
doc1 doc2 doc3
$ ls doc[B-E]
docB docD
```

You can combine the brackets with other special characters to form very flexible matching operators. Suppose you only want to list file names ending in either a .c or .o extension, but no other extension. You can use a combination of the asterisk and brackets: ***[co]**. The asterisk matches all file names, and the brackets match only file names with extension .c or .o.

```
$ ls *.[co]
main.c  main.o  calc.c
```

There may be times when a special character is part of a file name. In these cases, you need to quote the special character by preceding it with a backslash in order to reference the file. In the next example, the user needs to reference a file that ends with the **?** character, **answers?**. The **?** is, however, a special character and would match any file name beginning with "answers" that has one more characters. In this case, the user quotes the **?** with a preceding backslash in order to reference the file name.

```
$ ls answers\?
answers?
```

You can combine a quoted character with special characters in your file name. In the next example, the user lists all files beginning with "answers?" that have an extension.

```
$ ls answers\?.*
answers?.quiz  answers?.mid  answers?.final
```

Standard Input/Output and Redirection

When Unix was designed, a decision was made to distinguish between the physical implementation and logical organization of a file. Physically, Unix files are accessed in randomly arranged blocks. Logically, all files are organized as a continuous stream of bytes. Linux, as a version of Unix, has this same organization. Aside from special system calls, the user never references the physical structure of a file. To the user, all files have the same organization—a byte stream. Any file can be easily copied or appended to another because all files are organized in the same way. In this sense, there is only one standard type of file in Linux, the byte-stream file. Linux makes no implementational distinction between a character file and a record file, or a text file and a binary file.

This logical file organization extends to input and output operations. The data in input and output operations is organized like a file. Data input at the keyboard is placed in a data stream arranged as a continuous set of bytes. Data output from a command or program is also placed in a data stream and arranged as a continuous set of bytes. This input data stream is referred to in Linux as the *standard input*, and the output data stream is called the *standard output*.

Because the standard input and standard output have the same organization as that of a file, they can easily interact with files. Linux has a redirection capability that lets you easily move data in and out of files. You can redirect the standard output so that, instead of displaying the output on a screen, you can save it in a file. You can also redirect the standard input away from the keyboard to a file, so that input is read from a file instead of from your keyboard.

When a Linux command is executed that produces output, this output is placed in the standard output data stream. The default destination for the standard output data stream is a device, in this case, the screen. *Devices*, such as the keyboard and screen, are treated as files. They receive and send out streams of bytes with the same organization as that of a byte-stream file. The screen is a device that displays a continuous stream of bytes. By default, the standard output will send its data to the screen device, which will then display the data.

For example, the **ls** command generates a list of all file names and outputs this list to the standard output. This stream of bytes in the standard output is then directed to the screen device. The list of file names is then printed on the screen. The **cat** command also sends output to the standard output. The contents of a file are copied to the standard output whose default destination is the screen. The contents of the file are then displayed on the screen. Figure 5-1 shows the basic relationship between the standard input and the keyboard device, and between the standard output and the screen device.

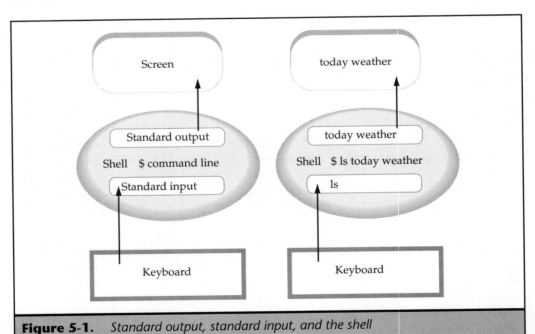

Figure 5-1. *Standard output, standard input, and the shell*

Redirecting the Standard Output: > and >>

Suppose that instead of displaying a list of files on the screen, you would like to save this list in a file. In other words, you would like to direct the standard output to a file rather than the screen. To do this, you place the output redirection operator, **>** (greater-than sign), and the name of a file on the command line after the Linux command. Table 5-2 (found at the end of this chapter) lists the different ways you can use the redirection operators. In the next example, the output of the **cat** command is redirected from the screen device to a file. As shown in Figure 5-2, instead of the contents of the file **myletter** being printed to the screen, they are redirected to the file **newletter**.

```
$ cat myletter > newletter
```

The redirection operation creates the new destination file. If the file already exists, it will be overwritten with the data in the standard output. You can set the **noclobber** feature to prevent overwriting an existing file with the redirection operation. In this case, the redirection operation on an existing file will fail. You can overcome the **noclobber** feature by placing an exclamation point after the

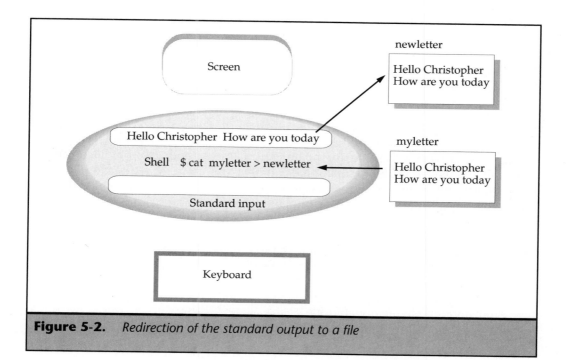

Figure 5-2.   *Redirection of the standard output to a file*

redirection operator. The next example sets the **noclobber** feature for the BASH shell and then forces the overwriting of the **oldletter** file if it already exists.

```
$ set -o noclobber
$ cat myletter >! oldletter
```

Redirection File Creation

Though the redirection operator and file name are placed after the command, the redirection operation is not executed after the command. In fact, it is executed before the command. The redirection operation creates the file and sets up the redirection before it receives any data from the standard output. If the file already exists, it will be destroyed and replaced by a file of the same name. In effect, the command generating the output is executed only after the redirected file has been created.

In the next example, the output of the **ls** command is redirected from the screen device to a file. First the **ls** command lists files, and in the next command, **ls** redirects its file list to the **listf** file. Then the **cat** command displays the list of files saved in **listf**. Notice that the list of files in **listf** includes the **listf** file name. The list of file names generated by the **ls** command will include the name of the file created by the redirection operation, in this case, **listf**. The **listf** file is first created by the redirection operation, and then the **ls** command lists it along with other files. This file list output by **ls** is then redirected to the **listf** file, instead of being printed on the screen.

```
$ ls
mydata intro preface
$ ls > listf
$ cat listf
mydata intro listf preface
```

Errors occur when you try to use the same file name for both an input file for the command and the redirected destination file. In this case, since the redirection operation is executed first, the input file, since it exists, is destroyed and replaced by a file of the same name. When the command is executed, it finds an input file that is empty.

In the **cat** command shown next, the file **myletter** is the name for both the destination file for redirected output and the input file for the **cat** operation. As shown in the next example, the redirection operation is executed first, destroying the **myletter** file and replacing it with a new and empty **myletter** file. Then the **cat** operation is executed and attempts to read all the data in the **myletter** file. However, there is now nothing in the **myletter** file.

```
$ cat myletter > myletter
```

Appending the Standard Output: >>

You can also *append* the standard output to an existing file using the **>>** redirection operator. Instead of overwriting the file, the data in the standard output is added at the end of the file. In the next example, the **myletter** and **oldletter** files are appended to the **alletters** file. The **alletters** file will then contain the contents of both **myletter** and **oldletter**.

```
$ cat myletter >> alletters
$ cat oldletter >> alletters
```

The Standard Input

Many Linux commands can receive data from the standard input. The standard input itself receives data from a device or a file. The default device for the standard input is the keyboard. Characters typed into the keyboard are placed in the standard input, which is then directed to the Linux command.

The **cat** command without a file name argument reads data from standard input. When you type in data on the keyboard, each character will be placed in the standard input and directed to the **cat** command. The **cat** command will then send the character to the standard output—the screen device—which displays the character on the screen.

When you try this, you will find that as you enter a line, that line will immediately be displayed on the screen. This is due to the line buffering method used in many Linux systems. *Line buffering* requires that a user type in an entire line before any input is sent to the standard input. The **cat** command receives a whole line at a time from the standard input, and it will immediately display the line. In the next example, the user executes the **cat** command without any arguments. As the user types in a line, it is sent to the standard input, which the **cat** command reads and sends to the standard output:

```
$ cat
This is a new line
This is a new line
for the cat
for the cat
command
command
^D
$
```

The **cat** operation will continue until a CTRL-D character (**^D**) is entered on a line by itself. The CTRL-D character is the end-of-file character for any Linux file. In a sense, the user is actually creating a file at the keyboard and ending it with the end-of-file character. Remember, the standard input, as well as the standard output, have the same format as any Linux file.

If you combine the **cat** command with redirection, you have an easy way of saving what you have typed to a file. As shown in the next example, the output of the **cat** operation is redirected to the **mydat** file. The **mydat** file will now contain all the data typed in at the keyboard. The **cat** command, in this case, still has no file arguments. It will receive its data from the standard input, the keyboard device. The redirection operator redirects the output of the **cat** command to the file **mydat**. The **cat** command has no direct contact with any files. It is simply receiving input from the standard input and sending output to the standard output.

```
$ cat > mydat
This is a new line
for the cat
command
^D
$
```

Redirecting the Standard Input: <

Just as with the standard output, you can also redirect the standard input. The standard input may be received from a file rather than the keyboard. The operator for redirecting the standard input is the less-than sign, **<**. In the next example, the standard input is redirected to receive input from the **myletter** file rather than the keyboard device. The contents of **myletter** are read into the standard input by the redirection operation. Then the **cat** command reads the standard input and displays the contents of **myletter**.

```
$ cat < myletter
hello Christopher
How are you today
$
```

You can combine the redirection operations for both standard input and standard output. In the next example, the **cat** command has no file name arguments. Without file name arguments, the **cat** command receives input from the standard input and sends output to the standard output. However, the standard input has been redirected to receive its data from a file, and the standard output has been redirected to place its data in a file.

```
$ cat < myletter > newletter
```

Pipes: |

You will find yourself in situations in which you need to send data from one command to another. In other words, you will want to send the standard output of a command to another command, not to a destination file. Suppose you want to send a list of your file names to the printer to be printed. You need two commands to do this: the **ls** command to generate a list of file names and the **lpr** command to send the list to the printer. In effect, you need to take the output of the **ls** command and use it as input for the **lpr** command. You can think of the data as flowing from one command to another. To form such a connection in Linux, you use what is called a pipe. The *pipe operator*, |, (vertical bar character) placed between two commands forms a connection between them. The standard output of one command becomes the standard input for the other. The pipe operation receives output from the command placed before the pipe and sends this data as input to the command placed after the pipe. As shown in the next example, you can connect the **ls** command and the **lpr** command with a pipe. The list of file names output by the **ls** command is piped into the **lpr** command.

```
$ ls | lpr
```

You can combine the pipe operation with other shell features such as special characters to perform specialized operations. The next example prints only files with a .c extension. The **ls** command is used with the asterisk and ".c" to generate a list of file names with the .c extension. Then this list is piped to the **lpr** command.

```
$ ls *.c | lpr
```

Whereas redirection simply places output in a file, pipes send output to another Linux command. You may wonder why this cannot be accomplished with redirection. You need to keep in mind the difference between a file and a command: A file is a storage medium that holds data. You can save data on it or read data from it. A command is a program that executes instructions. A command may read or save data in a file, but a command is not in itself a file. For this reason, a redirection operation operates on files, not on commands. Redirection can send data from a program to a file, but it cannot send data from a program to another program. Only files can be the destination of a redirection operation, not other programs.

You can, however, simulate the piping process through a series of redirection operations. You could send the output of one command to a file. Then, on the next line, you could execute a command using that file as redirected input. The next example uses two redirection operations in two separate commands to print a list of file names. This same task was performed in the previous examples using a single pipe operation. The pipe operation literally takes the standard output of one command and uses it as standard input for another command.

```
$ ls *.c > tempfile
$ lpr < tempfile
```

Up to this point we have been using a list of file names as input, but it is important to note that pipes operate on the standard output of a command, whatever that might be. The contents of whole files or even several files can be piped from one command to another. In the next example, the **cat** command reads and outputs the contents of the **mydata** file, which are then piped to the **lpr** command.

```
$ cat mydata | lpr
```

Suppose you want to print out data you are typing in from the keyboard instead of data from a file. Remember that the **cat** command without any arguments reads data from the standard input. In the next example, **cat** takes input from the keyboard instead of a file and pipes the output to the **lpr** command. The **cat** command is executed before the **lpr** command, so you first enter your data for the **cat** command on the keyboard, ending with the end-of-file, CTRL-D. The input for a piped byte stream may come from any source.

```
$ cat | lpr
This text will
be printed
^D
$
```

Linux provides **cat** with a **-n** option that outputs the contents of a file, adding line numbers. If you want to print your file with line numbers, you must first use the **cat** command with the **-n** option to output the contents of the file with line numbers added. You then pipe this output to the **lpr** command for printing, for example:

```
$ cat -n  mydata | lpr
```

You do much the same thing for displaying a file with line numbers. In this case, the numbered output is usually piped to the **more** command for screen-by-screen examination. You can even specify several files at once and pipe their output to the **more** command, examining all the files. In the next example, both **mydata** and **preface** are numbered and piped to the **more** command for screen-by-screen examination.

```
$ cat -n mydata preface | more
```

Linux has many commands that generate modified output; the **cat** command with the **-n** option is only one. Another is the **sort** command. The **sort** command takes the contents of a file and generates a version with each line sorted in alphabetic order. It works best with files that are lists of items. Commands like **sort** that output a modified version of its input are referred to as filters. Filters are discussed in detail in Chapter 14. They are often used with pipes. In the next example, a sorted version of **mylist** is generated and piped into the **more** command for display on the screen. Note that the original file, **mylist**, has not been changed and is not itself sorted. Only the output of **sort** in the standard output is sorted.

```
$ sort mylist | more
```

You can, of course, combine several commands, connecting each pair with a pipe. The output of one command can be piped into another command, which, in turn, can pipe its output into still another command. Suppose you have a file with a list of items that you want to print out both numbered and in alphabetic order. To print the numbered and sorted list, you can first generate a sorted version with the **sort** command and then pipe that output to the **cat** command. The **cat** command with the **-n** option then takes as its input the sorted list and generates as its output a numbered, sorted list, which can then be piped to the **lpr** command for printing. The next example shows the command, and in Figure 5-3 a sorted and numbered version of the **mylist** file is printed.

```
$ sort mylist | cat -n | lpr
```

You can accomplish the same task in a more cumbersome way, using redirection and a series of separate commands. In this case, two new temporary files (**sfile** and **nfile**) are needed to hold the output of each operation.

```
$ sort mylist > sfile
$ cat -n < sfile > nfile
$ lpr < nfile
```

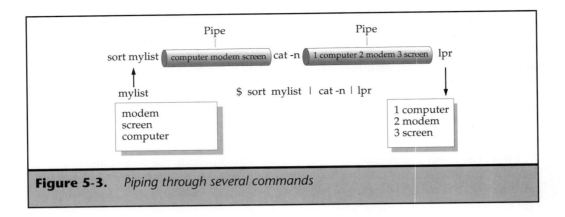

Figure 5-3. *Piping through several commands*

The standard input piped into a command can be more carefully controlled with the standard input argument, **-**. When you use the dash as an argument for a command, it represents the standard input. Suppose you would like to print a file with the name of its directory at the top. The **pwd** command outputs a directory name, and the **cat** command outputs the contents of a file. In this case, the **cat** command needs to take as its input both the file and the standard input piped in from the **pwd** command. The **cat** command will have two arguments: the standard input as represented by the dash and the file name of the file to be printed.

In the next example, the **pwd** command generates the directory name and pipes it into the **cat** command. For the **cat** command, this piped-in standard input now contains the directory name. As represented by the dash, the standard input is the first argument to the **cat** command. The **cat** command copies the directory name and the contents of the **mylist** file to the standard output, which is then piped to the **lpr** command for printing. If you want to print the directory name at the end of the file instead, simply make the dash the last argument and the file name the first argument, as in **cat mylist -** .

```
$ pwd | cat - mylist | lpr
```

Pipes and Redirection: tee

Suppose you want to redirect the standard output to a file and, at the same time, display the contents of that output on the screen so that you can see what you are saving. You can do this with the **tee** command. The **tee** command copies the standard output to a file. It takes as its argument the name of the new file to which the standard output is copied. The standard output continues on its way, but as it passes through the **tee** command, its contents are copied to a file. It is as if the standard output were split into two copies, one being redirected to a file and the other continuing on its way, often to the screen. The next example copies the contents of the file **mylist** to the file **newlist** and displays the contents on the screen.

```
$ cat mylist | tee newlist
```

The **tee** command is handy when you are modifying output and you would like to save the modified output in a file and also see what the modifications look like. In the next example, the file **mylist** is again sorted and the sorted output is piped to the **tee** command. The **tee** command then both saves the sorted output in a file called **sfile** and displays it on the screen.

```
$ sort mylist | tee sfile
computer
modem
screen
$
```

You could use redirection to save the output in a file first and then later print out the file:

```
$ sort mylist > sfile
$ cat sfile
computer
modem
screen
$
```

Suppose, however, you need to save your output in a file as well as print it. In this case, the standard output needs to continue to another command. You need to use **tee** to copy the output to another file while allowing the standard output to be piped into the next command. In the next example, the output of the **sort** command is first piped to **tee**, which copies the output to the file **sfile**. The output itself is then piped into the **lpr** command to be printed.

```
$ sort mylist | tee sfile | lpr
```

Be careful when you use redirection with pipes. A standard output redirection specifies a destination for the standard output. The standard output is saved and stored in that destination file. Once saved, there is no output to be piped into another command. Though redirection can take place at the end of a series of pipe operations, it cannot take place *within* pipe operations. The next example is a valid use of pipes and redirection. The output of the **sort** command is piped to the **cat** command with the **-n** option to number lines, and then the result is saved in the **nfile** file.

```
$ sort mylist | cat -n > nfile
```

What if you need to save the result in **nfile** and print it out? You cannot do something like this:

```
sort mylist | cat -n > nfile | lpr      ERROR
```

The only way to save the output in a file and print it is to use the **tee** command:

```
$ sort mylist | cat -n | tee nfile | lpr
```

You can use **tee** anywhere in the piping sequence. The next example saves a sorted version of the list while printing the numbered version.

```
$ sort mylist | tee sfile | cat -n | lpr
```

Redirecting and Piping the Standard Error: >&, 2>

When you execute commands, it is possible that an error could occur. You may give the wrong number of arguments, or some kind of system error could take place. When an error occurs, the system will issue an error message. Usually such error messages are displayed on the screen, along with the standard output. However, Linux distinguishes between standard output and error messages. Error messages are placed in yet another standard byte stream called the *standard error*. In the next example, the **cat** command is given as its argument the name of a file that does not exist, **myintro**. In this case, the **cat** command will simply issue an error:

```
$ cat myintro
cat : myintro not found
$
```

Because error messages are in a separate data stream than the standard output, error messages will still appear on the screen for you to see even if you have redirected the standard output to a file. In the next example, the standard output of the **cat** command is redirected to the file **mydata**. However, the standard error, containing the error messages, is still directed to the screen.

```
$ cat myintro > mydata
cat : myintro not found
$
```

Like the standard output, you can also redirect the standard error. This means that you can save your error messages in a file for future reference. This is helpful if you need a record of the error messages. Like the standard output, the standard error's default destination is the screen device, but you can redirect the standard error to any file or device that you choose using special redirection operators. In this case, the error messages will not be displayed on the screen.

Redirection of the standard error relies on a special feature of shell redirection. You can reference all the standard byte streams in redirection operations with numbers. The numbers 0, 1, and 2 reference the standard input, standard output, and standard error, respectively. By default, an output redirection, **>**, operates on the standard output, 1. However, you can modify the output redirection to operate on the standard error by preceding the output redirection operator with the number 2. In the next example, the **cat** command again will generate an error. The error message is redirected to the standard byte stream represented by number 2, the standard error.

```
$ cat nodata 2> myerrors
$ cat myerrors
cat : nodata not found
$
```

You can also append the standard error to a file by using the number 2 and the redirection append operator, **>>**. In the next example, the user appends the standard error to the **myerrors** file, which then functions as a log of errors.

```
$ cat nodata 2>> myerrors
$ cat compls 2>> myerrors
$ cat myerrors
cat : nodata not found
cat : compls not found
$
```

To redirect both the standard output and the standard error, you need a separate redirection operation and file for each. In the next example, the standard output is redirected to the file **mydata**, whereas the standard error is redirected to **myerrors**. If **nodata** actually exists, **mydata** will hold a copy of its contents.

```
$ cat nodata 1> mydata 2> myerrors
$ cat myerrors
cat : nodata not found
$
```

If, however, you want to save your errors in the same file as that used for the redirected standard output, you need to redirect the standard error into the standard output. In the BASH shell, you can reference a standard byte stream by preceding its number with an ampersand: **&1** references the standard output. You can use such a reference in a redirection operation to make a standard byte stream a destination file. The redirection operation **2>&1** redirects the standard error into the standard output. In effect, the standard output becomes the destination file for the standard error. Conversely, the redirection operation **1>&2** redirects the standard input into the standard error.

In the next example, the **cat** command has as its argument the name of a file that does not exist, **nodata**. The resulting error message is redirected to the file **mydata**. Both the contents of the standard error and the standard output will be saved in the same file, **mydata**. The message is not displayed on the screen but, instead, saved in a file. To see the error message, simply display the contents of the **mydata** file. If the **nodata** file actually existed, then **mydata** would hold the contents of that file instead of error messages.

```
$ cat nodata 1> mydata 2>&1
$ cat mydata
cat : nodata not found
```

The default output stream for a **>&** operation is the standard output, and the default input stream is the standard error. If the preceding operation is written without using numbers, as shown in the next example, any error messages will be redirected into the standard output and saved in the same destination file for the standard output.

```
$ cat nodata >& mydata
```

Shell Variables

You define variables within a shell, and such variables are known—logically enough—as *shell variables*. There are many different shells. Some utilities, such as the mailx utility, have their own shells with their own shell variables. You can also create your own shell using what are called shell scripts. You have a user shell that becomes active as soon as you log in. This is often referred to as the login shell. Special system variables are defined within this login shell. Shell variables exist as long as your shell is active, that is, until you exit the shell. For example, logging out will exit the login shell. When you log in again, any variables that you may need in your login shell will have to be defined once again.

Definition and Evaluation of Variables: =, $, set, unset

You define a variable in a shell when you first use the variable's name. A variable's name may be any set of alphabetic characters, including the underscore. The name may also include a number, but the number cannot be the first character in the name. A name may not have any other type of character, such as an exclamation point, an ampersand, or even a space. Such symbols are reserved by the shell for its own use. Also, a name may not include more than one word. The shell uses spaces on the command line to distinguish different components of a command such as options, arguments, and the name of the command.

You assign a value to a variable with the assignment operator, **=**. You type in the variable name, the assignment operator, and then the value assigned. Do not place any spaces around the assignment operator. The assignment **operation poet = Virgil**, for example, will fail. (The C-shell has a slightly different type of assignment operation that is described in the section on C-shell variables later in this chapter.) You can assign any set of characters to a variable. In the next example, the variable **poet** is assigned the string **Virgil**.

```
$ poet=Virgil
```

Once you have assigned a value to a variable, you can then use the variable name to reference the value. Often you use the values of variables as arguments for a command. You can reference the value of a variable using the variable name preceded by the **$** operator. The dollar sign is a special operator that uses the variable name to reference a variable's value, in effect, evaluating the variable. Evaluation retrieves a variable's value, usually a set of characters. This set of characters then replaces the variable name on the command line. Wherever a **$** is placed before the variable name, the variable name is replaced with the value of the variable. In the next example, the shell variable **poet** is evaluated and its contents, **Virgil**, are then used as the argument for an **echo** command. The **echo** command simply echoes or prints a set of characters to the screen.

```
$ echo $poet
Virgil
```

You must be careful to distinguish between the evaluation of a variable and its name alone. If you leave out the **$** operator before the variable name, all you have is the variable name itself. In the next example, the **$** operator is absent from the variable name. In this case, the **echo** command has as its argument the word "poet", and so prints out "poet".

```
$ echo poet
poet
```

The contents of a variable are often used as command arguments. A common command argument is a directory path name. It can be tedious to retype a directory path that is being used over and over again. If you assign the directory path name to a variable, you can simply use the evaluated variable in its place. The directory path you assign to the variable is retrieved when the variable is evaluated with the **$** operator. The next example assigns a directory path name to a variable and then uses the evaluated variable in a copy command. The evaluation of **ldir** (which is **$ldir**) results in the path name **/home/chris/letters**. The copy command evaluates to **cp myletter /home/chris/letters**.

```
$ ldir=/home/chris/letters
$ cp myletter $ldir
```

You can obtain a list of all the defined variables with the **set** command. The next example uses the **set** command to display a list of all defined variables and their values.

```
$ set
poet    Virgil
ldir    /home/chris/letters/old
$
```

If you decide that you do not want a certain variable, you can remove it with the **unset** command. The **unset** command "undefines" a variable. The next example undefines the variable **poet**. Then the user executes the **set** command to list all defined variables. Notice that **poet** is missing.

```
$ unset poet
$ set
ldir   /home/chris/letters/old
$
```

Variable Values: Strings

The values that you assign to variables may consist of any set of characters. These characters may be a character string that you explicitly type in, or the result obtained from executing a Linux command. In most cases, you will need to quote your values using either single quotes, double quotes, backslashes, or back quotes. Single quotes, double quotes, and backslashes allow you to quote strings in different ways. Back quotes have the special function of executing a Linux command and using the results as arguments on the command line.

Quoting Strings: Double Quotes, Single Quotes, and Backslashes

Although variable values can be made up of any characters, problems occur when you want to include characters that are also used by the shell as operators. Your shell has certain special characters that it uses in evaluating the command line. As mentioned earlier, a space is used to parse arguments on the command line. The asterisk, question mark, and brackets are special characters used to generate lists of file names. The period represents the current directory. The dollar sign is used to evaluate variables, and the greater-than and less-than characters are redirection operators. The ampersand is used to execute background commands, and the vertical bar pipes execute output. If you want to use any of these characters as part of the value of a variable, you must first quote them. Quoting a special character on a command line makes it just another character. It is not evaluated by the shell.

Double and single quotes allow you to quote several special characters at a time. Any special characters within double or single quotes are quoted. A backslash quotes a single character—the one that it precedes. If you want to assign more than one word to a variable, you need to quote the spaces separating the words. You can do so by enclosing the words within double quotes. You can think of this as creating a character string to be assigned to the variable. Of course, any other special characters enclosed within the double quotes will also be quoted.

The following examples show three ways of quoting strings. In the first example, the double quotes enclose words separated by spaces. Because the spaces are enclosed within double quotes, they are treated as characters, not as delimiters used to parse command line arguments. In the second example, single quotes also enclose a period, treating it as just a character. In the third example, an asterisk is also enclosed within the double quotes. The asterisk is considered just another character in the string and is not evaluated.

```
$ notice="The meeting will be tomorrow"
$ echo $notice
"The meeting will be tomorrow"

$ message='The project is on time.'
$ echo $message
The project is on time

$ notice="You can get a list of files with ls *.c"
$ echo $notice
You can get a list of files with ls *.c
```

Double quotes, however, do not quote the dollar sign—the operator that evaluates variables. A **$** next to a variable name enclosed within double quotes will still be evaluated, replacing the variable name with its value. The value of the variable will then become part of the string, not the variable name. There may be times when you want a variable within quotes to be evaluated. In the next example, the double quotes are used so that the winner's name will be included in the notice.

```
$ winner=dylan
$ notice="The person who won is $winner"
$ echo $notice
The person who won is dylan
```

On the other hand, there may be times when you do not want a variable within quotes to be evaluated. In that case, you would have to use the single quotes. Single quotes suppress any variable evaluation and treat the dollar sign as just another character. In the next example, single quotes prevent the evaluation of the winner variable.

```
$ winner=dylan
$ result='The name is in the $winner variable'
$ echo $result
The name is in the $winner variable
```

If, in this case, the double quotes were used instead, an unintended variable evaluation would take place. In the next example, the characters "$winner" are interpreted as a variable evaluation.

```
$ winner=dylan
$ result="The name is in the $winner variable"
$ echo $result
The name is in the dylan variable
```

You can always quote any special character, including the **$** operator, by preceding it with a backslash. The backslash is useful when you want to evaluate variables within a string and also include **$** characters. In the next example, the backslash is placed before the dollar sign in order to treat it as a dollar sign character, **\$**. At the same time, the variable **$winner** is evaluated since double quotes do not themselves quote the **$** operator.

```
$ winner=dylan
$ result="$winner won \$100.00""
$ echo $result
dylan won $100.00
```

Values from Linux Commands: Back Quotes

Though you can create variable values by typing in characters or character strings, you can also obtain values from other Linux commands. However, to assign the result of a Linux command to a variable, you first need to execute the command. If you place a Linux command within back quotes on the command line, that command is first executed and its result becomes an argument on the command line. In the case of assignments, the result of a command can be assigned to a variable by placing the command within back quotes to first execute it. Think of back quotes as a kind of expression that contains both a command to be executed and its result, which is then assigned to the variable. The characters making up the command itself are not assigned.

In the next example, the command **ls *.c** is executed and its result is then assigned to the variable **listc**. The command **ls *.c** generates a list of all files with a **.c** extension, and this list of files will then be assigned to the **listc** variable.

```
$ listc=`ls *.c`
$ echo $listc
main.c prog.c lib.c
```

Keep in mind the difference between single quotes and back quotes. Single quotes treat a Linux command as a set of characters. Back quotes force execution of the Linux command. There may be times when you accidentally enter single quotes when you mean to use back quotes. The following examples illustrate the difference. In the first example, the assignment for the **lscc** variable has single quotes, not back quotes, placed around the **ls *.c** command. In this case, **ls *.c** are just characters to be assigned to the variable **lscc**. In the second example, back quotes are placed around the **ls *.c** command, forcing evaluation of the command. A list of file names ending in **.c** is generated and assigned as the value of **lscc**.

```
$ lscc='ls *.c'
$ echo $lscc
ls *.c
$ lscc='ls *.c`
$ echo $lscc
main.c  prog.c
```

Quoting Commands: Single Quotes

There are times when you may want to use single quotes around a Linux command. Single quotes allow you to assign the written command to a variable. If you do so, you can then use that variable name as another name for the Linux command. Entering the variable name preceded by the **$** operator on the command line will execute the command. In the next example, a shell variable is assigned the characters that make up a Linux command to list files, **'ls -F'**. Notice the single quotes around the command. When the shell variable is evaluated on the command line, the Linux command that it contains will become a command line argument and will be executed by the shell.

```
$ lsf='ls -F'
$ $lsf
mydata /reports /letters
$
```

In effect, you are creating another name for a command, like an alias. You will see in later chapters on the specific shells that you can use a special alias command to do this for you.

TCSH Shell Variables

There is only a slight difference between variables in the TCSH shell and those in the BASH shell. In the TCSH shell, you assign a value to a variable with the **set** command and the assignment operator. To assign a value to a variable, first type **set**, then the variable name, the assignment operator, and the value assigned. The assignment operator must have either a space on both sides or no spaces. It cannot have a space on one side and not the other. For example, `> set poet =Virgil` is an error. Here, the variable **poet** is assigned the string **Virgil**:

```
> set poet=Virgil
```

Like the BASH shell, the TCSH shell also uses the dollar sign to evaluate variables. Evaluation retrieves a variable's value, usually a set of characters. This set of characters then replaces the variable name in the shell command. In the next example, the shell variable **poet** is evaluated, and its contents, **Virgil**, are then used as the argument for an **echo** command.

```
> echo $poet
Virgil
```

As with the BASH shell, double quotes, single quotes, and a backslash will suppress the evaluation of special characters. Also, back quotes can be used to assign the results of commands to variables. In the next example, the double quotes suppress the **?** special character.

```
> set notice = "Is the meeting tomorrow?."
> echo $notice
Is the meeting tomorrow?
>
```

Shell Scripts: User-Defined Commands

You can place shell commands within a file and then have the shell read and execute the commands in the file. In this sense, the file functions as a shell program, executing shell commands as if they were statements in a program. A file that contains shell commands is called a *shell script*.

You enter shell commands into a script file using a standard text editor such as the Vi editor. The **sh** or **.** command used with the script's file name will read the script file and execute the commands. In the next example, the text file called **lsc** contains an **ls** command that displays only files with the extension **.c**.

lsc

```
ls *.c
```

```
$ sh lsc
main.c calc.c
$ . lsc
main.c calc.c
```

You can dispense with the **sh** and **.** commands by setting the executable permission of a script file. When the script file is first created by your text editor, it is only given read and write permission. The **chmod** command with the **+x** option will give the script file executable permission. (Permissions are discussed in Chapter 7.) Once it is executable, entering the name of the script file at the shell prompt and pressing ENTER will execute the script file and the shell commands in it. In effect, the script's file name becomes a new shell command. In this way, you can use shell scripts to design and create your own Linux commands. You only need to set the permission once. In the next example, the **lsc** file's executable permission for the owner is set to on. Then the **lsc** shell script is directly executed like any Linux command.

```
$ chmod u+x lsc
$ lsc
main.c calc.c
```

Just as any Linux command can take arguments, so also can a shell script. Arguments on the command line are referenced sequentially starting with **1**. An argument is referenced using the **$** operator and the number of its position. The first argument is referenced with **$1**, the second with **$2**, and so on. In the next example, the **lsext** script prints out files with a specified extension. The first argument is the extension. The script is then executed with the argument **c** (of course, the executable permission must have been set).

lsext

```
ls *.$1
```

```
$ lsext c
main.c calc.c
```

In the next example, the commands to print out a file with line numbers have been placed in an executable file called **lpnum**, which takes a file name as its argument. The command to print out the line numbers is executed in the background.

lpnum

```
pr -t -n $1 | lp &
```

$ **lpnum mydata**

You may need to reference more than one argument at a time. The number of arguments used may vary. In **lpnum** you may want to print out three files at one time and five files at some other time. The **$** operator with the asterisk, **$***, references all the arguments on the command line. Using **$*** allows you to create scripts that take a varying number of arguments. In the next example, **lpnum** is rewritten using **$*** so that it can take a different number of arguments each time you use it.

lpnum

```
pr -t -n $* | lp &
```

$ **lpnum mydata preface**

Using a shell script is another way to create an alias for a command. In the next example, the **rmi** shell script contains an **rm** command that has the **-i** option. The **rm** command will first ask for approval from the user before erasing a file.

rmi

```
rm -i $*
```

$ **rmi mydata doc1**

Jobs: Background, Kills, and Interruptions

In Linux, you not only have control over a command's input and output but also over its execution. You can run a job in the background while you execute other commands. You can also cancel commands before they have finished executing. You can even interrupt a command, starting it up again later from where you left off. Background operations are particularly useful for long jobs. Instead of waiting at the terminal until a command has finished execution, you can place it in the background. You can then continue executing other Linux commands. You can, for example, edit a file while other files are printing.

Canceling a background command can often save you a lot of unnecessary expense. If, say, you execute a command to print out all your files and then realize you have some very large files you do not want to print out, you can reference that execution of the print command and cancel it. Interrupting commands is rarely used, and sometimes, it is unintentionally executed. You can, if you want, interrupt an editing session to send mail, and then return to your editing session, continuing from where you left off. The background commands as well as commands to cancel and interrupt jobs are listed in Table 5-2.

In Linux, a command is considered a *process*—a task to be performed. A Linux system can execute several processes at the same time, just as Linux can handle several users at the same time. There are commands to examine and control processes, though they are often reserved for system administration operations. Processes actually include not only the commands a user executes but also all the tasks the system must perform to keep Linux running.

The commands that users execute are often called jobs in order to distinguish them from system processes. When the user executes a command, it becomes a job to be performed by the system. The shell provides a set of job control operations that allow the user to control the execution of these jobs. You can place a job in the background, cancel a job, or interrupt one.

Background and Foreground: &, fg, bg

You execute a command in the background by placing an ampersand on the command line at the end of the command. When you do so, a user job number and a system process number are displayed. The user job number, placed in brackets, is the number by which the user references the job. The system process number is the number by which the system identifies the job. In the next example, the command to print the file **mydata** is placed in the background.

```
$ lpr mydata &
[1]   534
$
```

You can place more than one command in the background. Each is classified as a job and given a name and a job number. The command **jobs** will list the jobs being run in the background. Each entry in the list will consist of the job number in brackets, whether it is stopped or running, and the name of the job. The **+** sign indicates the job currently being processed, and the **–** sign indicates the next job to be executed. In the next example, two commands have been placed in the background. The **jobs** command then lists those jobs, showing which one is currently being executed.

```
$ lpr intro &
[1]   547
$ cat *.c > myprogs &
[2]   548
$ jobs
[1]   +   Running   lpr intro
[2]   -   Running   cat *.c > myprogs
$
```

If you wish, you can place several commands at once in the background by entering the commands on the command line, separated by an ampersand, **&**. In this case, the **&** both separates commands on the command line and executes them in the background. In the next example, the first command to **sort** and redirect all files with a **.l** extension, is placed in the background. On the same command line, the second command, to print all files with a **.c** extension, is also placed in the background. Notice that the two commands each end with **&**. The **jobs** command then lists the **sort** and **lpr** commands as separate operations.

```
$ sort *.l > ldocs & lpr *.c &
[1]   534
[2]   567
$ jobs
[1]   +   Running   sort *.l > ldocs
[2]   -   Running   lpr
$
```

After you execute any command in Linux, the system will tell you what background jobs, if you have any running, have been completed so far. The system will not interrupt any operation, such as editing, to notify you about a completed job. If you want to be notified immediately when a certain job ends, no matter what you are doing on the system, you can use the **notify** command to instruct the system to tell you. The **notify** command takes as its argument a job number. When that job is finished, the system will interrupt what you are doing to notify you that the job has ended. The next example tells the system to notify the user when job 2 has finished.

```
$ notify %2
```

You can bring a job out of the background with the foreground command, **fg**. If there is only one job in the background, the **fg** command alone will bring it to the foreground. If there is more than one job in the background, you must use the job's number with the command. You place the job number after the **fg** command, preceded with a percent sign. In the next example, the second job is brought back into the foreground. You may not immediately receive a prompt again because the second command is now in the foreground and executing. When the command is finished executing, the prompt will appear, and you can execute another command.

```
$ fg %2
cat *.c > myprogs
$
```

There is also a **bg** command that places a job in the background. This command is usually used for interrupted jobs and is discussed shortly, under "Interruptions: CTRL-Z."

Canceling Jobs: kill

If you want to stop a job that is running in the background, you can force it to end with the **kill** command. The **kill** command takes as its argument either the user job number or the system process number. The user job number must be preceded by a percent sign, **%**. You can find out the job number from the **jobs** command. In the next example, the **jobs** command lists the background jobs; then job 2 is canceled.

```
$ jobs
[1]  +  Running  lpr intro
[2]  -  Running  cat *.c > myprogs
$ kill %2
$
```

You can also cancel a job using the system process number, which you can obtain with the **ps** command. The **ps** command displays a great deal more information than the **jobs** command does. It is discussed in detail in the chapter on systems administration. The next example lists the processes a user is running. The PID is the system process number, also known as the process ID. TTY is the terminal identifier. The time is how long the process has taken so far. COMMAND is the name of the process.

```
$ ps
PID     TTY      TIME      COMMAND
523     tty24    0:05        sh
567     tty24    0:01       lpr
570     tty24    0:00        ps
```

You can then reference the system process number in a **kill** command. Use the process number without any preceding percent sign. The next example kills process 567.

```
$ kill 567
```

Interruptions: CTRL-Z

You can interrupt a job and stop it with the CTRL-Z command. This places the job to the side until it is restarted. The job is not ended; it merely remains suspended until you wish to continue. When you're ready, you can continue with the job in either the foreground or the background using the **fg** or **bg** command. The **fg** command will restart an interrupted job in the foreground. The **bg** command will place the interrupted job in the background.

There will be times when you need to place a job that is currently running in the foreground into the background. However, you cannot move a currently running job directly into the background. You first need to interrupt it with CTRL-Z, and then place it in the background with the **bg** command. In the next example, the current command to list and redirect **.c** files is first interrupted with a CTRL-Z. Then that job is placed in the background.

```
$ cat *.c > myprogs
^Z
$ bg
```

Often, while in the Vi editor, you may make the mistake of entering a CTRL-Z instead of a SHIFT-ZZ to end your session. The CTRL-Z will interrupt the Vi editor and return you to the Linux prompt. The editing session has not ended; it has only been interrupted. You may not detect such a mistake until you try to log out. The system will not allow you to log out while an interrupted job remains. To log out, you must first restart the interrupted job with the **fg** command. In the case of the Vi editor interruption, the **fg** command will place you back in the Vi editor. Then a ZZ editor command will end the Vi editor job and you can log out. In the next example, the

jobs command shows that there are stopped jobs. The **fg** command then brings the job to the foreground.

```
$ jobs
[1]  +  Stopped  vi mydata
$ fg %1
```

Delayed Execution: at

With the **at** command, you can execute commands at a specified time. Instead of placing a job immediately in the background, you can specify a time when you want it executed. You can then log out and the system will keep track of what commands to execute and when to execute them.

The **at** command takes as its argument a time when you want commands executed. The time is a number specifying the hour followed by the keywords a.m. or p.m. You can also add a date. If no date is specified, today's date is assumed. The **at** command will then read in Linux commands from the standard input. You can enter these commands at the keyboard, ending the standard input with a CTRL-D. You can also enter the commands into a file, which you can then redirect through the standard input to the **at** command. In the next example, the user decides to execute a command at 4:00 a.m.

```
$ at 4am
lpr intro
^D
$
```

In the next example, the user places several commands in a file called **latecmds** and then redirects the contents of this file as input to an **at** command. The **at** command will execute the commands at 6:00 p.m.

latecmds

```
lpr intro

cat *.c > myprogs
```

```
$ at 6pm < latecmds
```

You have a great deal of leeway in specifying the time and date. The **at** command assumes a 24-hour sequence for the time unless modified by the keywords a.m. or p.m. You can specify minutes in an hour by separating the hour and minutes with a colon, for example, 6:30. The **at** command also recognizes a series of keywords that specify certain dates and times. The keyword noon specifies 12 p.m. You can use the keyword midnight instead of 12 a.m. In the next examples, the user executes commands using a minute specification and then the keyword noon.

```
$ at 8:15pm < latecmds
$ at noon < latecmds
```

The date can be specified as a day of the month or a day of the week. The day of the month consists of the number of the day and a keyword representing the month. Months can be represented by three-letter abbreviations, for example, January is written as Jan. The day of the month follows the month's name. If there is no name, then the current month is assumed. Feb 14 specifies the fourteenth of February; 21 by itself specifies the twenty-first day of the current month. In the next example, the user first executes commands on the 15th of this month and then on the 29th of October.

```
$ at 8:15pm  15 < latecmds
$ at noon Oct 29 < latecmds
```

If you only want to run a job within your current week, you need only specify the day of the week instead of the day of the month. Each day of the week is represented by its name. Thus, entering tuesday as your date will run your commands on Tuesday. You can also use the keywords today and tomorrow for your date. In the next examples, the user executes commands on Friday and then tomorrow.

```
$ at 8:15pm  friday < latecmds
$ at noon tomorrow < latecmds
```

With either the time or date, you can specify an increment. For example, you could have commands executed one week from today or two months from Friday. You specify an increment using the **+** operator followed by a keyword denoting a segment of time. Segments of time keywords are: minutes, hours, days, weeks, months, or years. The plural *s* can be left off to denote one segment, for example, week is one week. The increment is added to the time or date that you specify. For example, to run commands one month from the 19th, you would enter **19 + month** for the date. One week from tomorrow is tomorrow + week. Two weeks from today is **today +2 weeks**. In the next example, the user executes commands 6 weeks from Monday and then 3 months from today.

```
$ at 8:15pm monday +6 weeks < latecmds
$ at noon today +3 months < latecmds
```

The **at** command has options that allow you to list the **at** jobs you have waiting, and to cancel any of those **at** jobs. Each time you execute an **at** command, the Linux commands you specify for late execution are queued and listed as an **at** job. You can obtain a list of your **at** jobs by entering the **at** command with the **-l** option. Each job will have a number with which you can reference it.

```
$ at -l
732893802.a     Fri Sept 27 20:15:00  1996
732893803.a     Tue Sept 24 12:00:00  1996
```

You can cancel your **at** jobs using the **-r** option. To cancel a specific job, you need to enter the job's number after the **-r** option. In the next example, the user cancels **at** job 732893802.a.

```
$ at -r 732893802.a
$ at -l
732893802.a     Tue Sept 24 12:00:00  1996
```

Ordinarily, the **at** command will not notify you when a job has been executed. However, with the **-m** option, you can request that you be notified by mail when an **at** job finishes execution. You can specify a particular job number to receive mail just for that job. In the next example, you will be notified by mail when **at** job 732893803.a has executed.

```
$ at -m 732893803.a
```

Summary: Shell Operations

The shell is a command interpreter that provides an interface between the user and the operating system. You enter commands on a command line that are then interpreted by the shell and sent as instructions to the operating system. The shell has sophisticated features, such as special characters, redirection, pipes, scripts, and job control.

The shell has three special characters, *, ?, [], which allow you to generate a list of file names for use as arguments on the command line. The * will match any possible sequence of characters, the ? matches any one character, and the [] matches a specified set of characters. You can even combine the special characters to compose complex matches.

In Linux, files and devices, as well as input and output from commands, all have the same structure—a byte stream. All input for a command is placed in a data stream called the standard input, and all output is placed in a data stream called the standard output. Because the standard input and standard output have the same structure as that of files, they can easily interface with files. Using redirection operators, you can redirect the standard input or the standard output from and to a file. With the > redirection operator, you can redirect the standard output from a command to a file. With the < redirection operator, you can redirect the standard input to be read from a file. You can also use the redirection append operator, >>, to append standard output to a file that already exists.

Since the input and output for commands has the same standard format, you can easily use the output of one command as input for another. Pipes allow you to take the standard output of one command and pipe it to another command as standard input. On the same command line, you can string together several commands, each receiving their input from the output of another command.

Using an editor, you can create files that contain shell commands and variable definitions. Such files are known as shell scripts. A shell script can even have argument variables that will receive arguments typed in at the command line. By setting the executable permission of the shell script, you can treat the name of the shell script file as if it were another command.

You can also define variables in the shell and assign them values. You evaluate a variable by placing a $ before the variable name. You can use variables as arguments in commands. They can hold directory path names, or even commands to be executed.

When you execute a command, it is treated by Linux as a job to be performed. You can instruct Linux to execute a job in the background, allowing you to continue executing other commands. Placing the & background operator at the end of the command line instructs the system to run this command in the background. You can list the jobs that you have in the background using the **jobs** command. With the **fg** command, you can bring a job in the background into the foreground. You can also cancel background jobs using the **kill** command, or interrupt jobs using the CTRL-Z command.

Standard Error Redirection Symbols	Execution
ENTER	Executes a command line
;	Separates commands on the same command line
`` `command` ``	Executes a command
*	Matches on any set of characters in file names
?	Matches on any single character in file names
[]	Matches on a class of possible characters in file names
\	Quotes the following character. Used to quote special characters
>	Redirects the standard output to a file or device, creating the file if it does not exist and overwriting the file if it does exist
>!	Forces the overwriting of a file if it already exists. This overrides the **noclobber** option
<	Redirects the standard input from a file or device to a program
>>	Redirects the standard output to a file or device, appending the output to the end of the file
|	Pipes the standard output of one command as input for another command
&	Executes a command in the background
!	History command
Standard Error Redirection Symbols	**Execution**
2>	Redirects the standard error to a file or device
2>>	Redirects and appends the standard error to a file or device
2>&1	Redirects the standard error to the standard output

Table 5-1. *Shell Symbols*

Standard Error Redirection Symbols	Execution
>&	Redirects the standard error to a file or device
|&	Pipes the standard error as input to another command

Table 5-1. *Shell Symbols* (continued)

Command	Execution
ENTER	Executes a command line
;	Separates commands on the same command line
command\ opts args	Enters backslash before carriage return in order to continue entering a command on the next line
`command`	Executes a command
BACKSPACE CTRL-H	Erases the previous character
CTRL-U	Erases the command line and starts over
CTRL-C	Interrupts and stops a command execution

Special Characters for Filename Generation	Execution
*	Matches on any set of characters
?	Matches on any single characters
[]	Matches on a class of possible characters
\	Quotes the following character. Used to quote special characters

Redirection	Execution
command > filename	Redirects the standard output to a file or device, creating the file if it does not exist and overwriting the file if it does exist

Table 5-2. *The Shell Operations*

Redirection	Execution
command **<** *filename*	Redirects the standard input from a file or device to a program
command **>>** *filename*	Redirects the standard output to a file or device, appending the output to the end of the file
command **>!** *filename*	In the C-shell and Korn shell, the exclamation point forces the overwriting of a file if it already exists. This overrides the **noclobber** option
command **2>** *filename*	Redirects the standard error to a file or device in the Bourne shell
command **2>>** *filename*	Redirects and appends the standard error to a file or device in the Bourne shell
command **2>&1**	Redirects the standard error to the standard output in the Bourne shell
command **>&** *filename*	Redirects the standard error to a file or device in the C-shell

Pipes	Execution
command **|** *command*	Pipes the standard output of one command as input for another command
command **|&** *command*	Pipes the standard error as input to another command in the TCSH-shell

Background Jobs	Execution
&	Executes a command in the background
fg *%jobnum*	Brings a command in the background to the foreground or resumes an interrupted program
bg	Places a command in the foreground into the background
CTRL-Z	Interrupts and stops the currently running program. The program remains stopped and waiting in the background for you to resume
notify *%jobnum*	Notifies you when a job ends

Table 5-2. *The Shell Operations* (continued)

Background Jobs	**Execution**
`kill` %*jobnum* `kill` *processnum*	Cancels and ends a job running in the background
`jobs`	Lists all background jobs. Not available in the Bourne shell, unless it is using the jsh shell
`ps`	Lists all currently running processes including background jobs

`at` *time date*	Executes commands at a specified time and date; *time* can be entered with hours and minutes and qualified as am or pm
	     hour:minutes am pm
	date is specified as a day of the month or day of the week
	
	     month day
	month can be represented by a three-letter abbreviation
	`Jan`, `Feb`, etc.
	day is specified by a name
	`monday tuesday wednesday`, etc.
	
	Keywords can be used to specify the date and time
	`am`, `pm`, `now`, `noon`, `midnight`, `today`, `tomorrow`
	
	You can increment from a date or time by a time segment using the **+** operator. A number after the **+** operator specifies how many time segments
	
	     date **+***num time-segment*
	time-segment can be
	`hours minutes days weeks months years`
	
	The **next** keyword increments by a time segment from the current date or time
	next *time-segment*
	`next week`

Table 5-2. *The Shell Operations* (continued)

Background Jobs

`options`

l *jobnum* (lists current **at** jobs)
r *jobnum* (cancels a job)
m *jobnum* (notification by mail when job finishes)

Table 5-2. *The Shell Operations (continued)*

Chapter Six

The Linux File Structure

In Linux, all files are organized into directories that, in turn, are hierarchically connected to each other in one overall file structure. A file is referenced not just according to its name but also to its place in this file structure. You can create as many new directories as you want, adding more directories to the file structure. The Linux file commands can perform sophisticated operations such as moving or copying whole directories along with their subdirectories. You can use file operations such as **find**, **cp**, **mv**, and **ln** to locate files and copy, move, or link them from one directory to another.

Together, these features make up the Linux file structure. This chapter will first examine different types of files as well as file classes. Then the chapter examines the overall Linux file structure and how directories and files can be referenced using path names and the working directory. The last part of the chapter discusses the different file operations such as copying, moving, and linking files.

Linux Files

You can name a file using any alphabetic characters, underscores, and numbers. You can also include periods and commas. However, a number cannot begin a file name, and except in certain special cases, you should never begin a file name with a period. Other characters, such as slashes, question marks, or asterisks, are reserved for use as special characters by the system and cannot be part of a file name. File names can be as long as 256 characters.

You can include an extension as part of a file name. A period is used to distinguish the file name proper from the extension. Extensions can be useful for categorizing your files. You are probably familiar with certain standard extensions that have been adopted by convention. For example, C source code files always have an extension of **.c**. Files that contain compiled object code have a **.o** extension. You can, of course, make up your own file extensions. The next examples are all valid Linux file names.

```
preface
chapter2
New_Revisions
calc.c
intro.bk1
```

There are also special initialization files that are used to hold shell configuration commands. These are the hidden, or dot files, referred to in Chapter 5 that begin with a period. Dot files have predetermined names. Recall that when you use **ls** to display your file names, the dot files will not be displayed. To include the dot files, you need to use **ls** with the **-a** option. Dot files are discussed in more detail in Chapter 14.

File Types

As you know from Chapter 5, all files in Linux have one physical format—a byte stream. A byte stream is just a sequence of bytes. This allows Linux to apply the file concept to every data component in the system. Directories are classified as files, and so are devices. Treating everything as a file allows Linux to organize and exchange data more easily. The data in a file can be sent directly to a device such as a screen, because a device interfaces with the system using the same byte-stream file format as regular files.

This same file format is used to implement other operating system components. The interface to a device such as the screen or keyboard is designated as a file. Other components, such as directories, are themselves byte-stream files, but they have a special internal organization. A directory file contains information about a directory, organized in a special directory format. Since these different components are treated as files, they can be said to constitute different *file types*. A character device is one file type. A directory is another file type. The number of these file types may vary according to your specific implementation of Linux. However, there are four common types of files: ordinary files, directory files, character device files, and block device files. Though you may rarely reference a file's type, it can be useful when searching for directories or devices. Later in the chapter, you will see how to use the file type in a search criteria with the **find** command to specifically search for directory or device names.

File Classifications: the file and od Commands

Though all ordinary files have a byte-stream format, they may be used in different ways. The most significant difference is between binary and text files. Compiled programs are examples of binary files. However, even text files can be classified according to their different uses. You can have files that contain C programming source code or shell commands, or even a file that is empty. The file could be an executable program or a directory file. The Linux **file** command helps you determine what a file is used for. It examines the first few lines of a file and tries to determine a classification for it. The **file** command looks for special keywords or special numbers in those first few lines, but it is not always accurate. In the next example, the **file** command examines the contents of two files and determines a classification for them.

```
$ file monday reports
monday:      text
reports:     directory
```

To illustrate the variety of classifications, the **file** command, in the next example, examines a C source code file, an executable file, and an empty file.

```
$ file calc.c proj newdata
calc.c:     C program text
proj:       executable
newdata:    empty
```

The **file** command also takes a **-f** option that allows you to read file names from a file rather than entering them on the command line. In the next example, the file names are read from the file **myfiles**.

```
$ cat myfiles
calc.c proj newdata

$ file -f myfiles
calc.c:     C program text
proj:       executable
newdata:    empty
```

If you need to examine the entire file byte-by-byte, you can do so with the **od** command. The **od** command performs a dump of a file. By default, it prints out every byte in its octal representation. However, you can also specify a character, decimal, or hexadecimal representation. The **od** command is helpful when you need to detect any special character in your file, or if you want to display a binary file. If you perform a character dump, then certain nonprinting characters will be represented in a character notation. For example, the carriage return will be represented by a **\n**. Both the **file** and **od** commands with their options are listed in Table 6-1 at the end of the chapter.

The File Structure

Linux organizes files into a hierarchically connected set of directories. Each directory may contain either files or other directories. In this respect, directories perform two important functions. A directory holds files, much like files held in a file drawer, and a directory connects to other directories, much like a branch in a tree is connected to other branches. With respect to files, directories appear to operate like file drawers, with each drawer holding several files. To access files, you open a file drawer. However, unlike file drawers, directories can contain not just files, but other directories. In this way, a directory can connect to another directory.

Because of the similarities to a tree, such a structure is often referred to in computer terminology as a *tree structure*. However, it could more accurately be thought of as an upside-down bush, rather than a tree. There is no trunk. The tree is represented upside down, with the root at the top. Extending down from the root are the branches. Each branch grows out of only one branch, but it can have many lower branches. In this respect, it can be said to have a *parent-child structure*. In the same way, each directory is itself a subdirectory of one other directory. Each directory may contain many subdirectories, but is itself the child of only one parent directory.

Figure 6-1 illustrates the hierarchical file structure. Beginning with the *root* directory at the top, other directories branch out. Each directory has several other directories or files, but a directory can only have one parent directory. The directory **chris**, for example, has two subdirectories: **reports** and **programs**. However, **chris** itself is connected to only one parent directory, the directory called **home**.

The Linux file structure branches into several directories beginning with a root directory, /. Within the root directory there are several system directories that contain files and programs that are features of the Linux system. The root directory also contains a directory called **home** that may contain the home directories of all the users in the system. Each user's home directory, in turn, will contain the directories the user has made for his or her own use. Each of these could also contain directories. Such nested directories would branch out from the user's home directory; see Figure 6-2.

Home Directories

When you log into the system, you are placed within your home directory. The name given to this directory by the system is the same as your login name. Any files you create when you first log in will be organized within your home directory. However, within your home directory, you can create more directories. You can then change to these directories and store files in them. The same is true for other users on the system. Each user has his or her own home directory identified by the appropriate login name. They, in turn, can create their own directories.

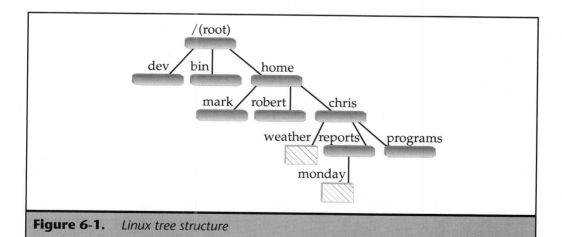

Figure 6-1.   *Linux tree structure*

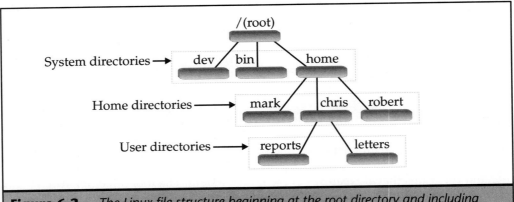

Figure 6-2.   *The Linux file structure beginning at the root directory and including system, home, and user directories*

You can access a directory either through its name or by making it the default directory. Each directory is given a name when it is created. You can use this name in file operations to access files in that directory. You can also make the directory your default directory. If you do not use any directory names in a file operation, then the default directory will be accessed. The default directory is referred to as the *working directory*. In this sense, the working directory is the one you are currently working from.

When you log in, the working directory is your home directory, usually having the same name as your login name. You can change the working directory by using the **cd** command to designate another directory as the working directory. As the working directory is changed, you can move from one directory to another. Another way to think of a directory is as a corridor. In such a corridor, there are doors with names on them. Some doors lead to rooms; others lead to other corridors. The doors that open to rooms are like files in a directory. The doors that lead to other corridors are like other directories. Moving from one corridor to the next corridor is like changing the working directory. Moving through several corridors is like moving through several directories.

Path Names

The name that you give to a directory or file when you create it is not its full name. The full name of a directory is its *path name*. The hierarchically nested relationship among directories forms paths, and these paths can be used to unambiguously identify and reference any directory or file. In Figure 6-3, there is a path from the root directory, /, through the **home** directory to the **robert** directory. There is another path from the root directory through the **home** and **chris** directories to the **reports** directory. Though parts of each path may at first be shared, at some point they differ. Both the directories **robert** and **reports** share the two directories, root and **home**. Then they differ. In the **home** directory, **robert** ends with **robert**, but the directory **chris** then

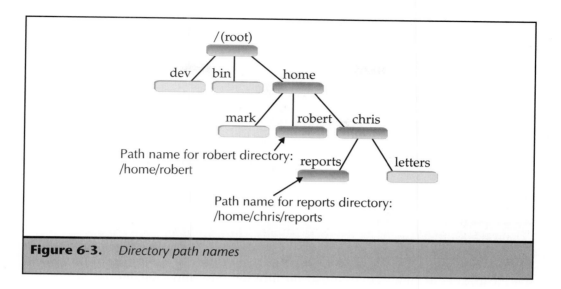

Figure 6-3. *Directory path names*

leads to **reports**. In this way, each directory in the file structure can be said to have its own unique path. The actual name by which the system identifies a directory will always begin with the root directory and consist of all directories nested above that directory.

In Linux, you write a path name by listing each directory in the path separated by a forward slash. A slash preceding the first directory in the path represents the root. The path name for the **robert** directory is **/home/robert**. The path name for the **reports** directory is **/home/chris/reports**.

Path names also apply to files. When you create a file within a directory, you give the file a name. However, the actual name by which the system identifies the file is the file name combined with the path of directories from the root to the file's directory. In Figure 6-4, the path for the **weather** file consists of the root, **home**, and **chris** directories and the file name **weather**. The path name for **weather** is **/home/chris /weather** (the root directory is represented by the first slash).

Path names may be absolute or relative. An *absolute path name* is the complete path name of a file or directory beginning with the root directory. A *relative path name* begins from your working directory; it is the path of a file relative to your working directory. Using the directory structure described in Figure 6-4, if **chris** is your working directory, the relative path name for the file **monday** is **/reports/monday**. The absolute path name for **monday** is **/home/chris/reports/monday**.

System Directories

The root directory that begins the Linux file structure contains several system directories. The system directories contain files and programs used to run and maintain the system. Many contain other subdirectories with programs for executing

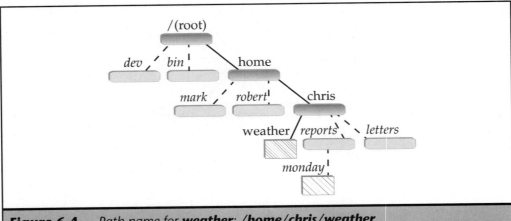

Figure 6-4.   *Path name for **weather**: **/home/chris/weather***

specific features of Linux. For example, the directory **/user/bin** contains the various Linux commands that users execute, such as **cp** and **mv**. The directory **/bin** holds interfaces with different system devices, such as the printer or the terminal. Table 6-2 lists the basic system directories, and Figure 6-5 shows how they are organized in the tree structure.

Listing, Displaying, and Printing Files: ls, cat, more, and lpr

One of the primary functions of an operating system is the management of files. You may need to perform certain basic output operations on your files, such as displaying

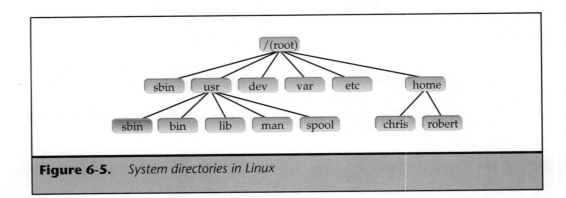

Figure 6-5.   *System directories in Linux*

them on your screen or printing them out. The Linux system provides a set of commands that perform basic file management operations such as listing, displaying, and printing files, as well as copying, renaming, and erasing files. These commands are usually made up of abbreviated versions of words. For example, the **ls** command is a shortened form of "list" and lists the files in your directory. The **lpr** command is an abbreviated form of "line print" and will print a file. The **cat** and **more** commands display the contents of a file on the screen. Table 6-3 lists these commands with their different options.

When you log into your Linux system, you may want a list of the files in your **home** directory. The **ls** command, which outputs a list of your file and directory names, is useful for this. The **ls** command has many possible options for displaying file names according to specific features. These are discussed in detail in Chapter 5.

Displaying Files: cat and more

You may also need to look at the contents of a file. The **cat** and **more** commands display the contents of a file on the screen. **cat** stands for "concatenate." It is actually a very complex and versatile command, as described in Chapter 7. Here it is used in a very limited way, displaying the text of a file on the screen:

```
$ cat mydata
computers
```

The **cat** command outputs the entire text of a file to the screen at once. This presents a problem when the file is large because its text quickly speeds past on the screen. The **more** command is designed to overcome this limitation by displaying one screen of text at a time. You can then move forward or backward in the text at your leisure. You invoke the **more** command by entering the command name followed by the name of the file that you want to view.

```
$ more mydata
```

When **more** invokes a file, the first screen of text is displayed. To continue to the next screen, you press the **f** key or the SPACEBAR. To move back in the text, you press the **b** key. You can quit at any time by pressing **q**.

Printing Files: lpr, lpq, and lprm

When you need to print files, use the **lpr** command to send files to the printer connected to your system. In the next example, the user prints the **mydata** file.

```
$ lpr mydata
```

If you want to print out several files at once, you can specify more than one file on the command line after the **lpr** command. In the next example, the user prints out both the **mydata** and **preface** files.

```
$ lpr mydata preface
```

Printing jobs are placed in a queue and printed one at a time in the background. You can continue with other work as your files print. You can see the position of a particular printing job at any given time with the **lpq** command. **lpq** gives the owner of the printing job (the login name of the user who sent the job), the print job ID, the size in bytes, and the temporary file in which it is currently held. In this example, the owner is **chris** and the print ID is 00015.

```
$ lpq
Owner      ID      Chars      Filename
chris      00015      360      /usr/lpd/cfa00015
```

Should you need to cancel an unwanted printing job, you can do so with the **lprm** command. **lprm** takes as its argument either the ID number of the printing job or the owner's name. **lprm** will then remove the print job from the print queue. For this task, **lpq** is very helpful, for it will provide you with the ID number and owner of the printing job that you need to use with **lprm**. In the next example, the print job 15 is canceled.

```
$ lprm   00015
```

You can have several printers connected to your Linux system. One of these will be designated the default printer, and it is to this printer that **lpr** will print, unless another printer is specified. With **lpr** you can specify the particular printer you want your file printed on. Each printer on your system will have its own name. You can specify which printer to use with the **-P** option followed by that printer's name. In the next example, the file **mydata** is printed on the evans1 printer.

```
$ lpr -Pevans1 mydata
```

Managing Directories: mkdir, rmdir, ls, cd, and pwd

As described in Chapter 4, you can create and remove your own directories, as well as change your working directory, with the **mkdir**, **rmdir**, and **cd** commands. Each of these commands can take as their argument the path name for a directory. The **pwd** command will display the absolute path name of your working directory. In addition to these commands, the special characters represented by a single dot, a double dot, and a tilde can be used to reference the working directory, the parent of the working directory, and the **home** directory. Taken together, these commands allow you to manage your directories. You can create nested directories, move from one directory to another, and use path names to reference any of your directories. Those commands commonly used to manage directories are listed in Table 6-4.

Creating and Removing Directories: mkdir and rmdir

You create and remove directories with the **mkdir** and **rmdir** commands. In either case, you can also use path names for the directories. In the next example, the user creates the directory **reports**. Then the user creates the directory **letters** using a path name.

```
$ mkdir reports
$ mkdir /home/chris/letters
```

You can remove a directory with the **rmdir** command followed by the directory name. In the next example, the user removes the directory **reports** with the **rmdir** command. Then the directory **letters** is removed using its path name.

```
$ rmdir reports
$ rmdir /home/chris/letters
```

Listing Directories: ls

You have seen how to use the **ls** command to list the files and directories within your working directory. However, to distinguish between file and directory names, you need to use the **ls** command with the **-F** option. A slash is then placed after each directory name in the list.

```
$ ls
weather reports letters
```

```
$ ls -F
weather reports/ letters/
```

The **ls** command will also take as an argument any directory name or directory path name. This allows you to list the files in any directory without having to first change to that directory. In the next example, the **ls** command takes as its argument the name of a directory, **reports**. Then the **ls** command is executed again, only this time the absolute path name of **reports** is used.

```
$ ls reports
monday tuesday
$ ls /home/chris/reports
monday tuesday
$
```

Path Names: the pwd Command

Within each directory, you can create still other directories, in effect, nesting directories. Using the **cd** command, you can change from one directory to another. However, there is no indicator that tells you what directory you are currently in. To find out what directory you have changed to, use the **pwd** command to display the name of your current working directory. The **pwd** command displays more than just the name of the directory—it displays the full path name, as shown in the next example. The path name displayed here consists of the **home** directory, **dylan**, and the directory it is a part of, **home**. Each directory name is separated by a slash. The root directory is represented by a beginning slash.

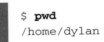

```
$ pwd
/home/dylan
```

Change Directory: the cd Command

As you already know, you can change directories with the **cd** command. Changing to a directory makes that directory the working directory, which is your default directory. File commands such as **ls** and **cp**, unless specifically told otherwise, will operate on files in your working directory.

When you log into the system, your working directory is your **home** directory. When a user account is created, the system also creates a **home** directory for that user. When you log in, you are always placed in your **home** directory. The **cd** command allows you to make another directory the working directory. In a sense, you can move from your **home** directory into another directory. This other directory then becomes the default directory for any commands and any new files created. For example, the **ls** command will now list files in this new working directory.

The **cd** command takes as its argument the name of the directory you want to change to.

```
$ cd directory-name
```

In the next example, the user changes from the **home** directory to the **props** directory. The user issues a **pwd** command to display the working directory.

```
$ pwd
/home/dylan
$ cd props
$ pwd
/home/dylan/props
$
```

You can also change to another directory by using its full path name. In the next example, the **cd** command takes as its argument the path name for the **letters** directory.

```
$ cd /home/chris/letters
$ pwd
/home/chris/letters
$
```

Notice that when you create a new directory, you are already in a working directory. Any directories that you then create are nested within that working directory. The working directory within which you create a new directory and the new directory itself take on a parent-child relationship. The working directory is the parent of the newly created directory. If, within the **home** directory, the user creates a **props** directory, then the **home** directory is the parent of the **props** directory, and **props** is the child of the **home** directory.

You can use a double dot symbol, **. .**, to represent a directory's parent. It literally represents the path name of the parent directory. You can use the double dot symbol with the **cd** command to move back up to the parent directory, making the parent directory the current directory. In the next example, the user moves to the **props** directory and then changes back to the **home** directory.

```
$ cd props
$ pwd
/home/dylan/props
$ cd ..
```

```
$ pwd
/home/dylan
```

If you want to change back to your **home** directory, you only need to enter the **cd** command by itself, without a file name argument. You will change directly back to the **home** directory, making it once again the working directory. In the next example, the user changes back to the **home** directory.

```
$ cd
```

In the next example, the **cd** command returns to the user's **home** directory, **chris**, and **pwd** displays the path name for that **home** directory.

```
$ pwd
/home/chris/letters
$ cd
$ pwd
/home/chris
```

You will find yourself changing from your **home** directory to another directory and back again frequently. In the next example, the user changes from his **home** directory, **dylan**, to the **props** directory. The user then changes back to his **home** directory with the **cd** command alone. Before each change, the user issues a **pwd** command to display the working directory.

```
$ pwd
/home/dylan
$ cd props
$ pwd
/home/dylan/props
$ cd
$ pwd
/home/dylan
```

Nested Directories

Let's see how the **cd** command can be used to progress through a series of nested directories. In the next example, the **cd** command changes to the **letters** directory. The **mkdir** command then makes a new subdirectory for **letters** called **thankyou**. Using the **cd** command again, the user changes to the **thankyou** directory. Within that directory, yet another subdirectory is created called **birthday**. The user then changes to that directory. Each time, the **pwd** command displays the path name. At the end, the **cd** command with no arguments returns to the **home** directory. The **ls** command with the **-R** option will print out all nested subdirectories below the working directory.

```
$ pwd
/home/chris
$ cd letters
$ pwd
/home/chris/letters
$ mkdir thankyou
$ cd thankyou
$ pwd
/home/chris/letters/thankyou
$ mkdir birthday
$ cd birthday
$ pwd
/home/chris/letters/thankyou/birthday
$ cd
$ pwd
/home/chris
$ ls -R
letters:
thankyou
letters/thankyou
birthday
letters/thankyou/birthday
$
```

Referencing the Working and Parent Directories: . and . .

A directory will always have a parent (except, of course, for the root). For example, in the last listing, the parent for **thankyou** is the **letters** directory. When a directory is created, two entries are made: one represented with a dot, **.**, and the other represented by a double dot, **. .** . The dot represents the path names of the directory, and the double dot represents the path name of its parent directory. The double dot, used as an argument in a command, references a parent directory. The single dot references the directory itself. In the next example, the user changes to the **letters** directory. The **ls** command is used with the **.** argument to list the files in the **letters** directory. Then the **ls** command is used with the **..** argument to list the files in the parent directory of **letters**, the **chris** directory.

```
$ cd letters
$ ls .
thankyou
$ ls ..
weather letters
$
```

Figure 6-6 illustrates the use of the dot and double dot representations for the parent and working directories. As in the previous example, the parent is the **home** directory, **chris**, and the working directory is **letters**.

You can use the single dot to reference your working directory, instead of using its path name. For example, to copy a file to the working directory retaining the same name, the dot can be used in place of the working directory's path name. In this sense, the dot is another name for the working directory. In the next example, the user copies the **weather** file from the **chris** directory to the **reports** directory. The **reports** directory is the working directory and can be represented with the single dot.

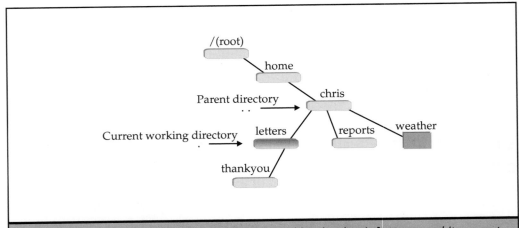

Figure 6-6. *The working directory, represented by the dot, is **letters**, and its parent, **chris**, represented by the double dot, is the **home** directory*

```
$ cd reports
$ cp /home/chris/weather  .
```

The **. .** symbol is often used to reference files in the parent directory. In the next example, the **cat** command displays the **weather** file in the parent directory. The path name for the file is the **. .** symbol followed by a slash and the file name.

```
$ cat ../weather
raining and warm
```

You can use the **cd** command with the **. .** symbol to step back through successive parent directories of the directory tree from a lower directory. In the next example, the user is placed in the **thankyou** directory. Then the user steps back up to the **chris** directory by continually using the command **cd . .** .

```
$ pwd
/home/chris/letters/thankyou
$ cd ..
$ pwd
/home/chris/letters
$ cd ..
$ pwd
/home/chris
```

There are many times when you will use both the **. .** and **.** as arguments to a command. For example, with **letters** as the working directory, **weather** can be copied down to **letters** referencing the **chris** directory with **. .** and the **letters** directory with **.** .

```
$ cp ../weather .
```

Using Absolute and Relative Path Names: ~

As mentioned earlier, you can reference files and directories using absolute and relative path names. However, each has its limitations. Though an absolute path name can reference any file or directory, it is usually lengthy and complex, making it difficult to use. A relative path name is often simpler and easier to use, but it is limited in the number of files it can reference. Usually, you will use relative path names whenever possible and absolute path names only when necessary. Some shells provide a way to abbreviate part of an absolute path name.

The relative path name starts from the working directory. In the next example, the **ls** command is used first with the relative path name and then with the absolute path name of **thankyou**. The working directory is the user's **home** directory, **chris**, and the relative path name of the **thankyou** directory is **letters/thankyou**. The absolute path name of the **thankyou** directory is **/home/chris/letters/thankyou**.

```
$ ls letters/thankyou
larisa
$ ls /home/chris/letters/thankyou
larisa
$
```

Relative path names can only reference files in subdirectories of the working directory. The subdirectories can be nested to any depth, but their paths must branch from the working directory. Suppose you need to reference a directory that is higher up in the directory tree or off in another branch from the working directory. For example, given **letters** as the working directory, suppose you want to display a file in a directory that is not a subdirectory of **letters**, say, the **reports** directory. In this case, you have to use the absolute path name for **reports**. In the next example, the user references the file **monday** in the **reports** directory using its absolute path name.

```
$ cat /home/chris/reports/monday
```

You also need to use an absolute path name when referencing directories higher in the directory tree than the working directory. Given **thankyou** as the working directory, suppose the user wants to display a file in your **home** directory, **/home/chris**. The **chris** directory is not a subdirectory of **thankyou** and cannot be referenced with a relative path name. In this case, the user would have to use the absolute path name to reference a file in his **home** directory. In the next example, the user is in the **thankyou** directory and wants to display a file **weather** in the **home** directory, **/home/chris**. To do so, the user needs to use an absolute path name for **weather**.

```
$ pwd
/home/chris/letters/thankyou
$ cat /home/chris/weather
raining and warm
$
```

The absolute path name from the root to your **home** directory could be especially complex and, at times, even subject to change by the system administrator. To make it easier to reference, you can use a special character, the tilde **~**, which represents the absolute path name of your **home** directory. In the next example, the user references the **weather** file in the **home** directory by placing a tilde and slash before **weather**.

```
$ pwd
/home/chris/letters/thankyou
$ cat ~/weather
raining and warm
$
```

You must specify the rest of the path from your **home** directory. In the next example, the user references the **monday** file in the **reports** directory. The tilde represents the path to the user's **home** directory, **/home/chris**, and then the rest of the path to the **monday** file is specified.

```
$ cat ~/reports/monday
```

File and Directory Operations: find, cp, mv, rm, and ln

As you create more and more files, you may want to back them up, change their names, erase some of them, or even give them added names. Linux provides you with several file commands that allow you to search for files, copy files, rename them, or remove files. If you have a large number of files, you can also search them to locate a specific one. The commands are shortened forms of full words, consisting of just two characters. The **cp** command stands for "copy" and copies a file, **mv** stands for "move" and will rename or move a file, **rm** stands for "remove" and will erase a file, and **ln** stands for "link" and will add another name for a file. One exception to this rule is the **find** command, which performs searches of your file names to find a file. Table 6-5 lists these different operations, including their options.

Searching Directories: find

Once you have a large number of files in many different directories, you may need to search them to locate a specific file or files of a certain type. The **find** command allows you to perform such a search. The **find** command takes as its arguments directory names followed by several possible options that specify the type of search and the criteria for the search. **find** then searches within the directories listed and their subdirectories for files that meet this criteria. The **find** command can search for a file based on its name, type, owner, and even the time of the last update.

```
$ find directory-list -option  criteria
```

The **-name** option has as its criteria a pattern and instructs **find** to search for the file name that matches that pattern. To search for a file by name, you use the **find** command with the directory name followed by the **-name** option and the name of the file.

```
$ find directory-list -name filename
```

The **find** command also has options that merely perform actions, such as outputting the results of a search. If you want **find** to display the file names it has found, you simply include the **-print** option on the command line along with any other options. The **-print** option instructs **find** to output to the standard output the names of all the files it locates. In the next example, the user searches for all the files in the **reports** directory with the name **monday**. Once located, the file, with its relative path name, is printed out.

```
$ find reports -name monday -print
reports/monday
```

The **find** command will print out the file names using the directory name specified in the directory list. If you specify an absolute path name, the absolute path of the found directories will be output. If you specify a relative path name, only the relative path name is output. In the previous example, the user specified a relative path name, **reports**, in the directory list. Located file names were output beginning with this relative path name. In the next example, the user specifies an absolute path name in the directory list. Located file names are then output using this absolute path name.

```
$ find /home/chris -name monday -print
/home/chris/reports/monday
```

If you want to search your working directory, you can use the dot in the directory path name to represent your working directory. The double dot would represent the parent directory. The next example searches all files and subdirectories in the working directory, using the dot to represent the working directory. If you are located in your **home** directory, this is a convenient way to search through all of your own directories. Notice that the located file names are output beginning with a dot.

```
$ find . -name weather -print
./weather
```

You can use shell special characters as part of the pattern criteria for searching files. However, the special character must be quoted in order to avoid evaluation by the shell. In the next example, all files with the **.c** extension in the **programs** directory are searched for.

```
$ find programs -name '*.c' -print
```

Search Criteria

You can also use the **find** command to locate other directories. In Linux, a directory is officially classified as a special type of file. Though all files have a byte-stream format, some files, such as directories, are used in special ways. In this sense, a file can be said to have a file type. The **find** command has an option called **-type** that searches for a file of a given type. The **-type** option takes a one-character modifier that represents the file type. The modifier that represents a directory is a **d**. In the next example, both the directory name and the directory file type are used to search for the directory called **thankyou**.

```
$ find /home/chris -name thankyou -type d -print
/home/chris/letters/thankyou
$
```

As noted previously, file types are not really so much different types of files as they are the file format applied to other components of the operating system, such as devices. In this sense, a device is treated as a type of file, and you can use **find** to search for devices, directories, as well as ordinary files. Table 6-6 lists the different types available for the **find** command's **-type** option.

The **find** command includes many different types of search criteria. You can search for a file by size, the time it was last accessed, the number of links it has, or the group it belongs to, as well as many other criteria. The different search criteria are listed in Table 6-6. Two of the more commonly used options are the **-size** and **-mtime** options. Each takes a number as its argument. By default, the **-size** option measures in blocks, but if you place a **c** after the number, it will measure in characters (bytes). You can modify the number with a **+** or **-** to look for a file greater than or less than the given size. For example, **+100c** will select files greater than 100 characters.

The **-mtime** option searches for files by how many days ago they were last modified. For example, using this option, you could locate all the files you worked on two days ago. In the next example, the **find** command uses the **-size** option to locate all files whose size is greater than 10 bytes. In the second example, **find** uses the **-mtime** option to search for those files modified three days ago.

```
$ find . -size +10c -print
.weather
./reports/monday

$ find . -mtime +3 -print
./weather
```

Complex Searches

When options are listed on the command line, they form an implied AND operation. Only files that meet all the criteria for the search have their names listed. However, using quoted parentheses and logical OR and NOT operators, you can construct complex search queries. The **find** command's NOT operator is an exclamation mark, **!**. A **!** placed before any search criteria negates the criteria. If the criteria is false, then the file is a match. For example, the following command prints out all files that do not have a **.c** extension.

```
$ ls
main.c lib.o today
$ find . ! -name "*.c" -print
lib.o today
```

The **find** command's logical OR operator is a **-o** . A **-o** placed between two search criteria treats the search criteria as part of an OR expression. If a file meets one or the other of the criteria, it is considered a match. You need to place the **-o** operation with its search criteria operands within quoted parentheses. Parentheses are quoted by putting a backslash before them and placing a space before and after them. The next command searches for files that have the name **weather**, as well as any directories. Notice the spaces around the quoted parentheses.

```
$ find . \( -name weather -o -type d \) -print
./weather
./reports
./letters
./letters/thankyou
```

You can form complex logical operations by combining search criteria using quoted parentheses. The next example searches for a directory named **reports** and any files that have a file size greater than 10 bytes. Quoted parentheses are placed around the **-name** and **-type** AND operation as well as the **-size** OR operation. The logical operations in the command can be formulated as:

```
((name = reports) AND (file = directory type)) OR (size > 10)

$ find . \( \( -name reports -type d \) -o -size+10 \) -print
./reports
./weather
```

Copying Files

To make a copy of a file, you simply give **cp** two file names as its arguments. The first file name is the name of the file to be copied—the one that already exists. This is often referred to as the source file. The second file name is the name you want for the copy. This will be a new file containing a copy of all the data in the source file. This second argument is often referred to as the destination file. The syntax for the **cp** command follows:

```
$ cp source-file destination-file
```

In the next example, the user copies a file called **proposal** to a new file called **oldprop**.

```
$ cp proposal oldprop
```

When the user lists the files in that directory, the new copy will be among them.

```
$ ls
proposal  oldprop
```

It is possible that you could unintentionally destroy another file with the **cp** command. The **cp** command generates a copy by first creating a file and then copying data into it. If another file has the same name as the destination file, then that file is destroyed and a new file with that name is created. In a sense, the original file is overwritten with the new copy. In the next example, the **proposal** file is overwritten by the **newprop** file. The **proposal** file already exists.

```
$ cp newprop  proposal
```

In Chapter 15 you will learn how you can configure your system to detect this overwrite condition. Until then, it may be safer to use the **cp** command with the **-i** option. With this option, **cp** will first check to see if the file already exists. If it does, you will then be asked if you wish to overwrite the existing file. If you enter **y**, the existing file will be destroyed and a new one created as the copy. If you enter anything else, it will be taken as a negative answer, and the **cp** command will be interrupted, preserving the original file.

```
$ cp -i  newprop  proposal
Overwrite proposal?  n
$
```

Copying Files to Directories

To copy a file from your working directory to another directory, you only need to use that directory name as the second argument in the **cp** command. The name of the new copy will be the same as the original, but the copy will be placed in a different directory. Files in different directories can have the same names. Because they are in different directories they are registered as different files.

```
$ cp filenames directory-name
```

To copy a file from the **home** directory to a subdirectory, simply specify the directory's name. In the next example, the file **newprop** is copied from the working directory to the **props** directory.

```
$ cp newprop props
```

The **cp** command can take a list of several file names for its arguments, so you can copy more than one file at a time to a directory. Simply specify the file names on the command line, entering the directory name as the last argument. All the files are then copied to the specified directory. In the next example, the user copies both the files **preface** and **doc1** to the **props** directory. Notice that **props** is the last argument.

```
$ cp preface doc1 props
```

You can use any of the special characters described in Chapter 5 to generate a list of file names to use with **cp** or **mv**. For example, suppose you need to copy all your C source code files to a given directory. Instead of listing each one individually on the command line, you could use a ***** special character with the **.c** extension to match on and generate a list of C source code files (all files with a **.c** extension). In the next example, the user copies all source code files in the current directory to the **sourcebks** directory.

```
$ cp *.c sourcebks
```

If you want to copy all the files in a given directory to another directory, you could use ***.*** to match on and generate a list of all those files in a **cp** command. In the next example, the user copies all the files in the **props** directory to the **oldprop** directory. Notice the use of a **props** path name preceding the ***.*** special characters. In this context, **props** is a path name that will be appended before each file in the list that ***.*** generates.

```
$ cp props/*.* oldprop
```

You can, of course, use any of the other special characters, such as **.**, **?**, or **[ ]**. In the next example, the user copies both source code and object code files (**.c** and **.o**) to the **projbk** directory.

```
$ cp *.[oc] projbk
```

When you copy a file, you may want to give the copy a different name than the original. To do so, place the new file name after the directory name, separated by a slash.

```
$ cp filename directory-name/new-filename
```

In the next example, the file **newprop** is copied to the directory **props** and the copy is given the name **version1**. The user then changes to the **props** directory and lists the files. There is only one file and it is called **version1**.

```
$ cp newprop props/version1
$ cd props
$ ls
version1
```

When you want to copy a file from a child directory such as **props** to a parent directory, you need to specify the name of the child directory. The first argument to **cp** is the file name to be copied. This file name must be preceded by the name of the child directory and separated by a slash. The second argument is the name the file will have in the parent directory.

```
$ cp child-directory-name/filename    new-filename
```

In the next example, the file **version1** is copied from the directory **props** up to the **home** directory.

```
$ cp props/version1    version1
```

Suppose, however, you have changed your working directory to that of a child directory and then want to copy a file from the child directory up to the parent. You need some way to reference the parent. You can do so using the double dot symbol, which represents the path name of the parent directory.

```
$ cp filename ..
$ cp filename ../new-filename
```

For example, if **props** is your current working directory and you want to copy the file **version1** from **props** up to its parent (in this case, the user's **home** directory), you need to use the double dot symbol in the second argument of the **cp** command.

```
$ cp version1 ..
```

If you want to give the copy of **version1** a new name, add the new name in the second argument, preceding it with a slash.

```
$ cp version1   ../newversion
```

Moving Files

You can use the **mv** command either to change the name of a file or to move a file from one directory to another. When using **mv** to rename a file, you simply use the new file name as the second argument. The first argument is the current name of the file that you are renaming.

```
$ mv original-filename    new-filename
```

In the next example, the **proposal** file is renamed with the name **version1**.

```
$ mv proposal version1
```

As with **cp**, it is very easy for **mv** to accidentally erase a file. When renaming a file, you might accidentally choose a file name that is already used by another file. In this case, that other file will be erased. The **mv** command also has a **-i** option that will check first to see if a file by that name already exists. If it does, then you will be asked first if you want to overwrite it. In the next example, a file already exists with the name **version1**. The overwrite condition is detected and you are asked whether or not you want to overwrite that file.

```
$ ls
proposal version1
$ mv -i  version1  proposal
Overwrite proposal?  n
$
```

You can move a file from one directory to another by using the directory name as the second argument in the **mv** command. In this case, you can think of the **mv** command as simply moving a file from one directory to another, rather than renaming the file. After you move the file, it will have the same name as it had in its original directory, unless you specify otherwise.

```
$ mv filename directory-name
```

In the next example, the file **newprop** is moved from the **home** directory to the **props** directory.

```
$ mv newprop props
```

Should you want to rename a file when you move it, you can specify the new name of the file after the directory name. The directory name and the new file name are separated by a forward slash. In the next example, the file **newprop** is moved to the directory **props** and renamed as **version1**.

```
$ mv newprops props/version1
$ cd props
$ ls
version1
```

A file can just as easily be moved from a child directory back up to the parent directory by specifying the child directory's name before the file name.

```
$ mv props/version1   version1
```

Suppose, however, you have changed your working directory to that of a child directory and then want to move a file from the child directory up to the parent. As with the **cp** command, you can use the double dot symbol to reference the parent directory.

```
$ mv filename ..
$ mv filename ../new-filename
```

If **props** is your current working directory and you want to move **version1** from **props** up to its parent, the **home** directory, then you can use the double dot symbol as the second argument of the **mv** command.

```
$ mv version1 ..
```

If you want to give the **version1** file a new name in the parent directory, you need to add the new name in the second argument, preceding it with a slash.

```
$ mv version1 ../oldprop
```

The actual name of a file is its file name preceded by its directory path. When **tuesday** was moved to the **reports** directory, its path name was actually changed. The full name of the **monday** file changed from **/home/chris/tuesday** to **/home/chris/reports/tuesday**. Its path name now includes the directory **reports**. In this sense, renaming a file is more like moving it.

You could just as easily use an absolute path name. In the next example, **today** is moved to the **reports** directory and given a new name, **tuesday**. Notice that the absolute path name is used for the file name argument in both the **mv** and **ls** commands.

```
$ mv today /home/chris/reports/tuesday
$ ls /home/chris/reports
monday tuesday
$
```

As with the **cp** command, the **mv** command can also move several files at once from one directory to another. You only need to enter the file names on the command line. The destination directory is always the last name you enter. In the next example, the user moves both the files **wednesday** and **friday** to the **lastweek** directory.

```
$ cp wednesday friday lastweek
```

You can also use any of the special characters described in Chapter 5 to generate a list of file names to use with **mv**. In the next example, the user moves all source code files in the current directory to the **newproj** directory.

```
$ mv *.c newproj
```

If you want to move all the files in a given directory to another directory, you can use ***.*** to match on and generate a list of all those files. In the next example, the user moves all the files in the **reports** directory to the **repbks** directory.

```
$ mv reports/*.*  repbks
```

Moving and Copying Directories

You can also copy or move whole directories at once. Both **cp** and **mv** can take as their first argument a directory name, allowing you to copy or move subdirectories from one directory into another. The first argument is the name of the directory to be moved or copied, and the second argument is the name of the directory within which it is to be placed. The same path name structure that is used for files applies to moving or copying directories.

You can just as easily copy subdirectories from one directory to another. To copy a directory, the **cp** command requires that you use the **-r** option. The **-r** option stands for "recursive." It directs the **cp** command to copy a directory as well as any subdirectories it may contain. In other words, the entire directory sub-tree, from that directory on, will be copied. In the next example, the **thankyou** directory is copied to the **oldletters** directory. There are now two **thankyou** subdirectories, one in **letters** and one in **oldletters**.

```
$ cp -r letters/thankyou oldletters
$ ls -F letters
/thankyou
$ ls -F oldletters
/thankyou
```

Suppose that, instead of copying a directory, making it a subdirectory of another directory, you just want to copy its files over. To copy all the files in one directory to another, you need to specify their file names. The asterisk special character will match all the file and directory names within a directory. To copy all the files in the **letters** directory to **oldletters**, you use the asterisk as your first argument in order to generate a list of all the file names in **letters**. If you need to specify a path name for the first argument, you can do so and place the asterisk at the end. In the next example, all the files in the **letters** directory are copied to the **oldletters** directory. A path name is specified for **letters**, and the asterisk at the end of the path name matches all files in the **letters** directory.

```
$ cp letters/* oldletters
```

In order to include the subdirectories in **letters** in the copy operation, you need to use the **-r** option with **cp**.

```
$ cp -r letters/* oldletters
```

The ~ Special Character

You have already seen how you can use the tilde to represent the absolute path name of the **home** directory. For example, to copy a file from a lower directory back to the **home** directory, you can use the tilde in place of the **home** directory's absolute path name. In the next example, the user changes to the **reports** directory and then copies the file **monday** from the **reports** directory up to the **home** directory.

```
$ cd reports
$ cp monday ~
```

To give a new name to the copied file when copying up to the **home** directory, place the new name after a **~/**. In the next example, the file **monday** is copied back up to the **home** directory and the copy is given the name **today**.

```
$ cp monday ~/today
```

The tilde is used in the same way for arguments in the **mv** command. In the next example, the file **monday** is moved from the **reports** directory back up to the **home** directory.

```
$ mv monday ~
```

If you are renaming a file while moving it to the **home** directory from a lower directory, the new name of the file is preceded by a tilde and a slash, **~/**. In the next example, there is a change to the **reports** directory, and then the file **monday** is moved back up to the **home** directory and renamed as **today**.

```
$ cd reports
$ mv monday ~/today
```

The tilde can be used wherever you would use the path name for the **home** directory. In the next example, a previously described **mv** and **ls** command are executed with the tilde.

```
$ mv weather ~/reports/monday
$ ls ~/reports
monday
$
```

Erasing a File: the rm Command

As you use Linux, you will find that the number of files you use increases rapidly. It is easy to generate files in Linux. Applications such as editors, and commands such as **cp**, easily create files. Eventually, many of these files may become outdated and useless. You can then remove them with the **rm** command. In the next example, the user erases the file **oldprop**.

```
$ rm oldprop
```

The **rm** command can take any number of arguments, allowing you to list several file names and erase them all at the same time. You just list them on the command line after you type **rm**.

```
$ rm proposal version1 version2
```

Be careful when using the **rm** command. It is irrevocable. Once a file is removed, it cannot be restored. Suppose, for example, you enter the **rm** command by accident while meaning to enter some other command, such as **cp** or **mv**. By the time you press ENTER and realize your mistake, it is too late. The files are gone. To protect against this kind of situation, you can use the **rm** command's **-i** option to confirm that you want to erase a file. With the **-i** option, you are prompted separately for each file and asked whether or not to remove it. If you enter **y**, the file will be removed. If you enter anything else, the file is not removed. In the next example, the **rm** command is instructed to erase the files **proposal** and **oldprop**. It then asks for confirmation for each file. The user decides to remove **oldprop** but not **proposal**.

```
$ rm -i proposal oldprop
Remove proposal? n
Remove oldprop? y
$
```

Links: the ln Command

You can give a file more than one name using the **ln** command. You might want to reference a file using different file names to access it from different directories. The added names are often referred to as links.

The **ln** command takes two arguments: the name of the original file and the new, added file name. The **ls** operation will list both file names, but there will be only one physical file.

```
$ ln original-file-name added-file-name
```

In the next example, the **today** file is given the additional name **weather**. It is just another name for the **today** file.

```
$ ls
today
$ ln today weather
$ ls
today weather
```

You can give the same file several names by using the **ln** command on the same file many times. In the next example, the file **today** is given both the names **weather** and **weekend**.

```
$ ln today weather
$ ln today weekend
$ ls
today weather weekend
```

You can use the **ls** command with the **-l** option to find out if a file has several links. **ls** with **-l** lists several pieces of information, such as permissions (described in the next chapter), as well as the number of links a file has, its size, and the date it was last modified. In this line of information, the first number, which precedes the user's login name, specifies the number of links a file has. The number before the date is the size of the file. The date is the last time a file was modified. In the next example, the user lists the full information for both **today** and **weather**. Notice that the number of links in both files is 2. Furthermore, the size and date are the same. This suggests that both files are really different names for the same file.

```
$ ls -l today weather
-rw-rw-r-- 2   chris   group 563   Feb   14   10:30   today
-rw-rw-r-- 2   chris   group 563   Feb   14   10:30   weather
```

This still does not tell you specifically what file names are linked. You can be somewhat sure if two files have exactly the same number of links, sizes, and modification dates, as in the case of the files **today** and **weather**. However, to be certain, you can use the **ls** command with the **-i** option. With the **-i** option, the **ls** command lists the file name and its *inode* number. An inode number is a unique number used by the system to identify a specific file. If two file names have the same inode number, they reference the exact same file. They are two names for the same file. In the next example, the user lists **today**, **weather**, and **larisa**. Notice that **today** and **weather** have the same inode number.

```
$ ls -i today weather larisa
1234 today     1234 weather    3976 larisa
```

The added names, or links, created with **ln** are often used to reference the same file from different directories. A file in one directory can be linked to and accessed from another directory. Suppose you need to reference a file that is in the **home** directory from within another directory. You can set up a link from that directory to the file in the **home** directory. This link is actually another name for the file. Because the link is in another directory, it can have the same name as the original file.

To link a file in the **home** directory to another directory, use the name of that directory as the second argument in the **ln** command.

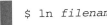

```
$ ln filename directory-name
```

In the next example, the file **today** in the **chris** directory is linked to the **reports** directory. The **ls** command will list the **today** file in both the **chris** directory and the **reports** directory. In fact, there is only one copy of the **today** file, the original file in the **home** directory.

```
$ ln today reports
$ ls
today reports
$ ls reports
today
$
```

Just as with the **cp** and **mv** commands, you can give another name to the link. Simply place the new name after the directory name, separated by a slash. In the next example, the file **today** is linked to the **reports** directory with the name **wednesday**. There is still only one actual file, the original file called **today** in the **chris** directory. However, **today** is now linked to the directory **reports** with the name **wednesday**. In this sense, **today** has been given another name. In the **reports** directory, the **today** file goes by the name **wednesday**.

```
$ ln today reports/wednesday
$ ls
today reports
$ ls reports
wednesday
$
```

You can easily link a file in any directory to a file in another directory by referencing the files with their path names. In the next example, the file **monday** in the **reports** directory is linked to the directory, **chris**. Notice that the second argument is an absolute path name.

```
$ ln monday /home/chris
```

To erase a file, you need to remove all of its links. The name of a file is actually considered a link to that file. Hence the command **rm** that removes the link to the file. If you have several links to the file and remove just one of them, the others stay in place and you can reference the file through them. The same is true even if you remove the original link—the original name of the file. Any added links will work just as well. In the next example, the **today** file is removed with the **rm** command. However, there is a link to that same file called **weather**. The file can then be referenced under the name **weather**. See Figure 6-7.

```
$ ln today weather
$ rm today
$ cat weather
The storm broke today
and the sun came out.
$
```

Symbolic Links and Hard Links

Linux supports what are known as symbolic links. Links, as they have been described so far, are called *hard links*. Though hard links will suffice for most of your needs, they suffer from one major limitation. A hard link may fail when you try to link to a file on some other user's directory. This is because the Linux file structure can be physically segmented into what are called file systems. A file system can be made up of any physical memory device or devices, from a floppy disk to a bank of hard disks. Though the files and directories in all file systems are attached to the same overall directory tree, each file system will physically manage its own files and directories. This means that a file in one file system cannot be linked by a hard link to a file in another file system. If you try to link to a file on another user's directory that is located on another file system, your hard link will fail.

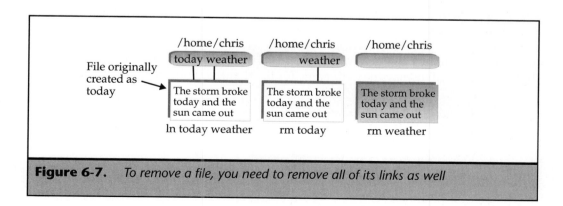

Figure 6-7.   *To remove a file, you need to remove all of its links as well*

To overcome this restriction, you use symbolic links. A *symbolic link* holds the path name of the file it is linking to. It is not a direct hard link, but rather information on how to locate a specific file. Instead of registering another name for the same file as a hard link does, a symbolic link can be thought of as another symbol that represents the file's path name. It is another way of writing the file's path name.

You create a symbolic link using the **ln** command with the **-s** option. In the next example, the user creates a link called **lunch** to the file **/home/george/veglist**.

```
$ ln -s lunch /home/george/veglist
```

If you list the full information about a symbolic link and its file, you will find that the information displayed is different. In the next example, the user lists the full information for both **lunch** and **/home/george/veglist** using the **ls** command with the **-l** option. The first character in the line specifies the file type. Symbolic links have their own file type represented by a **l**. The file type for **lunch** is **l**, indicating that it is a symbolic link, not an ordinary file. The number after the term "group" is the size of the file. Notice that the sizes differ. The size of the **lunch** file is only 4 bytes. This is because **lunch** is only a symbolic link—a file that holds the path name of another file—and a path name takes up only a few bytes. It is not a direct hard link to the **veglist** file.

```
$ ls lunch /home/george/veglist
lrw-rw-r-- 1  chris   group 4    Feb  14   10:30   lunch
-rw-rw-r-- 1  george  group 793  Feb  14   10:30   veglist
```

To erase a file, you need to remove only its hard links. If there are any symbolic links left over, they will not be able to access the file. In this case, a symbolic link would hold the path name of a file that no longer exists.

Unlike hard links, you can use symbolic links to create links to directories. In effect, you can create another name with which you can reference a directory. However, if you use a symbolic link for a directory name, bear in mind that the **pwd** command always displays the actual directory name, not the symbolic name. In the next example, the user links the directory **thankyou** with the symbolic link **gifts**. When the user uses **gifts** in the **cd** command, the user is actually changed to the **thankyou** directory. **pwd** will display the path name for the **thankyou** directory.

```
$ ln -s /home/chris/letters/thankyou   gifts
$ cd gifts
$ pwd
/home/chris/letters/thankyou
$
```

If you want to display the name of the symbolic link, you can access it in the **cwd** variable. The **cwd** variable is a special system variable that holds the name of a directory's symbolic link, if there is one. Variables such as **cwd** are discussed in Chapter 15. You display the contents of **cwd** with the command: **echo $cwd**.

```
$ pwd
/home/chris/letters/thankyou
$ echo $cwd
/home/chris/gifts
```

Summary: The Linux File Structure

In Linux, files are organized into directories. Directories themselves are connected hierarchically to each other, forming a treelike structure. Each directory contains files and other directories. At the top of the hierarchy is the root directory, which branches out into system directories and users' home directories. System directories contain utilities used to run the Linux system, and home directories are the users' login directories.

The nesting of directories forms a path from a higher directory to a lower one and vice versa. The set of directories from the root to a given directory is the directory's path name. In fact, each file has a path name consisting of the set of directories from the root to the file's directory. This path name together with the file's name constitutes the absolute path name of the file.

You can easily manage directories—creating new ones, removing old ones, and changing from one directory to another. Within a directory you can create other directories, nesting them to any depth. While logged into the system, you are always working within a default directory. This default directory is known as your working directory. Any files you create will be placed in this directory, unless otherwise specified. You can change your default directory with the **cd** command. In this sense, you can move from one directory to another. When you first log into the system, your default directory is your **home** directory.

You can perform file operations between directories or on the directories themselves. You can move files from one directory to another, as well as copy files to other directories. You can even move or copy entire directories. You can also create links for files. A link is another name for a file. You can have a link in one directory that references a file in another directory.

Command	Execution
`file`	Examines the first few lines of a file to determine a classification
`-f` *filename*	Reads the list of file names to be examined from a file
`od`	Prints out the contents of a file byte-by-byte in either octal, character, decimal, or hexadecimal; octal is the default
`-c`	Outputs character form of byte values; nonprinting characters have a corresponding character representation
`-d`	Outputs decimal form of bytes values
`-x`	Outputs hexadecimal form of bytes values
`-o`	Outputs octal form of bytes values

Table 6-1. *The `file` and `od` Commands*

Directory	Function
/	Begins the file system structure—called the root
/home	Contains users' **home** directories
/bin	Holds all the standard commands and utility programs
/usr	Holds those files and commands used by the system; this directory breaks down into several subdirectories
/usr/bin	Holds user-oriented commands and utility programs
/usr/sbin	Holds system administration commands
/usr/lib	Holds libraries for programming languages
/usr/doc	Holds Linux documentation
/usr/man	Holds the online manual **man** files
/usr/spool	Holds spooled files, such as those generated for printing jobs and network transfers
/sbin	Holds system administration commands for booting the system
/var	Holds files that vary, such as mailbox files
/dev	Holds file interfaces for devices such as the terminal and printer
/etc	Holds system configuration files and any other system files

Table 6-2.   *Standard System Directories in Linux*

Command or Option	Execution
`ls`	This command lists file and directory names `$ ls`
`cat`	This filter can be used to display a file. It can take file names for its arguments. It outputs the contents of those files directly to the standard output, which, by default, is directed to the screen `$ cat` filenames
`more`	This utility displays a file screen-by-screen. It can take file names for its arguments. It outputs the contents of those files to the screen, one screen at a time `$ more` filenames
`+`*num*	Begins displaying the file at page *num*
`num`**f**	Skips forward *num* number of screens
`num`**b**	Skips backward *num* number of screens
`d`	Displays half a screen
`h`	Lists all **more** commands
`q`	Quits **more** utility
`lpr`	Sends a file to the line printer to be printed; a list of files may be used as arguments
`-P` *printer-name*	Selects a specific printer
`lpq`	Lists the print queue for printing jobs
`lprm`	Removes a printing job from the printing queue

Table 6-3. *Listing, Displaying, and Printing Files*

Command	Execution
`mkdir`	Creates a directory `$ mkdir reports`
`rmdir`	Erases a directory `$ rmdir letters`

`ls -F`	Lists directory name with a preceding slash
	`$ ls -F`
	`today reports/letters/`

`ls -R`	Lists working directory as well as all subdirectories

`cd` *directory name*	Changes to the specified directory, making it the working directory; **cd** without a directory name changes back to the home directory
	`$ cd reports`
	`$ cd`

`pwd`	Displays the path name of the working directory
	`$ pwd`
	`/home/chris/reports`

directory name **/** *filename*	A slash is used in path names to separate each directory name. In the case of path names for files, a slash separates the preceding directory names from the file name
	`$ cd /home/chris/reports`
	`$ cat /home/chris/reports/mydata`

`..`	References the parent directory. You can use it as an argument or as part of a path name
	`$ cd ..`
	`$ mv ../larisa oldletters`

`.`	References the working directory. You can use it as an argument or as part of a path name
	`$ ls .`
	`$ mv ../aleina .`

`~` **/** *pathname*	The tilde is a special character that represents the path name for the **home** directory. It is useful when you need to use an absolute path name for a file or directory
	`$ cp monday ~/today`
	`$ mv tuesday ~/weather`

Table 6-4.   *Directory Commands*

Command	Execution
cp *filename filename*	Copies a file. **cp** takes two arguments: the original file and the name of the new copy. You can use path names for the files in order to copy across directories `$ cp today reports/monday`
cp -r *dirname dirname*	Copies a subdirectory from one directory to another. The copied directory will include all its own subdirectories `$ cp -r letters/thankyou oldletters`
mv *filename filename*	Moves (renames) a file. **mv** takes two arguments: the first is the file to be moved. The second argument can be the new file name or the path name of a directory. If it is the name of a directory, then the file is literally moved to that directory, changing the file's path name. `$ mv today /home/chris/reports`
mv *dirname dirname*	Moves directories. In this case, the first and last arguments are directories. `$ mv letters/thankyou oldletters`
ln *filename filename*	Creates added names for files referred to as links. A link can be created in one directory that references a file in another directory `$ ln today reports/monday`
rm *filenames*	Removes (erases) a file. Can take any number of file names as its arguments. Literally removes links to a file. If a file has more than one link, you need to remove all of them in order to finally erase a file `$ rm today weather weekend`

Table 6-5. *File Operations*

Command or Option	Execution
`find`	Searches directories for files based on a search criteria. This command has several options that specify the type of criteria and actions to be taken
`-name` *pattern*	Searches for files with the *pattern* in the name
`-group` *name*	Searches for files belonging to this group *name*
`-size` *num*c	Searches for files with the size *num* in blocks. If **c** is added after *num*, then the size in bytes (characters) is searched for
`-mtime` *num*	Searches for files last modified *num* days ago
`-newer` *pattern*	Searches for files that were modified after the one matched by *pattern*
`-print`	Outputs the result of the search to the standard output. The result is usually a list of file names, including their full path names
`-type` *filetype*	Searches for files with the specified file type
b	Block device file
c	Character device file
d	Directory file
f	Ordinary (regular) file
p	Named pipes (fifo)
l	Symbolic links

Table 6-6.   *The* `find` *Command*

Chapter Seven

File Management Operations

Linux provides several features for managing your files and directories. You can find out detailed information about files, such as when they were last updated and how many links they have. You can also control access to your files. Each file in Linux has permissions that determine who has access to it, as well as what kind of access they can have. You can allow other users to access given files or restrict access to just yourself.

Files reside on physical devices such as hard drives, CD-ROMS, or floppy disks, and, on each device, they are organized into a *file system*. To access files on a device, you attach its file system to a specified directory. This is called *mounting* the file system. For example, to access files on a floppy disk, you first mount its file system to a particular directory. This chapter discusses how you can access CD-ROMs, floppy disks, and hard disk partitions. You can even access an MS-DOS hard drive partition or floppy disk, as well as file systems on a remote server.

You can also back up your files into an archive, storing them for later retrieval, or you can combine them into an archive file for transfer across a network to another system. You can also compress your files, preparing them for more efficient transfer or to just take up less space for backups. Archiving and compression are used extensively for online software packages. You can download a compressed and archived software package, then decompress it and expand the archive. You are then ready to install the new software package on your system. This is a very common way to obtain new Linux software.

This chapter will first examine the different file and directory permissions, then will discuss accessing file systems. Finally, it will present archiving and compression methods. The commands and options discussed here are listed at the end of the chapter in Tables 7-1 through 7-10.

Displaying File Information: ls -l

As shown in Figure 7-1, the **ls -l** command displays detailed information about a file. First the permissions are displayed, followed by the number of links, the owner of the file, the name of the group the user belongs to, the file size in bytes, the date and time the file was last modified, and the name of the file. The group name indicates the group that is being given group permission. In Figure 7-1, the file type for **mydata** is that of an ordinary file. There is only one link, indicating that the file has no other names, no other links. The owner name is **chris**, the same as the login name, and the group name is **weather**. There are probably other users who also belong to the **weather** group. The size of the file is 207 bytes. It was last modified on February 20, at 11:55 a.m. The name of the file is **mydata**.

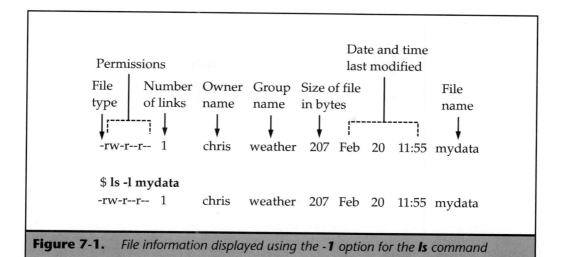

Figure 7-1. *File information displayed using the **-1** option for the **ls** command*

If you want to display this detailed information for all the files in a directory, simply use the **ls −1** command without an argument.

```
$ ls -1
-rw-r--r--  1  chris weather 207  Feb 20  11:55  mydata
-rw-rw-r--  1  chris weather 568  Feb 14  10:30  today
-rw-rw-r--  1  chris weather 308  Feb 17  12:40  monday
```

File and Directory Permissions: chmod

Each file and directory in Linux contains a set of permissions that determines who can access them and how. You set these permissions to limit access in one of three ways. You can restrict access to yourself alone. You can allow users in a predesignated group to have access. Or you can permit anyone on your system to have access. You can also control how a given file or directory is accessed. A file and directory may have read, write, and execute permission. When a file is created, it is automatically given read and write permissions for the owner, allowing you to display and modify the file. You may change these permissions to any combination you want. A file could have read-only permission, preventing any modifications. A file could also have execute permission, allowing it to be executed as a program.

There are three different categories of users that can have access to a file or directory: the owner, the group, or others. The owner is the user who created the file. Any file that you create, you own. You can also permit your group to have access to a file. Often users are collected into groups. For example, all the users for a given class or project could be formed into a group by the system administrator. It is possible for a user to give access to a file to other members of the group. Finally, you can also open up access to a file to all other users on the system. In this case, every user on your system could have access to one of your files or directories. In this sense, every other user on the system makes up the others category.

Each category has its own set of read, write, and execute permissions. The first set controls the user's own access to his or her files—the owner access. The second set controls the access of the group to a user's files. The third controls the access of all other users to the user's files. The three sets of read, write, and execute permissions for the three categories—owner, group, and others—make a total of nine types of permissions.

As you saw in the previous section, the **ls** command with the **-l** option displays detailed information about the file, including the permissions. In the next example, the first set of characters on the left is a list of the permissions that have been set for the **mydata** file.

```
$ ls -l mydata
-rw-r--r--  1  chris weather 207 Feb  20  11:55   mydata
```

An empty permission is represented by a dash, **-**. The read permission is represented by the **r**, write by **w**, and execute by **x**. Notice that there are ten positions. The first character indicates the file type. In a general sense, a directory can be considered a type of file. If the first character is a dash, a file is being listed. If it is a **d**, information about a directory is being displayed.

The next nine characters are arranged according to the different user categories. The first set of three characters is the owner's set of permissions for the file. The second set of three characters is the group's set of permissions for the file. The last set of three characters is the other users' set of permissions for the file. In Figure 7-2, the **mydata** file has the read and write permissions set for the owner category, the read permission only set for the group category, and the read permission set for the other users category. This means that, though anyone in the group or any other user on the system can read the file, only the owner can modify it.

You use the **chmod** command to create different permission configurations. **chmod** takes two lists as its arguments—a list of permission changes and a list of file names. You can specify the list of permissions in two different ways. One way uses permission symbols and is referred to as the symbolic method. The other uses what is known as a binary mask and is referred to either as the absolute or relative method. Of the two, the symbolic method is the more intuitive and will be presented first. Table 7-1 at the end of the chapter lists the options for the **chmod** command.

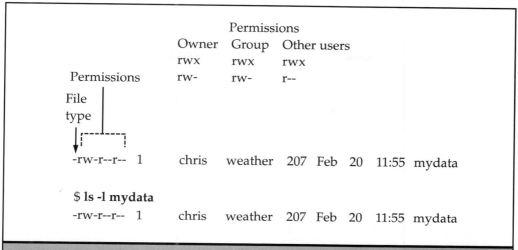

$ **ls -l mydata**
-rw-r--r-- 1   chris   weather   207   Feb   20   11:55   mydata

Figure 7-2.   *Owner, group, and other file permissions:* **r** *stands for read permission,* **w** *for write, and* **x** *for execute; a dash is a permission that is off*

Setting Permissions: Permission Symbols

As you might have guessed, the symbolic method of setting permissions uses the characters **r**, **w**, and **x** for read, write, and execute, respectively. Any of these permissions can be added or removed. The symbol to add a permission is the plus sign, **+**. The symbol to remove a permission is the minus sign, **–**. In the next example, the **chmod** command adds the execute permission and removes the write permission for the **mydata** file. The read permission is not changed.

```
$ chmod +x-w mydata
```

There are also permission symbols that specify each user category. The owner, group, and others categories are represented by the **u**, **g**, and **o** characters, respectively. Notice that the owner category is represented by a **u** and can be thought of as the user. The symbol for a category is placed before the read, write, and execute permissions. If no category symbol is used, all categories are assumed, and the permissions specified are set for the user, group, and others. In the next example and in Figure 7-3, the first **chmod** command sets the permissions for the group to read and write. The second **chmod** command sets permissions for other users to read. Notice that there are no spaces between the permission specifications and the category. The permission list is simply one long phrase, with no spaces.

```
$ chmod g+rw mydata
$ chmod o+r mydata
```

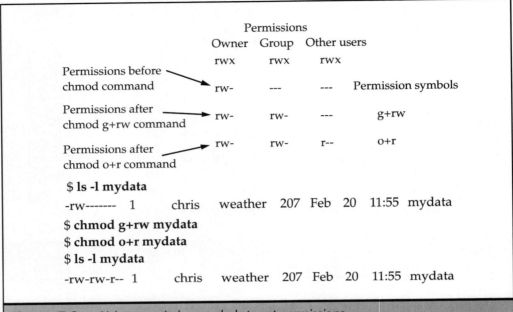

Figure 7-3. *Using permission symbols to set permissions*

A user may remove permissions as well as add them. In the next example, the read permission is set for other users, but the write and execute permissions are removed.

```
$ chmod o+r-wx mydata
```

There is another permission symbol, **a**, that represents all the categories. The **a** symbol is the default. In the next example, both commands are equivalent. The read permission is explicitly set with the **a** symbol denoting all types of users: other, group, and user.

```
$ chmod a+r mydata
$ chmod +r mydata
```

One of the most common permission operations is setting a file's executable permission. This is often done in the case of shell program files, which are discussed in Chapters 15 and 16. The executable permission indicates that a file contains executable instructions and can be directly run by the system. In the next example, the file **lsc** has its executable permission set and then executed.

```
$ chmod u+x lsc
$ lsc
main.c lib.c
$
```

Absolute Permissions: Binary Masks

Instead of permission symbols, many users find it more convenient to use the absolute method. The absolute method changes all the permissions at once, instead of specifying one or the other. It uses a binary mask that references all the permissions in each category. The three categories, each with three permissions, conform to an octal binary format. Octal numbers have a base eight structure. When translated into a binary number, each octal digit becomes three binary digits. A binary number is a set of 1 and 0 digits. Three octal digits in a number translates into three sets of three binary digits, which is nine altogether and the exact number of permissions for a file.

You can use the octal digits as a mask to set the different file permissions. Each octal digit applies to one of the user categories. You can think of the digits matching up with the permission categories from left to right, beginning with the owner category. The first octal digit applies to the owner category, the second to the group, and the third to the others category.

The actual octal digit that you choose will determine the read, write, and execute permissions for each category. At this point, you need to know how octal digits translate into their binary equivalents. The following table is a chart showing how the different octal digits, 0 to 7, translate into their three-digit binary equivalents. You can think of the octal digit first being translated into its binary form, and then each of those three binary digits being used to set the read, write, and execute permissions. Each binary digit is then matched up with a corresponding permission, again moving from left to right. If a binary digit is 0, the permission is turned off. If the binary digit is 1, the permission is turned on. The first binary digit sets the read permission on or off, the second sets the write permission, and the third sets the execute permission. For example, an octal digit 6 translates into the binary digits 110. This would set the read and write permission on, but set the execute permission off.

Octal	Binary
0	000
1	001
2	010
3	011
4	100

Octal	Binary
5	101
6	110
7	111

When dealing with a binary mask, you need to specify three digits for all three categories as well as their permissions. This makes it less versatile than the permission symbols. To set the owner execute permission on and the write permission off for the **mydata** file, as well as retain the read permission, you need to use the octal digit 5 (101). At the same time, you need to specify the digits for group and other users access. If these categories are to retain read access, you need the octal number 4 for each (100). This gives you three octal digits, 544, which translate into the binary digits 101 100 100. In Figure 7-4, these permissions are set for the **mydata** file.

```
$ chmod 544 mydata
```

Instead of painstakingly working out the octal-to-binary conversion in order to figure out what numbers you should use, there is a simple alternative. The read (**r**), write (**w**), and execute (**x**) permissions can be associated with the numbers 4, 2, and 1, respectively (see the table below). To find out what octal number you need to specify for a certain category, just add the associated numbers for the permission you want turned on. If you want to give a category a read and write permission, simply add 4 (read) and 2 (write) to give you 6. This is your octal number. To give a category read

Octal Binary Translation

				Permisions		
Octal digits	5	4	4	Owner	Group	Other users
Binary digits	101	100	100	rwx	rwx	rwx
				101	100	100
				r-x	r--	r--

$ chmod 544 mydata

$ ls -l mydata

-r-xr--r--	1	chris	weather	207	Feb	20	11:55	mydata

Figure 7-4. *Using octal digits to set permissions*

and execute permission, just add 4 (read) and 1 (execute) to give you 5. To set all the permissions, you would add 4 (read), 2 (write), and 1 (execute) to get 7, which is the equivalent of a binary 111. The next example uses this method to calculate the permissions used in the previous example. The owner is given read and execute permission, and the group and other users are given only read permission.

```
owner      rx        4 + 1 = 5
group      r      4         4
others     r      4         4
                           544          101 100 100
$ chmod 544 mydata
```

For example, to give members of your group both read and write permission to a given file, and deny access to any other users on the system, you need the octal digit 6 (110) for the group and 0 for the other users. Using 6 also for the owner retains read and write permission for the owner. You could also calculate the read and write permissions by adding 4 (read) and 2 (write) to get 6. Since you do not want any permissions for other users, you give them 0. This gives you the octal digits 660, which translate into the binary digits 110 110 000. Notice that an octal 0 will set all permissions off, using a binary 000.

```
$ chmod 660 mydata
```

Permission	Number	Binary
r	4	100
w	2	010
x	1	001

One of the most common uses of the binary mask is to set the execute permission. Remember, you can create files that contain Linux commands. Such files are called shell scripts. To have the commands in a shell script executed, you must first indicate that the file is an executable file—it contains commands that the system can execute. There are several ways to do this, one of which is to set the executable permission on the shell script file. Suppose you just completed a shell script file and need to give it executable permission in order to run it. You also want to retain read and write permission, but deny any access by the group or other users. The octal digit 7 (111) will set all three permissions, including execute (you can also add 4-read, 2-write, and 1-execute to get 7). Using 0 for the group and other users denies them access. This gives you the digits 700, which are equivalent to the binary digits

111 000 000. In the next example, the owner permission for the **myprog** file is set to include execute permission.

```
$ chmod 700 myprog
```

If you want others to be able to execute the file as well as read it, but not change it, you can set the read and execute permissions and turn off the write permission with the digit 5 (101). In this case, you would use the octal digits 755, having the binary equivalent of 111 101 101.

```
$ chmod 755 myprog
```

Directory Permissions

You can also set permissions on directories. The read permission set on a directory allows the list of files in a directory to be displayed. The execute permission allows a user to change to that directory. The write permission allows a user to create and remove his or her own files in that directory. If you allow other users to have write permission on a directory, they can add their own files to it. When you create a directory, the directory is automatically given read, write, and execute permission for the owner. You may list the files in that directory, change to it, and create files in that directory.

Like files, directories have sets of permissions for the owner, the group, and all other users. Often you may want to allow other users to change to and list the files in one of your directories, but not let them add their own files to it. In this case, you would set read and execute permissions on the directory, but not write permission. This would allow other users to change to the directory and list the files in it, but not create new files or copy any of their files into it. The next example sets read and execute permission for the group for the **thankyou** directory but removes the write permission. Members of the group may enter the **thankyou** directory and list the files there, but they may not create new ones.

```
$ chmod g+rx-w letters/thankyou
```

Just as with files, you can also use octal digits to set a directory permission. To set the same permissions as in the previous example, you would use the octal digits 750, which has the binary equivalent of 111 101 000.

```
$ chmod 750 letters/thankyou
```

As you know, the **ls** command with the **-1** option will list all files in a directory. To list only the information about the directory itself, you add a **d** modifier. In the next example, **ls -1d** displays information about the **thankyou** directory. Notice that the first character in the permissions list is **d**, indicating that it is a directory.

```
$ ls -ld thankyou
drwxr-x---  2  chris 512 Feb 10 04:30  thankyou
```

If you have files that you want other users to have access to, you not only need to set permissions for that file, but you also need to make sure that the permissions are set for the directory that the file is in. Another user, in order to access your file, must first access the file's directory. The same applies to parents of directories. Though a directory may give permission to others to access it, if its parent directory denies access, the directory cannot be reached. In this respect, you have to pay close attention to your directory tree. To provide access to a directory, all other directories above it in the directory tree must also be accessible to other users.

In Figure 7-5, the user wants to open up the **thankyou** directory to all other users. To do so, other users need access to the **chris** and **letters** directories. This is done by setting the execute permission on in the other category for each directory. Notice that

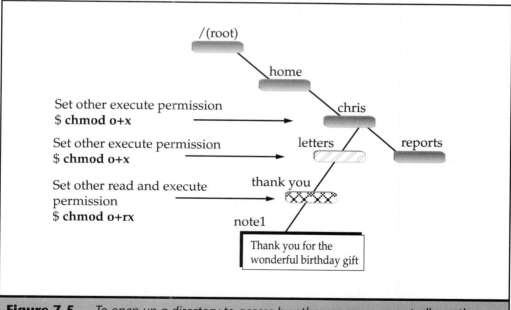

Figure 7-5. *To open up a directory to access by other users, you must allow other access to any of its parent directories as well*

only the execute permission needs to be set, not the read or write. Other users will not be allowed to list files or add files to either **letters** or **chris**. They can only change to those directories or reference their subdirectories.

Changing a File's Owner or Group: chown and chgrp

Though other users may be able to access a file, only the owner can change its permissions. If, however, you want to give some other user control over one of your file's permissions, you can change the owner of the file from yourself to the other user. The **chown** command transfers control over a file to another user. The **chown** command takes as its first argument the name of the other user. Following the user name, you can list the files you are giving up. In the next example, the user gives control of the **mydata** file to Robert.

```
$ chown robert mydata
$ ls -l mydata
-rw-r--r--  1  robert weather 207  Feb  20 11:55  mydata
```

You can also, if you wish, change the group for a file, using the **chgrp** command. **chgrp** takes as its first argument the name of the new group for a file or files. Following the new group name, you then list the files that you want changed to that group. In the next example, the user changes the group name for **today** and **weekend** to the forecast group. The **ls -l** command then reflects the group change.

```
$ chgrp forecast today weekend
$ ls -l
-rw-r--r--  1  chris weather 207  Feb  20 11:55  mydata
-rw-rw-r--  1  chris forecast 568  Feb  14 10:30  today
-rw-rw-r--  1  chris forecast 308  Feb  17 12:40  monday
```

File Systems: mount and umount

Though all the files in your Linux system are connected into one overall directory tree, the files themselves reside on storage devices such as hard drives or CD-ROMs. The Linux files on a particular storage device are organized into file systems. Your Linux directory tree may encompass several file systems, each on different storage devices. The files themselves are organized into one seamless tree of directories beginning from the root directory. Though the root may be located in a file system on your hard drive partition, there will be a path name directly to files located on the file system for your CD-ROM.

The files in a file system remain separate from your directory tree until you specifically connect them to it. A file system has its files organized into its own directory tree. You can think of this as a subtree that must be attached to the main directory tree. For example, a floppy disk with Linux files will have its own tree of directories. You need to attach this subtree to the main tree on your hard drive partition. Until they are attached, you will not be able to access the files on your floppy disk.

Remember that attaching a file system on a storage device to your main directory tree is called mounting the device. You mount a device with the **mount** command. To access files on a CD-ROM, first you have to mount the CD-ROM. The mount operation will attach the directory tree on the storage device to a directory that you specify. You can then change to that directory and access those files. Mounting file systems can only be done as the **root** user. It is a systems administration task and cannot be performed by a regular user. To mount a file system, be sure to log in as the **root** user. The syntax for the **mount** command follows. *mountpoint* is the directory on your main directory tree where you want the files on the storage device attached.

```
# mount device mountpoint
```

For a file system to be accessible it must be mounted. Even the file system on your hard disk partition has to be mounted with a **mount** command. However, when you install your Linux system and create the Linux partition on your hard drive, your system is automatically configured to mount your main file system whenever it starts. Your system will also automatically mount a CD-ROM if it is in your CD-ROM drive when the system starts up. Floppy disks, however, have to be explicitly mounted.

Before you can shut down your system, all your mounted file systems have to be unmounted. Your main file system is automatically unmounted for you. However, should you want to replace a mounted file system with another, you must first explicitly unmount the one already mounted. Say that you have mounted a floppy disk and now you want to take it out and put in a new one. You must unmount that floppy disk before you can put in and mount the new one. You unmount a file system with the **umount** command. **umount** takes as its arguments a device name and the directory where it was mounted. Here is the syntax:

```
# umount device mountpoint
```

The file systems on each storage device are formatted to take up a specified amount of space. For example, you may have formatted your hard drive partition to take up 300MB. Files installed or created on that file system will take up part of the space, and the remainder will be available for new files and directories. To find out how much space you have free on a file system, you can use the **df** command. It will list all your file systems by their device names and how much memory they take up as well as where they are mounted. **df** is also a very safe way to obtain a listing of all your partitions, instead of using **fdisk**.

```
$ df
Filesystem      1024-blocks   Used Available Capacity Mounted on
/dev/hda3          297635    169499    112764    60%    /
/dev/hda1          205380    182320     23060    89%    /mnt/dos
/dev/hdc           637986    637986         0   100%    /mnt/cdrom
```

You can also use **df** to tell you what file system a given directory belongs to. Just enter **df** with the directory name, or **df .** for the current directory.

```
$ df dirname
```

To make sure nothing is wrong with a given file system, you can use the **fsck** command to check it. Enter **fsck** and the device name that references the file system. The following examples check the disk in the floppy drive, the primary hard drive partition, and the CD-ROM currently in the CD-ROM drive.

```
# fsck    /dev/fd0
# fsck    /dev/hda1
# fsck    /dev/cd0
```

Mounting and Formatting Floppy Disks

Alternatively, you can explicitly reference the device and directory names when you mount and unmount them, as you would in any version of Linux. The device name for your floppy drive is **fd0**, and it is located in the directory **/dev**. **/dev/fd0** references your floppy drive. Notice the number 0 after **fd**. If you have more than one floppy drive, they will be represented by **fd1**, **fd2**, and so on. You can mount to any directory you want. However, your Redhat installation already created a convenient directory to use for floppy disks, **/mnt/floppy**. The following example mounts the floppy disk in your floppy drive to the **/mnt/floppy** directory.

```
# mount /dev/fd0  /mnt/floppy
```

Bear in mind that you are mounting a particular floppy disk, not the floppy drive. You cannot just remove the floppy disk and put in another one. The **mount** command has attached those files to your main directory tree, and your system expects to find those files on a floppy disk in your floppy drive. If you take out the disk and put another one in, you will get an error when you try to access it.

To change disks, you must first unmount the floppy disk already in your disk drive; then, after putting in the new disk, you must explicitly mount that new disk. To do this, you use the **umount** command. Notice that there is no *n* in the **umount** command.

```
# umount   /dev/fd0   /mnt/floppy
```

You can now remove the floppy disk and put in the new one. Then issue the command:

```
# mount   /dev/fd0     /mnt/floppy
```

When you shut down your system, any disk you have mounted will be automatically unmounted. You do not have to explicitly unmount it.

Before a floppy disk can be mounted, it must be formatted as a Linux file system. You format a floppy disk with the **mkfs** command. This takes as its arguments the device name and the number of memory blocks on the disk. At 1000 bytes per block, 1400 formats a 1.44MB disk. You do not mount the blank disk; you simply put it in your floppy drive and enter the **mkfs** command with its arguments. This example formats a 1.44MB floppy disk:

```
# mkfs   /dev/fd0   1400
```

Mounting CD-ROMs

You can also explicitly reference CD-ROMs and CD-ROM drives. For Redhat Linux, the device name for your CD-ROM drive is **hdc**, and it is located in the directory **/dev**. **/dev/hdc** references your CD-ROM drive. On other Linux systems, the device name for your CD-ROM may be **cd0**. The following example mounts the disc in your CD-ROM drive to the **/etc/mnt** directory.

```
# mount /dev/hdc   /etc/mnt
```

As with floppy disks, keep in mind that you are mounting a particular CD-ROM, not the CD-ROM drive. You cannot just remove the CD-ROM and put in a new one. The **mount** command has attached those files to your main directory tree, and your system expects to find those files on a disc in your CD-ROM drive.

To change discs, you have to unmount the CD-ROM that is already in your CD-ROM drive; then, after putting in the new disc, you must explicitly mount that new CD-ROM.

```
# umount   /dev/hdc   /dev/mnt
```

You can now remove the CD-ROM and put in the new one. Then issue a **mount** command to mount it:

```
# mount   /dev/hdc    /dev/mnt
```

File systems can be configured with entries in the **/etc/fstab** file. Your Redhat installation of Linux has configured your CD-ROM entry in such a way as to make it easier for you to mount and unmount your CD-ROMs. The directory **/mnt/cdrom** has been reserved for CD-ROM file systems. To mount a CD-ROM, all you have to do is enter the command **mount** and the directory **/mnt/cdrom**. You do not need to specify the device name. Then change to the **/mnt/cdrom** directory to access your CD-ROM.

```
# mount /mnt/cdrom
```

Mounting Hard Drive Partitions: Linux and MS-DOS

You can mount either Linux or MS-DOS hard drive partitions with the **mount** command. However, it is much more practical to have them mounted automatically using the **/etc/fstab** file as described in the next section. The Linux hard disk partitions you created during installation are already automatically mounted for you. To mount a Linux hard disk partition, you enter the **mount** command with the device name of the partition and the directory you want to mount it to. To find the device name, you can use **df** to display your hard disk partitions. The next example mounts the Linux hard disk partition on **/dev/hda4** to the directory **/mnt**.

```
# mount /dev/hda4   /mnt
```

You can also mount an MS-DOS partition and directly access the files on them. As with a Linux partition, you use the **mount** command, but you also have to specify the file system type as MS-DOS. For that you use the **-t** option and the type **msdos**. In the next example, the user mounts the MS-DOS hard disk partition **/dev/hda1** to the Linux file structure at directory **/mnt/dos**. **/mnt/dos** is a common designation for MS-DOS file systems, though you can mount it in any directory. Be sure that you have already created the directory.

```
# mount -t msdos  /dev/hda1  /mnt/dos
```

If you want to mount a new partition from either a new hard drive or your current drive, you must first create that partition using either the Linux **fdisk** or **cfdisk** and format it with **mkfs**. Once created and formatted, you can then mount it on your system. To start **cfdisk**, you enter **fdisk** on the command line. This will bring up an interactive program that you can use to create your Linux partition. Be very careful using Linux **fdisk**. It can literally erase your entire hard disk if you are not careful.

fdisk operates much as described in the installation process discussed in Chapter 2. The command **n** will create a new partition, and the command **t** will allow you to set its type to that of a Linux type, 83.

Hard disk partitions are named with **hd** followed by an alphabetic letter indicating the hard drive, and then a number for the partition on the hard drive. They can belong to any operating system such as MS-DOS, OS/2, or Windows NT, as well as Linux. The first partition created is called **hda1**—the first partition on the first hard drive, **a**. If you add another partition, it will have the name **hda2**. If you add a new hard drive, its first partition will have the name **hdb1**.

Once you have created your partition, you have to format it. For this, you use the **mkfs** command and the name of the hard disk partition. A hard disk partition is a device with its own device name in the /**dev** directory. You have to specify its full path name with the **mkfs** command. For example, the second partition on the first hard drive will have the device name /**dev/hda5**. The next example formats that partition.

```
# mkfs  /dev/hda5
```

You can now mount your new hard disk partition, attaching it to your file structure.

Automatically Mounting File Systems: The fstab File

When adding a new hard disk partition to your Linux system, you will most likely want to have it automatically mounted on startup, and unmounted when you shut down. Otherwise, you will have to mount and unmount the partition explicitly each time you boot up and shut down your system. To have Linux automatically mount the file system on your new hard disk partition, you only need to add its name to the **fstab** file. You can do this by directly and carefully editing the **fstab** file to type in a new entry, or you can use the **fstool** as described in the next section. The **fstab** file is located in the /**etc** directory. It lists the file systems that are mounted by the **mount** command with the **-a** option. This **mount -a** command is in your **/etc/rc.d/rc.sysinit** file. The commands perform system initialization operations. They are executed every time you boot your system. When you shut down your system an **umount -a** command is executed which unmounts all the file systems listed in **fstab**. The **umount -a** command is found in your **/etc/rc.d/init/halt** file which contains commands to be executed whenever you shut down your system. In this way, any file system you specify in your **/etc/fstab** file is automatically mounted when the system starts, and automatically unmounted when your system shuts down. **/etc/rc.d/rc.sysinit** is a Redhat implementation. Other systems such as Slackware may put the **mount -a** command in a file name, **/etc/rc.d/rc.local**.

An entry in a **fstab** file contains several fields, each separated by a space or tab. The first field is the name of the file system to be mounted. This usually begins with **/dev** such as **/dev/hda3** for the third hard disk partition. The next field is the directory in your file structure where you want the file system on this device to be attached. The third field is the type of file system being mounted. Table 7-2 is a list of the **mount** options and Table 7-3 provides a list of all the different types you can mount. The type for a standard Linux hard disk partition is **ext2**. The next example shows an entry for the main Linux hard disk partition. It is mounted at the root directory, /, and has a file type of **ext2**.

```
/dev/hda3  /  ext2  defaults  0  1
```

The field after the file system type lists the different options for mounting the file system. There is a default set of options that you can specify by simply entering **defaults**. You can list specific options next to each other separated by a comma (no spaces). The **defaults** option specifies that a device is read/write, asynchronous, block, that ordinary users cannot mount on it, and programs can be executed on it. By contrast, a CD-ROM only has a few options listed for it, **ro** and **noauto**. **ro** specifies that this is read-only, and **noauto** that it is not automatically mounted. The **noauto** option is used with both CD-ROMs and floppy drives, so they won't automatically mount since you do not know if you will have anything in them when you start up. At the same time, the entries for both the CD-ROM and the floppy drive specify where they are to be mounted when you start up if you do decide to mount them. An example of CD-ROM and floppy drive entries follows. Notice that the type for a CD-ROM file system is different from a hard disk partition, **iso9660**. The floppy drive also has all the default options of the hard disk partitions.

```
/dev/fd0   /mnt/floppy  ext2     defaults,noauto  0  0
/dev/hdc   /mnt/cdrom   iso9660  ro,noauto        0  0
```

The last two fields consist of an integer value. The first one is used by the **dump** command to determine if a file system needs to be dumped, backing up the file system. The last one is used by **fsck** to see if a file system should be checked and in what order. If the field has a value of 1, it indicates a boot partition. The 0 value means that the **fsck** does not have to check the file system.

A copy of an **/etc/fstab** file is shown here. Notice that the first line is a comment. All comment lines begin with a **#**. The entry for the **/proc** file system is a special entry used by your Linux operating system for managing its processes. It is not an actual device.

/etc/fstab

# <device>	<mountpoint>	<filesystemtype>	<options>	<dump>	<fsckorder>
/dev/hda3	/	ext2	defaults	0	1
/dev/hdc	/mnt/cdrom	iso9660	ro,noauto	0	0
/dev/fd0	/mnt/floppy	ext2	defaults,noauto	0	0
/proc	/proc	proc	defaults		
/dev/hda2	none	swap	sw		
/dev/hda1	/mnt/dos	msdos	defaults	0	0

To make an entry in the **/etc/fstab** file, you can either edit the **/etc/fstab** file directly or use the utility **fstool** that will prompt you for information and then make the correct entries into your **/etc/fstab** file.

As noted earlier, you can mount MS-DOS partitions used by your MS-DOS operating system onto your Linux file structure, just as you would mount any Linux file system. You only have to specify the file type of MS-DOS. You may find it convenient to have your MS-DOS partitions automatically mounted when you start up your Linux system. To do this, you just have to put an entry for your MS-DOS partitions in your **/etc/fstab** file. You make an entry for each MS-DOS partition you want to mount. You specify the device name for the MS-DOS partition, followed by the directory that you want to mount it in. The directory, **/mnt/dos**, would be a logical choice (be sure that the **dos** directory has already been created in **/mnt**). For the file system type, you enter **msdos**. The next example shows a standard MS-DOS partition entry for an **/etc/fstab** file. Notice that the last entry in the **/etc/fstab** file example is an entry for mounting an MS-DOS partition.

```
/dev/hda1 /mnt/dos  msdos  defaults  0  0
```

Redhat Linux File System Manager: fstool

On your root user Caldera Network Desktop you will find an icon for the **fstool** program. This program is the Linux Redhat File Systems Manager. It opens a window and lists the contents of your **/etc/fstab** file. Using buttons and menus, you can mount and unmount file systems, add new file systems to your **/etc/fstab** file, and change any options for your file systems. Figure 7-6 shows the **fstool** window.

The entries for the file systems listed in the **fstab** file are displayed in the center window pane. The top row provides a heading for each field. Five buttons across the bottom descibe various operations you can carry out on each file system. Just click on the file system entry and it will highlight. Then click on the button. Clicking on the Info button will open a window that displays detailed information about the file system, including the number of bytes still unused. The Check button checks the file system for error. The Mount and Unmount buttons both mount and unmount selected file systems. The Format button formats a file system, and the Edit button allows you to change certain fields such as file system options. Be very careful when using **fstool**. You don't want to unmount a system that you need access to, nor do you want to unintentionally format a file system, thereby losing all your data on it.

The upper left-hand corner of the window holds two menus, one configuring your File Systems Manager (FSM), and one for Network File Systems (NFS). NFS file systems are described in the next section. You can configure the file systems manager to display more information in the window, such as the percentage of unused memory on your file systems. You also use the FSM menu to add and remove file systems from your **/etc/fstab** file. The Add entry will let you add a file system and the Delete entry will remove it. For example, to add an MS-DOS file system on a hard disk partition to the **/etc/fstab** file, you would select Add from the FSM menu and then enter the device name for the file system.

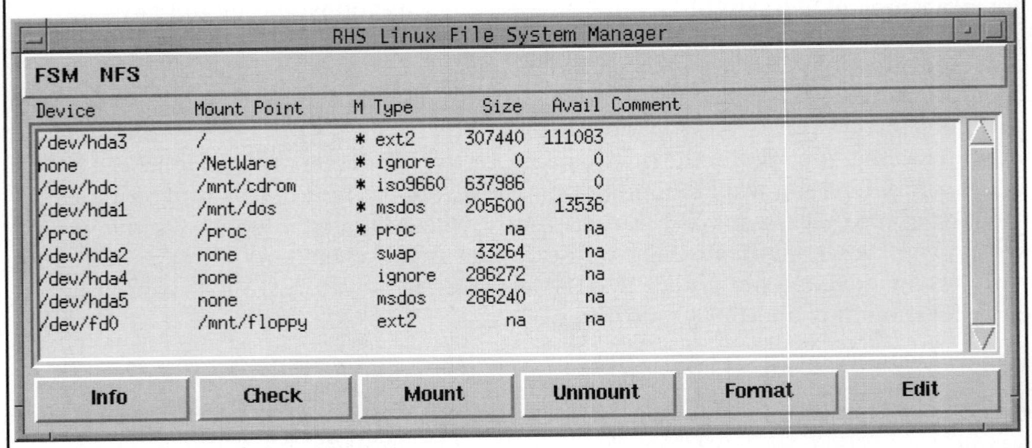

RHS Linux File System Manager

FSM NFS

Device	Mount Point	M	Type	Size	Avail	Comment
/dev/hda3	/	*	ext2	307440	111083	
none	/NetWare	*	ignore	0	0	
/dev/hdc	/mnt/cdrom	*	iso9660	637986	0	
/dev/hda1	/mnt/dos	*	msdos	205600	13536	
/proc	/proc	*	proc	na	na	
/dev/hda2	none		swap	33264	na	
/dev/hda4	none		ignore	286272	na	
/dev/hda5	none		msdos	286240	na	
/dev/fd0	/mnt/floppy		ext2	na	na	

| Info | Check | Mount | Unmount | Format | Edit |

Figure 7-6.   *The **fstab** window*

Network File Systems: NFS

The Network File Systems (NFS) allows you to mount a file sytem on a remote computer as if it were local to your own system. You can then directly access any of the files on that remote file system. This has the advantage of allowing different systems on a network to directly access the same files, without each having to keep their own copies. There would be just one copy on a remote file system that each computer can then access.

NFS operates over a TCP/IP network. The remote computer that holds the file system makes it available to other computers on the network. It does so by exporting the file system, which entails making entries in an NFS configuration file called **/etc/exports**, as well as running two daemons to support access by other systems, **rpc.mountd** and **rpc.nfsd**. An entry in the /etc/exports file specifies the file system to be exported and the computers on the network that can access it. For the file system, you enter its mount point, the directory it was mounted to. This is followed by a list of computers that can access this file system. A comma-separated list of mount options placed within a set of parentheses may follow each computer. For example, you might want to give one computer read-only access, and another read and write access. A complete list of NFS mount options can be found in the **man** pages for **mount**.

Once an NFS file system is made available, then different computers on the network have to first mount it before they can use it. You can mount an NFS file system either by an entry in the **/etc/fstab** file, or by an explicit **mount** command. An NFS entry in the **/etc/fstab** file has a mount type of **nfs**. An NFS file system name consists of the host name of the computer it is located on followed by the path name of the directory where it is mounted. The two are separated by a colon. For example, **rose.berkeley.edu:/home/project** specifies a file system mounted at **/home/project** on the **rose.berkeley.edu** computer.

There are also several NFS specific mount options that you can include with your NFS entry. You can specify the size of datagrams sent back and forth, and the amount of time your computer will wait for a response from the host system. You can also specify whether a file system is to be hard mounted or soft mounted. For a hard mounted file system, your computer will continually try to make contact, if, for some reason, the remote system fails to respond. A soft mount, after a specified interval, will give up trying to make contact and issue an error message. A hard mount is the default. The **man** pages for **mount** contains a complete listing of these NFS client options. They differ from the NFS server options indicated previously.

An example of an NFS entry follows. The remote system is **rose** and the file system is mounted on **/home/projects**. This file system is to be mounted on the local system's **/home/richlp** directory. The type of system is **nfs** and the **timeo** option specifies that the local system will wait up to 20 tenths of a second for a response, two seconds.

```
rose:/home/projects    /home/richlp    nfs    timeo=20
```

You can also use the **mount** command with the **-t nfs** option to explicitly mount a NFS file system. To explicitly mount the previous entry, you use the following command.

```
# mount -t nfs -o timeo=20   rose:/home/projects   /home/richlp
```

Archive Files and Devices: tar

The **tar** utility creates archives for files and directories. With **tar**, you can archive specific files, update them in the archive, and add new files, as you wish, to that archive. You can even archive entire directories with all their files and subdirectories, all of which can be restored from the archive. **tar** was originally designed to create archives on tapes. The term *tar* stands for *tape archive*. You can create archives on any device, such as a floppy disk, or you can create an archive file to hold the archive. **tar** is an ideal utility for making backups of your files or combining several files into a single file for transmission across a network.

On Linux, **tar** is often used to create archives on devices or files. You can direct **tar** to archive files to a specific device or a file by using the **f** option with the name of the device or file. The syntax for the **tar** command using the **f** option is shown in the next example. The device or file name is often referred to as the archive name. When creating a file for a **tar** archive, the file name is usually given the extension **.tar**. This is a convention only and is not required. You can list as many file names as you wish. If a directory name is specified, then all of its subdirectories will be included in the archive.

```
$ tar optionsf archive-name.tar directory-and-file-names
```

To create an archive, you use the **c** option. Combined with the **f** option, **c** will create an archive on a file or device. You enter this option before and right next to the **f** option. Notice that there is no preceding dash before a **tar** option. In the next example, the directory **mydir** and all of its subdirectories are saved in the file **myarch.tar**.

```
$ tar cf myarch.tar mydir
```

The user can later extract the directories from the tape using the **x** option. The **xf** option extracts files from an archive file or device. The **tar** extraction operation will generate all subdirectories. In the next example, the **xf** option directs **tar** to extract all the files and subdirectories from the **tar** file **myarch.tar**.

```
$ tar xf myarch.tar
```

You use the **r** option to add files to an archive that has already been created. The **r** option appends the files to the archive. In the next example, the user appends the files in the **letters** directory to the **myarch.tar** archive.

```
$ tar rf myarch.tar letters
```

Should you change any of the files in your directories that you have previously archived, you can use the **u** option to instruct **tar** to update the archive with any modified files. **tar** compares the time of the last update for each archived file with those in the user's directory and copies into the archive any files that have been changed since they were last archived. Any newly created files in these directories will be added to the archive as well. In the next example, the user updates the **myarch.tar** file with any recently modified or newly created files in the **mydir** directory.

```
$ tar uf myarch.tar mydir
```

If you need to see what files are stored in an archive, you can use the **tar** command with the **t** option. The next example will list all the files stored in the **myarch.tar** archive.

```
$ tar tf myarch.tar
```

To back up the files to a specific device, you specify the device as the archive. In the next example, the user creates an archive on the floppy disk in the **/dev/fd0** device and copies into it all the files in the **mydir** directory.

```
$ tar cf /dev/fd0 mydir
```

To extract the backed up files on the disk in the device, you use the **xf** option.

```
$ tar xf /dev/fd0
```

If the files you are archiving take up more space than would be available on a device such as a floppy disk, you can create a **tar** archive that uses multiple labels.

The **M** option instructs **tar** to prompt you for a new storage component when the current one is filled. When archiving to a floppy drive with the **M** option, **tar** will prompt you to put in a new floppy disk when one becomes full. You can then save your **tar** archive on several floppy disks.

```
$ tar cfM /dev/fd0 mydir
```

The **tar** operation will not perform compression on archived files. Should you want to compress the archived files, you can instruct **tar** to invoke the **gzip** utility to compress them. With the lowercase **z** option, **tar** will first use **gzip** to compress files before archiving them. The same **z** option will invoke **gzip** to decompress them when extracting files.

```
$ tar cfz  myarch.tar mydir
```

Keep in mind that there is a difference between compressing individual files in an archive and compressing the entire archive as a whole. Often an archive is created for transferring several files at once as one **tar** file. To shorten transmission time, the archive should be as small as possible. You can use the compression utility **gzip** on the archive **tar** file to compress it, reducing its size, and then send the compressed version. The person receiving it can decompress it, restoring the **tar** file. Using **gzip** on a **tar** file often results in a file with the extension **.tar.gz**. The **.gz** is added to a compressed **gzip** file. The next example creates a compressed version of **myarch.tar** using the same name with the extension **.gz**.

```
$ gzip myarch.tar
$ ls
myarch.tar.gz
```

Should you have a default device specified, such as a tape, and you want to create an archive on it, you can simply use **tar** without the **f** option and a device or file name. This can be helpful for making backups of your files. The name of the default device is held in a file called **/etc/default/tar**. The syntax for the **tar** command using the default tape device is shown in the following example. If a directory name is specified, then all of its subdirectories will be included in the archive.

```
$ tar option directory-and-file-names
```

In the next example, the directory **mydir** and all of its subdirectories are saved on a tape in the default tape device.

```
$ tar c mydir
```

In this example, the **mydir** directory and all of its files and subdirectories are extracted from the default tape device and placed in the user's working directory.

```
$ tar x  mydir
```

File Compression: gzip

There are several reasons for reducing the size of a file. The two most common are to save space, or, if you are transferring the file across a network, to save transmission time. The **gzip** utility is the GNU compression utility used to compress and decompress files. To compress a file, you enter the command **gzip** and the file name. This will replace the file with a compressed version of it with the extension **.gz**.

```
$ gzip mydata
$ ls
mydata.gz
```

To decompress a **gzip** file, you use either **gzip** with the **–d** option or the command **gunzip**. These commands will decompress a compressed file with the .gz extension and replace it with a decompressed version with the same root name, but without the .gz extension. When you use **gunzip**, you do not even have to type in the .gz extension. **gunzip** and **gzip –d** will assume it.

```
$ gunzip mydata.gz
$ ls
mydata
```

Suppose you want to display or print the contents of a compressed file without first having to decompress it. The command **zcat** will generate a decompressed version of a file and send it to the standard output. You can then redirect this output to a printer or display utility such as **more**. The original file will remain in its compressed state.

```
$ zcat mydata.gz | more
```

You can also compress archived **tar** files. This will result in files with extensions **.tar.gz**. Compressed archived files are often used for transmitting very large files across networks.

```
$ gzip myarch.tar
$ ls
myarch.tar.gz
```

You can compress **tar** file members individually using the **tar z** option that invokes **gzip**. With the **z** option, **tar** will invoke **gzip** to compress a file before placing it in an archive. However, archives with members compressed with the **z** option cannot be updated, nor can they be added to. All members have to be compressed and all have to be added at the same time.

You can also use the **compress** and **uncompress** commands to create compressed files. They generate a file that has a **.Z** extension and use a different compression format than **gzip**. **compress** and **uncompress** are not that widely used, but you may run across **.Z** files from time to time. Although you can use the **uncompress** command to decompress a **.Z** file, **gunzip** will also decompress a **.Z** file. **gzip** is the standard GNU compression utility and should be used instead of **compress**.

Installing Software from Compressed Archives: .tar.gz

Linux software programs are available at different sites on the Internet. You can download any of this software and install it on your system. You download software using the **ftp** program described in Chapter 10. The software is usually downloaded in the form of a compressed archive file. This is an archive file that was created with **tar** and then compressed with **gzip**. To install such a file, you have to first decompress it with the **gunzip** utility and then use **tar** to extract the files and directories making up the software package. Instead of **gunzip**, you could also use **gzip –d**. The next example decompresses the **videoteXt-0.6.tar.gz** file, replacing it with a decompressed version called **videoteXt-0.6.tar**.

```
$ ls
videoteXt-0.6.tar.gz
$ gunzip videoteXt-0.6.tar.gz
$ ls
videoteXt-0.6.tar
```

First, use **tar** with the **t** option to check the contents of the archive. If the first entry is a directory, then that directory will be created and the extracted files placed in it. If the first entry is not a directory, you should first create one and then copy the archive file to it. Then extract the archive within that directory. If there is no directory as the first entry, files will be extracted to the current directory. You have to create a directory yourself to hold these files.

```
$ tar tf videoteXt-0.6.tar
```

Now you are ready to extract the files from the **tar** archive. You use **tar** with the **x** option to extract files, the **f** option and the name of the archive file, and the **v** option to display the path names of files as they are extracted.

```
$ tar xvf  videoteXt-0.6.tar
```

Installation of your software may differ for each package. Instructions are usually provided along with an installation program.

Installing Software from Online Sources

Installing software from online sources is complicated by the fact that you first have to obtain software from remote sites. To do this, you need to know the site where the software is located and then use either Netscape or the **ftp** utility to download the package. The software is usually compressed, so, once downloaded, you use the **gunzip** command to decompress it. Some packages may not use an **rpm** format. Instead, they may be archived. Others may be both archived and have the **rpm** format. To open archived files, you have to use the **tar** command. If you download a package that has an **rpm** at the end of its name, you have to use the **rpm** command to install it.

In the next example, the user uses **ftp** to connect to the **sunsite.unc.edu** Linux **ftp** site. For the login ID the user enters **anonymous,** and for the password the user enters his or her's internet address. The download mode is set to binary by entering the keyword **binary**. With the **cd** command, the user changes to the **pub/packages/info-systems/WWW** directory where Web software is located. Then, the user changes to the **clients/Netscape/navigator/2.01/unix** directory to get the Netscape software package. The **get** command then downloads the package. The **close** command cuts the connection and **quit** leaves the ftp utility.

```
# ftp sunsite.unc.edu
Connected to fddisunsite.oit.unc.edu.
220 helios FTP server (Version wu-2.4(39) Tue May 16 01:34:21 EDT
    1995) ready.
Name (sunsite.unc.edu:root): anonymous
331 Guest login ok, send your complete e-mail address as password.
Password: (enter e-mail address here)
230 Guest login ok, access restrictions apply.
```

```
Remote system type is UNIX.
Using binary mode to transfer files.
ftp> binary
200 Type set to I.
ftp> cd pub/packages/info-systems/WWW
250 CWD command successful.
ftp> cd clients/Netscape/navigator/2.01/unix
250 CWD command successful.
ftp> pwd
257 "/pub/packages/info-systems/WWW/clients/Netscape/navigator/2.01
    /unix" is current directory.
ftp> ls
200 PORT command successful.
150 Opening ASCII mode data connection for /bin/ls.
total 97874
drwxr-xr-x   2 0        0             1536 Mar 16 04:49 .
drwxr-xr-x   6 0        0              512 Mar 16 03:39 ..
-r--r--r--   1 0        0            12905 Mar  9 20:29 LICENSE
-r--r--r--   1 0        0             8726 Mar  9 20:29 README
-r--r--r--   1 0        0          2737058 Mar 10 08:14
        netscape-v201-export.hppa1.1-hp-hpux.tar.gz
-r--r--r--   1 0        0          1648574 Mar 10 07:59
        netscape-v201-export.i386-unknown-bsd.tar.gz
-r--r--r--   1 0        0          2025581 Mar 10 09:07
        netscape-v201-export.i486-unknown-linux.tar.gz
-r--r--r--   1 0        0          2596214 Mar  9 20:31
        netscape-v201-export.mips-sgi-irix5.2.tar.Z
  (continues to list all current unix versions)
226 Transfer complete.
ftp> get netscape-v201-export.i486-unknown-linux.tar.gz
200 PORT command successful.
150 Opening BINARY mode data connection for
        netscape-v201-export.i486-unknown-linux.tar.gz (2025581 bytes).
226 Transfer complete.
2025581 bytes received in 625 secs (3.2 Kbytes/sec)
ftp> close
221 Good-bye.
ftp> quit
#
```

Alternatively, you could just use Netscape to access, browse through, and download software without having to bother with all the **ftp** commands. Be sure to precede an **ftp** site name with the term **ftp://** instead of the usual **http://**. For **sunsite** you would enter: **ftp://sunsite.unc.edu**. Once you have selected the software you want, you double-click on it to download it.

Once downloaded, any file that ends with a **.Z** or **.gz** is a compressed file that has to be decompressed. You would use the **gunzip** command followed by the name of the file.

```
# gunzip netscape-v201-export.i486-unknown-linux.tar.gz
```

If the file then ends with **.tar**, it is an archived file that has to be opened up. You use the **tar** command. First, use **tar** with the **t** option to check the contents of the archive to see if the first entry is a directory. If so, then that directory will be created and the extracted files placed in it. If the first entry is not a directory, you should first either create one or decide which directory you want the software in, and then copy the archive file to it. Then extract the archive within that directory. If there is no directory as the first entry, then files will be extracted to the current directory.

```
# tar tf netscape-v201-export.i486-unknown-linux.tar
```

Now you are ready to extract the files from the **tar** archive. You use **tar** with the **x** option to extract files, the **f** option and the name of the archive file, and the **v** option to display the path names of files as they are extracted.

```
# tar xvf netscape-v201-export.i486-unknown-linux.tar
```

Installation of your software may differ for each package. Instructions are usually provided along with an installation program. If the file ends with **rpm**, you have to use the **rpm -i** command to install it. Downloaded software will usually include readme files or other documentation. Be sure to consult them.

The mcopy Utilities: MS-DOS

Your Linux system provides a set of utilities known as **mtools** that let you easily access a floppy disk formatted for MS-DOS. The **mcopy** command allows you to copy files to and from an MS-DOS floppy disk in your floppy drive. No special operations, such as mounting, are required. With **mtools**, you do not have to mount an MS-DOS partition to access it. For an MS-DOS floppy disk, you just place the disk in your floppy drive and you can then use **mtool** commands to access those files. For example, to copy a file from an MS-DOS floppy disk to your Linux system, you use the **mcopy** command. You specify the MS-DOS disk with **a:** for the A drive. The next example copies the **mydata** file to the MS-DOS disk and then copies the **preface** file from the disk to the current Linux directory.

```
$ mcopy mydata a:
$ mcopy a:\preface
```

You can use the **mdir** command to list files on your MS-DOS disk, and you can use the **mcd** command to change directories on it. The next example lists the files on the MS-DOS disk in your floppy drive and then changes to the **docs** directory on that drive.

```
$ mdir a:
$ mcd a:\docs
```

Most of the standard MS-DOS commands are available as **mtool** operations. You can create MS-DOS directories with **mmd** and erase MS-DOS files with **mdel**. A list of **mtool** commands is provided in Table 7-10. For example, to display a file on drive **b:** on an MS-DOS 5 1/4-inch floppy drive, you use **mtype** and the the name of the file preceded by **b:**.

```
$ mtype b:\readme
```

Access to MS-DOS partitions is configured by the **/etc/mtools** file. This file lists the different MS-DOS partitions and how they are configured. The file has six fields: the drive, its device name, FAT, cylinders, heads, and offset. If an entry has 0 for the last three fields, then **mtools** will configure the values itself. Floppy drives usually have a FAT of 12 and hard disk partitions have a FAT of 16. The following is an example of an **/etc/mtools** file. With the Redhat version of Linux, the **/etc/mtools** file is already configured for both 3 1/2- and 5 1/4-inch floppy drives.

/etc/mtools

# drive	device	FAT	cylinders	heads	offset
A	/dev/fd0	12	80	2	18
A	/dev/fd0	12	0	0	0
A	/dev/fd0	12	40	2	9
B	/dev/fd1	12	0	0	0
B	/dev/fd1	12	40	2	9

Command	Execution
chmod	Changes the permission of a file or directory
Options	
+	Adds a permission
–	Removes a permission
r	Sets read permission for a file or directory. A file can be displayed or printed. A directory can have the list of its files displayed
w	Sets write permission for a file or directory. A file can be edited or erased. A directory can be removed
x	Sets execute permission for a file or directory. If the file is a shell script, it can be executed as a program. A directory can be changed to and entered
u	Sets permissions for the user who created and owns the file or directory
g	Sets permissions for group access to a file or directory
o	Sets permissions for access to a file or directory by all other users on the system
a	Sets permissions for access by the user, group, and all other users
chgrp *groupname filenames*	Changes the group for a file or files
chown *user-name filenames*	Changes the owner of a file or files
ls –l *filename*	Lists a file name with its permissions displayed
ls –ld *directory*	Lists a directory name with its permissions displayed
ls –l	Lists all files in a directory with its permissions displayed

Table 7-1.   *File and Directory Permission Operations*

Options	Effect
-f	Fakes the mounting of a file system; you use it to check if a file system can be mounted
-v	Verbose mode; **mount** displays descriptions of the actions it is taking; use with **-f** to check for any problems mounting a file system
-w	Mounts the file system with read and write permission
-r	Mounts the file system with only read permission
-n	Mounts the file system without placing an entry for it in the **mstab** file
-t *type*	Specifies the type of file system to be mounted; see Table 7-4 for valid file system types
-a	Mounts all file systems listed in **/etc/fstab**
-o *option-list*	Mounts the file system using a list of options; this is a comma-separated list of options following **-o** (see Table 7-6 for a list of options and the **man** pages for **mount** for a complete listing)

Table 7-2. *The* **mount** *Command*

Option	Description
async	All I/O to the file system should be done asynchronously
auto	Can be mounted with the **-a** option
defaults	Use default options: **rw**, **suid**, **dev**, **exec**, **auto**, **nouser**, and **async**
dev	Interprets character or block special devices on the file system
noauto	Can only be mounted explicitly; the **-a** option will not cause the file system to be mounted
exec	Permits execution of binaries
nouser	Forbids an ordinary (i.e., non-root) user to mount the file system

Table 7-3. **mount** *Options for File Systems: -o and* **/etc/fstab**

Option	Description
remount	Attempts to remount an already-mounted file system; this is commonly used to change the mount flags for a file system, especially to make a read-only file system writeable
ro	Mounts the file system read-only
rw	Mounts the file system read-write
suid	Allows set-user-identifier or set-group-identifier bits to take effect
sync	All I/O to the file system should be done synchronously
user	Allows an ordinary user to mount the file system; ordinary users always have the following options activated: **noexec**, **nosuid**, and **nodev**
nodev	Does not interpret character or block special devices on the file system
nosuid	Does not allow set-user-identifier or set-group-identifier bits to take effect

Table 7-3.   **mount** *Options for File Systems:* **–o** *and* **/etc/fstab** *(continued)*

Option	File System
minux	Minux file systems; file names limited to 30 characters
ext	Earlier version of Linux file system, no longer in use
ext2	Standard Linux file system supporting large file names and file sizes
xiaf	Xiaf file system
msdos	File system for MS-DOS partitions
hpfs	File system for OS/2 high-performance partitions
proc	Used by operating system for processes
nfs	NFS file system for mounting partitions from remote systems
umsdos	UMS-DOS file system

Table 7-4.   *File System Types*

Option	File System
swap	Linux swap partition or swap file
sysv	Unix System V file system
iso9660	File system for mounting CD-ROMs

Table 7-4. *File System Types (continued)*

Command	Effect
a	Sets and unsets the bootable flag for a partition
c	Sets and unsets the DOS compatibility flag
d	Deletes a partition
l	Lists partition types
m	Displays a listing of **fdisk** commands
n	Creates a new partition
p	Prints the partition table, listing all the partitions on your disk
q	Quits without saving changes; use this to abort an **fdisk** session if you made a mistake
t	Selects the file system type for a partition
v	Verifies the partition table
w	Writes partition table to disk and exits; at this point the changes are made, irrevocably
x	Displays listing of advanced **fdisk** commands; with these commands you can set the number of cylinders, sectors, and heads, print raw data, and change the location of data in the partition table

Table 7-5. **fdisk** *Commands*

Option	Description
blocks	Number of blocks for the file system; 1440 blocks for 1.44 floppy disk
-t *file-system-type*	Specifies the type of file system to format; the default is the standard Linux file system type, **ext2**
fs *-options*	Options for the type of file sytem specified
-V	Verbose mode; displays description of each action **mkfs** takes
-v	Instructs the file system builder program that **mkfs** invokes to show actions it takes
-c	Checks a partition for bad blocks before formatting it
-l *file-name*	Reads list of bad blocks

Table 7-6.   **mkfs** *Options*

Option	Description
file-system	Specifies the file system to be checked; uses file system's device name such as **/dev/hda3**
-A	Checks all file systems listed in **/etc/fstab** file
-V	Verbose mode; lists actions that **fsck** takes
-t *file-system-type*	Specifies the type of file system to be checked
-a	Automatically repairs any problems
-l	Lists the names of all files in the file sytem
-r	Asks for confirmation before repairing file system
-s	Lists superblock before checking file system

Table 7-7.   **fsck** *Options for Checking and Repairing File System*

Command or Option	Execution
tar *options files*	Backs up files to tape, device, or archive file
tar *options***f** *archive_name* *filelist*	Backs up files to specific file or device specified as *archive_name*; *filelist* can be file names or directories
c	Creates a new archive
t	Lists the names of files in an archive
r	Appends files to an archive
u	Updates an archive with new and changed files; adds only those files that have been modified since they were archived or files that are not already present in the archive
w	Waits for a confirmation from the user before archiving each file; allows you to update an archive selectively
x	Extracts files from an archive
m	When extracting a file from an archive, does not give it a new time stamp
M	Creates multiple volume archive that may be stored on several floppy disks
f *archive-name*	Saves the tape archive to the file *archive-name* instead of to the default tape device; when given an *archive-name*, the **f** option saves the **tar** archive in a file of that name
f *device-name*	Saves a **tar** archive to a device such as a floppy disk or tape; **/dev/fd0** is the device name for your floppy disk; the default device is held in **/etc/default/tar-file**
v	Displays each file name as it is archived
z	Compresses or decompresses archived files using **gzip**

Table 7-8.   *Archives:* **tar**

Option	Execution
-c	Sends compressed version of file to standard output; each file listed is separately compressed $ **gzip -c mydata preface** > **myfiles.gz**
-d	Decompresses a compressed file; alternatively, you can use **gunzip** $ **gzip -d myfiles.gz** $ **gunzip myfiles.gz**
-h	Displays help listing
-l *file-list*	Displays compressed and uncompressed size of each file listed $ **gzip -l myfiles.gz**
-r *directory-name*	Recursively searches for specified directories and compresses all the files in them; the search begins from the current working directory; when used with **gunzip**, compressed files of a specified directory will be uncompressed
-v *file-list*	For each compressed or decompressed file, displays its name and the percentage of its reduction in size
-num	Determines the speed and size of the compression; the range is from -1 to -9. A lower number gives greater speed but less compression, resulting in a larger file that compresses and decompresses quickly; -1 gives the quickest compression, but with the largest size; -9 results in a very small file that takes longer to compress and decompress. The default is -6

Table 7-9. **gzip** *Options*

Summary: File Management Operations

You can set permissions on a file or directory to control access by other users. A file or directory can be set for read, write, and execute permissions. Either the owner, the group, or all other users can have access. The command **chmod** sets these permissions, and the **ls** command with the **-l** option lists files and directories with their current permissions.

The various storage devices each contain their own file system that you can mount and access. You can access CD-ROMs, floppy disks, and hard disk partitions. You can also mount MS-DOS hard drive partitions and access them directly from your Linux system. By placing an entry for a file system in the **/etc/fstab** file, you can have a file

Command	Description
mcopy *filename filename*	Copies file to and from MS-DOS disk and your Linux system; the following copies file from MS-DOS diskette to your Linux system
	mcopy a: *filename directory-or-filename*
	The following copies file from Linux for MS-DOS diskette in your floppy drive
	mcopy *filename* **a:** *filename*
mcd *directory-name*	Changes directory on your MS-DOS file system
mdir	Lists files on MS-DOS disk
mattrib	Changes the attribute of MS-DOS file
mdel *filename*	Deletes MS-DOS file
mformat	Adds MS-DOS file system to a diskette
mlabel	Makes a volume label
mmd *directory-name*	Makes MS-DOS directory
mrd *directory-name*	Removes MS-DOS directory
mread *filename filename*	Low level reads (copies) MS-DOS file to Unix
mren *filename filename*	Renames MS-DOS file
mtype *filename*	Displays contents of MS-DOS file
mwrite *filename filename*	Low level writes (copies) Unix file to MS-DOS

Table 7-10.   *MS-DOS Access Commands*

system mounted automatically when you boot. If you are on a network, you mount and access file systems on a remote server.

To transmit files or to back them up, you can archive and compress them. The **tar** command archives files, and the **gzip** command compresses them. Most software packages available online are both archived and compressed. They usually have file names that end with **tar.gz**. You can download them and use **gunzip** to decompress them, then **tar xf** to expand the archive. You can then install the software using **rpm**.

PART THREE

Networking

Chapter Eight

Electronic Mail

Your Linux system has electronic mail utilities that allow you to send messages to other users on your system or other systems, such as those on the Internet. You can send and receive messages in a variety of ways, depending on the electronic mail utility you use. This book presents two of the most popular electronic mail utilities available on Linux: Mail and Elm. Each of these defines a different type of interface. Though all electronic mail utilities perform the same basic tasks of receiving and sending messages, they tend to have very different interfaces. The Mail utility employs a basic command line interface, operating within its own shell. It is found on most Linux systems and is considered a standard. The Elm utility uses a full screen interface and employs single key commands much like those used for the Vi editor. Both are provided by your Caldera Network Desktop enclosed with this book.

In addition to sending messages by electronic mail, you can also use the Write and Talk utilities to communicate directly with other users who are currently logged in. These utilities set up a direct connection with another user, allowing you to communicate as you would over a radio or telephone.

Local and Internet Addresses

Each user on a Linux system has a mail address, and whenever you send mail, you will be required to provide the address of the user to whom you are sending the message. For users on your local Linux system, addresses can consist of only the user's login name. However, when sending messages to users on other systems, you need to know not only the login name but also the address of the system they are on. Internet addresses require that the system address be uniquely identified.

Most systems have Internet addresses that you can use to send mail. Internet addresses use a form of addressing called domain addressing. A system is assigned a domain name, which, when combined with the system name, gives the system a unique address. This domain name is separated from the system name by a period and may be further qualified by additional domain names. Here is the syntax for domain addresses:

```
login-name@system-name.domain-name
```

Systems that are part of a local network are often given the same domain name. The domain name for both the **garnet** and **violet** systems at U.C. Berkeley is **berkeley.edu**. To send a message to **chris** on the **garnet** system, you simply include the domain name:

chris@garnet.berkeley.edu.

In the next example, a message is sent to **chris**, located on the **garnet** system, using domain addressing.

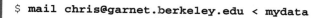

```
$ mail chris@garnet.berkeley.edu < mydata
```

Early domain names reflect the fact that the Internet was first developed in the United States. They qualify Internet addresses by category such as commercial, military, or educational systems. The domain name **.com** indicates a commercial organization, whereas **.edu** is used for educational institutions. As the Internet developed into a global network, a set of international domain names were established. These domain names indicate the country in which a system is located, for example, **.fr** represents France, **.jp** represents japan, and **.us** represents the United States. Table 8-1 lists several common international domain names.

Mail Transport Agents: deliver, sendmail, smail

Mail is transported to and from destinations using mail transport agents. The **deliver** agent handles mail exchanged between users on your own local system. **sendmail** and **smail** send and receive mail from destinations on the Internet or at other sites on a network. To send mail over the Intenet they use the Simple Mail Transport Protocol (SMTP). For the more direct UUCP connections they use the UUCP protocols. **sendmail** is a smaller agent that is easy to configure, whereas **smail** is more complex as well as more powerful. Your Caldera Network Desktop automatically installs and configures **sendmail** for you. Upon starting up your Caldera system you can send and receive messages over the Internet. If you are using a different Linux distribution, you may have to install and configure the Mail Transport Agents yourself. You can also download updated versions of these agents from Linux ftp sites and install them yourself.

Before users on your system can send and receive mail locally you have to configure a loopback interface. This will enable your system to address itself, allowing it to send and receive mail to and from itself. A loopback interface uses the host name **localhost** and a special IP address that is reserved for use by local systems, **127.0.0.1**. The Caldera Network Desktop package already has such a loopback interface installed.

You can examine your **/etc/hosts** file to see if your loopback interface has been configured as the local host. You will see **localhost 127.0.0.1** listed as the first entry. If there is no entry for "localhost", you may have to create a loopback interface yourself using the **ifconfig** and **route** commands as shown here. **lo** is the term for loopback.

```
ifconfig lo 127.0.0.1
route add -net 127.0.0.0
```

Check to see if these commands are in your network initialization file, **rc.inet1**, in the **/etc/rc.d/** directory. If not, you should add them. Once added, the loopback interface will automatically be created every time you start up your system. For the Redhat version of Linux the initialization file is **inet** in the **/etc/rc.d/init/** directory. See Chapter 20 on Network Administration for a detailed discussion of these commands and files.

The Mail Utility

With the Mail utility, you can easily send and receive messages to and from other users. Sending a message is as simple as typing in a login name followed by the text of the message. Receiving messages is merely a matter of selecting a message from a list of received messages. When sending messages in Mail, there are commands for modifying the message text and what is known as the message header. When receiving messages, you can reply to them, save them in files, or simply delete them. There is a special initialization file, **.mailrc**, that configures your Mail utility with special features such as aliases.

What is known now as the Mail utility was originally created for BSD Unix and called, simply, **mail**. Later versions of Unix System V adopted the BSD **mail** utility and renamed it **mailx**. Most Linux systems, including Redhat Linux, use this **mailx** utility and simply refer to it as Mail.

Sending Messages

The message you send in Mail can be something you type in at the keyboard, or it can be the contents of a file. While you are entering a message at the keyboard, you can edit it using special tilde commands. These commands allow you to save a message, redisplay what you have written, or invoke an editor with which to edit the message.

To send a message, type **mail** along with the address of the person to whom you are sending the message. Press ENTER and you will be prompted for a subject. Enter the subject of the message and press ENTER again. At this point, you are placed in input mode. Anything typed in is taken as the contents of the message. Pressing ENTER adds a new line to the text. When you have finished typing your message, press CTRL-**d** on a line of its own to end the message and send it. You will see EOT (end-of-transmission) displayed after you press CTRL-**d**.

In the next example, the user sends a message to another user whose address is **robert**. The subject of the message is "Birthday." After typing in the text of the message, the user presses CTRL-**d**.

```
$ mail robert
Subject: Birthday
    Your present is in the mail
    really.
```

```
^D
EOT
$
```

Standard Input and Redirection

The Mail utility receives input from the standard input. By default, the standard input is taken from what the user enters on the keyboard. However, with redirection, standard input can be taken from a file. Therefore, with redirection, you can use the contents of a file as the message for the Mail program. You can create and edit a text file with the Vi editor and then use that text file as redirected input for the Mail utility. In the next example, the file **mydata** is redirected as input for the Mail utility and sent to **robert**.

```
$ mail robert < mydata
```

Notice that when you mail a file through redirection, you do not have a chance to enter a subject for the actual mail message. However, the **mail** command has a **-s** option that allows you to specify the subject of a message on the command line. This subject will then show up in the header list of the person who receives the file. Table 8-2 lists several other Mail options that are discussed later in the chapter. In the next example, Robert sends the file **mydata** and specifies the subject as "party."

```
$ mail -s party chris < mydata
```

Sending Mail to Several Users

You can send a message to several users at the same time by listing those users' addresses as arguments on the command line following the **mail** command. In the next example, the user sends the same message to both **chris** and **aleina**.

```
$ mail chris aleina
Subject: Birthday
    Your present is in the mail
    really.
^D
EOT
$
```

You can also use redirection to send the contents of a file to several users at once. In the next example, the contents of the **mydata** file is sent to both **robert** and **aleina**.

```
$ mail robert aleina < mydata
```

Copying a Message to a File

You may also want to save a copy of the message you are sending for yourself. You can copy a mail message to a file in your account by specifying a file name on the command line after the addresses. The file name must be a relative or full path name, containing a slash. A path name identifies an argument as a file name to which mail will save a copy of the message being sent. In the next example, the user saves a copy of the message to a file called **birthnote**. A relative path name is used, with the period denoting the current working directory: **./birthnote**.

```
$ mail robert ./birthnote
Subject: Birthday
Your present is in the mail
really.
^D
EOT
$ cat birthnote
Subject: Birthday
    Your present is in the mail
    really.
$
```

The technique works equally as well when using redirection and multiple addresses:

```
$ mail robert aleina < mydata ./birthnote
```

Editing Mail Messages: The Tilde Commands

There are two components to a message: the header and the text. The header contains information about the message, such as the addresses of people to whom the message is to be sent and the subject. The addresses are specified as arguments of the **mail** command. The Mail utility then prompts the user to enter the subject of the message. After entering the subject, the user enters the text of the message.

A set of message commands known as tilde commands allow you to perform editing operations both on the header and the text. A tilde command consists of a one-character command preceded by a tilde that is entered on a line of its own. The tilde (which functions as a special character) and the command are not taken as part of the message. Should you need to enter the tilde as a character in the message, you can do so by entering two tildes next to each other, **~~**. The set of commonly used tilde commands are listed in Table 8-2. You can also obtain a listing of the tilde commands with the **~?** tilde command.

There are then three basic kinds of operations you perform in sending a message: you enter header information, you enter the text of the message, and you enter tilde commands to perform operations on either the header or the text. Tilde commands for the header allow you to change address and subject information. The tilde commands for the text allow you to redisplay, save, and use an editor to modify the text.

Tilde Commands for the Message Text

Unlike an editor, there is no command mode when entering the text of a mail message. Once you have entered the subject and pressed ENTER, you are placed into an input mode in which you enter the text of the message. The input mode for the Mail utility is subject to all the same restrictions of the input mode in the Vi editor. You are simply typing in a stream of characters. The only kind of correction you may perform is BACKSPACE, which will erase the character to the immediate left of the cursor on that line. No other type of correction is allowed. You may not move the cursor or perform any other type of editing operation.

You can overcome all the restrictions of the Mail input mode by invoking the Vi editor with the **~v** command. You enter the **~v** command on a line by itself, followed by ENTER. Once you have accessed the Vi editor, your message can be edited like any other text. In effect, you are using the Vi editor to compose your message instead of relying on the Mail input mode. In the Vi editor, the message you have typed in so far will be displayed as text to be edited.

The Vi editor's save commands will save to the Mail message, not to a file. When you exit the Vi editor with the **ZZ** command, you save to the Mail message and return to the input mode of the Mail utility. However, the text of the message will not be redisplayed. Instead, the word "continue" in parentheses is displayed on the screen. You can then enter more text, execute other tilde commands, or end and send the message with CTRL-**d**.

Though the invocation of the Vi editor is one of the most useful tilde commands, you may also want to perform basic operations on the text such as redisplaying it, saving the text to a file, or reading in text from another file.

You can redisplay your message at any time with the **~p** tilde command, which prints out the message entered so far. When you enter the **~p** command on a line by itself and press ENTER, everything you have typed in will be displayed. It is sometimes reassuring to enter the **~p** command after returning from the Vi editor. If you do so, you will notice that all the text edited and entered while in the Vi editor is displayed as the message.

```
$ mail aleina
Subject: Files
     This is a list of all the
     students in my class.
~p
_____
Message contains:
To: aleina
Subject: Files
     This is a list of all the
     students in my class.
(continue)
^D
EOT
$
```

There are also tilde commands that allow you to save your message to a file, or to read the contents of a file into your message. The **~w** tilde command will save your message, and **~r** will read in text from another file, making it part of the message. You enter the **~w** command with the name of the file the message is to be written to. The **~r** command is entered with the name of the file to be read. In the next example, **~w mydata** saves the input message to the file **mydata**. The **~r** command then reads the contents of the file **mynames** and inserts it into the Mail message.

```
$ mail aleina
Subject: Files
     This is a list of all the
     students in my class.
~w mydata
"mydata" 2/48
~r mynames
"mynames" 3/15
~p
_____
Message contains:
To: aleina
Subject: Files
     This is a list of all the
     students in my class.
mary
```

```
joe
harold
(continue)
^D
EOT
$
```

Should you change your mind and decide that you do not want to send the message, you can quit Mail with either the **~x** or the **~q** tilde command. The message is abandoned and you are returned to the shell. If you use the **~q** command, the text is saved in a file called **dead.letter**.

```
$ mail aleina
Subject: Files
    This is a list of all the
    students in my class.
~x
$
```

You can also process the text of your message through filters. You can use the current text of your message as input to a filter whose output will then replace the text of your message. For example, if your message consists of a list, you can pipe the list to the **sort** filter, and then have the contents of the message replaced by the sorted output. The ~| tilde command allows you to pipe your text through a filter. ~| takes as its argument a filter. The text of the message becomes the standard input that is piped into the filter. The output of the filter then replaces the message. In the next example, the user makes use of the ~| sort command to sort the list in the message.

```
$ mail george
Subject: Names
    mary
    joe
    harold
~| sort
~p
_____
Message contains:
To: george
Subject: Names
```

```
        harold
        joe
        mary
(continue)
^D
EOT
```

One very helpful filter, **fmt**, was designed especially to format Mail messages. Often, when you are entering a message, the lines of text are not of an even length, as they are in a word processor. The **fmt** filter will format your lines so that they all have a standard length of approximately 72 characters. Lines beginning with spaces or tabs are taken as the beginning of paragraphs. In the next example, the user makes use of **fmt** to format the message.

```
$ mail george
Subject: Title
George,
    Have you thought of a new
title for the
project we were discussing
last month?
It should have a new theme based on
the realistic expectations of
our target audience.
~| fmt
(continue)
~p
_____
Message contains:
To: george
Subject: Title
George,
    Have you thought of a new title for the project we were
discussing last month?  It should have a new theme based on the
realistic expectations of our target audience.
(continue)
^D
EOT
$
```

Tilde Commands for the Message Header

Other tilde commands allow you to change components of the message header. There are four possible components of a message header: the address list, the subject, the carbon copy list, and the blind carbon copy list. The two carbon copy components are optional. You must always have an address list and, though you may leave the subject empty, you will usually be prompted to type in something for it.

The list of addresses to whom the message is being sent is initially entered on the command line when Mail is invoked. If, while you are entering your message, you want to add more addresses, you can do so with the **~t** tilde command.

The **~s** command allows you to enter a new subject for your message. To change your subject entry, type the **~s** command followed by the new subject. In the next example, both the subject and the address list are changed. The addressee **larisa** is added to the address list. Now the message will be sent to both **larisa** and **aleina**. Then the subject is changed from "Files" to "Class Roster."

```
$ mail aleina
Subject: Files
This is a list of all the
students in my class.
~t larisa
~s Class Roster
_____

Message contains:
To: aleina larisa
Subject: Class Roster
    This is a list of all the
    students in my class.
(continue)
^D
EOT
$
```

You may want to send an associate a copy of a message you sent to someone else. That copy would contain the address of the person it was sent to. In effect, you are giving someone a carbon copy of a message you sent out, including the header, not just the text. To do this, you create a carbon copy list of addresses with the **~c** command. Enter **~c** and the list of addresses that will receive a copy of the message.

Everyone receiving the copy and those receiving the original message will have this carbon copy list printed at the end of the message. If you do not wish to have a person's address printed in this list, and yet still have that person receive a copy of the message, you can send the carbon copy using a blind carbon copy list. Enter the **~b** command followed by the addresses that you do not want printed at the end of the message. Only those addresses on the normal carbon copy list will appear on the message. In the next example, **larisa** and **marylou** will receive carbon copies and have their addresses listed at the end of each copy of the message. **valerie**, on the other hand, will also receive a carbon copy, but will not have her address listed in any of the copies.

```
$ mail aleina
Subject: Files
This is a list of all the
students in my class.
~c larisa marylou
~b valerie
~p
_____
Message contains:
To: aleina
Subject: Files
Cc: larisa marylou
Bcc: valerie
     This is a list of all the
     students in my class.
(continue)
^D
EOT
$
```

If you should need to change all the header components, you can use the **~h** command to change them all at once. You will first be prompted for a new address list, then a new subject, and finally, a new carbon copy list.

Receiving Mail: The Mail Shell

As messages are sent to you, they are placed in your mailbox. A mailbox is really a file filled with recently received messages that remain there until you retrieve them. To retrieve messages, you invoke the Mail utility by typing **mail** by itself on the command line. The Mail utility is a complex program for managing messages with its own shell and its own set of commands and prompt. Upon invoking the Mail utility, you enter the Mail shell, where you can receive messages, reply to messages, and even send new messages. The commonly used Mail commands are listed in Table 8-3.

If there is no mail waiting in the mailbox, a notice saying that there is no mail will be displayed. You only enter the Mail shell if messages are waiting. In the next example, the user attempts to enter the Mail shell. However, since there are no messages waiting, a simple notice is displayed, and the user remains in his login shell.

```
$ mail
Sorry, no mail
$
```

When you first enter the Mail shell, a list of header summaries for each message is displayed. Summary information is arranged into fields beginning with the status of the message and the message number. The status of a message is indicated by a single uppercase letter, usually **N**, for "new," or **U**, for "unread." A message number, used for easy reference to your messages, follows the status field. The next field is the address of the sender, followed by the date and time it was received, and then the number of lines and characters in the message. The last field contains the subject the sender gave for the message. After the header summaries, the Mail shell displays its prompt, a question mark, **?**. At the Mail prompt, you enter commands that operate on the messages. Here is an example of a Mail header summary:

```
$ mail
Mail version 5.5-kw 5/30/95. Type ? for help.
"/var/spool/mail/chris": 3 messages 3 new
>N 1 valerie    Tue Feb 11 10:14:32 5/44    "Budget"
 N 2 aleina     Wed Feb 12 12:30:17 28/537  "Birthday"
 N 3 robert     Fri Feb 14  8:15:24 16/293  "Homework"
?
```

Message Lists and the Current Message Marker

Mail references messages either through a message list or through the current message marker (**>**). The greater-than sign is placed before a message that is considered the current message. The current message is referenced by default when no message number is included with a Mail command. For example, in the preceding header summaries, if no message number is given in the command, then message 1 will be referenced, since it is the current message. When a message is referenced in a command, it automatically becomes the current message, and the current message marker moves to its header. If you were to display message 2, then message 2 would become the new current message.

You can also reference a message using a message list. Many Mail commands can operate on several messages. You reference several messages in a Mail command using a message list consisting of several message numbers. You can also specify a range of messages by entering the number of the first message in the range followed by a dash and then the message number of the last message in the range. Given the messages in the previous example, you can reference all three messages with **1-3**.

You can also use special characters to reference certain messages. The **^** references the first message; for example, **^-3** specifies the range of messages from the first message to the third message. The **$** references the last message; so **4-$** would reference messages from 4 to the last message. **$** by itself just references the last message. The period, **.**, references the current message. And the asterisk, *****, references all messages. For example, to display all messages, you could use the command **p ***.

You can also select a group of messages based on the addresses of senders or the subject. An address by itself constitutes a message list that references all messages sent by the user with that address. **robert** is a message list referencing all messages sent by Robert. A slash followed by a pattern references all messages whose subject field contains that pattern. For example, **/birthday** is a message list referencing all messages with the subject "birthday."

You can also reference messages according to their status by entering a colon followed by a character representing the status of the messages you want. The characters are lowercase versions of the uppercase status codes used in the header summaries. For example, **n** represents new messages that are indicated with a status code **N** in header summaries. **:n** is a message list that references all new messages. The command **p :n** would display all new messages; **:u** would reference all unread messages—those with a status code of **U**.

Displaying Messages

Another set of commands is used to display messages. Simply entering the number of the message by itself will display that message. The message will then be output, screen by screen. Press the SPACEBAR or the ENTER key to continue to the next screen. If you enter the number 1 at the Mail prompt, the first message will be displayed for you.

If you want to look at several messages, one after the other, you need only enter their message numbers at the Mail prompt. Other commands allow you to reference and display messages according to their position with respect to the current message. You can display the message before the current message with the – command. If you use a number with the – command, you can reference a message positioned several messages before the current message. If message 6 were the current message, **-4** would reference message 2. You can also reference messages after the current message. The **+** and **n** commands and the ENTER key all display the next message after the current message.

If you want to display a range of messages, you need to use the **p** and **t** commands. These commands, like most other commands in Mail, take as their argument a message list. In a message list you can specify a set of messages to be referenced or a range of messages, as well as a single message. You specify a set of messages by listing their numbers one after the other, separated by a space, for example, **1 3** will reference messages 1 and 3. **p 1 3** will display messages 1 and 3. You specify a range using a dash; for example, **1-3** will reference messages 1, 2, and 3, and **p 1-3** will display all three messages.

The **p** or **t** command without a message list will display the current message, **>**. You can also use **+** or **–** with either command to display the messages before or after the current message. In the next example, the **p** command without a message number prints out the current message, message 1. Then the second message is displayed using the **p** command and the message number.

```
Mail version 5.5-kw 5/30/95. Type ? for help.
"/var/spool/mail/chris": 3 messages 3 new
>N  1 valerie    Tue Feb 11 10:14:32 5/44    "Budget"
 N  2 aleina     Wed Feb 12 12:30:17 28/537 "Birthday"
 N  3 robert     Fri Feb 14  8:15:24 16/293 "Homework"
& p
From valerie Wed Feb 11 10:14:17 PST 1996
To: chris
Subject: Budget
Status: R

You are way under budget
so far.
Congratulations

        Val

& p 2
From aleina Wed Feb 11 10:14:17 PST 1996
To: chris
Subject: Birthday
Status: R

Yes, I did remember your present

        Aleina

&
```

The following table lists several examples of the **p** command using differently composed message lists. Remember the use of special characters **^**, **$**, and ***** to reference the first, last, and all messages, as well as the **:** to reference special types of messages. You can also reference by addresses or subjects.

Command	Function
p $	Displays the last message
p *	Displays all messages

Command	Function
p ^-3	Displays from the first to the third message
p .-$	Displays from the current message to the last message
p n	Displays the next message, not the current one
p +2	Displays second message down from the current message
p /budget	Displays messages with the pattern "budget" in their subject field
p dylan	Displays messages sent by the user with the address "dylan"
p :n	Displays newly received messages
p :u	Displays previously unread messages
p :r	Redisplays the messages you have already read

After a message has been displayed, you are again given the Mail prompt, **&**. However, the header summaries are not automatically redisplayed. Using the **h** command (for "headers"), you can redisplay the header summaries at any time. In the next example, the user enters the **h** command to redisplay the list of message headers.

```
& h
>N 1 valerie    Tue Feb 11 10:14:32 5/44    "Budget"
 N 2 aleina     Wed Feb 12 12:30:17 28/537 "Birthday"
 N 3 robert     Fri Feb 14  8:15:24 16/293 "Homework"
&
```

Sometimes the list of headers will be so long that it will take up more than one screen. In that case, the **h** command will only display the first screen of headers. The command **z+** and **z-** move forward and backward to the next and previous screen of headers. If you know the number of the particular message header you want, you can use the **h** command with that number to display the header. **h12** will display the header for message 12, as well as the headers before and after it.

Deleting and Undeleting Messages

Unless you instruct Mail to erase a message, any messages you have read will be automatically saved when you leave the Mail shell. You can erase a message using the delete command, **d**. Entering the **d** command with a message number deletes that message. The command **d2** deletes message 2. You can delete several messages at once by listing a set or a range of message numbers: **d 2-4** deletes messages 2, 3, and 4. If you enter the **d** command without a message number, then the current message, **>**, is deleted. In the next example, the user deletes the third message.

```
Mail version 5.5-kw 5/30/95. Type ? for help.
"/var/spool/mail/chris": 3 messages 3 new
>N  1 valerie     Tue Feb 11 10:14:32 5/44     "Budget"
 N  2 aleina      Wed Feb 12 12:30:17 28/537 "Birthday"
 N  3 robert      Fri Feb 14  8:15:24 16/293 "Homework"
& d 3
& h
>N  1 valerie     Tue Feb 11 10:14:32 5/44     "Budget"
 N  2 aleina      Wed Feb 12 12:30:17 28/537 "Birthday"
&
```

Before leaving the Mail shell, if you change your mind and want some of the deleted messages to be saved, you can do so using the **u** command. The **u** command lets you restore a message that has been deleted within a given Mail session. The delete command does not immediately erase a message. All messages are held until you quit the Mail shell. Again, you can specify several messages or a range of messages. The command **u3** restores message 3; **u 2-4** restores messages 2, 3, and 4. For example:

```
& h
>N  1 valerie     Tue Feb 11 10:14:32 5/44     "Budget"
 N  2 aleina      Wed Feb 12 12:30:17 28/537 "Birthday"
& u 3
& h
>N  1 valerie     Tue Feb 11 10:14:32 5/44     "Budget"
 N  2 aleina      Wed Feb 12 12:30:17 28/537 "Birthday"
 N  3 robert      Fri Feb 14  8:15:24 16/293 "Homework"
&
```

Replying to Messages and Sending New Messages: R, r, m, and v

While receiving messages, you can also send your own messages. You can either reply to messages that you have just received or send entirely new messages, just as you would using the **mail** command and an address. In replying to a message, Mail allows you to automatically make use of the header information in a received message. You need only specify the message that you are replying to and then type in your reply.

You use the **R** and **r** commands to reply to a message you have received. The **R** command entered with a message number will generate a header for sending a message and then place you into the input mode to type in the message. The header will consist of the address of the sender and the subject specified by the sender. The subject header will also have the added title **Re:**, to indicate a reply. Simply type in your reply and end with CTRL-**d** on a line of its own. The reply will be immediately sent to the sender.

```
Mail version 5.5-kw 5/30/95. Type ? for help.
"/var/spool/mail/chris": 3 messages 3 new
>N 1 valerie     Tue Feb 11 10:14:32 5/44    "Budget"
 N 2 aleina      Wed Feb 12 12:30:17 28/537 "Birthday"
 N 3 robert      Fri Feb 14  8:15:24 16/293 "Homework"

& R 2
To: aleina
Subject: RE: Birthday
Is it a really big present?
^D
EOT
&
```

Suppose the sender has sent the message you received to several users. You can use the **r** command to send your reply not only to the sender, but also to all the users the message was sent to. Be careful of the **r** command. You may not want your reply sent to all the people who received the message. If you only want your reply sent to the sender alone, you need to use the **R** command.

You can also create and send a new message using the **m** command. Messages are sent just as they are sent from your login shell, except that the **m** command is used instead of **mail**. In the next example, the user sends a new message to **cecelia**.

```
Mail version 5.5-kw 5/30/95. Type ? for help.
"/var/spool/mail/chris": 3 messages 3 new
>N 1 valerie     Tue Feb 11 10:14:32 5/44    "Budget"
 N 2 aleina      Wed Feb 12 12:30:17 28/537 "Birthday"
 N 3 robert      Fri Feb 14  8:15:24 16/293 "Homework"

& m cecelia
Subject: Birthday
Did you remember my present?
oops
```

> **^D**
> EOT
> &

As with any Mail message, you can use the tilde commands for both message replies and new messages sent from the Mail shell. With the **~v** tilde command, you can edit a message reply in the Vi editor and then return to the input mode of the message reply. Upon sending the reply with a CTRL-**d**, you return to the Mail shell prompt.

Suppose that in sending a message, you wish to include the contents of one of the messages that you have received. For example, in composing a reply to someone, you may want to include the text of the message that the user sent you. Or you may want to include a message you received from one person in a reply to another, in effect, forwarding the message. With the **~m** and **~f** tilde commands, you can read the contents of a message into the message you are sending. The **~m** and **~f** tilde commands take as their argument a message list, usually a message number. For example, the tilde command **~m 2** reads the contents of the second message into the new message you are currently composing. The **~m** and **~f** commands differ in that the **~m** command will indent each line of the message it reads in, distinguishing it from the rest of your message. The **~f** command performs no indentation, inserting the message as is.

You can also use the **v** command to directly edit a message that you received. For example, you might want to annotate a message with your own comments before you save it. Or you might want to add your comments directly to the message and then use **~m** to use it in a reply or to send to someone else. To edit a specific message, you simply specify the message number after the **v** command: **v 3** will edit the third message.

Quitting the Mail Shell

The **q** command quits the Mail utility and returns you to the login shell command line. Messages that you have read are placed in a file called **mbox** in your home directory. The Mail utility notifies you of how many messages were saved in your **mbox** file. By default, these messages are removed from your incoming mailbox. If for some reason you do not want a message removed, use the command **pre** with the message number before you quit. The message will remain in your incoming mailbox file.

If you quit before reading a message, the message remains in your incoming mailbox file, waiting for the next time you enter the Mail utility to read messages. The next time you enter the Mail shell, these messages are displayed in the message list with the letter **U** placed before them. This indicates that they are previously received messages that are as yet unread.

```
Mail version 5.5-kw 5/30/95. Type ? for help.
"/var/spool/mail/chris": 3 messages 2 new
>N 1 valerie    Tue Feb 11 10:14:32 5/44    "Budget"
 N 2 cecelia    Wed Feb 12 12:30:17 28/537 "Birthday"
& q
Saved 1 message in mbox
$
```

You can also exit the Mail shell with the **x** command. The **x** command is like a generalized undo command. Any messages that you have deleted during this Mail session will be undeleted.

Saving and Accessing Messages in Mailbox Files: s and S

Instead of saving messages in the **mbox** file, you can use the **s** command to explicitly save a message to a file of your choice. However, the **s** command saves a message with its header, in effect, creating another mailbox file. You can then later access this mailbox file using the Mail utility, much the same way that **mail** accesses waiting messages.

You save a message with the **s** command by typing **s** with the message number, followed by the name of the file to which the message is to be saved. If the file already exists, the message will simply be appended to the end of the file. In the next example, the command **s2 family_msgs** saves the second message to the **family_msgs** file. More than one message can be saved to the same file by specifying a set or range of message numbers: **s1-3 family_msgs** saves messages 1, 2, and 3 to the file **family_msgs**.

```
Mail version 5.5-kw 5/30/95. Type ? for help.
"/var/spool/mail/chris": 3 messages 3 new
>N 1 valerie    Tue Feb 11 10:14:32 5/44    "Budget"
 N 2 aleina     Wed Feb 12 12:30:17 28/537 "Birthday"
 N 3 robert     Fri Feb 14  8:15:24 16/293 "Homework"
& s 2 family_msgs
```

You can save messages to whatever files that you specify. Often it helps to organize messages from a specific sender into one file and name that file with the sender's address. For example, all messages from **robert** could be saved in a file called **robert**. Instead of the **s** command, you can use the **S** command to do this automatically for you. The **S** command followed by a message list will save that message to a file that has the name of the message's sender. If the file does not exist, **S** will create it. In the next example, the user saves message 3 to a file named after the message's sender, in this case **robert**.

```
Mail version 5.5-kw 5/30/95. Type ? for help.
"/var/spool/mail/chris": 3 messages 3 new
>N 1 valerie    Tue Feb 11 10:14:32 5/44     "Budget"
 N 2 aleina     Wed Feb 12 12:30:17 28/537 "Birthday"
 N 3 robert     Fri Feb 14  8:15:24 16/293 "Homework"
& S 3
& q
$ ls
mbox robert
$
```

Saving messages to a file with their message headers creates a mailbox file that you can read and manage using the Mail utility. The headers provide the Mail utility with information it needs to reference messages by a message number, display a header list, delete messages, and execute any other Mail commands. You can access a mailbox file either by invoking the Mail utility with the **-f** option and the mailbox file name, or, if you are already using Mail, by executing the **folder** command that switches to a specified mailbox file. For example, the command **mail -f family_msgs** accesses the mailbox file **family_msgs**. Each message in the **family_msgs** mailbox file will then be displayed in a message list. The Mail commands such as **d** and **p** will work on these messages.

```
$ mail -f family_msgs
Mail version 5.5. Type ? for help.
"family_msgs": 1 message
 >  1 aleina     Wed Feb 12 12:30:17 28/537 "Birthday"
&
```

Mail is designed to operate on any mailbox file that you specify. By default, when you invoke Mail, you automatically begin to operate on your incoming mailbox where the system places newly received mail. You can, however, switch to another mailbox file at any time and operate on the messages there. You can switch to yet another mailbox file, and so on, as you wish, or switch back to your incoming mailbox. To switch to another mailbox file, you enter the **folder** command followed by the name of the mailbox file. The header summaries for this mailbox file will then be displayed, and you can perform operations on those messages. To switch back to your incoming mailbox, you enter **folder** followed by the symbol **%**, which represents the name of your incoming mailbox. You can also switch back and forth between two mailboxes using the **#** symbol for the mailbox file name. **#** represents the previous mailbox file accessed.

In the next example, the user begins Mail with the incoming mailbox and then uses the **folder** command to switch to the **family_msgs** mailbox file. The user then switches back to the incoming mailbox with the **folder %** command.

```
$ mail
Mail version 5.5-kw 5/30/95. Type ? for help.
"/var/spool/mail/chris": 2 messages 2 new
>N 1 valerie    Tue Feb 11 10:14:32 5/44    "Budget"
 N 2 robert     Fri Feb 14  8:15:24 16/293 "Homework"
& folder family_msgs
Held 2 messages in /var/spool/mail/chris
"family_msgs": 1 message
>  1 aleina      Wed Feb 12 12:30:17 28/537 "Birthday"
& folder %
"/var/spool/mail/chris": 2 messages 2 new
>N 1 valerie    Tue Feb 11 10:14:32 5/44    "Budget"
 N 2 robert     Fri Feb 14  8:15:24 16/293 "Homework"
```

As mentioned previously, when you quit the Mail utility, the messages that you have read are saved with their headers in the **mbox** file. If the **mbox** file already exists, the new messages are appended to the end. You may want to go back and access a previously read message saved in **mbox**. Since the **mbox** file contains the message headers, it is a mailbox file that you can access with the Mail utility. You can access the **mbox** file either by invoking Mail with a **-f** option followed by the name **mbox**, (**mail -f mbox**), or by switching to **mbox** using the **folder** command and the symbol **&**, which represents the name of the file used to save your read messages (**folder &**). A list of header summaries for all your previously read messages is displayed with the headers. Mail commands such as **p** and **d** can display or delete them. You can even send replies to messages using the **R** or **r** commands. In the next example, the user invokes Mail to access previously read messages.

```
$ mail -f mbox
Mail version 5.5-kw 5/30/95. Type ? for help.
"/var/spool/mail/chris": 2 messages
>  1 marylou    Mon Feb 10 09:24:22 24/976   "Trip"
   2 dylan      Fri Feb  8 11:15:12 17/834   "Food"
&
```

Saving Message Text in Files: Sending and Receiving Files

Suppose you want to save only the text of a message without the header information. In this case, you use the **w** command to save a message to a file without the header. Its syntax is the same as that of the **s** command. **w1 newbudget** writes message 1 without its header to the file **newbudget**. The file **newbudget** is a standard text file, not a mailbox file. It cannot be accessed by the Mail utility.

```
Mail version 5.5-kw 5/30/95. Type ? for help.
"/var/spool/mail/chris": 3 messages 3 new
>N 1 valerie    Tue Feb 11 10:14:32 5/44    "Budget"
 N 2 aleina     Wed Feb 12 12:30:17 28/537 "List"
 N 3 robert     Fri Feb 14  8:15:24 16/293 "Homework"
& w 1 newbudget
```

You can make use of this feature to receive full documents from other users, instead of just messages. Any user can send you a text file through the Mail utility using redirection. Then you can use the **w** command to receive and save that text file. In turn, you can send a text file to another user who can then use the **w** command to receive that file.

To send a text file through the Mail utility, you must use redirection. The Mail utility's input mode accepts standard input. Standard input, in turn, can be redirected to receive input from a text file. In the next example, the user sends the file **complist** to **chris**.

```
$ mail chris < complist
```

When you receive the text file, a Mail header is attached to the file. To save the file without the Mail header, you use the **w** command. If the **complist** file was received as message 1, then the command **w1 complist** saves the message as a text file without the Mail header:

```
$ mail
Mail version 5.5-kw 5/30/95. Type ? for help.
"/var/spool/mail/chris": 1 message 1 new
>N 1 aleina     Tue Feb 11 10:14:32 5/44
& w 1 complist
```

Sending files through Mail has one major limitation. You can only send character files, not binary files. The Mail utility will corrupt a binary file in the transmission process as well as insert a header. However, there are special file transfer utilities such as ftp that you can use to send binary files. These are discussed in Chapter 11. Such utilities are far more reliable than Mail for transferring very large files as well as binary files.

Mail Aliases, Options, and the Mail Shell Initialization File: .mailrc

The Mail utility has its own initialization file, called **.mailrc**, that is executed each time Mail is invoked, either for sending or receiving messages. Within it you can define Mail options and create Mail aliases. You can set options that add different features to mail, such as changing the prompt or saving copies of messages that you send. With a Mail alias, you can easily send a message to several users. You will find this very useful for broadcasting different messages to the same group of users.

Mail Aliases

You may often need to send—or broadcast—messages to the same group of users. For example, suppose you are part of a study group. You will want to send the same messages, such as when you are meeting next, to every person in the group. Ordinarily, each time you send a message to this group of users, you would have to type in all their addresses. However, it is possible to define an alias for a set of addresses so that, instead of listing all the addresses each time you broadcast, you could use the alias. The alias replaces the list of addresses on the command line.

To define an alias, you enter the keyword **alias**, followed by the alias you have chosen, and then the list of addresses it represents. There's one catch: to alias addresses for use in Mail commands, you need to define the alias within the Mail shell. Each time you leave and then reenter the Mail shell, you need to redefine the alias. This can be done automatically by placing the alias definition in the Mail shell initialization file, **.mailrc**. To enter an alias into the **.mailrc** file, first edit the **.mailrc** file with a text editor such as Vi. Then enter the **alias** command, followed by the alias and the list of addresses. Be sure there is no new line character splitting up the list of addresses. In the next example, the alias **myclass** is defined in the **.mailrc** file.

.mailrc

```
alias myclass  chris dylan aleina justin larisa
```

When the Mail utility is invoked, the **.mailrc** file is automatically executed, defining the alias. When you use Mail to send a message, you can use the alias in place of the list of addresses on the command line. You could also use the alias when sending messages within the Mail shell. In either case, the **.mailrc** file is executed, defining the alias. In the following example, the **myclass** alias is used in place of the addresses. The contents of the file **homework** are sent to all the users whose addresses are aliased by **myclass**.

```
$ mail myclass < homework
```

Mail Options

Mail also provides a set of options that you can define in the **.mailrc** file that will be active each time you use Mail. For example, you could define the Mail prompt to be something other than the **&**. Table 8-4 lists several of the more common Mail options. You set a Mail option using the keyword **set** followed by the option name and then, if called for, an equal sign and a string. For example, **set prompt="*"** will set the Mail prompt to an asterisk. When **.mailrc** is executed, it will then set all the options that you have specified in it.

One useful option is **sign**, which specifies a signature that you can insert into your message using the **~a** tilde command. Often the **sign** option is set to your name and can include other information, such as your phone number or network address. The next example sets the signature to "Robert and Valerie."

```
set sign="Robert and Valerie"
```

You can then use the **~a** tilde command to insert your signature in any message:

```
$ mail aleina
Subject: Dinner
Lets have ice cream for dessert
OK?
~a
Robert and Valerie
^D
EOT
$
```

Another useful option is the **record** option. This option instructs Mail to automatically save any messages that you create and send. In setting the **record** option, you need to specify what file Mail will save your sent messages to. In the next example, the user sets the **record** option and has sent messages saved in a file called **outbox**. If no absolute path name is specified, the file is placed in your home directory.

```
set record="outbox"
```

Organizing Your Mailbox Files: folder, MBOX, and outfolder

You will notice that mailbox files that you create with your **s** and **S** commands, as well as your **mbox** file, can often end up scattered throughout different directories on your system. Mailbox files that you create with the **s** command are placed in your current working directory, whatever that may be at the time you invoke Mail. Mailbox files that you create with the **S** command, as well as your **mbox** file, are placed in your home directory. Instead of your home directory or working directory, you could place all your mailbox files in one specified directory. To do so, you need to make use of three special options: **folder**, **MBOX**, and **outfolder**.

First you need to create the directory that you want to hold your mailbox files. Then you set the **folder** option in your **.mailrc** file, assigning to it the path name of that directory. This directory is often referred to as the **folder** directory. The **folder** option performs two tasks. First, any mailbox files that you create using the **S** command will be placed in the directory assigned to **folder**. Second, setting the **folder** option activates the **+** symbol as a special character in Mail file names that represents the **folder** directory. When using the **s** command, you can precede a mailbox file name with the **+** symbol to save it to the **folder** directory, along with the other mailboxes. When using the **folder** command to switch to another mailbox file, you can precede the file name with a **+** symbol so that Mail will search for the file in the **folder** directory.

In the next example, the user has created a directory called **/home/chris/mail** and has assigned this path name to the variable **folder**. Now any mailbox files that the user creates using the **S** command are placed in that directory. You can give the directory any name you wish. In this case, it is simply called **mail**.

```
set folder="/home/chris/mail"
```

In the following example, the user saves message 2 to a mailbox file called **family_msgs**. The file name is preceded by a **+** symbol, which represents the directory held by the **folder** option. Given the setting of the **folder** option in the preceding example, the file name **+family_msgs** will save the **family_msgs** mailbox file to the directory **/home/chris/mail**, along with any other mailbox files. Then the user switches to another mailbox file in the **folder** directory, making sure to precede the mailbox file name with a **+** symbol so that Mail will search for it in the **folder** directory, and not the current working directory.

```
Mail version 5.5-kw 5/30/95. Type ? for help.
"/var/spool/mail/chris": 3 messages 3 new
>N  1 valerie     Tue Feb 11 10:14:32 5/44    "Budget"
 N  2 aleina      Wed Feb 12 12:30:17 28/537 "Birthday"
 N  3 robert      Fri Feb 14  8:15:24 16/293 "Homework"
& s 2 +family_msgs
"/usr/mail/chris/mail/family_msgs" [Appended]
& folder +family_msgs
Held 2 messages in /usr/mail/chris
"+family_msgs": 1 message 1 new
>   1 aleina      Wed Feb 12 12:30:17 28/537 "Birthday"
```

Your **mbox** file will not, however, be automatically placed in the **folder** directory. The name for the **mbox** file is held in a special variable called **MBOX**. You can have **mbox** placed in your **folder** directory by assigning the name **mbox** preceded by a **+** sign to the **MBOX** variable: **+mbox**. As in the case of the **folder** option, you would normally make the **MBOX** assignment in your **.mailrc** file.

```
set MBOX=+mbox
```

You can also specify that the file you have designated for saving outgoing messages be placed in your **folder** directory. You need to have already defined your **record** option, assigning the name of the file for your outgoing messages. Then to have this file placed in your **folder** directory, you set the **outfolder** option, as shown here:

```
set outfolder
```

You could also simply assign to the **record** option, the file name for your outgoing messages preceded by a **+** symbol:

```
set record=+outbox
```

Having set these three options, all your mailbox files will be kept in one designated directory. All settings should be placed in your **.mailrc** file. A sample **.mailrc** file follows, incorporating Mail aliases as well as many of the variable and option assignments.

.mailrc

```
alias myclass  chris dylan aleina justin larisa
set sign="Robert and Valerie"
set folder="/home/chris/mail"
set MBOX=+mbox
set record=outbox
set outfolder
set prompt="*"
```

The Elm Utility

Another popular mail utility, Elm, was developed by Dave Taylor. Though it is not an official standard mail utility, it has become widely used. Unlike Mail, which is command line oriented, Elm has a screen-oriented, user-friendly interface that makes mail tasks easy to execute. Messages are displayed one screen at a time, and you can move back and forth through the message, screen by screen. Instead of entering commands on a command line, the keys on your keyboard become single-letter commands that execute mail operations, just as single-letter Vi commands execute editing operations. Many of the commands used in Elm bear a similarity to commands used in utilities such as **more** and Vi. Table 8-5 lists the different Elm commands.

Sending Mail with Elm

With Elm, you send a message to any user by using the **elm** command. The message can be something you type in at the keyboard, or it can be the contents of a file. When you are entering a message at the keyboard, you are actually using a standard editor, such as Vi.

To send a message, type **elm** along with the address of the person to whom you are sending the message. When you press ENTER, Elm will display the name of the person to whom you are sending the message, and then prompt you for the subject. Elm displays the actual name of the person, not the address. It obtains the user's name from online information much the same way that the **finger** command can obtain the name of a user.

```
$ elm robert


Send only mode [ELM 2.4 PL20]
```

```
To: Robert Petersen
Subject of message: Birthday
Copies to:



Invoking editor...
```

At the subject prompt, you enter a subject. Then Elm prompts you for a carbon copy list. You can then enter the addresses of other users whom you want to have a copy of the message, or you can simply press ENTER if you do not want any carbon copies sent. Upon pressing ENTER at this point, you are placed in the standard editor, usually Vi, and you can use the editor to enter your message. Remember that you are in the Vi editor—to actually enter text, you first have to enter the Vi input mode with either the **a** or **i** command. Then, after entering your text, you press ESC to return to the Vi command mode. When you have finished entering your message, you save and exit Vi with the **ZZ** command.

```
Your present is in the mail
really
~
~
~
~
~
~
```

After editing the message, Elm will prompt you for an action, at which time you can send it, quit without sending, edit the message again, or edit its headers. Each option is listed with a single-letter command. Simply press the key, just as you would press a Vi editor command key. There is no command line in which you enter the letter and press ENTER.

```
Please choose one of the following options by parenthesized
letter:
e)dit message, edit h)eaders, s)end it, or f)orget it
```

When you invoke the Elm utility, you can specify the subject on the command line using the **-s** option. In the next example, the subject "Tonight's celebration" is specified on the command line. The user will then not be prompted for the subject by Elm.

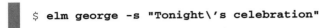

```
$ elm george -s "Tonight\'s celebration"
```

The **h** option displayed in the Elm message menu is for editing the header. With this option, you can change any of the entries in your message header, and you can enter other header values, such as addresses for blind carbon copies. When you press **h**, a message header edit screen is displayed, listing a prompt for each header field. To edit or add values to a header field, simply enter the first character of the header prompt. At the bottom of the screen you will be prompted with the name of the field, and you can then enter a new value. Press ENTER and the new value is displayed in the header field.

For example, to change the subject, press **s**, and you will be prompted to enter a new subject. After entering the new subject and pressing ENTER, the new value for the subject field is displayed in the header. You can then edit another header field. To add addresses to the blind carbon copy, press **b**, type in the addresses, and press ENTER. You leave the Message Header Edit Screen by pressing ENTER, instead of the first character of a header prompt. This places you back at the message menu. Figure 8-1 shows a sample of the Message Header Edit Screen.

Receiving Mail Using Elm

To receive mail using Elm, you invoke the Elm utility the same way you do to send mail—you enter **elm** by itself on the command line. The Elm utility then displays a list of message headers representing messages you have received. The headers are displayed from the top of the screen. At the bottom of the screen is an information menu listing the different commands you can perform on the screen of message headers. This list of headers is referred to in Elm as the *index*. The message headers are displayed on the screen much like text in a Vi editor. If you have more than one screen of message headers, you can move to the next screen with the **+** key. You can also move back a screen with the **-** key.

The Elm message headers look just like the headers in Mail. An Elm header displays the status, message number, date, name of the sender, number of lines in the message, and the subject. As in Mail, the message status is represented by a letter code. An **N** indicates a newly received message, and **O** indicates an old message, one that is still unread. The message number can be used to reference the message in Elm commands. Figure 8-2 shows an example of an Elm message header. All the messages are newly received. The first message is from Gabriel Matoza and was sent on Feb 11. It contains 5 lines, and its subject is "Budget." Notice that the full name of the sender is displayed, not simply the address.

The current header is either preceded by an arrow, **->**, or highlighted by the background. To perform an operation on a message, you must make that message's

Message Header Edit Screen

T)o: robert (Robert Petersen)
C)c:
B)cc:
S)ubject Birthday

R)eply to:
A)ction: E)xpires:
P)riority: Precede(n)ce:
I)n-reply to:

Choose header, u)ser defined header, d)omainize
!)shell, or {enter}

Choice:

Figure 8-1.   *Elm's message editing screen*

Mailbox is '/var/spool/mail/chris' with 3 messages
N1 Gabriel Matoza   Feb 11   (5)   "Budget"
N2 Aleina Petersen   Feb 12   (28)   "Birthday"
N3 Marylou Carrion   Feb 14   (16)   "Homework"

You can use any of the following commands by pressing the first character:
d)elete or u)ndelete mail, m)ail a message, r)eply or f)orward mail, q)uit
 To read a message, press {enter}. j = move down, k = move up, ? = help

Command:

Figure 8-2.   *Elm headers*

header the current header. You can do this in several ways. You can enter its message number and press ENTER. You can also make a header the current header by moving to it on the screen using the movement commands, **j** and **k**. **j** moves up to the previous header, and **k** moves down to the next header. You can also use the UP and DOWN ARROW keys. The arrow or highlight indicating the current header will move as you press the **j** or **k** commands, moving to the next or previous message header. If the first header is the current header, then pressing the **j** key twice will make the third header the current header.

To display the current message, you simply press ENTER. To display a specific message, either move to that message with the **k** or **j** keys or enter the message number, and then press ENTER. A new screen will appear in which the message is displayed. If the message is larger than a screen, you can move through it, screen by screen, using the same commands as those in the **more** utility. Pressing the SPACEBAR moves you to the next screen, and pressing **b** moves you back a screen. You can even search for particular patterns in the message.

```
Message 1/3 From Aleina Petersen        Feb 11, 96 04:13:56 am -0300


Subject: Birthday
To: robert (Robert Petersen)
Date: Mon, 12 Feb 1996 10:14:17 -0700 (PDT)


Yes, I did remember your present

        Aleina



Command ('i' to return to index):
```

Once you have examined your message, you can use the **i** command to return to the header screen. Simply press the **i** key. The **i** stands for index, which is the term Elm uses to refer to the list of headers.

You can print messages by pressing the **p** key. Press **p** alone to print the message for the current message header, or type a message number followed by **p** to print a particular message.

If you want to perform an operation on several messages at once, you can first tag them using the **t** command, and then the next Elm command that you enter will operate on all of them. To tag a message, you move to that message header and press **t**. A **+** sign will appear before that message header. Suppose you want to print several messages. You could tag the headers for those messages using the **t** command and then press **p** to print them. In the next example, the user has tagged the first two messages. If the user then presses **p**, messages 1 and 2 will both be printed.

```
+N 1  Gabriel Matoza     Feb 11  (5)    "Budget"
+N 2  Aleina Petersen    Feb 12  (28)   "Birthday"
 N 3  Marylou Carrion    Feb 14  (16)   "Homework"
```

Elm also allows you to select a current header by using pattern searches. There are several Elm commands that search different parts of a message for a specified pattern. The **/** command searches the address and subject fields of a header for a particular pattern. A double slash command, **//**, searches the text of a message for a pattern. If you enter a **/** command, you are then prompted to enter a pattern. Upon pressing ENTER, Elm searches address and subject fields in each message for that pattern. It stops at the first occurrence it finds and makes that header the current header. Using the previous example, if you searched for a header that has the pattern "birth", you would locate and make message 2 the current header.

A **//** command will search the text of your messages for a pattern. You enter a **//** command, and then Elm prompts you to enter a pattern. Elm searches the text of all your messages and makes the header of the first message with that pattern in its text the current header. For example, if the user enters a **//** and the pattern **congratulations**, then Elm will match on the pattern "congratulations" in the text of the first message, making that the current header:

```
->N 1  Gabriel Matoza    Feb 11  (5)    "Budget"
  N 2  Aleina Petersen   Feb 12  (28)   "Birthday"
  N 3  Marylou Carrion   Feb 14  (16)   "Homework"
```

Other search commands perform specific operations, such as the CTRL-**t** command that tags headers with a certain pattern, or the CTRL-**d** command that deletes headers with a pattern. You can use the CTRL-**t** command to tag all messages from a certain user or messages that deal with a certain topic. You could then perform an operation on those messages, such as printing them out. For example, to print all messages that deal with the subject "birthday," you first enter CTRL-**t** and the pattern **birthday** to tag all messages that deal with birthdays, and then press the **p** command to print those messages.

Quitting the Elm Utility

You can quit the Elm utility by pressing the **q** key. Before you leave Elm, you will be asked whether or not you wish to save your read messages in your received mailbox file. The name of the received mailbox file is contained in the Elm variable called

received. You will also be asked whether you want to keep unread messages in your incoming mailbox so that you can read them later. If not, they will be deleted. Also, if you have deleted any messages during this session, you will be asked to confirm the delete. In the next example, the user confirms deleted messages, saves read messages in the received mailbox, and keeps unread messages for later access.

```
Delete message? (y/n) n
Move read messages to "received" folder? (y/n) y
Keep unread messages in incoming mailbox? (y/n) y
Keeping 2 messages and storing 1
```

There are several other commands that you can use to quit Elm. A **Q** command will quit without any prompts for received and unread messages. Preset defaults will be used to determine whether messages are to be saved or not. The **x** and CTRL-**q** commands will quit the Elm utility, leaving the incoming mailbox as you found it. Any deletions, read or unread messages, will be ignored.

Deleting and Undeleting Messages: d and u

To delete the message whose header is the current header, simply press **d**. This will mark the status of the message with a **D** and will delete it when you exit the Elm utility. To delete a message whose header is not the current header, use either the **j** or **k** key to move to that header or enter the message number, and then press the **d** key. To delete message 5 press **5** and then d. To delete several messages at once, first tag them with the **t** command, and then press the **d** key. In the next example, the user has deleted the second message. Its status is now marked with a **D**.

```
   N 1  Gabriel Matoza    Feb 11  (5)   "Budget"
->D 2  Aleina Petersen   Feb 12  (28)  "Birthday"
   N 3  Marylou Carrion   Feb 14  (16)  "Homework"
```

You can also use the CTRL-**d** command to select a set of headers to be deleted that contain a specified pattern in their addresses or subjects. You can use this feature to select and delete messages from a certain user or messages that deal with a specific topic. In the next example, the user decides to delete all messages from Aleina. The user presses CTRL-**d** and is prompted for a pattern, in this case "Aleina." The second and fourth messages are matched in their address field and marked for deletion.

```
   N 1  Gabriel Matoza    Feb 11  (5)   "Budget"
   D 2  Aleina Petersen   Feb 12  (28)  "Birthday"
   N 3  Marylou Carrion   Feb 14  (16)  "Homework"
->D 4  Aleina Petersen   Feb 16  (32)  "Party"
```

To undelete a message, move to its header or enter its message number, and then press the **u** key. The status of the message will change from **D** to **U**, indicating an undelete. Whereas the **u** key undeletes the current message or tagged messages, the CTRL-**u** command will undelete any messages with a certain pattern in their address or subject fields. CTRL-**u** works the same way as CTRL-**d**.

Replying to Messages

While in the Elm utility, you can send a reply to any messages that you receive. Elm will use the header information in a message to determine the address of the sender. The **r** command sends a reply to a message. You reply to a message by first making its header the current header or by entering the message number, and then pressing the **r** key. Upon pressing **r**, Elm first asks if you want to include a copy of the message in your reply. You enter **y** or **n**. Elm then opens up a screen with the sender's name and subject displayed at the top. The cursor is positioned at the subject so that you can modify it if you wish. Press ENTER to continue. You are then prompted for any carbon copies that you want to send. Upon pressing ENTER, you then enter a standard editor such as Vi in which you type the text of your reply. Just as with a regular message, to enter text, you must first enter the input mode with an **a** command. You exit the input mode with ESC. Then the **ZZ** command saves the text and returns you to Elm. The menu for sending messages is displayed. You then press the **s** key to send the message.

Sending Messages from Elm

You send messages while in the Elm utility with the **m** command. Upon pressing the **m** key, you are prompted for the address of the user to whom you want to send the message. You enter the address and are then prompted for the subject. After the subject, you are asked if you want to send any carbon copies. If not, press ENTER. You are then in the Vi editor and can edit and input your message. Upon exiting the editor, you can send the message with the **s** command.

Saving Messages in Elm

You can save a message to a mailbox file using the **s** command. Either make the message you want to save the current header or enter the message number, and then press the **s** key. At the bottom of the screen, Elm gives you a save prompt with a default mailbox file name. This name is the name of the sender of the message. Elm assumes that you may want to organize the messages that you save into different mailbox files according to the person who sent them. To save your message in the mailbox file for the sender displayed at the save prompt, just press ENTER. If, instead, you want to save the message to a file of your own choosing, at the save prompt, enter an **=** sign followed immediately by the name of the file. For example, to save your message in the file **birthdays**, enter **=birthdays**.

If you want to save several messages to the same mailbox file, you could first tag the message headers and then press the **s** key. The mailbox file that you then specify will have all the tagged messages saved in it.

Elm also provides two special mailbox files whose names are referenced in the Elm variables **received** and **sent**. The **received** mailbox file operates like the **mbox** file in Mail. Messages that you read are automatically saved in this file when you exit Elm. The **sent** file usually holds messages you have sent. You can specifically save your message in the **received** mailbox file by entering a **>** at the save prompt. A **<** will save the message in the **sent** mailbox.

Reading Mailbox Files with Elm

While in Elm, you can switch over to reading a specific mailbox file instead of incoming messages. The **c** command will prompt you for the name of a mailbox file. Simply press the **c** key and the prompt appears. The prompt will display the name of the mailbox file used to hold received messages from the sender in the current message header. You can specify your own mailbox file by entering the name of the file preceded by an **=** sign. **=birthdays** will specify the **birthdays** mailbox file. In the next example, the current header is a message sent by the user called **aleina**. When the user presses the **c** command, the "Change folder" notice is displayed at the Command prompt, and, as a default, the name of the user who sent the current message is displayed at the "Change to which folder" prompt. In this case, the user's name is **aleina**.

```
Command: Change folder
Change to which folder: =aleina
The user then enters the new folder name at the prompt,
overwriting =aleina:

Command: Change folder
Change to which folder: =birthdays
```

Once you have changed to the other folder, the headers for all the messages in this mailbox file will be displayed, and you can display the messages, delete them from the file, or send replies. The folder's name will be displayed at the top of the screen.

You can change to any other folder you wish by entering a name at the folder prompt. Entering a **!** will change back to the incoming mailbox. Pressing **>** will change to the **received** files folder, and **<** to the **sent** files folder.

Elm Aliases: Alias Menu and aliases.text

You can create an alias using either the Elm alias menu within the utility, or by entering aliases into a special Elm initialization file called **aliases.text**. The alias menu is by far the easiest and most efficient way to manage your Elm aliases. However, if you wish to create group aliases, such as those used by Mail, you will need to know how to enter an alias directly into the **aliases.text** file.

Elm Aliases: Alias Menu

To create an alias within the Elm utility, you use the **a** command, which displays an alias menu. You can enter commands in the menu to create an alias, delete an alias, or list all aliases or particular aliases. To create a new alias, you select the new alias option by pressing the **n** key. Elm then prompts you for the alias, the user's name, and the user's address. It then automatically installs and adds the alias to the **aliases.text** file.

```
Aliases [ELM 2.4 PL20]



You can use any of the following commands by pressing the first
    character;
a)lias current message, n)ew alias, d)elete or u)ndelete an alias,
    m)ail to alias, or r)eturn to main menu.  To view an alias,
    press <enter>.
j = move down, k = move up, ? = help

Alias: n
Add a new alias to database..
Enter alias name: mark
```

The following prompts will all be displayed on the same line, one after the other. After entering the name of the alias, that prompt and name are replaced by a prompt for the last name of the person for whom you are making the alias. The prompt for the first name then replaces the one for the last name, and so on, for the address. Finally, you are asked if you want to accept the new prompt. You can enter either **y** or **n**.

```
Enter last name for mark: Petersen
Enter first name for mark: Mark
Enter optional comment for mark:
Enter address for mark: mark@violet.berkeley.edu
```

```
Messages addressed as: mark@violet.berkeley.edu (mark petersen)
New alias: mark is 'Mark Petersen'. Accept new alias? (y/n) y
```

You can also create an alias for the sender of the message referenced by the current message header. In this case, you press the **a** command at the Elm alias menu. Elm will then prompt you for an alias name but take the user's name and the user's address from the message header. The alias will be automatically installed and added to **aliases.text**. This is perhaps the easiest way to create an alias.

You can delete an alias by pressing the **d** key. Elm prompts you for the alias name and then deletes the alias from the **aliases.text** file. You can also list aliases with the **l** command or list a particular alias with its name and address using the **p** command.

Elm Aliases: .elm and aliases.text

Elm maintains a **.elm** directory in your own home directory with which it will configure your use of Elm. Each time you invoke Elm, it generates a shell for your own use, within which you can define your own aliases and configuration variables. The **.elm** directory contains special initialization files in which you can place alias or variable definitions. These initialization files operate like the **.mailrc** file, configuring your Elm utility just as **.mailrc** configures Mail.

You can define Elm aliases in the **aliases.text** file in the .elm directory. The syntax for an Elm alias is the alias followed by an **=** sign and the user's name followed by another **=** sign and the user's address.

```
alias = user name = user address
```

In the next example, the user creates an alias for Gabriel Matoza whose address is **gabriel@garnet.berkeley.edu**.

```
gabe = Gabriel Matoza = gabriel@garnet.berkeley.edu
```

You can have more than one alias for the same person. You just list the aliases, separated by a colon. In the next example, the user creates two aliases for Robert Petersen at **robert@violet.fallon.edu**.

```
robert, bob = Robert Petersen = robert@violet.fallon.edu
```

Once you have created individual aliases, you can use them to create group aliases. A group alias operates in the same way as aliases used in Mail's **.mailrc** file. When you send a message to a group alias, the message is sent to every user in that group. You define a group alias with the following syntax. The *alias-list* contains the previously defined aliases that reference individual users, separated by commas.

```
group alias = group name = alias-list
```

In the next example, the user creates a group alias using "gabe" and "robert," defined previously. The alias group is called **myclass** and the group name is "photography class". If the user sends a message to **myclass**, it will go to **robert@violet.fallon.edu** and to **gabriel@garnet.berkeley.edu**.

```
myclass = photography class = robert, gabe
```

An example of the **alias.text** file follows. Notice that the individual aliases are defined first, followed by the group aliases that make use of them.

```
alias.text
gabe = gabriel matoza = valerie@garnet.berkeley.edu
robert, bob = robert petersen = robert@violet.eugene.edu
myclass = photography class = robert, val
```

Whenever you add new aliases to the **alias.text** file, you must install them in the Elm utility by executing the command **newalias**.

Elm Options: .elmrc

Elm has a number of different options with which to configure your Elm shell. These options are variables that you can turn on or off, or assign values to. Some Elm options are simple switches that you turn on or off using the special values **YES** and **NO**. For example, the assignment **alwaysstore = YES** will set the option to always store received mail in the **received** mailbox file. Other Elm options hold string values. For example, the assignment **receivedmail = mybox** assigns the string "mybox" to the **receivedmail** option. This option holds the file name of the file used as the received mail file. In this case, received mail will be saved to the **mybox** file.

You set options either by entering assignments to the .elmrc file in your .elm directory, or by using the options menu within the Elm utility. Within Elm, the command **o** brings up the options menu. The options menu only displays the more commonly used options. To change an option, you press the first character of one of the options displayed, and then you are prompted to enter a new value.

Mailing Binaries and Archives

Internet mail operations are set up to handle only text messages; that is, those consisting of a sequence of characters. Binary files such as compiled programs cannot be sent through the mail utilities—if sent, they will arrive corrupted and unusable. The same is true for archived or compressed files. A set of files that you archive into one file using **tar** cannot be sent through the mail. Nor can you send a file that you compressed using a compression utility such as **gzip**. There is a way, however, for you to convert binary and archived files into character files that you can then send through mail utilities. The **uuencode** program translates a binary file into one that is character equivalent, which can then be sent through a mail utility such as **mail** or **elm**. The person receiving such an encoded file can then convert it back to a binary file using the **uudecode** program.

The **uuencode** program is designed to work on either the standard input or on a particular file. In either case you have to provide a name for the file that will be created when the encoded data is converted back to binary. **uuencode** outputs the encoded binary data to the standard output. **uuencode** has the following syntax:

```
uuencode file  name
```

where *name* is the name to be given to the decoded binary data and *file* is the name of a binary file to be encoded. Keep in mind that since **uuencode** sends the encoded data to the standard output, you should redirect this output to a file; then you can send that file.

The **uudecode** program takes as its argument the file that holds the encoded data. It will generate a binary file using the name you provided in the **uuencode** operation. The basic steps are shown here:

```
uuencode file name > datafile
mail address < datafile
& s msg-num datafile
uudecode datafile
```

The file is encoded and mailed as a message. When that message is received, it is saved as a file that is then decoded, generating a binary file called *name*.

In the next example, the user encodes the picture file called **dylan.gif**. Picture files such as gif and jpeg files are binary files and have to be translated to character format before they can be mailed. In this case, the name of the binary file and the name to be used for the decoded version of the file are the same. The encoded output is redirected to a file called **dylanpic**:

```
$ uuencode dylan.gif  dylan.gif  > dylanpic
```

dylanpic is the file that contains only character data, although this character data is encoded binary data. The user can then send **dylanpic** through the mail system:

```
$ mail larisa@ix.com < dylanpic
```

Once received, you simply use **uudecode** to convert the encoded data back to its binary form. **uudecode** will create a binary file, giving it the name specified for **uuencode**. In the following example, the data from **dylanpic** file has been received as a message. The receiver then saves this message as **dylanpic**. **uudecode** then converts this message to the original binary format and places it in a file called **dylan.gif**. The name that the receiver saves the message as does not have to be the same as the one the sender used. You can use any name, but you must use that same name with **uudecode**.

```
$ mail
Mail version 5.5-kw 5/30/95.  Type ? for help.
"/var/spool/mail/chris": 1 message 1 unread
>U  1 robert              Mon Apr  8 00:06 236/14104
& s 1 dylanpic
"dylanpic" [New file]
& q
$ uudecode dylanpic
$ ls
dylan.gif
```

You can do the same for archived and compressed files. For example, you could send several gif picture files in the same message by first combining them into one archived file and then compressing it. Then, you could encode the compressed archived file with **uuencode** and mail it as a message. The person receiving it can decode the message to a compressed archived file that can then be decompressed in order to extract the gif pictures. You can do this for entire directories and their subdirectories as well. In the following two examples, the entire **birthday** directory is archived by **tar** and compressed with **gzip**. The compressed archive is then encoded into character data and saved in a file called **birthdaydir**. The name given to the binary data is **birthday.tar.gz**. The file is sent as a message through **mail**. The receiver saves this message in a file called **birthd**. **uudecode** then decodes the **birthd** file, generating the **birthday.tar.gz** file that can then be decompressed and extracted to create the **birthday** directory in its entirety.

```
$ tar cvf birthday.tar   birthday
$ gzip birthday.tar
$ uuencode birthday.tar.gz birthday.tar.gz > birthdaydir
$ mail aleina@pango1.com  < birthdaydir
```

```
$ mail
Mail version 5.5-kw 5/30/95.   Type ? for help.
"/var/spool/mail/chris": 1 message 1 new
>N  1 robert                Mon Apr  8 00:10 236/14162
& s 1 birthd
"birthd" [New file]
& q
$ uudecode birthd
```

Since the **uuencode** program can receive binary data from the standard input, you
could combine the archive, compression, encoding, and mailing operations into one
pipe sequence as shown here:

```
$ tar cf - birthday | gzip | uuencode birthday.tar.gz | mail
  aleina@pango1.com
```

The – in the **tar** operation represents the standard output and will instruct **tar** to
send its output to the standard output instead of a file. Notice that the name to be used
for the decoded binary file is still included as an argument to **uuencode**. **uudecode**,
when applied to this message, will generate a binary file called **birthday.tar.gz**.

The **uudecode** and **uuencode** programs are in the **sharutils.4.1-2** software
package on your Caldera CD-ROM. If you choose a minimum install for your Linux
system, they will not be installed. You will have to use **glint** or **rpi -i** to install the
package. Table 8-6 shows some mail and communication utilities.

Notifications of Received Mail: From and biff

As your mail messages are received, they are automatically placed in your mailbox
file, but you are not automatically notified when you receive a message. To find out if
you have any messages waiting, you can either use the Mail utility to retrieve the
messages, or you can use the From and biff utilities simply to tell you if you have any
mail waiting.

The From utility tells what messages you have received and are waiting to be read. For each waiting message, it lists the senders' addresses and times that each message was received. To use From, you enter the keyword **from** and press ENTER.

```
$ from
1 From valerie Sun Feb 11 10:14:32 1996
  Subject: Budget
2 From aleina Mon Feb 12 12:30:17 1996
  Subject: Birthday
3 From robert Wed Feb 14  8:15:24 1996
  Subject: Homework
$
```

The biff utility notifies you immediately when a message is received. It is helpful when you are expecting a message and want to know as soon as it arrives. Biff automatically displays the header and beginning lines of messages as they are received. To turn on biff, you enter **biff y** on the command line. To turn it off, you enter **biff n**. To find out if biff is on or not, enter **biff** alone. It displays a message notification whenever a message arrives, no matter what you may be doing at the time. You could be in the middle of an editing session and biff will interrupt it to display the notification on your screen. You can then return to your editing session. In the next example, the user first sets biff on. Then biff notifies the user that a message has been received. The user then checks to see if biff is still on.

```
$ biff y
$
New mail for chris has arrived:
--Date: Sun Feb 11 12:30:21
From: dylan
To: chris
Subject: Food
    Chris,
        Have you tried the chocolate
...more...
$
$ biff
is y
$
```

You can temporarily block biff by using the **mesg n** command to prevent any message displays on your screen. **mesg n** will not only stop any Write and Talk messages, it will also stop biff and Notify messages. Later you can unblock biff with a

mesg y command. A **mseg n** command comes in handy should you not want to be disturbed while working on some project.

Communications with Other Logged-in Users: Write and Talk

You may, at times, want to communicate immediately with other users on your Linux system and not wait for them to read their mail. You can do so with the Write and Talk utilities, provided that the other user is also logged into your Linux system. The Write utility operates like radio communication, allowing you to contact someone already logged in and display a message on their screen. The Talk utility operates like a telephone, allowing you to have a direct two-way conversation with another user.

Direct Connections: The Write Utility

The Write utility lets you send real-time messages to another user. The message the sender types is immediately displayed on the receiver's screen. In this sense, Write is guaranteed to get someone's immediate attention. However, Write has one important limitation. It can only connect to users who are already logged in. If you are not sure if someone is logged in, you can use the **who** command to find out.

Write is not like the standard mail operation. It does not send messages that are placed in a mailbox file; it displays a message directly on another user's screen. When you enter the **write** command followed by a user's login name, a connection to that user is opened. You can then enter text that is displayed on the receiver's screen. To end the connection, enter CTRL-**d** on a line of its own. The receiver, meanwhile, will first have a notice displayed on his or her screen saying that a message was sent by you and giving the date and time. Immediately after this, the message itself will be displayed.

In the next example, a user writes a message to **cecelia**. After entering the message, the user presses CTRL-**d** to cut the connection.

```
$ write cecelia
How are you today?
^D
```

cecelia receives a message header followed by the message. The CTRL-**d** entered by the sender shows up as EOT.

```
Message from gabriel [Tues July 5 10:31]
How are you today?
EOT
```

You can also use Write to establish two-way communication between you and another user. You issue the **write** command followed by a login name. The user receiving the Write notice responds with a **write** command of his or her own, with the sender's login name. The messages sent back and forth by you and the other user are displayed on both terminal screens.

Interactive Write communication should be handled as if you were talking over a radio. First one user sends a message and then indicates that the message is finished, and then the other user responds. A common convention adopted by many Linux and Unix users is to indicate the end of a message by pressing **o**, for "over." Press **oo**, "over and out," to indicate that you are finished communicating and wish to sign off. You physically end the connection with CTRL-**d**. However, both users must enter CTRL-**d**. Your CTRL-**d** cuts your connection with the other user, and the other user's CTRL-**d** ends that user's connection with you.

A Write communication will be displayed on your screen no matter what you are doing. If you do not want to be interrupted by Write messages suddenly being displayed on your screen, you can suppress them with the **mesg** command. The **mesg** command takes two possible options, **y** or **n**. **mesg -n** suppresses reception of a Write message; **mesg -y** restores reception of write messages.

Interactive Communication: The Talk Utility

You can use the Talk utility to set up an interactive two-way communication between you and another user. Unlike Write, Talk operates more like a phone call—both you and the other user can type in messages simultaneously. The **talk** utility operates more like a phone call where two people are constantly talking back and forth to each other.

You initiate the communication by entering the **talk** command followed by the other user's address, usually the login name. This displays a message on the other user's screen asking if he or she wants to **talk** and giving your address. The user then responds with a **talk** command of his or her own using your address. Both your screen and the other user's screen then split into two segments. The top segment displays what you type, and the bottom segment displays what the other user types. Either user can end the session with an interrupt character, usually CTRL-**c**.

Summary: Mail

With electronic mail utilities, you can send messages to other users on your system. A user's login name constitutes his or her address. Two commonly used electronic mail utilities with very different interfaces are described in this chapter: Mail and Elm.

Mail is the standard electronic mail utility found on most Linux and Unix systems. It has a simple command line interface with its own set of commands that operate within a special Mail shell. The different Mail commands for sending and receiving messages can be thought of as defining the basic mail operations found in all electronic mail utilities. When sending a message with Mail, you can perform operations such as redisplaying the message, saving the message to a file, or invoking the Vi editor to edit the message. You can also create a message in an editor, save it in a file, and then send the contents of the file as a message. For Mail, this involves using redirection to use the contents of a file as input for the **mail** command.

To receive messages, you invoke the Mail utility with the command **mail**. You are first given a list of message headers. Each header provides information about a message, including the person who sent it and the subject of the message. Different Mail commands allow you to read, print, save, or delete a message. You can even reply to a message, sending a response immediately.

You can send a message to more than one user at a time by listing the user addresses on the command line next to the **mail** command. Instead of listing all the addresses, you can create an alias for them in the .mailrc file. The .mailrc file contains commands executed whenever the **mail** command is executed. When you send a message to those users, you can use the alias instead of the list of their addresses.

The Elm utility uses a full screen interface with single key commands to perform much the same operations for sending, receiving, and saving messages, as well as creating aliases for addresses. The full screen interface often makes Elm much easier to use than Mail.

The **write** and **talk** commands establish direct communications with another user who is currently logged in. No messages are actually sent. Instead, whatever you type is displayed immediately on another user's terminal. The **write** command is like a radio communication in which one user talks and then waits for the other's reply. The **talk** command is like a phone call in which both users can talk simultaneously.

Internet Addresses	Description
login-name@system . domain	Internet mail addresses `chris@garnet.rose.edu`
Standard Domains	
`com`	Commercial organization
`edu`	Educational institution
`gov`	Government organization
`int`	International organization
`mil`	Military
`net`	Networking organization
`org`	Non-profit organization
International Domains	
`at`	Austria
`au`	Australia
`ca`	Canada
`ch`	Switzerland
`de`	Germany
`dk`	Denmark
`es`	Spain
`fr`	France
`gr`	Greece
`ie`	Ireland
`jp`	Japan
`nz`	New Zealand
`uk`	United Kingdom (Britain)
`us`	United States

Table 8-1.   *Internet Domains*

Mail Command Options	Description
-f *mailbox-filename*	Invokes the Mail utility to read messages in a mailbox file in your directory rather than your mailbox of waiting messages
-H	Displays only the list of message headers
-s *subject*	When sending messages, specifies the subject
-v	Displays the sequence of Mail operations used to send a message
Tilde Commands for Message Header	
~h	Prompts the user to enter addresses, subject, and carbon copy list
~s *subject*	Enters a new subject
~t *addresses*	Adds addresses to the address list
~c *addresses*	Adds addresses to the carbon copy list
~b *addresses*	Adds addresses to the blind carbon copy list
Tilde Commands for Message Text	
~v	Invokes the Vi editor; changes are saved to the message text
~p	Redisplays the text of the message
~q	Quits the message and leaves the Mail utility
~w *filename*	Saves the message in a file
~r *filename*	Reads the contents of a file into the message text
~e	Invokes the default text editor
~	*filter*	Pipes the contents of a message to a filter and replaces the message with the output of that filter

Table 8-2.　*Mail Commands for Sending Messages*

Tilde Commands for Message Text	Description
~m *message-list*	When sending messages or replying to received mail, inserts the contents of a received message; the contents are indented; used when receiving messages
~f *message-list*	When sending messages or replying to received mail, inserts the contents of a received message; unlike **~m**, there is no indentation; used when receiving messages
General Tilde Commands	
~?	Displays a list of all the tilde commands
~~	Enters a tilde as a character into the text
~! *command*	Executes a shell command while entering a message

Table 8-2.   *Mail Commands for Sending Messages (continued)*

Status Codes	Description
N	Newly received messages
U	Previously unread messages
R	Reads messages in the current session
P	Preserved messages, read in previous session and kept in incoming mailbox
D	Deleted messages; messages marked for deletion
O	Old messages
*	Messages that you have saved to another mailbox file

Table 8-3.   *Mail Commands for Receiving Messages*

Display Messages	Description
h	Redisplay the message headers
z+ z-	If header list takes up more than one screen, scrolls header list forward and backward
t *message-list*	Displays a message referenced by the message list; if no message list is used, the current message is displayed
p *message-list*	Displays a message referenced by the message list; if no message list is used, the current message is displayed
n or +	Displays next message
-	Displays previous message
top *message-list*	Displays the top few lines of a message referenced by the message list; if no message list is used, the current message is displayed
Message Lists	
message-number	References message with message number
num1-*num2*	References a range of messages beginning with *num1* and ending with *num2*
.	Current message
^	First message
$	Last message
*	All the messages waiting in the mailbox
/*pattern*	All messages with pattern in the subject field
address	All messages sent from user with address

Table 8-3. *Mail Commands for Receiving Messages* (continued)

Message Lists	Description
: *c*	All messages of the type indicated by *c*; message types are as follows: **n** newly received messages **o** old messages previously received **r** read messages **u** unread messages **d** deleted messages
Deleting and Restoring Messages	
d *message-list*	Deletes a message referenced by the indicated message list from your mailbox
u *message-list*	Undeletes a message referenced by the indicated message list that has been previously deleted
q	Quits the Mail utility and saves any read messages in the **mbox** file
x	Quits the Mail utility and does *not* erase any messages you deleted; this is equivalent to executing a **u** command on all deleted messages before quitting
pre *message-list*	Preserves messages in your waiting mailbox even if you have already read them
Sending and Editing Messages	
r	Sends a reply to all persons who received a message
R	Sends a reply to the person who sent you a message
m *address*	Sends a message to someone while in the Mail utility
v *message-list*	Edits a message with the Vi editor
Saving Messages	
s *message-list filename*	Saves a message referenced by the message list in a file, including the header of the message
S *message-list*	Saves a message referenced by the message list in a file named for the sender of the message

Table 8-3.   *Mail Commands for Receiving Messages* (continued)

Saving Messages	Description
w *message-list filename*	Saves a message referenced by the message list in a file without the header; only the text of the message is saved
folder *mailbox-filename*	Switches to another mailbox file
%	Represents the name of incoming mailbox file **folder %** switches to incoming mailbox file
#	Represents name of previously accessed mailbox file **folder #** switches to previous mailbox file
&	Represents name of mailbox file used to save your read messages automatically; usually called **mbox** **folder &** switches to **mbox** file
General Commands	
?	Displays a list of all the Mail commands
! *command*	Executes a user shell command from within the Mail shell

Table 8-3. *Mail Commands for Receiving Messages* (continued)

Options	Description
alias *name address-list*	Creates an alias for a list of addresses alias myclass chris aleina larisa **$ mail myclass**
asksub	Prompts for subject **set asksub**
askcc	Prompts for carbon copy addresses **set askcc**
prompt=*string*	Redefines Mail prompt **set prompt="&"**

Table 8-4. *Mail Options*

Options	Description
sign=*string*	Defines string to be inserted by the **~a** tilde command into a message that you are inputting **set sign**="Robert and Valerie"
folder=*directory*	Saves any mailbox files created by the **s** or **S** command to the directory assigned to it **set folder=$HOME/mail**
record=*filename*	Automatically saves a copy of any message that you create and send; messages are saved in a file specified when you set the **record** option **set record=$HOME/outbox**
outfolder	Places record file in folder directory; in the following example, outbox will be a file in the directory defined by **folder** **set record=outbox** **set outfolder**
MBOX=*filename*	Holds the name of the **mbox** file to which read messages are automatically saved; by default, **mbox** is placed in your home directory; to put it in the **folder** directory, place a + sign before the **mbox** name **set MBOX=+mbox**

Table 8-4. *Mail Options (continued)*

Sending Messages	Description
elm *address*	Sends a message using Elm
s	Sends the message
e	Edits the message
f	Forgets the message, quits, and does not send
h	Edits the header of the message

Table 8-5. *Elm Commands*

Receiving Messages	**Description**
elm	Invokes the Elm utility

?	Invokes help; press key used for a command to display information about that command
	    ? Displays a list of all commands
	    . Returns to Elm index

q	Quits the Elm utility with prompts for saving read and unread messages, and deleting messages marked for deletion
Q	Quits the Elm utility with no prompts
x and CTRL-**q**	Quits the Elm utility leaving your mail as you found it; no deletions are made or messages saved; messages remain as you found them
+	Displays next index screen if headers take up more than one screen
−	Displays previous index screen if headers take up more than one screen
Selecting a Message	
j	Moves down to the next message header, making it the current message
k	Moves up to the previous message header, making it the current message
message-number	Makes the header whose message number is *message-number* the current message
/*pattern*	Searches for the pattern in the subject or address headers, making the first header with a match the current message
//*pattern*	Searches for the pattern in the text of messages, making the first message with a match the current message
t	Tags the current message; a + sign appears before the message; you can tag several messages and then perform an operation on them all at once

Table 8-5.   *Elm Commands (continued)*

Selecting a Message	Description
CTRL-**t**	Searches address and subject headers for a pattern and tags all messages that match
Operations on Messages	
ENTER	Displays the current message
i	Returns to headers (index)
p	Prints the current message
d	Deletes the current message; the header is marked with a D and deleted when you exit Elm
CTRL-**d**	Searches address and subject headers for a pattern and deletes all messages that match
u	Undeletes the current message
CTRL-**u**	Searches address and subject headers for a pattern and undeletes all messages that match
r	Replies to the current message; the address and subject are taken from the current message's header; you then compose and send your reply as you would any other message
s	Saves the current message or tagged messages in a mailbox file; by default, the message is saved to a mailbox file using the address of the user who sent the message; you can specify your own mailbox file by entering the name of the file preceded by an = sign =*mailbox-filename* You can also save the message to received or sent mailbox files using the following commands: > Saves message to received mailbox file < Saves message to sent mailbox file
Operations	
m	Sends a message from the Elm utility; you compose and send a message

Table 8-5. *Elm Commands* (continued)

Operations	Description
c	Uses Elm to operate on a specific mailbox file; the command switches from incoming mail to any other mailbox file with messages
a	Manages Elm aliases; upon pressing the **a** command, the alias menu is displayed with the following options:
	a Creates an alias using the name and address of the current message
	m Creates an alias using a name and address that you enter
	d Deletes an alias
	l Lists aliases
	p Displays the name and address of particular aliases
	s Displays any system aliases
	r Returns to Elm main menu

Table 8-5. *Elm Commands* (continued)

Utility	Description
mail	Mail utility for sending and receiving mail
elm	Mail utility for sending and receiving mail
uuencode *filename*	Encodes a binary file into a character format allowing it to be sent through a mail system; redirects to a file and sends that file **uuencode** *filename* **>** *datafile*
uudecode *file*	Decodes a uuencoded file, generating a binary file with the name designated by **uuencode**
from	Tells you what messages you have received
biff	Notifies you of received mail
write *address*	Displays a message on a logged-on user's terminal
talk *address*	Sets up two-way communication with a logged-on user

Table 8-6. *Mail and Communication Utilities*

Chapter Nine

Usenet and Newsreaders

Usenet is an open mail system on which users post news and opinions. It operates like a systemwide mailbox that any user on your Linux system can read or send messages to. Users' messages are incorporated into Usenet files, which are distributed to any system signed up to receive them. Each system that receives Usenet files is referred to as a site. Certain sites perform organizational and distribution operations for Usenet, receiving messages from other sites and organizing them into Usenet files that are then broadcast to many other sites. Such sites are called backbone sites and they operate like publishers, receiving articles and organizing them into different groups.

To access Usenet news, you need access to a news server. A news server receives the daily Usenet newsfeeds and makes them accessible to other systems. Your network may have a system that operates as a news server. If you are using an Internet Service Provider, a news server is probably maintained for your use. To read Usenet articles, you use a newsreader, a client program that connects to a news server and accesses the articles. On the Internet and in TCP/IP networks, news servers communicate with newsreaders using the Network News Transport Protocol (NNTP) and are often referred to as nntp news servers.

Alternatively, you could also create your own news server on your Linux system to run a local Usenet news service or to download and maintain the full set of Usenet articles. Several Linux programs, called News Transport Agents, can be used to create such a server.

Usenet News

Usenet files were originally designed to function like journals. Messages contained in the files are referred to as articles. A user could write an article, post it in Usenet, and have it immediately distributed to other systems around the world. Someone could then read the article on Usenet instead of waiting for a journal publication. Usenet files themselves were organized as journal publications. Since journals are designed to address specific groups, Usenet files were organized according to groups called newsgroups. When a user posts an article, it is assigned to a specific newsgroup. If another user wants to read that article, he or she looks at the articles in that newsgroup. You can think of each newsgroup as a constantly updated magazine. For example, to read articles on computer science, you would access the Usenet newsgroup on computer science.

More recently, Usenet files have also been used as bulletin boards on which people carry on debates. Again, such files are classified into newsgroups, though their articles read more like conversations than journal articles.

Each newsgroup has its own name, which is often segmented in order to classify newsgroups. Usually the names are divided into three segments: a general topic, subtopic, and specific topic. The segments are delimited by periods. For example, you may have several newsgroups that deal with the general topic **rec**, which stands for recreation. Of those, some newsgroups may deal with only the subtopic **food**. Again, of those, there may be a group that only discusses a specific topic, such as **recipes**. In this case, the newsgroup name would be **rec.food.recipes**.

Many of the bulletin board groups are designed for discussion only, lacking any journal-like articles. Many of these begin with either **alt** or **talk** as their general topic. For example, **talk.food.chocolate** may contain conversations about how wonderful or awful chocolate is thought to be, and **alt.food.chocolate** may contain informal speculations about the importance of chocolate to the basic structure of civilization as we know it. Here are some examples of Usenet newsgroup names:

```
comp.ai.neural-nets
comp.lang.pascal
sci.physics.fusion
rec.arts.movies
rec.food.recipes
talk.politics.theory
```

Linux has newsgroups on various topics. Some are for discussion, others are sources of information about recent developments. On some you can ask for help for specific problems. A current list of some of the popular Linux newsgroups is provided here. For a more compete list see Chapter 1.

comp.os.linux.announce	Announcements of Linux developments
comp.os.linux.admin	System adiministration questions
comp.os.linux.misc	Special questions and issues
comp.os.linux.setup	Installation problems
comp.os.linux.help	Questions and answers for particular problems

You read Usenet articles with a newsreader, such as **trn** or **tin**, which allows you first to select a specific newsgroup and then read the articles in it. A newsreader operates like a user interface, allowing you to browse through and select available articles for reading, saving, or printing. **trn**, perhaps the most widely used newsreader today, is a more recent and powerful version of an earlier newsreader called **rn**. It employs a sophisticated retrieval feature called threads that pulls together articles on the same discussion or topic.

You can create articles of your own that you can then add to a newsgroup for others to read. Adding an article to a newsgroup is called posting the article. You post an article using a separate utility called Pnews.

Installing trn and tin

Before you can use **trn** and **tin**, you must install them. Neither one is automatically installed by the Caldera Express Install procedure. You first have to log in as the root user. Before you install, make sure you have mounted your Linux CD-ROM with the following command:

```
$ mount /mnt/cdrom
```

To install **trn** and **tin**, you can either use the **glint** installation program available on your Caldera Desktop, or issue an **rpm** command on the command line. With **glint**, first open the window for your available packages. Then locate and click on the Applications icon. Locate the News icon and click on it. You will then see the **trn** and **tin** packages displayed. Click to select them, and then choose Install.

Alternatively, from the command line, you can change to the **/mnt/cdrom/RedHat /RPMS** directory. Then issue the commands:

```
$ rpm -i trn-3.6.1.i386.rpm
$ rpm -i tin-1.22-1.i386.rpm
```

Both **tin** and **trn** can read Usenet news provided on remote news servers that use the Network News Transport Protocol (NNTP). Many such remote news servers are available through the Internet. To connect to a remote news server, first assign the Internet address of the news sever to a shell variable called **NNTPSERVER**, and then export that variable. The assignment and export of **NNTPSERVER** can be done in a login initialization file such as **.bash_profile**.

```
$ NNTPSERVER=news.servername.com
$ export NNTPSERVER
```

To connect to the remote news server using **tin**, either invoke **tin** with the **-r** option, or use the **rtin** command.

```
$ tin -r
```

News Transport Agents

Usenet news is provided over the Internet as a daily newsfeed of articles for over 10,000 newsgroups. This newsfeed is sent to sites that can then provide access to the news for other systems through newsreaders. These sites operate as news servers, and the newsreaders used to access them are their clients. The news server software, called News Transport Agents, is what provides newsreaders with news, allowing you to read newsgroups and post articles. For Linux, three of the popular News Transport Agents are INN, nntp, and Cnews. Both Cnews and nntp are smaller, simpler, and useful for small networks. INN is more powerful and complex, and was designed with large systems in mind.

Daily newsfeeds on Usenet are often very large and consume much of a news server's resources in both time and memory. For this reason, you may not want to set up your own Linux system to receive such newsfeeds. If you are operating in a network of Linux systems, you can designate one of them as the news server and install the News Transport Agent on it to receive and manage the Usenet newsfeeds. Users on other systems on your network can then access that news server with their own newsreaders.

If your network already has a news server, you do not need to install a news transport agent at all. You just have to use your newsreaders to remotely access that server (see **NNTPSERVER** in the previous section). In the case of an Internet Service Provider, such providers will often operate their own news servers, which you can also remotely access using your own newsreaders, such as **trn** and **tin**. Bear in mind though that **trn** and **tin** will have to take the time to download all the articles for selected newsgroups as well as updated information on all the newsgroups.

You can also use News Transport Agents to run local versions of news for just the users on your system or your local network. To do this, you would install nntp or Cnews and configure them just to manage local newsgroups. Users on your system could then post articles and read local news. You could also use INN, though the other agents would be adequate for local networks.

INN

The InterNetNews (INN) News Transport Agent, which is on your Caldera CD-ROM, provides full news server capabilities. Use **glint** or **rpm** to install it from your Caldera CD-ROM, or you can download it from any Linux ftp site, such as **sunsite.unc.edu**. Be sure to select the Redhat version of the INN package so you can use **rpm** to install it. The next example uses **rpm** to install INN.

```
$ rpm -i inn-3.6.1.i386.rpm
```

This will install the INN programs as well as configuration files in the appropriate directories.

In your **/usr/doc** directory, you will find a directory of HOW-TO documents. INN is configured to start automatically whenever you start your system. The primary program for INN is **innd**. The **d** stands for daemon, a program that is loaded at system startup and continues running in the background as you do your work. Various INN configuration files can be found in **/etc/news**. Among these are **inn.conf**, which sets options for INN, and **host.nntp**, which controls access to your system's news. You can edit any of these configuration files should you need to. **man** pages will be installed for all the INN programs and many of the configuration files, such as **innd**, **inn.conf**, **rnews**, and **host.nntp**. Correct configuration of INN can be a complex and time-consuming process. Be sure to consult reference and online resources such as the HOW-TO documents on your CD-ROM in **/docs/HTML/news.html**.

The trn Newsreader

With the popular **trn** newsreader, you can scroll through a list of newsgroups, select one, and then read the articles in it. The **trn** interface has several powerful features, such as pattern searches for groups of articles. The **trn** newsreader is an enhancement of **rn** that allows you to display and search articles by subject, article, or threads. The *t* in **trn** stands for "threaded." A thread is any connection between articles, such as articles that share the same subject or follow-up articles to a previously posted article. You can still use the standard **rn** commands to move from one article to the next. However, **trn**'s special interface, called a selector, allows you to move through a threaded set of articles. For example, if you are reading an article on a particular subject and you give an **n** command to go to the next article, you go to the next article on that subject (in the thread), not to the next sequentially posted article as you would normally do. Instead of moving through a newsgroup's articles according to their posted order, you can move through them using different threads, examining articles according to different subjects. The same is true for an article and its follow-up articles. An article and its follow-ups are threaded so that upon reading an article, pressing the **n** command will move you to the first follow-up to that article, not to the next sequentially posted article. Using threads, you can use the **n** command to read an article with all of its follow-ups, instead of searching separately for each one. The **trn** newsreader commands are listed in Table 9-1.

trn operates on two levels: the newsgroup list and the article list. When you first execute **trn**, you select a newsgroup from a list of newsgroups. Commands move you from one newsgroup to another in the list. Once you have found the one you want, you can then select articles to read in that newsgroup. When you have finished reading, you can leave that newsgroup and select another in the newsgroup list. You use the **trn** selector to display, organize, and move through the article list, though you can also use the standard **rn** commands to manage the article list.

The **trn** newsreader distinguishes between those newsgroups with unread news and those with no unread news. You can use certain **trn** commands to search for and select only those newsgroups with unread news. The term "unread news" refers to articles that you personally have not read in a newsgroup. **trn** keeps track of what a user has read or not read by means of a **.newsrc** file placed in the user's account. Each user has his or her own **.newsrc** file, which consists of a list of all the newsgroups provided by the Usenet server. Each entry is used to keep track of whether there is read or unread news in it.

The **trn** newsreader also allows you to subscribe or unsubscribe to a newsgroup. When you first use **trn**, you will be given access to all newsgroups provided by your Usenet server, automatically subscribing you to all newsgroups. However, there may be many newsgroups that you have no interest in. Instead of having them clutter up your **trn** interface, you can unsubscribe to them. You can subscribe to them again later, if you change your mind. The **.newsrc** file keeps track of those newsgroups that you subscribe to.

Newsgroup List

You enter the **rn** newsreader by typing the command **rn** at your Linux prompt. **rn** will initially display a short list of newsgroup headers. However, before doing so, **trn** will first check an official list of new newsgroups with those listed in your **.newsrc** file. If there are any new newsgroups not yet listed in your **.newsrc** file, then **trn** will ask, one by one, if you want to subscribe to them. At each prompt, you can enter **y** to add the newsgroup and **n** not to add it.

There can, at times, be a great many new newsgroups to decide on. Should you want to skip this initial subscription phase, you can do so by invoking **trn** with the **-q** option. With **-q**, **trn** will go directly to displaying the newsgroup headers, skipping any new newsgroup queries.

```
$ trn -q
```

After the subscription phase, **trn** checks to see if there are any newsgroups listed in your **.newsrc** file that have unread news in them. If so, the newsgroup headers for the first few of these are displayed. Each newsgroup header tells how many unread articles remain in a given newsgroup. **trn** then prompts you as to whether you want to read articles in the first newsgroup. If not, you can enter the **n** command to move to the next newsgroup. The **p** command moves you back to the previous newsgroup.

To list articles in a newsgroup, you enter **+** at the prompt. This displays the **trn** selector from which you can select the article you want to display. If you enter **y**, you will skip the list of articles and display the first article in the newsgroup. You will then be prompted to read the next article or quit and return to the newsgroup list. You can leave the newsgroup and return to the newsgroup list by entering **q** at the prompt.

In the next example, the user enters the **trn** interface, and a list of newsgroup headers is displayed. The user is then prompted for the first header, which the user skips with the **n** command. At the next header, the user enters a **+** command to list articles in the **comp.os.linux.misc** newsgroup.

```
$ trn
comp.ai.language                    3 articles
```

```
comp.os.linux.misc            1    article
rec.arts.movies               7    articles
rec.food.recipes            245  articles
sci.physics.fusion           32   articles
talk.politics.theory        126  articles
 etc.

====== 3 unread articles in comp.ai.language -- read now? [+ynq] n
====== 1 unread articles in comp.os.linux.misc -- read now? [ynq] +
```

trn has a variety of commands for moving through the list of newsgroups. You can move to the first or last newsgroup, the next or previous newsgroup, or the newsgroup whose name has a specific pattern. For example, a **$** will place you at the end of the newsgroup list. Many commands are designed to distinguish between read and unread newsgroups. The **^** places you at the first newsgroup with unread news, whereas the number 1 places you at the first newsgroup in the list, whether it is read or not. The lowercase **n** and **p** commands place you at the next and previous unread newsgroups. To move to the next or previous newsgroup regardless of whether it is read or not, you use the uppercase **N** and **P** commands.

When you first start using **trn**, many of your newsgroups will have a vast number of unread articles in them. Instead of reading each one, you could simply start with a clean slate by marking them all as read. The **c** command entered at the newsgroup prompt will mark all articles in the newsgroup as read. Then, unread-sensitive commands such as **n** and **p** cannot select the newsgroup until new articles are posted for it.

Often, you will know the name of a newsgroup that you want to access. Instead of stepping through newsgroups one at a time with **n** and **p** commands to get to the one you want, you can use pattern searches to move directly to it. The pattern searching commands give **trn** great versatility in locating newsgroups. To perform a pattern search for a newsgroup, at the prompt you enter a **/** followed by the pattern. The **/** performs a forward search through the list of newsgroups. The **?** performs a backward search. In the next example, the user searches for the newsgroup on food recipes.

```
$ trn
comp.ai.language              3    articles
comp.os.linux.misc            1    article
rec.arts.movies               7    articles
rec.food.recipes            245  articles
sci.physics.fusion           32   articles
```

```
talk.politics.theory                           126 articles
  etc.


====== 3 unread articles in comp.ai.language -- read now? [+ynq]
/food.recipes
  Searching...
====== 245 unread articles in rec.food.recipes -- read now?
[+ynq] +
```

You can also locate a newsgroup by its full name. The **g** command followed by a newsgroup's name will locate that newsgroup.

```
====== 3 unread articles in comp.ai.language -- read now? [+ynq]
g rec.food.recipes
Searching...
====== 245 unread articles in rec.food.recipes -- read now? [+ynq]
```

The **trn** list and search commands reference only those newsgroups that you have subscribed to. With the **l** command you can list or search for unsubscribed newsgroups. The **l** command by itself lists all newsgroups that you have not subscribed to. Followed by a pattern, the **l** command searches unsubscribed newsgroups for that pattern, listing those matched. For example, **ltrek** searches for unsubscribed newsgroups with the pattern "trek" in their names.

You can subscribe to a newsgroup with the **a** command. Enter **a** followed by the name of the newsgroup you want. You can unsubscribe from a newsgroup with the **u** command. For example, **u rec.foods.recipes** will unsubscribe that newsgroup. If you tried to select it with search commands such as **/** or **g**, you would not find it. Of course, the **l** command would locate it: **l rec.foods.recipes**. To once again subscribe to this newsgroup, you would use the command **a rec.foods.recipes**.

The trn Selector

As mentioned earlier, typing **+** at the **trn** prompt enters the selector, which allows you to use threads. The selector consists of a screen that lists each article's author, thread count, and subject. Any follow-up articles are preceded by a **>** symbol. Articles are grouped according to the threads they belong to. The first article in each thread is preceded by an ID consisting of a lowercase alphabetic character or a single digit, starting from *a*. A sample **trn** selector screen is shown here:

```
rec.food.recipes       258 articles (moderated)

a    Dylan Chris        1    Fruit Salad
b    Cecelia Petersen   1    Fudge Cake
d    Richard Leland     2    Chocolate News
     Larisa@atlash
     Aleina Petersen    1    >White chocolate
     Maryann Price      1    >Chocolate Fudge
     mark@pacific       1    >
     Justin G.          1    >Chocolate
e    George Petersen    1    Apple Muffins
f    Marylou Carrion    1    REQUEST: romantic dinners
g    Valerie Fuller     1    REQUEST: Dehydrated Goodies
i    Carolyn Blacklock  1    REQUEST: Devonshire Cream
     Bill Bode          1    >
j    Bonnie Matoza      1    Sauces
l    Gabriel Matoza     1    Passion Fruit
o    Ken Blacklock      1    REQUEST: blackened (red)fish
     augie@napa         3    >blackened (red)fish
     John Carrion
     Anntoinnete

-- Select threads (date order) -- 24%
```

Upon entering the selector, the first screen of articles is displayed, and the first thread is preceded with an *a*. To display the next screen of articles, you press either the SPACEBAR or the > key. You can display the previous screen by pressing the < key. Upon displaying the next screen, threads will again be listed beginning from *a*. The ID preceding a thread is unique to that thread only for that screen; they are simply a screen device for referencing threads displayed on the screen at that time.

To read an article, you first select the thread for that article, and then instruct the selector to display it. You select a thread by pressing the key corresponding to its ID. For example, pressing **d** selects the thread that has a *d* at the beginning of its first line. You will notice that upon selecting a thread, a **+** symbol appears before its ID. Once you have selected the thread, you can then display its articles by pressing either the ENTER key or uppercase **z**. The first article in the thread will be displayed. Pressing the **n** key moves you to the next article in the thread. Once you have found the article you want, you can read it using any of the standard **trn** commands for displaying articles. If the article takes up more than one screen, you can display the next screen by pressing the SPACEBAR.

You can return to the selector any time by pressing the **+** key. Should you no longer want to read articles in a given thread, you need to deselect the thread. You do so by again pressing the key that corresponds to its ID. You will notice that a **+** symbol appears before the ID of a selected thread. Upon deselecting the thread, this **+** symbol will disappear.

You can also use cursor commands to select a thread. When the selector screen first appears, the cursor is placed at the *a* before the first thread. Using the cursor **n** and **p** commands or arrow keys, you can move to the next thread or back to the previous thread. The **n** command moves down to the next thread, and the **p** command moves back to the previous thread. You can also use the UP and DOWN ARROW keys. To start displaying articles in a particular thread, you can simply move the cursor to that thread's ID and press ENTER or **z**.

If you want to examine several threads, you can mark each one by pressing the key corresponding to the ID displayed before the thread. To select the thread preceded by *b*, just press the **b** key. Then move on to the next thread you want, and do the same. A **+** symbol will appear after each thread that you have selected. You can move from one screen to another, selecting the threads you want, and then begin displaying articles based on those threads.

Selector Display Modes: Article, Subject, and Thread

The selector has three display modes: article, subject, and thread, which correspond to how the selector displays articles. You can easily choose the mode you want by pressing the **S** command and entering **a** for article, **s** for subject, or **t** for thread. You can also switch back and forth between the different modes by pressing the **=** key.

Each mode can be thought of as a kind of thread. When using the subject mode, articles are grouped according to their subject entries. A subject is whatever a user enters into the subject field of an article's header. Articles with the same subject entry are threaded together. Subject groupings are limited to those articles that share exactly the same subject entries in their header. Articles that have even slightly different subject entries will not be grouped together.

When using the thread mode, articles are grouped with any posted follow-ups, as well as with articles of the same subject. The follow-up articles are preceded by a **>** symbol. The thread mode differs from the subject mode in that it will include all follow-up articles, even though such articles may have different subject entries. The article mode does not display threads. Articles are listed individually, each preceded by its own ID, in posted sequence.

The selector screen will appear differently depending on the display mode you are using. In the subject mode, the selector displays the author of each article, grouping them into subject categories. With the first author in a subject category, the number of articles in the category is displayed, followed by the category's subject. The subject is listed only once, followed by a list of authors, each representing an article. An ID is placed only before the first article in the subject category. In the subject mode, an ID references a subject, not a particular article. On the screen, IDs are placed only at the beginning of different subject groupings. To select a subject, press the key corresponding to its ID. The subject mode provides easy access to articles on different topics, and the list of subject headings also provides a quick summary of topics being discussed in the newsgroup.

In the next example, the selector is in the subject mode. Notice that item **d** specifies the subject Chocolate News. There are two articles in this subject category, one with the author Richard Leland and another with the author Larisa@atlash. The article count specifies two articles. The same is true for item **i**, except that the second article is a follow-up article, as indicated with a **>** symbol. Item **u** specifies a subject category of three articles, all of which are follow-ups. Notice that these are actually follow-ups to item **o**, though item **o** has a slightly different subject title.

```
rec.food.recipes               258 articles (moderated)

a     Dylan Chris         1     Fruit Salad
b     Cecelia Petersen    1     Fudge Cake
d     Richard Leland      2     Chocolate News
      Larisa@atlash
e     George Petersen     1     Apple Muffins
f     Marylou Carrion     1     REQUEST: romantic dinners
g     Valerie Fuller        1    REQUEST: Dehydrated Goodies
i     Carolyn Blacklock   1     REQUEST: Devonshire Cream
      Bill Bode           1     >
j     Bonnie Matoza       1     Sauces
l     Gabriel Matoza      1     Passion Fruit
o     Ken Blacklock       1     REQUEST: blackened (red)fish
r     dylan@sf            1     REQUEST: Cheese Toast
s     Penny Bode          1     REQUEST: Sausage Recipes
t     gloria@stlake       1     Biscuit Recipe
u     augie@napa          3     >blackened (red)fish entree
      John Carrion
      Anntoinnete
v     John Gunther        1     Oatmeal Cookies

-- Select subjects (date order) -- 24%
Selector mode:  Threads, Subjects, Articles? [tsa] s
```

In the thread mode, the selector displays articles that are connected either by follow-up or by subject. In other words, the thread mode groups articles that are in any way connected to each other. Follow-up articles are listed below the original article and preceded by a **>** sign. A grouping of this sort is often referred to as a thread. Using the thread mode, you can easily access an article and all follow-ups posted on it to check out any discussion or comments. Articles related by subject will be in the same thread, along with their own follow-ups. Each thread will have its own ID. To select a thread, just press the corresponding key for its ID.

In the next example, the **trn** selector is in the thread mode. Notice how the screen differs from the subject mode. Item **d** now includes follow-up articles as well as articles on the same subject. Item **d** represents a thread consisting of six articles. The first two share the same subject, and the remaining four are follow-up articles to them, as indicated by the > symbol. Many of these follow-up articles have different subject titles, while two of them, Maryann Price and mark@pacific, are two follow-up articles that have the same subject. Notice that the **o** item represents a thread beginning with the Ken Blacklock article and includes its three follow-ups, augie@napa, John Carrion, and Anntoinette. The three follow-ups all have the same subject, though it is different from the initial article in the thread.

```
rec.food.recipes      258 articles (moderated)

a     Dylan Chris         1     Fruit Salad
b     Cecelia Petersen    1     Fudge Cake
d     Richard Leland      2     Chocolate News
      Larisa@atlash
      Aleina Petersen     1     >White chocolate
      Maryann Price       2     >Chocolate Fudge
      mark@pacific
      Justin G.           1     >Chocolate
e     George Petersen     1     Apple Muffins
f     Marylou Carrion     1     REQUEST: romantic dinners
g     Valerie Fuller      1     REQUEST: Dehydrated Goodies
i     Carolyn Blacklock   1     REQUEST: Devonshire Cream
      Bill Bode           1     >
j     Bonnie Matoza       1     Sauces
l     Gabriel Matoza      1     Passion Fruit
o     Ken Blacklock       1     REQUEST: blackened (red)fish
      augie@napa          3     >blackened (red)fish entree
      John Carrion
      Anntoinete

-- Select threads (date order) -- 24%
Selector mode:  Threads, Subjects, Articles? [tsa] t
```

In the next example, the articles are simply arranged by posted order, each article having its own ID. Notice how items **d** and **e** have the same subject. No threads are active in the article mode. Articles and their follow-ups are scattered throughout the display. For example, though the article augie@napa is a follow-up to Ken Blacklock, each has its own ID in different parts of the display, **r** and **v**.

```
rec.food.recipes              258 articles (moderated)

a    Dylan Chris           Fruit Salad
b    Cecelia Petersen      Fudge Cake
d    Richard Leland        Chocolate News
e    Larisa@atlash         Chocolate News
f    George Petersen       Apple Muffins
g    Marylou Carrion       REQUEST: romantic dinners
i    Valerie Fuller        REQUEST: Dehydrated Goodies
j    Carolyn Blacklock     REQUEST: Devonshire Cream
l    Bonnie Matoza         Sauces
o    Gabriel Matoza        Passion Fruit
r    Ken Blacklock         REQUEST: blackened (red)fish
s    dylan@sf              REQUEST: Cheese Toast
t    Penny Bode            REQUEST: Sausage Recipes
u    gloria@stlake         Biscuit Recipe
v    augie@napa            >blackened (red)fish
w    John Gunther          Oatmeal Cookies
x    Margaret              REQUEST: Potato Salad
y    Frank Moitoza         REQUEST: Sesame Chicken
z    maryann@sebast        >Summer desserts

-- Select subjects (date order) -- 24%
Selector mode:  Threads, Subjects, Articles? [tsa] a
```

Displaying Articles: trn Thread Trees

When you select an article, its header is displayed followed by a **(more)** prompt and the first page of the text. The article will be displayed screen by screen, just as files are displayed screen by screen with the More utility. To continue to the next screen, you press the SPACEBAR. You can move backward one page at a time by pressing the **b** key. The **q** command allows you to quit before reading the whole article. You can also search the text of the article for a pattern. The **g** command followed by a pattern will locate the first occurrence of that pattern in the text. You can repeat the search with the **G** command.

```
rec.food.recipes (moderated) #7155 (229 more)                    (1)
From: richpete@garnet.berkeley.edu (Richard Petersen)
[1] Spelling Cookies
```

```
Followup-To: poster
Date: Mon Dec 20 04:48:01 PST 1995
Organization: University of California, Berkeley
Lines: 43


Spelling Cookies
                        INGREDIENTS
        1 cup flour
        2 teaspoons single acting baking powder, or 1 teaspoon double
            acting baking powder, or 1 teaspoon baking soda
        1/2 teaspoon nutmeg
        1/4 teaspoon cinnamon
        3/4 cup butter  (or 1 1/2 sticks)
        1 cup brown or dark brown sugar
        1/2 cup regular sugar
        1 egg
        1 teaspoon vanilla extract
        1/4 cup milk
--MORE--(44%)
```

Upon pressing the SPACEBAR the next screen of the message is displayed.

```
rec.food.recipes (moderated) #7155 (229 more)
[1] Spelling Cookies

    12 ounces semisweet chocolate chips
    pecan or walnut bits
    3/4 cup wheat germ
    2 3/4 cups rolled oats (Old Fashioned Quaker Oats)

                    STEPS
    1. Mix brown and regular sugars together.
    2. Cream butter, then mix in sugars. Then mix in egg, vanilla
extract, and milk until creamy.
    3. Separately mix flower, cinnamon, nutmeg, baking powder (or
baking soda), salt (if wanted).
    4. Mix in flower concoction into butter/sugar concoction
until creamy.
    5. With spatula add in wheat germ, then nuts, then chocolate
chips, then oats.
```

```
     6. Preheat oven to about 300 degrees.  Spoon out onto cookie
sheets. Cook for about 20 minutes or so.  Watch carefully.  When
top of cookies begin to brown they are done.
     7.  Eat immediately or refrigerate.  Aging only improves
taste.
     8.  These are called spelling cookies because when I gave the
recipe to a friend in my class her daughter found so many
spelling mistakes that she called them spelling cookies.
     9.  Eat at your own risk.   Good luck.

End of article 7155 (of 7158) -- what next? [npq] +
```

At the end of the article you will be presented with a prompt asking what you want to do next. The choices **n**, **p**, and **q** will be displayed in brackets. Pressing **n** will display the next article in the newsgroup, and **p** will display the previous article. To return to your selector screen of newsgroup articles, you press **+**, as shown in the next example. Pressing **q** will return to the newsgroup list.

```
End of article 7155 (of 7158) -- what next? [npq] +
```

When you display the first article in a thread, a thread tree will appear in the upper-right corner of the screen. A thread tree represents the connections between articles in a thread. Each unread article is represented by a number starting from 1, with each enclosed in brackets. Lines connect the different article numbers. The number representing the article you are currently displaying is highlighted in the thread tree. Once you read an article and move on to another, the read article's number is enclosed in parentheses, and the next article's number is highlighted.

A thread tree illustrates the relationship between articles. The first article in a thread is located in the upper-left corner of the tree. Branching to the right and down, the next column, are any follow-up articles to that article. Follow-up articles are connected to each other by lines. For example, the follow-up articles for the first article in the thread are arranged as a column of bracketed numbers set to the right of the first article's number. A line connects the article's number to its first follow-up. Any other follow-up articles are arranged in a column below this first follow-up, each connected by a line. The last follow-up article will be connected by a slanted line. Figure 9-1 shows such a thread tree.

A follow-up article may, in turn, have its own follow-ups. People may respond to another person's response, carrying on a conversation or debate on a particular point. The number of a second follow-up is positioned to the right of the follow-up's number. That second follow-up may also have its own follow-up, and the number will be positioned to the right of that follow-up's number. You could have a whole string of sequential follow-ups, arranged in a horizontal line, as shown in Figure 9-2.

Any given follow-up could have more than one follow-up of its own. These follow-ups are arranged in a column below the first follow-up. Thus, a thread tree can

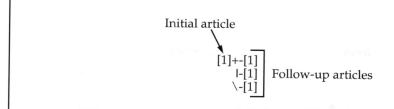

Figure 9-1.   *Thread tree showing initial article and follow-up articles*

extend horizontally and vertically. Horizontally the thread lists a follow-up that responds to previous follow-ups and that may, in turn, have a follow-up responding to it. Vertically the thread lists several follow-ups that are all responses to one particular follow-up.

Articles related by subject are listed below the first article. These are not connected by lines. Looking at the thread tree, the left-most column of article numbers indicates subject groupings, and any articles branching to the right are follow-up articles. As shown in Figure 9-3, articles that share the same subject are arranged in the outer column.

The numbers that represent articles in the thread tree indicate whether articles share the same subject. The first article, represented by the number 1, indicates the initial subject of the thread. Articles that share the same subject will have the same number. Other articles with the number 1 share the same subject as the first article. Many times, however, articles in the same thread may have different subjects, and these will be represented with a different number. Any subsequent articles with that same subject will share that same number. The first article with a different subject will be represented by a number 2, and any other articles with a number 2 will share that same subject. As different subjects in the thread are encountered, they are incrementally given a new number. Such a numbering system allows you to identify different subtopics in the thread. It is like detecting different parts of a conversation

```
                      Follow-ups to follow-ups
                               |
          [1]+-[1]     ┌───────────────┐
           |-[1]--[1]--[1]
           \-[1]
```

Figure 9-2.   *Thread tree showing articles that are follow-ups to follow-ups*

Articles with the same subject
```
[1] +-[1]
    |-[1]--[1]--[1]
    \-[1]
[1] +-[1]
[1]
```

Figure 9-3. `trn` *thread tree showing subject articles*

that veer off into different topics. Also, should part of a thread contain a subject you are not interested in, you can easily identify what articles in the thread to avoid. Figure 9-4 shows a thread tree with different subjects. The first follow-up article is represented by a number 2, indicating that this article has a different subject from that of the first article. Again, the article below it is represented by a number 3, indicating that it has yet another subject.

You can use the thread tree to move from one article to another in the thread, going directly to any article without having to display any intervening articles. You can even move backward in the thread. Thread trees are a very easy way to move back and forth to different articles in a thread. You use the arrow keys to move up and down and across the thread tree, highlighting different article numbers as you go. For example, if you press a DOWN ARROW key, you move from the current article number to the one below it, highlighting it. Pressing the RIGHT ARROW key moves you to the article number on the right. Repeatedly pressing the RIGHT ARROW key moves you to article numbers farther on the right. The LEFT ARROW key will move you back to the left, and the UP ARROW will move you up. The article for the number you have currently highlighted will be displayed. As you move through the thread tree, different articles are displayed.

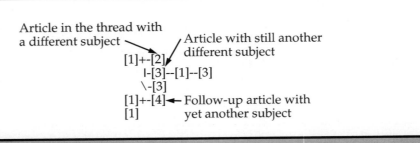

Figure 9-4. `trn` *thread tree showing articles with different subjects*

Saving Articles

You can save any article that you have read. After displaying the article, enter the **s** command with a file name. If the file does not yet exist, you will be asked if you want to use a mailbox file format for it. If you enter **y**, the file will be a mailbox file, and the article will be saved as one message in that mailbox. You can then use the **mailx** command with the **-f** option to read the articles saved in that file. If, however, you simply press ENTER, the file will have a standard text file format.

```
rec.food.recipes (moderated) #7155 (229 more)                    (1)
From: richpete@garnet.berkeley.edu (Richard Petersen)
Subject: Spelling Cookies
Followup-To: poster
Date: Mon Dec 20 04:48:01 PST 1995
Organization: University of California, Berkeley
Lines: 43


Spelling Cookies
                        INGREDIENTS
        1 cup flour
        2 teaspoons single acting baking powder, or 1 teaspoon double
            acting baking powder, or 1 teaspoon baking soda
        1/2 teaspoon nutmeg
        1/4 teaspoon cinnamon
        3/4 cup butter  (or 1 1/2 sticks)
        1 cup brown or dark brown sugar
        1/2 cup regular sugar
        1 egg
        1 teaspoon vanilla extract
        1/4 cup milk
End of article 7155 (of 7158) -- what next? [npq] s spellcookies

File /h/garnet_d/richpete/News/spellcookies doesn't exist--
        use mailbox format? [ynq] y
Saved to mailbox /h/garnet_d/richpete/News/spellcookies

End of article 7155 (of 7158) -- what next? [npq]
```

Other articles that you save to an already existing file will simply be appended to it. In the case of mailbox files, the added articles will become new messages. When saving more than one article in the same file, the mailbox format has several advantages. You can easily access particular articles using Mail. You can also mail replies to authors of articles using the **R** command, and you can easily incorporate an article in messages to other users.

Replying to Articles in trn: Follow-ups and Messages

You can reply to a specific article either by posting a follow-up article of your own or by sending the author a message by mail. A follow-up article is an article that you post on Usenet in response to another article you have read, and anyone on Usenet can read it. A mail message, on the other hand, is a private message that you send using Linux mail. The **f** and **F** commands will post a follow-up article, and the **r** and **R** commands send a reply message.

Posting Follow-ups

You post a follow-up article from within the **trn** newsreader. While you are reading an article, you can post a follow-up to it by entering the **f** or **F** commands. These commands invoke Pnews, which actually enters and posts your follow-up article. The **F** command will include the text of the article you are responding to in your follow-up. The text will be displayed indented with each line preceded by a **>** sign.

You can also post a follow-up by locating the article you want to respond to and pressing the **f** command. You are then placed in the editor with the header for your follow-up. You can enter the text of your article and edit the header fields if you want. Upon exiting the editor, you are prompted to either send, abort, edit, or list the follow-up article. The **send** command posts the article for you.

You can see how follow-ups allow you to carry on discussions about an article in your newsgroup. You can not only read an article, you can also read what other people think of it in follow-up articles. As described earlier, you can even post follow-ups to the follow-ups, carrying on discussions with other users about an article. You post a follow-up of a follow-up by locating the follow-up article and then pressing **f** and posting your response.

When responding to an article, it is often helpful to include the original text in your follow-up. You can do so using the **F** command. Each included line of article text is preceded by a **>** sign. You do not have to keep the entire text of the article in your follow-up. Suppose you only want to respond to one part of the article. While in the editor, you can delete all but that part of the article, and your follow-up article will then list only that part of the original article and any comments that you decide to add. You can even use the editor to insert your own comments throughout the included text of the original article, providing a kind of annotated version of it. Use the **F** command to make your follow-ups clearer and avoid having to retype others' comments.

The **F** command is very useful when posting follow-ups to follow-ups. It is often clearer to include those comments a user has made that you are responding to. Instead of painstakingly typing them in yourself, the **F** command will include the follow-up article text automatically for your own follow-up.

Mailing Replies to Authors

Instead of posting a follow-up for everyone to read, you can simply mail a reply directly to the author of an article. You do so with either the **r** and **R** commands. First locate the article you want to send a reply to, and then press **r**. The article header is displayed, and the mail program is invoked. You are placed in your editor, and you can then enter your message. The header will also be included so that you can change your subject entry or summary line if you want. When you leave the editor, you are asked if you want to send, abort, edit, or list the message. The **send** command will mail the message to the author of the article.

Should you want to include a copy of the article's text in your message, you use the **R** command. As with the **F** command, the **R** command will include the text of the article with each line preceded by a **>** sign. In the editor, you can then delete, copy, or move the text as you wish.

Marking Articles

Once you have read an article, **trn** will no longer display its header in the article list, and you will no longer be able to access it at a later date through **trn**. If you want to be able to come back to the article at a later date, you can mark the article as unread so that **trn** will continue to display its header in the article list. To mark an article as unread, enter the **m** command when you read it. If you only want to read it during the next session, use the **M** command.

Article Selections

You can select a group of articles based on pattern searches or number references. A pattern search followed by a colon and one of the **trn** commands will apply that command to every article with that pattern, not just to the next article. In effect, a pattern search followed by a colon will select a group of articles upon which you can perform operations. For example, if you want to save all articles dealing with the subject "cookies" you could issue the command **/cookies/:s cookfile**, as shown in the next example.

```
End of article 6914 (of 7158) -- what next? [npq] /cookies/:s
cookfile
Searching...7094
File /h/garnet_d/richpete/News/cookfile doesn't exist--
       use mailbox format? [ynq] y
Saved to mailbox /h/garnet_d/richpete/News/cookfile
7128    Appended to mailbox /h/garnet_d/richpete/News/cookfile
```

```
7155     Appended to mailbox /h/garnet_d/richpete/News/cookfile
done
End of article 6914 (of 7158) -- what next? [npq]
```

The ^ symbol is a special pattern that represents all articles. To save all articles to a file, you use the command:

```
/^/:s myfile
```

When used with the = command, a pattern can provide you with a listing of articles on a certain topic. The = command lists the number and subject of each article. When qualified by a pattern, it only lists those articles on that subject. The next example lists the numbers and subjects of all unread articles on cookies.

```
/cookies/:=
```

If you want to include all read articles in your list, you need to qualify the pattern with **r**. The next example provides a listing of all articles on cookies, including read ones:

```
/cookies/r:=
```

By default, a pattern only searches the subject field of an article. When used with the **a** qualifier, a pattern searches throughout the entire text of an article. The next example provides a list of all recipes that use chocolate. The results of this particular query is often too long to print out.

```
/chocolate/a:=
```

You can also reference a group of articles by listing their numbers separated by commas. End the list with a colon followed by a command applied to those articles. Since articles are consecutively numbered, you can include number ranges in your list, for example, **3-5** references articles 3, 4, and 5. To save articles 34, 17, and 9-12, you would use the command:

```
34,17,9-12:s myfile
```

In the next example, the user saves articles 7155 and 7128 to the file **goodcook**:
7155, 7128:s goodcook.

```
End of article 6919 (of 7158) -- what next? [npq] 7155,7128:s
goodcook
7155      Appended to mailbox /h/garnet_d/richpete/News/goodcook
7128      Appended to mailbox /h/garnet_d/richpete/News/goodcook

End of article 6919 (of 7158) -- what next? [npq]
```

In both pattern and number references, you can append other commands to be applied to the group of articles. Just separate each command with a colon. In the next example, articles 34, 17, and 9-12, are both saved and printed.

```
34,17,9-12:s myfile: | lp
```

trn Options

You can use a number of options with **trn**. With the **-n** option you can specify a newsgroup or type of newsgroup that you want to read. With the **-l** option you can list just newsgroup headers. In the next example, the user lists the newsgroup headers for the **rec.food.recipes** newsgroups.

```
$ trn -l -n rec.food.recipes
```

With the **-q** option you can skip the subscription phase and move directly to reading your newsgroups.

```
$ trn -q rec.food.recipes
```

Article List : the rn Newsreader

As an alternative to the **trn** selector, you can use **rn** commands to display and select items in your article list. The **rn** commands for moving through the newsgroup list and the article list are often the same. Depending on what type of list you are operating on, you will either move through newsgroups or articles. For example, the **n** command for the newsgroup list moves you to the next newsgroup, whereas the **n** command for the article list moves you to the next article. The **rn** newsreader commands are listed in Table 9-2.

Once you have located the newsgroup you want, you enter the article level and select the article in that newsgroup that you want to read. Upon pressing **y** at the newsgroup prompt, you enter the article level, and the header of the first article in the newsgroup is displayed. You can then read the first article or use article-level commands to move to another article in the newsgroup. The article-level commands are the same as those described earlier for moving through the newsgroup list. To move to the next article, you use the **n** command. The **p** command moves you back an article. The **^** command moves to the first unread article, and the **$** command moves to the last article.

You can also move to a particular article by entering its number. Articles in a newsgroup are numbered consecutively. You can obtain a list of unread article titles and their numbers by pressing the **=** sign. Each line will list the number of the article, its title, and its subject. Entering the number of the article will move you to it.

```
End of article 7155 (of 7158) -- what next? [npq] 7155
rec.food.recipes (moderated) #7155 (229 more)                    (1)
From: richpete@garnet.berkeley.edu (Richard Petersen)
```

With **rn** you can also use pattern searches at the article level to locate an article. The **/** command, followed by a pattern, searches forward in the article list for an article with that pattern in the subject field of its header. The **?** command will search backward. In the next example, the user searches the subject field of articles for the pattern "cookies."

```
End of article 7050 (of 7158) -- what next? [npq] /cookies
Searching...
```

Using qualifiers with the pattern search, you can specify whether you want to search the text of articles, the entire header, or articles you have already read. The **a** qualifier searches the entire text of articles for a pattern. The **h** qualifier searches the entire header, and the **r** qualifier includes read articles in the search. In the next example, the user searches the headers of articles for the pattern "richpete," including any articles that have already been read.

```
End of article 6914 (of 7158) -- what next? [^Nnpq] /richpete/hr
Searching...
```

You can also search for articles that have the same subject. To do so, you first locate an article with the subject you are looking for. To locate the next article with that same subject, you press CTRL-**n**. You then move to that article. Consecutive CTRL-**n**'s will find the next articles with the same subject. CTRL-**p** searches backward for the previous article with the same subject.

Posting Articles: Pnews

You can post your own articles for a newsgroup of your choice. Perhaps the most commonly used utility for posting articles is Pnews. It prompts you for certain header information, places you in an editor in which you can type in your article, and then prompts you either to send, edit, save, or quit the article.

To begin, enter the **Pnews** command at your Linux prompt. You are then prompted to enter the newsgroup for the article. To see the full list of newsgroups, enter a **?** at the newsgroups prompt. It is, however, a good idea to have already decided on what newsgroups you want. You can obtain a listing of newsgroups at any time from the newsgroups file located in the **news** directory on your system.

After selecting your newsgroups, you are asked to specify distribution. Distribution can be made at ever widening areas. You can post your article for local viewing for users on your own system, or you can post it for worldwide viewing. There are various intermediate levels of distribution, such as North America, the United States, or a specific state or city. Pnews will first list possible prefixes, and then you enter the one you want at the distribution prompt. For the United States you would enter **usa**.

Next you are asked to enter a title or subject of the article. This will be used to classify the article and will be searched in pattern searches. You are then asked if you really want to post the article. To continue, enter **y**. You are then asked if you have a prepared file to include in your article. Often it is easier to write your article and save it to a file first, using a standard editor. Once it is ready, you can post the contents of that file. The contents of the file you specify are then read into the article that is being posted. If you do not enter a file name at this point, Pnews will automatically place you in an editor where you can type in your article.

Finally, Pnews prompts you either to send, abort, edit, or list the article. You need enter only the first character of a command to execute it. For example, if you change your mind and decide not to post the article, you just enter **a** at this prompt, quitting Pnews without sending the article. On the other hand, you can enter **e** at the prompt to edit the article, in case you notice any mistakes or want to add something. You would then be placed in the standard editor with the contents of the article displayed. Here, you can make the changes you want and return to the Pnews prompt upon exiting the standard editor (**zz** for Vi). To post the article, enter **s**, for send, at this prompt. The article is sent to the Usenet manager and posted in the appropriate newsgroup.

If you want to use the standard editor to type the text of the article, you simply press ENTER when asked for a prepared file to include. You are then asked to enter an editor. Within brackets, Pnews will display the default standard editor it uses—often Vi—and you can simply press ENTER to use it. Pnews then places you in the default editor and displays the header information. You are free to change fields in the header if you want. You can change your subject or even your newsgroup. You then use standard editing commands to type the text of your article. When finished, exit the editor (if you are using Vi, press **ZZ**). Pnews prompts you to send, abort, edit, or list your article. You can, of course, edit your article again by typing **e** at this prompt. To finally post the article, you enter **s** at the prompt.

Pnews Signatures: The .signature File

You usually end an article with the same standard signature information, such as your name, Internet address or addresses, and a polite sign-off. As you write more articles, it is helpful to have your signature information automatically added to your articles. To do so, you need to create a file called **.signature** in your home directory and enter your signature information in it. Pnews will read the contents of the **.signature** file and place them at the end of your article. You can use any standard editor to create your **.signature** file.

The tin Newsreader

The **tin** newsreader operates using a selector that is much like the one used in the **trn** newsreader. However, **tin** has a screen selector for both newsgroups and articles. When you enter **tin**, the selector displays the screen listing your newsgroups. You can then select the newsgroup you want and display a screen for its articles.

One set of screen movement commands are used for all screens, whether for newsgroups, article lists, or article text. CTRL-**d**, CTRL-**f**, and SPACEBAR all move you forward to the next screen. CTRL-**u**, CTRL-**b**, and **b** all move you backward to the previous screen. The UP ARROW and the **k** key move you up a line on the screen, and the DOWN ARROW and **j** key move you down a line. The **q** command will move you back from one selector to another. For example, if you are in the article selector, pressing **q** will move you back to the newsgroup selector. **Q** will quit the **tin** newsreader entirely.

tin also has a set of editing and history commands that you can use to edit any commands that you enter. ESC will always erase a command you have entered and let you start over. The editing commands are a subset of the Emacs commands. CTRL-**d** deletes a character, CTRL-**f** and the RIGHT ARROW key move right one character. CTRL-**b** and the LEFT ARROW key move back one character. To insert new text, move your cursor to the position you want and start typing. **tin** also keeps a history of the commands you enter. You can recall the previous commands with CTRL-**p**, moving back, one by one, through a list of your previously entered commands. CTRL-**n** moves you forward through the list. You can find a complete listing of all **tin** commands in the **tin** manual pages, which you can invoke by typing **man tin**. The **tin** newsreader commands are listed in Table 9-3.

When you start **tin**, it first displays a screen of newsgroups. The term "Group Selection" will be shown at the top of the screen. To its right will be "h=help." Pressing the **h** key will bring up a help menu. The newsgroups are listed with a selection number that identifies the newsgroup, followed by the number of unread articles, and then the name of the newsgroup.

To select a newsgroup, you must first move to it. You can do this in a variety of ways. If you see your newsgroup displayed on the screen, you can just use your UP and DOWN ARROW keys to move to it. CTRL-**d** will move you to the next screen, and CTRL-**u** will move you back. Instead of using the arrow keys, you can move directly to a newsgroup by entering its index number. You can also locate a newsgroup by using pattern searches. You enter the **/** followed by a pattern. **?** performs a backward search.

Once you have located the newsgroup you want, press ENTER to display a list of its articles. A list of commonly used commands are displayed at the bottom of the screen. The **s** command will subscribe to a new newsgroup, and the **u** command will unsubscribe.

```
Group Selection (agate.berkeley.edu 3230)        h=help

    1    3       comp.ai.language
    2    1       comp.os.linux.misc
    3    7       rec.arts.movies
    4    24      rec.food.recipes
    5    32      sci.physics.fusion
    6    126     talk.politics.theory


    <n>=set current to n, TAB=next unread, /=search pattern,
c)atchup,
  g)oto, j=line down, k=line up, h)elp, m)ove, q)uit, r=toggle
all/unread,
      s)ubscribe, S)ub pattern, u)nsubscribe, U)nsub pattern,
y)ank in/out

search forwards > rec.food
```

The **tin** newsreader displays the subject and author of each article in the newsgroup preceded by an index number and, if unread, a **+**. The **+** sign indicates all unread articles. Working from the selector, you can choose articles you want to display. You select an article by moving the cursor to that article and pressing ENTER. Both the newsgroup and article selector screens use many of the same commands. The UP and DOWN ARROW keys will move you from one article to the next. If there is more than one screen of articles, you can move back and forth through them using CTRL-**u** or

CTRL-**d**. You can also move to an article by typing its index number. An example of the **tin** article selector screen follows.

```
rec.food.recipes (119T 124A 0K 0H R)              h=help

65    +    Fruit Salad                  Dylan Chris
66    +    Fudge Cake                   Cecelia Petersen
67    +    Chocolate News               Richard Leland
68    +    Chocolate News               Larisa@atlash
69    +    Apple Muffins                George Petersen
70    +    REQUEST: romantic dinners    Marylou Carrion
71    +    REQUEST: Dehydrated Goodies  Valerie Fuller
72    +    REQUEST: Devonshire Cream    Carolyn Blacklock
73    +    Sauces                       Bonnie Matoza
74    +    Passion Fruit                Gabriel Matoza
75    +    REQUEST: blackened (red)fish Ken Blacklock
76    +    REQUEST: Cheese Toast        dylan@sf
77    +    REQUEST: Sausage Recipes     Penny Bode
78    +    Biscuit Recipe               gloria@stlake
79    +    >blackened (red)fish         augie@napa
80    +    Oatmeal Cookies              John Gunther
81    +    REQUEST: Potato Salad        Margaret
82    +    REQUEST: Sesame Chicken      Frank Moitoza
83    +    >Summer desserts             maryann@sebast

    <n>=set current to n, TAB=next unread, /=search pattern,
^K)ill/select,
  a)uthor search, c)atchup, j=line down, k=line up, K=mark read,
l)ist thread,
    |=pipe, m)ail, o=print, q)uit, r=toggle all/unread, s)ave,
t)ag, w=post
```

The commonly used commands for accessing articles are displayed at the bottom of the screen. You can search articles for a specified pattern with the **/** command. The **a** command allows you to search for articles by a specified author. The **s** command will save an article. You can post an article of your own to the newsgroup by pressing the **w** command. You will be prompted for header information, and then you enter the text of your message. Once you have selected and displayed an article, you will also be able to post follow-ups and send replies.

Once you have selected an article, it is displayed. If the article takes up more than one screen, you can move forward by pressing the SPACEBAR and backward by pressing the **b** key. With the **B** command you can search the article for a specified pattern, and with the **s** command you can save it. With the **f** command you can post a follow-up to the article, and with the **r** command you can send a message to the author.

```
Mon, 20 Dec 1995 04:48:o1    rec.food.recipes   Thread   33 of   119
Lines 43                     Spelling Cookies   No responses
richpete@garnet.berkeley.edu. Richard Petersen at University of
California

Spelling Cookies
                        INGREDIENTS
        1 cup flour
        2 teaspoons single acting baking powder, or 1 teaspoon
           double acting baking powder, or 1 teaspoon baking soda
        1/2 teaspoon nutmeg
        1/4 teaspoon cinnamon
        3/4 cup butter   (or 1 1/2 sticks)
        1 cup brown or dark brown sugar
        1/2 cup regular sugar
        1 egg
        1 teaspoon vanilla extract
        1/4 cup milk


  <n>=set current to n, TAB=next unread, /=search pattern,
^K)ill/select,
        a)uthor search, B)ody search, c)atchup, f)ollowup, K=mark
read,
          |=pipe, m)ail, o=print, q)uit, r)eply mail, s)ave, t)ag,
w=post

    --More--(44%)   [46/100]
```

You can also automatically select articles and newsgroups by moving to their entries and pressing +. A ***** will appear before the automatically selected entries. These are known as *hot items*. You can reference these automatically selected items in the various **tin** commands such as the **same** or **mail** commands.

Encoded Binaries: uuencode and uudecode

Certain newsgroups specialize in encoded binary files. In these newsgroups, articles consist of encoded binary files such as **jpeg** pictures. Newsgroups as well as mail utilities cannot handle binary files. They can only handle character files. However, you can translate a binary file into a character format and then post or send that version. To do so, you need to use the **uuencode** and **uudecode** programs. **uuencode** translates a binary file into a character file. You can then post that character file to a newsgroup or send it to another user through email. **uudecode** will decode a file that has been encoded with **uuencode**. You can save a uuencoded file from a newsgroup and then translate it back into a binary file using **uudecode**. See Chapter 8 for a discussion of these two programs.

Newsgroups that specialize in binary files usually have the word "binaries" in their names. For example, **alt.binaries.pictures** holds articles consisting of uuencoded **jpeg** or **gif** pictures. **alt.binaries.multimedia** has uuencoded **mpeg** or **mov** files. Many times binary files will be posted in several parts, one per article. You would need to download all the articles making up the binary file, and then use **uudecode** to decode and combine them back into one binary file.

Summary: Usenet and Newsreaders

Usenet can be thought of as an online electronic news service containing journal articles, recent bulletins, and discussions on different topics. Usenet is divided by topic into different newsgroups. You can access a newsgroup and read the articles in it. You can also compose and post articles of your own to a particular newsgroup. You can respond to an article either by posting your response in the same newsgroup for everyone to read or by sending your response as a message directly to the article's author.

To access Usenet articles, you can use one of several available newsreader programs. Two of the more popular programs are **trn** and **tin**. **trn** allows you to search newsgroups and articles using pattern searches, as well as copy articles and post articles of your own. **trn** also distinguishes between read and unread articles, giving you easy access to newly posted articles in a newsgroup. **trn** makes use of an interface called a selector that lists articles grouped according to threads, allowing you to reference articles by subject or by related follow-up articles. You can select the group of articles you want to examine and then move through these related articles. When displaying articles in a thread, you can make use of a thread tree that delineates the relationship of follow-up articles. Using the tree, you can move from one article to any other article in the thread.

The **tin** newsreader uses selectors for both newsgroups and for articles within a newsgroup. It shares many of the same features of **trn**. Newsgroups are accessed through a selector, allowing easy reference.

Option	Function/Description
-c	Checks for any unread newsgroups
-r	Restarts in previous newsgroup
-q	Skips new newsgroup selection when starting
-O*mode sort-order*	
Mode	
a	Article mode
s	Subject mode
t	Thread mode
Sort-order	
d	Date
s	Subject
a	Author
c	Article count
g	Subject-date groups
Selecting Newsgroups	
y	Selects the current newsgroup
n	Moves to the next newsgroup with unread articles
N	Moves to the next newsgroup
p	Moves to the previous newsgroup with unread articles
P	Moves to the previous newsgroup
-	Moves to the previously selected newsgroup
^	Moves to the first newsgroup with unread articles
num	Moves to newsgroup with that number
$	Moves to the last newsgroup

Table 9-1.   `trn` *Commands*

Option	Function/Description
g_newsgroup-name_	Moves to newsgroup with that name
/_pattern_	Searches forward to the newsgroup with that pattern
?_pattern_	Searches backward to the newsgroup with that pattern
L	Lists subscribed newsgroups
l_pattern_	Lists unsubscribed newsgroups
u _newsgroup-name_	Unsubscribed newsgroups
a _newsgroup-name_	Subscribed to a newsgroup
c	Marks articles in a newsgroup as read
Displaying Selector	
+	Enters the selector from the **trn** line prompt, or leaves the selector and returns to the **trn** line prompt

S	Selects selector mode: subject, thread, or article
	`Selector Mode: Threads, Subjects,`
	`    Articles? [tsa]`
	s Subject mode, displays articles by subject
	a Article mode, displays individual articles
	t Thread mode, displays articles by threads

=	Switches between article and subject/thread selector

O	Sorts selector items by date, author, thread count, or subject. User is prompted to enter **d**, **a**, **n**, or **s**. (Note that this command is an uppercase O.) The options differ depending on whether you are in the subject or thread modes
	`Subject  Order by Date, Subject, or`
	`    Count? [dscDSC]`
	`Thread  Order by Date, Subject, Author,`
	`    subject-date Groups?`

L	Sets selector item display to short, medium, or long forms
E	Exclusive mode; displays only selected articles
k	Removes an article or subject from the selector display

Table 9-1.   **trn** _Commands_ (continued)

Option	Function/Description
U	Displays unread articles
Moving Through Selector	
SPACEBAR	Displays the next screen of articles
>	Displays the next screen of threads
<	Displays the previous screen of articles
$	Displays the last screen of articles
^	Displays the first screen of articles
Selecting Articles in the Selector	
id	Selects/deselects an article thread
id★	Selects/deselects articles with the same subject as ID
n	Moves to the next thread ID
p	Moves to the previous thread ID
z	Begins displaying selected articles; returns to newsgroup screen when finished
X	Begins displaying selected articles, but moves to the next newsgroup when finished

/*pattern*	Searches forward to the article with that pattern in each article's subject field
	Modifiers
	h Searches forward to the article with that pattern in the header
	   /*pattern*/**h**
	a Searches forward to the article with that pattern in either the header or the text
	   /*pattern*/**a**
	r Includes read articles in your search
	   /*pattern*/**r**
	c Makes search case sensitive
	   /*pattern*/**c**

Table 9-1.   **trn** *Commands* (continued)

Option	Function/Description
?pattern?	Searches backward to the article with that pattern in each article's subject field **Modifiers** **h** Searches backward to the article with that pattern in the header *?pattern?***h** **a** Searches forward to the article with that pattern in either the header or the text **r** Includes read articles in your search **c** Makes search case sensitive
/	Repeats previous forward search
?	Repeats previous backward search
/*pattern***:***command*	Selects a group of articles matching the pattern and applies the **trn** command to all
*id,id***:***command*	Selects a group of articles referenced by the numbers and applies the **trn** command to all

Displaying Articles

SPACEBAR	Displays the next screen of the article
ENTER	Scrolls to the next line of the article
d	Scrolls to the next half screen of the article
b	Displays the previous screen of the article
v	Redisplays article from the beginning
q	Displays last screen of the article
g *pattern*	Searches for pattern in the text
G	Repeats pattern search in the text

Saving Articles

:w	Saves selected article

Table 9-1.   **trn** *Commands* (continued)

Option	Function/Description
:s	Saves selected article to a mailbox file
Replying to Articles	
r	Replies to current article
R	Replies to current article and includes article text in the reply
f	Posts a follow-up to the current article
F	Posts a follow-up including the text of the current article
Marking Articles	
m	Marks current article as read
n	Marks current article as read and moves to next article
j	Marks current article as read and displays end of article
c	Marks all articles as read in the current newsgroup
trn Option Variables	
EDITOR	Editor for composing replies
MAILPOSTER	Mail utility for sending replies
PAGER	Page utility for reading articles
SAVEDIR	Directory in which to save articles
NAME	Your full name to be used for article headers that you post
ORGANIZATION	Your organization name for article headers that you post
NNTPSERVER	NNTP remote news server address

Table 9-1. trn *Commands* (continued)

Selecting Articles	Function
y	Displays the current article
n	Moves to the next article with unread articles
N	Moves to the next article
p	Moves to the previous article with unread articles
P	Moves to the previous article
–	Moves to the previously selected article
^	Moves to the first article with unread articles
num	Moves to article with that number
$	Moves to the last article
CTRL-n	Moves to the next article with the same subject as the current one
CTRL-p	Moves to the previous article with the same subject as the current one

Table 9-2.   **rn** *Article List Commands for* **trn**

Screen Movement Commands

Screen Movement Commands	Effect/Description
DOWN ARROW, **j**	Moves down a line
UP ARROW, **k**	Moves up a line
$	Goes to last line
CTRL-**U**, CTRL-**B**, **b**, PAGE UP	Goes to previous screen
CTRL-**D**, CTRL-**F**, SPACEBAR, PAGE DOWN	Goes to next screen
CTRL-**L**	Redraws screen
q	Returns to previous level
Q	Quits **tin**

Command Editing and History

Command Editing and History	
CTRL-**f**, RIGHT ARROW	Moves to next character
CTRL-**b**, LEFT ARROW	Moves to previous character
CTRL-**d**, BACKSPACE, DEL	Deletes character
CTRL-**p**	Previously entered command in history list
CTRL-**n**	Next entered command in history list
ESC	Erases command entered

Newsgroup Selector

Newsgroup Selector	
num	Goes to newsgroup with that index number
ENTER	Selects current newsgroup
TAB	Goes to next unread newsgroup
/	Searches forward
?	Searches backward
g	Chooses a new group by name

Table 9-3. **tin** *Newsreader Commands*

Newsgroup Selector	Effect/Description
K	Marks article/thread as read and goes to next unread
l	Lists articles within current thread
C	Marks all articles as read and goes to next unread group
c	Marks all articles as read and goes to group selection menu
s	Subscribes to a newsgroup
u	Unsubscribes to a newsgroup
S *pattern*	Subscribes to newsgroups with *pattern*
U *pattern*	Unsubscribes to newsgroups with *pattern*
M	Displays menu of configurable options
v	Shows version information
h	Help command
CTRL-K	Kill/Auto select current newsgroup
H	Toggles mini-help menu
I	Toggles inverse video
Article Selector	
num	Goes to article with that index number
$	Goes to last article
ENTER	Selects current article
TAB	Goes to next unread article
a	Author forward search
A	Author backward search
/	Subject forward search
?	Subject backward search

Table 9-3. `tin` *Newsreader Commands* (continued)

Article Selector	Effect/Description
n	Goes to next group
p	Goes to previous group
N	Goes to next unread article
P	Goes to previous unread article
d	Toggles display of subject or subject and author
r	Toggles display to show all/only unread articles
u	Toggles display of unthreaded and threaded articles
z	Marks article as unread
Z	Marks thread as unread
X	Marks all unread articles that have not been selected as read
t	Tags current article for cross-posting/mailing /piping/printing/saving
U	Untags all tagged articles
s	Saves article/thread/hot/pattern/tagged articles to file
m	Mails article/thread/hot/pattern/tagged articles to someone
o	Outputs article/thread/hot/pattern/tagged articles to printer
w	Posts an article to current group
W	Lists articles posted by user
x	Cross-posts current article to another group
*	Selects thread
.	Toggles selection of thread
@	Reverses all selections (all articles)
~	Undoes all selections (all articles)

Table 9-3.   `tin` *Newsreader Commands (continued)*

Article Selector	Effect/Description
+	Performs auto-selection on groups or articles creating hot items; these items will have a * displayed before them
=	Marks threads selected if at least one unread article is selected
!	Escapes shell
–	Shows last message
|	Pipes article/thread/hot/pattern/tagged articles into command
Displaying Article	
b	Moves back a page
SPACEBAR	Moves forward a page
B	Article body search
;	Marks threads selected if at least one unread article is selected
s	Saves article/thread/hot/pattern/tagged articles to file
m	Mails article/thread/hot/pattern/tagged articles to someone
o	Outputs article/thread/hot/pattern/tagged articles to printer
w	Posts an article to current group
f	Posts follow-up for current article
r	Sends reply to author of article
tin Option Variables	
VISUAL	Editor for composing replies
NNTPSERVER	NNTP remote news server address

Table 9-3. tin *Newsreader Commands* (continued)

Chapter Ten

Internet Tools

The Internet is a network of computers around the world that you can access with an Internet address and a set of Internet tools. Many computers on the Internet are configured to operate as servers, providing information to anyone who requests it. The information is contained in files that you can access and copy. Each server, often referred to as a site, has its own Internet address by which it can be located. Linux provides a set of Internet tools that you can use to access sites on the Internet and then locate and download information from them.

To access Internet sites, your computer must be connected to the Internet. You may be part of a network that is already connected to the Internet. If you have a stand-alone computer, such as a personal computer, you can obtain an Internet connection from an Internet Service Provider (ISP). Once you have an Internet address of your own, you can configure your Linux system to connect to the Internet and use various Internet tools to access different sites. Chapter 12 describes how to configure your Linux system to make such a connection.

The Internet tools telnet and ftp allow you to connect to another Internet site. telnet performs a remote login to another computer connected on the Internet. You could use it to search the Library of Congress online catalogue, for example. ftp connects to a site and allows you to perform file transfers both from and to it. You can connect to a site that has Linux software and download software directly to your computer using ftp.

Finding out what information is available and on what system it is located, as well as where on the system it is stored, can be an overwhelming task. Ordinarily you would need to know the location of the file ahead of time. However, two Internet tools, Archie and Gopher, allow you to search for files on the network. Using Archie is like searching on an online catalogue; just as you can use keywords to search for a title of a book, with Archie you can use patterns to search for the name of a file. Gopher operates more like a reference librarian. It provides you with a series of menus listing different topics. You move from one menu to the other, narrowing your topic until you find the information you want. Using Gopher, you can then directly transfer your information without having to resort to ftp.

In the last few years, the Web Browsers have become the primary tool for accessing information on the Internet. However, Web Browsers rely on underlying Internet tools that actually retrieve and transfer information. telnet, ftp, Archie, and Gopher are all tools developed to locate and access Internet sites and to retrieve information from them. Web Browsers make use of these tools to obtain information on the Internet, but they often hide their use from the user, making for smoother interaction. Most of the tasks you perform on the Internet may be done easily with a Web Browser. You may only need to use the Internet tools described in this chapter for more specialized tasks, such as downloading files from a specific ftp site. For example, you would use ftp if you wanted to download a new Linux software program from a Linux ftp site.

Internet Addresses

The Internet uses a set of network protocols called TCP/IP, which stands for Transmission Control Protocol/Internet Protocol. In a TCP/IP network, messages are broken into small components called datagrams that are then transmitted through various interlocking routes and delivered to their destination computers. Once received, the datagrams are reassembled into the original message. Datagrams are also referred to as packets. Sending messages as small components has proven to be far more reliable and faster than sending them as one large bulky transmission. With small components, if one is lost or damaged, only that component has to be re-sent, whereas if any part of a large transmission is corrupted or lost, the entire message has to be re-sent.

On a TCP/IP network such as the Internet, each computer is given a unique address called an IP address. The IP address is used to identify and locate a particular host—a computer connected to the network. An IP address consists of a set of four segments, each separated by a period. The segments consist of numbers that range from 0 to 255, with certain values reserved for special use. The IP address is divided into two parts, one that identifies the network and the other that identifies a particular host. The number of segments used for each is determined by the class of the network. On the Internet, networks are organized into three classes depending on their size—classes A, B, and C. A class A network will use only the first segment for the IP address and the remaining three for the host, allowing a great many computers to be connected to the same network. Most IP addresses reference smaller, class C, networks. For a class C network, the first three segments are used to identify the network, and only the last segment identifies the host. The syntax looks like this:

```
net.net.net.host
```

In a class C network, the first three numbers identify the network part of the IP address. This part is divided into three network numbers, each identifying a subnet. Networks on the Internet are organized into subnets beginning with the largest and narrowing to small subnetworks. The last number is used to identify a particular computer that is referred to as a host. You can think of the Internet as a series of networks with subnetworks, and these subnetworks have their own subnetworks. The rightmost number identifies the host computer, and the number preceding it identifies the subnetwork that the computer is a part of. The number to the left of that identifies the network that the subnetwork is part of, and so on. The Internet address 192.18.187.4 references the fourth computer connected to the network identified by the number 187. Network 187 is a subnet to a larger network identified as 18. This larger network is itself a subnet of the network identified as 192. Here's how it breaks down:

192.18.187.4	IP address
192.18.187	Network identification
4	Host identification

An IP address is officially provided by the Network Information Center (NIC) that administers the Internet. You can obtain your own Internet address from the NIC, or if you are on a network already connected to the Internet, your network administrator can assign you one. If you are using an Internet Service Provider, the ISP may obtain one for you or, each time you connect, may temporarily assign one from a pool they have on hand.

Certain numbers are reserved. The numbers 127, 0, or 255 cannot be part of an official IP address. The address 127.0.0.0 is the loopback address that allows users on your computer to communicate with each other. The number 255 is a special broadcast identifier that you can use to broadcast messages to all sites on a network. Using 225 for any part of the IP address references all nodes connected at that level. For example, 192.18.255.255 broadcasts a message to all computers on network 192.18, all its subnetworks, and their hosts. The address 192.18.187.255 broadcasts to every computer on the local network. If you use 0 for the network part of the address, the host number will reference a computer within your local network. For example, 0.0.0.6 references the sixth computer in your local network. If you want to broadcast to all computers on your local network, you can use the number 0.0.0.255.

All hosts on the Internet are identified by their IP addresses. When you send a message to a host on the Internet, you must provide its IP address. However, using a sequence of four numbers of an IP address can be very difficult. They are hard to remember, and it's easy to make mistakes when typing them. To make it easier to identify a computer on the Internet, the Domain Name Service (DNS) was implemented. The DNS establishes a domain name address for each IP address. The domain name address is a series of names separated by periods. Whenever you use a domain name address it is automatically converted to an IP address that is then used to identify that Internet host. The domain name address is far easier to use than its corresponding IP address.

A domain name address needs to be registered with the NIC so that each computer on the Internet will have a unique name. Creating a name follows specified naming conventions, as discussed earlier in Chapter 8. The domain name address consists of the hostname, the name you gave to your computer, a domain name, the name that identifies your network, and an extension that identifies the type of network you are on. Here is the syntax for domain addresses:

```
host-name.domain-name.extension
```

In the following example, the domain address references a computer called sunsite on a network referred to as unc, and it is part of an educational institution, as indicated by the extension edu.

```
sunsite.unc.edu
```

The conversion of domain addresses to IP addresses used to be performed by each individual host. And for a few frequently used addresses for which you know the IP address, this can still be done. However, there are now so many computers connected to the Internet that domain name conversion has to be performed by special servers known as Domain Name Servers or simply nameservers. A nameserver holds a database of domain name addresses and their IP addresses. Local networks will sometimes have their own nameservers. If a nameserver does not have the address, then it may call on other nameservers to perform the conversion. A program on your computer called a resolver will obtain the IP address from a nameserver and then use it in the application where you specified the domain name address.

With the **whois** and **nslookup** commands, you can obtain information for domain nameservers about different networks and hosts connected to the Internet. Enter **whois** and the domain name address of the host or network, and **whois** will display information about the host, such as the street address and phone number as well as contact persons.

```
$ whois   domain-address
```

The **nslookup** command takes a domain address and finds its corresponding IP address.

```
$ nslookup   domain-address
```

nslookup has an interactive mode that you enter by not specifying any domain name. You can then use **nslookup** to search for other kinds of information about a host. For example, the HINFO option will find out what type of operating system a host uses. The **nslookup** man page specifies a list of different options and how to use them.

Remote Login: telnet

You use the **telnet** command to log in remotely to another system on your network. The system can be on your local area network or available through an Internet connection. telnet operates as if you were logging into another system from a remote terminal. You will be asked for a login name and, in some cases, a password. In effect, you are logging into another account on another system. In fact, if you have an account on another system, you could use telnet to log into it.

Usually, telnet is used to connect to hosts on the Internet that provide certain public services, such as the Library of Congress and its online catalogue, or sites that provide you with Archie indexes. Such sites allow guest logins, meaning that they do not require any specific login name or password. Anyone can log in. However, such sites are specially designed to handle public access, presenting you with menus of options that control your access to the system.

You invoke the telnet utility with the keyword **telnet**. If you know the name of the site you want to connect with, you can just enter **telnet** and the name of the site on the Linux command line. In the next example, the user specifies the garnet system.

```
$ telnet garnet.berkeley.edu
Connected to garnet
login:
```

telnet also has a command mode with a series of commands that you can use to configure your connection. You can enter the telnet command mode either by invoking telnet with the keyword **telnet** or by pressing CTRL-] during a session. The telnet **help** command will list all the telnet commands that you can use. Table 10-1 provides a list of commonly used telnet commands, and a comprehensive list is available on the man pages (**man telnet**). In the next example, the user first invokes the telnet utility. Then a prompt is displayed, indicating the command mode, **telnet>**. The telnet command **open** then connects to another system.

```
$ telnet
telnet> open garnet.berkeley.edu
Connected to garnet.berkeley.edu
login:
```

Once connected, you follow the login procedure for that system. If you are logging into a regular system, you will have to provide a login name and password. Once logged in, you will be provided with the operating system prompt that, in the case of Linux or Unix, will either be **$** or **%**. You are then directly connected to an account on that system and can issue any commands you want.

When you have finished your work, you log out. This will break the connection and return you to the telnet prompt on your own system. You can then quit telnet with the **quit** command.

```
telnet> quit
```

When using telnet to connect to a site that provides public access, you will not need to provide a login name or password. Access is usually controlled by a series of menus that restricts what you can do on that system. Figure 10-1 shows a telnet session accessing the online catalog of the Library of Congress at **locis.loc.gov**.

```
$ telnet locis.loc.gov
```

If you are logging into a specific account on another system, you can use the **-1** option to specify the login name of that account. This allows you to skip the login prompt. You can use the **-1** option with either the telnet invocation on the command line or with the **open** command, as shown in the next examples. Here the user is logging into a specific account called richpete on the **rose.berkeley.edu** system.

```
$ telnet rose.berkeley.edu -1 richpete
telnet> open rose.berkeley.edu -1 richpete
```

```
        L O C I S :  LIBRARY OF CONGRESS INFORMATION SYSTEM

            To make a choice: type a number, then press ENTER

    1   Library of Congress Catalog      4   Braille and Audio

    2   Federal Legislation              5   Organizations

    3   Copyright Information            6   Foreign Law
    *   *   *   *   *   *   *   *   *   *   *   *
    7   Searching Hours and Basic Search Commands
    8   Documentation and Classes
    9   Library of Congress General Information
   10   Library of Congress Fast Facts
   11   * * Announcements * *



   12   Comments and Logoff
        Choice:
```

Figure 10-1.   *Library of Congress telnet connection*

Certain online software, such as Gopher or Web Browsers, will, when called for, make telnet connections to public sites automatically. In such cases, you may suddenly find yourself presented with a simple menu of options rather than the detailed graphics interface of a Web Browser or page display of a Gopher. At this point, you are remotely logged into another site with telnet, using that site's interface to obtain controlled access to its resources. Simply follow the menu options, and when you leave the site, you will be returned to your Web Browser or Gopher page.

Network File Transfer: ftp

One of the most widely used Internet tools is ftp. You can use ftp to directly transfer very large files from one site to another. It can handle both text and binary files. ftp stands for File Transfer Protocol. It operates on systems connected to networks that use the TCP/IP protocols, such as the Internet. ftp has its own set of commands, listed in Table 10-2, that you can use to manage your file transfers.

ftp performs a remote login to another account on another system connected to you on a network such as the Internet. Once logged into that other system, you can transfer files to and from it. To log in you will need to know the login name and password for the account on the remote system. For example, if you have accounts at two different sites on the Internet, you can use ftp to transfer files from one to the other. However, there are also many sites on the Internet that allow public access using ftp. Many sites serve as depositories for very large files that anyone can access and download. Such sites are often referred to as ftp sites, and in many cases their Internet address will begin with the word "ftp". One such site is **sunsite.unc.edu**, which specializes in Linux files. These public sites allow anonymous ftp login from any user. For the login name you use the word "anonymous," and for the password you use your Internet address. You can then transfer files from that site to your own system.

You invoke the ftp utility with the command **ftp**. If there is one specific site that you want to connect to, you can include the name of that site on the command line after the **ftp** keyword. Otherwise, you will need to connect to the remote system with the ftp command **open**. You are then prompted for the name of the remote system with the prompt (to). Upon entering the remote system name, ftp connects you to the system and then prompts you for a login name. The prompt for the login name will consist of the word "Name" and, in parentheses, the system name and your local login name. Sometimes the login name on the remote system is the same as the login name on your own system. If they are the same, just press ENTER at the prompt. If they are different, enter the remote system's login name. After entering the login name, you are prompted for the password. In the next example, the user connects to the remote system garnet and logs into the robert account.

```
$ ftp
ftp> open
(to) garnet
Connected to garnet.berkeley.edu.
220 garnet.berkeley.edu FTP server (ULTRIX Version 4.1 Sun May 16
10:23:46 EDT 1996) ready.
Name (garnet.berkeley.edu:root): robert
password required
Password:
user robert logged in
ftp>
```

To save a step, you can directly specify the remote system on the command line when you invoke ftp. This connects you to that system without the need of the **open** command. The login procedure then begins.

```
$ ftp garnet.berkeley.edu
Connected to garnet.berkeley.edu.
220 garnet.berkeley.edu FTP server (ULTRIX Version 4.1 Sun May 16
10:23:46 EDT 1996) ready.
Name (garnet.berkeley.edu:root):
```

To access a public ftp site, you have to perform an anonymous login. Instead of a login name, you enter the keyword **anonymous**. Then, for the password, you enter your Internet address. Once the ftp prompt is displayed, you are ready to transfer files. You may need to change to the appropriate directory first or set the transfer mode to binary. The following example is a complete ftp session in which the user performs an anonymous login and then downloads the Archie software package. The site access is the **sunsite.unc.edu** ftp site. After changing to the **/pub/Linux/system /Network/info-systems** directory, the user downloads the Archie software with the **get** command.

```
$ ftp sunsite.unc.edu
Connected to fddisunsite.oit.unc.edu.
220 helios FTP server (Version wu-2.4(39) Tue May 16 01:34:21 EDT
1996) ready.
```

```
Name (sunsite.unc.edu:root): anonymous
331 Guest login ok, send your complete e-mail address as password.
Password:
230 Guest login ok, access restrictions apply.
Remote system type is UNIX.
Using binary mode to transfer files.
ftp> cd  /pub/Linux/system/Network/info-systems
250 CWD command successful.
ftp> ls
200 PORT command successful.
150 Opening ASCII mode data connection for /bin/ls.
total 1130
drwxrwxr-x   4 67        1002        512 Jan 16 02:54 .
drwxr-xr-x  20 67        1002       1024 Sep  5  1995 ..
drwxr-xr-x   2 67        1002        512 Jul 21  1994 .cap
-rw-r--r--   1 67        1002        570 Jan 16 02:55 INDEX
-rw-r--r--   1 67        1002        586 Apr  8  1995
  archie-1.4.1.linux.lsm
-rw-r--r--   1 67        1002      24335 Apr  9  1995
  archie-1.4.1.linux.tar.gz
-rw-r--r--   1 67        1002     109147 Sep 25  1995
  archie-1.4.1.src.tar.gz
226 Transfer complete.
ftp> binary
200 Type set to I.
ftp> get archie-1.4.1.linux.tar.gz
200 PORT command successful.
150 Opening BINARY mode data connection for
  archie-1.4.1.linux.tar.gz (24335 bytes).
226 Transfer complete.
24335 bytes received in 7.87 secs (3 Kbytes/sec)
ftp> close
221 Good-bye.
ftp> quit
```

Once logged in, you can execute Linux commands on either the remote system or your local system. You execute a command on your local system in ftp by preceding the command with an exclamation point. Any Linux commands without an exclamation point are executed on the remote system. In the next example, the first command lists files in the remote system, and the second command lists files in the local system.

```
ftp> ls
ftp> !ls
```

There is one exception to this rule. Whereas you can change directories on the remote system with the **cd** command, to change directories on your local system, you need to use a special ftp command called **lcd** (local **cd**). In the next example, the first command changes directories on the remote system, and the second command changes directories on the local system.

```
ftp> cd
ftp> lcd
```

You close your connection to a system with the **close** command. You can then open another connection if you wish. To end the ftp session, use the **quit** or **bye** command.

```
ftp> close
ftp> bye
Good-bye
$
```

To transfer files to and from the remote system, use the **get** and **put** commands. The **get** command will receive files from the remote system to your local system, and the **put** command will send files from your local system to the remote system. In a sense, your local system **get**s files *from* the remote and **put**s files *to* the remote. In the next example, the file **weather** is sent from the local system to the remote system using the **put** command.

```
ftp> put weather
PORT command successful.
ASCII data connection
ASCII Transfer complete.
ftp>
```

You can transfer files in character mode or binary mode. The character mode is the default. The command **ascii** sets the character mode, and the command **binary** sets the binary mode. If you are transferring either programs or compressed files, be sure to set the binary mode first. A program is a binary file and must be transferred in binary mode. Most software packages available at Internet sites are archived and compressed files. These you will also have to download in binary mode. In the next example, the transfer mode is set to binary, and the archived software package **life.tar.gz** is sent from the remote system to your local system using the **get** command.

```
ftp> binary
ftp> get life.tar.gz
PORT command successful.
Binary data connection
Binary Transfer complete.
ftp>
```

Often you may want to send several files, specifying their names with special characters. **put** and **get**, however, operate only on a single file and do not work with special characters. To transfer several files at a time, you have to use two other commands, **mput** and **mget**. When you use **mput** or **mget**, you will be prompted for a file list. You can then either enter the list of files or a file-list specification using special characters. For example, ***.c** would specify all the files with a .c extension, and ***** would specify all files in the current directory. In the case of **mget**, each file will be sent, one by one, from the remote system to your local system. Each time, you will be prompted with the name of the file being sent. You can type **y** to send the file or **n** to cancel the transmission. You will then be prompted for the next file. The **mput** command works in the same way but sends files from your local system to the remote system. In the next example, all files with a .c extension are sent to your local system using **mget**.

```
ftp> mget
(remote-files) *.c
mget calc.c? y
PORT command successful
ASCII data connection
ASCII transfer complete
mget main.c? y
PORT command successful
ASCII data connection
ASCII transfer complete
ftp>
```

Archie

On the Internet there are a great many sites that are open to public access. They contain files that anyone can obtain using file transfer programs such as ftp. However, unless you already know where a file is located, it can be very difficult finding it. There are so many sites to check out. Archie is designed to search for files and tell you where they can be found. Once you know the site, you can use ftp to access it and download the file. You can think of Archie as an online index of all the files available at different Internet sites.

Archie has a database of all the file names and their sites that is updated monthly. Copies of this database are located at different Archie sites that operate as Archie servers. You can query these sites, searching for specific file names, and the Archie server will give you the results, listing different files and the sites where they reside.

You can access an Archie server either through an interactive telnet session or by using an Archie client installed on your own system. An Archie client will automatically access an Archie server for you, perform your query, and retrieve the results. Because of the potential demand on Archie, users are encouraged to use an Archie client if available, instead of interactively logging in. However, if you do not have an Archie client, you will have to telnet to an Archie server and perform your queries directly on that server. Because of demand, many Archie servers may limit the number of users that can access it at any one time, as well as the time a user can take making queries. Table 10-3 lists the options for an Archie client and the commands used for Archie servers.

Archie client software is not included with your Caldera Network Desktop. However, you can download it from the **ftp.mcgill.ca** ftp site or from **sunsite.unc.edu** and its mirror sites. At **sunsite.unc.edu**, Archie is currenly located in the directory **/pub/Linux/system/Network/info-systems**. The current Archie software package is named **archie-1.4.1.linux.tar.gz**. Once downloaded you unzip and extract it with **gunzip** and **tar xvf**. This creates a directory called **/archie-1.4.1** that holds the source code files (the previous ftp example shows an actual download of the Archie client software). You compile your Archie client by changing to that directory and entering the command **make**. This will create an Archie client program called **archie**. You then copy this Archie program to the **/bin** or **/usr/local/bin** directories. The **INSTALL** file holds more detailed instructions on how to create your Archie client program.

Archie Client

If your system has an Archie client, you can execute an Archie by entering the keyword **archie** followed by an option and a pattern. The pattern is then used to search for matching file names. Here is the syntax for an Archie command:

```
$ archie -option pattern
```

If you enter a pattern without an option, Archie treats the pattern as a full file name. In the next example, the user searches for a file with the file name **recipe**.

```
$ archie recipe
```

Different Archie options allow you to create more powerful queries. The options cannot be combined. Should you do so, only the last one will be used. The **-c** option will treat the pattern as an incomplete pattern and search for its occurrence anywhere in a file name. In the next example, the user searches for any file name with the pattern **recipe** in it. It will match on **recipe**, **cookie_recipe**, and **oldrecipes**.

```
$ archie -c recipe
```

The **-s** option performs the same kind of pattern search as a **-c** option but ignores case. It will match either upper- or lowercase versions of a pattern. In the next example, the user will match on file names such as **recipe**, **Recipe**, and **oldRecipes**.

```
$ archie -s recipe
```

The **-r** option allows you to use regular expressions. This means that you can use special characters to match on variations of a file name. Suppose, for example, that you want to make an exact search for a file name in which only the first character may or may not be capitalized. The regular expression **[Rr]ecipe** searches for file names beginning with either upper- or lowercase *r*: **recipe** or **Recipe**. Also, an **s*** placed at the end will search for file names with or without an ending *s*: **recipes** or **recipe**.

```
$ archie -r [Rr]ecipes*
```

Other options control Archie's output. The **-m** option followed by a number limits the number of matched items that are output. If you want to see only the first ten items, you can use **-m10**. The **-t** option will output items sorted by date, beginning with the most recent.

```
$ archie -m10 -t java

Host sun.rediris.es
    Location: /docs/faq/comp/lang
        DIRECTORY drwxr-xr-x          512   Mar 30 02:18   java

Host sunsite.rediris.es
```

```
    Location:/software/linux/distributions/jurix/source/networking/www
        DIRECTORY drwxr-xr-x        512  Mar  4 02:52  java
    Location: /software/linux/networking/net-sources/www
        DIRECTORY drwxr-xr-x        512  Mar  3 08:13  java

Host kobra.efd.lth.se
    Location: /pub/languages
        DIRECTORY drwxr-xr-x        512  Jan 24 13:51  java

Host sunsite.rediris.es
    Location: /software
        DIRECTORY drwxr-xr-x        512  Dec 13 17:36  java
```

To save your results you can redirect them to a file using the **-o** option with a file name. In the following example, the results of the Archie search are placed in a file named **javares**.

```
$ archie -m50 -t java -o javares
```

Archie Servers

Several Archie public servers are available on the Internet. Their addresses usually begin with the word "archie". For example, **archie.sura.net**, **archie.internic.net**, and **archie.doc.ic.ac.uk** are all popular Archie servers. Archie servers are located around the world, with several in the United States. You should only use an Archie server if, for some reason, you do not have access to an Archie client. On your own system you should install and use your Archie client. Archie servers are helpful if you have to perform a search, but you are using a system that has no Archie client.

To use an Archie server, you need to log into it first using telnet. When you are prompted for a login name, you enter the keyword **archie**. Once logged in, you will receive an Archie prompt: **archie>**. At the prompt you can execute searches or set parameters. You execute searches with the command **prog** followed by the string to search for. The following example searches for files with the file name **Linux**.

```
archie> prog Linux
```

As with the Archie client, you can qualify your search using regular expressions or a partial pattern match. To do so, you set the feature search to a specific option using the **set** command.

```
archie> set search option
```

The **rgex** option searches using a regular expression, and the **sub** option searches with a partial pattern. In the next example, the user searches for file names that contain the pattern "Linux".

```
archie> set search sub
archie> prog Linux
```

The following example uses a regular expression to perform a search. The regular expression **[Rr]ecipes*** searches for file names beginning with either upper- or lowercase *r* and ending with or without an *s*: **recipes** or **Recipe**.

```
archie> set search regex
archie> prog [Rr]ecipes*
```

In addition, you can set options that control your output. For example, you can limit the number of retrieved items by setting **maxhits**. The variable **sortby** is used to output items sorted on a specified field. You set a variable using the keyword **set** followed by the variable name and then the variable value. In the next example, the user limits the items output to ten and **sorts** the output by the name of the host.

```
archie> set maxhits 10
archie> set sortby hostname
```

Once you have finished your session, you can log out using the **quit** command.

```
archie> quit
```

An Internet User Interface: Gopher

Gopher is a user-friendly, menu-driven catalogue of Internet services and resources. It operates as a user interface for Internet services. Gopher combines the capabilities of telnet, ftp, and Archie, allowing you to browse through and select different available databases, files, and online information services. The Gopher interface uses a top-down menu system that moves from more general to more specific topics. You work your way down from one menu to another until you locate the item you want.

Gopher is designed to place at your fingertips information distributed throughout a network. It was originally created at the University of Minnesota to provide a campuswide distributed information service connecting different university departments. Each department maintained its own Gopher information server that anyone using a Gopher client could access. This distributed model was quickly adopted for use across the Internet to provide easy access to the numerous information services available there. Many universities maintain Gopher servers that can be used both within their campuses and across the Internet.

To access Gopher servers, you need to use a Gopher client program. The Gopher client provides a menu interface through which you make your requests and then carries out your requests, whether it be to connect to another service or transfer a file. There are several Gopher clients commonly available. Your Caldera CD-ROM has a copy of **xgopher**, an X-Windows-based Gopher client with buttons and drop-down menus that allow you to move through Gopher menus. You can also download the University of Minnesota line-based Gopher client from **boombox.micro.umn.edu** in the **/pub/gopher** directory ftp site. You can also obtain it as well from **sunsite.unc.edu** and its mirror sites in the **/pub/packages/info-systems/gopher /boombox/unix** directory. The current software package is named **gopher2_3.tar.gz**. You do not need X-Windows to run it and consequently it tends to be very fast. This client is part of a larger Gopher software package that includes a Gopher server, described in Chapter 12. When you decompress and extract this package, a directory called **gopher2_3** will be created. To create your Gopher client, change to this directory and execute the command **configure**. This detects your system configurations and creates makefiles tailored to it. You then enter the command **make client**. This will create your Gopher client program. The **INSTALL** file in the **/doc** directory has more detailed information about the installation procedure.

When you invoke the Gopher client, you can specify the Gopher server to access. The following example accesses the **gopher.tc.umn.edu** Gopher server.

```
$ gopher gopher.tc.umn.edu
```

The names of many Gopher servers begin with the word "gopher". If you do not specify a Gopher server, then the default server will be accessed. In this case you just enter the term **gopher** on the command line. You can determine the default server by pressing the **O** command once you have started your Gopher program. This will bring up an options menu from which you can configure your Gopher client. The options menu saves its information in a configuration file called **.gopherrc** that is kept in your home directory.

It is also possible to use telnet to access one of several available Gopher public clients such as **gopher.uiuc.edu**. Use telnet to access the server's address and log in using the first name of the address, usually **gopher**. As with Archie, it is strongly recommended that you use your own Linux system's Gopher client if possible.

Gopher Menus

A Gopher menu consists of a list of menu items that can represent files, other menus, databases, or telnet connections. Each type of item is indicated by a qualifier placed at the end of the entry. Items that are files end with a period qualifier. Items that are other menus end with a slash. Database items end with the symbols **<?>**. The qualifier **<CSO>** indicates a CSO nameserver used to search for user addresses and information. The **<TEL>** qualifier indicates a telnet connection. The **<Picture>**, **<Movie>**, and **<)** qualifiers reference images, video, and sound files, respectively. Figure 10-2 shows a Gopher menu.

When a Gopher menu is first displayed, an arrow will appear before the first menu item. You use the arrow to select the menu item you want. You move the arrow from one menu item to another by using the arrow keys on your keyboard. The UP ARROW moves the arrow up to the previous item, and the DOWN ARROW moves the arrow to the next item. The next example shows the top Gopher menu. The first three items have a / qualifier, indicating that these are other menus. The first item ends in a period, indicating that it is a text file. Notice the arrow placed before the first menu item.

Once you have positioned the arrow at the menu item you want, you can select and display the item by pressing ENTER. Alternatively, you could enter the number of

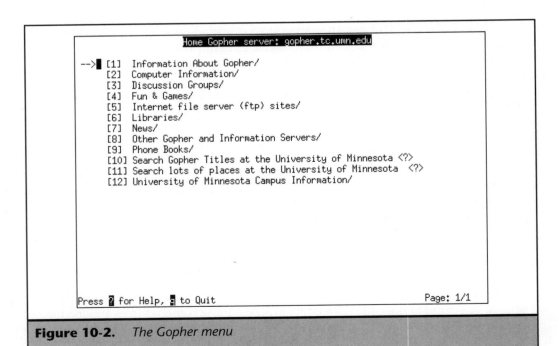

Figure 10-2. *The Gopher menu*

the menu item followed by pressing ENTER. You can continue moving from one menu to another until you find the item you want. Should you want to move back to a previous menu, you can press the **u** key. You can quit Gopher at any time by pressing the **q** key. Table 10-4 lists the Gopher commands.

A Gopher menu can be very lengthy, often consisting of many pages. To move to the next screen, you simply press the SPACEBAR. The **b** command moves you back to the previous screen in the menu. The number of the screen you are currently on, as well as the total number of screens in the menu, are displayed in the lower-right corner.

To locate an item, you could page through all the screens one by one, or you could use Gopher's menu item search capability. Gopher can perform a pattern search on the text of each menu item. To perform a search, you press the slash key, **/**. A box will open in the middle of the screen, prompting you to enter a search pattern. After you enter the pattern, you press ENTER to execute the search. The text of each menu item will be searched for the pattern. You can cancel the search at any time by pressing CTRL-**g**. Upon pressing ENTER, a search is made and the results displayed. You can continue searching through menus until you reach the item you want. To display the item, select it and press ENTER. Once you have displayed an item, Gopher will prompt you as to whether you want to save, mail, or print the information, or simply return to your last Gopher menu.

```
Press <RETURN> to continue, <m> to mail, <s> to save, or <p> to print:
```

The save option is the equivalent of an ftp operation. The file containing the information just displayed is transferred to your own account. Alternatively, you can simply mail information to yourself or to some other user who can then retrieve the information as a mail message. You could also simply print the information without saving it.

The xgopher client works much the same way with just a few differences. Instead of positioning an arrow, you can use your mouse to click on a menu item. A double-click will select an item. Buttons and drop-down menus move you back and forth through the Gopher menus. Figure 10-3 shows the xgopher client.

Using Gopher to Access Services

You can just as easily use Gopher to access information services such as online library catalogues. Such a service will be represented by a menu item qualified by a **<TEL>** at the end. When you choose the item, Gopher will telnet to the service for you. For example, you can use Gopher to log into the Library of Congress. First you select the Libraries menu from the Gopher menu. This brings up another Gopher menu listing possible online libraries that you can access. Select the item that brings up a Gopher menu for the Library of Congress. From this menu you can select the item that

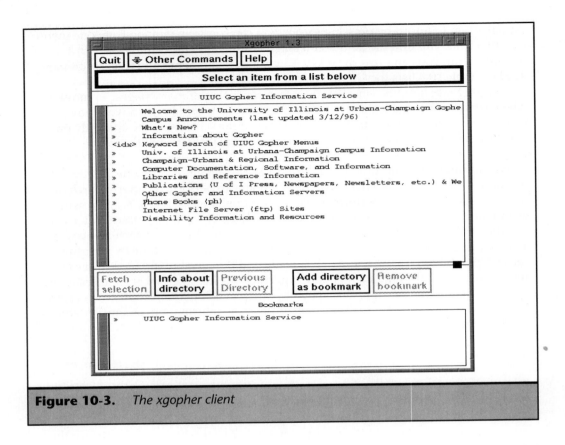

Figure 10-3. *The xgopher client*

displays another Gopher menu listing online systems. Notice that some of these items are files, others are yet more Gopher menus, and two are online information services as indicated with the **<TEL>** qualifier. You then select the item to connect to the Library of Congress online catalogue. The Gopher client then makes the telnet connection, warning you that you are now leaving Internet and Gopher and entering an online service.

Once logged into an online information service, you are operating according to whatever interface and commands that service provides. In the case of the Library of Congress, you are given a menu and asked to qualify your search. You can then perform searches using keywords and display the results. To end the session, you simply log off.

Gopher Bookmark Menu

As you search through Gopher for different items, you may want to save certain menus or menu items for later access. Say, for example, you follow the progress of the latest NASA shuttle mission over the next several days. Ordinarily, each time you need to access the Gopher menus on NASA, you would have to start from the top menu and work your way down. Instead, you could use the Gopher bookmark capability to place the NASA item in a special bookmark menu that you can access directly. In a sense, you can create your own customized Gopher menu.

You add a menu or menu item to your bookmark list using the **A** and **a** commands. The **A** command adds the whole menu you are currently displaying to your bookmark list. The lowercase **a** command adds a menu item that you have selected to your bookmark list. Having added the menu or menu item to your bookmark list, you can then access them in your bookmark menu. The bookmark list is used to generate a bookmark menu whose items consist of those in the bookmark list. You then access the bookmark menu with the **v** command.

In the case of the NASA example, as shown in Figure 10-4, the user only needs to locate it once in the Gopher menus and then add it to the bookmark list using the **A** or **a** command. Whenever the user wants to access the NASA item, he or she displays the bookmark menu and selects the NASA menu item displayed there.

You can add as many items to your bookmark list as you wish. In Figure 10-5, the user has added the weather report for San Francisco to the bookmark menu. The user first located the weather report for San Francisco by moving through several menus, starting with the News menu. From the News menu, the user moved to the National Weather Service Forecasts menu, which lists states. The user chose California and

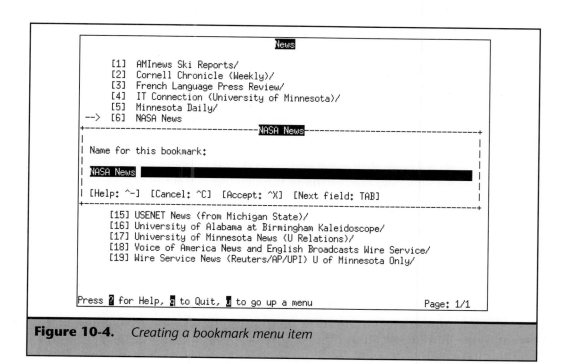

Figure 10-4. *Creating a bookmark menu item*

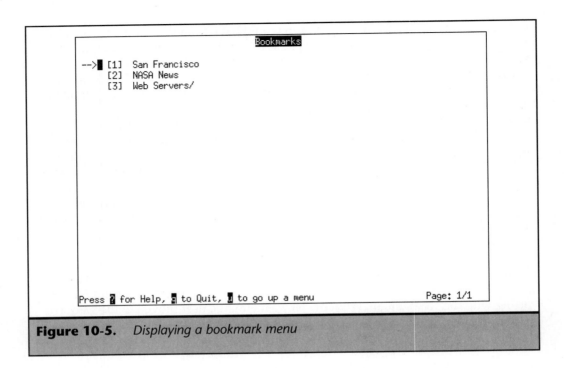

Figure 10-5. *Displaying a bookmark menu*

moved to the California menu, which lists the cities in California. Finally, the user moved the arrow to the item for San Francisco. The user then pressed the **a** key to add the San Francisco menu item to his or her bookmark menu. A box opened up in the middle of the screen with a prompt for the name this menu item will have in the bookmark menu. The name of the selected menu item is already displayed as the default name, in this case, San Francisco. The user then added the word "Weather," making the name of this new menu item in the bookmark menu "San Francisco Weather." Now, to find the weather for San Francisco, the user only needs to press the **v** key to bring up the bookmark menu and select the menu item San Francisco Weather. The user no longer needs to move through the long series of menus from News, to Forecasts, to State, and finally to City.

When you no longer need to access an item or menu in your bookmark list directly, use the **d** command to remove it. For example, once the user no longer needs to access the NASA menu item, he or she can simply delete it from the bookmark menu by selecting it and pressing the **d** key.

Just as you can save items, you can also save entire menus in your bookmark list. You add a menu to your bookmark list using the **A** command. The **A** command adds the whole menu you are currently displaying to your bookmark menu. Say, for example, you are going to be referencing weather reports for cities in California over the next several weeks. You could use the Gopher bookmark capability to place the

California weather report menu as an item in your bookmark menu. Whenever you need to access the California weather report menu, you display your bookmark menu and select the California weather menu item displayed there.

Such a feature is particularly useful in saving the results of Archie searches made through Gopher. In the main Gopher menu, the item for ftp searches allows you to perform an Archie search for files that you can then have downloaded to your account. The result of the search is listed as another Gopher menu. Each menu item is a file located on an anonymous ftp server. Selecting such a menu item will instruct Gopher to access the ftp server and transfer the file to your system.

The Gopher menu that results from such Archie searches is temporary. Should you want to save it for further use and reference, you need to place it in your bookmark menu. Simply give the **A** command when displaying this Gopher menu, and it will be added to your bookmark menu. You can then use your bookmark menu to access this menu containing your Archie search results.

Veronica

Resources on a given topic can be widely dispersed through the Internet. You could end up having to search, one by one, for each resource on a given topic, working through different Gopher menus each time. The Veronica utility was designed to streamline this process. Veronica will search all Gopher menus for menu items, using keywords provided by the user. Veronica will then generate a customized menu consisting of all the menu items it has found. In effect, with Veronica, you can create temporary Gopher menus on specialized topics. You can then select the menu item you want, just as you would on any standard Gopher menu.

To use Veronica, you first need to access the Veronica menu on Gopher. The Veronica menu lists different Veronica servers that you can use to search Gopher menus. The second and third menu items provide more information about Veronica. The first menu item is always empty. There is a **<?>** qualifier at the end of each server menu item, indicating a database to be queried by keywords. Select a server and press ENTER. A box will open up in the middle of the screen, prompting you to enter keywords for the search. Upon pressing ENTER, Veronica performs the search. The result is a customized Gopher menu consisting of all the menu items Veronica was able to locate. You can then move to the menu item you want and select it. If you want to know where exactly a menu item comes from, you can simply move to the menu item and press = to display information about it.

Though the menus generated by Veronica are temporary, you can save a menu by adding it as an item to your bookmark list. While displaying your Veronica-generated menu, give the **A** command to add it to your bookmark list. You can then later access the menu through your bookmark menu, which you display with the **v** command. You can save as many Veronica searches as you want, making them items in your bookmark menu. You can also save particular items in your Veronica-generated menu by selecting the items one by one and giving the lowercase **a** command.

WAIS

WAIS (Wide Area Information Servers) is an information service designed to search available databases on the Internet. Throughout the Internet there are many WAIS databases, which consist of articles covering such diverse topics as movies and programming. A WAIS database is any collection of documents that have been indexed using WAIS indexing software. WAIS servers set up indexes that can be used to search documents.

To search WAIS databases, you use either a WAIS client utility such as **waisq**, **swais,** or **xwais**, or a Web Browser such as Netscape. **waisq** uses a simple command line interface. **swais** provides a full-screen interface. **xwais** is designed for X-Windows interfaces. The **swais** commands and options are listed in Table 10-5. A WAIS client allows you to select a WAIS database and perform searches using complex Boolean queries. The results are then listed and numbered. You then choose the number of the article in this list that you want. This will display the article, and you can save or print it. You can also use your Web browser to access WAIS sites such as **www.wais.com**. There, you can perform searches on many different topics or move to other WAIS sites.

Unlike searches in other information services, WAIS both performs full text searches of database articles and ranks its results. WAIS searches the entire text of each article, not just the article title or a predetermined list of index words. In this respect, the content of each article is examined, providing a more comprehensive search. The results of a WAIS search are ranked from 0 to 1,000, beginning with those articles that best respond to the search having the highest scores. You can use these results to further expand or narrow your search.

If you want to use a WAIS client, you will have to first download it and install it. These are complete packages that include the WAIS server, an indexer, as well as both **swais** and **xwais** clients. A free version of WAIS called freeWAIS has been made available by the Clearinghouse for Network Information Discovery and Retrieval (CNIDR). Their Web site at **ftp.cnidr.org** has a Linux version of freeWAIS already compiled and ready to use. You can also download the source code and compile it yourself. freeWAIS is also available at **sunsite.unc.edu** and its mirror sites in the **/pub/packages/info-systems/wais** directory.

To directly access WAIS databases, you need to install WAIS source files onto your system. A WAIS source file contains the Internet address of a WAIS database as well as information about it. A source file has the extension **.src** and should be placed in your **/usr/lib/wais-sources** directory. You may have to create this directory. You can obtain a set of WAIS source files for commonly accessed WAIS databases from **sunsite.unc.edu**.

In the **/pub/packages/info-systems/wais** directory, first locate and download the file **wais-servers.tar.Z.**, then place this file in the **/usr/lib/wais-sources** directory. Decompress and extract the file with **gunzip** and **tar**. A large number of WAIS source files will be extracted. One in particular, called the **directory-of-servers.src**, references the WAIS server at **quake.think.com**, which holds the main directory of WAIS servers. The next time you start up **swais** you will be presented with a long list of databases to choose from. Each of these databases has its own WAIS source file in **/usr/lib/wais-sources**. Press the / key to search the database names or use the arrow keys to move from one to another. Once you have found the one you want, press ENTER to select it. You can choose everything from artworks in the Smithsonian to kitchen recipes.

You can also create your own WAIS database using the freeWAIS server software. You can then set up a collection of documents, index them, and make them available for searching by other users on the Internet. The freeWAIS server software is described in Chapter 12.

Summary: Accessing the Internet

Linux has a set of Internet tools that you can use to locate and access information sites on the Internet. With telnet you can remotely log into another computer connected on the Internet. For example, you could directly connect to the online catalogue for the Library of Congress and perform queries on it. With ftp you can download files from an ftp site to your own computer. With Archie you can find out where certain files may be located. Gopher combines all these features into a powerful and easy-to-use interface for browsing the Internet. Information is organized into a series of menus that you can move through until you find the information you want. Finally, you can use WAIS for comprehensive searches on a variety of databases.

telnet Command mode	Effect
-d	Sets the debug toggle to TRUE
-a	Attempts automatic login using USER variable as set by ENVIRON option
-n *tracefile*	Opens *tracefile* for recording trace information
-l *user*	Connects to a remote system with user as the login name
-e escape char	Sets telnet escape character
telnet Command Mode	
close	Closes a telnet session and returns to command mode
open *host* [[-l] *user*][-port]	Opens a connection to the specified host

Table 10-1. *telnet Options and Commands*

telnet Command mode	Effect
quit	Closes any open telnet session and exits telnet
! *command*	Executes a Linux command
status	Shows the current status of telnet
? *command*	With no arguments, displays a help summary; if a command is specified, displays the information for that command
set *variable value* **unset** *variable value*	Sets different telnet variables; see **man** pages for a complete list
toggle arguments ...	Toggles different flags between true and false; see **man** pages for complete list of flags

Table 10-1. *telnet Options and Commands* (continued)

Command	Effect
ftp	Invokes ftp program
open	Opens a connection to another system
close	Closes connection to a system
quit or **bye**	Ends ftp session
get *filename*	Sends file from remote system to local system
put *filename*	Sends file from local system to remote system
mget *regular-expression*	Allows you to download several files at once from a remote system; you can use special characters to specify the files; you will be prompted one by one for each file transfer in turn
mput *regular-expression*	Allows you to send several files at once to a remote system; you can use special characters to specify the files; you will be prompted one by one for each file to be transferred

Table 10-2. *ftp Commands*

Command	Effect
`binary`	Transfers files in binary mode
`ascii`	Transfers files in ascii mode
`cd` *directory*	Changes directories on the remote system
`lcd` *directory*	Changes directories on the local system
`help` or `?`	Lists ftp commands

Table 10-2. *ftp Commands (continued)*

Archie Client Option	Description/Effect
`archie` *options search-string*	
`-e`	Exact pattern match (default)
`-c`	Searches file names for occurrence of pattern
`-s`	Searches file names ignoring case
`-r`	Pattern is a regular expression
`-t`	Sorts the results by date
`-l`	Outputs results as a record that can be parsed by programs
`-o` *filename*	Places result of search in *filename*
`-h` *hostname*	Queries the hostname Archie server
`-m`*num*	Limits the maximum number of results (matches)
`-N`*num*	Estimates number of results of a query (default 0)
`-L`	Lists the known Archie servers
-V	Verbose option; Archie notifies user of progress in long searches

Table 10-3. *Archie Commands*

Public Server Commands	Description/Effect
prog	Searches file names for occurrence of pattern
list	Lists the known Archie servers
site	Lists files at a particular host
mail	Mails results of search
quit	Logs out of Archie server
help	Displays help
set *variable value*	Sets Archie variables
show	Displays current values of Archie variables
unset	Removes variables

Server Variables

autologout *num*	Number of minutes that Archie waits idle before automatically logging you out of the Archie server; the default is usually 15 minutes **set autologout** 10
mailto *address*	Mail address to which results are sent **set mailto richpete@garnet.berkeley.edu**
maxhits *num*	Limits the maximum number of results (matches) **set maxhits** 10
pager	Uses the default pager utility, such as More, to display your results **set pager** **unset pager**

search *option*	Type of search
	set search subcase
	  search options
	  sub Pattern search within file names
	  subcase Pattern search that distinguishes between upper- and lowercase
	  exact Exact pattern match
	  regex Uses regular expressions

Table 10-3.   *Archie Commands* (continued)

Server Variables	Description/Effect
sortby *option*	Type of sort for output
	set sortby *filename*
	sortby options
	none No sort
	filename Sorts the results alphabetically by file name
	hostname Sorts the results by hostname
	time Sorts the results from most recent date
	size Sorts the results from largest size
	rfilename Reverses alphabetical file name sort
	rhostname Reverses alphabetical hostname sort
	rtime Sorts the results from oldest date
	rsize Sorts the results from smallest size
status	Issues status reports on searches as they are performed
	set status
	unset status
term *terminal-id*	Type of terminal you are using
	set term vt100

Table 10-3. *Archie Commands* (continued)

Option	Effect
gopher [**-sb**] [**-t** *title*] [**-p** *path*] [*hostname port*]	
-p *string*	Specifies a selector string to send to the root-level server on startup
-t *string*	Sets the title of the initial screen for the Gopher client
Menu Item Qualifiers	
.	File
/	Menu
<CSO>	CSO nameserver

Table 10-4. *Gopher Commands*

Menu Item Qualifiers	Effect
`<TEL>`	telnet connection
`<Picture>`	Graphic, such as gif or jpeg
`<)`	Sound file
`<Move>`	Video, such as mov or avi
`<HTML>`	Hypertext document
`<Bin>`	Binary file
`<HCX>`	Macintosh BinHexed file
`<PC Bin>`	DOS binary file
`<MIME>`	Multipurpose Internet Mail extensions file
`<?>`	Database with keyword search
Moving to and Selecting Menu Items	
k and UP ARROW	Moves up to previous menu item
j and DOWN ARROW	Moves down to next menu item
num	Moves to *num* item in menu
l, RIGHT ARROW, ENTER	Press one of these to select the current menu item
Searching a Menu for an Item	
/ *pattern*	Searches menu items for pattern and moves to first item with that pattern
n	Repeats previous search of menu items
Operations Performed on Menu Items	
=	Displays information about a menu item
s	Saves the current item to a file
m	Mails the current item to a user
p	Prints the current item

Table 10-4. *Gopher Commands* (continued)

Moving Through Menu Screens	Effect
>, +, SPACEBAR	Moves to next menu screen
<, -, b	Moves back to previous menu screen
Return to Previous Menus	
u, .	Moves back to previous menu
m	Returns to top main menu
Bookmark Commands	
a	Adds selected item to bookmark list
A	Adds current menu to bookmark list
d	Removes a bookmark from the bookmark list
v	Displays bookmark list
Options, Quit, and Help Commands	
q	Quits Gopher
Q	Quits Gopher without prompt
?	Help
O	Displays and changes options for Gopher
Environment Variables	
PAGER	Client will use that to display files to the user
GOPHER_MAIL	Program to send mail (must understand -s option)
GOPHER_PLAY	Program to play sound
GOPHER_TELNET	Program to contact telnet services
GOPHER_HTML	Program to display HTML documents
GOPHER_PRINTER	Program to print from a pipe

Table 10-4. *Gopher Commands* (continued)

Option	Description/Effect
-s *sourcename*	Selects *sourcename* for search; sources are discussed in Chapter 12
-S *sourcedir*	Specifies a source directory; default is ~/**wais-sources**
-C *sourcedir*	Specifies a common source directory; default is **/usr/lib/wais-sources**
-h	Help message

Command

Command	
j, DOWN ARROW, **^N**	Moves down one source
k, UP ARROW, **^P**	Moves up one source
J, **^V**, **^D**	Moves down one screen
K, ESC **v**, **^U**	Moves up one screen
###	Position to source number ###
/sss	Searches for source *sss*
SPACEBAR, **.** (period)	Selects current source
=	Deselects all sources
v, **,** (comma)	Views current source info
<ret>	Performs search
s	Selects new sources (refresh sources list)
w	Selects new keywords
X, **-**	Removes current source permanently
o	Sets and shows **swais** options
h, **?**	Shows this help display
H	Displays program history
q	Leaves this program

Table 10-5.   *WAIS Client Commands*

Chapter Eleven

The World Wide Web

The World Wide Web (WWW) is a hypertext database of different types of information distributed across many different sites on the Internet. A hypertext database consists of items that are linked to other items, that in turn may be linked to yet other items, and so on. Upon retrieving an item, you can then use that item to retrieve any related items. For example, you could retrieve an article on the Amazon rain forest and then use it to retrieve a map of the rain forest or a picture of the rain forest. In this respect, a hypertext database is like a web of interconnected data that you can trace from one data item to another. Information is displayed in pages known as Web pages. On a Web page certain keywords are highlighted that form links to other Web pages or to items such as pictures, articles, or files.

The World Wide Web links data across different sites on the Internet throughout the world. It is often referred to as WWW or simply as the Web. The World Wide Web originated in Europe at CERN research laboratories. CERN remains the original WWW server. An Internet site that operates as a Web server is known as a Web site. Such Web sites are often dedicated to specialized topics or institutions, for example, the Smithsonian Web site or the NASA Web site. These Web sites usually have an Internet address that begins with www, as in **www.caldera.com**, the Web site for Caldera. Once connected to a Web site, you can use hypertext links to move from one Web page to another.

To access the Web you use a client program called a Browser. There are many different Web Browsers to choose from. There are Browsers available for use on Unix, Windows, the Mac, and for Linux. Certain Browsers, such as Netscape and Mosaic, have versions that operate on all such systems. On your Linux system you can choose from several Web Browsers. Your Caldera Network Desktop comes with a trial version of the Netscape Browser, the most popular Browser currently in use. Netscape is already installed on your system and is accessible from your desktop. In addition to Netscape, you have the Lynx Browser. This is a line-mode Browser that displays only lines of text. You can download several other Browsers to your system at no charge. For example, Mosaic and Arena are X-Windows-based Browsers that provide full picture, sound, and video display capabilities. Both are available under a free public license.

URL Addresses

An Internet resource is accessed using a Universal Resource Locator (URL), shown in Figure 11-1. A URL is composed of three elements: the transfer protocol, the hostname, and the path name. The transfer protocol and hostname are separated by a colon and two slashes, `://`. The path name always begins with a single slash.

```
transfer-protocol://host-name/path-name
```

The transfer protocol is usually **http** (HyperText Transfer Protocol), indicating a Web page. Other possible transfer protocols are **gopher**, **ftp**, and **file**. As their

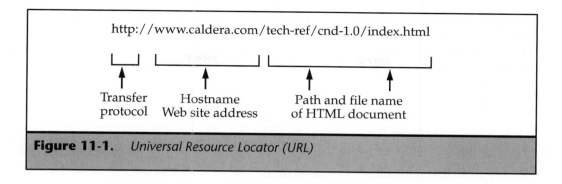

Figure 11-1.   *Universal Resource Locator (URL)*

names suggest, **gopher** and **ftp** initiate Gopher and ftp sessions. **file** displays a text or a directory file, as well as an HTML file. Table 11-1 lists the various transfer protocols.

The hostname is the computer that a particular Web site is located on. You can think of this as the address of the Web site. By convention most hostnames begin with www. In the next example, the URL locates a Web page called **toc.html** on the **home.netscape.com** Web site.

```
http://home.netscape.com/toc.html
```

If you do not want to access a particular Web page, you can leave it out, and you will automatically access the Web site's home page. To access a Web site directly, you can just use its hostname. The default name for a Web site's home page is **index.html**, located in the site's top directory. A Web site can override the default and specify a particular file as the home page. However, if no file is specified, the **index.html** file is taken to be the home page. In the next example, the user brings up the Caldera home page.

```
http://www.caldera.com/
```

The path name specifies the directory where the resource can be found on the host system, as well as the name of the resource's file. For example, **/pub/Linux/newdat.html** references an HTML document called **newdat** located in the **/pub/Linux** directory. As you move to other Web pages on a site you may move more deeply into the directory tree. In the following example, the user accesses the **faq.html** document in the directory **/tech-ref/cnd-1.0/faq**.

```
http://www.caldera.com/tech-ref/cnd-1.0/faq/faq.html
```

As just explained, should you specify a directory path name without a particular Web page file, your Web Browser will look for a file called **index.html** in that directory. An **index.html** file in a directory operates as the default Web page for that directory. In the next example, the **index.html** Web page in the **/tech-ref/cnd-1.0** directory is displayed.

```
http://www.caldera.com/tech-ref/cnd-1.0/index.html
```

You can use this technique to access local Web pages on your system. For example, once installed, the demo Web pages for Java are located in **/usr/local/java/**. Since it is on your local system you do not need to include a hostname. There is an **index.html** page in the **/usr/local/java/** directory that will be automatically displayed when you specify the directory path. You can do the same for your system documentation, which is in Web-page format located in the **/usr/doc/HTML/ldp** directory.

```
file:/usr/local/java
file:/usr/doc/HTML/ldp
```

If you reference a directory that has no **index.html** file, the Web server will create one for you, and your Browser will then display it. This index will simply list the different files and directories in that directory. You can click on an entry to display a file or move to another directory. The first entry will be a special entry for the parent directory.

The resource file's extension indicates the type of action to be taken on it. A picture will have a **.gif** or **.jpeg** extension and will be converted for display. A sound file will have a **.au** or **.wav** extension and will be played. The following URL references a **gif** file. Instead of displaying a Web page, your Browser will invoke a graphics viewer to display the picture. Table 11-2 provides a list of the different file extensions.

```
http://www.train.com/engine/engine1.gif
```

Web Pages

A Web page is a specially formatted document that can be displayed by any Web Browser. You can think of a Web page as a word processing document that can display both text and graphics. Within the Web page, links can be embedded that call up other Internet resources. An Internet resource can be a graphic, a file, a telnet connection, or even another Web page. The Web page acts as an interface for accessing different Internet tools, such as ftp, to download files, or telnet, to connect to an online catalog or other remote service.

When you first start your desktop, you will notice the Caldera Info icon displayed, as shown here. This is the icon that your desktop uses to display HTML pages.

Web pages display both text and graphics. Text is formatted with paragraphs and can be organized with different headings. Graphics of various sizes may be placed anywhere in the page. Throughout the page there will usually be anchor points that you can use to call up other Internet resources. Each anchor point is associated with a particular Internet resource. One anchor point may reference a picture, another a file; others may reference other Web pages or even other Web sites. These anchor points are specially highlighted text or graphics that usually appear in a different color from the rest of the text. Whereas ordinary text may be black, text used for anchor points may be green, blue, or red. You select a particular anchor point by moving your mouse pointer to that text or picture and then clicking on it. The Internet resource associated with that anchor point will then be called up. If it is a picture, the picture will be displayed. If it is another Web page, that Web page is displayed. If the Internet resource is on another Web site, that site will be accessed. The color of an anchor point indicates its status and the particular Web Browser you are using. Both Mosaic and Netscape use blue for anchors that you have not yet accessed. Netscape uses purple for anchors you have already accessed, and Mosaic uses red. All these colors can be overridden by a particular Web page.

Your Web Browser will keep a list of the different Web pages that you accessed for each session. You will be able to move back and forth easily in that list. Having called up another Web page, you can use your Browser to move back to the previous one. Web Browsers construct their lists according to the sequence in which you displayed your Web pages. They keep track of the Web pages you are accessing, whatever they may be. However, on many Web sites, several Web pages are meant to be connected in a particular order, like chapters in a book. Such pages usually have buttons displayed at the bottom of the page that reference the next and previous pages in the sequence. Clicking on the Next button will display the next Web page for this site. The Home button will return you to the first page for this sequence.

Web Browsers

Most Web Browsers are designed to access several different kinds of information. They can access a Web page on a remote Web site or a file on your own system. Some Browsers can also access a remote news server or an ftp site. The type of information for a site is specified by the keyword **http** for Web sites, **nntp** for news servers, **ftp** for ftp sites, and **file** for files on your own system.

To access a Web site you enter **http://** followed by the Internet address of the Web site. If you know a particular Web page you want to access on that Web site, you can add the path name for that page, attaching it to the Internet address. Then simply press ENTER. The Browser will connect you to that Web site and display its home page or the page you specified.

You can just as easily use a Web Browser to display Web pages on your own system by entering the term **file** followed by a colon, **file:**, with the path name of the Web page you want to display. You do not specify an Internet site. Remember, all Web pages have the extension **.html**. Links within a Web page on your own system can connect you to other Web pages on your system or to Web pages on remote systems. When you first start a Web Browser on your Caldera Network Desktop, your Browser displays a local Web page on your own system that has links to the Caldera Web site where you can obtain online support. If you wish, you can create your own Web pages, with their own links, and make one of them your default Web page.

Web pages on a Web site will often contain links to other Web pages, some on the same site and others at other Web sites. Through these links you can move from one page to another. As you move from Web page to Web page, using the anchor points or buttons, your Browser will display the URL for the current page. Your Browser keeps a list of the different Web pages you have accessed in a given session. Most Browsers have buttons that allow you to move back and forth through this list. You can move to the Web page you displayed before the current one, and then move back further to the one before that. You can move forward again to the next page and so on.

To get to a particular page you may have moved through a series of pages, using links in each to finally reach the Web page you want. To access any Web page, all you need is its URL address. If you want to access a particular page again, you can enter in its URL address and move directly to it, without moving through the intervening pages as you did the first time. Instead of writing down the URL addresses and entering them yourself, most Web Browsers can keep a hotlist—a list of favorite Web pages you want to access directly. When you are displaying a Web page you want to access later, just instruct your Browser to place it on the hotlist. The Web page will usually be listed in the hotlist by its title, not its URL. To access that Web page later, select the entry in the hotlist.

Most Web Browsers can also access ftp and Gopher sites. You may find that using a Web Browser to access an ftp site is easier than using the ftp utility. Directories and files are automatically listed, and selecting a file or directory is just a matter of clicking on its name. First enter **ftp://** and the Internet address of the ftp site. The contents of a directory will be displayed, listing files and subdirectories. To move to another directory, just click on it. To download a file, click on its name. You will see an entry listed as **..**, representing the parent directory. You can move down the file structure from one subdirectory to another and move back up one directory at a time by selecting **..**. To leave the ftp site, just return to your own home page. You can also use your Browser to access Gopher sites. Enter **gopher://** followed by the Internet address of the Gopher site. Your Web Browser will display the main Gopher menu for that site. You can then move from one Gopher menu to the next.

Most Browsers can connect to your news server to access specified newsgroups or articles. This is a local operation, accessing the news server you are already connected to. You enter **nntp** followed by a colon and the newsgroup or news article. Some Browsers, such as Netscape, have an added Newsreader Browser that allows them to access any remote news servers.

As noted previously, there are several popular Browsers available for Linux. Four distinctive ones are described here; the Netscape Navigator, Mosaic, Arena, and Lynx. Netscape and Mosaic are X-Windows-based Web Browsers capable of displaying graphics, video, and sound, as well as operating as newsreaders and mailers. Arena is a Browser designed to support the development of new features of HTML 3, the Markup language that Web pages are written in. Lynx is a command line-based Browser with no graphics capabilities. But in every other respect it is a fully functional Web Browser. Arena and Lynx are both provided with your Caldera Lite Network Desktop. You can easily download and install versions of Netscape and Mosaic. You can also download more recent versions of Arena and Lynx. Netscape is a commercial product available for a 90-day free trial. Mosaic, Arena, and Lynx are all free of charge.

Netscape Navigator

Hypertext databases are designed to access any kind of data, whether it is text, graphics, sound, or even video. Whether you can actually access such data depends to a large extent on the type of Browser you use. One of the more popular Web Browsers is the Netscape Navigator. Versions of Netscape operate on different graphical user interfaces such as X-Windows, Microsoft Windows, and the Macintosh. Using X-Windows, the Netscape Browser can display graphics, sound, video, and Java-based programs (you will learn about Java a little later in the chapter). You can obtain more information about Netscape on its Web site: **www.netscape.com**.

To obtain a copy of Netscape, you need to download it from a Netscape ftp site. There are several ftp sites for Netscape, as well as many mirror sites that also carry it. The address of the Netscape ftp site is **ftp2.netscape.com**. Other sites are **ftp3.netscape.com** through **ftp8.netscape.com**. If these sites are busy, a list of alternative mirror sites will be displayed for you to access. The current version of the Netscape Navigator for Linux is **netscape-v201-export.i486-unknown-linux**, usually located in the **pub/navigator/2.01/unix** directory. The **pub/navigator** directory will hold more recent beta versions of the Netscape Navigator for you to choose from. If you are not sure what directory the Linux version of the Netscape Browser is kept in, you can use **ls** within ftp to display the files and directories of the current directory, and then use **cd** to move through the directory structure until you find it. The Linux version is usually located within a directory called **unix**. Be sure to download the file in binary mode.

```
# ftp ftp4.netscape.com
Connected to ftp4.netscape.com.
220 ftp4 FTP server (Version wu-2.4(3) Tue Dec 27 17:53:56 PST 1994) ready.
```

```
Name (ftp4.netscape.com:root): anonymous
331 Guest login ok, send your complete e-mail address as password.
Password:

230 Guest login ok, access restrictions apply.
Remote system type is UNIX.
Using binary mode to transfer files.
ftp> cd pub/navigator/2.01/unix
250 CWD command successful.
ftp> ls
200 PORT command successful.
150 Opening ASCII mode data connection for /bin/ls.
total 97455
drwxr-xr-x    2 999        995             1024 Mar 14 03:05 .
drwxr-xr-x    6 999        995              512 Mar 14 03:05 ..
-rw-r--r--    1 999        995             1298 Mar 14 00:01 .message
-rw-r--r--    1 999        995            12905 Mar  9 15:29 LICENSE
-rw-r--r--    1 999        995             8726 Mar  9 15:29 README
-rw-r--r--    1 999        995          1648574 Mar 10 02:59
netscape-v201-export.i386-unknown-bsd.tar.gz
-rw-r--r--    1 999        995          2813035 Mar 10 04:08
netscape-v201-export.i486-unknown-linux.tar.Z
-rw-r--r--    1 999        995          2025581 Mar 10 04:07
netscape-v201-export.i486-unknown-linux.tar.gz
-rw-r--r--    1 999        995          2152042 Mar 10 03:10
netscape-v201-export.sparc-sun-solaris2.3.tar.gz
226 Transfer complete.
ftp> binary
200 Type set to I.
ftp> get netscape-v201-export.i486-unknown-linux.tar.gz
200 PORT command successful.
150 Opening BINARY mode data connection for
netscape-v201-export.i486-unknown-linux.tar.gz (2025581 bytes).
226 Transfer complete.
2025581 bytes received in 634 secs (3.1 Kbytes/sec)
ftp> close
221 Good-bye.
ftp> quit
#
```

Once you have downloaded the Netscape file, you place it in the directory you want to start it from, such as **/usr/local**. Notice that the Netscape file ends in **.tar.gz**. This is a gzip compressed and tar archived file. You first use **gunzip** to decompress the file. Then it will only have a **.tar** extension. Next use **tar** to generate the Netscape program files.

```
# gunzip netscape-v201-export.i486-unknown-linux.tar.gz
# tar xvf netscape-v201-export.i486-unknown-linux.tar
README
LICENSE
netscape
Netscape.ad
(continues list of package files)
#
```

Once you have generated your Netscape Browser, you are ready to use it. Netscape Navigator is an X-Windows application that you have operated from your desktop. If you haven't done so already, start your desktop with the **startx** command. Then use a directory window to open the directory you placed Netscape Navigator in. Find the Netscape icon and double-click on it. You may want to move the Netscape icon onto the desktop for easy access. The Netscape Navigator icon looks like this:

Netscape Navigator displays an area at the top of the screen for entering a URL address and a series of buttons for various Web page operations (see Figure 11-2). Drop-down menus provide access to Netscape features. To access a Web site, you enter its address in the URL area and press ENTER.

The icon bar, shown in Figure 11-3, across the top of the Browser, holds buttons for moving from one page to another and performing other operations. The Back-arrow and Forward-arrow buttons move you back and forth through the list of Web pages you have already accessed in a given session. The Home button (picture of house) exits a Web site and places you back in your own system. There is also a Stop button, in the form of a stop sign, that becomes active when you are linking to and displaying a new Web page. If the Web page is taking too long to display, you may want to click on the Stop button to stop the process.

Netscape refers to the URLs of Web pages you want to keep in a hotlist as bookmarks, marking pages you want to access directly. The Bookmarks menu lets you add your favorite Web pages to a hotlist. You can then view your bookmarks and select one to move to.

Through the Mail item in the Windows menu you can open a fully functional mail client with which you can send and receive messages over the Internet. The News item, also in the Windows menu, opens a fully functional newsreader with which you

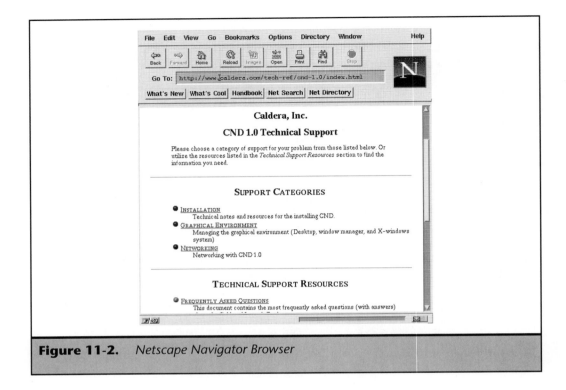

Figure 11-2. *Netscape Navigator Browser*

can read and post articles in Usenet newsgroups. In this respect, your Netscape Navigator is more than just a Web Browser. It is also a Mail program and a newsreader.

Other items in the Windows menu enhance your Web Browser operations. In the address book you can keep a list of Web site URLs. The Bookmark item lets you edit your list of bookmarks, adding new ones or removing old ones. The History item is a list of previous URLs you have accessed. If you want to go back to a Web page that you did not save as a bookmark, you can find it in the history list. You can then use Netscape to receive and send mail as well as access Usenet newsgroups.

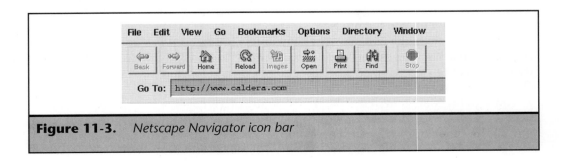

Figure 11-3. *Netscape Navigator icon bar*

The Options menu in the Netscape Navigator lets you set several different kinds of preferences for your Browser. You can set preferences for mail and news, the network, and security, as well as general preferences. In general preferences you can determine your home page and how you want the toolbar displayed. For mail and news you can enter the mail and news servers you use on the Internet. Netscape can be set to access any number of news servers that you subscribe to and that use the NNTP transfer protocols. You can switch from one news server to another if you wish.

If you are on a network that connects to the Internet through a firewall, you will have to use the Proxies screen to enter the address of your network's firewall gateway computer. A *firewall* is a computer that operates as a controlled gateway to the Internet for your network. There are several types of firewalls. One of the most restrictive uses programs called *proxies* that receive Internet requests from users and then makes those requests on their behalf. There is no direct connection to the Internet. From the Options menu select Network, then choose the Proxies screen. Here, enter the IP address of your network's firewall gateway computer.

To save a Web page, select the Save As entry in the File menu. This opens a dialog box with a default directory specified. There are three boxes. The top box is for a filter. The bottom box is the name of the file. The middle box lists different directories in the current directory. You can enter a path and file name of your own, or you can click on the . . entry in the middle box to move back through the directory tree, and then click on directory names to move into those directories. When you have reached the directory you want, you can save your Web page.

Mosaic

Mosaic, which can display graphics, sound, and video data, was the first graphics-based Browser developed for the Web. Unlike Netscape, it is available free to anyone. There are versions of Mosaic for different graphical user interfaces such as X-Windows, Microsoft Windows, and the Macintosh. It was developed by the National Center for Supercomputing Applications (NCSA) at the University of Illinois at Urbana-Champaign. More information about Mosaic is available at the NCSA Web site: **www.ncsa.uiuc.edu**. You can download a copy of Mosaic from the Mosaic ftp site at **ftp.ncsa.uiuc.edu** in the directory **/Web/Mosaic/Unix/binaries**. This directory will display directories for different version numbers. Those with a **b** in the directory name are new beta versions currently being tested. The current version of Mosaic is 2.6, located in directory **2.6**. There is also a beta version of 2.7 available in directory **2.7b**. Change to a directory and use the **get** command to download the Linux version.

```
# ftp ftp.ncsa.uiuc.edu
Connected to ftp.ncsa.uiuc.edu.
220 curley FTP server (Version wu-2.4(25) Thu Aug 25 13:14:21 CDT 1994) ready.
Name (ftp.ncsa.uiuc.edu:root): anonymous
331 Guest login ok, send your complete e-mail address as password.
Password:
```

```
230-
230-Welcome to NCSA's new anonymous FTP server! I hope you find what you are
230-  looking for. If you have any technical problems with the server,
230-  please e-mail to ftpadmin@ncsa.uiuc.edu. For other questions regarding
230-  NCSA software tools, please e-mail softdev@ncsa.uiuc.edu.
230 Guest login ok, access restrictions apply.
Remote system type is UNIX.
Using binary mode to transfer files.
ftp> cd /Web/Mosaic/Unix/binaries
250 CWD command successful.
ftp> cd 2.6
250-Please read the file README-2.6
250-  it was last modified on Fri Jul  7 14:31:14 1995 - 267 days ago
250 CWD command successful.
ftp> ls
200 PORT command successful.
150 Opening ASCII mode data connection for /bin/ls.
total 22596
drwx------    2 101        10           2048 Jul  7  1995 .
drwxr-xr-x    6 12873      wheel        2048 Oct 25 17:51 ..
-rw-r--r--    1 101        10         797705 Jul  7  1995 Mosaic-ibm-2.6.Z
-rw-r--r--    1 101        10         915718 Jul  7  1995 Mosaic-indy-2.6.Z
-rw-r--r--    1 101        10         903973 Jul  7  1995 Mosaic-linux-2.6.Z
-rw-r--r--    1 101        10         648431 Jul  7  1995 Mosaic-sgi-2.6.Z
-rw-r--r--    1 101        10        1708074 Jul  7  1995
   Mosaic-solaris-23-2.6.Z
-rw-r--r--    1 101        10           1835 Jul  7  1995 README-2.6
ftp> binary
200 Type set to I.
ftp> get Mosaic-linux-2.6.Z
200 PORT command successful.
150 Opening BINARY mode data connection for Mosaic-linux-2.6.Z (903973 bytes).
226 Transfer complete.
903973 bytes received in 276 secs (3.2 Kbytes/sec)
ftp> get README-2.6
200 PORT command successful.
150 Opening BINARY mode data connection for README-2.6 (1835 bytes).
226 Transfer complete.
1835 bytes received in 0.74 secs (2.4 Kbytes/sec)
ftp> close
221 Good-bye.
ftp> quit
# exit
```

The file will be a **.Z** compressed file, not an archived and gzip compressed file (**.tar.gz**) as the Netscape file was. To decompress it you just use **gunzip**, not **tar**. This will result in a file called **Mosaic-linux-2.6**. Use **chmod** to change the permissions on the file to be executable, 755. Then place this file in the directory you want to access it from. In the next example, the user decompresses the file, makes it executable, and moves the Mosaic Browser to the **/usr/local** directory.

```
$ gunzip Mosaic-linux-2.6.Z
$ chmod 755 Mosaic-linux-2.6.Z
$ mv Mosaic-linux-2.6.Z /usr/local
```

Like Netscape, Mosaic is an X-Windows application. You must have your desktop running before you can use it. Within your desktop, open the directory where you placed your Mosaic Browser, find its icon, and click on it. For easier access you can drag the Mosaic icon onto your desktop. The Mosaic window will open, displaying your home Web page (see Figure 11-4).

The Mosaic window has two boxes at the top. The first displays the title of the current Web page. The second is for entering URLs. The contents of the Web page are then displayed. At the bottom of the window are a series of buttons for navigating the Web pages you access. The Back and Forward buttons move you back and forth through a list of Web pages you have accessed. The Home button returns you to your own home page. The Save As button saves the current Web page on your own system.

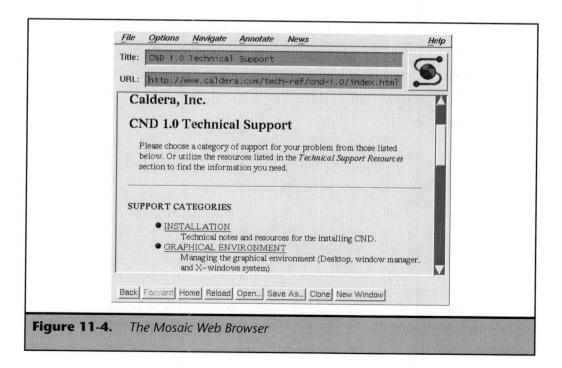

Figure 11-4. *The Mosaic Web Browser*

When you attempt to access a Web page, the globe image in the upper-right corner will spin. Once the Web page is displayed, the globe will stop spinning. Should you decide not to access the Web page while the globe is spinning, you can stop the access by clicking on the globe. In this respect, the globe functions as a stop button. Sometimes, attempts to access a Web page may take a great deal of time. You can simply cancel your request by clicking on the spinning globe.

The menus across the top of the Mosaic window allow you to manage your Web searches. With the Navigate menu, you maintain a hotlist of favored Web sites. The Options menu has several entries for configuring your Mosaic Browser. You can set your home page or specify mail or news servers. You can also set default colors used for the background and for URL links. The News menu lets you use your Mosaic Browser to access Usenet newsgroups, displaying and saving articles. Mosaic also has built-in security features that can protect your system.

Arena

Arena is an experimental browser designed as a testbed for the new HTML 3 language and the WC3 libraries. Arena supports tables, mathematical formulas, and style sheets. It is not meant to be a full-featured Web Browser; rather, it is intended as a tool for the development of HTML 3 Web pages. Arena is installed on your Caldera Lite Desktop as your default Web Browser. It presents a screen with buttons at the top for commands, followed by a URL entry area, and then the Web page display area.

A series of buttons across the top of the Arena Browser controls movement and executes commands (see Figure 11-5). To enter a new URL in the URL area, you first click on the Open button. This will clear the area and you can then enter your new URL. Use CTRL-**h** to backspace. The Abort button to the left of the URL entry area will cancel a Web access operation. The Forward button moves you forward a page and the Back button moves you back to a previously displayed page. The Home button returns you to your Home page. The other buttons function exactly as they do in other Windows applications.

One helpful command for those developing HTML 3 pages is the View button. When you click on the View button, the Web page is displayed as an HTML document, an ASCII text with HTML tags embedded in it. This way you can see how your Web pages are constructed. If you want to see how a particular effect was done, you can click on view to see the HTML tags used.

You can set your Home Web page, the default editor, and any proxies, by corresponding shell environment variables. To change your Home page, you set the **WWW_HOME** variable to the URL of that Web page. To set the default editor, you set the **EDITOR** variable to the name of the editor you want to use. If you need to specify a proxy, you can set the **http_proxy** variable to the URL of the proxy. Shell environment variables are usually set in your **.bash_profile** or **.bschrc** file. In the BASH shell you also have to export the variables. The following shows several examples. If you are using the C-shell, you have to use the **setenv** command.

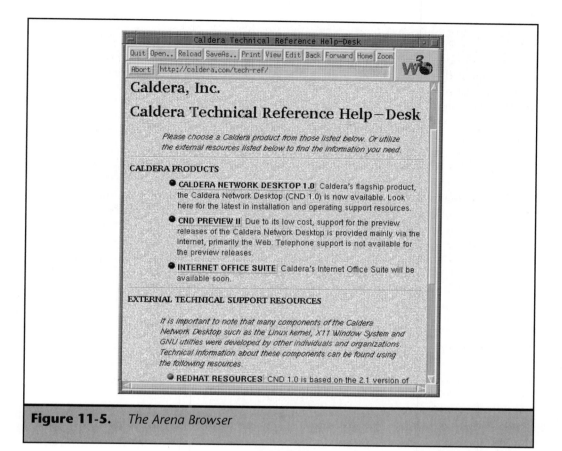

Figure 11-5.   *The Arena Browser*

```
WWW_HOME=file://home/httpd/html/myfile.html
EDITOR=vi
http_proxy=pango1.train.com
export WWW_HOME  EDITOR  http_proxy
```

To find out more about the Arena project, click on the Help button. This connects you to the Arena Home page at **www.w3.org/hypertext/WWW/Arena/**. Here you can find a discussion of the project as well as tutorials on HTML 3. You can also download more current versions of Arena from the **ftp.w3.org** ftp site in the **/pub/arena** directory. The current version of Arena for Linux is in the file **arena-beta-2b-linux.tar.gz**.

Lynx: Line-Mode Browser

Lynx is a line-mode Browser that you can use without X-Windows (see Figure 11-6). A Web page is displayed as text only. A text page can contain links to other Internet resources, but will not display any graphics, video, or sound. To start the Lynx Browser, you enter **lynx** on the command line and press ENTER.

    $ **lynx**

The links are displayed in bold and dispersed throughout the text of the Web page. A selected link is highlighted in reverse video with a shaded rectangle around the link text. The first link is automatically selected. You can then move sequentially from one link to the next on a page by pressing the DOWN ARROW key. The UP ARROW key moves you back to a previous link. To choose a link, you first highlight it and then press either ENTER or the RIGHT ARROW key. If you want to go to a specific site, press **g**. This opens a line at the bottom of the screen with the prompt **URL to open:**. There, you can enter the URL for the site you want. Pressing **m** will return you to your Home page. The text of a Web page is displayed one screen at a time. To move to the next screen of

```
                                    Caldera Technical Reference Help-Desk (p1 of 3)

  [IMAGE]

                            CALDERA, INC.

                  CALDERA TECHNICAL REFERENCE HELP-DESK


       Please choose a Caldera product from those listed below. Or utilize the external
       resources listed below to find the information you need.


       ------------------------------------------------------------------------------

CALDERA PRODUCTS
          [INLINE] CALDERA NETWORK DESKTOP 1.0
                   Caldera's flagship product, the Caldera Network Desktop (CND 1.0) is
                   now available. Look here for the latest in installation and operating
                   support resources.

          [INLINE] CND PREVIEW II
                   Due to its low cost, support for the preview releases of the Caldera
                   Network Desktop is provided mainly via the Internet, primarily the
                   Web. Telephone support is not available for the preview releases.

          [INLINE] INTERNET OFFICE SUITE
                   Caldera's Internet Office Suite will be available soon.
-- press space for next page --
  Arrow keys: Up and Down to move. Right to follow a link; Left to go back.
 H)elp O)ptions P)rint G)o M)ain screen Q)uit /=search [delete]=history list
```

Figure 11-6.   *The Lynx Browser*

text, you can either press SPACEBAR or PAGE DOWN. PAGE UP displays the previous screen of text. Pressing DOWN and UP ARROW will move to the next or previous links in the text, displaying the full screen of text around the link. To display a description of the current Web page with its URL, press the = key.

Lynx keeps a list of all the Web pages you access in a session. LEFT ARROW moves you back to a previously displayed page. RIGHT ARROW moves you forward to the next page in the list. Lynx refers to this list of Web pages as a *history list*. You can directly display this history list by pressing DEL. You can then use your UP and DOWN ARROW, keys to select a particular Web page link and use RIGHT ARROW or ENTER to access it. Lynx also supports bookmarks. By pressing **a**, you automatically add the current Web page to a bookmark file. Press **v** to display the list of bookmarks. As with a history list, you can use the UP and DOWN ARROW to select a bookmark link. Pressing either RIGHT ARROW or ENTER will move to and display that Web page.

Lynx uses a set of one letter commands to perform various Browser functions. By pressing the **?** key at any time, you can display a list of these commands. For example, pressing the **d** key will download a file. The **h** key will bring up a help menu. To search the text of your current Web page, you press the **/** key. This opens up a line at the bottom of the screen where you enter your search pattern. Lynx will then highlight the next instance of that pattern in the text. By pressing **n**, Lynx will display the next instance. The **** key will toggle you between a source and rendered version of the current Web page, showing you the HTML tags or the formatted text.

Except for the display limitations, Lynx is a fully functional Web Browser. You can use Lynx to download files or make telnet connections. All information on the Web is still accessible to you. Since it does not require much of the overhead that graphics-based Browsers need, Lynx can operate much faster, quickly displaying Web page text. This feature makes it ideal for public Web clients. You can telnet to a public Web client, such as **info.cern.ch**, and use its line-mode Browser to access the Web, rather than accessing from your own system. Of course, since you are operating from a remote system, you will not be able to download any files. This is a simple way to access the Web if you do not have access to a Web Browser on your current system.

Web Search Utilities

Finding the particular Web page on the Internet that you want can be a very slow process. Often, you have to move from one link to another with your Browser until you track down a Web page on a particular topic. Web page links are very restrictive in this respect. To search for a Web page, you can either use an index or a program that will search the Web for you. An index acts as a kind of yellow pages for the Internet, allowing you to search for Web pages using complex queries. One of the most popular indexes is located at the Yahoo site, http://www.yahoo.com. Here you can search for pages on any given topic.

You can also use programs known as *spiders* that are designed to search the Web directly, site by site. Some popular spiders are the WebCrawler and the World Wide Web Worm (WWWW). A spider not only lists pages on a given topic, but also lists the links from those pages to others with associated topics. In addition, a spider can show you not only a page you are looking for, but its links to other pages on the Web. You can obtain the WWWW spider from:

```
www.cs.colorado.edu/home/mcbryan/WWWW.html
```

The WebCrawler is available from:

```
www.biotech.washington.edu/WebCrawler/WebCrawler.html
```

Java

Java is a freely available enhancement to Web Browsers that allows you to run programs on a Web site. Without Java, a Web site can only offer you preset data such as you would find in a book or magazine. The information is preset. You move from one display to another looking at text and pictures. However, with Java, you can interact with the information on a Web site. For example, with Java you can actually play games by entering responses, and the game reacts to you. You are executing your own program on the Web site.

Java is distributed free by Sun. You can download a copy from an ftp site and install it on your Linux system. At present, only the Netscape Browser supports Java, but newer versions of other Browsers are expected to support it. Java has become an industry standard for Internet access. You can find the Linux version of Java at the blackdown ftp site located at **ftp.blackdown.org** in the directory **/pub/Java/linux**. The Linux version of Java requires two files, java-common and either java-motif-static or java-motif-dynamic. Of the two motif files, most users will need the static file. The files are named **linux.jdk-1.0.1-try1.common.tar.gz** and **linux.jdk-1.0.1-try2.static-motif.tar.gz**. You should also download the **README** file for more up-to-date information.

```
# ftp ftp.blackdown.org
Connected to ftp.blackdown.org.
220-Local time is now 20:00 and the load is 1.47.
220 You will be thrown out after 900 seconds of inactivity.
Name (ftp.blackdown.org:root): anonymous
230-Welcome to the Blackdown Organization public FTP server.
230-Please note we have no user restrictions in place on the ftp server
230-at the moment.
230-Thank you.
230 Anonymous user logged in, no need to bother with a password.
Remote system type is UNIX.
Using binary mode to transfer files.
ftp> binary
```

```
200 Only 8-bit binary mode is supported.
ftp> cd  /pub/Java/linux
250-Welcome to the Java-Linux Porting Project public FTP site.
250-Please visit http://www.blackdown.org/java-linux.html for
250-a wealth of information on the port and Java in general.
250 Changed to /pub/Java/linux
ftp> ls
200 Connected to 205.187.212.47 port 1096
150 Opening data connection
-rw-rw-r--   1 chapman   java        1406 Oct  7  1995 COPYRIGHT
drwxr-xr-x   2 chapman   java        1024 Jan 22  1996 HOWTO
drwxr-xr-x   2 chapman   java        1024 Jan 16  1996 HOWTO.old
-rw-rw-r--   1 chapman   java        1279 Dec 11  1995 README
-rw-rw-r--   1 chapman   java         226 Feb 14  1996 README.try4
drwxr-xr-x   2 chapman   java        1024 Feb  4  1996 beta1
-rw-r--r--   1 chapman   java     1701324 Mar 25  1996
linux.jdk-1.0.1-try1.common.tar.gz
-rw-r--r--   1 chapman   java      411695 Mar 26  1996
linux.jdk-1.0.1-try2.shared-motif.tar.gz
-rw-r--r--   1 chapman   java     1429153 Mar 26  1996
linux.jdk-1.0.1-try2.static-motif.tar.gz
226 That's all
ftp> get linux.jdk-1.0.1-try1.common.tar.gz
200 Connected to 205.187.212.47 port 1098
150 Opening data connection
226-File written successfully
226 517.572 seconds (measured here), 3.11 Kbytes per second
1701324 bytes received in 525 secs (3.2 Kbytes/sec)
ftp> get linux.jdk-1.0.1-try2.static-motif.tar.gz
200 Connected to 205.187.212.47 port 1100
150 Opening data connection
226-File written successfully
226 437.950 seconds (measured here), 3.07 Kbytes per second
1429153 bytes received in 443 secs (3.1 Kbytes/sec)
ftp> get README
200 Connected to 205.187.212.47 port 1101
150 Opening data connection
226 File written successfully
1279 bytes received in 1.21 secs (1 Kbytes/sec)
ftp> close
221-Good-bye.  You uploaded 0 and downloaded 3073 kbytes.
221 CPU time spent on you: 1.830 seconds.
ftp> quit
#
```

Place these files in the directory **/usr/local**. These are gzip compressed and tar archived files, so you will first have to use **gunzip** to decompress them and then **tar**

xvf to generate the Java program files from the archive. This will create a directory called **/usr/local/java** with the Java applications and sample files. Be sure to place the archived tar files in the **/usr/local** directory before you extract them. The Java software is already configured to operate from **/usr/local**.

```
# mv linux.jdk-1.0.1-try1.common.tar.gz  /usr/local
# mv linux.jdk-1.0.1-try2.static-motif.tar.gz  /usr/local
# cd /usr/local
# gunzip linux.jdk-1.0.1-try1.common.tar.gz
# gunzip linux.jdk-1.0.1-try2.static-motif.tar.gz
# tar xvf linux.jdk-1.0.1-try1.common.tar
java/
java/COPYRIGHT
java/README
(extracts the demo, include, and lib directories)
# tar xvf linux.jdk-1.0.1-try2.static-motif.tar
java/
java/COPYRIGHT
java/HOWTO
(extracts the bin and lib directories)
# cd /usr/local/java
# ls
COPYRIGHT include HOWTO index.html README README.jdk bin lib demo
    src.zip
#
```

Once installed, you can now use the Netscape Browser to view Web pages with Java resources. Your **/usr/local/java/demo** directory will contain many examples of Web pages that make use of Java applications. In your Netscape Browser enter **file://usr/local/java/**. From there you can link to different Web page examples. There are interactive resources, such as animations you can run or games to play. You can also create your own Java applications. Documentation is provided in the **/usr/local/java** directory.

If you are using an older version of Linux, you will need to obtain the newer version of the **ld.so** library and install it with **ldconfig**. Java requires the use of a **ld.so** library of version 11 or above. Details on how to do this are located at the **www.blackdown.org** Web site. Redhat 2.1, which is installed with your Caldera Network Desktop, already uses a newer version.

Using Linux as a Web Server

Linux systems are ideal for creating your own Web site. To do this you have to configure your Linux system as a server (described in Chapter 12). You will also need to create the Web pages and resources that you want to make up your Web site. Web pages are not difficult to create. Links from one page to another will move users through your Web site. You can even create links to Web pages or resources on other sites.

Network Configuration as a Web Server

Your Caldera Network Desktop is already configured to operate as a Web server. The httpd software for managing a Web server is already installed and running. All you need to do is perform the necessary network server configurations and then designate the files and directories open to remote users. If you are using another version of Linux, you may need to obtain and install a Web server. Table 11-3 lists several popular Web servers.

Creating Your Own Web Site

To create your own Web site you will first have to obtain an Internet address and connect your system to the Internet. Having done this, all you have to do is start your Web server daemons and have the correct directories set up for use by your Web site users. Your Caldera Network Desktop has already installed the Web server daemon and has set up the appropriate directories. All you have to do to have a working Web site is to connect to the Internet and create your Web pages. The directory set up by your Caldera Web server for your Web site pages is **/home/httpd/html**. Place the Web pages that you create in that directory. You can make other subdirectories with their own Web pages to which these can link. There are many excellent texts on Web page creation and management, in particular, *The World Wide Web: The Complete Reference* by Rick Stout. A brief description of Web page construction is provided here. You can obtain up-to-date information on current developments in HTML at the following Web page.

    http://www.w3.org/hypertext/WWW/MarkUp/MarkUp.html

Creating Web Pages with HTML

Web pages are created using HTML, the HyperText Markup Language that is a subset of SGML (the Standard Generalized Markup Language). Creating an HTML document is a matter of inserting HTML tags in a text file. In this respect, creating a Web page is as simple as using a tag-based word processor. You use the HTML tags to format text for display as a Web page. The Web page itself is a text file that you can create using any text editor, such as Vi. For those familiar with tag-based word processing on Unix systems you will find it conceptually similar to nroff. There are HTML tags to indicate headings, lists, and paragraphs, as well as to reference Web resources. Table 11-4 lists many of the commonly used HTML tags.

There are alternatives to manually creating a Web page. The Linux version of WordPerfect can automatically generate a Web page from a WordPerfect document. You could create your Web page using all the word processing features of WordPerfect. There are also special Web page creation programs such as **tkWWW**, that easily help you create very complex Web pages without ever having to explicitly type any HTML tags. Everything is done with objects in a window interface (see Table 11-3). Keep in mind though that no matter what tool you use to create your Web page, the Web page itself will be an HTML document.

Page and Text Format

An HTML tag consists of a keyword enclosed in angle brackets, for example, the tag for paragraph is <P>. Tags are usually used in pairs, with the end tag the same as the beginning but with a preceding slash. So you would begin a paragraph with the <P> tag and end the paragraph with the corresponding </P> tag. All Web pages are enclosed with the <HTML> tag. The first entry in your Web page should be <HTML>, and the last </HTML>. You can divide your Web page into sections for the heading and the body. The heading contains the title for your Web page. The body contains the contents.

Formatting Text

In the body of your Web page you can use formatting tags to organize your text headings, paragraphs, or lists. You enter a heading with the tag <Hn>, where n refers to the level of the heading. <H1> is a top-level heading, <H2> is the next level, and so on. Depending on the Browser used, the subheading may be indented or portrayed in a smaller or different font. Each head has to be terminated with its own ending tag—<H1> with </H1>, and <H2> with </H2>.

You use the UL and LI tags to display a list of items. At the beginning and end of the list, you insert <UL> and </UL>. Each item within the list is entered with it own <LI> and </LI> tags. UL displays a bulleted list. For a numbered list you can use OL.

You can position components such as pictures or paragraphs at either the top, bottom, or middle of your Web page using the TOP, BOT, and MID tags.

Referencing Internet Resources: HREF

You can designate certain text or pictures in your Web page as links to other Web pages or to items such as pictures or documents. The items can be on your system or at other Web sites. When the user chooses the text referencing a link, that item or Web page will be retrieved. To create a link, you associate certain text or pictures in your

Web page with a URL of an Internet resource. This resource can be another Web page, an item such as a picture or file, or even another Internet tool, such as ftp or telnet. You use an HREF anchor tag to create such a link. The HREF anchor tag begins with <A HREF=. The URL is entered following the = sign and is enclosed within double quotes. A closing > ends the opening HREF anchor tag. After the opening HREF tag, you enter the text that is displayed on your Web page to reference this URL. The closing </A> anchor tag ends the text. When the Web page is displayed on a Browser, you will see this text set to a special color to indicate that it references a URL. You can also include an image reference, in which case the user can click on the image to reference the URL. Its syntax is as follows:

```
<A HREF="URL">text</A>
```

In the following example, the HREF anchor tag will connect to a Web page on the www.caldera.com system. The text "Caldera's documentation on the Internet" will be displayed in color, usually blue. When the user clicks on that text, the URL **www.caldera.com/doc** will be accessed. As the transfer protocol is http, this resource will be displayed as a Web page.

```
<A HREF="http://www.caldera.com/doc/"> Caldera's documentation on
the Internet</A>
```

If you include an image reference in the text portion, users can click on the image to reference the URL. Image references are discussed in the next section. In the next example, an image reference to the **books.gif** image file will display that image on the Web page. The user can then click on the books image to reference the URL. The image reference is **<IMG SRC="book2.gif">**.

```
<H3><A HREF="http://www.caldera.com/doc/gs/gs.html"><IMG
SRC="book2.gif">
Getting Started with the Network Desktop (Internet)</A></H3>
```

To access a Web page on your own system you do not need the transfer protocol or the hostname. You only have to specify the path name. The path name can be a relative path name from the directory in which the current Web page is located. In the next example, the Web page **desktop.html** is located in the subdirectory **lg** on your own system.

```
<H3><A HREF="lg/desktop.html">Desktop User's Guide</A></H3>
```

Instead of referencing a separate Web page, you can reference certain labeled text on the same page that you have identified by a specific name. This is referred to as a hypertext target or named element. An HREF anchor can then access this target, jumping to that text. To reference such a target in an HREF anchor, you precede its name with a # sign. In the following HREF anchor, the text "The newest engine" will be displayed on the Web page. When the user clicks on this text, the target on the Web page labeled with the name engine1 will be displayed. The target can be a heading, a picture, or any text segment.

```
<A HREF="#engine1">The newest engine</A>
```

There are currently several ways you can create a hypertext target. You can simply use the NAME anchor tag with a target name followed by the text of the target. In the next example, the target name is engine1 and the target text is "This is the newest engine on the block". The name can be used in HREF anchors to identify the particular hypertext target.

```
<A NAME="engine1"> This is the newest engine on the block</A>
```

Given both the HREF anchor and the NAME anchor, you can use the HREF anchor to reference the text specified in the NAME anchor. When the user clicks on the text, "The newest engine", specified by the HREF anchor, he or she will be moved to the part of the Web page beginning with the text "This is the newest engine on the block", as specified by the NAME anchor. This technique is often used to move users to different headings, with each heading starting a different segment of the page's topic. To name a heading, you need to enclose the entire heading within NAME anchor tags.

```
<A NAME="Heading-name">
<Hn>Heading text<\Hn>
</A>
```

You can then jump to the text using the name you gave to the heading.

```
<A HREF="#Heading-name">some text</A>
```

In the next example, engine1 now references a heading, not just text.

```
<A NAME="engine1">
<H2>This is the newest engine on the block<\H2>
</A>
```

With the most recent version of HTML, called HTML 3, you can use the ID tag to create targets. You can make anything a target, including pictures.

```
<Hn ID="name"> Heading text<\Hn>
```

Images and Sounds

You can also use HTML commands to display pictures on your Web page. The picture is either a gif or jpeg file, usually in the same directory as the Web page. The <IMG SRC=*filename*> tag will display a specified picture. For example, to display a picture called **books.gif,** you place it within the IMG tag.

```
<IMG SRC="books.gif">
```

The IMG tag displays the picture as part of the Web page. You can, however, display an image externally using a separate image display program. To do so you reference the graphics file with an HREF tag. In effect you are linking to the picture file and the application that displays it.

```
<HREF="engine.gif">The greatest engine in the world<\A>
```

You use the same method to play sound and video files. These files rely on outside applications to run them. An HREF tag will link to the sound or video file and run its associated application.

```
<HREF="whistle.au">Steam melody<\A>
```

Web Page Example

The **cald1.html** file shown here is a shortened form of the **/usr/doc/HTML/calderadoc /caldera.html** file on your system. It illustrates many of the features discussed concerning Web page construction. The entire page is enclosed in <HTML> and

</HTML> tags. The title of the page is defined within the <TITLE> tags, which are placed within the <HEAD> tags. The <BODY> tags mark the text that will be displayed on the Web page. The <H1> tag prints a heading in very large text. <P> tags format the following text into paragraphs. <H2> and <H3> tags display progressively smaller headings. The <HR> tag draws a line across the page. Anchor tags with URL references, <A HREF>, are embedded within both paragraphs and headings. The anchor tags within headings include images that can be used to reference the URL. Many of the URLs reference local files and others reference Web pages on remote sites. For example, <A HREF="crisp/crisp.html"> references a local Web page called **crisp.html** in the subdirectory **crisp**. <A HREF="http://home.netscape.com/eng /mozilla/2.0/handbook/"> references the **handbook** directory on the home.netscape.com Web site. Figure 11-7 shows how the **cald1.html** will be displayed.

cald1.html

```
<HTML>
<HEAD>
<TITLE>Caldera Network Desktop Online Documentation</TITLE>
</HEAD>
<BODY>
<H1>Caldera Network Desktop Online Documentation</H1>
<P>
Welcome to the Caldera Network Desktop, Release 1.0. We encourage you to
begin with the <A HREF="file:/etc/README">README</A> file for this
release.
<P>
Many of these manuals are regularly updated on Caldera's WWW server.
For the most current documentation, see <A HREF="http://www.caldera
.com/doc/"> Caldera's documentation on the Internet</A>
<HR>
<H2>Online Manuals</H2>
<H3><A HREF="http://www.caldera.com/doc/gs/gs.html">
<IMG SRC="book2.gif"> Getting Started with the Network Desktop
(Internet)</A></H3>
<H3><A HREF="lg/desktop.html"><IMG SRC="books.gif">Desktop User's
Guide</A></H3>
<H3><A HREF="crisp/crisp.html"><IMG SRC="books.gif">CRiSPlite Editor
User's Guide </A></H3>
<H3><A HREF="http://home.netscape.com/eng/mozilla/2.0/handbook/">
<IMG SRC="book2.gif">Netscape Navigator Handbook (Internet)</A></H3>
</BODY>
</HTML>
```

Taking what you have learned so far, you can easily create your own Web page. All you need is a text editor. The **index.html** file shown next is an example of a Web page you can create yourself. The **/usr/doc/HOWTO/ldp** directory holds numerous Web pages that are documentation for various topics. There are Web pages for the PPP protocols and printing configuration. Currently there is no index for these different Web pages. You have to find the beginning page for each group. For example, the file **Sound-HOWTO.html** is itself an index referencing a set of HTML files beginning with **Sound-HOWTO-1.html**. The following **index.html** file creates an index that you can use to access any of these HTML files directly. Each HOWTO Web page has a heading with an embedded anchor referencing it. For example, <H2><A HREF="PPP-HOWTO.html">PPP HOWTO </A></H2> references the file **PPP-HOWTO.html**. The text PPP HOWTO is displayed on the Web page. When you click on this text, the PPP-HOWTO Web page will be displayed.

/usr/doc/HOWTO/ldp/index.html

```
<HTML>
<HEAD>
<TITLE>Index of HOWTO Documents</TITLE>
</HEAD>
<BODY>
<H1>List of HOWTO Documents</H1>
<H2>by Dylan Petersen</H2>
<P>
v.1.0, 5 April 1996
<P>
<H2><A HREF="Printing-Usage-HOWTO.html">Printing
HOWTO</A></H2>
<H2><A HREF="Sound-HOWTO.html">Sound HOWTO</A></H2>
<H2><A HREF="NET-2-HOWTO.html">Network HOWTO</A></H2>
<H2><A HREF="PPP-HOWTO.html">PPP HOWTO</A></H2>
<H2><A HREF="News-HOWTO.html">News HOWTO</A></H2>
<H2><A HREF="Mail-HOWTO.html">Mail HOWTO</A></H2>
<H2><A HREF="UUCP-HOWTO.html">UUCP HOWTO</A></H2>
<H2><A HREF="Hardware-HOWTO.html">Hardware HOWTO </A></H2>
<H2><A HREF="Ethernet-HOWTO.html">Ethernet HOWTO</A></H2>
</BODY>
</HTML>
```

Once you have created this Web page you can display it using your Web Browser. First make sure you have placed the **index.html** file in the **/usr/doc/HTML/ldp** directory. Then enter the URL, `file:/usr/doc/HTML/ldp/index.html`, in your

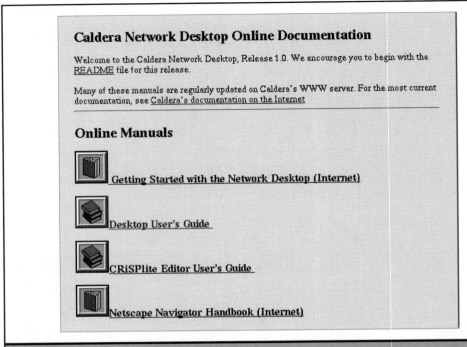

Figure 11-7. *The **cald1.html** Web page for Online Documentation*

Web Browser. You will see your Web page displayed. Click on a HOWTO heading to bring up its Web page. Figure 11-8 shows you what the **index.html** page looks like.

There is currently no way to return to the index page once you have accessed a HOWTO page. You could, of course, just click on the Back button on your Web Browser until you come to it. However, you can place an HREF anchor within a Web HOWTO page that will return you to the index page. A possible anchor is shown here:

```
<A HREF="index.html">Return to Main Index</A>
```

Common Gateway Interfaces

A Common Gateway Interface (CGI) is a program that a Web server at a Web site can use to interact with Web Browsers. When using a Browser to display a Web page at a particular Web site, the Web page may call up CGI programs to provide you with certain real-time information or to receive information from you. For example, a Web

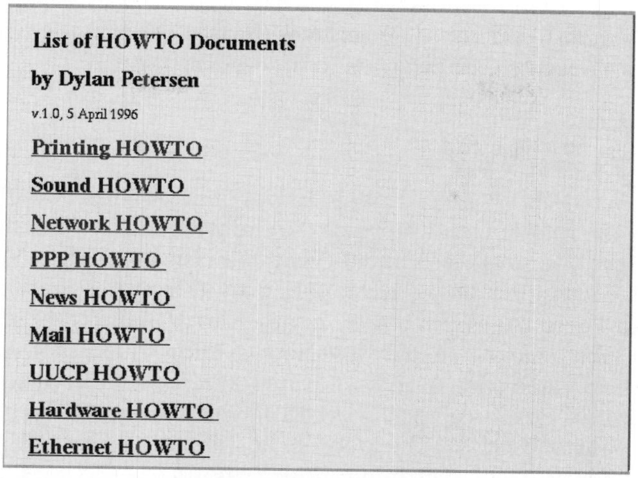

List of HOWTO Documents

by Dylan Petersen

v.1.0, 5 April 1996

Printing HOWTO

Sound HOWTO

Network HOWTO

PPP HOWTO

News HOWTO

Mail HOWTO

UUCP HOWTO

Hardware HOWTO

Ethernet HOWTO

Figure 11-8. *The index.html Web page for HOWTO pages*

page may execute the server's **date** command to display the current date whenever the Web page is accessed.

A CGI script can be a Linux shell script or a program. For the shell script you can use the BASH or TCSH shell commands described in Chapters 15 and 16. Programs can be developed using a programming language such as C. There are also two special HTML operations that are considered CGI scripts: query text and forms. Both receive and process interactive responses from particular users.

You have seen how a user can use a Browser to display Web pages at a given Web site. In effect the user is receiving information in the form of Web pages from the Web site. A user can also, to a limited extent, send information back to the Web site. This is usually information specifically prompted for in a Web page displayed by your Browser. The Web server then receives and processes that information using the CGI programs.

On a Web page you can use a single field to prompt for a one-line response from the user, or use a form that has a collection of fields. The <ISINDEX> tag displays a single edit box in which a user can type text. This is usually used to obtain keywords for a search and is referred to as a document-based query.

A form is a Web page that holds several input fields of various types. These can be input boxes for entering text or check boxes and radio boxes that users simply click on. The text boxes can be structured, allowing a certain number of characters to be entered, as in a phone number. It can also be unstructured, allowing users to type in sentences as they would for a comment. Forms are referred to as form-based queries.

After entering information into a form, the user sends it back to the server by clicking on a Submit button. The server receives the form and, along with it, instructions to run a specific CGI program to process the form.

Summary: WWW

The World Wide Web (WWW) links different types of information distributed worldwide across the Internet, and presents that information in an easy-to-use format known as Web pages. These are documents written in the HyperText Markup Language (HTML). A single Web page can link to another Web page, that in turn can link to yet another. These pages can be at the same site or at different sites. More importantly, each Web page can display a variety of information that you can access such as text, pictures, video, and sound. Information resources on the Internet are identified by Universal Resource Locators (URL), which are made up of three components: the transfer protocol, the Web site hostname, and the file name of the resource. The transfer protocol determines how a resource is accessed: http accesses a Web page, whereas ftp initiates a file transfer. URLs can be used to access Web pages or resources at other sites.

You use Web Browsers to display Web pages at Web sites throughout the Internet. Web Browsers will keep track of the different Web pages that you access in a session, allowing you to move back and forth among these pages. You can also keep a hotlist of Web pages you like and use the Browser to directly access them. Many Web Browsers also have the capability to operate as newsreaders and mailers. There are several popular Web Browsers available for Linux such as the Netscape Navigator and Mosaic.

Your Linux system can also operate as a Web server, and the details of configuring a Web server are discussed in Chapter 12 (the Caldera Network Desktop already has a Web server installed and configured). Using Web server software, you can set up your own Web site. Once you have your Web server software, you then need to create the Web pages for your site. Since a Web page is a text file that contains HTML tags that are used to format the page, composing a Web page is a matter of entering text with the appropriate HTML tags. HREF anchor tags are used to reference Internet resources with URLs. You can have several Web pages distributed in different subdirectories, each having links to Web pages on your system or at other Web sites. Within directories, a Web page (usually named **index.html**) operates as a table of contents with links to other pages in the directory.

Protocol	Description
`http`	Hypertext Transfer Protocol for Web site access
`gopher`	Access Gopher site
`ftp`	File Transfer Protocol for anonymous ftp connections
`telnet`	Makes a telnet connection
`wais`	Access WAIS site
`news`	Reading Usenet news; uses Net News Transfer Protocol (NNTP)

Table 11-1.   *Web Transfer Protocols*

File Type	Description
.html	Web page document formatted using HTML, the HyperText Markup Language
Graphics Files	
.gif	Graphics, using gif compression
.jpeg	Graphics, using jpeg compression
Sound Files	
.au	Sun (Unix) sound file
.wav	Microsoft Windows sound file
.aiff	Macintosh sound file
Video Files	
.QT	Quicktime video file, multiplatform
.mpeg	Video file
.avi	Microsoft Windows video file

Table 11-2.   *Web Resource File Types*

Web Browsers	Location
Netscape Navigator	ftp3.netscape.com/pub/navigator/*n.n*/unix ftp3.netscape.com through ftp8.netscape.com are available as well as many mirror sites
NCSA Mosaic	ftp.ncsa.uiuc.edu/Web/Mosaic/unix/
Arena	http://www.w3.org/hypertext/WWW/Arena/Status.html ftp.w3.org/pub/arena
Lynx	ftp://ftp2.cc.ukans.edu/pub/lynx (included with most distributions)
HTML Editors	
Phoenix	http://www.bsd/uchicago.edu/ftp/pub/phoenix
tkWWW	http://www.w3.org/hypertext/WWW/tkWWW ftp.aud.alcatel.com/pub/tcl/extensions
Web Servers	
Apache	http://www.apache.org
CERN httpd	ftp://info.cern.ch/pub/www.bin
NCSA httpd	ftp.ncsa.uiuc.edu http://boohoo.ncsa.uiuc.edu
Plexus	http://www.bsdi.com/2.2.1/dist/Plexus.html
Netscape Server	ftp3.netscape.com/pub/server/*n.n*/unix
Web Utilities	
Java	ftp.blackdown.org/pub/Java/linux
WebCrawler	http://www.biotech.washington.edu/WebCrawler /WebCrawler.html
World Wide Web Worm	http://www.cs.colorado.edu/home/mcbryan/WWWW.html http://info.cern.ch/WWW/Tools

Table 11-3. *Tools for Using the Web*

Basic Tags	Description
<HTML> *Web page***</HTML>**	Place <HTML> as the first entry in your Web page and </HTML> as the last
<HEAD> *Head of Web page* **</HEAD>**	The head segment of a Web page; includes any configuration entries and the title entry
<TITLE>*title text***</TITLE>**	The title of the Web page; this will be used in hotlists to identify the page easily
<BODY> *Text of Web page* **</BODY>**	The body of the Web page; this is the material that is displayed as the Web page
<ADDRESS> *Address of creator* **<\ADDRESS>**	Internet address of Web page creator
<BASE=Href" *Web page path name"***>**	Path name of Web page that serves as base path name for any relative path names on that page

Format

<H*n***>***Heading title***<\H***n***>**	Headers; n is sequential subhead level, as in <H1> for top level, <H2> for subheads, etc.
<P>*paragraph text***</P>**	Paragraphs
<CENTER>	Center text
<BLINK>	
** **	Line break
<PRE> *Preformatted text* **</PRE>**	Displays the following text as it appears with no formatting
<HR>*Horizontal rule***</HR>**	Displays a line across the page
<CLEAR>	Forces break in text

Images

<IMAGE SRC="*file.gif*"	Image to be displayed in Web page

Table 11-4.   *HTML Codes for Web Pages*

Images	Description
ALIGN="*position*"	Positions images or text on the Web page; *position* can be **Bottom**, **Top**, **Left**, or **Right**
WIDTH=	Sets width for display of image
HEIGHT=	Sets height
Anchors	
<A*Anchor tag* **/A>**	Anchor tag, such as URL reference
HREF="*URL address*"> *reference text*	URL reference; ties the specified text to the URL address
<A NAME="*text*">*Anchor text*< **/A>**	Creates an anchor reference for text in the Web page
<A NAME="*Heading text*"> **<H***n*>*Heading text*<**\H***n*> **</A>**	Makes a heading an anchor reference in the Web page
ID="*Anchor text*"	Uses ID instead of NAME to create anchor text in the Web page
<H*n* **ID**="*Anchor text*" >*Heading text*<**\H***n*>	Uses ID to make a heading an anchor text
<A HREF="**#***Anchor text*" >*Text displayed in page*</A>	A reference to anchor text in the Web page
<LINK REL=*Relationship* **HREF**="*URL reference*">	Creates a link to other Web pages making up the Web site; displays buttons at top and bottom of Web page with relationship described by **REL**

REL=Relationship
Relationship of current Web page to others:

Previous	HRL for previous Web page
Next	HRL for next Web Page
Home	HRL for home Page
Banner	HRL for banner displayed for all Web pages

Table 11-4.   *HTML Codes for Web Pages* (continued)

Lists | Description

\<LH\>_List header_**\</LH\>**	Name for the list
\<LI\>_List item text_**\</LI\>**	List item
\<UL\>_List item entries_**\</UL\>**	Unordered list
\<OL\>_Ordered list entries_**\</OL\>**	Ordered list, usually numbered
\<DL\>_List entries_**\</DL\>**	Definition list; a list of terms and an explanation of each called a definition; a _term_ is a word that you specify
\<DT\>_Definition term_**\</DT\>**	Term for a definition list entry
\<DD\>_Definition_**\</DD\>**	Text associated with a definition term

Tables

\<TABLE\>_Table entries_**\</TABLE\>**	Displays a table
\<TC\>_Table caption_**\</TC\>**	
\<TR\>_Table row_**\</TR\>**	
\<TH\>_Table head_**\</TH\>**	
\<TD\>_Table cell_**\</TD\>**	

Configuration

BGCOLOR=rrggbb	Background color; hexadecimal number representing color; rr = red, gg = green, bb = blue; all 0s = no color (black); all 1s = white, FFFFFF; it is set in the **BODY** tag **\<BODY BGCOLOR=**_137HF2_**\>**
TEXT=rrggbb	Color of text; it is set in the **BODY** tag
BACKGOUND=_file.gif_	Picture to use as background for Web page; it is set in the **BODY** tag

Table 11-4. _HTML Codes for Web Pages_ (continued)

Entities	Description
&lt	<
&gt	>
&amp	&
&quot	"

Table 11-4.   *HTML Codes for Web Pages* (continued)

Chapter Twelve

Internet Servers

R eflecting the close relationship between Unix and the development of the Internet, Linux is particularly good at providing Internet services such as Web, WAIS, ftp, and Gopher. But instead of just accessing other sites, you can set up your own Linux system to be a Web site or an ftp site. Other people can then access your system using Web pages you created or download files you provide for them. A system that operates this way is called a server and is known by the service it provides. You can set up your system to be a Web server or an ftp server, connecting it to the Internet and turning it into a site that others can access. A single Linux system can provide several different services. Your Linux system can be a Web server and an ftp server as well as a Gopher and WAIS server, all at the same time. One user could download files using your ftp services while another reads your Web pages. All you have to do is install and run the appropriate server software for each service. Each one operates as a continually running daemon looking for requests for its particular services from remote users.

The Caldera Network Desktop is already a Web, ftp, and Gopher server. It was designed with Internet servers in mind. Normally you would have to obtain and install server software yourself, but when you install your Caldera Network Desktop, the server software for these two services is automatically installed and configured for you. Every time you start the Caldera Network Desktop you also start the Web and ftp server daemons. To turn your Linux system into a Web server, all you have to do is create Web pages. For an ftp server, you only have to place the files you want to make available in the ftp directories. A Gopher server is also automatically installed.

To operate your Linux system as an Internet server, you must obtain a connection to the Internet and provide access to your system for remote users. Access is usually a matter of allowing anonymous logins to directories reserved for server resources. Your Caldera Network Desktop is already configured to allow such access for Web and ftp users. Connections to the Internet that can accommodate server activity can be difficult to come by. You may need a dedicated connection, or you may need to use a connection set up by an Internet Service Provider. You are no longer connecting only yourself to the Internet, but you are allowing many other users to make what could be a great many connections to you through the Internet.

If you only want to provide the services to a local area network, you will not need a special connection. Also, you can provide these services to users by allowing them to connect over a modem and log in directly. Users could dial into your system and use your Web pages or use ftp to download files. In whatever situation you want to use these services, you will need the appropriate server software installed and running.

This chapter examines Internet servers for the four different services: Web, ftp, WAIS, and Gopher. As the Web and ftp servers are already installed, you will not have to perform the installation procedures described. However, these sections will tell you in what directories the services are set up and how to place files such as Web pages in them. WAIS and Gopher are not set up on your Caldera Network Desktop, so you will have to obtain the server software and install it as described in this chapter.

Starting Servers

A server is a daemon that runs concurrently with your other programs, continuously looking for a request for its services either from other users on your system or from remote users connecting to your system through a network. When it receives a request from a user, it starts up a session to provide its services. For example, if users want to download a file from your system, they can use their own ftp client to request that your ftp server start an ftp session for them. In the session, they can access and download files from your system.

You have to have your server running for a user to access its services. If you set up a Web site on your system with HTML files, you first have to have the httpd Web server program running before users can access your Web site and display those files.

There are several ways to start a server. You can do it manually from the command line by entering the name of the server program and its arguments. Upon pressing ENTER, the server will start, although your command line prompt will reappear. The server will be running concurrently as you go on to do other tasks. To see if your server is running, you can enter the following command to list all currently running processes. You should see a process for the server program you started up.

```
# ps -ax
```

Instead of manually executing all the server programs each time you boot your system, you can have your system automatically start the servers. There are two ways to do this, depending on how you want to use a server. You can have a server running continuously from the time you start your system until you shut it down, or you can have the server start only when it receives a request from a user for its services. If a server is being used frequently, you may want to have it running all the time. If it is used rarely, you may just want it to start when a request comes in. For example, if you are running a Web site, your Web server will be receiving requests all the time from remote hosts on the Internet. However, for an ftp site, you may receive requests infrequently, in which case you may want to have the ftp server start only when it receives a request, instead doing nothing much of the time it is running. Of course certain ftp sites receive frequent requests, which would warrant a continually running ftp server.

To have a server start automatically with the system, you use a startup script in the **/etc/rc.d/init.d** directory. To have the server start only when a request for its services is received, you configure it for use by the **inetd** daemon. **inetd** looks for server requests and then starts up the server when a request comes through for its services. The Caldera Network Desktop has already configured the Web server to start automatically and run continuously. There is a script for it in the **/etc/rc.d/init.d** directory called **httpd.init**. The ftp server is configured to run under **inetd**. It will start only when someone initiates an ftp session with your system. You will find an entry for the ftp server in the **inetd.conf** configuration file, but there is no script for it in **/etc/rc.d/init.d** as there is for the Web server.

Server init Scripts

The Redhat distribution of Linux used by the Caldera Network Desktop uses a method of implementing startup files that may not be found on other distributions. For other distributions you only have to place the server command in a system initialization file such as **rc.local**. For your Caldera Network Desktop, you have to create special startup scripts in the **/etc/rc.d/init.d** directory.

The **/etc/rc.d/init.d** directory holds shell scripts that are executed automatically whenever you boot your system. These shell scripts have commands to execute particular programs such as servers. You will find one there already for the Web server called **httpd.init**. Be careful never to touch or modify any of the other scripts. These start essential programs such as your network interface and your printer daemon. A sample startup script, called the **skeleton** script, is provided in this directory. To create a new startup script for a server, you can begin by copying the **skeleton** script or the **httpd.init** script. Then edit this new script and place the server path name and the server command in the appropriate places. As an example, the **httpd.init** script is shown here. The name of the Web server program is **httpd**. Notice the line for checking the existence of this program.

httpd.init

```
#!/bin/sh
# httpd       This shell script takes care of starting and stopping httpd.
# Source function library.
. /etc/rc.d/init.d/functions
# Source networking configuration.
. /etc/sysconfig/network
# Check that networking is up.
[ ${NETWORKING} = "no" ] && exit 0
[ -f /usr/sbin/httpd ] || exit 0
# See how we were called.
case "$1" in
  start)
      # Start daemons.
      echo -n "Starting httpd: "
      daemon httpd
      echo
      ;;
  stop)
      # Stop daemons.
```

```
        echo -n "Shutting down httpd: "
         killproc httpd
        echo "done"
        rm -f /var/run/httpd.pid
        ;;
  *)
        echo "Usage: httpd {start | stop}"
        exit 1
esac
exit 0
```

The Web server is executed with the following line found in this script.

```
daemon httpd
```

Once the startup script is created, you then have to create a symbolic link to it from the **/etc/rc.d/rc3.d** directory. In the **/etc/rc.d** directory, there is a set of subdirectories whose names have the format **rcN.d**, where *N* is a number referring to a runlevel. The **rc** script will detect the runlevel that the system was started in and then execute only the startup scripts specified in the subdirectory for that runlevel. The default runlevel is 3, the multiuser level. When you start your system, the **rc** script will execute the startup scripts specified in the **rc3.d** directory. The **rc3.d** directory holds symbolic links to certain startup scripts in the **/etc/rc.d/init.d** directory (see Chapter 6 for a discussion on symbolic links). So the **httpd.init** script in the **/etc/rc.d/init.d** directory is actually called through a symbolic link in the **rc3.d** directory. The symbolic link for the **/etc/rc.d/httpd.init** script in the **rc3.d** directory is **S85httpd**. So to have a server automatically start, you first create a startup script for it in the **/etc/rc.d/init.d** directory and then create a symbolic link to that script in the **/etc/rc.d/rc3.d** directory.

Suppose that you have installed the Gopher server on your system and now want to have it started automatically. The name of the University of Minnesota Gopher server program is **gopherd**. The easiest way to create a startup script for the **gopherd** Gopher server program, is to first make a copy of the **httpd.init** script, naming the copy **gopherd.init**. Both **httpd** and **gopherd** are network servers and use much the same script.

```
# cp httpd.init  gopherd.init
```

You then edit the **gopherd.init** script and replace all references to **httpd** with **gopherd**. There is a line that checks to see if the server exists, before executing it. Here

you should have the path name for the **gopherd** server program, probably
/usr/sbin/gopherd.

```
[ -f /usr/sbin/gopherd ] || exit 0
```

The following line executes the **gopherd** server. Notice that the command
includes arguments such as the directory for Gopher files. Argument requirements
vary from server to server. The **httpd** Web server program has no arguments.

```
daemon gopherd /usr/lib/gopher-data
```

Now you change to the **/etc/rc.d/rc3.d** directory and make a symbolic link to that
/etc/rc.d/init.d/gopherd.init script. The **ln** command with the **-s** option creates a
symbolic link.

```
ln -s /etc/rc.d/init.d/gopherd.init    S94gopherd
```

Now when you start your system, the **gopherd** server is automatically started up,
running concurrently and waiting for requests.

Instead of copying the **httpd.init** script, you could also have copied the **skeleton**
script. This would require you to replace lines referencing **skeleton** with the lines to
check, start and shut down the **gopherd** server. You would also have to add lines to
execute the **/etc/sysconfig/network** script and to check that networking is operating.

You will notice that there is no script for the ftp server. As implemented by the
Caldera Network Desktop, the ftp server is managed by the **inetd** program, as
described in the next section. If you should want to have the ftp server running all the
time, you could make an **init** script for it and a symbolic link, just as described for the
gopherd server. The name of the ftp server program is **in.ftpd**. You would also
have to disable **inetd** management of the ftp server by commenting out its entry in
the **inetd.conf** file.

inetd Server Management

If your system averages only a few requests for a specific service, you do not need the
server for that service running all the time. You only need it when a remote user is
accessing its service. The **inetd** daemon manages Internet servers, invoking them
only when your system receives a request for their services. **inetd** checks
continuously for any requests by remote users for a particular Internet service, and
when it receives a request it then starts the appropriate server daemon. For example,
when **inetd** receives a request from a user to access ftp, it starts **ftpd**, the ftp
daemon. **ftpd** then handles the request, allowing the remote user to download files.

For **inetd** to call the appropriate server daemon, it must be configured for that service. You place entries for that server in the **/etc/services** and the **/etc/inetd.conf** files. The **/etc/services** file lists services available on your system. An entry in **/etc/services** consists of the name of the service followed by its port and protocol separated by a slash. Entries for ftp as they appear in your Redhat **/etc/service** file are shown here. Other distributions may require only one entry for ftp.

```
ftp-data        20/tcp
ftp             21/tcp
```

The **/etc/inetd.conf** file is the **inetd** configuration file. For this entry you specify the service, its protocol, and the server program to invoke. An entry for ftp is shown here. Server paths and arguments may vary according to different Linux distributions.

```
# <service> <sock_type> <proto> <flags> <user>  <server_path>    <args>
ftp          stream      tcp     nowait  root    /usr/sbin/ftpd   ftpd
```

On other Linux distributions, the configuration lines may be there, but they may be commented out with a preceding **#** symbol. Just remove the **#**. If there are no configuration entries, you will have to add them.

tcpd

You can use the **tcpd** daemon to add another level of security to **inetd** managed servers. You can set up **tcpd** to monitor a server connection made through **inetd**. **tcpd** will verify remote user identities and check to make sure they are making valid requests. With **tcpd** you can also restrict access to your system by remote hosts. Lists of hosts are kept in the **hosts.allow** and **hosts.deny** files. Entries in these files have the format **service:hostname:domain**. The domain is optional. For the service you can specify a particular service such as ftp or you can enter **ALL** for all services. For the hostname you can specify a particular host, or **ALL** for all hosts. In the following example, the first entry allows access by all hosts to the Web service, **http**. The second entry allows access to all services by the **pango1.train.com** host. The third and fourth entries allow **rose.berkeley.edu** and **caldera.com** ftp access.

```
http:ALL
ALL:pango1.train.com
ftp:rose.berkeley.edu
ftp:caldera.com
```

The **hosts.allow** file holds hosts that you allow access to. If you want to allow access to all but just a few specific hosts, you can specify **ALL** for a service in the **hosts.allow** file, but list the one you are denying access in the **hosts.deny** file. The **tcpd** man pages (**man tcpd**) provide more detailed information about **tcpd**.

To have **tcpd** monitor a server, you have to place the path name for **tcpd** in the path name field of a server's entry for the **inetd.conf** file. This is what your Caldera Network Desktop has already done for the **ftpd** server entry. Instead of the path name for the **ftpd** program, **/usr/sbin/in.ftpd**, there is the path name for the **tcpd** daemon, **/usr/sbin/tcpd**. The argument field that follows then lists the **in.ftpd** server program.

```
# <service> <sock_type> <proto> <flags> <user> <server_path>   <args>
ftp         stream      tcp     nowait  root   /usr/sbin/tcpd  in.ftpd
```

When **inetd** receives a request for an ftp service, it calls the **tcpd** daemon which then takes over and monitors the connection. Then it starts up the **in.ftpd** server program. By default, **tcpd** will allow all requests. To allow all requests specifically for the ftp service you would enter in the following in your **/etc/hosts.allow** file. The entry **ALL:ALL** opens up your system to all hosts for all services.

```
ftp:ALL
```

ftp Server

Your Caldera Network Desktop has already installed an ftp server and has created the directories where you can place files for ftp access. The directories have already been configured to control access by remote users, restricting use to just the ftp directories and any subdirectories. The directory reserved for your ftp files is **/home/ftp**. You just have to place the files you want to allow access to in that directory. You can also create subdirectories and place files there. Once connected to a network, a remote user can ftp to your system and download files you have placed in **/home/ftp** or any of its subdirectories.

Although your Caldera Network Desktop has already been configured as an ftp site, it may be helpful to understand how it is set up. Also, if you are using another system, you will need to know the following procedures to install an ftp server and create its data directories. However, for the Caldera Network Desktop, it has all been done for you already. You do not need to do any of this.

Ftp server software is available at different Linux ftp sites. At **sunsite.unc.edu** and its mirror site, ftp server software is located in the **/pub/Linux/systems/Network/file-transfer** directory. The Washington University ftp server is a file called **wu-ftpd-2.4-fixed.tar.gz**.

In the future you may want to download a new version of your ftp server software from such a site and use it to upgrade your server. If you download an ftp server from an ftp site, you will have to decompress the file and extract the archive. Several directories will be created for documentation and source code. The server package will include installation instructions for creating your server directories and compiling your software.

The ftp server, **ftpd**, must be running to allow ftp access by remote users. (**ftpd** options are shown in Table 12-1.) As with other servers, you can start the ftp server at boot time, through **inetd** when a request is received, or directly from the command line. The use of **inetd** for the ftp server is described in detail in the previous section, "Starting Servers." To start the ftp server when you boot your system, you have to set up an **init** script for it in the **/etc/rc.d/init.d** directory, as was described for the Web server. To start the ftp server from the command line, you enter the **ftpd** command with any options or arguments. The **ftpd** server can be called with several options. Usually it is called with the **-l** option that allows logins. The **-t** and **-T** options set timeouts for users, cutting off those that have no activity after a certain period of time. The **-d** option displays debugging information, and **-u** sets the umask value for uploaded files. The command name for the ftp server installed on your Caldera Desktop is **in.ftpd**—use it to invoke the ftp server directly.

The ftp User Account

To allow anonymous ftp access by other users to your system you must create a user account named ftp. You can then place restrictions on the ftp account to keep any

Option	Effect
-d	Writes debugging information to the syslog
-l	Logs each ftp session in the syslog
-t_seconds_	Sets the inactivity timeout period to specified seconds (default is 15 minutes)
-T_seconds_	The maximum timeout period allowed when timeout is set by user (default is two hours)
-a	Enables use of the ftpaccess(5) configuration file
-A	Disables use of the ftpaccess(5) configuration file
-L	Logs commands sent to the **ftpd** server to the syslog
-i	Logs files received by **ftpd** to xferlog
-o	Logs files transmitted by **ftpd** to the syslog

Table 12-1. _ftpd Options_

remote ftp users from accessing any other part of your system. You must also modify the entry for this account in your **/etc/passwd** file to prevent normal user access to it. The following is the entry that you will find in your **/etc/passwd** file on your Caldera Network Desktop that sets up an ftp login as an anonymous user.

```
ftp:*:14:50:FTP User:/home/ftp:
```

The asterisk in the password field blocks the account, which prevents any other users from gaining access to it and thereby gaining control over its files or access to other parts of your system. The user ID, 14, is a unique ID. The comment field is "FTP User". The login directory is **/home/ftp**. When ftp users log into your system, this is the directory they will be placed in. If a home directory has not been set up, create one and then change its ownership to the ftp user with the **chown** command.

The group ID is the ID of the **ftp** group, which is set up just for anonymous ftp users. You can set up restrictions on the **ftp** group, thereby restricting any anonymous ftp users. Here is the entry for the **ftp** group that you will find in the **/etc/group** file. For other Linux distributions, if you do not have one, you should add it.

```
ftp::50:
```

The permissions for the **/home/ftp** directory should deny write access. You do not want ftp users creating and deleting directories. You use the **chmod** command with the permission 555 to turn off write access: **chmod 555 /home/ftp**.

The **/home/ftp** directory and its permission, password, and group entries have already been set up on your Caldera Network Desktop. If you are setting up an ftp server on another distribution, you will have to set up **/home/ftp** yourself.

ftp Server Directories

To protect your system from any unwanted access by ftp users, you should create a restricted set of directories attached to the ftp directory, in this case, **/home/ftp**. A list of directories is provided in Table 12-2. An important part of protecting your system is preventing remote users from using any commands or programs that are not in the restricted directories. For example, you would not let a user use your **ls** command to list file names since **ls** is located in your **/bin** directory. At the same time, you want to let the ftp user list file names using an **ls** command. To do this you make a new bin directory in the **/home/ftp** directory and then make a copy of the **ls** command and place it in **/home/ftp/bin**. This bin directory would be restricted to use by ftp users, and whenever they use the **ls** command, they are using the one in **/home/ftp/bin**, not the one you use in **/bin**. Do this for any commands you want to make available to ftp users. Other commands you will need are **cd** to allow users to change directories and **more** to let them display text files. Your Caldera Network Desktop has already created

/home/ftp	ftp server directory; owned by root (on some distributions this may be **/usr/local/ftp**); all directories and subdirectories would have permissions of 555 or 755 to restrict other and group access to read and execute only
/home/ftp/bin	ftp bin directory to hold commands that ftp remote users can execute, such as **ls** and **cd**
/home/ftp/etc	ftp etc directory to hold configuration files such as its own **passwd** file
/home/ftp/pub	ftp directory where the files you are making available for downloading are placed; you can set up any subdirectories you wish
/home/ftp/lib	ftp lib directory used if the **ls** command needs the **ld.so.1** file

Table 12-2. *ftp Directories*

the **/home/ftp/bin** directory and installed a basic set of commands in it. You can add others if you wish.

You will also need a **/home/ftp/etc** directory, which holds a copy of your **passwd** and **group** files. Again the idea is to prevent any access to the original files in the **/etc** directory by ftp users. The **/home/ftp/etc/passwd** file should be edited to remove any entries for regular users on your system. All other entries should have their passwords set to * to block access. For the **group** file remove all user groups and set all passwords to *.

```
# cat /home/ftp/passwd
root:*:0:0:::
bin:*:1:1:::
operator:*:11:0:::
ftp:*:14:50:::
nobody:*:99:99:::

# cat /home/ftp/group
root::0:
bin::1:
daemon::2:
sys::3:
adm::4:
ftp::50:
```

A directory called **/home/ftp/pub** holds the files you are making available for downloading by remote ftp users. When ftp users log in, they will be placed in the **/home/ftp** directory and can then change to the **/home/ftp/pub** directory to start accessing those files. Within **/home/ftp/pub** you can add as many files and directories as you wish. You can even designate some directories as upload directories, allowing ftp users to transfer files to your system.

Some Linux systems require that the **ls** command have access to the **libc.so.1** and **rld** files in order to work. These are usually located in your **/lib** directory. Since you do not want to provide even indirect access to your system by ftp users, you have to create a **/home/ftp/lib** directory and then make a copy of these files and place the copies in there. In addition, since **rld** uses the **/dev/zero** file, you also have to create a **/home/ftp/dev** directory and use **mknod** to make a copy of the **/dev/zero** device file and place it in this directory.

Permissions

To restrict ftp users to the **/home/ftp** directory and its subdirectories, you have to hide the rest of the file structure from it. In effect, you have to make the **/home/ftp** directory appear to be the root directory as far as ftp users are concerned. The real root directory, **/**, and the rest of the directory structure remain hidden. You use the **chroot** command to make the **/home/ftp** directory appear as a root directory, with the ftp user as the argument.

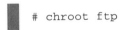

```
# chroot ftp
```

Now when ftp users issue a **cd /** command to change to the root, they will always change to the **/home/ftp** directory.

As a further restriction, all the directories that hold commands in **/home/ftp**, as well as the commands themselves, should be owned by the root, not by the ftp user. In other words, no ftp user should have any control over these directories. You change the ownership of a directory using the **chown** command. The following example changes the ownership of the **/home/ftp/bin** directory and the **/home/ftp/bin/ls** command to the root. The root has to own **/home/ftp/bin**, **/home/ftp/etc**, and all the files they contain. The Caldera Network Desktop has already done this for you. For other distributions you may have to set the ownership yourself.

```
# chown root  /home/ftp/bin
```

Permissions for the ftp directories should be set to allow access for ftp users. Recall that there are three sets of permissions—read, write, and execute for the owner, the group, and others. To allow access by ftp users, the group and other permissions for directories should be set to both read and execute. The execute permission allows ftp users to access that directory, and the read permission allows listing the contents of the directory. Directories should not allow write permission by ftp users. You don't want them to be able to delete your directories or make new ones. For example, the **/home/ftp/bin** directory needs both read and execute permissions since ftp users have to access and execute its commands. This is particularly true for directories such as **/home/ftp/pub**, which holds the files for downloading. It must have both read and execute permissions set.

You as the owner of the directories will need write permission to be able to add new files or subdirectories. Of course, you only need this when you are making changes. To add further security, you could set these directories at just read and execute even for the owner when you are not making changes. You can set all permissions to read and execute with the **chmod** command and the number 555 followed by the directory name. This sets the owner, group, and other permissions to read and execute. The permissions currently in place for the ftp directories on your Caldera Network Desktop are designated by the number 755, giving the owner write permission.

```
# chmod 555 /home/ftp/bin
```

Permissions for files within the **/home/ftp/bin** and other special ftp directories can be more restrictive. Some files only need to be read, while others have to be executed. Files such as **ls** and **rld** in the **/home/ftp/bin** or **/home/ftp/lib** directories only have to be executed. These could have their permissions set to 555. Files in the **/home/ftp/etc** directory such as **passwd** and **group** could have their permissions set to 111. They only have to be read. You always use the **chmod** command to set permissions for files, as shown in the following example. These permissions are already set on your Caldera Network Desktop. For other distributions you may have to set them yourself.

```
# chmod 111 /home/ftp/etc/passwd
```

ftp Files

In each directory set up under **/home/ftp/pub** to hold ftp files, you should create a **readme** file and an **index** file as a courtesy to ftp users. The **readme** file contains a brief description of the kind of files held in this directory. The **index** file should contain a listing of the files and a description of what each one holds.

Web Server

The Caldera Network Desktop automatically installs the Apache Web server on your system during installation, with all the necessary directories and configuration files. Your Caldera Network Desktop is already a fully functional Web site. Every time you start your system, the Web server starts up also, running continuously. The directory reserved for your Web site data files is **/home/httpd/html**. Place your Web pages in this directory or in any subdirectories. Apache provides online support and tutorials for its Web server at **http://www.apache.org**. There is also online support available from Caldera at **http://www.caldera.com**. You can obtain more detailed information there on developing your Web site and any problems you may encounter.

There is nothing more you have to do. Once connected to a network, remote users will be able to access your Web site. It may be helpful to understand how a Web site is set up. Also, if you are using another system, you will need to know the following procedures to install a Web server and create its supporting directories.

The Web server installed on your Caldera Network Desktop sets up your Web site in the **/home/httpd** directory. It also sets up several directories for managing the site, as listed in Table 12-3. **cgi-bin** holds the gateway interfaces, and the **icons** file holds

Web Server Directories	Description
/home/httpd	Location of your Web server directories
/home/httpd/cgi-bin	Common gateway interfaces and scripts
/home/httpd/icons	Icons for home pages
/home/httpd/html	The Web pages for your Web site
/etc/httpd/conf	Holds your Web server configuration files
httpd Option	
−d *directory*	Allows you to specify a directory for the httpd program if it is different from the default directory
−f *config-file*	Allows you to specify a configuration file different from **httpd.conf**
−v	Displays the version

Table 12-3. *Web Server Directories and httpd Options*

the icons used for your home page. Your Web pages are to be placed in the **/home/httpd/html** directory. You will already find your home page located there, **index.html**. Your configuration files are located in a different directory, **/etc/httpd/conf**.

There are also other Web servers freely available that you could also use if you wish. The NCSA httpd Web server was one of the first servers developed. Apache is very similar and corrects some of the problems with the NCSA httpd server. You can download server software from most Linux ftp sites. At **sunsite.unc.edu** and its mirror site, Web server software is located in the **/pub/Linux/systems/Network/info-systems /www/server** directory. You can use ftp or Netscape to access this directory. In the future you may want to download a new version of your Web server software from such a site and use it to upgrade your server.

If you download a Web server from an ftp site, you will have to decompress the file and extract the archive. Many of the same directories will be created, with added ones for documentation and source code. The server package will include installation instructions for creating your server directories and compiling your software.

Configuring Your Web Server

You configure your Web server software using several configuration files in the **/etc/httpd/conf** directory. Configuration varies depending on whether you want to run the Web server continuously as a daemon, or have it called when needed by **inetd**. If you are expecting a great deal of use, you should just run it directly as a daemon.

The **httpd.conf-dist** file configures the Web server daemon. It lists a set of variables and their values. Each entry consists solely of a variable name followed by a value, separated by a space. These variables set different features of your Web server. Some require path names, whereas others just need to be turned on or off with the keywords **on** and **off**. These variables are already set for the Caldera Network Desktop. You can, however, add to the list or change the ones already there. Table 12-4 provides a complete listing of the different variables you can place in the **httpd.conf-dist** file. Many of the entries are preceded by comments explaining their purpose. The following is an example of the ServerAdmin variable used to set the address where users can send mail for administrative issues. You replace the you@your.address entry with the address you want to use to receive system administration mail.

```
# ServerAdmin: Your address, where problems should be e-mailed.
ServerAdmin you@your.address
```

Only a few of the variables are set in this file. You do not need to set all of them. Some require specific information about your system. For example, ServerName specifies a separate hostname for your Web server. It must be a valid hostname in its own right. Suppose the hostname of your system was **richlp.ix.com**. You could have a separate hostname for your server called **www.ix.com**. Notice that the entry is commented with a preceding **#**. Just remove the **#** and type your Web server's hostname in place of **new.host.name**.

```
# ServerName allows you to set a hostname which is sent back to clients for
# your server if it's different than the one the program would get (i.e. use
# "www" instead of the host's real name).

#ServerName new.host.name
```

The **srm.conf** file configures the Web server's resources. It lists a set of variables and their values. Entries are usually preceded by commented explanations. Some already have values assigned, others you may need to enter yourself. You can change entries using a standard text editor. A list of these variables is provided in Table 12-5. The next example shows the entry for DocumentRoot. A commented explanation precedes the entry. The entry itself consists of the variable name followed by the value—in this case a directory path name.

```
DocumentRoot /usr/local/etc/httpd/htdocs
```

The **access.conf-dist** file determines the services that will be made available to users in the directories your server has access to. This file consists of a series of directives, each encased in a set of directory tags. The beginning tag is the word "Directory" with a directory path name, encased within less-than and greater-than symbols, <Directory *pathname*>. The ending tag uses the same <> symbols but with a slash preceding the term "Directory", </Directory>. Within the tags you can have several directives.

With the Options directive you can enable certain features such as use of symbolic links. With AllowOverride you can determine to what extent an **.htaccess** file in the directory can override the features set by a directive.

With the Limit directive, you can modify the **access.conf-dist** file to control access to your system by Web users. The Limit directive uses a set of tags just like the Directory tags. <Limit> begins a Limit directive and </Limit> ends it. The Limit directive specifies who can have access to your Web server. There are several options

Variable	Description
AccessConfig	Location of **access.conf** file (default is **conf/access.conf**)
AgentLog	Log file for actions (default is **logs/agent_log**)
ErrorLog	The location of the error log file; if this does not start with /, ServerRoot is prepended to it (default is **logs/error_log**)
Group	Group ID server runs when operating as a daemon
IdentityCheck	Checks identity of remote users
MaxClients	Limits total number of servers running, i.e., limits the number of clients who can simultaneously connect; if this limit is ever reached, clients will be locked out (default is 150)
MaxRequestsPerChild	Number of requests each child process is allowed to process before the child dies (default is 30)
PidFile	The file the server should log its pid to (default is **/logs/httpd.pid**)
Port	Port to wait for requests
ResourceConfig	Location of **srm.conf** file (default is **conf/srm.conf**)
ServerAdmin	Administrator's email address
ServerName	Separate hostname for the server
ServerRoot	The root directory for users of the Web server; also the directory where the server's config, error, and log files are kept (default is **/usr/local/etc/httpd**)
ServerType	Either stand-alone or **inetd**
StartServers	Number of servers to start with (default is 5)
TimeOut	Number of seconds to wait for a user request; if none is received in that time period, the user is logged out (default is 400)
TransferLog	Path to logs (default is **logs/access_log**)
TypesConfig	Location of MIME configuration file (default is **conf/mime.conf**)
User	User ID of the server

Table 12-4.   *Variables for **httpd.conf-dist***

Variable	Description
AccessFileName	File in each directory that holds access control information (**.htaccess** is the default)
AddDescription	Short description of file placed in server-generated indexes
AddEncoding *extensions-list*	Allows certain browsers with the capability to decompress files as they retrieve them; the extensions list contains extensions used to designate different types of compressions, such as **.gz** for **gzip** **AddEncoding x-gzip gz**
AddIcon *image file file-extensions*	Icons to use for particular file types; you specify the image file followed by a list of file name extensions, such as **.mpg**, **.bin**, or **.ps** **AddIcon /icons/movie.gif .mpg .qt**
AddIconByEncoding	Specifies icon and adds encoding information
AddIconByType	Uses MIME type to determine icon use
AddLanguage *language extension*	Allows you to specify the language of a document; you can then use content negotiation to give a browser a file in a language it can understand, then specify the language and an extension **AddLanguage en .en**
AddType *type/subtype extension*	Allows you to override MIME types without actually editing them, and designate specified files as certain types; commented entries are listed in the Apache **srm.conf-dist** file for enabling use of files such as map files
Alias *alias-name path-name*	Creates aliases for different path names **Alias /icons/ /usr/local/etc/httpd/icons/**
DefaultType	The default MIME type used for documents that the server cannot find the type of from file name extensions (default is **text/html**)
DefaultIcon	Which icon to show for files that do not have an icon
DirectoryIndex	File names for your Web site indexes; these are files to use as a prewritten HTML directory index; separate multiple entries with spaces (default is **index.html**)

Table 12-5. *Variables for **srm.conf***

Variable	Description
`DocumentRoot`	The directory out of which you will serve your documents; by default, all requests are taken from this directory, but symbolic links and aliases may be used to point to other locations (default is **/usr/local/etc/httpd/htdocs**)
`FancyIndexing`	Adds icons and file name information to file list for indexing; set on or off
`HeaderName`	File that should be appended to directory indexes (default is HEADER)
`IndexIgnore` *file-list*	Set of file names that directory indexing should ignore; these are files such as README or HEADER
`IndexOptions`	Indexing options
`LanguagePriority` *language-list*	Allows you to give precedence to some languages; content negotiation is ambiguous `LanguagePriority en fr de`
`OldScriptAlias`	Same as `Alias`
`ReadmeName`	The name of the README file the server will look for by default (default is README)
`Redirect`	Tells users where to find documents that are no longer on your server
`ScriptAlias` *alias-name path-name*	Controls which directories contain server scripts `ScriptAlias /cgi-bin/` `/usr/local/etc/httpd/cgi-bin/`
`UserDir`	The name of the directory that is appended to a user's home directory if a ~user request is received (default is **public_html**)

Table 12-5. *Variables for* **srm.conf** *(continued)*

you can use. For example, the **allow** option followed by a list of hostnames restricts access to just those users. The **deny** option with a list of hostnames denies access by those systems. Table 12-6 lists the different directives and their options.

Directory Tag	Description
`<Directory` *path-name>* `</Directory>`	Specifies directory to set controls for; ends with `</Directory>`

Directives

`Options` *feature-list*	Server options for specified directories; placed within Directory or Limit directives	
	All	Enables all features
	ExecCGI	CGI scripts executable
	FollowSymLinks	Enables symbolic links
	Includes	Allows use of include files
	IncludeNoExec	Allows include files but disables exec option
	Indexes	Allows users to retrieve indexes
	None	All features are disabled
	SymLinksIfOwnerMatch	Checks user ID before using symbolic links
`AllowOverride` *feature-list*	Controls options that the **.htaccess** files in directories can override	
	All	Unrestricted access
	AuthConfig	
	AuthName	Authorization name of directory
	AuthType	Authorization type of directory
	AuthUserFile	File containing user names and passwords
	AuthGroupFile	File containing allowable group names
	FileInfo	Enables AddType and AddEncoding directives
	Limit	Enables Limit directive
	None	No access allowed
	Options	Enables Options directive
`<Limit>` `</Limit>`	Controls access to your Web server using the following designations; the term **all** refers to all hosts	
	`allows` *host-list* `-host-list`	Permits specified hosts in the host-list access
	`denies` *host-list* `host-list`	Denies specified hosts in host-list from access
	`orders` *options*	Order in which deny and allow list are evaluated, as in: `order deny,allow`
	`requires` *host-list* `host-list`	Requires authentication using the AuthUserFile file

Table 12-6. *Directives for access.conf-dist*

You will find two Directory entries already in your **access.conf** file. The first Directory is meant to apply to the Directory that is your Web site root. This is where your Web pages are located. Check to see that the path name used in this first Directory entry is in fact the path name of your Web site root directory. If not, be sure to change it. An example of a Directory entry follows.

```
# This should be changed to whatever you set DocumentRoot to.
<Directory /home/httpd/htdocs>
Options Indexes FollowSymLinks
AllowOverride All
# Controls who can get stuff from this server.
<Limit GET>
order allow,deny
allow from all
</Limit>
</Directory>
# Place any directories you want access information for after this one.
```

Starting the Web Server

Before you start your Web server, you have to copy the configuration files ending with the extension **.conf-dist** to files with the same prefix but with just the extension **.conf**. The Web server reads configuration information only from files with a **.conf** extension. You have to copy the **httpd.conf-dist** file to **httpd.conf**.

You start your Web server with the command **httpd**. This command has several options. The **-d** option allows you to specify a directory for the **httpd** program if it is different from the default directory. With the **-f** option you can specify a configuration file different from **httpd.conf**. The **-v** option displays the version.

As noted previously in the discussion of **init** scripts, your Caldera Network Desktop runs the Web server daemon continuously, invoking it whenever you start your system. A startup script for the Web server called **httpd.init** is in the **/etc/rc.d/init.d** directory. A symbolic link through which the **rc** program runs is in the **/etc/rc.d/rc3.d** directory and is called **S85httpd**. For systems using other Linux distributions, you can place the Web server command in a system startup script such as **rc.local** or **rc.sysinit**.

If you want to have **httpd** called by the **inetd** daemon, place an entry for **httpd** in the **/etc/services** and **/etc/inetd.conf** files. **/etc/services** lists the different services available on your system. For a Web server you enter **http** with a port/tcp specification.

```
http    80/tcp
```

The Web server entry in the **/etc/inetd.conf** file is similar to the entry for the ftp server. The path name for the Web server installed on your Caldera Network Desktop is **/usr/sbin/httpd**. **httpd** takes no arguments.

```
http stream tcp nowait nobody /usr/sbin/httpd  httpd
```

To have Web server requests monitored and controlled by **tcpd**, you place the **/usr/sbin/tcpd** path name in place of the **/usr/sbin/httpd** path name.

```
http stream tcp nowait nobody /usr/sbin/tcpd  httpd
```

You also have to specify the **inetd** value for the ServerType variable in your **httpd.config-dist** file.

```
# ServerType is either inetd, or standalone.
ServerType inetd
```

The Caldera Network Desktop is not configured to run your Web server from **inetd**. If you want this done, you will have to place the appropriate entries in **/etc/services** and **/etc/inetd.conf** as well as comment out or remove the invocation of **httpd** in the **/etc/rc.d/init.d/httpd.init** file. To comment out the **httpd** command, you edit the **httpd.init** file and enter a **#** at the beginning of the line where the **httpd** command is called.

To check your Web server, you just start your Web Browser and enter the Internet domain name address of your system. For the system **pango1.train.com** the user enters **http://pango1.train.com**. This should display and the home page you placed in your Web root directory. A simple way to do this is to use **lynx**, the command line Web browser. Just start **lynx** and then press **g** to open a line where you can enter a URL for your own system. Then **lynx** will display your Web site's home page.

You can also use telnet to check to see if your Web server is operating. Use telnet, the hostname of your system, and the port that your Web server is operating off of.

```
telnet  pango1.train.com 80
```

Gopher Server

A Gopher server presents a highly organized way to access Internet resources such as data files or graphics. Unlike ftp, with Gopher you can present users with a menu of items from which they can choose. One menu can lead to another menu or to another

Gopher site. In this respect, Gopher is like the Web, allowing you to move from one site to another in search of resources, but it is like ftp in that only the resources are listed. There is no text or graphics to give you explanations.

Gopher uses a TCP/IP protocol called the Gopher protocol. It provides for the very fast transmission of Gopher menu files. Gopher information is held in these files, which contain lists of items accessible at certain sites. Each item is organized into five fields specifying the information about the item and where it can be found. The fields are separated by tabs: type, display name, selector string, hostname, and port.

The type can be one of several possible Gopher codes, as listed in Table 12-7. The display name is a description of the item as it will appear on the Gopher menu. The selector string is the item's unique identifier. The hostname is the hostname of the system where the item is located, and the port is the port to use when accessing this host system (usually 70).

File Type	Description
0	Text file
1	Gopher directory
2	CSO phone book server
3	Error
4	BinHex Macintosh file, HQX
5	Binary DOS file
6	Unix UUencoded file
7	Full text index (Gopher menu file)
8	Telnet session, includes the remote host's address
9	Binary file
g	GIF image file
h	HTML file
I	Graphic image file (other than GIF)
M	MIME multipart mixed message
P	Adobe PDF file
s	Sound file
T	TN3270 telnet session

Table 12-7. *Gopher File Types*

Gopher was developed at the University of Minnesota where it is currently supported, with new versions continually being developed. You can obtain a copy of Gopher from the University of Minnesota Gopher ftp site at **boombox.micro.umn.edu** in the directory **/pub/gopher/unix**. You can also obtain the Gopher server software from most Linux ftp sites. A copy is available at **sunsite.unc.edu** and its mirror sites in the **/pub/Linux/systems/Network/info-systems/gopher** directory or in **/pub/packages/info-systems/gopher/boombox-mirror/unix**. There is also a GNU Public Licensed Gopher server available called GN Gopher. It is already on your Caldera CD-ROM as the **gn-2.22-1.i386.rpm** package. Use rpm or glint to install and configure your GN Gopher server. The University of Minnesota provides the Gopher software free to any educational institution and for noncommercial uses. It does ask a license fee for commercial users or anyone charging a fee for information accessed through a version of their Gopher server. The GN Gopher server is provided free to anyone, commercial or not. The University of Minnesota also has a more advanced version of Gopher called Gopher+ that it is currently provided as a commercial product.

The procedures for creating GN and the University of Minnesota Gopher servers are different. Examples in this chapter use the 2.3 version of the University of Minnesota Gopher and the 2.20 version of GN Gopher, currently available at most Linux ftp sites. You will probably be able to obtain more recent versions. The University of Minnesota Gopher software package includes Gopher clients in addition to the sever. The GN Gopher software package includes only the server. The **gopher** client is a very fast line-mode client. There are, however, many other Gopher clients available from other sources, such as the **xgopher** client, a package on your Caldera CD-ROM that runs on your desktop.

The Gopher User Account and Data Directory

You will have to have a data directory for your Gopher data files as well as a user account and group specifically for Gopher access. Although the Caldera Network Desktop has already created the Gopher user, it has not created the data directory. If you are using another distribution you will also have to create the Gopher user.

Gopher User Account

To better control access by other Gopher users to your system, you should have an account named **gopher**. Your Caldera Network Desktop has already created the Gopher account and has fully configured it. The following is the entry that you will find in your **/etc/passwd** file on your Caldera Network Desktop for the Gopher user.

```
gopher:*:13:30:gopher:/usr/lib/gopher-data:
```

The asterisk in the password field blocks the account, which prevents any other users from gaining access to it and thereby gaining control over its files or access to other parts of your system. The user ID, 13, is a unique ID. The comment field is "gopher". The login directory is **/usr/lib/gopher-data**. When Gopher users log into your system, this is the directory they will be placed in.

For other distributions you will have to create the Gopher account. You can then place restrictions on it to keep any remote Gopher users from accessing any other part of your system. You would also have to modify the entry for this account in your **/etc/passwd** file to prevent normal user access to it by placing an asterisk in the password entry field of the Gopher password.

The group ID is the ID of the **gopher** group, which is set up just for Gopher users. You can set up restrictions on the **gopher** group, thereby restricting any Gopher users. Here is the entry for the **gopher** group that you will find in the **/etc/group** file. For other Linux distributions, if you do not have one, you should add it.

```
gopher::30:
```

Gopher Data Directory

Although the Caldera Network Desktop has specified that the **/usr/lib/gopher-data** is to be used as the Gopher data directory, this directory does not yet exist. You will have to create it. The data directory for your Gopher files should be the same as the home directory for the Gopher user account. After you create the directory, change its ownership to that of the Gopher user with the **chown** command. When you configure your Gopher server software, be sure to specify **/usr/lib/gopher-data** as your Gopher data directory. Otherwise, your server will not be able to find your Gopher files.

The University of Minnesota Gopher

In the following examples, the user has downloaded the University of Minnesota Gopher software package for Linux, which is called **gopher2_3.tar.gz**. The package is first unzipped with **gunzip** and then the files and directories are extracted using **tar**. This creates a directory called **gopher2_3**. Within this directory are different subdirectories for documentation and the applications. The **gopherd** directory holds your source code for the Gopher server, and the **gopher** directory holds the source code for your Gopher client. The **doc** directory has the documentation, including your man documents.

```
# gunzip gopher2_3.tar.gz
# ls
gopher2_3.tar
# tar xvf gopher2_3.tar
# ls
gopher2_3      gopher2_3.tar
# cd gopher2_3
```

```
# ls -F
Copyright MANIFEST Makefile.config.in Makefile.in README conf.h
config.guess config.h.in config.sub configure configure.in
copyright doc/ gopher/ gopherd/ gophfilt/ install-sh make.com
object/ patchlevel.h
```

To install the Gopher server, you first specify options in certain configuration files located in the **gopherd** directory. You have to provide information such as the directory where you want to place your Gopher menu files. You then compile the Gopher software. Compiling the software is merely a matter of entering the command **make** in your Gopher source code directory. **make** uses a Makefile to correctly compile the Gopher program for you. With version 2.3, University of Minnesota Gopher has a **configure** utility that automatically detects how your system is configured and creates Makefiles tailored to your specific system. Any system specific information has to be explicitly set in configuration files.

Configuring the University of Minnesota Gopher Server

Before you create your Gopher server, you have to configure it using entries in the **gopherd.conf** and **gopherdlocal.conf** file. In the University of Minnesota Gopher version these are found in the **gopherd** subdirectory. **gopherd.conf** is designed to configure system specific features such as the number of connections permitted. **gopherdlocal.conf** customizes your Gopher server providing information like the name of the administrator and controlling access by specified remote systems.

gopherd.conf   The **gopherd.conf** and **gopherdlocal.conf** files contain the configuration specifications for your Gopher server. A set of commented default specifications are already listed in the file. You just need to uncomment the ones you want by deleting the **#** at the beginning of the line, and then change any values if you wish.

You can set options such as the maximum number of users allowed or the compression method for transmitting files. Options are entered with the option's specification and a colon followed by a space and the option's value. The following example sets the maximum number of users.

```
MaxConnections: 15
```

You have to specify an alias for the Gopher service on your system. You do this with the **hostalias:** entry. Usually this is just the full hostname of your system, though some systems may identify it with the host part of the name as **gopher**. In the next example, the **hostalias** is the full hostname, **garnet.train.com**.

```
hostalias: garnet.train.com
```

You may also have to set the full path name for the **gopherdlocal.conf** file. There is an entry that begins with the **include** command and specifies the location of the **gopherdlocal.conf** file. On your Caldera Network Desktop, your **gopherd** server along with the **gopherd.conf** and **gopherdlocal.conf** files should be installed in the **/usr/sbin** directory. When the **gopherd** server is run, it reads the **gopherd.conf** file for configuration information, which in turn reads the **gopherdlocal.conf** file for specific configuration information. The **include** operation in **gopherd.conf** may need to have the full path name for **gopherdlocal.conf**, which in this case would be **/usr/sbin/gopherdlocal.conf**.

```
include: /usr/sbin/gopherdlocal.conf
```

With the **ignore** and **ignore_patt** options you can restrict the files that are accessible to Gopher users. **ignore** will deny access to any file with a specified extension, for example, **ignore: conf** denies access to any file with a .conf extension. **ignore_patt** restricts any file with the specified pattern, for example, **ignore_patt bin** denies access to any file whose file name contains the pattern "bin".

gopherdlocal.conf   The **gopherdlocal.conf** file is designed to hold local customizations. Its entries will override comparable entries in the **gopherd.conf** file. In the **gopherdlocal.conf** file you specify management information such as the name of the system administrator and the description of your Gopher service. There are two entries in the **gopherdlocal.conf** file for the system administrator: Admin: and AdminEmail:. Use the Admin: entry to add the system administrator's name. You can also add other information, such as a phone number. Use the AdminEmail: entry for the system administrator's email address.

```
Admin: Richard Petersen
AdminEmail:  rp@richlp.com
```

A series of entries provide information about your Gopher server. The Abstract: entry is a notice displayed to any user who uses your system. It briefly describes what your Gopher server provides. The Language: entry is used to tell users what language most of your files are in. These are both entries you should make. Other informational entries are options. For the Org: entry you can enter your organization, and for Loc:

you can enter your address. The BummerMsg: entry specifies the message that is displayed when users make an error or cannot get onto your site because it is already in use by the maximum number of users.

With the access: option you can restrict access by other systems. An access: entry has the following format:

```
access: hostname permission-list num
```

The hostname is the domain name or IP address of either a network or a remote system. The num setting specifies how many users from that network or system can have access at any one time. The permission list sets the permissions for users from that network or system. There are four possible permissions: browse, ftp, read, and search. To turn off a permission you precede it with an exclamation point (!). The browse permission allows users to list files in directories, ftp allows your system to be used as an ftp gateway, read allows access to files, and search allows access to indexes.

For the hostname you can specify a network address, the address of a particular system, or a default entry that allows access by any system. The default entry uses the keyword **default** for the hostname. In the next example, the Gopher server is open to any user with the read and search permissions enabled, but with the browse and ftp permissions denied. No single network or system can have more than 15 of their users on your Gopher server at one time.

```
access: default  !ftp read search !browse  15
```

To control access from a particular network you can use an access: entry with the network's domain name. In the next example, up to 5 users from the network **train.com** can access your Gopher server, but they have no browse capability.

```
access: train.com  ftp read search !browse  5
```

Instead of a domain name you can use an IP address for a network or system. For the network you specify only the network portion of an IP address. Don't forget to end the address with a period. In the next example, the network with the address 199.189. is denied use of your system as an ftp gateway. Only 7 users are allowed on at one time.

```
access: 199.189.  !ftp read search browse  7
```

To provide access by a particular system you enter that system name for the host. In the next example, the system with the IP address of 204.166.189.21 has full access to your Gopher system. If the system is a stand-alone PC used by one person, you could specify that only one user from that system can have access.

```
access: 204.166.189.21 ftp read search browse   1
```

Makefile.config and conf.h   Before you compile your Gopher server, you should check your **Makefile.config** and **conf.h** files for certain configurations. In the **Makefile.config** file first check the directory path that the Gopher program expects to operate from. This is assigned to a variable called PREFIX. If you want to operate Gopher out of a different directory, modify the default path name that is assigned to the PREFIX variable. The Caldera Network Desktop expects to find server programs in the **/usr/sbin** directory. You should move PREFIX to this directory. You can also modify other directory variables if you wish.

```
PREFIX=/usr/sbin
```

You should also check the entries for the DOMAIN, SERVERPORT, SERVERDATA, and SERVEROPTS variables. The DOMAIN variable specifies the network portion of your hostname. For **richlp.ix.com** the network portion would be **.ix.com**. Be sure to include the preceding period. If your hostname command displays your fully qualified domain name, then you can just leave this blank.

```
DOMAIN=.ix.com
```

The SERVERPORT variable is set to 70, and you should leave it at this for general access. The SERVERDATA variable holds the path name for the directory where your Gopher data files are kept. By default this is **/gopher-data**. If you want to use another directory, you have to assign it to SERVERDATA. For the Caldera Network Desktop you should set this to **/usr/lib/gopher-data**. The SERVEROPTS variable is assigned a list of options used to control your Gopher service. You can add the date and time to titles or set the maximum number of users. A list of these options can be found in Table 12-8.

```
SERVERDATA=/usr/lib/gopher-data
```

In the **conf.h** file you can set values for features such as the length of timeouts and the programs to use for certain operations such as viewing a graphics file. The **conf.h** file contains a list of define entries familiar to those with C programming experience. An entry begins with **#define** followed by an uppercase term and then a value. To change a value for a specific term, carefully use your text editor to delete the value

Makefile.config	Description
PREFIX	The base path name for installing software (default is **/usr/local**)
CLIENTDIR	Directory where Gopher client is installed (default is **/usr/local/bin**)
CLIENTLIB	Gopher client help files
MAN1DIR	Directory where the man pages for the Gopher client are installed
MAN8DIR	Directory where the man pages for **gopherd** server are installed
SERVERDIR	Directory where Gopher server and configuration files are installed (**gopherd** and **gopherd.conf**—default is **/usr/local/etc**)

CLIENTOPTS	Options for the Gopher client program
	  -DONOMAIL Remote users cannot mail files
	  -DAUTOEXITONU Treat q and u as the same, and automatically exit from the top menu (useful if Gopher called from another application)

DOMAIN	If your system does not return the fully qualified domain name, you have to specify the network address of your system; otherwise, leave null
SERVERPORT=*num*	Sets port that Gopher server uses to wait for requests, usually 70
SERVERDATA=*pathname*	Location of the Gopher data files to be made available by the Gopher server; for the Caldera Network Desktop this directory is **/usr/lib/gopher-data**
SERVEROPTS=*options-list*	
Options for Gopher Server	-DADD_DATE_AND_TIME Adds date and time to Gopher titles -DDL Sets up support for dl database utility -DCAPFILES Provides compatibility with **.cap** directories -DLOADRESTRICT Restricts user access -DSETPROCTITLE Sets process title displayed by ps

Table 12-8.   *University of Minnesota Gopher **Makefile.config** and **conf.h***

Makefile.config	Description
DLPATH	Path to dl database
conf.h	
CLIENT1_HOST	Host to contact first (default host listed here) **#define CLIENT1_HOST "gopher.tc.umn.edu"**
CLIENT2_HOST	Host to contact **#define CLIENT2_HOST "gopher2.tc.umn.edu"**
CLIENT1_PORT	Port to contact first (default is 70) **#define CLIENT1_PORT 70**
CLIENT2_PORT	Port to contact (default is 70)
PAGER_COMMAND	Command to page through text
MAIL_COMMAND	Command for Gopher users to send mail (default is **/bin/mail**)
TELNET_COMMAND	Command to use for telnet sessions (default is telnet)
PRINTER_COMMAND	Command to use for printing (default is **lpr**)
PLAY_COMMAND	Command to use for playing sounds (default is **/bin/false**)
IMAGE_COMMAND	Command to use for viewing graphics (default is **xloadimage**)
HTML_COMMAND	Command to use for viewing Web pages (no default, but can specify **lynx**)
MAXLOAD	Load average at which to restrict connections (default is 10.0)
READTIMEOUT	Timeout in seconds for network reads (default is 1 * 60)
WAISMAXHITS	Maximum number of retrieved items to return from a WAIS query (default is 40)
NOMAIL	If defined, restricts users from mailing or downloading files (currently commented out with enclosing /* */, remove comments to enable)
GOPHERHELP	Online Gopher help file
TN3270_COMMAND	Command for TN3270 sessions

Table 12-8.   *University of Minnesota Gopher **Makefile.config** and **conf.h** (continued)*

conf.h	
MIME_COMMAND	Command for MIME operations (default is metamail -P)
AFTP_HOST	Sets ftp gateway (currently set to **gopher-gw.micro.umn.edu**)
CONF_FILE	Sets the location of the **gopherd.conf** file; the default is **/usr/local/etc/gopherd.conf**; for the Caldera Network Desktop you have to change this to **/usr/sbin** **#define CONF_FILE /usr/sbin**
DELETE_BOOKMARKS_ONLY	Restricts **delete** command to deleting bookmarks (currently commented out)

Table 12-8. *University of Minnesota Gopher* **Makefile.config** *and* **conf.h** *(continued)*

and type the new one in its place. Default values are already entered. The next example sets the print operations to the **lpr** command.

```
#define PRINTER_COMMAND "lpr"
```

For the Gopher client you use the CLIENT1_HOST entry to specify the Gopher server to which it will be connected by default. The next example connects to **gopher.tc.umn.edu**, the original Gopher Internet site.

```
#define CLIENT1_HOST  "gopher.tc.umn.edu"
```

The **conf.h** file can be confusing. This is a C program file, not a shell script file. It looks different from other configuration files. In most configuration files, a **#** is a comment, but in the **conf.h** file it is the beginning of a define directive. In **conf.h** a comment is anything encased by an opening **/*** and a closing ***/**. Such entries are commented out, disabling them. To enable them you remove the **/*** and ***/** symbols around them.

Though the default entries for the **conf.h** file should work fine, you can change them if you wish. However, be careful to change entries used for Linux systems. Linux uses any entries not reserved for other systems. If you see an entry preceded by a **#if defined(***system***)**, where system is the name of an operating system, then the following entries only apply to that operating system, until the next **#endif**. Thus,

`#if defined(sun)` applies only to Sun systems. There is a large section devoted entirely to the VMS operating system. Most entries that apply to Linux are at the end of the **conf.h** file, with a few at the beginning.

You are now ready to compile your Gopher software. You can compile both the Gopher client and the Gopher server with the following command.

```
# make install
```

To compile just one or the other, use the **make** command with either the term "client" or "server".

```
# make client
# make server
```

This creates a server program called **gopherd**. You can then invoke **gopherd** directly or from **inetd**.

Starting the University of Minnesota Gopher

Before you start your Gopher server, you should first create some Gopher menu files as described in the next section. As noted in a prior section, "Starting Servers," you can start the Gopher server from the command line, or at boot time automatically using an **init** script, or through **inetd** when a request for the Gopher service is received. The University of Minnesota Gopher Server options are listed in Table 12-9.

The Caldera Network Desktop has already configured your system to run Gopher through **inetd**. This configuration expects to locate the Gopher data directory in **/usr/lib/gopher-data**. In the **/etc/services** file you will find an entry for Gopher as shown here. It specifies the name of the service with the port number and the protocol. On other distributions you may have to enter it.

```
gopher   70/tcp
```

There is already an entry for Gopher in the **/etc/inetd.conf** file. The entry currently references the GN Gopher server, **gn**. You will have to modify it for the **gopherd** server. In place of the entry for **gn** you enter **gopherd** with the **-I** option and the path name for the Gopher data directory. The **-I** option specifies that **gopherd** is to be called with **inetd**. You can also add the port number, in this case, 70. This entry is also set up to use the **tcpd** to monitor and control access by remote users. Your entry should look like the following example. The Gopher data files are in **/usr/lib/gopher-data**, and the port is 70. The arguments, including the name of the **gopherd** program are **gopherd -I /usr/lib/gopher-data 70**.

```
gopher stream tcp nowait root  /usr/sbin/tcpd  gopherd -I
/usr/lib/gopher-data 70
```

Should you not want to use **tcpd**, you can replace it with the path name for the **gopherd** server program.

```
gopher stream tcp nowait root  /usr/sbin/gopherd gopherd -I
/usr/lib/gopher-data 70
```

If you want to start the **gopherd** server on the command line, you enter **gopherd** and as its arguments the path name of the directory for the Gopher data files and the port number. **gopherd** has several possible options, as listed in Table 12-10. As a precaution you can use the **-u** option to specify an owner other than root to run **gopherd**. You have to first create the user and enter a * in the password field of its **passwd** entry. The user's home directory will be the gopher data directory. The Caldera Network Desktop has already created a user called gopher. In the following

Option	Description
-C	Disables caching of directory requests
-c	Runs without **chroot** restrictions; allows access to files outside Gopher data root through symbolic links, such as system man files; potential security risk, should use with **-u** *username* option
-D	Enables debugging
-I	Uses **inetd** to invoke Gopher
-L *num*	Specifies maximum load average
-l *logfile*	Logs connections to log file
-o *conf-file*	Specifies alternate **gopherd.conf** configuration file
-u *username*	Runs **gopherd** under username; provides added restrictions for security purposes
-U *userid*	Runs **gopherd** under userid; provides added restrictions for security purposes (same as **-u**)

Table 12-9. *University of Minnesota Gopher Server Options*

gopherd.conf	Description
hostalias: *DNS-alias-name*	Uses this hostname instead of the system's; hostname must be a valid DNS name; used to reference Gopher servers on a system such as **gopher.ix.com** **hostalias: gopher.turnip.com**
cachetime: *seconds*	Seconds that a cache file used to cache Gopher directories remains valid
viewext: *extension* *Gophertype Prefix* *Gopher+Type [Language]*	Maps a file name extension onto a particular Gopher type; most of these are already set for you in the **gopherd.conf file**. The first argument is an extension such **.gif**; the second argument is the single character Gopher type (1, 0, I, etc.); the third argument is a prefix that will be appended to the normal file name path; the fourth argument is the Gopher+ view attribute or Internet Media Type (formerly called MIME Content Types), such as image/gif; the optional fifth argument is a language to use for the file instead of the default language **viewext: .jpg I 9 image/JPEG** **viewext: .html h 0 text/html**
ignore: *extension*	Ignores files with specified extension; these files are not presented to Gopher users **ignore: bin**
ignore_patt: *regular-expression*	Ignores files that match the regular expression; these files are not presented to Gopher users
blockext: *extension*	Maps files with specified extension to attribute blocks
decoder: *extension program*	The specified program will be run on files with the indicated extension when the file is retrieved; used with compressed files **decoder: .gz /usr/gnu/bin/zcat**
pids_directory: *path-name*	A scratch directory to store pid files in

Table 12-10.   *gopherd.conf and gopherdlocal.conf Entries*

gopherd.conf	Description
`maxconnections:` *num*	The number of concurrent connections that the Gopher server can handle at the same time

gopherdlocal.conf

`admin:` *administrator-name-and-info*	The administrator's name and added information such as a phone number
`adminemail:` *email-address*	Email address of Gopher server administrator
`site:` *site-description*	Descriptive name of the site
`loc:` *address*	Address of site—street, city, etc.
`geog:`	Longitude and latitude for site
`language:` *default-language*	Default language used by the site
`secureusers:` *filename*	Specifies file listing authorized hosts and networks
`bummermsg:`	Message displayed when a client is denied access
`access:` *domain name access-list*	Allows you to determine who can browse directories, read files, and search your system. The first argument is a domain name, IP address, or default; the second argument is a list of comma-separated words determining access; the words are: browse, read, search, and ftp. Each can be preceded by a ! to deny access; **default !browse, read, search, !ftp** sets the default to deny browsing and ftp, but allow reading and searching. If you set the default first, it will be inherited by following entries and you only need to specify the access that differs. Optionally, you can base the access on the number of concurrent transactions in an added argument **access: default browse,read,search,ftp 5**

Table 12-10. *gopherd.conf* and *gopherdlocal.conf* Entries (continued)

example, the full path name for the **gopherd** server program is **/usr/sbin/gopherd**, the Gopher data files are in **/usr/lib/gopher-data**, and the port is 70.

```
/usr/sbin/gopherd -u gopher /usr/lib/gopher-data 70
```

To have the Gopher server start automatically whenever you boot, you can create an **init** script for it in the **/etc/rc.d/init.d** directory. The section on **init** scripts at the beginning of this chapter provides a detailed description on how to do this for the **gopherd** server.

GN Gopher Server

Your Caldera Linux system is already configured for your GN Gopher server. The GN Gopher server is automatically installed if you choose the Complete Install option, but with the Recommended Install option, you have to use rpm or glint to install the **gn-2.22-1.i386.rpm** package. In either case, your Gopher server is ready to use. You can start adding Gopher files and menus to the **/usr/lib/gopher-data** directory. However, if you are using another version of Linux, you will have to download the standard GN Gopher server package, **gn-2.20.tar.gz**, from a Linux ftp site, and then configure and install it. Unzipping and extracting this file will create a directory called **gn-2.20** that holds the GN Gopher server sources and documentation.

The GN Gopher package contains source code that you need to configure for Linux before you compile it. There is one configuration file, **config.h**, and a Makefile that holds compiler directives. The **INSTALL** file in the **docs** subdirectory has detailed instructions on how to create your GN server, as well as setting up a Gopher site. The **docs/examples** directory has numerous examples of GN Gopher menus.

Configuring the GN Gopher Server

To configure the GN Gopher server, you modify entries in the **config.h** file and the Makefile. There are certain entries that are compulsory, that you have to specify. These are clearly indicated at the beginning of the file with the heading "Compulsory items to fill in". You have to enter your hostname and the path name of the Gopher data directory, as well as specify that you are using a Linux system. You can make any other customizations you want. An entry in the **config.h** file has the format of a **#define** term followed by the item and then the value you want for it. You can change the value, not the item. The following entries are valid for the Caldera Network Desktop distribution of Linux. In place of the hostname **garnet.train.com** you should have your own system's hostname.

```
#define GN_HOSTNAME     "garnet.train.com"
#define ROOT_DIR  "/usr/lib/gopher-data"
#define LINUX
#define MAINTAINER      "mailto:justin@garnet.train.com"
#define ROOT_MENU_NAME  "GN -- A Gopher/HTTP Server"
#define GN_LOGFILE  "/var/log/gn.log"       /* "/path/to/gn.log" */
#define MIME_TYPE_FILE  "/usr/local/gn_mime.types"
#define WAISGN  "/usr/sbin/waisgn"
```

Following the compulsory items there are several other items that you also change if you wish, though the defaults should work fine. Should you want to use a different port you can specify it in the DEFAULTPORT entry. You can set the time out with the TIMEOUT entry and set the maximum depth of menu searches in the MAXDEPTH entry. In the Makefile you have to specify the type of C compiler you are using and the directories where you want your server program placed. You will find two entries for the CC which designates the type of C compiler to use. The one specifying **gcc** will be commented out with a preceding #. The one for **cc** will not. You have to comment the **cc** entry by placing a # before it and remove the # from the **gcc** entry. This sets the CC entry to the **gcc** compiler. Also, in the Makefile you can set SERVERBINDIR, which holds the directory path where you want to place the server program. BINDIR is the directory for the **mkcache** an **uncache** programs. Set these to the directories where you want those programs placed such as **/usr/sbin**. On your Caldera Network Desktop using the Redhat distribution, the SERVERFINDER directory should be set to **/usr/sbin**, the directory that holds daemons. Though the **mkcache** and **uncache** programs can go anywhere, it may be best to also place them together with the GN server by also setting BINDIR to **/usr/sbin**.

Just below these variables, you will find the following entry for **include** directories. Uncomment the one for Linux by removing the preceding # so that it reads

```
# INCLUDES= -I.. -I../gn
# For Linux use
INCLUDES= -I.. -I../gn -I/usr/include/bsd
```

Further down in the Makefile you will find an empty entry for the Libraries as shown here.

```
#    Libraries to be included.
LIBS    =
```

Following this entry will be comments specifying libraries for different systems. The Linux specification will look like this:

```
#For Linux use
#LIBS = -lbsd
```

You can either uncomment this LIBS entry by removing the preceding #, or type in the -lbsd value in the prior empty LIBS entry.

```
LIBS = -lbsd
```

Once configured, you can then create the server by entering **make**. This creates two executable server programs called **sgn** and **gn**. **gn** is for use with **inetd**, while **sgn** is the stand-alone daemon that you can run directly. It also creates two utility programs, **mkcache** and **uncache**. Then enter **make install** to install these programs on your system.

Starting the GN Gopher Server

You are now ready to start the server. However, before you start your Gopher server, you should first create some Gopher menu files as described in the next section. You can either run the server as a stand-alone daemon or through **inetd**. See Tables 12-11 and 12-12.

The Caldera Network Desktop has already configured your system to run the GN Gopher server through **inetd**. After creating and installing the GN Gopher server, all you have to do to have a fully functioning Gopher server is to create your Gopher data files and place them in the **/usr/lib/gopher-data** directory.

To use **inetd**, there have to be entries for the Gopher server in the **/etc/services** and /etc/inetd.conf files. The Caldera Network Desktop has already placed those entries. You will find the following entry in the **/etc/services** file.

```
gopher 70/tcp
```

In the **/etc/inetd.conf** file, you will find the following entry for the GN Gopher server. Notice that the GN Gopher server is invoked with **gn**. This is the version of the GN server that works through **inetd**. Also, **tcpd** is used to monitor and control Gopher access.

```
gopher stream tcp nowait root /usr/sbin/tcpd  gn
```

You can also start the GN Gopher at boot time with an **init** script or directly from the command line. In both cases, the server has to be run as a stand-alone daemon using the **sgn** version of the GN Gopher. If you want to start Gopher at boot time, you have to create an **init** script for it in the **/etc/rc.d/init.d** directory as described in a

GN_HOSTNAME	Sets the hostname for your server; this is the hostname of your system
ROOT_DIR	Sets the Gopher data directory; for the Caldera Network Desktop this is **/usr/lib/gopher-data**
LINUX	Defines Linux as your operating system; the default here will be SUN_OS; you have to replace it with LINUX
MAINTAINER	Mail address of administrator
ROOT_MENU_NAME	Name you want displayed as the title of your Gopher menu; default is "GN — A Gopher/HTTP Server"
GN_LOGFILE	Location for a GN log file
MIME_TYPE_FILE	Location of MIME configuration file; default is **/usr/local/gn_mime.types**; you place this file anywhere, but be sure to set this path name accordingly
WAISGN	Path name of the **waisgn** program that handles WAIS indexes **/usr/sbin/waisgn**
DEFAULTPORT	Sets the default port for Gopher access, currently 70
TIMEOUT	Sets the timeout waiting for requests
MAXDEPTH	Sets the maximum depth of menu searches
USERID	The user ID that the GN server will be run as for security purposes
GROUPID	The group ID that the GN server will be run as for security purposes
DECOMPRESS	Program used to decompress files; default is **/usr/local/bin/zcat**
MENUFNAME	Sets the name used for menu files; the default is **menu**
TEMPDIR	Sets the temporary directory; default is **/tmp**

Table 12-11.   *The GN Server config File*

previous section, "Starting Servers." You enter **sgn** with arguments specifying the path name of the directory for the Gopher data files and the port number (usually 70). The port number is specified with the **-p** option. As a precaution **sgn** will automatically run as the user specified in the USERID entry in the **config.h** file.

```
sgn -p 70 /usr/lib/gopher-data
```

CC	Sets the C compiler; default setting is cc; you have to change it to gcc; CC = gcc
INCLUDE	Sets Include directories; should be set to use **/usr/include/bsd**
SERVBINDIR	Directory for your GN and SGN server programs; default is **../bin**; should be set to **/usr/sbin**
BINDIR	Directory for cache support programs; default is **../b**; should be set to **/usr/sbin**
LIBS=	Sets the library used; uncomment the one for Linux by removing #; should be set to **-lbsd**

Table 12-12.   *The GN Server Makefile*

Testing the Gopher Server

Once your Gopher server is running, you can test it using either telnet or a Gopher client. With telnet, you telnet into your own system specifying the port used for Gopher. The following command tests a Gopher server on the **garnet.train.com** system. Startup messages will be displayed.

```
telnet garnet.train.com 70
```

If you then press ENTER, the menu items for the main Gopher directory on your server will be displayed, output in the following format:

```
type display-name   selector   hostname   port
```

Here is an example of a test of a Gopher server:

```
# telnet garnet.train.com 70
Trying 127.0.0.1...
Connected to garnet.train.com.
Escape character is '^]'.

0About My Weather Site  0/intro     garnet.train.com    70    +
1California Weather Information    1/calif    garnet.train.com    70    +
1New York Weather this week    1/newyork    garnet.train.com    70    +
1The Weather in Hawaii     1/weather/hawaii/
garnet.train.com    70
.
```

You can also use your Gopher client to access your own Gopher server. In the next example, the Gopher client on **garnet.train.com** is used to access the Gopher server on the same system. The main Gopher menu for the Gopher server will be displayed and the user can then select and access items.

```
gopher garnet.train.com
```

Gopher Directories

A Gopher menu that you see displayed when you access a Gopher site, is generated using special files contained within a Gopher directory. Gopher menus are designed to operate by directory, listing the different files available within a directory or referencing another directory. Special Gopher menu configuration files within each directory provide information about the different data files available and how to access them. The University of Minnesota Gopher server uses **.cap** directories and link files to organize Gopher menus. The GN Gopher server uses a **menu** and **.cache** file. However, the entries for the link and GN menu files are much the same.

Gopher Cap and Link Files

By default any files and subdirectories in a Gopher directory are automatically displayed in a Gopher menu in alphabetical order. Data files are given a type 0, and directories a type 1. The name used for each menu item is the name of the file or directory. You can override this listing by using cap files.

Your Gopher data files can have any name you wish to give them. However, Gopher files are usually described in a Gopher menu using a descriptive sentence. By selecting that menu item, the file associated with that sentence is selected. The association between this descriptive sentence and the Gopher data file is carried out either by special files in a **.cap** directory or by entries in an extended link file.

Each directory of Gopher data files can have its own **.cap** directory, which holds files of the same name as those in the Gopher data directory. If you have a Gopher data file called **engine.1**, there will be a file in the **.cap** directory also called **engine.1**. A file in the **.cap** directory contains three entries: Name, Type, and Numb. Name is assigned the descriptive sentence used for the menu item that references the Gopher data file. The Type entry specifies the type of Gopher resource. 1 is a directory and 0 is a text file. The Numb entry is assigned the number of your Gopher entry in the Gopher menu; for example, Numb=3 indicates that this is the third item in the Gopher menu.

.cap/engine.1

```
Name=The best engine in the world
Type=0
Numb=1
```

When displayed on the Gopher menu this entry will appear as the first entry. Selecting it will select the **engine.1** Gopher data file.

```
1. The best engine in the world.
```

Although **.cap** files can be used to reference data files in your directory, they do not reference files in other directories or at other Gopher sites. For this you use a link entry in a link file. There is one link file in a directory that has several link entries to different Gopher resources. A link file is any file beginning with a period. A common name for a link file is **.links**.

Each entry for a link has five variables set: Name, Type, Port, Path, and Host. You can also add an entry for the menu order, NUMB. The Name entry is the descriptive sentence used in the menu item. The Port is the port used for connection to a remote system and is usually set to 70. The Type is the type of resource that the menu item references. A resource could be a file, but it can also be a telnet session or a graphics file. Gopher can reference files other than data files. The Path variable holds the path name for the resource that the menu item references. The path name here is the path starting from the Gopher data directory. The directory **/usr/lib/gopher-data/calif** would have a path name of **/calif**, where **/usr/lib/gopher-data** is the Gopher data directory. The path name can also be preceded by the Type. The **calif** directory could be entered as **1/calif**, 1 being the type for a directory. Host holds the hostname where the resource is to be found. For your own system this will be your own hostname. If the resource is located on another system, it will have that system's hostname. A **+** sign for the Port and Host entries will indicate the current port and hostname. For files and directories on your own system, it is best to leave out the Port and Hostname entries.

.links

```
Name=The best engine in the world
Type=1
Port=70
Path=1/engines
Host=richlp.ix.com
```

You may also use links to set up ftp or WAIS connections to other systems to access files or information from them. In this case the service you are using and its arguments are specified in the Path entry. Both Host and Port have a + entry. The format for an ftp link is shown here:

```
Name=ftp-file-or-directory
Type=1
Path=ftp:hostname/path/
Host=+
Port=+
```

For example, to set up an ftp link to access the file **caboose1** on **chris.train.com**, you would set the path as shown in the following example. The current port and hostname are indicated by + for their entries.

```
Name=The last caboose
Type=0
Port=+
Path=ftp:pango1.train.com/usr/lib/gopher-data/caboose1
Host=+
```

For a WAIS link you can access WAIS resources on your own system or on a remote system. For your own system you use **waisrc:** followed by the path to the WAIS resource. For a remote system you include the hostname after **waisrc:**, for example:

```
waisrc:pango1.train.com/usr/wais/data.
```

You can also set up a link to execute shell scripts, rather than just accessing a resource. In this case the Path variable is set to **exec:** followed by the script arguments and name. The arguments are enclosed in double quotes, and if there are none you just use an empty set of quotes. The argument and script are separated by a colon.

```
Path=exec:"arguments":script
```

Instead of maintaining separate **.cap** files in each directory along with a separate link file, you can use an extended link file to hold both the local file entries and the link entries. A common name for a link file is **.names**. The **.names** would list each Name and Numb entry along with a Path entry to specify the location of the file. The

.names file also has an Abstract entry that allows you to enter a brief description of the file's contents. In the **.names** file shown here the first entry references a local file in the directory whereas the second entry references a remote Gopher site.

.names

```
Path=/engines
Name=The best engine in the world
Numb=1
Abstract=A discussion of the best steam engine ever built.

Name=The oldest train running
Type=1
Port=70
Path=1/museums
Host=pango1.train.com
```

GN Gopher Directories

GN Gopher directories place their menu entries in a file called **menu**. Each Gopher directory will have its own **menu** file with the entries for each menu item. GN Gopher uses the same set of entries as described for the University of Minnesota Gopher with a few exceptions. Within the **menu** file you list the Path, Name, Numb, and Abstract for each menu item. However, before the path name in the Path entry you have to specify the Gopher type. This is usually a one digit number such as 0 for text files and 1 for directories.

```
Name=About My Weather Site
Path=0/intro
Type=0
Numb=1
Abstract=Important Weather Information.
```

GN Gopher requires the creation of a **.cache** file for each directory. You make a **.cache** file by executing the **mkcache** program within that directory. You can do this to each **gopher** directory, or just execute **mkcache** with the **-r** option from the main **gopher-data** directory. The **mkcache -r** command will make the **.cache** files for the current directory and any of its nested subdirectories. On your Caldera Network Desktop, you can run **mkcache -r** from your **/usr/lib/gopher-data** directory to create **.cache** files for all your Gopher directories.

GN Gopher also fully supports Web pages. It can display Web pages and use Web page HREF references in its menu items. See the GN documentation for a detailed discussion on these capabilities.

Gopher Indexes: gopherindex

With the **gopherindex** command you can create full text indexes of your Gopher data documents. **gopherindex** is provided as part of the University of Minnesota Gopher software package, and uses **waisindex** to perform its indexing, so you must have WAIS installed to use it. It takes as its arguments several possible options and a Gopher data directory. All the documents in the data directory will be indexed. The **-N** option specifies a description of the index file to be used in a Gopher menu. The following example indexes all the files in **/home/gopher/gopher-data/baseball**.

```
/usr/sbin/gopherindex -v -N "Search CIS Services Short Courses"
/usr/lib/gopher-data/baseball
```

Instead of using **gopherindex** you can use **waisindex** directly and then create a link for the index file.

```
waisindex -r /usr/lib/gopher-data/baseball
```

You create the link entry for the index file in that directory's link or menu file. Type 7 is a WAIS index type of document.

```
Type=7
Name=Baseball Index
Host=+
Port=+
Path=7/.index/index
```

A Gopher Example

Here is a simple Gopher example. It is a Gopher site with files that hold weather information for several states. The files for each state are placed in their own directories. You begin with a Gopher menu in the Gopher data directory. The items in this menu are defined in the **.names** file (for GN Gopher this would be named the menu file). Most of the menu items are references to other Gopher directories. One is a file with general introductory information about the Gopher site. In the main Gopher directory there is only this intro file and the **.names** file. The next two items link to local Gopher directories, **calif** and **newyork**. The last item links to another Gopher site located at **rose.ix.com**.

.names

```
Path=/intro
Name=About My Weather Site
Numb=1
Type=0
Abstract=Important Weather Information.

Name=California Weather Information
Numb=2
Type=1
Path=/calif

Name=New York Weather this week
Numb=3
Type=1
Path=/newyork

Name=The Weather in Hawaii
Numb=4
Type=1
Port=70
Path=/usr/lib/weather/hawaii/
Host= garnet.train.com
```

The California menu item references the **calif** subdirectory. Here are located the files with information on California weather. The **calif** directory lists two data files, a link file, and a **.caps** directory. In the **.caps** directory there are two files, each having the name of a data file in the **calif** directory. For the **surf.data** and **storm.data** files in the **calif** directory, there is also a **surf.data** and **storm.data** file in the **.caps** directory. These **.caps** directory files are shown here.

surf.data

```
Name=Surfing Conditions
Numb=1
Type=0
```

storm.data

```
Name=Storm Advisory
Numb=2
Type=0
```

In the **calif** directory, the **.links** file lists an entry to access a file on a remote system.

.links

```
Name=The Weekend Snowpack
Numb=3
Type=0
Port=+
Path=ftp:rose.net.com/usr/lib/weather/snow/current.txt
Host=+
```

For the GN gopher, the menu file looks very similar with the exception that each path name must be preceded by the type of the file (0 for text files and 1 for directories).

menu

```
Name=About My Weather Site
Path=0/intro

Name=California Weather Information
Path=1/calif

Name=New York Weather this week
Path=1/newyork

Name=The Weather in Hawaii
Path=0/usr/lib/weather/hawaii/
```

WAIS Server

WAIS (Wide Area Information Service) searches a database of documents using keywords and displays the documents it finds with a ranking of their importance. It is a very effective way to make information available throughout a network. WAIS was developed by Thinking Machines and is now managed by WAIS Inc. A free version of WAIS, called freeWAIS, is available through the Clearinghouse for Networking Information Discovery and Retrieval (CNIDR). You can obtain a Linux version of freeWAIS from CNIDR and Linux ftp sites.

The freeWAIS package includes clients, a server, and an indexer program. (See Tables 12-13 and 12-14.) The clients are called **swais**, **xwais**, and **waissearch**. They are used to enter requests and display results. The indexer is called **waisindex**. You use it to create indexes of keywords for your WAIS documents, providing fast and effective search capabilities. The server is called **waisserver**. With it you can create your own WAIS site and allow other users to perform searches on your WAIS documents.

You can obtain freeWAIS from the **ftp.cnidr.org** site or most Linux ftp sites. The ftp site at **ftp.cnidr.org** has a Linux version of freeWAIS already compiled and ready to use. For Linux the current package is freeWAIS–0.5–linux.tar.gz located in the **/pub/CNDIR.tools/freewais** directory. You can also download the source code and

Option	Description
-p *portnum*	Listens to the port; if the *portnum* is supplied, then that port number is used
-s	Listens to standard I/O for queries
-d *directory*	Uses this directory as the default location of the indexes
-e *path-name*	Redirects error output to *path-name*, if supplied, or to **/dev/null**

-1 *log_level*	Sets logging level 0, 1, 5 and 10
	   0 logs nothing (silent)
	   1 logs only errors and warnings
	   5 logs messages of MEDIUM priority
	 10 logs everything

-u *user*	Runs the server as the user specified
-v	Displays current version and date of server

Table 12-13. *The WAIS Server: z3950*

waisindex Files	**Description**
index-name.**doc**	Information about the document, including the size and name
index-name.**dct**	Dictionary file with list of each unique word cross-indexed to inverted file
index-name.**fn**	List of all files created for the index
index-name.**hl**	Table of all headlines; headlines are the titles and are displayed when in retrieved results
index-name.**inv**	The inverted file containing a table of words, a ranking of their importance, and their connection to the indexed documents
index-name.**src**	A source description file that contains information about the index, what system it is located on, the topic it deals with, who maintains it, etc.
index-name.**status**	Contains user-defined information
waisindex Options	
-a	Appends index to an existing one
-contents	Indexes the contents of a file (default)
-d *path-name*	Specifies a path name for index files; the path name will be appended to the front of the index's file name
-e *logfile*	Redirects error messages to *logfile*
-export	Adds hostname and TCP port to source description files to allow Internet access; otherwise, no connection information will be included and the files will be accessed locally

-l *num*	Sets logging level 0, 1, 5 and 10
	    0 logs nothing (silent)
	    1 logs only errors and warnings
	    5 logs messages of MEDIUM priority
	    10 logs everything

-mem	The amount of memory to use during indexing
-M	Links different types of files

Table 12-14.   **waisindex**: *Options and File Types*

`waisindex` Options	Description
`-contents` `-nocontents`	Determines whether to index the contents of a document; **`-contents`** indexes the entire document; **`-nocontents`** indexes only the header and file name, not the contents
`-pairs` `-nopairs`	How to treat consecutive capitalized words; **`-pairs`** (the default) treats capitalized words as one term; **`-nopairs`** treats them as separate terms
`-pos` `-nopos`	Whether to include word's position information in the index; **`-pos`** includes this information allowing proximity searches, but increasing the size of the index; **`-nopos`** does not include this information
`-r`	Recursively indexes subdirectories
`-register`	Registers indexes with WAIS Directory of Services
`-t`	Specifies the type of document file
`-T`	Sets the type of document

Document File Types

`filename`	The text type that uses the file name as the headline
`first_line`	The text type that uses the first line in the file as the headline
`one_line`	The text type that indexes each sentence
`text`	The text type that indexes the document; headline is the path name
`ftp`	Contains ftp code for accessing other systems
`GIF`	GIF image file
`PICT`	PICT image file
`TIFF`	TIFF image file
`MPEG`	MPEG file
`MIDI`	MIDI file
`HTML`	HTML file used for Web pages

Table 12-14. *`waisindex`: Options and File Types (continued)*

waisindex **Options**	**Description**
`mail_or_rmail`	Indexes the mbox mailbox file
`mail_digest`	Indexes email using the subject as the headline
`netnews`	Indexes USENET news
`ps`	Postscript file

Table 12-14.   `waisindex`: *Options and File Types* (continued)

compile it yourself. This package is called simply freeWAIS–0.5.,tar.Z. This is one source code package that can be configured for different systems. freeWAIS is also available at **sunsite.unc.edu** and its mirror sites in the **/pub/packages/info-systems/wais** directory. Several versions will be listed.

Create a directory where you want to place freeWAIS, usually **/home/wais**. It is recommended that you download the package of precompiled binaries for Linux, freeWAIS–0.5–linux.tar.gz. You then unzip the file with **gunzip** and extract the archive with **tar xvf**. This will create a directory called **freeWAIS-0.5–linux**. This directory will hold those binaries. All you have to do is install them in an appropriate directory such as **/usr/bin**. The source code, however, has to first be configured before you can create its binaries, and if you downloaded the source code and want to compile freeWAIS yourself, you must first configure the software.

Configuring and Installing freeWAIS Source Code: Makefile and ir.h

If you downloaded the source code, this directory will hold several subdirectories: **doc** for documentation and **src** for source code. One in particular, **wais-test**, holds test files for your server.

You will first have to set the TOP variable in the Makefile. TOP is assigned the path name of the directory where the freeWAIS source code is located. Enter the full path name of the directory that your WAIS source is located in.

Besides the Makefile, there are several specialized Makefiles each with an extension for a particular operating system. The **Makefile.linux** file holds the **make** commands for creating a Linux version of freeWAIS. This file is already configured for Linux. There are, however, several options you can specify or remove, and there are detailed descriptions of each option. These options are assigned to the CFLAGS variable. A set of default options are already included. Here is a sample of the CFLAGS entry. This is the only line you should ever change.

```
CFLAGS = -Wall -m486 -fwritable-strings -Who-unused -I$(INCLUDE)
-DTELL_USER -DUSG -DSECURE_SERVER -DRELEVANCE_FEEDBACK -DBOOLEANS
-DPARTIALWORD -DLITERAL -DSOUND -DBIBDB -DLINUX
```

Here is a list of other useful options:

Makefile Option	Description
-DBIO	Allows indexing on biological symbols
-DBOOLEANS	Enables Boolean searches using AND, OR, and NOT
-DBINGINDER	Used for indexing large sets of documents
-DLITERAL	Literal string search
-DPARTIALWORD	Enables the use of the ***** in pattern matches to match on any variation of a pattern, for example, **hum*** matches human, hummingbird
-DRELEVANCE_FEEDBACK	Allows you to select relevant documents from a search and use them as the basis for new searches
-DSECURE_SERVER	Provides better server security
-DTELL_USER	Tells the server who is connecting
-DUSE_SYSLOG	Logs in using syslog

You can, if you wish, restrict access to your WAIS service by only certain selected networks or systems. To do this, create a **SERV_SEC** file and enter the domain names and IP addresses of allowable networks and systems. The **SERV_SEC** file is defined in an entry for the **ir.h** file in the **include** directory, as shown here:

```
#define SERVSECURITYFILE   "SERV_SEC"
```

An entry in the **SERV_SEC** file consists of the domain name followed by the IP address. The IP address is optional, for example:

```
pango1.train.com   204.166.189.21
```

You can further refine access to specific databases, allowing only specified networks and systems access to certain databases. To do this you set up a **DATA_SEC** file. This file is defined in an entry for the **ir.h** file in the include directory, as shown here:

```
#define DATASECURITYFILE   "DATA_SEC"
```

Each entry in the **DATA_SEC** file first lists the database followed by the domain name and an optional IP address. To allow access by all users to a certain database you use a ***** for the domain name. The next example shows entries in the **DATA_SEC** file. The second entry opens the **oldata** database to all users.

```
mydata   pango1.train.com   204.166.189.21
oldata        *                  *
```

Once you are ready to compile freeWAIS, you issue the following **make** command with the term "linux". This will create your WAIS clients, indexer, and server programs for your Linux system. First, run **xmkmf** in the **src/x** directory to create the Makefile for **xwais**.

```
#  make linux
```

Creating Indexes

To use WAIS, you have to create indexes for the documents you want to make available. This indexing process is carried out by the **waisindex** command that creates a particular WAIS database. You can index a single file, a group of files, or whole directories and subdirectories of files. The data files together with their index form a WAIS data base. You can separately index different files or groups of files, setting up several different WAIS databases on your server. The WAIS databases should be located in the WAIS data directory that was specified when the WAIS server was invoked.

waisindex creates an inverted file index, referencing every word in the designated files. This allows keyword searching on the full text of documents. **waisindex** takes several options followed by the name of the file, group of files, or directory to be indexed as the last argument. With the **-d** option you can specify a name for the index. **waisindex** creates several index files for a document that are used to manage the index. Each will have its own extension indicating its function, but all will have the index name specified by the **-d** option as the prefix. If you do not specify a name, the term "index" will be used as the prefix. Also, if you want to have your database accessible to other users on the Internet, you have to add the **-export**

option. Without this option, your database is accessible only to other users on your system. The **-export** option is discussed in the next section. The **waisindex** options and the index files are listed in Table 12-14.

```
waisindex -d index-file -export file-list
```

If you list more than one file to be indexed, all those files will be referenced by the single index. If you want to index all the files in a subdirectory, you use the **-r** option followed by the directory name.

```
waisindex -d index-file -export -r directory-name
```

To add a file or directory to an existing database, you index it with the **-a** option. You also have to use the **-d** option and the database name to add the indexing of this file to that database. You can add several files by listing them on the command line. If you want to add a directory of files, you have to use the **-r** option followed by the directory name.

```
waisindex -d index-file -a -export file-list
```

In the next examples, the user first indexes the files **cookies** and **cakes**, creating an index called **recipes** for that group of files. Queries on **recipes** will search both **cookies** and **cakes**. In the next example, the user indexes the **pies** file and adds it to the **recipes** index. The WAIS **recipes** database now includes the files **cookies**, **cakes**, and **pies**. Now the user indexes the **snacks** directory, including all its files as well as files in any of its subdirectories. The name of the index is **junkfood**. In the final example, indexing is carried out again on the **snacks** array, but this time the indexing is added to the **recipes** database. The **junkfood** database still exists and references the **snacks** directory.

```
# waisindex -d recipes -export cookies cakes
# waisindex -d recipes -export -a pies
# waisindex -d junkfood -export -r snacks
# waisindex -d recipes -export -a -r snacks
```

With the **-t** option you are able to index different types of files. You can index images, mailbox files, and even HTML pages, as well as standard text documents. The different document types are listed in Table 12-14. For text documents, you can refine your indexing by specifying the one_line type. If you index by line, WAIS will indicate the line in the document where a keyword is found. In the next example, the user indexes each line of the document **breads** and creates the index, called **cereals**.

```
#  waisindex -d cereals -t one_line breads
```

The **waisindex** command can also associate different types of files with a specified document. For example, if you have image, video, or sound files that you want to associate with a specific text document, you can have **waisindex** link those files together. When a user retrieves the text document, the associated image, video, or sound files will also be retrieved. As the user reads the text she or he can also display a picture or play a sound. Associated files must have the same prefix as the document they are linked to. For example, if you have a document called **train.txt**, you can have a picture of a train in a file called **train.gif** and the sound of a train in **train.midi**. You use the **-M** option and a list of file types with the **-export** option to link a set of files to an index.

```
# waisindex -d train -M text, tiff, mpeg, midi  -export
/user/waisdata/train/*
```

To integrate WAIS with your Web resources, you need to create WAIS indexes for your Web pages. You use **waisindex** with the **-T HTML** option, specifying that the type of document being indexed is an HTML document. The name of the index could be something like **myweb**. This allows WAIS to search Web HTML documents. In the next example, the user indexes Web pages located in the **/home/httpd/html** directory. The name of the index is **myweb** and the type is HTML. The full contents of each Web page are indexed as specified by the **-contents** option. The **-export** option will include hostname information for easy Internet access.

```
# waisindex -d myweb -T HTML  -contents -export -r
/home/httpd/html/*.html
```

Your WAIS Sources

When you index files to make a database accessible, **waisindex** will create a source file for the database—the source file is the means by which other users can reach your database; it provides information such as the name of the database. Some WAIS databases will charge for access, specifying a cost, and the source file will show this information. You will see the address of the maintainer where you can send comments. The source file ends with a short description of the WAIS database.

If you specified the **-export** option when the database was created with **waisindex**, several fields will be added to allow users on other systems access to your database. Two fields for Internet address information are added, one for the IP name and the other for the IP address of your host system. Another field is added to specify the port (usually 210) to be used to access the WAIS database on your computer (the host computer). If you did not use the **-export** option, these fields will be absent. In this case, only users on your system will be able to access the database.

If necessary, you can modify any of the fields in a source file. The entire source is enclosed in parentheses, with each field on a line of its own beginning with a colon and the field name. You can edit the source file and add more to the description. Notice that the description is enclosed in double quotes, with the first quote following the term "description" and the closing quote on a line by itself after the descriptive text. The following example is a source for zipcodes in a file called **zipcodes.src**.

```
(:source
  :version  3
  :ip-address "192.31.181.1"
  :ip-name "quake.think.com"
  :tcp-port 210
  :database-name "/proj/wais/db/sources/zipcodes"
  :cost 0.00
  :cost-unit :free
  :maintainer "wais@quake.think.com"
  :description "
WAIS index of USA Zip Code database.
The full Zipcodes file may be obtained via FTP using the URL:
<ftp://obi.std.com/obi/ZIPCODES/zipcode.txt>
  "
)
```

Other users use the source file to access its WAIS database. The source file tells a user which host it is located on and what it is called. You can think of it as a URL for WAIS databases. The remote user has to first have the source file in order to access the database. You can either send the source file to a user who then can insert their host's wais-sources directory, or register the source file with a WAIS server that maintains a directory of servers such as **quake.think.com** and **cnidr.org**. Your source will be placed there with other sources. Using a WAIS client such as **swais**, users can access this directory of servers and find your WAIS database listed there. Then they can select and query your database.

You register a database when you create it by including the **-register** option when indexing the files with **waisindex**. You can also wait and register it later, perhaps after you've tested it. Use the **waisindex** command with the **-d** option and the index name, followed by the **-register** option.

```
waisindex -d recipes -register
```

Testing Your WAIS Server

In the freeWAIS-0.5 source code package, there is a directory called **test-wais** that holds a set of test files you can use to test indexing and server access. Within the directory you will find a shell script called **test.waisindex**. If you examine this shell script, you will find several **waisindex** commands, creating several different databases using test files. This creates four test indexes. The test-Bool index tests Boolean search capabilities. The test-Comp index tests the handling of compressed files. The test-Docs index tests recursive searches using the documentation in the **docs** directory, and test-Multi checks the handling of different types of files such as GIF graphics files. (The commands have a preceding **../bin/** path before their name. If you have downloaded WAIS binaries and already installed them, you should remove the preceding **../bin/**.)

You will notice that a source file is created for each test database: a **boolean.src** and a **doc.src**. To locally test your server, copy these source files to the directory that your WAIS clients use for their WAIS sources. For example, if **swais** uses **/usr/lib/wais-sources** as its sources directory, then copy the **test-boolean.src** (source) file to it. Now start your WAIS server either through **inetd** or directly (if you start it up directly, be sure to place an ampersand at the end). Use the path of the **test-wais** directory as your WAIS data directory. When you start up **swais**, it will list all the sources in its source directory, including the test-boolean source and the other test sources. You can then select and query your test sources which will then access your WAIS server and return the results. Try searching on the keyword "boolean". You can also simply move the wais-test directory to your WAIS data directory. To make one overall database you can index wais-test with the **-r** option.

Starting freeWAIS

You can have WAIS run continuously or have it called by **inetd** when needed. To start the WAIS server you use the command **waisserver** with several possible options. You can use the **-d** option to specify the default location of your WAIS indexes. You can also set the port with **-p** or the user name with **-u**. Be sure to add an ampersand at the end of the command. When called directly, **waisserver** has to be run in the background. To run WAIS as a continuous daemon, you should enter the **waisserver** command in an **rc.d/init** initialization file, such as **wais.init**. The following is an example of the **waisserver** command.

```
waisserver -d /usr/wais/wais_index &
```

To provide your WAIS service with more security, it's a good idea to run **waisserver** as a user other then root. Create a user and place a * in its **passwd** entry. Then use the **-u** option with that user name when you start **waisserver**. In the following example, **waisserver** runs as the user **sports**.

```
waisserver -u sports -d /usr/wais/wais_index &
```

To have **inetd** start the WAIS server you must place the appropriate entries in the **/etc/services** and **/etc/inetd.conf** files. For the **/etc/services** file you place the following entry.

```
z3590          210/tcp      # Z39_50 protocol for WAIS
```

Then in the **inetd.conf** file you place the entry to invoke the WAIS server. When **waisserver** is called as **waisserver.d**, it knows it is being run under **inetd**. For this reason, the first argument in the argument list is **waisserver.d**.

```
z3590   stream   tcp   nowait   root   /usr/sbin/waisserver
waisserver.d   /home/wais -e server.log
```

Summary: Internet Servers

You can set up your Linux system to operate as a server for various Internet services. All you need is the appropriate server software and securely organized directories. Server software is freely available for setting up your Linux system as an ftp server, a Web server, a Gopher server, or a WAIS server. The Caldera Network Desktop automatically installs the Web and ftp server software during installation. With the desktop, you are immediately ready to operate your Linux system as a Web site or an ftp site.

You can have all the different Internet servers running at the same time. They operate as daemons, waiting for requests from remote users. When a request for a particular service is received, the appropriate server processes the request. One remote user could connect to your ftp server and download files, while another could connect to your Web server and view your Web pages. Depending on how often a server is used, you can have it running continuously, or use the **inetd** daemon to call it only when it is needed. To run a server continuously you simply invoke its server program. With **inetd**, you have to place entries in the **/etc/services** and **/etc/inet.conf** files and then run the **inetd** daemon.

The Internet server software is freely available online at different Linux sites. See Chapter 1 for some of these sites. At **sunsite.unc.edu** and its mirror sites, most server software is currently kept in directories located in **/pub/Linux/systems/info-systems**. You should keep this in mind for downloading and installing more current versions in the future. The Caldera Network Desktop currently has installed the Apache Web server and the wa-ftpd ftp server.

Chapter Thirteen

Remote Access

Linux provides the ability to access other Linux or Unix systems remotely. You can copy files or execute Linux commands, as well as log in remotely to accounts on those systems. Instead of working through an interface, such as ftp or Gopher, you can execute remote access commands within your own shell that will then perform actions on a remote system.

Remote access commands operate across network connections. There are two different types of network connections that Unix and Linux systems can use, each with its own protocols. The TCP/IP protocols used with the Internet (see Chapter 10) can also be used for local networks. Networks using TCP/IP often have dedicated connections, such as Ethernet connections. The UUCP protocols are an alternative set of protocols that provide network communication between Linux and Unix systems. However, UUCP is an older protocol that was designed to operate between systems that were not already connected on a network. With UUCP, one system can connect to another across phone lines at a predetermined time, sending a batched set of communications all at once. UUCP is very helpful for making a direct connection to a particular system, transferring data, and then cutting the connection. UUCP allows you to set up direct modem-to-modem communication with another system.

TCP/IP and UUCP each has its own set of remote access commands, reflecting the strengths and weaknesses of each. The remote access commands for TCP/IP are referred to as remote or simply **r** commands. Common command names are preceded by an *r* to indicate that their operations are remote. For example, **rcp** is the command to copy a file remotely from one system to another. The **r** commands have the advantage of performing real-time operations. For systems on your network that allow you access, you can copy files and execute commands, and the operations will be carried out immediately. It is very easy, with **r** commands, to copy whole directories from one system to another. However, you can only access systems with connections that support TCP/IP, such as Ethernet, CSLIP, or PPP.

With UUCP you can dial across regular phone lines into any system that will permit you access. UUCP operates in batches. Users on a system submit their requests for copying files or executing commands on a remote system. Those requests are then gathered together and sent all at once when a connection is made to the remote system. The remote system receives the requests, executes them, and then makes another connection to your system to send back responses. Some requests may be to copy files from the remote system to your own. In this case, those files will be sent by the remote system to yours when it responds. Needless to say, execution of remote operations can be very time-consuming with UUCP. A user has to wait for the system to send the request, and then for the remote system to respond.

TCP/IP Remote Access Operations: rwho, rlogin, rcp, and rsh

The TCP/IP network communications package makes use of remote access commands first developed at UC Berkeley for Arpanet. They allow you to log in remotely to another account on another system and to copy files from one system to another. You can also obtain information about another system, such as who is currently logged on. When a system address is called for, these remote access commands use domain name or IP addressing. Domain addressing was originally designed for use on Arpanet, as were the TCP/IP remote access commands. The TCP/IP remote access commands are listed in Table 13-1.

Many of the TCP/IP commands have comparable network communication utilities used for the Internet. For example, the TCP/IP command **rlogin**, which remotely logs into a system, is similar to telnet. The **rcp** command, which remotely copies files, performs much the same function as ftp. The TCP/IP commands differ in the ease of use and control they provide to users. You easily access other accounts you may have on different Unix or Linux systems, and you can control access by other users to your account without having to give out your password. In effect, you can provide a kind of group permissions to your account for different users.

TCP/IP Network System Information: rwho, ruptime, and ping

There are several TCP/IP commands that you can use to obtain information about different systems on your network. You can find out who is logged in, get information about a user on another system, or find out if a system is up and running. For example, the **rwho** command functions in the same way as the **who** command. It displays all the users currently logged into each system in your network.

```
$ rwho
violet      robert:tty1     Sept 10 10:34
garnet      chris:tty2      Sept 10 09:22
```

The **ruptime** command displays information about each system on your network. The information shows how each system has been performing. **ruptime** shows whether a system is up or down, how long it has been up or down, the number of users on the system, and the average load on the system for the last 5, 10, and 15 minutes.

```
$ ruptime
violet      up    11+04:10,    8 users,   load 1.20 1.10   1.00
garnet      up    11+04:10,   20 users,   load 1.50 1.40   1.30
```

The **ping** command detects whether or not a system is up and running. The **ping** command takes as its argument the name of the system you want to check. The next example checks to see if violet is up and connected to the network.

```
$ ping violet
violet is alive
$
```

If the system you want to check is down, you will get a response like that in the next example. In this case, garnet is down and disconnected from the network.

```
$ ping garnet
no answer from garnet
$
```

Remote Access Permission: .rhosts

You use a **.rhosts** file to control access to your account by users using TCP/IP commands. Users create the **.rhosts** file on their own accounts using a standard editor such as Vi. It must be located in the user's home directory. In the next example, the user displays the contents of a **.rhosts** file.

```
$ cat .rhosts
garnet chris
violet robert
```

The **.rhosts** file is a simple way to allow other people access to your account without giving out your password. To deny access to a user, simply delete the system's name and the user's login name from your **.rhosts** file. If a user's login name and system are in a **.rhosts** file, then that user can directly access that account without knowing the password. This type of access is not necessary for remote login operations to work (you could use a password instead); the **.rhosts** file is required for other remote commands, such as remotely copying files or remotely executing Linux commands. If you want to execute such commands on an account in a remote system, that account must have your login name and system name in its **.rhosts** file.

The type of access **.rhosts** provides allows you to use TCP/IP commands to access other accounts directly that you may have on other systems. You do not have to log into them first. In effect, you can treat your accounts on other systems as extensions of the one you are currently logged into. Using the **rcp** command, you can copy any files from one directory to another no matter what account they are on. With the **rsh** command, you can execute any Linux command you wish on any of your other accounts.

Remote Login: rlogin

It is possible that you could have accounts on different systems in your network, or be permitted to access someone else's account on another system. You could access an account on another system by first logging into your own and then remotely logging in across your network to the account on the other system. You can perform such a remote login using the **rlogin** command. The **rlogin** command takes as its argument a system name. The command will connect you to the other system and begin login procedures.

Login procedures using **rlogin** differ from regular login procedures in that the user is not prompted for a login name. **rlogin** assumes that the login name on your local system is the same as the login name on the remote system. Upon executing the **rlogin** command, you are immediately prompted for a password. After entering the password, you are logged into the account on the remote system.

rlogin assumes the login name is the same because most people use **rlogin** to access accounts they have on other systems with their own login name. However, when the login name on the remote system is different from the one on the local system, the option, **-l** allows you to enter a different login name for the account on the remote system. The syntax is shown here:

```
$ rlogin system-name -l login-name
```

In the next example, the user logs into a system called violet using the login name robert.

```
$ rlogin violet -l robert
password
$
```

Once logged into a remote system, you can execute any command you wish. You can end the connection with either **exit**, CTRL-**d**, **~.**, or **logout** (TCSH or C-shell).

Remote File Copy: rcp

You can use the **rcp** command to copy files to and from remote and local systems. **rcp** is a file transfer utility that operates like the **cp** command, but across a network connection to a remote system. The **rcp** command requires that the remote system have your local system and login name in its **.rhosts** file. The **rcp** command begins with the keyword **rcp** and has as its arguments the source file and copy file names. To specify the file on the remote system, you need to place the system name before the file name, separated by a colon, as shown here:

```
$ rcp system-name:source-file    system-name:copy-file
```

When copying to a remote system, the copy file will be a remote file and require the remote system's name. The source file is one on your own system and does not require a system name:

```
$ rcp source-file    remote-system-name:copy-file
```

In the next example, the user copies the file **weather** from his own system to the remote system violet and renames the file **monday**.

```
$ rcp weather violet:monday
```

When copying a file on the remote system to your own, the source file is a remote file and will require the remote system's name. The copy file will be a file on your own system and does not require a system name:

```
$ rcp remote-system-name:source-file    copy-file
```

In the next example, the user copies the file **wednesday** from the remote system violet to his own system and renames the file **today**.

```
$ rcp violet:wednesday today
```

You can also use **rcp** to copy whole directories to or from a remote system. The **rcp** command with the **-r** option will copy a directory and all its subdirectories from one system to another. Like the **cp** command, **rcp** requires a source and copy directory. The directory on the remote system requires the system name and colon placed before the directory name. When you copy a directory from your own system to a remote system, the copy directory will be on the remote system and requires the remote system's name.

```
$ rcp -r source-directory    remote-system-name:copy-directory
```

In the next example, the user copies the directory **letters** to the directory **oldnotes** on the remote system violet.

```
$ rcp -r letters violet:oldnotes
```

When you copy a directory on a remote system to one on your own system, the source directory is on the remote system and requires the remote system name:

```
$ rcp -r remote-system-name:source-directory  copy-directory
```

In the next example, the user copies the directory **birthdays** on the remote system violet to the directory **party** on his own system.

```
$ rcp -r violet:birthdays party
```

You may, at times, want to use special characters such as asterisks for file name generation, or the dot to reference the current directory. Shell special characters are evaluated by your local system, not by the remote system. If you want a special character to be evaluated by the remote system, you must quote it. To copy all the files with a **.c** extension in the remote system to your own, you will need to use the asterisk special character: ***.c**. You must be careful to quote the asterisk special character. In the next example, the files with a **.c** extension on the violet system are copied to the user's own system. Notice that the asterisk is quoted with a backslash. The dot, indicating the current directory, is not quoted. It will be evaluated to the current directory by the local system.

```
$ rcp violet:\*.c .
```

The next example copies the directory **reports** from the user's own system to the current directory on the remote system. Notice that the dot is quoted. It will be evaluated by the remote system.

```
$ rcp -r reports violet:\.
```

Remote Execution: rsh

At times, you may need to execute a single command on a remote system. The **rsh** command will execute a Linux command on another system and display the results on your own. Your system name and login name must, of course, be in the remote system's **.rhosts** file. The **rsh** command takes two general arguments, a system name and a Linux command. The syntax is as follows:

```
$ rsh remote-system-name  Linux-command
```

In the next example, the **rsh** command executes an **ls** command on the remote system violet to list the files in the **/home/robert** directory on violet.

```
$ rsh violet ls /home/robert
```

Special characters are evaluated by the local system unless quoted. This is particularly true of special characters that control the standard output, such as redirection operators or pipes. The next example lists the files on the remote system and sends them to the standard output on the local system. The redirection operator is evaluated by the local system and redirects the output to **myfiles**, which is a file on the local system.

```
$ rsh violet ls /home/robert > myfiles
```

If you quote a special character, it becomes part of the Linux command evaluated on the remote system. Quoting redirection operators will allow you to perform redirection operations on the remote system. In the next example, the redirection operator is quoted. It becomes part of the Linux command, including its argument, the file name **myfiles**. The **ls** command then generates a list of file names that is redirected on the remote system to a file called **myfiles**, also located on the remote system.

```
$ rsh violet ls /home/robert '>' myfiles
```

The same is true for pipes. The first command shown next prints out the list of files on the local system's printer. The standard output is piped to your own line printer. In the second command, the list of files is printed on the remote system's printer. The pipe is quoted and evaluated by the remote system, piping the standard output to the printer on the remote system.

```
$ rsh violet ls /home/robert | lpr
$ rsh violet ls /home/robert '|' lpr
```

Unix to Unix CoPy: uucp

There are a set of remote commands that you can use with the UUCP to perform operations on other systems. For example, the **uucp** command will copy a file from one system to another. Just as you can access files on your own system, you can also access files on other systems. UUCP commands, however, are subject to the same permission restrictions as your own local commands. Protected files and directories cannot be accessed. Only files and directories with the other user permission set can be accessed.

You can think of UUCP commands as referencing files on other Linux systems through a mail system. These commands are designed to operate using point-to-point communication. It is as if you were using the mail capability of different systems to implement a network. When you issue a UUCP command for a given system, the command is queued and collected with other commands for that same system. The commands are then mailed to that system for execution. Once that system receives the commands and executes them, it mails back any results. Several systems can arrange to receive and send commands to each other, forming a UUCP network. The entire process then depends on each system in the network sending and receiving commands to and from other systems. In this respect, the network is only as strong as its weakest link. On the other hand, it requires no special structure, only the sending and receiving of what are essentially messages.

There are four major UUCP commands: **uuto**, **uupick**, **uucp**, and **uux**. The **uuto** command mails files to other systems, and **uupick** receives those files. These commands are used for sending and receiving large files. The **uucp** command copies files from one system to another. The **uux** command remotely executes a Linux command on another system. Many of the UUCP commands correspond to the TCP/IP remote access commands. **uucp** operates much like **rcp** and **uux** like **rsh**.

Installing and Configuring UUCP

The UUCP package is not automatically installed on your Linux system. For the Caldera Network Desktop you need to mount your Caldera CD-ROM and then either use glint from the root user's desktop or the **rpm** command to install the UUCP package. Alternatively, you can download the package from Linux ftp sites, using **gunzip** to decompress it and then **tar** to install the files. Several versions of Linux UUCP are available. Configuration formats may vary in the different versions, so be sure to consult any included installation instructions. Two of the more popular are Taylor UUCP and HDP UUCP. Taylor UUCP is the version included here.

Once installed, you must configure UUCP. This can be a very complex process. Be sure to consult the documentation on UUCP, such as HOW-TO documents, and even texts on the subject. A simple configuration involves setting the configuration files located in **/usr/lib/uucp**. There are three configuration files: **Permissions**, **Devices**, and **Systems**. The **Permissions** file lists the different systems and the type of access they have to your system, as well as the systems you can access. The **Devices** file lists the modems you use for UUCP communications along with initialization information, such as speed. The **Systems** file lists dial-in and login information for the different Linux or Unix systems you can access, including phone numbers, login names, and passwords.

In the **Permissions** file you list a system you want to interact with along with permissions for that system. That system, in turn, must have a similar entry in its **Permissions** file permitting you access. Permissions are set by assigning values to certain variables. There is a set of variables set for each system, and they are all entered on the same line (you can use \ to escape the newline character if you want to enter them on separate lines). The variables are listed here.

MACHINE	Remote system you wish to access and that allows access from `MACHINE=rose`
LOGNAME	Permissions specified for this login name will apply to the remote system when it accesses yours `LOGNAME=uucp`
COMMANDS	Command that the remote system can execute on your system `COMMANDS=uucp:uux`
READ	Spool directories for holding transmission to be sent on to the remote system `READ=/usr/spool/uucppublic`
WRITE	Spool directories for holding transmissions received from remote system `WRITE=/usr/spool/uucppublic`
SENDFILES	Specifies whether you can send files to the remote system `SENDFILES=yes`
REQUEST	Specifies whether the remote system can request files from your system `SENDFILES=no`

A sample **Permissions** file is shown here. The remote system is called rose. The login name my system uses when accessing rose is uucp. The commands that rose can execute on my system are **uucp** and **uux**. Any transmissions that my system sends to rose are held in the **/usr/spool/uucppublic** directory. Any transmissions that rose sends my system are also placed in **/usr/spool/uucppublic**. My system can send files to rose, but rose cannot ask for files.

/usr/lib/uucp/Permissions

```
LOGNAME=uucp MACHINE=rose \
  READ=/usr/tmp:/usr/spool/uucp/uucppublic \
  WRITE=/usr/tmp:/usr/spool/uucp/uucppublic \
  SENDFILES=yes REQUEST=yes \
  COMMANDS=rmail:rnews:uucp
```

In the **Systems** file there is a separate line for each system's dial-in and login information. The line begins with the remote system name. Then you specify the modem to use. You can enter **Any** to let UUCP choose any available modem. You then specify the modem type, usually **ACU**, which stands for Automatic Calling Unit. Then you enter the modem speed. You can specify a range if you want. The telephone number follows. Then you specify the last few characters of the login prompt, such as **ogin:** followed by the login name. Do the same for the password, **word:** and then the password. A sample entry for the **/usr/lib/uucp/Systems** file is shown here.

```
rose Any  ACU 19200  5555555 "" \r ogin:  richlp word: mypass
```

The **Devices** file lists your modem type, the port it uses, its speed, and a driver file. You can have multiple entries for the same modem specifying different speeds and drivers. The modem type is usually ACU (Automatic Calling Unit), the type for modems that can dial numbers themselves. All modems currentlly made have this type. A sample entry for the **Devices** file follows. The port is cua4, the 4th serial port; the speed is 38400.

```
ACU cua4 - 38400 dialfast
```

UUCP Addressing

A UUCP network usually uses the path form of addressing, which reflects the UUCP point-to-point form of communications. Systems may be connected to other systems at different locations across the country, which in turn may be connected to other systems in other parts of the world. All these systems are not directly connected to each other—one system is connected to another system, which in turn is connected to yet another system, and so on. You can reach a system on the far end of a network by sending a message that is then passed along by intermediately connected systems. If the garnet system is connected to the stan system, for example, which in turn is connected to the bell system, then a user on garnet can reach a user on bell through stan. However, the communication is not made in real-time. A message is actually sent as part of a batched collection of messages that are sent from one system to another, being delivered as they reach their addressed systems.

In a path form of addressing, the system address is placed before the user's login name and separated by an exclamation point. Here is the syntax for path addressing:

```
system!login-name
```

In the next example, the mailx utility sends a message to the user chris on the Linux system called garnet. Chris's address is represented using a path format.

```
$ mailx garnet!chris < mydata
```

Within the C-shell, the path form of addressing requires that a backslash be placed before the exclamation point. The exclamation point by itself in the C-shell denotes the **history** command. The backslash will escape the exclamation point, treating it as an exclamation point character, not as a **history** command. The syntax for a C-shell path address, as well as an example of the C-shell path used in a **mailx** command, are shown here:

```
system\!login-name
> mailx garnet\!chris < mydata
```

In a path form of addressing, the address of a user on another system consists of the intermediate systems you have to go through to get to that user's system. Each intermediate system is written in the address sequentially before the user's system and separated by an exclamation point. If you are on garnet and want to send a message to robert on the bell system, then you have to specify any intermediate systems through which the message is to be sent. In the following example, the intermediate system is stan, giving an address of **stan!bell!robert**. There may be any number of intermediate systems. If, to send a message to aleina at rose, you have to go through three intermediate systems, you must specify those three intermediate systems in the address. In the next examples, messages are sent through intermediate systems to reach a final destination. In the first command, a message is sent to the stan system, which then passes it on to bell where robert is located. In the second command, the message is first sent to lilac, which passes it on to sf. sf then passes it on to rose where aleina is located.

```
$ mailx stan!bell!robert < mydata
$ mailx lilac!sf!rose!aleina < mydata
```

There are often several different intermediate paths of connected systems that you can specify. A network is connected together in many different ways. Some are shorter than others. Finding a correct sequence of systems with which to address a user can become very complicated very fast. The next two commands show two different paths to the same system. The first example travels through three systems before it arrives at rose: lilac, mac, and violet. The second example only travels through one system, sf.

```
$ mailx lilac!mac!violet!rose!aleina < mydata
$ mailx sf!rose!aleina < mydata
```

Connected Systems: uname

In a UUCP network you may be connected to many systems. The command **uname** will list the systems to which a user can remotely connect and perform remote commands such as **uucp** on. In the next example, the **uname** command lists all connected systems.

```
$ uname
garnet
rose
lilac
$
```

The **uname** command with the **-1** option will display the name of your own system.

```
$ uname -1
violet
$
```

The **uname** command generates a list of system names that are sent to the standard output. The list of names may be large, so you may want to save it in a file or print it out, instead of just displaying it on the screen. You can redirect this list of system names to a file to save it, pipe it to a printer to print it out, or filter it through a search filter to detect a specific system name. In the next example, the first command saves the list of system names in a file, the next command prints the list, and the last command uses **grep** to see if a specific system name is in the list.

```
$ uname > syslist
$ uname | lpr
$ uname | grep garnet
garnet
$
```

Making UUCP Connections: uucico and uuxqt

On your Linux system the uucico program handles all your UUCP communications. uucico stands for UUCP Call-In Call-Out. It is a daemon that waits for any incoming UUCP transmission, saving it in the directory **/usr/lib/uucp/uucppublic**. A follow-up program called uuxqt then interprets and executes the operations specified in the transmission. Both uucico and uuxqt are system administration operations that are performed only by the root user.

The uucico program also sends transmissions to other systems. UUCP requests are batched together and then sent by uucico to the next system on its UUCP network. Operations for a specified system will continue to be transmitted from one system to another in the UUCP network, until they reach their intended system.

As the root user, you can use uucico to dial into another system that is waiting for your connection. The program will then make the connection, transmit any **uucp** command requests, and then receive responses and other **uucp** requests from the other system. The syntax for using uucico is as follows:

```
uucico   -options   remote-name
```

Two helpful options are **-r** to suppress an automatic wait time for redialing, and **-x** with the number 9, which sets debugging so you can see the actions uucico is taking. In the next example, the root user makes a connection to the rose system.

```
$ uucico  -r -x 9  rose
```

Mail File Transfer: uuto and uupick

UUCP provides a mail facility for sending large files. The command **uuto** sends files, and the command **uupick** receives files. Together these commands operate much like the **mailx** command. The **uuto** command operates in a batch mode. Your request is queued along with other uuto requests on your system. When your request reaches the top of the queue, your file is sent. If, in the meantime, you change your file, then that changed file will be sent. The **uuto** command has an option that allows you to avoid such a conflict. The **-p** option will immediately copy your file to the system's spool directory and, when the time comes, send that copy. You can then modify the original as much as you wish. The **uuto** command also has a **-m** option that notifies you when the file has been sent. The options for **uuto** are listed in Table 13-2. The syntax for the **uuto** command and its options is shown here:

```
$ uuto filename address
$ uuto -m -p filename address
```

In the next example, the file **mydata** is sent to address marylou at violet.

```
$ uuto mydata violet!marylou
```

You receive files sent to you by the **uuto** command with the **uupick** command. To receive your files, you first enter **uupick** on the command line without arguments. The files received from other systems sent with the **uuto** command are then sequentially displayed. You are first prompted with the name of the first file received. The prompt ends with a question mark waiting for you to reply. You then enter a reply that specifies how you want to dispose of the received file. One common response is **m**, which moves the file into your current directory. To move the file to a specific directory, you can specify a directory path after **m**. Upon pressing ENTER, you are then prompted with the name of the next file received. You then enter a response and, upon pressing ENTER, are prompted with the name of the next file. This continues until you have processed the entire list of files sent to you with the **uuto** command. If you should just press ENTER with no response, then the file remains unreceived and will be prompted for again the next time you execute the **uupick** command. The different **uupick** commands are listed in Table 13-2.

In the next example, the **uupick** command prompts the user for three files received. The first file, **mydata**, is moved to the current directory. The size of the file in blocks is then displayed. The second file, **party**, is moved to the directory **birthdays**. The file **project** is not disposed of. It will be prompted for again the next time the user executes **uupick**.

```
$ uupick
from system violet: file mydata ? m
10 blocks
from system garnet: file party ? m /home/chris/birthdays
2 blocks
from system violet: file project ?
$
```

You may want to check on whether you received any files from someone on a specific system. The **uupick -s** option followed by a system name will prompt you only for files received from that system. In the next example, **uupick** will prompt only for those files received from violet.

```
$ uupick -s violet
```

Direct File Copy: uucp and uustat

Whereas the **uuto** command sends files from one account to another, the **uucp** command copies a file directly from one user's directory to another user's directory. With **uucp** it is as if the different accounts are only different directories on other systems, directories to which you have access. Like **cp**, **uucp** takes two arguments: the name of the source file and the name of the copy.

```
$ uucp source-file copy-file
```

You can use **uucp** to copy files from your directory to one on another system, or to copy a file on another system to your own directory. In either instance the copy name or the source name will include the name of the other system as well as the full path name of the file. In the next example, the file **mydata** is copied to the directory **george** on the violet system.

```
$ uucp mydata violet!/home/george/mydata
```

The **uucp** command operates in a batch mode in the background. Your **uucp** request is queued, and when it reaches the top of the queue, your file is copied. If you change your file in the meantime, then the current changed version is copied. You can overcome this conflict with the **-C** option. With the **-C** option, the file is copied to the system spool directory when you issue the **uucp** command. Then when it is time to actually perform the copy, the system uses the version in the spool directory. The different **uucp** options are listed in Table 13-2. In the next example, the **mydata** file will be copied to the spool directory and that version used in the **uucp** operation.

```
$ uucp -C mydata violet!/home/george/mydata
```

If the directory that you may designate in your **uucp** command does not actually exist in the remote user's file system, the **uucp** command will create it. However, the remote user may not want you creating such a directory in his or her system. In that case you can use the **-f** option, which will instruct **uucp** not to create a directory if it does not already exist. In the next example, the user copies a file to the **birthday** directory in george's home directory. In the first **uucp** command, the **birthday** directory will be created if it does not already exist. In the second **uucp** command, the **birthday** directory will not be created.

```
$ uucp party violet!/home/george/birthday/party
```

```
$ uucp -f party violet!/home/ george /birthday/party
```

There may be times when you only know the user's name, not the user's full path name beginning from the root. Yet, you need to specify the full path name of the file on the other system in order to reference it in a **uucp** command. You can use the UUCP tilde operator to find the full path name of that user. The tilde, **~**, takes as its argument a user name and evaluates to the full path name of that user's home directory. For example, **~george** evaluates to **/home/george**. You can then use the tilde and the user name as part of a path name, to provide you with a full path name for a file. In the next example, the tilde is used to specify a full path name, first for **mydata** and then for **party**. The second command copies the file **party** on the violet system to the user's own directory.

```
$ uucp mydata violet!~george/mydata
$ uucp violet!~george/party party
```

With **uucp**, you can also copy files from one remote system to another remote system. The next example copies **mydata** from a directory on violet to a directory on garnet.

```
$ uucp violet!~george/mydata  garnet!~robert/mydata
```

Remember that **uucp** commands are executed in batch mode. They may take some time to perform their task. The command **uustat** lists information about current **uucp** operations. With the **-u** option, you can display **uucp** jobs for a specific user. With the **-s** option, you can display jobs for a specific system. The next example displays the **uucp** jobs for robert that were directed to the system garnet.

```
$ uustat -urobert -sgarnet
```

You can also use **uustat** to kill **uucp** jobs. **uustat** will list the job number of each **uucp** job in progress. Add a **-k** option and the job ID to kill the **uucp** job.

```
$ uustat -k 795
```

Remote Execution: uux

With the **uux** command, you can remotely execute a command on files on other systems. In a **uux** command, files and commands are referenced using their paths. For example, **violet!~robert/filmdata** refers to the **filmdata** file in robert's home directory on the violet system. Commands and files on your own system are referenced with a preceding exclamation point, **!**, with no system name. **!mydata** refers to the **mydata** file on your own system. The same rule is applied to the command to be executed. To execute a command on your own system, you precede it with a single exclamation point. In the next example, the file **filmdata** in robert's home directory is displayed on the user's own terminal.

```
$ uux !cat violet!~robert/filmdata
```

In a **uux** command, you need to quote special characters, such as those used for redirection and pipes (**>**, **<**, **|**), in order to avoid their evaluation by your shell. You can quote them individually or place the entire command within quotes. In the next example, the **cat** command copies files and then pipes them to the printer.

```
$ uux '!cat violet!~george/party garnet!~robert/food | lpr'
```

If you want to use a command on a remote system, you need to precede it with its system path. For example, suppose you want to print a file on a remote system's printer instead of your own. You then precede the **lpr** command with the system's path. In the next example, the user prints the file **filmdata** on the remote system's printer.

```
$ uux "!cat violet!~robert/filmdata | violet!lpr"
```

Like **uucp** commands, **uux** commands are not executed right away. They are placed on a queue and executed when they reach the head of the queue. In the meantime, you may have changed some of the files your **uux** command operates on. In that case the changed files are operated on. As in the **uucp** command, you can avoid this conflict by using the **uux** command with the **-C** option. This option makes an immediate copy of the files involved and then operates on those copies when it is time to execute. A list of **uux** options is provided in Table 13-2.

Each particular Linux system will often restrict the commands that can be executed with **uux**. Commands such as **rm**, which erases files, are usually not allowed. The commands that can be executed with **uux** on a given system are listed in the permissions file, **/usr/lib/uucp/Permissions**.

Remote Login: cu and ct

The **cu** command (call Unix) allows you to log in remotely to another system. With the **cu** command, you can either dial into a system across a telephone line or connect across network lines. The **cu** command also allows you to transfer character files to and from a remote system.

The **cu** command is very much like the **rlogin** command used for TCP/IP. To connect to another Linux system, enter the **cu** command followed by the name of the system. You will then be prompted for a login name, and you can log into an account on that system. In the next example a user connects to the violet system.

```
$ cu violet
Connected
login:
```

A list of the systems to which you are connected is kept in the file **/usr/lib/uucp /Systems**. All UUCP remote access commands will reference this file to determine whether they are being instructed to access a connected system. If a system is not in the file, the **cu** command will fail. In the next example, the **cu** command fails because the peach system is not in the **/usr/lib/uucp/Systems** file—it is not registered as a connected system.

```
$ cu peach
Connection failed: SYSTEM NOT IN Systems FILE
$
```

You can also use **cu** to dial into another system using a telephone number. Many systems allow you to connect to them across telephone lines using a modem. If you use a telephone number as an argument to **cu**, the **cu** command will use a modem to dial into another system across a telephone line. In the next example the user dials a system with **cu**.

```
$ cu 6426870
```

You can also specify transmission features such as baud rate, duplex, and parity. The next example sets the baud rate to 9600 using the **-s** option.

```
$ cu -s9600 6426870
```

The **ct** command (call terminal) allows you to connect to a terminal through an auto-answer modem. In effect, it executes the login process in reverse. Your system initiates and sets up a login connection for you between your Linux account and the specified terminal. The **ct** command takes as its argument a telephone number. **ct** has the same options as **cu** for specifying transmission features such as baud rate and duplex. In the next example, the system connects to a terminal with the phone number 6427400.

```
$ ct -s9600 6427400
```

Once you have logged into your remote system, you can then execute any commands you wish. When you have finished, you log out from your remote system with the **~.** command. When you enter the period, **.**, the name of the remote system will be displayed within brackets.

```
$ ~[violet].
Disconnected
```

Once logged into another system, you may want to access your original system. The command sequence **~!** generates a shell that allows you to return to your local system temporarily without breaking your login connection. You then enter commands for your local system. When you are ready to return to your remotely logged in system, end the shell with the **exit** command. In the next example, the user temporarily returns to the local system and executes commands to list files and print a file. When the user hits the exclamation point in the **~!** command sequence, the name of the local system is displayed within brackets.

```
$ ~[garnet]!
$ ls
mydata newdocs
$ lpr mydata
$ exit
$
```

The **~!** command generates a new shell. This is not the same as the original shell in the local system. Changes in the new shell, such as directory changes or changes to local shell variables, will not be retained when the new shell is exited. If you return to the local system with the **!~** command and change directories, then you only change the working directory for the new shell, not the working directory for the original shell.

You can affect your local system's original shell with the **~%** command. The **~%** command effects a one command line escape to the local system. To change the directory of your local system's original shell, use the **~%** with the **cd** command. When you type the percent sign, the name of the local system will appear within brackets.

```
$ ~[garnet]% cd letters
```

The **cu** command also supports simple character file transfers between systems. The command sequence **~%** precedes the commands for sending and receiving files. The command **~%** **take** sends files from your remote system to the local system. The command **~%** **put** sends files from the local system to the remote system. The commands take as their argument the name of the file being transferred. If the file is to have a different name from the one on the other system, you can specify that as the second argument. The syntax for **take** and **put** are noted here:

```
$ ~% take remote-file
$ ~% put local-file
```

In the next example, a user sends the file **mydata** from the remote system, violet, to the local system, garnet, using the **take** command. Upon typing the percent sign, the name of the local system is displayed within brackets.

```
$ ~[garnet]% take mydata
```

In the next example, the file **party** is sent from the local system, garnet, to the remote system, violet, with the **put** command and given a new name, **birthday**.

```
$ ~[garnet]% put party birthday
```

Summary: Remote Access

You can access remote systems across a network using the remote commands for either the TCP/IP or UUCP network protocols. The TCP/IP remote commands allow you to log in remotely to accounts on other systems. You can also copy files and execute Linux commands on those systems. However, for your remote commands to work on a remote system, you must first be given access by that remote system. To provide such access, the remote system needs to have a **.rhosts** file that lists your system name and login name.

The UUCP protocol is an alternative to TCP/IP. It is simpler in design and use. It lacks some of the powerful features of a TCP/IP network, but is easier to implement. UUCP networks use a path form of addressing. One system may be connected to another system through several intervening systems. There are UUCP remote commands for sending files, copying files to and from remote systems, remotely executing commands, and remotely logging into other systems.

Command	Effect
rwho	Displays all users logged into systems in your network
ruptime	Displays information about each system on your network
ping	Detects whether a system is up and running
Remote Commands	
rlogin *system-name*	Allows you to log in remotely to an account on another system $ **rlogin violet**
-l	Allows you to specify the login name of the account $ **rlogin violet -l robert**
-x	Turns on DES encryption for all data transmitted
-d	Turns on socket debugging
-e	Sets escape character for **rlogin** session; by default escape is ~ character
-E	Prevents any character from being interpreted as an escape character
-8	Allows for 8-bit data path to permit special codes to be transmitted
-k *realm*	Obtains Kerberos tickets for the remote host in the specified realm instead of the remote host's realm

Table 13-1. *TCP/IP Remote Access Commands and Their Options*

Command	Effect
Remote Commands	
rcp *sys-name:file1* *sys-name:file2*	Allows you to copy a file from an account on one system to an account on another system; if no system name is given, the current system is assumed $ `rcp mydata violet:newdata`
-r	With the **-r** option, allows you to copy directories instead of just files $ `rcp -r newdocs violet:edition`
-p	Preserves the modification times and modes of source files
-d	Turns on socket debugging
-x	Turns on DES encryption for all data transmitted
-k *realm*	Obtains Kerberos tickets for the remote host in the specified realm instead of the remote host's realm
-K	Turns off Kerberos authentication
rsh *sys-name Linux-command*	Allows you to remotely execute a command on another system $ `rsh violet ls`
-l	Allows you to specify the login name $ `rsh -l ls`
-x	Turns on DES encryption for all data transmitted
-n	Redirects input from the null special device, **/dev/null**
-d	Turns on socket debugging
-k *realm*	Obtains Kerberos tickets for the remote host in the specified realm instead of the remote host's realm
-K	Turns off Kerberos authentication

Table 13-1. *TCP/IP Remote Access Commands and Their Options (continued)*

Command	Effect/Description
uucico *options remote-system*	Dials into and connects to a remote system; this is a systems administration action performed only as the root user `$ uucico -r -x rose`
-r	Starts in master mode (calls out to a system); implied
-s *system*	If no system is specified, calls any system for which work is waiting to be done
-r0 -s slave	Starts in slave mode; this is the default
-f	Ignores any required wait for any systems to be called
-l, -p	Prompts for login name and password using "login: " and "password:"
-p *port*	Specifies port to call out on or listen to
-c	Calls named system only if there is work for that system
-x *type*	Turns on debugging type; the number 9 turns on all types. Types are: abnormal, chat, handshake, uucp-proto, proto, port, config, spooldir, execute, incoming, outgoing. Debug information is placed in **/usr/spool/uucp/Debug**
uuxqt	Program called by uucico to execute **uux** requests
uname	Lists the systems to which yours is connected
uuto *filename address*	Mail command for sending large files to another system `$ uuto mydata violet!aleina`
-m	Notifies sender when file was sent
-p	Copies file to spool directory and sends the copy
uupick	Mail command that receives files sent to you using **uuto**; you are sequentially prompted for each file

Table 13-2.   *UUCP Commands and Options*

Command	Effect/Description
uupick	
m *dir*	Moves file received to your directory
a *dir*	Moves all files received to your directory
d	Deletes the file received
p	Displays the file received
ENTER	Leaves file waiting
q	Quits **uupick**
*	Lists **uupick** commands
! *cmd*	Executes a Linux command, escaping to your shell
uucp *sys-name* **!** *filename* *sys-name* **!** *filename*	Copies files from one system to another $ **uucp mydata violet!robert/newdata**
-m	Notifies the user when a **uucp** job is completed
-n *user*	Notifies the remote user when a **uucp** job is performed
-C	Copies file to spool directory and sends that copy
-c	Does not copy file to spool directory (default)
-f	Does not create destination directories
-g	Specifies grade of service (high, medium, low)
uustat	Lists current **uucp** jobs; with the **-k** option and the job number, you can delete a **uucp** job
-a	Lists all jobs for all users
-u *user*	Lists all jobs for specific user
-s *system*	Lists all jobs for specific system
-k *jobid*	Kills a **uucp** job
-c	The queue time for a job

Table 13-2.   *UUCP Commands and Options (continued)*

Command	Effect/Description
uux	Remotely executes a command on another system; file names and command name must be preceded with an exclamation point
-z	Notifies user the job is successful
-n	Suppresses notification of job's success
-C	Copies file to spool directory and sends that copy
-c	Does not copy file to spool directory (default)
-g	Specifies grade of service (high, medium, low)
cu	Remotely logs into an account on another system (call Unix)
-s	Specifies baud rate (transmission speed), such as 1200, 2400, 4800, 9600, 38400, etc.
-c	Selects local area network to be used
-l	Selects communications line to be used
-e	Sets even parity
-o	Sets odd parity
-h	Sets half-duplex
-n	Prompts for telephone number instead of entering it on the command line
~!	Temporarily returns to local system $ ~[garnet]!
exit	Ends use of local system and returns to remote
~%	A one-command escape to local system $ ~[garnet]% cd newdocs
~% **take** *remote-file*	Copies a file from remote system to local system $ ~[garnet]% take mydata
~% **put** *remote-file*	Copies a file from local system to remote system $ ~[garnet]% put party

Table 13-2. *UUCP Commands and Options* (continued)

Command	Effect/Description
`ct`	Remotely connects from your system to a terminal through an auto-answer modem (connect terminal); takes as an argument a telephone number of the terminal; has several options for specifying transmission features, such as baud rate and parity `$ ct 6427400`
`-s`	Baud rate `$ ct -s1200 6427400`

Table 13-2.   *UUCP Commands and Options* (continued)

PART FOUR

Shells

Chapter Fourteen

Filters

One of the more popular innovations of Unix that was carried over to Linux is the filter. Filters are commands that read data, perform operations on that data, and then send the results to the standard output. Filters generate different kinds of output, depending on their task. Some filters only generate information about the input, other filters output selected parts of the input, and still other filters output an entire version of the input, but in a modified way. Some filters are limited to one of these, while others have options that specify one or the other. You can think of a filter as operating on a stream of data, receiving data and generating modified output. As data is passed through the filter, it is analyzed, screened, or modified.

The data stream input to a filter consists of a sequence of bytes that can be received from files, devices, or the output of other commands or filters. The filter operates on the data stream but does not modify the source of the data. If a filter receives input from a file, the file itself is not modified. Only its data is read and fed into the filter.

The output of a filter is usually sent to the standard output. It can then be redirected to another file or device, or piped as input to another utility or filter. All the features of redirection and pipes apply to filters. Often data will be read by one filter and its modified output piped into another filter. Data could easily undergo several modifications as it is passed from one filter to another. However, it is always important to realize that the original source of the data is never changed.

This book organizes filters into three general categories: file filters, editing filters, and data filters. This chapter presents file and editing filters. You can find discussions of data filters in most Unix books. Detailed tables of all filters are provided at the end of this chapter that include the data filters.

First you will see how filters operate using redirection and pipes and look at different types of output that filters generate. Then the editing filters will be discussed, followed by an examination of regular expressions.

Using Redirection and Pipes with Filters: Outputting Files with cat, tee, head, and tail

Filters send their output to the standard output and so, by default, display their output on the screen. The simplest filters merely output the contents of files. You have already seen the **cat** and **tee** commands. What you may not have realized is that **cat** and **tee** are filters. They receive lines of data and output a version of that data. The **cat** filter receives input and copies it out to the standard output, which, by default, is displayed on the screen. The **tee** filter receives input and copies the output both to the standard output and to a specified file. In addition to **cat** and **tee**, two other filters output files: **head** and **tail**. The **head** filter outputs part of the beginning of a file, and **tail** outputs the end of the file.

You can save the output of a filter in a file or send it to a printer. To do so, you need to use redirection or pipes. To save the output of a filter to a file, you redirect it to a file using the redirection operation, **>**. To send output to the printer, you pipe the output to the **lpr** utility, which will then print it. In Figure 14-1, as in the next command, the **cat** command pipes its output to the **lpr** command, which then prints it.

```
$ cat complist | lpr
```

Other commands for displaying files, such as **more**, may seem to operate like a filter, but they are not filters. You need to distinguish between a filter and device-oriented utilities such as **lpr** and **more**. Filters send their output to the standard output. A device-oriented utility such as **lpr**, though it receives input from the standard input, sends its output to a device. In the case of **lpr**, the device is a printer; for **more**, the device is the terminal. Such device-oriented utilities may receive their input from a filter, but they can only output to their device.

All filters accept input from the standard input. In fact, the output of one filter can be piped as the input for another filter. However, many filters also accept input directly from files. Such filters can take file names as their arguments and read data directly from those files. The **cat** and **sort** filters operate in this way. They can receive input from the standard input or use file name arguments to read data directly from files. In Figure 14-1, the **cat** filter reads its input from the **complist** file, whose name was entered as an argument on the command line.

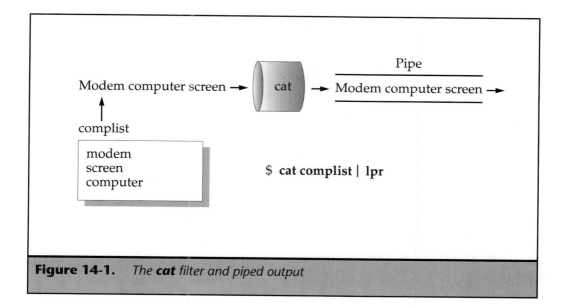

Figure 14-1. *The **cat** filter and piped output*

If you do not specify a file name when you use **cat**, the **cat** command will take its input from the standard input. Thus the **cat** command will wait for you to type something in and then read what you have typed as input. You end the standard input with a CTRL-D, the end of file character. **cat** will read this standard input and then output it to the standard output. In the next example, the **cat** command reads input from the standard input, in this case the keyboard, and redirects the output to a file called **mydata**.

```
$ cat > mydata
Hello Marylou
      How are you
today
^D
$
```

One of the more powerful features of **cat** is that it can combine the contents of several files into one output stream. This output can then be piped into a utility or even another filter, allowing the utility or filter to operate on the combined contents of files as one data stream. For example, if you want to view the contents of several files at once, screen by screen, you must first combine them with the **cat** filter and then pipe the combined data into the **more** filter. The **more** command is, then, receiving its input from the standard input. In the next example, the **cat** filter copies the contents of **veglist** and **fruitlist** into a combined output that is piped into the **more** command. The **more** filter then allows you to view the combined text, screen by screen.

```
$ cat veglist fruitlist | more
$ cat veglist fruitlist | lpr
$ cat veglist fruitlist > grocerylist
```

A filter can receive input from a pipe, as well as send output to one. You can pipe the output of a filter or utility into a given filter, which can then pipe output to still another filter. You can even set up a sequence of filters that pipes the output of one as input into another. You could pipe the output of the **cat** filter as input to another filter, instead of a utility. Notice that such a filter would then receive its input from the piped standard input, not from files. For example, suppose you want both to print the output of **cat** and save the output to another file. You can first save the output to a file by using the **tee** filter and then pipe it into the **lpr** utility for printing. **tee** is a filter that copies the standard input to a file and also sends it on to the standard output. Notice that **tee** receives its input from the piped output of the **cat** filter. In the next example, the **tee** filter first saves the output in the **grocerylist** file and then pipes it on to the **lpr** utility.

```
$ cat veglist fruitlist | tee grocerylist | lpr
```

Outputting the Beginning and End of a File: head and tail

Suppose that, instead of displaying the entire file, you only want to check the first few lines to see what the file is about. For this you can use another filter, the **head** filter. **head** displays the first few lines of either a file or the standard input. Like many filters, the **head** filter has different options that allow you to control the output. By default, the **head** filter displays the first ten lines of a file. You can specify the number of lines you want displayed as an option on the command line. Enter a dash followed by the number of lines that you want displayed. In the next example, first **cat** is used to output the **preface** file, and then the first three lines of the file are displayed, using **head**.

```
$ cat preface
A text file in Unix
consists of a stream of
characters.  An editor can
be used to create such
text files, changing or
adding to the character
data in the file.
$ head -3 preface
A text file in Unix
consists of a stream of
characters.  An editor can
```

If, instead, you want to see just the end of a file, you can use yet another filter—the **tail** filter. By default, **tail** displays the last ten lines of a file. As with the **head** filter, using a dash followed by a number specifies how many lines you want displayed. In the next example, the last three lines of the **preface** file are displayed.

```
$ tail -3 preface
text files, changing or
adding to the character
data in the file.
```

tail reads in data and outputs a filtered version of it, in this case, the last few lines of the data. Just as with **cat**, you can pipe the output of **tail** or **head** to the printer or redirect it to a file. In the next example, the **tail** filter pipes the last five lines of the **preface** file to the printer.

```
$ tail -5 preface | lpr
```

Types of Filter Output: wc, spell, and sort

The output of a filter may be a modified copy of the input, selected parts of the input, or simply some information about the input. Some filters are limited to one of these, while others have options that specify one or the other. The **wc**, **spell**, and **sort** filters illustrate all three kinds of output. The **wc** filter merely prints out counts of the number of lines, words, and characters in a file. The **spell** filter selects misspelled words and outputs only those words. The **sort** command outputs a complete version of the input, but in sorted order. These three filters are listed in Table 14-1 with their more commonly used options.

Counting Words: wc

The **wc** filter takes as its input a data stream, which is usually data read from a file. It then counts the number of lines, words, and characters (including the new line character, found at the end of a line) in the file and simply outputs these counts. In the next example, the **wc** command is used to find the number of lines, words, and characters in the **foodlist** file. Notice that the file has 49 printed characters, including spaces, and 4 new line characters, making a total of 53 characters.

foodlist

```
lowfat milk
fresh vegetebels
potatoes
vegetable soop
```

```
$ wc foodlist
4          7          53          foodlist
```

The **wc** command has three options that allow you to output any one of these specific counts: the line count, word count, or character count. With the **-1** option, **wc** counts only the number of lines. The -w option allows **wc** to count only words. And with the **-c** option, **wc** counts only characters. In the next example, the **wc** filter only outputs the number of words in the **foodlist** file.

```
$ wc -w foodlist
7              foodlist
```

You can combine the different options to output different combinations of the line, word, and character counts. You can, of course, either redirect the output to a file or pipe it to the printer. In the first example shown next, the **wc** filter pipes its output to the printer to be printed. In the second example, the **wc** filter redirects its output to a file. The **cat** command then displays it.

```
$ wc foodlist | lpr
$ wc foodlist > foodcount
$ cat foodcount
5              7              53              foodlist
$
```

Spell Checking: spell

The **spell** filter checks the spelling of words in its input and outputs only those words that are misspelled. In the next example, the words "vegetebels" and "soop" in the **foodlistsp** file are misspelled. The **spell** filter outputs those misspelled words.

foodlistsp

```
lowfat milk
fresh vegetebels
potatoes
vegetable soop
```

```
$ spell foodlistsp
soop
vegetebels
```

Using redirection, you can save those words in a file. With a pipe, you can print them out. In the next example, the user saves the misspelled words to a file called **misspell**.

```
$ spell foodlistsp > misspell
$ cat misspell
soop
```

```
vegetebels
$ spell foodlistsp | lpr
```

Remember that you can pipe the output of one filter into another filter, in effect applying the capabilities of several filters to your data. For example, suppose you only want to know how many words are misspelled. You could pipe the output of the **spell** filter into the **wc** filter, which would count the number of misspelled words. In the next example, the words in the **foodlistsp** file are spell-checked, and the list of misspelled words is piped to the **wc** filter. The **wc** filter, with its **-w** option, then counts those words and outputs the count.

```
$ spell foodlistsp | wc -w
2
$
```

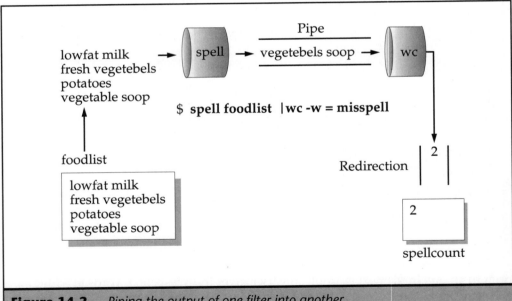

Figure 14-2.   *Piping the output of one filter into another*

You could then save the count of misspelled words to a file, or print it out. In the first command shown next, the user saves the count of misspelled words in the file **spellcount**. In the second command, the user prints the count of misspelled words.

```
$ spell foodlistsp | wc -w > spellcount
$ spell foodlistsp | wc -w lpr
```

Figure 14-2 illustrates the process of piping the output of one filter to another. The content of **foodlist** is read by **spell**, which then outputs the list of misspelled words. The **wc** filter then counts the list of misspelled words and outputs the count. Finally, the output of **wc** is redirected to the file **spellcount**.

Sorting Files: sort

The **sort** filter outputs a sorted version of a file. **sort** is a very useful utility with many different sorting options. These options are primarily designed to operate on files arranged in a database format. In fact, **sort** can be thought of as a powerful data manipulation tool, arranging records in a database-like file. This chapter examines how **sort** can be used to alphabetize a simple list of words.

The **sort** filter sorts, character by character, on a line. If the first character in two lines is the same, then **sort** will sort on the next character in each line. In the next example, the **sort** filter outputs a sorted version of **foodlist**. Notice in the second and third lines that the characters are the same up to the second word. **sort** will then sort starting with the characters in the second words, "vegetables" and "fruit."

foodlist

```
vegetable soup
fresh vegetables
fresh fruit
lowfat milk
```

```
$ sort foodlist
fresh fruit
fresh vegetables
lowfat milk
vegetable soup
```

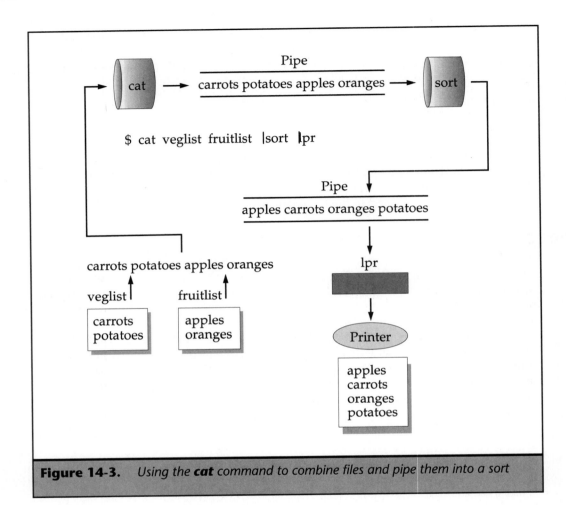

Figure 14-3. *Using the **cat** command to combine files and pipe them into a sort*

You can, of course, save the sorted version in a file or send it to the printer. In the next example, the user saves the sorted output in a file called **slist**. Then the user prints out the sorted output.

```
$ sort foodlist > slist
$ sort foodlist | lpr
```

The **sort** filter can also operate on the standard input. Suppose you want to combine the lines in several files and sort them all as one group. You can use the **cat** filter to combine the lines from files and then pipe these combined lines into the **sort** filter. **sort** will then output a sorted version that includes all the lines. In Figure 14-3, the contents of **veglist** and **fruitlist** are combined into the standard output by **cat** and piped to **sort**. The sorted version is then printed out.

```
$ cat veglist fruitlist | sort | lpr
```

You could also save the output by redirecting it to a file. In the next example, the sorted output of **veglist** and **fruitlist** is saved to a file called **clist**.

```
$ cat veglist fruitlist | sort > clist
```

Searching Files: grep and fgrep

The **grep** and **fgrep** filters search the contents of files for a pattern. They then inform you of what file the pattern was found in and print out the lines in which it occurred in each file. Preceding each line is the name of the file the line is in. **grep** can search for only one pattern, whereas **fgrep** can search for more than one pattern at a time. The **grep** and **fgrep** filters, along with their options, are described in Table 14-1.

The **grep** and **fgrep** filters are useful for locating files about certain topics. The patterns can be thought of as keywords that you use to search for files that contain those terms. In the case of **grep**, the searching capabilities are further enhanced by what are called regular expressions (**fgrep** does not allow regular expressions). These are expressions used in the Ed line editor and as discussed later in this chapter.

grep

The **grep** filter takes two types of arguments. The first argument is the pattern to be searched for; the second argument is a list of file names, which are the files to be searched. You enter the file names on the command line after the pattern. You can also use special characters, such as the asterisk, to generate a file list.

```
$ grep pattern filenames-list
```

In the next example, the **grep** command searches the lines in the **perishables** file for the pattern "veg". It finds two lines with this pattern and outputs them.

perishables

```
lowfat milk
fresh vegetables
potatoes
vegetable soup
```

```
$ grep veg perishables
fresh vegetables
vegetable soup
```

If you want to include more than one word in the pattern search, you enclose the words within single quotation marks. This is to quote the spaces between the words in the pattern. Otherwise the shell would interpret the space as a delimiter or argument on the command line, and **grep** would try to interpret words in the pattern as part of the file list. In the next example, **grep** searches for the pattern "fresh vegetables".

```
$ grep 'fresh vegetables' perishables
fresh vegetables
```

If you use more than one file in the file list, **grep** will output the name of the file before the matching line. In the next example, two files, **perishables** and **packaged**, are searched for the pattern "veg". Before each occurrence, the file name is output.

```
$ grep veg perishables packaged
perishables:fresh vegetables
perishables:vegetable soup
packaged:frozen vegetables
```

As mentioned earlier, you can also use shell special characters to generate a list of files to be searched. In the next example, the asterisk special character is used to generate a list of all files in your directory. This is a simple way of searching all of a directory's files for a pattern.

```
$ ls
breakfast brunch packaged perishables
$ grep veg *
breakfast:vegetables
```

```
brunch:vegetables
packaged:frozen vegetables
perishables:fresh vegetables
perishables:vegetable soup
```

The special characters are often useful for searching a selected set of files. For example, if you want to search all your C program source code files for a particular pattern, you can specify the set of source code files with a ***.c**. Suppose you have an unintended infinite loop in your program and need to locate all instances of iterations. The next example searches only those files with a **.c** extension for the pattern "while" and displays the lines of code that perform iterations.

```
$ grep while *.c
```

grep Options

The **grep** filter has a set of options that vary its output. You can add line numbers, output just the count of lines with pattern matches, output all the lines that do not have matches instead of those that do, or simply output the names of files in which a match has been made. You can also instruct **grep** to ignore upper- and lowercase. These options are listed in Table 14-1.

The ability to ignore upper- and lowercase is perhaps one of **grep**'s most widely used options. By default, a **grep** pattern search is case sensitive: lowercase and uppercase letters are separate characters. If you want to search for a pattern regardless of case, you add the **-i** option. In the next example, both the upper- and lowercase patterns of "soup" are matched.

```
$ grep -i soup perishables
chicken SOup
vegetable soup
```

You can also specify the line number of a matched line by using the **-n** option. This allows you to quickly locate a line later with the editor. In the next example, the user searches the files **perishables** and **packaged** for the pattern "milk". The output is the file name, line number, and the line where the pattern is found.

```
$ grep -n milk perishables packaged
perishables :1:lowfat milk
```

```
packaged:1:canned milk
packaged:4:chocolate milk
```

In some cases, you may want to invert the **grep** operation. Instead of finding lines that contain a specific pattern, you may need to find those lines that do *not* have the pattern. The **–v** option outputs all lines without the pattern. In the next example, the user wants to locate all items that are not milk products. Using the **–v** option and the pattern "milk" outputs all lines without the pattern "milk".

```
$ grep -v milk perishables packaged
perishables :fresh vegetables
perishables :potatoes
perishables :vegetable soup
packaged:frozen vegetables
packaged:tomato paste
```

You can, of course, combine these options to obtain specific information. Suppose you want to search both upper- and lowercase and also list the line number of each matched line. In that case, you could use the **–ni** options together:

```
$ grep -ni milk perishables packaged
perishables :1:lowfat milk
packaged:1:canned milk
packaged:4:chocolate Milk
```

fgrep

fgrep is faster than **grep** and can quickly search files for more than one pattern at a time. However, unlike **grep**, **fgrep** cannot search for regular expressions. **fgrep** will not evaluate special characters. It can only search explicit patterns.

You can enter the patterns on the command line, or with the **–f** option, you can read them in from a file. On the command line, as in a file, each pattern must be separated by a new line character. The entire pattern list is enclosed in double quotation marks, and each new line character separating each pattern is itself quoted by a backslash. In the next example, the user searches the **perishables** file for lines that have either the pattern "milk" or "soup". Notice that "milk" and "soup" are separated by a new line character, and that the new line character is quoted by a preceding backslash.

```
$ fgrep "milk\
soup" perishables
lowfat milk
vegetable soup
$
```

With the **-f** option, **fgrep** reads the pattern list from a file. The file contains a list of patterns, each on its own line. **fgrep** will search for those patterns in parallel. This strategy is helpful when you have a set of commonly used words that you often need to search for. In the next example, the user has placed the patterns to be searched in the **mypats** file. Then **fgrep** reads the patterns from **mypats**.

mypats

```
lowfat
veg
```

```
$ fgrep -f mypats perishables
lowfat milk
fresh vegetables
vegetable soup
$
```

fgrep is very helpful when you are searching for a topic that can be referenced by different keywords. For example, suppose you have an unintended infinite loop in your program and need to locate all instances of any kind of loop in your source code files. A loop can use the keywords "while" or "for". To locate all loops in your source code, you could search for both "while" and "for" at the same time, using **fgrep**. In the next example, the user searches for all instances of the keywords "while" and "for", reading them from the file **loopwords**.

loopwords

```
while
for
```

```
$ fgrep -f loopwords  *.c
```

Editing Filters

In Linux, as in Unix, text files are organized into a series of lines. For this reason, many editors and filters are designed to operate on a text file, line by line. The very first Unix editor, Ed, is a line editor whose commands reference and operate on a text file one line at a time. Other editing utilities and filters operate on text much the same way as the Ed line editor. In fact, the Ed editor and other editing filters use the same set of core line editing commands. The editing filters such as **sed** and **diff** use those same line editing commands to edit filter input.

Editing filters perform edit operations on filter input that is read from files or received from the standard input. Like the filters described previously, edit filters receive input, perform operations on it, and generate as output a modified version of the input. In a sense, the data is filtered. An edit filter receives lines of text as its input and performs line editing operations on them, outputting a modified version of the text.

There are three major edit filters: **tr**, which translates characters, **diff**, which outputs editing information about two files, and **sed**, which performs line editing operations on the input. As a filter, **sed** makes no modifications to any file. Instead, it generates an edited version of the file. The **diff** filter provides editing information in the form of line editing operations. It shows what line editing commands need to be performed in order to make one file the same as the other. The line editing operations themselves show how the two files are different.

The Stream Editor: sed

The **sed** filter performs line editing operations on input that is either read from files or received from the standard input. The name **sed** stands for stream editor. A **sed** command takes as its arguments a line editing operation and a file list. The **sed** command generates an edited version of the files in the file list and sends it to the standard output. The files are not themselves changed. All lines in the files are output whether they have been edited or not. In this sense, **sed** generates a complete, though edited, copy of the input files.

```
$ sed 'edit-command' file-list
```

The sed Editing Commands

The **sed** editor has a set of editing commands that are the same as those in the Ed line editor. The line editing command is placed within single quotes to prevent any special characters from being evaluated by the shell. The **sed** editing commands are listed in Table 14-2. In the next example, an edited version of **perishables** is generated by the **sed** command. The editing command **3 d** is the same as the Ed line editing command to delete line 3. The **sed** line editor command will modify the output by deleting the third line.

perishables

> lowfat milk
> fresh vegetables
> potatoes
> vegetable soup

```
$ sed '3 d' perishables
lowfat milk
fresh vegetables
vegetable soup
```

As in Ed, a **sed** editing command is a single letter. The **sed** command for deleting a line is the letter **d**. The **a** command appends text after a selected line. The **n** command outputs lines with line numbers. The **i** command inserts text before the line. The **c** command replaces the selected line or lines with new text. And the **s** command replaces the selected text on a line. All of these operate in the same way as their counterparts in the Ed line editor.

One of the more common line editing operations is pattern substitution. Like the Ed substitution command, the **sed** substitution command consists of an **s** followed by a pattern and replacement text. The substitution command substitutes the matched pattern in a line with replacement text. The command to substitute the pattern "milk" for "yogurt" is written as **s/milk/yogurt/**. The substitution command works on only the first instance of a pattern in a line. The **g** modifier applies the substitution to all instances of the pattern in the line. The command **s/milk/yogurt/g** changes all instances of the pattern "milk" to "yogurt" on a given line. In the next example, the user replaces the word "fresh" on the second line, with the word "canned".

```
$ sed '2 s/fresh/canned/' perishables
lowfat milk
canned vegetables
potatoes
vegetable soup
```

The **sed** command can execute several editor commands at the same time. You can either enter the editing commands on the command line or place them in a file to be read by **sed**. The **-e** option allows you to enter more than one editing command on the command line. Each editing command must have the **-e** option placed before it. The **-f** option allows a set of editing commands to be read from a file. The **-f** option is followed by the name of the file that contains the editing command. **sed** will then read a set of Ed line editor commands from that file. In the next example, the editing commands are read from the file **myed**.

```
$ sed -f myed perishables
fresh noodles
potatoes
noodle soup
```

myed

```
1d
s/vegetable/noodle/g
```

Though many of the **sed** editing commands are the same as those found in the Ed line editor, those commands that require more than one line to execute need to be read in from a file. Commands such as the **a** command, which appends text after a selected line, require that you enter more than one line. The first line is the **a** command and the following lines are the text to be added. When you do so, you need to quote the new line character at the end of each line. Doing so prevents the shell from interpreting that particular character as the end of a Linux command.

The **sed** command receives input as a stream of data. It can read this input stream either from the standard input or from files. If no files are specified for the **sed** command, then input is taken from the standard input. Line numbers will reference the place of a line in the input stream, whether the input comes from a file or the standard input. Through the standard input, **sed** can receive data piped in from the output of another Linux operation, or data typed in from the keyboard. Data may also be redirected from a file or a device. In all cases, the **sed** editor is editing a stream of data, and this is where it gets its name.

In the next example, **sed** receives its input from another filter. The **cat** filter first combines the **perishables** and **packaged** files into the standard output and pipes them into the **pr** filter, which generates a copy of the input with line numbers. The line-numbered output is then piped as input to the **sed** command, and the **sed** command replaces each instance of the pattern "milk" with "yogurt".

```
$ cat perishables packaged | pr -nt | sed 's/milk/yogurt/'
1 lowfat yogurt
2 fresh vegetables
3 potatoes
4 vegetable soup
5 canned yogurt
```

```
6 frozen vegetables
7 tomato paste
8 chocolate yogurt
```

You could think of the **sed** command as the **cat** command with editing capability. Like **cat**, **sed** can receive input either from the standard input or a file list. If files are listed as arguments to the **sed** command, then input is taken from those files. If no files are listed, then input is taken from the standard input. Like the **cat** command, **sed** then outputs a copy of the input to the standard output. However, unlike **cat**, editing operations are first performed on the output. The editing operations are line editing commands specified in the first argument to **sed**. These line editing operations are applied to the output, generating an edited version of the input. The original input, including files listed as arguments to **sed**, are left untouched. Only the standard output has been modified. The standard output may then be redirected by the redirection operation to a file, creating an edited version of the original input. In the next example, the modified output of **sed** is redirected to a file. The file **pfile** then contains an edited version of the **perishables** file.

```
$ sed '3 d' perishables > pfile
```

Like the Ed line editor, the **sed** stream editor can select lines to be edited either with a line number or a pattern match. The line number is often referred to as an address. As with the Ed editor, a line number or range of line numbers is placed before the editing command. The range of numbers specifies the set of lines to be operated on by the editing command. The first number is the first line in the range, and the second number is the last line. In the next example, a range of line numbers is specified by two numbers separated by a comma. The range **1,3** specifies lines 1, 2, and 3. The last line in a file may be referenced with the dollar sign special character, **$**. The range **3,$** specifies all lines from line 3 to the last line in the file. In the next example, the user deletes the last two lines.

```
$ sed '3,$ d' perishables
lowfat milk
fresh vegetables
```

You can also use a search pattern in place of a line number to select lines. The pattern match can be thought of as selecting a line by context rather than by address. A pattern in a **sed** command is encased in slashes. You can use a pattern to designate the first or last line in a range. You can also use a pattern to select all those lines that have the pattern. However, a **sed** pattern search command is applied by **sed** to every line in the input stream. This means that, unlike the Ed line editor, pattern searches in the **sed** editor are global. A pattern search will search all lines in the input stream. It will not stop at the first match. When you perform a pattern search with the **sed** editor, you are selecting a set of lines—all lines with that pattern. In this respect, a **sed** pattern search is comparable to the Ed global command **g**. Just as an Ed **g** command selects every line in the file with a given pattern, a **sed** pattern references all lines with that pattern. In the next example, the user deletes all lines that have the pattern "veg".

```
$ sed '/veg/ d' perishables
lowfat milk
potatoes
```

All **sed** commands have the same global scope as its pattern search. Any **sed** editing command, unless restricted by line numbers or patterns, will, by default, operate on every line in the data stream. In this sense, there is no current line at which you are positioned. The lines are read from the file, one by one, and fed into the **sed** editor. As a line is read, it is subjected to all the editing commands supplied to the **sed** editor when it was invoked. If, however, an editing command is preceded by a line number or pattern, it will be applied only to those lines referenced. In the next example, the substitution command is applied to every line in the input file. On each line, the substitution command will search for the pattern "vegetable" and, if found, will replace it with the pattern "noodle". Notice that both the first and last lines are changed, even though there is no specific global reference in the substitution command itself.

```
$ sed 's/vegetable/noodle/' perishables
lowfat milk
fresh noodles
potatoes
noodle soup
```

In the next example, the substitution operation is applied to only the second line in the input file. All the other lines, including the last line, are left untouched.

```
$ sed '2 s/vegetable/noodle/' perishables
lowfat milk
fresh noodles
potatoes
vegetable soup
```

You can just as easily use a pattern to reference a line. In the next example, the pattern "soup" is placed before the substitution command. The substitution command will only operate on those lines that hold the pattern, in this case the last line.

```
$ sed '/soup/ s/vegetable/noodle/' perishables
lowfat milk
fresh vegetables
potatoes
noodle soup
```

The **sed** editor, then, differs from other editors in two important ways. Unlike any of the standard editors such as Ed, all editing commands in the **sed** editor are, by default, global. Furthermore, whereas the Ed editor requires the **p** command to specifically print out a line, all lines input to the **sed** editor are by default output to the standard output, whether they have been edited or not.

You can, however, output only referenced lines. First use the **-n** option to suppress the **sed** command's automatic output of a line to the standard output. Then use the **p** command to overcome this suppression for referenced lines. The **p** command prints a line. The combination of the **-n** option and the **p** command has the effect of outputting only referenced lines in the input. In the next example, only those lines that match the pattern "/veg/" are sent to the standard output.

```
$ sed -n '/veg/ p' perishables
fresh vegetables
vegetable soup
```

Differences and Changes: diff

The **diff** filter compares two files and outputs those lines that are different. **diff** shows you not only what is different in two files, but also how they are different. The **diff** filter outputs line editing information that shows you how the first file can be changed to make it the same as the second. The editing changes that the first file would have to undergo define how it is different from the second file. In this sense, the output of the **diff** command is editing information.

This editing information can be useful to you when you are working on a document and you want to keep track of how the document has changed. You can keep an original version of the document and make changes to a copy of it. To see how your document has changed, use **diff** to compare the original with the current working copy.

diff compares a line in the first file to a line in the second file, one line at a time. It outputs only those lines that are different—in other words, lines that are unique to each file. Those lines unique to the first file are listed with a less-than sign placed before each line. Those lines unique to the second file are listed with a greater-than sign placed before each line. Lines that are the same in both files are not listed.

```
$ diff file1 file2
file1-linenums edit-command file2-linenums
< Differing line in file1
> Differing line in file2
```

Before the lines, **diff** outputs editing information that specifies how the first file must be changed to make it the same as the second file. The first file may need several different types of editing changes at different places in the file. Each change will begin with an editing directive and be followed by the differing lines from one or both of the files. Lines may need to be deleted, added, or changed in order to make the first file the same as the second. The editing directive takes the form of line numbers and three possible editing directives: **a**, **d**, and **c**. An **a** specifies lines that must be added from the second file to the first file. It is the same as the Ed line editing command **a**, which appends input. After the **a** command, **diff** lists the lines from **file2** that need to be added to **file1**.

The **d** command specifies lines that must be deleted from the first file to make it like the second file. It functions in the same way as the Ed line editing command **d**. After the **d** command, **diff** lists the lines in **file1** that need to be deleted. The **c** command indicates lines in the first file that need to be changed to lines in the second file. It is the same as the Ed line editing command **c**, which changes lines. In **diff**, the **c** command reads more like a replacement operation. It indicates the lines in the first file that must be replaced by lines in the second file. After the **c** command, **diff** will list both the lines in the first file that are to be replaced and the lines in the second file that will replace those lines in the first file. Both sets of lines are separated by a dashed line. The following examples list the syntax for each editing directive and the type of output that follows each.

```
f1-linenum a f2-line1, f2-line2         Append lines from
      file2 to after f1-linenum in file1.
> file2 lines

f1-line1, f1-line2 d f1-linenum         Delete the lines in
      file1.
< file1 lines

f1-line1, f1-line2 c f2-line1, f2-line2   Replace lines in file1
      with lines in file2.
< file1 lines
------------
> file2 lines
```

A line number or a range of line numbers is placed both before and after the editing directive. The line numbers placed before the editing directive reference lines in the first file. Line numbers placed after the editing directive reference lines in the second file. The editing directive is read from left to right and specifies how the first file must be changed to make it like the second file. For example, reading from left to right, the editing directive **5a10,14** specifies that after line 5 in the first file, you need to add lines 10 through 14 from the second file. This modification will make the first file the same as the second file. The editing directive **3 d** specifies that line 3 must be deleted from the first file to make it like the second. The command **4,6c9** specifies that lines 4 through 6 in the first file need to be changed to (replaced by) line 9 from the second file.

In the next example, there are two food lists: **breakfast** and **brunch**. The **diff** filter, when applied to **breakfast** and **brunch**, outputs the differing lines. The **diff** filter specifies how **breakfast** must be changed to make it like **brunch**. Lines 3 and 4 in **breakfast** must be changed to lines 3 through 5 in **brunch**.

breakfast

```
milk
vegetables
eggs
chocolate
```

brunch

```
milk
vegetables
bread
chips
cola
```

```
$ diff breakfast brunch
3,4c3,5
< eggs
< chocolate
------------------
> bread
> chips
> cola
```

The **diff** filter performs a strict character-by-character comparison on each line. Spaces, control characters, and tabs are all valid characters and may form part of a line. The **-b** option ignores blanks at the end of the line and treats differing sets of spaces as the same. The **-i** option ignores upper- and lowercase when comparing text. Table 14-2 lists the different **diff** options.

You could, if you want, save the output of **diff** by redirecting it to a file. In the next example, the user saves the differences between **doc.v1** and **doc.v5** to the file **changes5**. If you are dealing with changes to an original document, such a file can constitute a record of changes that you have made so far. In this example, you can think of **doc.v1** as the original document and **doc.v5** as the latest version of the original. **changes5**, then, contains all the changes to the original that were made to obtain the **doc.v5** version. As you make more changes, you can use **diff** to record them. Together, those files containing these changes will show you how you are developing your document.

```
$ diff -b doc.v1 doc.v5 > changes5
```

You may, at times, want to use the editing information that **diff** outputs to actually edit the first file and change it to a copy of the second file. The editing directives normally output by **diff** are not actual editing commands. However, the **diff** filter does have a **-e** option that actually generates a set of Ed editing commands. When executed, these commands change the first file into an exact copy of the second file. In the next example, the output of the **diff** command is an editing command to be performed on **breakfast** that will make it the same as **brunch**. Notice that the editing command is an Ed editing command, **c**. Preceding the **c** command are lines in the file to be replaced. Following the **c** command is the replacement text. The text is ended with a period on a line by itself. The replacement text consists of lines taken from the second file, **brunch**.

```
$ diff -e breakfast brunch
3,4 c
bread
chips
cola
.
```

The editing commands output by **diff** will be listed in reverse order. Those lines at the end of the file will be operated on first. This is to avoid any problems with line renumbering that may occur as a result of a change that an editing command may make. When a line is deleted from a file, all the remaining lines are immediately renumbered. The same is true for any added lines. If such changes were made at the beginning of a file first, then the remaining lines would be renumbered, and the line numbers used in later line editing commands would be out of sync.

Instead of simply executing these commands by hand, you can redirect them as input to the Ed editor. The Ed editor can receive editing commands from the standard input and will then execute those commands.

Regular Expressions

Many utilities and filters use patterns to locate and select specific text in your file. Sometimes you may need to use patterns in a more flexible and powerful way, searching for several different variations on a given pattern. There is a set of special characters that you can include in your pattern to enable a flexible search. A pattern that contains such special characters is called a *regular expression*. Regular expressions can be used in most filters and utilities that employ pattern searches such as Ed, **sed**, awk, **grep**, and **egrep**. Though many of the special characters used for regular expressions are similar to the shell special characters, they are used in a different way. Shell special characters operate on file names. Regular expressions search text.

Regular expressions allow you to match possible variations on a pattern, as well as patterns located at different points in the text. You can search for patterns in your text that have different ending or beginning letters, or you can match text that is at the beginning or end of a line. The regular expression special characters are the circumflex, dollar sign, asterisk, period, and brackets: ^, $, *, ., []. The circumflex and dollar sign match on the beginning and end of a line. The asterisk matches repeated characters, the period matches single characters, and the brackets match on classes of characters.

Matching the Beginning and End of a Line: ^, $

To match on patterns at the beginning of a line, you enter the ^ followed immediately by a pattern. The ^ special character makes the beginning of the line an actual part of the pattern to be searched. In the next example, **^orange** matches on the line beginning with the pattern "orange". Notice that even though the second line has the pattern "orange" in it, it is not matched.

```
^orange
    orange juice
    A new orange     no match
```

The next example uses the **$** special character to match patterns at the end of a line. The pattern **ice$** matches on two lines ending with "ice", but ignores the next one, even though the pattern "ice" occurs earlier in the line.

```
ice$
    orange juice
    shaved ice
    juice oranges    no match
```

When you combine the ^ and **$** special characters in the same pattern, you create a pattern that matches on an entire line. For example, the pattern **^fresh vegetables$** will only match on the line consisting entirely of those two words and nothing more. You can also use the combination of the ^ and **$** characters to match on empty lines. The pattern **^$** matches on a line that has no text, just a beginning and an end.

```
^$
    orange juice
            match on empty line
    A new orange
```

Matching Any Character: .

The period is a special character that matches any one character. Any character will match a period in your pattern. The pattern **b.d** will find a pattern consisting of three letters. The first letter will be *b*, the third letter will be *d*, and the second letter can be any character. It will match on "bid", "bad", "bed", "b+d", "b d", for example. Notice that the space is a valid character (so is a tab).

For the period special character to have much effect, you should provide it with a context—a beginning and ending pattern. The pattern **b.d** provides a context consisting of the preceding *b* and the following *d*. If you specified **b.** without a *d*, then any pattern beginning with *b* and having at least one more character would match. The pattern would match on "bid", "bath", "bedroom", "bump", as well as "submit", "habit", and "harbor".

You can use as many period special characters in a regular expression as you want. Using several periods side by side allows you to match on a pattern with the same prefixes or suffixes. For example, the pattern **box..** matches on text beginning with "box" and ending with any two characters. It will match on "boxes" and "boxer" as well as "boxed".

You can also combine the period special character with the ^ and **$** to match on the beginning and end of a line. Suppose you have a file whose lines end with file names and you want to match on files that begin with "week" and have only one more character, such as **week1, week2, weeka**, but not **weekend**. You can use the pattern **week.$** to match on any of those file names.

```
week.$
    reports on week4
    reports on week15        no match
    week1 weather       no match
```

Matching Repeated Characters: *

The asterisk special character, *****, matches on zero or more consecutive instances of a character. The character matched is the one placed before the asterisk in the pattern. You can think of the asterisk as an operator that takes the preceding character as its operand. The asterisk will search for any repeated instances of this character. Here is the syntax of the asterisk special character:

```
c*    matches on zero or more repeated occurrences of whatever
the character c is:   c cc ccc cccc  and so on.
```

The asterisk comes in handy when you need to replace several consecutive instances of the same character. The next example matches on a pattern beginning with *b* and followed by consecutive instances of the character *o*. This regular expression will match on "boooo", "bo", "boo", and "b".

```
bo*
    book
    born
    booom
    zoom    no match
```

It is necessary to provide a context for the ***** special character. The ***** matches zero or more instances of a character. Suppose you want to locate one or more instances of the character *b*. You are looking for the patterns "b", or "bb", or "bbb", and so on, in the text. You may think that the pattern **b*** will do the job. It will not. The ***** also matches on the zero occurrence of the character. Any other character in the line is preceded by a zero occurrence of the character you are matching on. **b*** matches on *b's* as well as the zero instance that precedes any other character in the line. In effect, the pattern will match on every character in every line. In the next example, the pattern **b*** matches ons every character. The characters in each line that are not *b* are each preceded by a zero instance of the character *b*. For example, the character *a* is preceded by a zero instance of *b*.

```
b*
    aaaa
    abb
    aabbb
```

To avoid this problem you need to provide a context for the * special character. In this case, the context you need is another *b*. The pattern **bb*** matches on one or more instances of the *b* character. First it matches on "b" and then zero or more consecutive instances of "b". Using the same example, the pattern **bb*** matches only on the sequence of *b*'s in the second and third lines:

```
bb*
    aaaa
    abb
    aabbb
```

Instead of searching for one specific repeated character, you may simply want to match a varying number of different characters within a certain context. Notice that the * special character does not require you to specify how many instances of a character you want to match. It will match a varying number of instances, whether it be 0, 2, or 20. You can make use of this capability in combination with the period special character to select words with suffixes of varying length, whole segments of characters on a line, and even the entire line itself. Suppose that instead of a specific character, you used the period special character as the character you want to find multiple instances of. What does it mean to have multiple instances of the period special character? The period matches on any character. Combined with the * special character, you are then matching multiple instances of any character. The pattern **.*** will match on any character. Used as the suffix for a pattern, you can then match patterns whose roots have suffixes of varying length. For example, using the root pattern "fish" you could use the pattern **fish.*** to match on "fishy", "fishing", "fished", and also just "fish".

The **.*** pattern used by itself will match on any character in the line; in fact, it selects the entire line. In the next example, the entire text of a line is matched.

```
.*
    oranges and fresh vegetables
    fresh vegetables from yesterday
```

Remember, however, that the * special character will match on zero instances of a character. In the case of the period, the * will match zero instances of any character—in other words, an empty line. If you want to match only on lines that have one or more characters in them, you can precede the period by another period and use the pattern **..***:

```
..*
    oranges and fresh vegetables
                            no match on empty line
    fresh vegetables from yesterday
```

If you have a context for **.***, you can match different segments of the line. A pattern placed before the **.*** special characters will match the remainder of the line from the occurrence of the pattern. A pattern placed after the **.*** will match the beginning of the line up until the pattern. The **.*** placed between patterns will match any intervening text between those patterns on the line. In the next example, the pattern **.*and** matches everything in the line from the beginning up to and including the letters "and". Then the pattern **and.*** matches everything in the line from and including the letters "and" to the end of the line. Finally, the pattern **/o.*F/** matches all the text between and including the letters *o* and *F*.

```
.*and      Hello to you and to them Farewell

and.*      Hello to you and to them Farewell

o.*F       Hello to you and to them Farewell
```

Because the ***** special character matches zero or more instances of the character, you can provide a context with zero intervening characters. For example, the pattern **I.*t** matches on "It" as well as "Intelligent".

Classes of Characters: [ ]

Suppose that instead of matching on a specific character or allowing a match on any character, you need to match only on a selected set of characters. For example, you might want to match on words ending with an *A* or *H*, as in "seriesA" and "seriesH", but not "seriesB" or "seriesK". If you used a period, you would match on all instances. Instead, you need to specify that *A* and *H* are the only possible matches. You can do so with the brackets special characters.

You use the brackets special characters to match on a set of possible characters. The characters in the set are placed within brackets and listed next to each other. Their order of listing does not matter. You can think of this set of possible characters as defining a class of characters, and characters that fall into this class are matched. You may notice that the brackets operate much like the shell brackets. In the next example, the user searches for a pattern beginning with "doc" and ending with either the letters *a, g,* or *N*. It will match on "doca", "docg", or "docN", but not on "docP".

```
doc[agN]
    List of documents
    doca docb
    docg docN docP
```

The brackets special characters are particularly useful for matching on various suffixes or prefixes for a pattern. For example, suppose you need to match on file names that begin with the pattern "week" and have several different suffixes, as in **week1**, **week2**, and so on. To match on just those files with suffixes 2, 4, and 5, you enclose those characters within brackets. In the next example, notice that the pattern **week[245]** matches on **week2** and **week4**, but not on **week1**.

```
week[245]
    week2 weather
    reports on week4
    week1 reports          no match
```

The brackets special characters are also useful for matching on a pattern that begins in either upper- or lowercase. Linux distinguishes between upper- and lowercase characters. The pattern "computer" is different from the pattern "Computer"; "computer" would not match on the version beginning with an uppercase *C*. To match on both patterns, you need to use the brackets special characters to specify both *c* and *C* as possible first characters in the pattern. Place the uppercase and lowercase versions of the same character within brackets at the beginning of the pattern. For example, the pattern **[Cc]omputer** searches for the pattern "computer" beginning with either an uppercase *C* or a lowercase *c*.

You can place the brackets anywhere in the pattern. They can be at the beginning, end, or even the middle of a pattern. For example, the pattern **week[235]1** looks for any text beginning with "week" and ending with either 21, 31, or 51. You can also use as many bracket class specifications in your pattern as you want. For example, you may want to match on a pattern beginning in both upper- and lowercase, as well as ending in a set of possible characters. The next example matches on patterns beginning with either *W* or *w* and ending in either 2, 4, or 8.

```
[Ww]eek[248]
    Week2 weather
    reports on week4
    week3 reports          no match
```

Finally, you can place bracket class specifications next to each other in a pattern. The following pattern matches on any text beginning with "week" and ending first with either the numbers 1 or 4 and followed by either the numbers 7 or 3.

```
week[14][73]
    week13 storm warning
    reports on week47
    week12 heat wave          no match
```

Exclusive Classes: ^

Sometimes, you may want to match most instances of a pattern but avoid certain exceptions. These exceptions can be thought of as forming an exclusive class of characters. To match on all characters except an exclusive class of characters, you use the brackets with a circumflex, **^**. The circumflex is placed within the brackets and before the characters. Instead of matching on the characters, any characters other than these will be matched. For example, to match on all file names beginning with the pattern "week", except those ending with 5 and 7, you use the following pattern:

```
week[^57]
    week7 weather          no match
    reports on week4
    week5 reports          no match
```

You can, if you wish, use both exclusive classes and regular classes in the same pattern. You place the different bracket class specifications next to each other in a pattern. For example, the pattern **week[14][^12]** matches on any text beginning with "week" and ending first with either the numbers 1 or 4 and followed by any number other than 1 or 2. **week41** is not matched, whereas **week43** or **week15** is.

Only the first circumflex in the brackets is special. Any following circumflex is a simple character. This feature allows you to include the circumflex as just one more character in your class specification. The pattern **doc[a^g]** matches on a pattern beginning with "doc" and ending in either ^, *a*, or *g*.

Should you want to specify the **^** character as part of an exclusive class, you would use two circumflexes in the class specification. The first **^** indicates an exclusive class, and the second **^** is simply the ^ character. The pattern **doc[^^]** matches on any pattern beginning with "doc" but not ending with a circumflex.

Notice that the circumflex is used in two different ways, as both the special character for the beginning of a line and the exclusive class specifier in class specifications. The pattern **^[^0-9]** searches for text at the beginning of a line that does not begin with a number. The first circumflex is a special character that references the beginning of the line, and the second circumflex is the exclusive class specifier.

Range of Characters: -

You can specify a range of characters within the brackets with the dash. Characters are ranged according to the character set that is being used. In the ASCII character set, lowercase letters are grouped together. Specifying a range with [a-z] selects all the lowercase letters. In the first example shown next, any lowercase letter will match the pattern. More than one range can be specified by separating the ranges with a comma. The ranges [A-Za-z] selects all alphabetic letters, both upper- and lowercase.

```
doc[a-z]      doca docg docN docP
doc[A-Za-z]   doca docg docN docP
```

Using ranges, the pattern **week[14][^12]** described previously can be more accurately rewritten as **week[14][3-9]**. The previous pattern matches on any characters other than 1 or 2, including alphabetic characters. By using the range **[3-9]**, only the numeric characters from 3 to 9 are matched.

```
week[14][3-9]
    week43 weather
    reports on week15
    week41 reports      no match
    week4g reports      no match
```

You can also use ranges to specify an exclusive class of characters. You place the circumflex before the range specification. The next example matches on patterns not ending in uppercase alphabetic characters or in numbers.

```
doc[^A-Z0-9]   doca docg docN docP doc2 docb
```

If you want to include the dash as a character in your class specification, you place it at the end of your list of characters and quote it with a preceding backslash. The pattern **doc[09\-]**, for example, matches on a pattern beginning with "doc" and ending in either a 0, -, or 9 character.

Classes and the * Special Character: [ ]*

You can combine brackets with other special characters to create highly effective matching patterns. If you combine the brackets with the asterisk, you can match on multiple instances of a specific set of characters. For example, the pattern **doc[123]*** searches for any pattern beginning with "doc" and ending with any combination of the characters 1, 2, or 3. The pattern would search for **doc221** as well as **doc3321311**. To search for any number, use the dash to specify the range 0-9 to select all numbers. The pattern **doc[0-9]*** matches any pattern beginning with "doc" and ending with a number. The pattern will locate **doc582** and **doc7834103**. You can also use the brackets and the asterisk to specify numbers beginning or ending with certain integers. The pattern **23[0-9]*** matches on all numbers beginning with 23, such as 235 or 2378945. The pattern **[0-9]*\.50** matches on any number ending with .50, such as 7.50 or 1000.50.

Using both ranges and the asterisk, you can specify patterns that have certain features. For example, you can match on patterns that are only in uppercase, or patterns that only contain numbers. In such cases, you need to be sure to provide a context for the asterisk special character. Remember that the ***** matches on zero or more instances of a character. To provide a context for a range of characters, simply specify the range again before the one used with the *****. The pattern **[0-9][0-9]*** will match on one or more instances of a numeric character. The pattern **[A-Z][A-Z]*** will match on one or more instances of an uppercase character.

```
[A-Z][A-Z]*      we sold 9645 IBM and DEC components

[0-9][0-9]*      we bought 9645 oranges today
```

Sometimes you may need to combine several special characters in a pattern (see the table here). For example, the pattern **^[^0-9]*** selects all text from the beginning of a line up to the first number. The pattern **[^0-9]*$** selects all text from the end of a line up to the first number.

```
^[^0-9]*         We bought 9645 oranges today

[^0-9]*$         We bought 9645 oranges today
```

Character	Match	Operation
^	Start of a line	References the beginning of a line
$	End of a line	References the end of a line
.	Any character	Matches on any one possible character in a pattern
*	Repeated characters	Matches on repeated characters in a pattern
[]	Classes	Matches on classes of characters (a set of characters) in the pattern

grep and Regular Expressions

Though shell special characters allow you to match on file names, regular expressions allow you to match on data within files. Using **grep** with regular expressions, you can locate files and the lines in them that match a specified pattern. You can use special characters in a **grep** pattern, making the pattern a regular expression. **grep** regular expressions use the *****, **.**, and **[]**, as well as the **^** and **$** special characters.

Suppose that you want to use the long form output of **ls** to display just your directories. One way to do this is to generate a list of all directories in the long form and pipe this list to **grep**, which can then pick out the directory entries. You can do this by using the **^** special character to specify the beginning of a line. Remember that in the long form output of **ls**, the first character indicates the file type. A **d** represents a directory, an **l** represents a symbolic link, and **a** represents a regular file. Using the pattern **^d**, **grep** will match only on those lines beginning with a *d*.

```
$ ls -l | grep '^d'
drwxr-x---  2  chris 512 Feb 10 04:30  reports
drwxr-x---  2  chris 512 Jan 6  01:20  letters
```

If you only want to list those files that have symbolic links, you can use the pattern **^l**:

```
$ ls -l | grep '^l'
lrw-rw-r-- 1  chris  group 4   Feb 14  10:30  lunch
```

You can also use the **$** special character with **grep** to match on data at the end of a line. Remember that the **finger** command outputs the location of a person's login as its last field. You could match on this last field in order to find out who has logged in from a certain location. In the next example, the user pipes the output of **finger** to a **grep** command that will match on lines that have the pattern "Lab" at the end. This will provide a list of all those who have logged into the system from the Lab location.

```
$ finger | grep 'Lab$'
marylou     Marylou Carrion    02         Mon 8:30     Lab
dylan     Dylan Petersen    06       Mon 9:15    Lab
```

With the *****, **.**, and **[]** special characters, you can match on actual variations on a pattern. For example, suppose you want to match on both the singular and plural forms of "cousin" ("cousin" and "cousins"). In effect, there could be zero or more instances of *s* after the word "cousin". As previously noted, the ***** character will match on zero or more instances of a character. The regular expression **cousins*** will match on both "cousin" and "cousins".

Be sure to distinguish between the shell special character and special characters used in the pattern. When you include special characters in your **grep** pattern, you need to quote the pattern. Notice that regular-expression special characters and shell special characters use the same symbols: the asterisk, period, and brackets. If you do not, then any special characters in the pattern will be interpreted by the shell as shell special characters. Without quotes, an asterisk would be used to generate file names rather than being evaluated by **grep** to search for repeated characters. Quoting the pattern guarantees that **grep** will evaluate the special characters as part of a regular expression.

In the next example, the asterisk special character is used in the pattern as a regular expression and in the file name list as a shell special character to generate file names. In this case, all files in the current directory will be searched for patterns with zero or more *s*'s after "report".

```
$ grep 'reports*' *
mydata: The report was sitting on his desk.
weather: The weather reports were totally accurate.
```

Special characters can help you to accurately select the pattern on the line that you want to match. Suppose you want to match a pattern that is located at a specific location on a line. Say, for example, you want to list those files that have read and write group access. In the output of **ls -l**, the read and write group permissions are listed four spaces from the beginning of an output line. The preceding four characters could be any character, so you need to be able to match on any possibilities. The period special character will match on any character. The pattern **^....** will match on any characters in the first four positions on a line, effectively skipping them. The pattern **^....rw** will then search for any files with group read and write access. The first four characters in the pattern are ignored, skipping the file type and owner permissions. The group permissions follow, beginning with the fifth character. In the next example, the user locates all files with other read and execute access.

```
$ ls -l | grep '^.......r.x'
-rw-r--r-x  1  chris weather 207  Feb 20  11:55  mydata
-rw-rw-r-x  1  chris weather 568  Feb 14  10:30  today
```

The brackets match on either a set of characters, a range of characters, or a non-match of those characters. For example, the pattern **doc[abc]** matches on the patterns "doca", "docb", and "docc", but not on "docd". The same pattern can be specified with a range: **doc[a-c]**. However, the pattern **doc[^ab]** will match on any pattern beginning with "doc", but not ending in *a* or *b*. Thus, "docc" will be retrieved but not "doca" or "docb". In the next example, the user finds all lines that reference "doca", "docb", or "docc".

```
$ grep 'doc[abc]' myletter
File letter doca and docb.
We need to redo docc.
```

You can combine the different special characters to increase the power of your regular expressions. You already know that a combination of the period and asterisk, **.***, will match on any set of characters. With the appropriate context, they can match on patterns of varying length. For example, suppose you want to list those users' files that were last updated between 10:00 and 11:00 a.m. You would need to construct a regular expression that skips everything from the end of the line to the next colon. After the colon is the hour in which the file was last updated. Files with an hour of 10 were updated between 10 and 11. Notice that because the length of file names varies, you do not know how many characters you will have to skip to reach the colon. The **.*** combination will skip any number of characters. The pattern **10:.*$** will skip any characters from the end of the line to the next colon followed by a 10:

```
$ ls -l | grep '10:.*$'
-rw-r--r--  1  chris weather 207  Jan 27  10:55  forecast
-rw-rw-r-x  1  chris weather 568  Feb 14  10:30  today
```

If you want to select files that were updated over several hours, say from 10 to 12, you could add a class special character specifying all the possible digits: 0,1, and 2.

```
$ ls -l | grep '1[012]:.*$'
-rw-r--r--  1  chris weather 207  Jan 27  10:55  forecast
-rw-rw-r--  1  chris weather 308  Feb 17  12:40  monday
-rw-r--r-x  1  chris weather 207  Feb 20  11:55  mydata
-rw-rw-r-x  1  chris weather 568  Feb 14  10:30  today
```

Full Regular Expressions and Extended Special Characters: |, ( ), +, and ?

Certain Linux utilities such as **egrep** and awk can make use of an extended set of special characters in their patterns. These special characters are |, ( ) +, and ?, and are listed here:

Character	Execution
pattern | *pattern*	Logical OR for searching for alternative patterns `'milk|soup'`
(*pattern*)	Parentheses for grouping patterns `(canned|lowfat) milk`
char+	Searches for one or more repetitions of the previous character `it+i`
char?	Searches for zero or one instance of the previous character `si?t`

The **+** and **?** are variations on the ***** special character, whereas **|** and **()** provide new capabilities. Patterns that can use such special characters are referred to as full regular expressions. The Ed and Ex standard line editors do not have these extended special characters. Only **egrep**, which is discussed here, and awk have extended special characters.

The **+** sign matches one or more instances of a character. For example, **t+** matches at least one or more *t*'s, just as **tt*** does. It will match on "sitting" or "biting", but not "ziing". The **?** matches zero or one instance of a character. For example, **t?** matches on one *t* or no *t*'s, but not "tt". The expression **it?i** will match on "ziing" and "biting" but not "sitting". In the next examples, repeated *n* characters followed by an *e* is searched for. With the **+** special character, the regular expression **an+e** will match on one or more instances of *n* preceded by *a* and followed by *e*. The "ane" is matched in "anew", and "anne" is matched on "canned". In the second example, the regular expression **an?e** searches for zero or one instance of *n* preceded by *a* followed by *e*. Thus "ane" in "anew" is matched, but not the "anne" in "canned".

```
an+e
    anew
    canned

an?e
    anew
    canned      no match
```

The **|** and **()** special characters operate on pattern segments, rather than just characters. The **|** is a logical OR special character that specifies alternative search patterns within a single regular expression. Though part of the same regular expression, the patterns are searched for as separate patterns. The search pattern **milk|soup** will search for either the pattern "milk" or "soup".

```
milk|soup
    lowfat milk
    vegetable soup
```

With the **()** special characters, you can specify segments of a pattern that can be operated on by special characters. For example, the pattern **(%-)*** would search for zero or more repeated instances of the pattern %-%-%-%-. Using the **+**, **(%-)+**, it would look for one or more repeated instances of the pattern. In the next examples, the user applies the **+** and **?** special characters to whole patterns. First the user searches for multiple occurrences of "He". The pattern "He" is enclosed in parentheses and immediately followed by the **+** special character. A match is made on the pattern "HeHe". In the next example, the user searches for either the pattern "Dickens" or "Mr. Dickens". In this case, the **?** special character searches for zero or one instance of "Mr." followed by "Dickens".

```
(He)+
    HeHe, I'm laughing

(Mr. )?Dickens
    Mr. Dickens is here
    Dickens wrote this
```

Parts of the pattern can be grouped with parentheses to create alternate prefixes or suffixes for a pattern. The pattern **'(high|low)fat'** searches for either the pattern "highfat" or "lowfat". In the first example that follows, the user searches for a pattern beginning with either "lowfat" or "chocolate" and followed by "milk". Either "lowfat milk" or "chocolate milk" will match the regular expression. In the following example, the user searches for either "shining" or "shined".

```
'(lowfat|chocolate) milk'
    lowfat milk is good
    chocolate milk is great

shin(ing|ed)
    The sun shined all day.
    Stop shining the light.
```

egrep and Full Regular Expressions

egrep combines the capabilities of **grep** and **fgrep**. Like **fgrep**, it can search for several patterns at the same time. Like **grep**, it can evaluate special characters in its patterns and it can search for regular expressions. However, unlike **grep**, it can evaluate extended special characters such as the logical OR operator, |. In this respect, **egrep** is the most powerful of the three search filters.

To search for several patterns at once, you can either enter them on the command line separated by a new line character as **fgrep** does, or you can use the logical OR special character in a pattern to specify alternative patterns to be searched for in a file. The patterns are actually part of the same regular expression, but they are searched for as separate patterns. The pattern **milk|soup egrep** will search for either the pattern "milk" or the pattern "soup".

```
$ egrep 'milk|soup' perishables
lowfat milk
vegetable soup
```

Parts of the pattern can be grouped with parentheses to create alternate prefixes or suffixes for a pattern. The pattern **'(canned|lowfat) milk'** searches for either the pattern "canned milk" or "lowfat milk".

```
$ egrep '(canned|lowfat) milk' perishables packaged
perishables:lowfat milk
packaged:canned milk
```

You can use groupings with any special characters, not just the |. Groupings allow you to create very flexible regular expressions. For example, suppose you want to match on both the singular and plural forms of a word, such as "box" and "boxes". Because the plural form of "box" uses two characters, "es", the * special character needs to operate on a sequence of characters, not just one. You can do just that by grouping the characters with parentheses and placing the * after them. The pattern **(es)*** will match on zero or more instances of "es". The pattern **box(es)*** will match on both "box" and "boxes".

```
$ egrep 'box(es)*' mydata
The boxes fell when
the heavy box was put on top.
```

Groupings can help you refine the selection of patterns. Take the example used earlier for **grep** in which the user wants to list those files that were updated during certain hours. Now suppose you want to select hours from 6:00 a.m. to 12:00 p.m. If you only used the classes special characters **[01][6-90-2]**, you would match not only 12 but also 02; not only 06 but also 16. Grouping with the | special character can help you overcome such a problem. The regular expression **(0[6-9]|1[0-2])** will successfully match only the hours from 6 to 12, as shown in the next example.

```
$ ls -l | egrep '(0[6-9]|1[0-2]):.*$'
-rw-r--r--  1  chris  weather 207  Jan 27  10:55  forecast
-rw-rw-r--  1  chris  weather 308  Feb 17  12:40  monday
-rw-r--r-x  1  chris  medical 789  Feb 06  06:45  roster
-rw-rw-r-x  1  chris  weather 942  Feb 12  08:20  storm
```

With the **+** and **?** special characters, you can make more refined matches than those available with the ***** special character. The **+** sign matches one or more instances of a character, and the **?** matches zero or one instance of a character. Take the example that was used for **grep** in which the user wants to match on both "cousin" and "cousins". The ***** will successfully perform such a match; however, it would also match on "cousinss", "cousinsss", and so on. What is called for is a match on only one *s* character or none at all. In this respect, **egrep** with the **?** special character provides a more accurate match. The regular expression **cousins?** will match on either "cousin" or "cousins", but not on "cousinss". In the next example, the user applies **egrep** to a file, searching for "cousin" and its plural.

```
$ egrep 'cousins?' birthday
Your cousins can
cousin from back east
```

When you include special characters in your **egrep** pattern, you need to quote the pattern. Notice that the **?** is a regular-expression special character for **egrep** and a shell special character for your shell. If you did not quote the pattern, then the **?** would be interpreted by the shell as the **?** shell special character. Quoting the pattern guarantees that **grep** will evaluate the **?** special character as part of a regular expression.

Summary: Filters

A filter takes, as its input, data from the standard input, examines it, and generates a filtered output. The original data is not affected. There are three general categories of filters: file filters, editing filters, and data filters. File filters perform basic operations such as displaying files and searching files for patterns. Editing filters perform editing operations, and data filters manipulate data fields in files. All can enhance their capabilities by using regular expressions to form powerful pattern matching operations.

Though many filters take file names as their arguments, all can receive data from the standard input. This allows you to pipe data from one filter to another. On a command line, you can specify a series of filters in which the output of one is piped as input to another. In this sense, the same data can be passed through several filters, the output being modified as it is passed along.

Filters generate different kinds of output, depending on their task. Some filters only generate reports, such as the **wc** filter that outputs the number of words in a file. Other filters output selected parts of a file. The **spell** filter outputs only misspelled words. The **head** and **tail** filters output only the beginning and ending lines in a file. The **cmp** filter outputs differing lines in a file. Still other filters output an entire version of the input, but in a modified way. The **pr** filter outputs files in a paginated format with headers and page numbers, and the **sort** filter outputs a sorted version of a file.

Most filters have a set of options that allow you to further modify the output. For example, the pr filter with the -n option outputs text with line numbers. The **tail** filter with a - and a number allows you to determine how many lines you want to display.

File Filters

The file filters perform basic operations on files, such as displaying files, comparing files, searching for patterns, generating a formatted version of a file, and backing up files. The **cat**, **head**, and **tail** filters display a file. **cat** displays the entire file, whereas **head** displays the beginning lines of a file, and **tail** displays the last lines of a file. The **tail** filter has several options that allow you to reverse lines or designate how much of the file is displayed.

The **cmp** and **comm** filters compare files. The **cmp** filter performs a character-by-character comparison and outputs the line number and first differing character. The **comm** filter performs more of a line-by-line comparison, outputting lines that are unique to each file and those that are the same.

The **grep** filter searches a file for a particular pattern. You can search several files at a time if you want. **grep** will output the file name and the line number in the file where the pattern is located. **grep** has several different options, one of which, **-n**, will output the line number along with any matched lines.

The **pr** filter outputs a file or files in a paginated format. **pr** has many options, such as designating a header with the **-h** option or setting the page width using the **-w** option. Of particular interest is the ability of **pr** to output line numbers using the **-n** option. Combined with the **-t** option to suppress headers, you can use **-n** to generate a simple text version of your file that has line numbers.

The **cpio** filter allows you to manage backups of your files. With **cpio** you can copy your files to an archive file and then later, extract copies. **cpio** does not directly access and archive files but makes use of redirection to read from and save to an archive file. The **cpio** filter has two major options: the **-i** option for archiving files and the **-o** option for extracting files. You can also back up directories to an archive file. But if you do so, you need to use the **find** command to first generate full path names of all the files in your directories.

Edit Filters

Linux text files are organized and referenced as a series of lines by many editing utilities such as line editors and edit filters. A core set of line editing commands is used in all these utilities to perform editing operations on lines of text. Text is referenced line by line, and then line editing commands operate on those lines. A line can be referenced with a line number or a pattern search. A pattern search locates and references the line that contains the pattern. Certain lines can also be referenced using special line references. The **$** references the last line in the file, and the period references the current line. In a line editor, such as Ed, the **+** symbol references the next line, and the **-** symbol references the previous line. You can mark a line using the **k** command followed by a single letter, and then reference the marked line using that letter preceded by a single quote.

Having referenced a line or lines, you can execute line editing commands to input lines, delete and replace lines, as well as copy and move lines. If you want to modify specific text within a line, you need to use the substitution command. The substitution command allows you to replace a pattern in a line with other specified text. Notice that a pattern is used both in searches to locate a line and in the substitution command to match text within a line.

The **tr**, **diff**, and **sed** filters perform editing operations on input read from files of the standard input. They are useful for generating a modified version of a text file. The edit filters receive input from files or standard input, and then output an edited form of that input. This output can then be directed to a file or a device such as a printer.

The **sed** filter is actually a stream editor that performs Ed line editing operations on the input, generating an edited form of the input. However, unlike other editors, the **sed** editing commands are, by default, global. You can restrict the application of **sed** editing commands by using line numbers and patterns. A pattern placed before a **sed** editing command restricts it to only those lines with that pattern.

The **diff** filter compares two files and outputs the lines that are different. It specifically outputs editing information, showing how the first file can be changed to become a copy of the second file. The **diff** filter with its **-e** option allows you to output line editing commands that you can then use to make the first file an exact copy of the second.

The **tr** filter will translate characters in the input stream. It can perform several translations at the same time using two character lists. A character from the first list is translated into a corresponding character in the second list. The **tr** filter also has options that allow you to delete characters or replace multiple instances of characters. One common use of **tr** is the simple encryption of files.

Regular Expressions

Searching text sometimes requires a more powerful and flexible pattern matching capability. Many of the utilities that have editing capabilities use a standard set of special characters designed for use in patterns that search text. A pattern that contains such special characters is called a regular expression. Though some of the special characters are similar to shell special characters, they do not do the same thing.

Regular-expression special characters are designed for text searches, whereas shell special characters match and generate file names.

With a regular-expression special character, you can reference the end or beginning of a line (**$** and **^**), repeated instances of a character (*****), any possible character and any possible class of characters (**.** and **[]**). You will find regular expressions used in many utilities that have editing capabilities. The **sed** and awk utilities make extensive use of regular expressions.

A special character is only special within a pattern. Outside of a pattern it may have a different meaning or simply be a character. For example, the dollar sign, **$**, in the line editor references the last line in a file. Within a pattern, the **$** is a special character referencing the end of a line, **/$/**. In the replacement text of the substitution command, the **$** is simply the dollar sign character.

The replacement text in a substitution command has its own separate set of special characters. They are used to construct the replacement text. If you want to use the character equivalent of a special character in either a pattern search or replacement text, you can quote the special character with a backslash. For example, searching for a pattern that contains a period requires that you quote the period with a backslash: **\.**.

The **grep** filter will perform pattern searches on files and output the lines where a specified pattern occurs. **grep** has numerous options with which you can output line numbers or file names as well as non-matches. There are two variations on the **grep** filter: **fgrep** and **egrep**. As noted in Chapter 8, **fgrep** can search for several matches at once but does not allow special characters in its patterns. **egrep** can also search for several patterns at once but does allow the use of special characters in its patterns. In fact, **egrep** also allows the use of extended special characters such as **|**, **+**, and **?**.

Data Filters

There is a set of filters that perform data operations on an input stream. These data filters, like other filters, operate on a stream of input, receiving data and generating modified output. The data filters are designed to operate on files whose text is organized into fields of data much like a single file database. Each line in the file is a record and each word in the line constitutes a field in that record. The data filter takes as its input a file containing such records, and it outputs records selected on the basis of a given criteria.

There are five data filters: **sort**, **cut**, **paste**, **join**, and **uniq** (see Table 14-3). The **sort** filter generates a sorted version of the file in which all records are sorted alphabetically according to a specified field. **sort** is also a more general purpose filter that you can use to sort lines in any text file. The **cut** filter outputs all entries for a selected field in a data file. The **paste** filter generates output that combines the records of several data files. The **join** filter generates output that combines the records in two files by comparing the values of specified fields. The **uniq** filter detects fields that have the same values. It allows you to count how many fields have the same values as well as eliminating any repetitions from its output.

Though the data filters cannot perform many of the complex operations found in professional database management software, you will find that they can perform many of the more common operations. You can sort data and selectively display fields. You can also selectively retrieve matching records in different files. You can even combine data filters to form complex queries. For example, you could use the **join** filter to combine selected records from different files and then pipe the output to the **sort** filter to sort the results.

Command	Execution
cat	Displays a file. It can take file names for its arguments. It outputs the contents of those files directly to the standard output, which, by default, is the screen $ **cat** *filenames*
tee	Copies the standard input to a file while sending it on to the standard output. It is usually used with another filter and allows you to save output to a file while sending the output on to another filter or utility. As with **cat**, if the standard output is not further redirected or piped, it will be sent to its default destination, the screen $ *filter* | **tee** *filename* | *utility* $ *filter* | **tee** *filename*
a	Appends to the file; does not overwrite it
head	Displays the first few lines of a file. The default is ten lines, but you can specify the number of lines $ **head** *filenames*
tail	Displays the last lines in a file. The default is ten lines, but you can specify the number of lines $ **tail** *filenames*
-*num*	With this option, **tail** displays the number of lines specified by *num* and starting from the end of the file
+*num*	With this option, **tail** displays the rest of the text, starting from page *num*
-c	With this option, **tail** displays by characters. This option is used with either *num* or +*num*, where *num* refers to a number of characters to be displayed

Table 14-1. *File Filters*

Command	Execution
-l	With this option, **tail** displays by line. This option is used with either *num* or **+***num*, where *num* refers to a number of lines to be displayed. This is the default option
-r	With this option, **tail** displays lines in reverse order. This option is used with either *num* or **+***num*, where *num* refers to a number of lines to be displayed in reverse. **+1r** displays the entire file in reverse order
wc	Counts the number of lines, words, and characters in a file and outputs only that number $ **wc** *filename*
c	With this option, **wc** counts the number of characters in a file
l	With this option, **wc** counts the number of lines in a file
w	With this option, **wc** counts the number of words in a file
spell	Checks the spelling of each word in a file and outputs only the misspelled words $ **spell** *filename*
+*filename*	Use this option with **spell** to specify your own user-defined dictionary of words to be searched $ **spell** **+mydict** *list1*
sort	Outputs a sorted version of a file $ **sort** *filename*
cmp	Compares two files, character by character, checking for differences. It stops at the first difference it finds and outputs the character position and line number $ **cmp** *file1 file2*
l	With this option, **cmp** outputs all the character positions of differing characters, as well as their respective octal values $ **cmp lunch dinner** **15 160 164** **17 164 155**
comm	Compares two files, line by line, and outputs both files according to lines that are similar and different for each $ **comm** *file1 file2*

Table 14-1.   *File Filters (continued)*

Command	Execution
1	With this option, **comm** suppresses output for lines unique to the first file. The **1** refers to the first column
2	With this option, **comm** suppresses output for lines unique to the second file. The **2** refers to the second column
3	With this option, **comm** suppresses output for lines common to both files. The **3** refers to the third column
grep	Searches files for a pattern and lists any matched lines `$ grep ` *pattern filenames*
i	With this option, **grep** ignores upper- and lowercase differences `$ grep -i milk perishables packaged`
c	With this option, **grep** only outputs a number—the count of the lines with the pattern `$ grep -c milk perishables`
l	With this option, **grep** only displays the names of the files that contain the matching pattern `$ grep -l milk perishables packaged`
n	With this option, **grep** outputs the line number along with the text of those lines with the matching pattern `$ grep -n milk perishables packaged`
v	With this option, **grep** outputs all those lines that do not contain the matching pattern `$ grep -v milk perishables packaged`
fgrep	Searches files in the file list for several patterns at the same time. It executes much faster than either **grep** or **egrep**; however, **fgrep** cannot interpret special characters. It cannot search for regular expressions `$ fgrep ` *patterns file-list* `$ fgrep milk perishables packaged`
f *filename*	With this option, **fgrep** reads its pattern list from a file called *filename* `$ fgrep -f mypats perishables packaged`

Table 14-1. *File Filters* (continued)

Command	Execution
egrep	Searches files in the file list for the occurrence of a pattern. Like **fgrep**, it can read patterns from a file. Like **grep**, it can use regular expressions, interpreting special characters. However, unlike **grep**, it can also interpret extended special characters such as **?**, **|**, and **+**.
-f *filename*	With this option, **egrep** reads its pattern list from *filename* `$ egrep -f mypats perishables`
pr	Outputs a paginated version of the input, adding headers, page numbers, and any other specified format `$ pr options` *filenames*
+*num*	This option instructs **pr** to output only from the page numbered *num*. Unlike other options, there is no preceding dash `$ pr +6 wreport	lpr`
-*num*	This option instructs **pr** to format the output into columns. The number of columns is designated by *num* `$ pr -2 wreport	lpr`
d	This option instructs **pr** to double-space the formatted output `$ pr -d wreport	lpr`
h*name*	This option replaces the default header with *name*. The default header is the file name `$ pr -h "Weather Report" wreport	lpr`
l*num*	This option sets the number of lines on a page `$ pr -120 wreport	lpr`
m	With this option, **pr** outputs several files at the same time, each in its own column. The output shows multiple columns, one for each file `$ pr -m mon tues	lpr`
n	This option instructs **pr** to number lines. The option can be modified with either a character or a number. The character represents a character to be placed between the line number and the line text. The number represents the minimum number of spaces between the line number and line text `$ pr -n wreport	lpr` `$ pr -n: wreport	lpr` `$ pr -n3 wreport	lpr`

Table 14-1.   *File Filters (continued)*

Command	Execution
t	This option instructs **pr** not to generate a header or trailer for the formatted output `$ pr -t wreport	lpr`
w*num*	This option sets the width of a page. *num* is the number of character columns. The default is 72 `$ pr -w25 wreport	lpr`
cpio	Copies files to an archive and extracts files from an archive. It has two modes of operation: one using the **-o** option to copy files to an archive, and the other using the **-i** option to extract files from an archive. When copying files to an archive, you need to first generate the list of file names using a command such as **ls** or **find** `$ ` *generated-filenames* `	cpio -o > ` *archive-file* `$ cpio -i ` *filenames* ` < ` *archive-file*
o	With this option, meaning out, **cpio** creates archived output that can be redirected to a file, making it an archive file. The operation effectively creates a backup for designated files. With this option, **cpio** takes as its input a list of file names. These files will have their contents read and copied into the standard output in an archived format. File names can be generated with the **ls** or **find** commands and piped to **cpio**. To archive directories, you must use the **find** command `$ ls	cpio -o > progarch` `$ find -name *	cpio -o > progarch`

i	With this option, meaning in, **cpio** extracts files from an archive. The archive is read from the standard input, which usually has been redirected from an archive file. The files to be extracted have their names listed as arguments to **cpio**. If no file names are listed, then all files are extracted. Extracted files are copied out of the archive. A copy of each is written to the current directory unless it was archived with a path name. In that case, the file is saved in the directory referenced by its path name
	`$ cpio -i < progarch`
	`$ cpio -i main.c < progarch`

d	This option, meaning directory, is used with the **-i** option to direct **cpio** to extract directories, creating new ones if needed `$ cpio -id < progarch`

Table 14-1.   *File Filters* (continued)

Command	Execution
u	This option, meaning unconditional, is used with the **-i** option to direct **cpio** to copy older files over their corresponding newer ones that already exist in your directory. By default, **cpio** will not overwrite files newer than those extracted from the archive `$ cpio -iu < progarch`

Table 14-1. *File Filters* (continued)

Command	Execution
sed	Outputs an edited form of its input. **sed** takes as an argument an editing command and a file list. The editing command is executed on input read from files in the file list. **sed** then outputs an edited version of the files. The editing commands are line editing commands similar to those used for the Ed line editor `$ sed` *editing-command file-list* `$ sed '1d' perishables`
n	With this option, **sed** does not output lines automatically. This option is usually used with the **p** command to output only selected lines `$ sed -n '/veg/ p' perishables`
f *filename*	With this option, **sed** reads editing commands *filename* `$ sed -f myed perishables`
Line Commands	(you need to quote any new line characters if you are entering more than one line)
a	Appends text after a line
i	Inserts text before a line
c	Changes text
d	Deletes lines

Table 14-2. *Edit Filters*

Command	Execution
p	Prints lines
w	Writes lines to a file
r	Reads lines from a file
q	Quits the **sed** editor before all lines are processed
n	Skips processing to next line
s / *pattern* / *replacement* /	Substitutes matched pattern with replacement text
g s / *pat* / *rep* / g	Global substitution on a line
p s / *pat* / *rep* / p	Outputs the modified line
w s / *pat* / *rep* / w *fname*	Writes the modified line to a file
/ *pattern* /	A line can be located and referenced by a pattern
diff	Compares two files and outputs the lines that are different as well as the editing changes needed to make the first file the same as the second file. With the **-e** option, **diff** will output Ed line editing commands that you can then use to actually make the first file the same as the second $ **diff** *file1 file2* $ **diff breakfast brunch**
f1-linenum **a** *f2-line1, f2-line2*	Appends lines from file2 to after *f1-linenum* in file1
f1-line1, f1-line2 **d** *f1-linenum*	Deletes the lines in file1
f1-line1, f1-line2 **c** *f2-line1, f2-line2*	Replaces lines in file1 with lines in file2
b	With this option, **diff** ignores any trailing or duplicate blanks $ **diff -b breakfast brunch**
c	With this option, **diff** outputs a context for differing lines. Three lines above and below are displayed $ **diff -c breakfast brunch**

Table 14-2.   *Edit Filters* (continued)

Command	Execution

e	With this option, **diff** outputs a list of Ed editing commands that, when executed, change the first file into an exact copy of the second file. You usually redirect this output to a file and then add the **w** and **q** commands to this file. Then the file can be used as redirected input for the Ed command
	`$ diff -e breakfast brunch > bchanges`
	`$ echo "w\nq" >> bchanges`
	`$ ed breakfast < bchanges`

tr	Outputs a version of the input in which characters in the first character list that occur in the input are replaced in the output by corresponding characters in the second character list. In effect, you can replace each occurrence of a character with another character `$ tr` *first-character-list second-character-list* `$ tr "abc" "xyz"`
[]	Specifies a range of characters `$ tr "[a-z]" "[A-Z]"`
d	With this option, **tr** deletes any character in the character list `$ tr -d "abc"`
c	With this option, **tr** replaces those characters not in the character list `$ tr -c "abc" "xyz"`
s	With this option, **tr** replaces multiple instances of characters in the character list with only one corresponding replacement character `$ tr -s "abc" "xyz"`

Table 14-2.   *Edit Filters* (continued)

Command	Execution

sort	Sorts the lines it receives as input. You use it to generate a sorted version of a file. You can perform alphabetic sorts, reverse sorts, and numeric sorts. You can sort on a given field or range of fields. The syntax for the **sort** filter is the keyword **sort** followed by any options and then a list of file names. **sort** can also receive its input from the standard input. You can pipe data into **sort** to be sorted
	`$ sort -option file-list`
	`$ sort -n listdata`

-o *filename*	Saves the output of **sort** in *filename*. You can use this option to safely overwrite the original input file, giving you a sorted file `$ sort listdata -o listdata`
c	Checks only to see if the file is sorted. If the file is not sorted, **sort** displays an error message; otherwise it displays nothing
m	Merges previously sorted files
u	Outputs repeated line only once
Sorting Data	
d	Dictionary sort ignores any characters in the character set that are not alphabetic, numbers, or blanks. Punctuation characters and control characters are ignored
f	Ignores case. Lowercase characters are folded into uppercase characters `$ sort -f listdata`
i	Ignores nonprinting characters `$ sort -f listdata`
M	Sorts months. Fields whose values are the names of the month are sorted. The first three characters of the name are examined and changed to uppercase for sorting: JAN, FEB, JUN, NOV. They are ordered according to the months of the year beginning with January

Table 14-3. *Data Filters*

Command	Execution
n	Sorts according to the numeric value of a field, not its character value. The **-b** option is automatically applied, ignoring any leading blanks `$ sort -n listdata`
-r	Sorts in reverse order `$ sort -r listdata`

Sorting Fields

Command	Execution
b	Ignores any leading blanks before a field `$ sort -b listdata`
+*num*	The number of fields to skip on a line. Sorting begins from the next field. **+2** skips the first two fields and begins sorting on the third field `$ sort +2 listdata`
–*num*	The number of the field where sorting on a line ends. –3 will stop a sort on a line at the third field. Fields after the third field would not be used in the sort. This option is often used with the **+** option to isolate a field and restrict the sort to that field. **+2 –3** sorts only on the third field. You can also specify a range of fields: **+1 –4** `$ sort +2 -3 listdata`
-t*c*	Specifies a new field delimiter, *c*. The default is a space
paste	Joins lines from different files into a new combined output `$ paste` *-option file-list* `$ paste -n costs foods`
-d*delimiter-list*	Allows you to specify your own delimiter for separating joined lines `$ paste -d% costs foods`
cut	Copies out specified fields or columns in a file. You must always use either the **-f** option or the **-c** option with **cut** `$ cut` *-option file-list* `$ cut -f2,3 listdataD`

Table 14-3.   *Data Filters (continued)*

Command	Execution
-f*num*	Specifies what fields you want copied out of a file. Fields are numbered from 1. You can specify more than one field by separating them with a comma, or you can specify a range of fields using a dash between numbers
-f*num1,* *num2*	Specifies fields to be cut out `$ cut -f1,3 listdata`
-f*num1 -num2*	Specifies a range of fields beginning with *num1* and ending with *num2* `$ cut -f2-4 listdata`
-c*num-num*	Allows you to specify columns of characters to be cut out `$ cut -c20-35 listdata`
-d*delimiter-list*	Allows you to specify your own delimiter to look for in a file `$ cut -d: -f2-4 listdata`
-s	Ignores any lines that do not have a delimiter in them. This option can only be used with the **-f** option. You use it to pass over lines with no data, such as headings, titles, or empty lines `$ cut -f2-4 -s listdata`

join	Joins the lines of different files if the values of a specified field in each file match
	`$ join -option file-list`
	`$ join -j1 2 -j2 1 foods counts`

-j*filenum fieldnum*	Specifies what fields in each file are to be compared. Each field is numbered from 1. If you are comparing the same field in each file, you need only one **-j** option and the *fieldnum*. If you are comparing different fields in each file, then you need a **-j** option and *filenum* as well as the *fieldnum* for each file. The *filenum* is the position of the file's name in the file list
-j*fieldnum*	Compares the same field in each file. There is a space between the **-j** option and the *fieldnum* `$ join -j 2 foods counts`

Table 14-3. *Data Filters* (continued)

Command	Execution
-j_filenum_ _fieldnum_	Compares different fields in each file `$ join -j1 2 -j2 1 foodtypes counts`

-o_filenum._ _fieldnum_	Specifies what fields in each file are to be output. The _filenum_ and _fieldnum_ are separated by a period. You can list several fields, separating each _filenum.fieldnum_ combination with a space
	`$ join -j1 2 -j2 1 -o 1.3 1.4 2.2 2.4`
	`foodtypes counts`

-t_delimiter_	Allows you to specify your own delimiter to look for in a file. This is the same as the **-d** option in the **cut** and **paste** filters `$ join -t: -j1 2 -j2 1 foodtypes counts`
-a_filenum_	Outputs lines whose fields from a specified file do not match, as well as matched fields from both files, and takes a _filenum_ to specify the file from which to output unmatched lines `$ join -j1 2 -j2 1 -a1 foodtypes counts`
uniq	Eliminates repeated lines from its input. You can also compare lines based on selected fields. Lines whose selected fields have the same values are considered repetitions and can be eliminated from the output `$ uniq` _options input-file output-file_ `$ uniq -d listdata newfile`
c	Allows **uniq** to output each line preceded by the number of times the line occurs in the input `$ uniq -c listdata`
d	With this option, **uniq** only outputs repeated lines `$ uniq -d listdata`
u	With this option, **uniq** only outputs lines that are not repeated `$ uniq -u listdata`
-num	The number of fields to be skipped for comparison. Only the remaining fields are compared `$ uniq -3 listdata`

Table 14-3.   _Data Filters_ (continued)

Command	Execution
+num	The number of characters to be skipped for comparison. Only the remaining characters are compared, including spaces `$ uniq +12 listdata`

Table 14-3. *Data Filters* (continued)

Chapter Fifteen

The Bourne Again Shell (BASH)

Three different major shells have been developed for Linux: the Bourne Again shell (BASH), the Public Domain Korn shell (PDKSH), and the TCSH shell. Both the BASH and TCSH shells are enhanced versions of their corresponding Unix shells. The BASH shell is an advanced version of the Bourne shell, which includes most of the advanced features developed for the Korn shell and C-shell. TCSH is an enhanced version of the C-shell that was originally developed for BSD versions of Unix. PDKSH is a subset of the Unix Korn shell. Though their Unix counterparts differ greatly, the Linux shells share many of the same features. In Unix, the Bourne shell lacks many capabilities found in the other Unix shells. However, in Linux, the BASH shell incorporates all the advanced features of the Korn shell and C-shell, as well as the TCSH shell.

All three shells are available for your use, though the BASH shell is the default. All examples so far in this book have used the BASH shell. You log into your default shell, but you can change to another shell by entering its name. **tcsh** invokes the TCSH shell, **bash** the BASH shell, and **ksh** the PDKSH shell. You can leave a shell with the CTRL-**d** or **exit** command.

You only need one type of shell to do your work. Chapter 5 discussed features common to all shells, while this chapter and the next discuss the BASH and TCSH shells. This book does not cover the PDKSH shell. PDKSH is a subset of the Korn shell, and most of the advanced features of the Korn shell have already been incorporated into the BASH shell.

Command and File Name Completion

The BASH command line has a built-in feature very similar to the TCSH shell's feature that performs command and file name completion. If you enter an incomplete pattern as a command or file name argument, you can then press TAB to activate the command and file name completion feature, which will complete the pattern. If there is more than one command or file with the same prefix, the shell will simply beep and wait for you to add enough characters to select a unique command or file name. In the next example, the user issues a **cat** command with an incomplete file name. Upon pressing TAB, the system searches for a match and, when it finds one, fills in the file name. The user can then press ENTER to execute the command.

```
$ cat pre tab
$ cat preface
```

The shell can also perform file name completion to list the partially matching files in your current directory. If you press ESC followed by a question mark, ESC **?**, the shell will list all the file names matching the incomplete pattern. In the next example, the ESC **?** after the incomplete file name generates a list of possible file names. The shell then redraws the command line, and you can type in the complete name of the file you want, or type in distinguishing characters and press TAB to have the file name completed.

```
$ ls
document docudrama
$ cat doc escape ?
document
docudrama
$ cat docudrama
```

Command Line Editing

The BASH shell has built-in command line editing capabilities that let you easily modify commands you have entered before executing them. If you make a spelling mistake when entering a command, rather than reentering the entire command, you can use the editing operations to correct the mistake before executing the command. This is particularly helpful for commands that use arguments with lengthy path names.

The command line editing operations are a subset of the Emacs editing commands. You can use CTRL-**f** or the RIGHT ARROW key to move forward a character, the CTRL-**b** or the LEFT ARROW key to move back a character. CTRL-**d** or DEL will delete the character the cursor is on. To add text, you just move the cursor to where you want to insert text and type in the new characters. At any time, you can press ENTER to execute the command. As described in the next section, you can also use the command line editing operations to modify history events—previous commands that you have entered.

History

In the BASH shell, the history utility keeps a record of the most recent commands you have executed. The commands are numbered starting at 1, and there is a limit to the number of commands remembered—the default is 500. The history utility is a kind of short-term memory, keeping track of the most recent commands you have executed. To see the set of your most recent commands, type **history** on the command line and press ENTER. A list of your most recent commands is then displayed, preceded by a number.

```
$ history
1 cp mydata today
2 vi mydata
3 mv mydata reports
```

```
4 cd reports
5 ls
```

Each of these commands is technically referred to as an event. An event describes an action that has been taken—a command that has been executed. The events are numbered according to their sequence of execution. The most recent event has the highest number. Each of these events can be identified by its number or beginning characters in the command.

The history utility lets you reference a former event, placing it on your command line and allowing you to execute it. The easiest way to do this is to use UP ARROW and DOWN ARROW to place history events on your command line one at a time. You do not need to display the list first with **history**. Pressing UP ARROW once will place the last history event on your command line. Pressing it again places the next history event on your command. Pressing DOWN ARROW will place the previous event on the command line.

The BASH shell also has a history event completion operation invoked by the ESC TAB command. Much like standard command line completion, you enter part of the history event that you want. Then you press ESC, followed by TAB. The event that matches the text you have entered will be located and used to complete your command line entry. If more than one history event matches what you have entered, you will hear a beep, and you can then enter more characters to help uniquely identify the event you want.

You can then edit the event displayed on your command line using the command line editing operations. The LEFT ARROW and RIGHT ARROW keys move you along the command line. You can insert text wherever you stop your cursor. With BACKSPACE and DEL, you can delete characters. Once the event is displayed on your command line, you can press ENTER to execute it.

You can also reference and execute history events using the ! history command. The ! is followed by a reference that identifies the command. The reference can be either the number of the event or a beginning set of characters in the event. In the next example, the third command in the history list is referenced first by number and then by the beginning characters.

```
$ !3
mv mydata reports
$ !mv
mv mydata reports
```

You can also reference an event using an offset from the end of the list. A negative number will offset from the end of the list to that event, thereby referencing it. In the next example, the fourth command, **cd mydata**, is referenced using a negative offset, and then executed. Remember that you are offsetting from the end of the list, in this case event 5, up toward the beginning of the list, event 1. An offset of 4 beginning from event 5 places you at event 2.

```
$ !-4
vi mydata
```

If no event reference is used, then the last event is assumed. In the next example, the command **!** by itself executes the last command the user executed, in this case, **ls**.

```
$ !
ls
mydata today reports
```

You can also use a pattern to reference an event. The pattern is enclosed with question marks. In the next example, the pattern **?myd?** references the third event, **vi mydata**.

```
> !?myd?
vi mydata
```

History Event Editing

You can also edit any event in the history list before you execute it. In the BASH shell there are two ways to do this. You can use the command line editor capability to reference and edit any event in the history list. You can also use a history **fc** command option to reference an event and edit it with the full Vi editor. Each approach involves two very different editing capabilities. The first is limited to the commands in the command line editor, which edits only a single line with a subset of Emacs commands. However, at the same time, it allows you to reference events easily in the history list. The second approach invokes the standard Vi editor with all of its features, but only for a specified history event.

With the command line editor, not only can you edit the current command, but you can also move to a previous event in the history list to edit and execute it. The CTRL-**p** command then moves you up to the prior event in the list. The CTRL-**n** command will move you down the list. The ESC **<** command moves you to the top of the list, and the ESC **>** command moves you to the bottom. You can even use a pattern to search for a given event. The slash followed by a pattern searches backward in the list, and the question mark followed by a pattern searches forward in the list. The **n** command repeats the search.

Once you have located the event you want to edit, you use the Emacs command line editing commands to edit the line. CTRL-**d** will delete a character. CTRL-**f** and the RIGHT ARROW move you forward a character, and CTRL-**b** or the LEFT ARROW move you back a character. To add text, you position your cursor and type in the characters you want. Table 15-1 lists the different commands for referencing the history list.

If, instead, you want to edit an event using a standard editor, you need to reference the event using the **fc** command and a specific event reference, such as an event number. The editor used is the one specified by the shell as the default editor for the **fc** command. The next example will edit the fourth event, **cd reports**, with the standard editor and then execute the edited event.

```
$ fc 4
```

You can select more than one command at a time to be edited and executed by referencing a range of commands. You select a range of commands by indicating an identifier for the first command followed by an identifier for the last command in the range. An identifier can be the command number or the beginning characters in the command. In the next example, the range of commands 2 through 4 are edited and executed, first using event numbers and then using beginning characters in those events.

```
$ fc 2 4
$ fc vi c
```

fc uses the default editor specified in the **FCEDIT** special variable. Usually, this is the Vi editor. If you want to use the Emacs editor instead, you use the **-e** option and the term **emacs** when you invoke **fc**. The next example will edit the fourth event, **cd reports**, with the Emacs editor and then execute the edited event.

```
$ fc -e emacs 4
```

Configuring History: HISTFILE and HISTSAVE

The number of events saved by your system is kept in a special system variable called **HISTSIZE**. By default this is usually set to 500. You can change this to another number by simply assigning a new value to **HISTSIZE**. In the next example, the user changes the number of history events saved to 10 by resetting the **HISTSIZE** variable.

```
$ HISTSIZE=10
```

The actual history events are saved in a file whose name is held in a special variable called **HISTFILE**. By default this file is the **.bash_history** file. However, you can change the file in which history events are saved by assigning its name to the **HISTFILE** variable. In the next example, the value of **HISTFILE** is displayed. Then a new file name is assigned to it, **newhist**. History events will then be saved in the **newhist** file.

```
$ echo $HISTFILE
.bash_history
$ HISTFILE="newhist"
$ echo $HISTFILE
newhist
```

Aliases

You use the **alias** command to create another name for a command. The **alias** command operates like a macro that expands to the command it represents. The alias does not literally replace the name of the command; it simply gives another name to that command.

An **alias** command begins with the keyword **alias** and the new name for the command, followed by an equal sign and the command that the alias will reference. There can be no spaces around the equal sign. In the next example, **list** becomes another name for the **ls** command.

```
$ alias list=ls
$ ls
mydata today
$ list
mydata today
$
```

You can also use an alias to substitute for a command and its option. However, you need to enclose both the command and the option within single quotes. Any command that you alias that contains spaces must be enclosed in single quotes. In the next example, the alias **lss** references the **ls** command with its **-s** option, and the alias **lsa** references the **ls** command with the **-F** option. **ls** with the **-s** option lists files and their sizes in blocks, and the **ls** with the **-F** option places a slash before directory names. Notice that single quotes enclose the command and its option.

```
$ alias lss='ls -s'
$ lss
```

```
mydata 14    today  6    reports  1
$ alias lsa='ls -F'
$ lsa
mydata today /reports
$
```

You may often use an alias to include a command name with an argument. If you find yourself executing a command that has an argument with a complex combination of special characters on a regular basis, you may want to alias it. For example, suppose you often list just your source code and object code files—those files ending in either a .c or .o. You would need to use as an argument for **ls**, a combination of special characters — ***.[co]**. Instead, you could alias **ls** with the ***.[co]** argument, giving it a simple name. In the next example, the user creates an alias called **lsc** for the command **ls*.[co]**.

```
$ alias lsc='ls *.[co]'
$ lsc
main.c main.o lib.c lib.o
```

You can also use the name of a command as an alias. This can be helpful in cases where you should only use a command with a specific option. In the case of the **rm**, **cp**, and **mv** commands, the **-i** option should always be used to ensure that an existing file is not overwritten. Instead of constantly being careful to use the **-i** option each time you use one of these commands, the command name can be aliased to include the option. In the next example, the **rm**, **cp**, and **mv** commands have been aliased to include the **-i** option.

```
$ alias rm='rm -i'
$ alias mv='mv -i'
$ alias cp='cp -i'
```

The **alias** command by itself provides a list of all aliases in effect and their commands. You can remove an alias by using the **unalias** command. In the next example, the user lists the current aliases and then removes the **lsa** alias.

```
$ alias
lsa=ls -F
list=ls
```

```
rm=rm -i
$ unalias lsa
```

Controlling Shell Operations

The BASH shell has several features that allow you to control the way different shell operations work. For example, setting the **noclobber** feature prevents redirection from overwriting files. You can turn these features on and off like a toggle, using the **set** command. The **set** command takes two arguments: an option specifying on or off and the name of the feature. To set a feature on, you use the **-o** option, and to set it off, you use the **+o** option. Here is the basic form:

```
$ set -o feature          turn the feature on
$ set +o feature          turn the feature off
```

Three of the most common features are described here: **ignoreeof**, **noclobber**, and **noglob**. Table 15-2 lists these different features as well as the **set** command.

ignoreeof

Setting **ignoreeof** enables a feature that prevents you from logging out of the user shell with a CTRL-**d**. CTRL-**d** is not only used to log out of the user shell, but also to end user input that is entered directly into the standard input. It is used often for the Mailx program or for utilities such as **cat**. You could easily enter an extra CTRL-**d** in such circumstances and accidentally log yourself out. The **ignoreeof** feature prevents such accidental logouts. In the next example, the **ignoreeof** feature is turned on using the **set** command with the **-o** option. The user can now only log out by entering the **logout** command

```
$ set -o ignoreeof
$ ctrl-d
Use exit to logout
$
```

noclobber

Setting **noclobber** enables a feature that safeguards existing files from redirected output. With the **noclobber** feature, if you redirect output to a file that already exists, the file will not be overwritten with the standard output. The original file will be preserved. There may be situations in which you use, as the name for a file to hold the redirected output, a name that you have already given to an existing file. The **noclobber** feature prevents you from accidentally overwriting your original file. In the next example, the user sets the **noclobber** feature on and then tries to overwrite an existing file, **myfile**, using redirection. The system returns an error message.

```
$ set -o noclobber
$ cat preface > myfile
myfile: file exists
$
```

There may be times when you want to overwrite a file with redirected output. In this case, you can place an exclamation point after the redirection operator. This will override the **noclobber** feature, replacing the contents of the file with the standard output.

```
$ cat preface >! myfile
```

noglob

Setting **noglob** enables a feature that disables special characters in the user shell. The characters *****, **?**, **[]**, and **~** will no longer expand to matched file names. This feature is helpful if you have special characters as part of the name of a file. In the next example, the user needs to reference a file that ends with the **?** character, **answers?**. First the user turns off special characters using the **noglob** feature. Now the question mark on the command line is taken as part of the file name, not as a special character, and the user can reference the **answers?** file.

```
$ set -o noglob
$ ls answers?
answers?
```

Environment Variables and Subshells: export

When you log into your account, Linux generates your user shell. Within this shell, you can issue commands and declare variables. You can also create and execute shell scripts. However, when you execute a shell script, the system generates a subshell. You then have two shells, the one you logged into and the one generated for the script. Within the script shell, you could execute another shell script, which would have its own shell. When a script has finished execution, its shell terminates and you return to the shell it was executed from. In this sense you can have many shells, each nested within the other.

Variables that you define within a shell are local to it. If you define a variable in a shell script, then, when the script is run, the variable is defined with that script's shell and is local to it. No other shell can reference it. In a sense, the variable is hidden within its shell.

You can define environment variables in all three major types of shells: BASH, PDKSH, and TCSH shells. However, the strategy used to implement environment variables in the BASH shell is very different from that of the TCSH shell. In the BASH shell, environment variables are exported. That is to say, a copy of an environment variable is made in each subshell. For example, if the myfile variable is exported, a copy is automatically defined in each subshell for you. In the TCSH shell, on the other hand, an environment variable is defined only once and can be directly referenced by any subshell.

In the BASH shell an environment variable can be thought of as a regular variable with added capabilities. To make an environment variable, you apply the **export** command to a variable you have already defined. The **export** command instructs the system to define a copy of that variable for each new shell generated. Each new shell will have its own copy of the environment variable. This process is called exporting variables.

In the next example, the variable myfile is defined in the **dispfile** script. It is then turned into an environment variable using the **export** command. The myfile variable will now be exported to any subshells, such as that generated when **printfile** is executed.

dispfile

```
myfile="List"
export myfile

echo "Displaying $myfile"
pr -t -n $myfile

printfile
```

printfile

```
echo "Printing $myfile"
lpr $myfile &
```

```
$ dispfile
Displaying List
1 screen
2 modem
3 paper
Printing List
$
```

It is a mistake to think of exported environment variables as global variables. A new shell can never reference a variable outside of itself. Instead, a copy of the variable with its value is generated for the new shell. You can think of exported variables as exporting their values to a shell, not themselves. For those familiar with programming structures, exported variables can be thought of as a form of call-by-value.

Configuring Your Login Shell with Special Shell Variables

As noted earlier, when you log into your account, the system generates a shell for you. This shell is referred to as either your login shell or your user shell. When you execute scripts, you are generating subshells of your user shell. You can define variables within your user shell, and you can also define environment variables that can be referenced by any subshells that you generate.

Linux sets up special shell variables that you can use to configure your user shell. Many of these special shell variables are defined by the system when you log in, but you define others yourself.

A reserved set of keywords are used for the names of these special variables. You should not use these keywords as the names of any of your own variable names. The special shell variables are all specified in uppercase letters, making them easy to identify. Special local variables are in lowercase. For example, the keyword **HOME** is used by the system to define the **HOME** variable. **HOME** is a special environment variable that holds the path name of the user's home directory. On the other hand, the keyword **noclobber**, covered earlier in the chapter, is used to define the **noclobber** variable. This special local variable prevents redirection from overwriting files.

Many of the special variables that are automatically defined and assigned initial values by the system when you log in can be changed, if you wish. However, there are some special variables whose values should not be changed. For example, the **HOME** variable holds the path name for your home directory. Commands such as **cd** reference the path name in the **HOME** special variable in order to locate your home directory. Some of the more common of these special variables are described in this section.

Other special variables are defined by the system and given an initial value that you are free to change. To do this, you redefine them and assign a new value. For example, the **PATH** variable is defined by the system and given an initial value; it contains the path names of directories where commands are located. Whenever you execute a command, the shell searches for it in these directories. You can add a new directory to be searched by redefining the **PATH** variable yourself so that it will include the new directory's path name.

There are still other special variables that the system does not define. These are usually optional features, such as the **EXINIT** variable that allows you to set options for the Vi editor. You must define and assign a value to such variables each time you log in. In this sense they can be described as user-defined special variables. These user-defined special variables are further broken down into environment and local variables.

There is no official classification for the three different types of special variables. This text applies a classification of its own, referring to the special variables you should not change as *system-determined* special variables, those you can change as *redefinable* special variables, and those you need to define yourself as *user-defined* special variables.

You can obtain a listing of the currently defined special variables using the **env** command. The **env** command operates like the **set** command, but only lists special variables.

```
$ env
USERNAME=chris
ENV=/home/chris/.bashrc
HISTSIZE=1000
HISTFILE=/home/chris/.bash_history
HISTFILESIZE=1000
HOSTNAME=garnet
LOGNAME=chris
HISTFILESIZE=1000
CDPATH=:$HOME/letters:$HOME/oldletters
MAIL=/var/spool/mail/chris
WWW_HOME=file:/usr/doc/calderadoc-0.80-1/Caldera_Info
TERM=linux
HOSTTYPE=i386
PATH=/sbin:/bin:/usr/sbin:/usr/bin:/usr/X11R6/bin:/home/chris/bin:
HOME=/home/chris
SHELL=/bin/bash
PS1=[\u@\h \W]\$
PS2=>
MAILCHECK=10000
```

```
MAILPATH=/home/mail/chris:/home/chris/projmsgs
CRPATH=/usr/lib/CRiSPlite/macros
OSTYPE=Linux
NNTPSERVER=nntp.ix.netcom.com
EXINIT='set nu ai'
TZ=PST5PDT
SHLVL=1
_=/usr/bin/env
```

You can automatically define redefinable and user-defined special variables using special shell scripts called initialization files. An initialization file is a specially named shell script executed whenever you enter a certain shell. You can edit the initialization file and place in it definitions and assignments for special variables. When you enter the shell, the initialization file will execute these definitions and assignments, effectively initializing special variables with your own values. For example, the BASH shell's **.bash_profile** file is an initialization file that is executed every time you log in. It contains definitions and assignments of special variables. However, the **.bash_profile** file is basically only a shell script, which you can edit with any text editor such as the Vi editor; changing, if you wish, the values assigned to special variables.

In the BASH shell, all the redefinable and user-defined special variables are designed to be environment variables. When you define or redefine a special variable, you also need to export it in order to make it an environment variable. This means that any change you make to a special variable must be accompanied by an **export** command. You shall see that at the end of the login initialization file, **.bash_profile**, there is usually an **export** command for all the special variables defined in it.

System-determined Special Variables

Three of the commonly used system-determined special variables, **HOME**, **LOGNAME**, and **TZ**, are described here. They are defined by the system and available for your use as soon as you log in, and should not be changed. All are environment variables, accessible to any subshells.

HOME

The **HOME** variable contains the path name of your home directory. Your home directory is determined by the system administrator when your account is created. The path name for your home directory is automatically read into your **HOME** variable when you log in. In the next example, the **echo** command displays the contents of the **HOME** variable.

```
$ echo $HOME
/home/chris
```

The **HOME** variable is often used when you need to specify the absolute path name of your home directory. In the next example, the absolute path name of **reports** is specified using **HOME** for the home directory's path.

```
$ ls $HOME/reports
```

LOGNAME

The **LOGNAME** variable holds only your login name, not a path name. A user with the login name chris would have chris as the value of his **LOGNAME** variable. You can use **LOGNAME** in certain situations in which you need to use just your login name. In the next example, the user knows that his mailbox directory will have the same name as his login name. He can either use his login name directly or simply reference it in the **LOGNAME** variable. The **LOGNAME** variable would be preferable if the user should decide to change his or her login name.

```
$ ls /usr/mail/$LOGNAME
```

TZ

The **TZ** variable specifies the time zone that your system is using. It is set by the system when you log in. **TZ** displays its value in three different fields. The first three letters represent the local time zone, the next letter is the number of hours the local time differs from Greenwich mean time, and the last three letters represent the local daylight saving time zone. In the next example, the **TZ** variable holds the value for Pacific standard time, which differs eight hours from Greenwich mean time, and uses Pacific daylight saving time.

```
$ echo $TZ
PST8PDT
```

BASH Shell Redefinable Special Variables

The redefinable special variables hold such information as the location of Linux commands, the location of your mailbox file, and even the symbol used for your prompt. You may modify any one of these variables through simple assignment operations.

Some of the more common of the redefinable special variables are **SHELL**, **PATH**, **PS1**, **PS2**, and **MAIL**. The **SHELL** variable holds the path name of the program for the type of shell that you log into. The **PATH** variable lists the different directories to be searched for a Linux command. The **PS1** and **PS2** variables hold the prompt symbols. The **MAIL** variable holds the path name of your mailbox file.

SHELL

In Linux, any one of the three shells—BASH, PDKSH, or TCSH—can be the type of shell you use when you log in. The **SHELL** variable holds the path name of this shell; in a sense, it is your default shell. The shell programs are held in the **/bin** directory. Here is a listing of the path names for the different shell programs:

```
BASH shell:   /bin/bash
PDKSH shell: /bin/pdksh
TCSH shell:   /bin/tcsh
```

In the next example, the contents of the **SHELL** variable are displayed.

```
$ echo $SHELL
/bin/sh
```

PATH

The **PATH** variable contains a series of directory paths separated by colons. Each time a command is executed, the paths listed in the **PATH** variable are searched one by one for that command. For example, the **cp** command resides on the system in the directory **/usr/bin**. This directory path is one of the directories listed in the **PATH** variable. Each time you execute the **cp** command, this path is searched and the **cp** command located. The system defines and assigns **PATH** an initial set of path names. In Linux the initial path names are **/usr/bin** and **usr/sbin**.

The shell can execute any executable file, including programs and scripts that you have created. For this reason, the **PATH** variable can also reference your working directory; so if you want to execute one of your own scripts or programs in your working directory, the shell can locate it.

There can be no spaces between the path names in the string. A colon with no path name specified references your working directory. Usually a single colon is placed at the end of the path names as an empty entry specifying your working directory. For example, the path name **/usr/bin:/usr/sbin:** references three directories: **/usr/bin**, **/usr/sbin**, and your current working directory.

```
$ echo $PATH
/usr/bin:/usr/sbin:
```

You can add any new directory path you wish to the **PATH** variable. This can be very useful if you have created several of your own Linux commands using shell scripts. You could place these new shell script commands in a directory you created and then add that directory to the **PATH** list. Then, no matter what directory you are in, you can execute one of your shell scripts. The **PATH** variable will contain the directory for that script, so that directory will be searched each time you issue a command.

You add a directory to the **PATH** variable with a variable assignment. You can execute this assignment directly in your shell. In the next example, the user chris adds a new directory called **mybin** to the **PATH**. Though you could carefully type in the complete path names listed in **PATH** for the assignment, you can also use an evaluation of **PATH**, **$PATH**, in their place. In this example, an evaluation of **HOME** is also used to designate the user's home directory in the new directory's path name. Notice the empty entry between two colons, which specifies the working directory.

```
$ PATH=$PATH:$HOME/mybin
$ export PATH
$ echo $PATH
/usr/bin:/usr/sbin::/home/chris/mybin
```

If you add a directory to **PATH** yourself while you are logged in, the directory would be added only for the duration of your login session. When you log back in, the login initialization file, **.bash_profile**, would again initialize your **PATH** with its original set of directories. The **.bash_profile** file is described in detail a bit later in the chapter. To permanently add a new directory to your **PATH**, you need to edit your **.bash_profile** file and find the assignment for the **PATH** variable. Then you simply insert the directory, preceded by a colon, into the set of path names assigned to **PATH**.

PS1 and PS2

The **PS1** and **PS2** variables contain the primary and secondary prompt symbols, respectively. The primary prompt symbol for the BASH shell is a dollar sign, **$**. You can change the prompt symbol by assigning a new set of characters to the **PS1** variable. In the next example, the shell prompt is changed to the **->** symbol.

```
$ PS1="->"
-> export PS1
->
```

You can change the prompt to be any set of characters, including a string, as shown in the next example.

```
$ PS1="Please enter a command: "
Please enter a command: export PS1
Please enter a command: ls
mydata /reports
Please enter a command:
```

The **PS2** variable holds the secondary prompt symbol, which is used for commands that take several lines to complete. The default secondary prompt is **>**. The added command lines will begin with the secondary prompt instead of the primary prompt. You can change the secondary prompt just as easily as the primary prompt, as shown here:

```
$ PS2="@"
```

Like the TCSH shell, the BASH shell provides you with a predefined set of codes that you can use to configure your prompt. With them you can make the time, your user name, or your directory path name a part of your prompt. You can even have your prompt display the history event number of the current command you are about to enter. Each code is preceded by a \ symbol. **\w** represents the current working directory, **\t** the time, and **\u** your user name. **\!** will display the next history event number. In the next example, the user adds the current working directory to the prompt.

```
$ PS1="\w $"
/home/dylan $
```

The codes must be included within a quoted string. If there are no quotes, the code characters are not evaluated and are themselves used as the prompt. **PS1=\w** will set the prompt to the characters **\w**, not the working directory. The next example incorporates both the time and the history event number with a new prompt.

```
$ PS1="\t \! ->"
```

The following table lists the codes for configuring your prompt.

\\ !	Current history number
\\ $	Use **$** as prompt for all users except the root user, which has the **#** as its prompt.
\\ d	Current date
\\ s	Shell currently active
\\ t	Time of day
\\ u	User name
\\ w	Current working directory

MAIL, MAILCHECK, and MAILPATH

The **MAIL** variable has the path name for your mailbox file in which the system places messages that are sent to you. The waiting messages that you read when you invoke Mailx are taken from this file. The mailbox files and the Mailx utility are described in Chapter 8. Though you can change the value of **MAIL**, you would rarely, if ever, do so. The system needs this path name in order to locate your mailbox file.

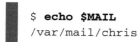

```
$ echo $MAIL
/var/mail/chris
```

The **MAILCHECK** variable sets the time interval in which you will be notified of new mail. If you are expecting mail and want to be notified as soon as possible when it arrives, you can shorten this time interval. If you do not want to be bothered, you can lengthen it. The default is 10 minutes, or 600 seconds. In the next example, the time interval is set to 1200 seconds (20 minutes).

```
$ MAILCHECK=1200
$ export MAILCHECK
```

The **MAILPATH** variable contains path names of other mailbox files that you may want checked for incoming mail. Unlike **MAIL** and **MAILCHECK**, **MAILPATH** is a user-defined special variable. To use it, you need to define it and assign a value. You would assign **MAILPATH** the path names of any other mailbox files you want checked. In the next example, the user specifies a mailbox file other than the one specified in **MAIL** to be checked for incoming mail.

```
$ MAILPATH=/home/mail/$lOGNAME
$ export MAILPATH
```

BASH Shell User-defined Special Variables

The user-defined special variables in the BASH shell hold information such as your current terminal type or the default configuration for your Vi editor. Many variables such as **TERM** and **CDPATH** enhance shell operations. Others are designed to work with special utilities. For example, the **EXINIT** variable configures the Vi and Ex editors. Both the redefinable and user-defined special variables for the BASH shell are listed in Table 15-2.

User-defined special variables are not defined by the system. If you want to use them, you need to define and assign values to them yourself. Three of the more common user-defined special variables are **CDPATH**, **TERM**, and **EXINIT**. The **CDPATH** variable holds the path names of the directories that the **cd** command can easily locate. The **TERM** variable holds the terminal name of the terminal that you are currently using. **EXINIT** holds configuration commands for the Vi and Ex editors.

CDPATH

If **CDPATH** is undefined, then when the **cd** command is given a directory name as its argument, it searches only the current working directory for that name. However, if **CDPATH** is defined, **cd** will also search the directories listed in **CDPATH** for that directory name. If the directory name is found, **cd** changes to that directory. This is helpful if you are working on a project in which you constantly have to change to directories in another part of the file system. To change to a directory that has a path name very different from the one you are in, you would need to know the full path name of that directory. Instead, you could simply place the path name of that directory's parent in **CDPATH**. Then **cd** will automatically search the parent directory, finding the name of the directory you want. Notice that you assign to **CDPATH** the path name of the parent of the directory you want to change to, not the path name of the directory itself.

In the next example, **CDPATH** is modified to include **/home/chris/letters**. **letters** is the parent for the **thankyou** directory. Whenever the **cd** command is entered with the argument **thankyou**, the directories in **CDPATH** will be automatically searched, including **letters**, and **thankyou** will be located.

```
$ CDPATH=$CDPATH:/home/chris/letters
$ export CDPATH
$ echo $CDPATH
:/home/chris/letters
$ cd thankyou
$ pwd
/home/chris/letters/thankyou
$
```

You can, of course, edit the **.bash_profile** file and permanently add a directory name to the **CDPATH** variable.

It is advisable to use the **HOME** variable to specify the home directory part of the path in any new path name added to **CDPATH**. This is because it is possible that your home directory path name could be changed by the system administrator in any reorganization of the file system. **HOME** will always hold the current path name of the home directory. In the next example, the path name **/home/chris/letters** is specified with **$HOME/letters**.

```
$ CDPATH=$CDPATH:$HOME/letters
$ export CDPATH
$ echo $CDPATH
:/home/chris/letters
```

TERM

The **TERM** variable holds the name of the terminal you are currently using. If you log in from a terminal, you are asked for your terminal's name, and the name you enter is placed in the **TERM** variable. Utilities such as the standard editors will use **TERM** to find out what your terminal type is. This allows them to map commands to your keyboard and screen. The following command will display your terminal type:

```
$ echo $TERM
tvi925
```

If you want to change your terminal type, you can do so by assigning another terminal name to the **TERM** variable. In the next example, the **TERM** variable is assigned the terminal type vt100. You then need to export the **TERM** variable to make it accessible throughout your shell.

```
$ TERM=vt100
$ export TERM
$
```

EXINIT

The **EXINIT** variable holds editor commands with which to configure the Ex and Vi editors. When you invoke these editors, the commands in the **EXINIT** variable are executed. These commands usually set other commands that specify such features as line numbering or indentation. They are discussed in detail in Chapter 17.

In the next example, the **EXINIT** variable is assigned an editor **set** command to execute. This **set** command sets line numbering and automatic indent. Notice that the two commands can be abbreviated and combined into one string.

```
$ EXINIT='set nu ai'
$ export EXINIT
```

BASH Shell Login Initialization File: .bash_profile

The **.bash_profile** file is the BASH shell's login initialization file. It is a script file that is automatically executed whenever a user logs in. The file contains shell commands that define special environment variables used to manage your shell. They may be either redefinitions of system-defined special variables or definitions of user-defined special variables. For example, when you log in, your user shell needs to know what directories hold Linux commands. It will reference the **PATH** variable in order to find the path names for these directories. However, first, the **PATH** variable must be assigned those path names. In the **.bash_profile** file there is an assignment operation that does just this. Since it is in the **.bash_profile** file, the assignment is executed automatically when the user logs in.

Special variables also need to be exported, using the **export** command, in order to make them accessible to any subshells you may enter. You can export several variables in one **export** command by listing them as arguments. Usually at the end of the **.bash_profile** file there is an **export** command with a list of all the variables defined in the file. If a variable is missing from this list, you may not be able to access it. Notice the **export** command at the end of the **.bash_profile** file in the example described next.

A copy of the standard **.bash_profile** file provided for you when your account is created is listed in the next example. Notice how **PATH** is assigned as is the value of **$HOME**. Both **PATH** and **HOME** are system special variables that the system has already defined. **PATH** holds the path names of directories searched for any command that you enter, and **HOME** holds the path name of your home directory. The assignment **PATH=$PATH:$HOME/bin** has the effect of redefining **PATH** to include your **bin** directory within your home directory. So your **bin** directory will also be searched for any commands, including ones you create yourself, such as scripts or programs. Notice that **PATH** is then exported so that it can be accessed by any subshells. Should you want to have your home directory searched also, you can use the Vi or Emacs editor to modify this line in your **.bash_profile** file to **PATH=$PATH:$HOME\bin:$HOME**, adding **:$HOME** at the end. In fact, you can change this entry to add as many directories as you want searched.

.bash_profile

```
# .bash_profile

# Get the aliases and functions
if [ -f ~/.bashrc ]; then
   . ~/.bashrc
fi

# User-specific environment and startup programs

PATH=$PATH:$HOME/bin
ENV=$HOME/.bashrc
USERNAME=""

export USERNAME ENV PATH
```

Your Linux system also has its own profile file that it executes whenever any user logs in. This system initialization file is simply called **.profile** and is found in the **/etc** directory, **/etc/profile**. It contains special variable definitions that the system needs to provide for each user. A copy of the system **.profile** file follows. Notice how **PATH** is redefined to include the **/usr/X11R6/bin** directory. This is the directory that holds the X-Windows commands that you execute when using the Caldera Desktop. **HISTFILE** is also redefined to include a larger number of history events.

/etc/profile

```
# /etc/profile

# Systemwide environment and startup programs
# Functions and aliases go in /etc/bashrc

PATH="$PATH:/usr/X11R6/bin"
PS1="[\u@\h \W]\\$ "

ulimit -c 1000000
umask 002

HOSTNAME='/bin/hostname'
HISTSIZE=1000
HISTFILESIZE=1000
# Default page for the arena browser
WWW_HOME=file:/usr/doc/calderadoc-0.80-1/Caldera_Info
# Default path for CRiSPlite
CRPATH=/usr/lib/CRiSPlite/macros

export PATH PS1 HOSTNAME HISTSIZE HISTFILESIZE WWW_HOME CRPATH
if [ "$TERM" = console ]
then
    MINICOM="-l -m -con -tmc" ; export MINICOM
fi
```

Your **. bash_profile** initialization file is a text file that can be edited by a text editor like any other text file. You can easily add new directories to your **PATH** by editing **.bash_profile** and using editing commands to insert a new directory path name in the list of directory path names assigned to the **PATH** variable. You can even add new variable definitions. If you do so, be sure, however, to include the new variable's name in the **export** command's argument list. For example, if your **.bash_profile** file does not have any definition of the **EXINIT** variable, you can edit the file and add a new line that assigns a value to **EXINIT**. The definition **EXINIT='set nu ai'** will configure the Vi editor with line numbering and indentation. You then need to add **EXINIT** to the **export** command's argument list. When the **.bash_profile** file executes again, the **EXINIT** variable will be set to the command **set nu ai**. When the Vi editor is invoked, the command in the **EXINIT** variable will be executed, setting the line number and auto-indent options automatically.

In the following example, the user's **.bash_profile** has been modified to include definitions of **EXINIT** and redefinitions of **CDPATH**, **PS1**, and **HISTSIZE**. The redefinition of **HISTSIZE** reduces the number of history events saved, from 1000 defined in the system **.profile** file, to 30. The redefinition of the **PS1** special variable changes the prompt to include the path name of the current working directory. Any changes that you make to special variables within your **.bash_profile** file will override those made earlier by the system's **.profile** file. All these special variables are then exported with the **export** command.

.bash_profile

```
# .bash_profile

# Get the aliases and functions
if [ -f ~/.bashrc ]; then
    . ~/.bashrc
fi

# User-specific environment and startup programs

PATH=$PATH:$HOME/bin:$HOME
ENV=$HOME/.bashrc
USERNAME=""
CDPATH=$CDPATH:$HOME/bin:$HOME
HISTSIZE=30
EXINIT='set nu ai'
PS1="\w \$"

export USERNAME ENV PATH CDPATH HISTSIZE EXINIT PS1
```

Though **.bash_profile** is executed each time you log in, it is not automatically reexecuted after you make changes to it. The **.bash_profile** file is an initialization file that is *only* executed whenever you log in. If you want to take advantage of any changes you make to it without having to log out and log in again, you can reexecute **.bash_profile** with the dot (**.**) command. **.bash_profile** is a shell script and, like any shell script, can be executed with the **.** command.

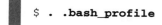

```
$ . .bash_profile
```

The BASH Shell Initialization File: .bashrc

The **.bashrc** file is an initialization file that is executed each time you enter the BASH shell or generate any subshells. If the BASH shell is your login shell, **.bashrc** is executed along with your **.bash_login** file when you log in. If you enter the BASH shell from another shell, the **.bashrc** file is automatically executed, and the variable and alias definitions it contains will be defined.

The **.bashrc** shell initialization file is actually executed each time you generate a shell, such as when you run a shell script. In other words, each time a subshell is created, the **.bashrc** file is executed. This has the effect of exporting any local variables or aliases that you have defined in the **.bashrc** shell initialization file. The **.bashrc** file usually contains the definition of aliases and any feature variables used to turn on shell features. Aliases and feature variables are locally defined within the shell. But the **.bashrc** file will define them in every shell. For this reason, the **.bashrc** file usually holds such aliases as those defined for the **rm**, **cp**, and **mv** commands. The next example is a **.bashrc** file with many of the standard definitions.

.bashrc

```
# Source global definitions
if [ -f /etc/bashrc ]; then
    . /etc/bashrc
fi
set -o ignoreeof
set -o noclobber

alias rm 'rm -i'
alias mv 'mv -i'
alias cp 'cp -i'
```

Linux systems usually contain a system **.bashrc** file that is executed for all users. This may contain certain global aliases and features needed by all users whenever they enter a BASH shell. This is located in the **/etc** directory, **/etc/.bashrc**. A user's own **.bashrc** file, located in the home directory, will contain commands to execute this system **.bashrc** file. The **./etc/bashrc** command in the previous example of **.bashrc** does just that.

You can add any commands or definitions of your own to your **.bashrc** file. If you have made changes to **.bashrc** and you want them to take effect during your current login session, you need to reexecute the file with either the **.** or the **source** command:

```
$ source .bashrc
```

The BASH Shell Logout Initialization File: .bash_logout

The **.bash_logout** file is also an initialization file, which is executed when the user logs out. It is designed to perform any operations you want done whenever you log out. Instead of variable definitions, the **.bash_logout** file usually contains shell commands that form a kind of shutdown procedure—actions you always want taken before you log out. One common logout command is to clear the screen and then issue a farewell message.

As with **.bash_profile**, you can add your own shell commands to **.bash_logout**. In fact, the **.bash_logout** file is not automatically set up for you when your account is first created. You need to create it yourself, using the Vi or Emacs editor. You could then add a farewell message or other operations. In the next example, the user has a **clear** and an **echo** command in the **.bash_logout** file. When the user logs out, the **clear** command will clear the screen, and then the **echo** command will display the message "Good-bye for now".

.bash_logout

```
clear
echo "Good-bye for now"
```

BASH Shell Programming

The BASH shell has programming-languagelike capabilities that allow you to create complex shell programs. A shell program combines Linux commands in such a way as to perform a specific task. The Linux shell provides you with many programming tools with which to create shell programs. You can define variables and assign values to them. You can also define variables in a script file and have a user interactively enter values for them when the script is executed. There are loop and conditional control structures that repeat Linux commands or make decisions on which commands you want to execute. You can also construct expressions that perform arithmetic or comparison operations. All these programming tools operate like those found in other programming languages.

You can combine shell variables, control structures, expressions, and Linux commands to form a shell program. Usually, the instructions making up a shell program are entered into a script file that can then be executed. You can create this script file using any standard editor. To run the shell program, you then execute its script file. You can even distribute your program among several script files, one of which will contain instructions to execute others. You can think of variables, expressions, and control structures as tools you use to bring together several Linux commands into one operation. In this sense, a shell program is a new, complex Linux command that you have created.

Shell Scripts: Commands and Comments

A shell script is a text file that contains Linux commands, which you enter using any standard editor. You can then execute the commands in the file by using the file name as an argument to any **sh** or dot command (**.**). They read the commands in shell scripts and execute them. You can also make the script file itself executable and use its name directly on the command line as you would use the name of any command.

You make a script file executable by setting its execute permission using the **chmod** command. The executable permission for the **chmod** command can be set using either symbolic or absolute references. The symbolic reference **u+x** sets the execute permission of a file. The command **chmod u+x hello** will set the execute permission of the **hello** script file. You can now use the script file name **hello** as if it were a Linux command. You only need to set the executable permission once. Once set, it remains set until you explicitly change it.

hello

```
echo "Hello, how are you"
```

```
$ chmod u+x hello
$ hello
Hello, how are you
$
```

An absolute reference will set read and write permission at the same time that it sets the execute permission. See Chapter 7 for a more detailed explanation of absolute and symbolic permission references. In brief, a 700 will set execute as well as read and write permission for the user; 500 will set only execute and read permission; 300 only execute and write permission; and 400 only execute permission. Users most often set 700 or 500. In the next example, the user sets the execute permission using an absolute reference.

```
$ chmod 750 hello
$ hello
Hello, how are you
$
```

It is often helpful to include in a script file short explanations describing what the file's task is as well as describing the purpose of certain commands and variables. You can enter such explanations using comments. A comment is any line or part of a line preceded by a sharp sign, #, with the exception of the first line. The end of the comment is the next new line character, the end of the line. Any characters entered on a line after a sharp sign will be ignored by the shell. The first line is reserved for identification of the shell, as noted in the following discussion. In the next example, a comment describing the name and function of the script is placed at the head of the file.

hello

```
# The hello script says hello

echo "Hello, how are you"
```

You may want to be able to execute a script that is written for one of the Linux shells while you are working in another. Suppose you are currently in the TCSH shell and want to execute a script you wrote in the BASH shell that contains BASH shell commands. First you would have to change to the BASH shell with the **sh** command, execute the script, and then change back to the TCSH shell. You can, however, automate this process by placing as the first characters in your script, **#!**, followed by the path name for the shell program on your system.

Your shell always examines the first character of a script to find out what type of script it is—BASH, PDKSH, or TCSH shell script. If the first character is a space, the script is assumed to be either a BASH or PDKSH shell script. If there is a **#** alone, the script is a TCSH shell script. If, however, the **#** is followed by a **!** character, then your shell reads the path name of a shell program that follows. A **#!** should always be followed by the path name of a shell program identifying the type of shell the script works in. If you are currently in a different shell, that shell will read the path name of the shell program, change to that shell, and execute your script. If you are in a different shell, the space or **#** alone is not enough to identify a BASH or TCSH shell script. Such identification works only in their own shells. To identify a script from a different shell, you need to include the **#!** characters followed by a path name.

For example, if you put **#!/bin/sh** at the beginning of the first line of the **hello** script, you could execute it directly from the TCSH shell. The script will first change to the BASH shell, execute its commands, and then return to the TCSH shell (or whatever type of shell it was executed from). In the next example, the **hello** script includes the **#!/bin/sh** command. The user then executes the script while in the TCSH shell.

hello

```
#!/bin/sh

# The hello script says hello

echo "Hello, how are you"
```

> **hello**
Hello, how are you

Variables and Scripts

In the shell, you can create shell programs using variables and scripts. Within a shell program, you can define variables and assign values to them. Variable definitions were discussed in detail in Chapter 5. A brief discussion is presented here since variable definitions are used in shell programs for many purposes.

Variables are used extensively in script input and output operations. The **read** command allows the user to interactively enter a value for a variable. Often **read** is combined with a prompt notifying the user when to enter a response. Another form of script input, called the Here document, allows you to use lines in a script as input to a command. This overcomes the need to always read input from an outside source such as a file.

Definition and Evaluation of Variables: =, $, set, unset

A variable is defined in a shell when you first use the variable's name. A variable name may be any set of alphabetic characters, including the underscore. The name may also include a number, but the number cannot be the first character in the name. A name may not have any other type of character, such as an exclamation point, ampersand, or even a space. Such symbols are reserved by a shell for its own use. A name may not include more than one word, because a shell uses spaces to parse commands, delimiting command names and arguments.

You assign a value to a variable with the assignment operator. You type the variable name, the assignment operator, =, and then the value assigned. Note that you cannot place any spaces around the assignment operator. Any set of characters can be assigned to a variable. In the next example, the greeting variable is assigned the string "Hello".

```
$ greeting="Hello"
```

Once you have assigned a value to a variable, you can then use that variable to reference the value. Often you use the values of variables as arguments for a command. You can reference the value of a variable using the variable name preceded by the **$** operator. The dollar sign is a special operator that uses a variable name to reference a variable's value, in effect, evaluating the variable. Evaluation retrieves a variable's value—a set of characters. This set of characters then replaces the variable name on the command line. Thus, wherever a **$** is placed before the variable name, the variable name is replaced with the value of the variable.

In the next example, the shell variable greeting is evaluated and its contents, "Hello", are then used as the argument for an **echo** command. The **echo** command simply echoes or prints a set of characters to the screen.

```
$ echo $greeting
Hello
```

You can obtain a list of all the defined variables with the **set** command. If you decide that you do not want a certain variable, you can remove it with the **unset** command.

NOTE: *Table 15-3 is a general collection of commands used in different places like* ***echo***, ***read***, *and* ***break***.

Script Input and Output: echo, read, and <<

Within a script you can use the **echo** command to output data and the **read** command to read input into variables. In addition, you can use a Here document to specify data within the script and redirect it to a command.

Within a script, the **echo** command will send data to the standard output. The data is in the form of a string of characters. As you have seen, the **echo** command can output variable values as well as string constants.

The **read** command reads in a value for a variable. It is used to allow a user to interactively input a value for a variable. The **read** command literally reads the next line in the standard input. Everything in the standard input up to the new line character is read in and assigned to a variable. In shell programs, you can combine the **echo** command with the **read** command to prompt the user to enter a value and then read that value into a variable. In the **greetvar** script in the next example, the user is prompted to enter a value for the greeting variable. The **read** command then reads the value the user typed and assigns it to the greeting variable.

greetvar

```
echo Please enter a greeting:
read greeting

echo "The greeting you entered was $greeting"
```

```
$ greetvar
Please enter a greeting:
hi
The greeting you entered was hi
$
```

When dealing with user input, you must consider the possibility that the user may enter shell special characters. Any special characters in a Linux command, whether within a script or not, will be evaluated unless quoted. If the value of a variable is a special character and the variable's value is referenced with a **$**, then the special character will be evaluated by the shell. However, placing the evaluated variable within quotes prevents any evaluation of special characters such as **$**. In the **greetvar** script, **$greeting** was placed within a quoted string, preventing evaluation of any special characters. However, if **$greeting** is not quoted, then any special characters it contains will be evaluated.

There are times when you want special characters evaluated. Suppose you want to retrieve the list of files beginning with characters the user enters. In this case, any special characters entered by the user need to be evaluated. In the **listfiles** script that follows, any special characters for generating file lists will be expanded. Notice that **$fref** is not quoted.

listfiles

```
echo Please enter a file reference:
read fref

echo The files you requested are: $fref
```

```
$ listfiles
Please enter a file reference:
*.c
The files you requested are: calc.c lib.c main.c
```

Normally, a shell script contains a series of commands. However, there may be times when you need to enter data as well as commands. You may want to type lines of data into the shell script and use the data as input for one of the commands. The Here operation allows you to do this. It is a redirection operation, redirecting data within a shell script into a command. It is called Here because the redirected data is here in the shell script, not somewhere else in another file. The Here operation is represented by two less-than signs, **<<**. The **<<** operator can be thought of as a kind of redirection operator, redirecting lines in a shell script as input to a command. The **<<** operator is placed after the command to which input is being redirected. Lines following the **<<** operator are then taken as input to the command. The end of the input can be specified by an end-of-file character, CTRL-**d**. Instead of using an end-of-file character, you can specify your own delimiter. A word following the **<<** operator on the same line is taken to be the ending delimiter for the input lines. The delimiter can be any set of symbols. All lines up to the delimiter are read as input to the command.

In the next example, a message is sent to the user mark. The input for the message is obtained from a Here operation. The delimiter for the Here operation is the word **myend**.

mailmark

```
mail mark << myend
Did you remember
the meeting
   robert
myend
```

Script Command Line Arguments

Like Linux commands, a shell script can take arguments. When you invoke a script, you can enter arguments on the command line after the script name. These arguments can then be referenced within the script using the **$** operator and the number of its position on the command line. Arguments on the command line are sequentially numbered from 1. The first argument is referenced with **$1**, the second argument with **$2**, and so on. The argument **$0** will contain the name of the shell script, the first word on the command line.

These argument references can be thought of as referencing read-only variables. For those familiar with programming terminology, you can think of words on the command line as arguments that are passed into argument variables, **$1** through **$9**. The argument variables are read-only variables. You cannot assign values to them. Once given the initial values, they cannot be altered. In this sense, argument variables function more as constants—constants determined by the command line arguments. Each word on the command line is parsed into an argument unless it is quoted. If you enter more than one argument, you can reference them with each corresponding argument number. In the next example, four arguments are entered on the command line.

greetargs

```
echo "The first argument is: $1"
echo "The second argument is: $2"
echo "The third argument is: $3"
echo "The fourth argument is: $4"
```

```
$ greetargs Hello Hi Salutations "How are you"
The first argument is: Hello
The second argument is: Hi
The third argument is: Salutations
The fourth argument is: How are you
$
```

A set of special arguments allows you to reference different aspects of command line arguments, such as the number of arguments or all the arguments together: **$***, **$@**, **$#**. The **$#** argument contains the number of arguments entered on the command line. This is useful when you need to specify a fixed number of arguments for a script. The argument **$*** references all the arguments in the command line. A command line may have more than nine arguments. The **$@** also references all the arguments on the command line, but allows you to separately quote each one. The difference between **$*** and **$@** is not clear until you use them to reference arguments using the **for-in** control structure. For this reason, they are discussed only briefly here and more extensively in the section on control structures later in the chapter.

In the next example, the command line arguments are displayed first using the **$*** special variable and then **$@**. The number of arguments is displayed using the **$#** special variable.

sargs

```
echo $*
echo $@
echo "There are $# arguments"
```

```
$ sargs Hello Hi Welcome
Hello Hi Welcome
Hello Hi Welcome
There are 3 arguments
```

Export Variables and Script Shells

When you execute a script file, you initiate a new process that has its own shell. Within this shell you can define variables, execute Linux commands, and even execute other scripts. If you execute another script from within the script currently running, the current script suspends execution, and control is transferred to the other script. All the commands in this other script are first executed before returning to continue with the suspended script. The process of executing one script from another operates much like a function or procedure call in programming languages. You can think of a script calling another script. The calling script waits until the called script finishes execution before continuing with its next command.

Any variable definitions that you place in a script will be defined within the script's shell and only known within that script's shell. Variable definitions are local to their own shells. In a sense, the variable is hidden within its shell. Suppose, however, you want to be able to define a variable within a script and use it in any scripts it may call. You cannot do this directly, but you can export a variable definition from one shell to another using the **export** command. When the **export** command is applied to a variable, it will instruct the system to define a copy of that variable for each new subshell generated. Each new subshell will have its own copy of the exported variable. In the next example, the myname variable is defined and exported.

```
$ myname="Charles"
$ export myname
```

It is a mistake to think of exported variables as global variables. A shell can never reference a variable outside of itself. Instead, a copy of the variable with its value is generated for the new shell. Exported variables export their values to a shell, not themselves. An exported variable operates to some extent like a scoped global parameter. It is copied to any shell derived from its own shell. Any shell script called directly or indirectly after the exported variable's shell will be given a copy of the exported variable with the initial value.

Arithmetic Shell Operations: let

The **let** command is the BASH shell command for performing operations on arithmetic values. With **let** you can compare two values or perform arithmetic operations such as addition or multiplication on them. Such operations are used often in shell programs to manage control structures or perform necessary calculations. The **let** command can be indicated either with the keyword **let** or with a set of double parentheses. The syntax consists of the keyword **let** followed by two numeric values separated by an arithmetic or relational operator, as shown here:

```
$ let value1 operator value2
```

You can use as your operator any of those listed in Table 15-4. The **let** command automatically assumes that operators are arithmetic or relational. You do not have to quote shell-like operators. **let** also automatically evaluates any variables and converts their values to arithmetic values. This means that you can write your arithmetic operations as simple arithmetic expressions. In the next example, the **let** command multiplies the values 2 and 7. The result is output to the standard output and displayed.

```
$ let 2*7
14
```

If you want to have spaces between operands in the arithmetic expression, you must quote the expression. The **let** command expects one string.

```
$ let "2 * 7"
```

You can also include assignment operations in your **let** expression. In the next example, the result of the multiplication is assigned to **res**.

```
$ let "res = 2 * 7"
$ echo $res
14
$
```

You can also use any of the relational operators to perform comparisons between numeric values, such as checking to see whether one value is less than another. Relational operations are often used to manage control structures such as loops and conditions. In the next example, **helloprg** displays the word "hello" three times. It makes use of a **let** less-than-or-equal operation to manage the loop, **let "again <= 3 "**, and to increment the again variable, **let "again = again + 1"**. Notice that when again is incremented, it does not need to be evaluated. No preceding **$** is needed. **let** will automatically evaluate variables used in expressions.

helloprg

```
again=1
while let "again <= 3"
        do
        echo $again Hello
        let "again = again + 1"
        done
```

```
$ helloprg
1 Hello
2 Hello
3 Hello
```

Control Structures

You can control the execution of Linux commands in a shell program with control structures. Control structures allow you to repeat commands and to select certain commands over others. A control structure consists of two major components: a test and commands. If the test is successful, then the commands are executed. In this way, you can use control structures to make decisions as to whether commands should be executed.

There are two different kinds of control structures: loops and conditions. A loop repeats commands, whereas a condition executes a command when certain conditions are met. The BASH shell has three loop control structures: **while**, **for**, and **for-in**. There are two condition structures: **if** and **case**.

The **while** and **if** control structures are more for general purposes, such as performing iterations and making decisions using a variety of different tests. The **case** and **for** control structures are more specialized. The **case** structure is a restricted form of the **if** condition and is often used to implement menus. The **for** structure is a limited type of loop. It runs through a list of values, assigning a new value to a variable with each iteration.

The **if** and **while** control structures have as their test the execution of a Linux command. All Linux commands return an exit status after they have finished executing. If a command is successful, its exit status will be 0. If the command fails for any reason, its exit status will be a positive value referencing the type of failure that occurred. The **if** and **while** control structures check to see if the exit status of a Linux command is 0 or some other value. In the case of the **if** and **while** structures, if the exit status is a zero value, then the command was successful and the structure continues.

The test Command

Often you may need to perform a test that compares two values. Yet the test used in control structures is a Linux command, not a relational expression. There is, however, a Linux command called **test** that can perform such a comparison of values. The **test** command will compare two values and return as its exit status a 0 if the comparison is successful.

With the **test** command, you can compare integers, strings, and even perform logical operations. The command consists of the keyword **test** followed by the values being compared, separated by an option that specifies what kind of comparison is taking place. The option can be thought of as the operator, but is written, like other options, with a minus sign and letter codes. For example, **-eq** is the option that represents the equality comparison. However, there are two string operations that actually use an operator instead of an option. When you compare two strings for equality you use the equal sign, **=**. For inequality you use **!=**. Table 15-5 lists all the options and operators used by **test**. The syntax for the **test** command is shown here:

```
test value -option value
test string = string
```

In the next example, the user compares two integer values to see if they are equal. In this case, you need to use the equality option, **-eq**. The exit status of the **test** command is examined to find out the result of the test operation. The shell special variable **$?** holds the exit status of the most recently executed Linux command.

```
$ num=5
$ test $num -eq 10
$ echo $?
1
```

Instead of using the keyword **test** for the **test** command, you can use enclosing brackets. The command **test $greeting = "hi"** can be written as

```
$ [ $greeting = "hi" ]
```

Similarly, the test command **test $num -eq 10** can be written as

```
$ [ $num -eq 10 ]
```

The brackets themselves must be surrounded by white spaces: a space, TAB, or ENTER. Without the spaces it would be invalid.

The **test** command is used extensively as the Linux command in the test component of control structures. Be sure to keep in mind the different options used for strings and integers. Do not confuse string comparisons and integer comparisons. To compare two strings for equality, you use **=**; to compare two integers, you use the option **-eq**.

Conditions: if, if-else, elif, case

The BASH shell has a set of conditional control structures that allow you to choose what Linux commands to execute. Many of these are similar to conditional control structures found in programming languages, but there are some differences. The **if** condition tests the success of a Linux command, not an expression. Furthermore, the end of an **if-then** command must be indicated with the keyword **fi**, and the end of a **case** command is indicated with the keyword **esac**. The condition control structures are listed in Table 15-6.

if-then

The **if** structure places a condition on commands. That condition is the exit status of a specific Linux command. If a command is successful, returning an exit status of 0, then the commands within the **if** structure are executed. If the exit status is anything other than 0, then the command has failed and the commands within the **if** structure are not executed.

The **if** command begins with the keyword **if** and is followed by a Linux command whose exit condition will be evaluated. This command is always executed. After the command, the keyword **then** goes on a line by itself. Any set of commands may then follow. The keyword **fi** ends the command. Often, you need to choose between two alternatives based on whether or not a Linux command is successful. The **else** keyword allows an **if** structure to choose between two alternatives. If the Linux command is successful, then those commands following the **then** keyword are executed. If the Linux command fails, then those commands following the **else** keyword are executed. The syntax for the **if-then-else** command is shown here:

```
if Linux Command
    then
        Commands
    else
        Commands
fi
```

The **elsels** script in the next example executes the **ls** command to list files with two different possible options, either by size or with all file information. If the user enters an **s**, files are listed by size, otherwise, all file information is listed.

elsels

```
echo Enter s to list file sizes,
echo otherwise all file information is listed.
echo –n "Please enter option: "
read choice

if [ "$choice" = s ]
   then
       ls -s
   else
           ls -l
fi
echo Good-bye
```

```
$ elsels
Enter s to list file sizes,
otherwise all file information is listed.
Please enter option: s
total 2
    1 monday     2 today
$
```

The **if** structure is often used to check whether the user entered the appropriate number of arguments for a shell script. The special shell variable **#** contains the number of arguments the user entered. Using **$#** in a test operation allows you to check whether the user entered the correct number of arguments.

If an incorrect number of arguments has been entered, you may need to end the shell script. You can do this with the **exit** command, which ends the shell script and returns an exit condition. **exit** takes a number argument. An argument of 0 indicates that the shell script ended successfully. Any other argument, such as 1, indicates that an error occurred. In the next example, the **ifarg** script takes only one argument. If the user fails to enter an argument, or enters more than one argument, then the **if** test will be true, and the error message will be printed out and the script exited with an error value.

ifarg

```
if [ $# -ne 1 ]
    then
        echo Invalid number of arguments
        exit 1
fi

echo $1
```

```
$ ifarg

Invalid number of arguments
```

The **elif** structure allows you to nest **if-then-else** operations. The **elif** structure stands for "else if." With **elif**, you can choose between several alternatives. The first alternative is specified with the **if** structure, followed by other alternatives, each specified by its own **elif** structure. The alternative to the last **elif** structure is specified with an **else**. If the test for the first **if** structure fails, control will be passed to the next **elif** structure, and its test will be executed. If it fails, control is passed to the next **elif** and its test checked. This continues until a test is true. Then that **elif** has its commands executed and control passes out of the **if** structure to the next command after the **fi** keyword.

The Logical Commands: && and ||

The logical commands perform logical operations on two Linux commands. The syntax is as follows:

```
command && command
```

```
command || command
```

In the case of the logical AND, **&&**, if both commands are successful, then the logical command is successful. For the logical OR, **||**, if either command is successful, then the OR is successful and returns an exit status of 0. The logical commands allow you to use logical operations as your test command in control structures.

case

The **case** structure chooses among several possible alternatives. The choice is made by comparing a value with several possible patterns. Each possible value is associated with a set of operations. If a match is found, the associated operations are performed. The **case** structure begins with the keyword **case**, an evaluation of a variable, and the keyword **in**. A set of patterns then follows. Each pattern is a regular expression terminated with a closing parenthesis. After the closing parenthesis, commands associated with this pattern are listed, followed by a double semicolon on a separate line, designating the end of those commands. After all the listed patterns, the keyword **esac** ends the **case** command. The syntax looks like this:

```
case string in
    pattern)
        commands
        ;;
    pattern)
        commands
        ;;
    *)
        default commands
        ;;
    esac
```

A pattern can include any shell special characters. The shell special characters are the *****, **[ ]**, **?**, and **|**. You can specify a default pattern with a single ***** special character. The ***** special character matches on any pattern and so performs as an effective default option. If all other patterns do not match, the * will. In this way, the default option is executed if no other options are chosen. The default is optional. You do not have to put it in.

A **case** structure is often used to implement menus. In the program **lschoice**, in the next example, the user is asked to enter a choice for listing files in different ways. Notice the default option that warns of invalid input.

lschoice

```
# Program to allow the user to select different ways of
#   listing files

echo  s. List Sizes
echo  l. List All File Information
echo  c. List C Files

echo -n "Please enter choice: "
read choice

case $choice in
   s)
      ls -s
      ;;
   l)
      ls -l
      ;;
   c)
      ls *.c
      ;;
   *)
      echo Invalid Option
   esac
```

```
$ lschoice
s. List Sizes
l. List All File Information
c. List C Files
Please enter choice: c
main.c    lib.c    file.c
$
```

Loops: while, for-in, for

The BASH shell has a set of loop control structures that allow you to repeat Linux commands. They are the **while**, **for-in**, and **for** structures. Like the BASH **if** structure, **while** and **until** test the result of a Linux command. However, the **for** and **for-in** structures do not perform any test. They simply progress through a list of values, assigning each value in turn to a specified variable. Furthermore, the **while** and **until** structures operate like corresponding structures found in programming languages, whereas the **for** and **for-in** structures are very different. The loop control structures are listed in Table 15-6.

while

The **while** loop repeats commands. A **while** loop begins with the keyword **while** and is followed by a Linux command. The keyword **do** follows on the next line. The end of the loop is specified by the keyword **done**. Here is the syntax for the **while** command:

```
while Linux command
    do
         commands
    done
```

The Linux command used in **while** structures is often a test command indicated by enclosing brackets. In the **myname** script, in the next example, you are asked to enter a name. The name is then printed out. The loop is controlled by testing the value of the variable again using the bracket form of the **test** command.

myname

```
again=yes

while [ "$again" = yes ]
do
   echo -n "Please enter a name: "
   read name
   echo "The name you entered is $name"

   echo -n "Do you wish to continue? "
   read again
done

echo Good-bye
```

```
$ myname
Please enter a name: George
The name you entered is George
Do you wish to continue? yes
Please enter a name: Robert
The name you entered is Robert
Do you wish to continue? no
Good-bye
```

for-in

The **for-in** structure is designed to reference a list of values sequentially. It takes two operands—a variable and a list of values. Each value in the list is assigned, one by one, to the variable in the **for-in** structure. Like the **while** command, the **for-in** structure is a loop. Each time through the loop, the next value in the list is assigned to the variable. When the end of the list is reached, the loop stops. Like the **while** loop, the body of a **for-in** loop begins with the keyword **do** and ends with the keyword **done**. The syntax for the **for-in** loop is shown here:

```
for variable in list of values
    do
    commands
    done
```

In the **mylistfor** script, the user simply outputs a list of each item with today's date. The list of items makes up the list of values read by the **for-in** loop. Each item is consecutively assigned to the grocery variable.

mylistfor

```
tdate='date +%D'

for grocery in milk cookies apples cheese
do
    echo "$grocery     $tdate"
done
```

```
$ mylistfor
milk        12/23/93
cookies     12/23/93
apples      12/23/93
cheese      12/23/93
$
```

The **for-in** loop is handy for managing files. You can use special characters to generate file names for use as a list of values in the **for-in** loop. For example, the ***** special character, by itself, generates a list of all files and directories, and ***.c** lists files with the **.c** extension. The special character ***** placed in the **for-in** loop's value list will generate a list of values consisting of all the file names in your current directory.

```
for myfiles in *
    do
```

The **cbackup** script makes a backup of each file and places it in a directory called **sourcebak**. Notice the use of the ***** special character to generate a list of all file names with a **.c** extension.

cbackup

```
for backfile in *.c
do
    cp $backfile sourcebak/$backfile
    echo $backfile
done
```

```
$ cbackup
io.c
lib.c
main.c
$
```

for

The **for** structure without a specified list of values takes as its list of values the command line arguments. The arguments specified on the command line when the shell file is invoked become a list of values referenced by the **for** command. The variable used in the **for** command is set automatically to each argument value in sequence. The first time through the loop, the variable is set to the value of the first argument. The second time, it is set to the value of the second argument.

The **for** structure without a specified list is equivalent to the list **$@**. **$@** is a special argument variable whose value is the list of command line arguments. In the next example, a list of C program files is entered on the command line when the shell file **cbackuparg** is invoked. In **cbackuparg**, each argument is automatically referenced by a **for** loop. **backfile** is the variable used in the **for** loop. The first time through the loop, **$backfile** holds the value of the first argument, **$1**. The second time through, it holds the value of the second argument, **$2**.

cbackuparg

```
for backfile
do
    cp $backfile sourcebak/$backfile
    echo "$backfile"
done
```

```
$ cbackuparg  main.c  lib.c  io.c
main.c
lib.c
io.c
```

Summary: BASH Shell

Three different types of shells have been developed for Linux: the BASH shell, the PDKSH shell, and the TCSH shell. The BASH shell incorporates most of the commands found in the PDKSH and TCSH shells, including features such as command line editing, the history utility, and aliasing. With history you can list and reference previous commands that you have executed. You can even edit those commands, executing the edited versions. The BASH shell **alias** command allows you to give another name to a command. The alias can reference a command or a command with its arguments.

The BASH shell also has a set of shell features that you can turn on and off. Three common features are **ignoreeof**, **noclobber**, and **noglob**. **ignoreeof** prevents accidental logouts. **noclobber** prevents the redirection operation from overwriting existing files. The **noglob** feature treats special characters as ordinary characters.

There is also a set of special variables used to configure your user shell. Some are defined by the system and can be redefined by you. Others are user-defined, and you must explicitly define them. Various special variables govern the configuration of different aspects of your environment. For example, the **PATH** special variable specifies what directories hold Linux commands. The **EXINIT** variable holds the default configuration for the Ex and Vi editors.

Special variables are assigned values in initialization files. Initialization files are shell scripts invoked automatically when a shell is entered. In the BASH shell, the login initialization file is called **.bash_profile**. In the C-shell it is called **.login**. The BASH shell also has a **.bash_logout** file that is automatically executed when you log out. All shells have shell initialization files. These are files that are executed each time you enter a shell. In the BASH shell this file is called the **.bashrc** file.

The BASH shell has a programming capability that operates like a programming language. You can define variables and assign values to them. You can also interactively read values into a variable. There are control structures that you can use to implement loops and conditions. You can enter shell programming statements into a script file and execute the script, just as you would do with a program.

You can define variables in the shell and assign them values. You evaluate a variable by placing a **$** before the variable name. You can use variables as arguments in commands. They can hold directory path names, or even commands to be executed.

Using an editor, you can create files that contain shell commands and variable definitions. Such files are known as shell scripts. A shell script can even have argument variables that will receive arguments typed in at the command line. By setting the executable permission of the shell script, you can treat the name of the shell script file as if it were another command.

Script input and output is controlled with the **echo** and **read** commands as well as the Here document. **echo** outputs data to the standard output. The **read** command allows you to read input into a variable interactively. The input is taken from the standard input, whether it is entered at the keyboard or redirected from a file. The

Here document allows you to use text directly typed in the script as input to a Linux command. The Here operator is **<<** followed by a user-defined delimiter. The delimiter is placed at the end of text to be input to a command.

Variables are text variables. They take as their values strings. Aside from equality, there are no operators that perform operations on variables. If you want to perform arithmetic or relational operations on variables, you need to use the **let** command. In the BASH shell, the **let** command allows you to use variables as if they were numeric. You can perform such operations as addition, subtraction, and multiplication.

The loop and condition control structures correspond to similar structures in programming languages. The loop structures are the **while**, **for-in**, and **for** loops. The condition structures are the **if** and **case** conditions. The **while** loop operates much like those in other languages. The loop continues until a test is false. However, in BASH shell control structures, the test is a Linux command. All commands in Linux return an exit status upon completing execution, denoting whether the command was successful or not. If the Linux command has an exit status of 0, the command was successful. If the exit status is any non-zero value, the command was unsuccessful. In the case of a **while** loop, a Linux command is the test. If the Linux command was successful, then the loop continues. If it fails, the loop stops.

A special Linux command called **test** can be used to implement programming-languagelike tests. The **test** command can compare two values, performing relational operations on them. If the relational operation is true, the exit status of the **test** command will be a 0—a success. If false, its exit status will be some other value. With the **test** command, you can control a loop using a relational operation that compares two operands.

The **if** control structure conditions the execution of commands upon a test. Like the **while** structure, this test is itself a Linux command. If the Linux command is successful, then the commands within the **if** are executed. The **if** structure can use the **test** command to implement programminglike conditional operations. The **test** command can perform relational operations between two variables, allowing the **if** to succeed if the relational operation is true. The **elif** and **else** structures allow you to construct nested **if** conditions. **elif**, like **if**, has as its test a Linux command.

The **case** structure works like a restricted version of the **if** structure—it compares a single value with a set of possible values. If a match is found, then operations associated with that matched value are executed. **case** is very useful for implementing menus, in which users make choices among several possible options.

The **for-in** structure runs through a list of values, assigning each value in turn to a specified variable. There is no test. The list of values can be generated by any of several Linux commands. For example, **ls** will generate a list of file names. A list of values can also be specified by a list of words. Each word is then a value assigned in turn to the **for** variable. The loop will always continue until all values have been assigned. The **for** structure uses as its list the command line arguments. There is no explicit list of values.

Command Line Editing	Effect
CTRL-**b** or LEFT ARROW	Moves left one character (backward to the previous character)
CTRL-**f** or RIGHT ARROW	Moves right one character (forward to the next character)
CTRL-**a**	Moves to beginning of a line
CTRL-**e**	Moves to end of a line
ESC **f**	Moves forward one word
ESC **b**	Moves backward one word
DEL	Deletes the character the cursor is on
BACKSPACE or CTRL-**h**	Deletes the character before the cursor
CTRL-**d**	Deletes the character after the cursor
CTRL-**k**	Removes (kills) the remainder of a line
History Commands	**Effect**
CTRL-**n** or DOWN ARROW	Moves down to the next event in the history list
CTRL-**p** or UP ARROW	Moves up to the previous event in the history list
ESC **<**	Moves to beginning of the history event list
ESC **>**	Moves to end of the history event list
ESC TAB	History event matching and completion

fc *event-reference*	Edits an event with the standard editor and then executes it
	   options
	   -l List recent history events; same as **history** command
	   -e *editor event-reference* Invokes a specified editor to edit a specific event

Table 15-1. *Command Line Editing, History Commands, and History Event References*

Command Line Editing	Effect
!*event num*	References an event with event number
!*characters*	References an event with beginning characters
!?*pattern*?	References an event with a pattern in the event
!-*event num*	References an event with an offset from the first event
!*num-num*	References a range of events

Table 15-1. *Command Line Editing, History Commands, and History Event References (continued)*

Shell Special Variables	Function
System-determined	
HOME	Path name for user's home directory
LOGNAME	Login name
USER	Login name
TZ	Time zone used by system
Redefinable Special Variables	
SHELL	Path name of program for type of shell you are using
PATH	List of path names for directories searched for executable commands
PS1	Primary shell prompt
PS2	Secondary shell prompt
IFS	Interfield delimiter symbol
MAIL	Name of mail file checked by mail utility for received messages
MAILCHECK	Interval for checking for received mail

Table 15-2. *BASH Shell Special Variables and Features*

Shell Special Variables	Function
User-defined Special Variables	
MAILPATH	List of mail files to be checked by mail for received messages
TERM	Terminal name
CDPATH	Path names for directories searched by **cd** command for subdirectories
EXINIT	Initialization commands for Ex/Vi editor
BASH Shell Features	
$ set -+o *feature*	Korn shell features are turned on and off with the **set** command; **-o** sets a feature on and **+o** turns it off **$ set -o noclobber** *set noclobber on* **$ set +o noclobber** *set noclobber off*
ignoreeof	Disabled CTRL-**d** logout
noclobber	Does not overwrite files through redirection
noglob	Disables special characters used for file name expansion: *****, **?**, **~**, and **[]**

Table 15-2. *BASH Shell Special Variables and Features* (continued)

BASH Shell Commands	Effect
break	Exits from **for**, **while**, or **until** loop
continue	Skips remaining commands in loop and continues with next iteration
echo	Displays values **-n** Eliminates output of new line
eval	Executes the command line

Table 15-3. *BASH Shell Commands and Arguments*

BASH Shell Commands	Effect
exec	Executes command in place of current process; does not generate a new subshell, uses the current one
exit	Exits from the current shell
export *var*	Generates a copy of *var* variable for each new subshell (call-by-value)
history	Lists recent history events
let *"expression"*	Evaluates an arithmetic, relational, or assignment expression using operators listed in Table 15-4. The expression must be quoted
read	Reads a line from the standard input
return	Exits from a function
set	Assigns new values for these arguments (when used with command line arguments); lists all defined variables (when used alone)
shift	Moves each command line argument to the left so that the number used to reference it is one less than before; argument 3$ would then be referenced by $2, and so on; $1 is lost
test *value option value* [*value option value*]	Compares two arguments; used as the Linux command tested in control structures **test 2 -eq $count** **[2 -eq $count]**
unset	Undefines a variable
Command Line Arguments	
$0	Name of Linux command
$n	The *n*th command line argument beginning from 1, $1-$n; you can use **set** to change them
$*	All the command line arguments beginning from 1; you can use **set** to change them
$@	The command line arguments individually quoted
$#	The count of the command line arguments

Table 15-3.   *BASH Shell Commands and Arguments* (continued)

BASH Shell Commands	Effect
Process Variables	
$$	The PID number, process ID, of the current process
$!	The PID number of the most recent background job
$?	The exit status of the last Linux command executed

Table 15-3. *BASH Shell Commands and Arguments* (continued)

Arithmetic Operators	Function
*	multiplication
/	division
+	addition
−	subtraction
%	modulo—results in the remainder of a division
Relational Operators	
>	greater-than
<	less-than
>=	greater-than-or-equal-to
<=	less-than-or-equal-to
=	equal in expr
==	equal in let
!=	not-equal
&	logical AND
		logical OR
!	logical NOT

Table 15-4. *Expression Operators: **let***

Integer Comparisons	Function
`-gt`	greater-than
`-lt`	less-than
`-ge`	greater-than-or-equal-to
`-le`	less-than-or-equal-to
`-eq`	equal
`-ne`	not-equal

String Comparisons	
`-z`	Tests for empty string
`-n`	Tests for string value
`=`	equal strings
`!=`	not-equal strings
`str`	Tests to see if string is not a null string

Logical Operations	
`-a`	Logical AND
`-o`	Logical OR
`!`	Logical NOT

File Tests	
`-f`	File exists and is a regular file
`-s`	File is not empty
`-r`	File is readable
`-w`	File can be written to, modified
`-x`	File is executable
`-d`	File name is a directory name
`-h`	File name is a symbolic link
`-c`	File name references a character device
`-b`	File name references a block file

Table 15-5.   *Test Command Operations*

Condition Control Structures: if, else, elif, case	Function

`if` *command* `then`
  command
`fi`
	`if` executes an action if its test command is true

`if` *command* `then`
  command
`else`
  command
`fi`
	`if-else` executes an action if the exit status of its test command is true; if false, then the `else` action is executed

`if` *command* `then`
  command
`elif` *command* `then`
  command
`else`
  command
`fi`
	`elif` allows you to nest `if` structures, enabling selection among several alternatives; at the first true `if` structure, its commands are executed and control leaves the entire `elif` structure

`case` *string* `in`
pattern `)`
  command `;;`
`esac`
	`case` matches the string value to any of several patterns; if a pattern is matched, its associated commands are executed

command `&&` *command*	The logical AND condition returns a true 0 value if both commands return a true 0 value; if one returns a non-zero value, then the AND condition is false and also returns a non-zero value
command `||` *command*	The logical OR condition returns a true 0 value if one or the other command returns a true 0 value; if both commands return a non-zero value, then the OR condition is false and also returns a non-zero value
`!` *command*	The logical NOT condition inverts the return value of the command

Table 15-6.   *BASH Shell Conditions and Loops*

Condition Control Structures: **if, else, elif, case**	**Function**
Loop Control Structures: while, until, for, for-in, select	
while *command* **do** *command* **done**	**while** executes an action as long as its test command is true
until *command* **do** *command* **done**	**until** executes an action as long as its test command is false
for *variable* **in** *list-values* **do** *command* **done**	**for-in** is designed for use with lists of values; the variable operand is consecutively assigned the values in the list
for *variable* **do** *command* **done**	**for** is designed for reference script arguments; the variable operand is consecutively assigned each argument value
select *string* **in** *item-list* **do** *command* **done**	**select** creates a menu based on the items in the *item-list*; then it executes the command; the command is usually a **case**

Table 15-6.   *BASH Shell Conditions and Loops (continued)*

Chapter Sixteen

The TCSH Shell

The TCSH shell is essentially a version of the C-shell with added features. It is fully compatible with the standard C-shell and incorporates all of its capabilities, including the shell language and the history utility. The C-shell, itself, was originally developed for use with BSD Unix. It incorporates all the core commands used in the original Bourne shell, but differs significantly in more complex features such as shell programming. The C-shell was developed after the Bourne shell and was the first to introduce new features such as command line editing, the history utility, and aliasing. The Korn shell later incorporated many of these same features, adding to them with more versatile command line and history editing. Similar improvements were then incorporated into the BASH and TCSH shells. TCSH has more advanced command line and history editing features than those found in the original C-shell.

The TCSH, BASH, and PDKSH shells all share the same set of basic shell operations, as described in Chapter 5. One notable difference for the TCSH shell is that it uses a different default prompt, the **>** instead of the **$**. This chapter focuses on the TCSH shell operations that differ from the other shells, namely, command line editing, history, and shell environment variables and initialization scripts. TCSH shell programming is also covered in this chapter. See Table 16-1 for the TCSH shell history commands.

Command Line Completion

The command line has a built-in feature that performs command and file name completion. If you enter an incomplete pattern as a file name argument, you can press TAB to activate this feature, which will then complete the pattern with a file name. If you press CTRL-D, it will expand to all file names matching a pattern. To use this feature, you type the partial name of the file on the command line and then press TAB. The shell will automatically look for the file with that partial prefix and complete it for you on the command line. In the next example, the user issues a **cat** command with an incomplete file name. When the user presses TAB, the system searches for a match and, upon finding one, fills in the file name.

```
> cat pre  tab
 > cat preface
```

If more than one file has the same prefix, the shell will match the name as far as the file names agree and then beep. You can then add more characters to select one or the other. For example:

```
> ls
document docudrama
> cat doc  tab
 > cat docu  beep
```

If, instead, you want a list of all the names that your incomplete file name matches, you can press CTRL-D on the command line. In the next example, the CTRL-D after the incomplete file name generates a list of possible file names.

```
> cat doc Ctrl-d
document
docudrama
> cat docu
```

The shell redraws the command line, and you can then type in the remainder of the file name, or type in distinguishing characters, and press TAB to have the file name completed.

```
> cat docudrama
```

History

As in the BASH and PDKSH shells, the TCSH shell's history utility keeps a record of the most recent commands you have executed. The history utility is a kind of short-term memory, keeping track of a limited number of the most recent commands. If the history utility is not automatically turned on, you first have to define it with a **set** command and assign to it the number of commands you want recorded. This is often done as part of your shell configuration, which is discussed in Chapter 14. In the next example, the history utility is defined and set to remember the last 5 commands.

```
> set history=5
```

The commands remembered are technically referred to as *events*. To see the set of your most recent events, enter **history** on the command line and press ENTER. A list of your most recent commands is displayed, preceded by an event number.

```
> history
1 ls
2 vi mydata
3 mv mydata reports
4 cd reports
5 ls -F
>
```

The history utility lets you reference a former event by placing it on your command line and allowing you to execute it. However, you do not need to display the list first with history. The easiest way to do this is to use your UP ARROW and DOWN ARROW keys to place history events on your command line one at a time. Pressing the UP ARROW key once will place the last history event on your command line. Pressing it again places the next history event on your command line. The DOWN ARROW key will place the previous command on the command line.

You can also edit the command line. The LEFT ARROW and RIGHT ARROW keys move you along the command line. You can then insert text wherever you stop your cursor. With the BACKSPACE and DEL keys, you can delete characters. CTRL-A moves your cursor to the beginning of the command line, and CTRL-E moves it to the end. CTRL-K deletes the remainder of a line from the position of the cursor, and CTRL-U erases the entire line.

Displaying the history list provides you with a more powerful interface for referencing history events. Each of these events can be referenced by either its event number, the beginning characters of the event, or a pattern of characters in the event. A pattern reference is enclosed in question marks, **?**. You can reexecute any event using the history command, **!**. The exclamation point is followed by an event reference such as an event number, beginning characters, or a pattern. In the next examples, the second command in the history list is referenced first by an event number, then by the beginning characters of the event, and then by a pattern in the event.

```
>  !2
vi mydata
>  !vi
vi mydata
>  !?myd?
vi mydata
```

You can also reference a command using an offset from the end of the list. Preceding a number with a minus sign will offset from the end of the list to that command. In the next example, the second command, **vi mydata**, is referenced using an offset.

```
>  !-4
vi mydata
```

An exclamation point is also used to identify the last command executed. It is equivalent to an offset of -1. In the next examples, both the offset of 1 and the exclamation point reference the last command, **ls -F**.

```
> !!
ls -F
mydata /reports

> !-1
ls -F
mydata /reports
```

History Event Substitutions

An event reference should be thought of as a representation of the characters making up the event. The event reference **!1** actually represents the characters "ls". As such, you can use an event reference as part of another command. The history operation is basically a substitution. The characters making up the event replace the exclamation point and event reference entered on the command line. In the next example, the list of events is first displayed. Then a reference to the first event is used as part of a new command. The event reference **!1** evaluates to **ls**, becoming part of the command **ls > myfiles**.

```
> history
1 ls
2 vi mydata
3 mv mydata reports
4 cd reports
5 ls -F

> !1 > myfiles
ls > myfiles
```

You can also reference particular words in an event. An event is parsed into separate words, each identified sequentially by a number starting from 0. An event reference followed by a colon and a number references only a word in the event. Using the preceding example, the event reference **!3:2** first references the third event, **mv mydata reports**, and the second word in that event, **mydata**. You can use such word references as part of a command. In the next example, **2:0** references only the first word in the second event, **vi**. The command evaluates to **vi preface**.

```
> !2:0 preface
vi preface
```

Using a range of numbers, you can reference several words in an event. The number of the first and last word in the range are separated by a dash. In the next example, **3:0-1** references the first two words of the third event, **mv mydata**.

```
> !3:0-1 oldletters
```

The special characters **^** and **$** represent the second word and the last word in an event. They are used to reference arguments of the event. If you needed just the first argument of an event, then **^** would reference it. The **$** references the last argument. The range **^-$** references all the arguments (the first word, the command name, is not included). In the next examples, the arguments used in previous events are referenced and used as arguments in the current command. First, the first argument (the second word) in the second event, **mydata**, is used as an argument in an **lp** command, printing the file. Then the last argument in the third event, **reports**, is used as an argument in the **ls** command, listing out the file names in **reports**. Then the arguments used in the third event, **mydata** and **reports**, are used as arguments in a **copy** command.

```
> lpr !2:^
lpr mydata
> ls !3:$
ls reports
> cp !3:^-$
cp mydata reports
```

The asterisk is a special symbol that represents all the arguments in a former command. It is equivalent to the range **^-$**. The last example just shown can be rewritten using the asterisk:

```
> cp !3*
cp mydata reports
```

In the C-shell as well as the TCSH shell, whenever the exclamation point is used in a command, it is interpreted as a history command reference. If you need to use the exclamation point for other reasons, such as an electronic mail address symbol, you have to escape the exclamation point by placing a backslash in front of it:

```
> mail garnet\!chris < mydata
```

Aliases

You use the **alias** command to create another name for a command. The alias operates like a macro that expands to the command it represents. The alias does not literally replace the name of the command; it simply gives another name to that command.

An **alias** command begins with the keyword alias and the new name for the command, followed by the command that the alias will reference. In the next example, the **ls** command is aliased with the name **list**. **list** becomes another name for the **ls** command.

```
> alias list ls
> ls
mydata intro
> list
mydata intro
>
```

Should the command you are aliasing have options, you will need to enclose the command and the option within single quotes. An aliased command that has spaces will need quotation marks as well. In the next example, **ls** with the **-l** option is given the alias **longl**:

```
> alias longl 'ls -l'
> ls -l
-rw-r--r--  1  chris weather 207 Feb  20  11:55   mydata
> longl
-rw-r--r--  1  chris weather 207 Feb  20  11:55   mydata
>
```

You can also use the name of a command as an alias. In the case of the **rm**, **cp**, and **mv** commands, the **-i** option should always be used to ensure that an existing file is not overwritten. Instead of constantly being careful to use the **-i** option each time you use one of these commands, you can alias the command name to include the option. In the next examples, the **rm**, **cp**, and **mv** commands have been aliased to include the **-i** option.

```
> alias rm 'rm -i'
> alias mv 'mv -i'
> alias cp 'cm -i'
```

The alias command by itself provides a list of all aliases in effect and their commands. An alias can be removed with the **unalias** command.

```
> alias
lss    ls -s
list   ls
rm     rm -i
> unalias lss
```

TCSH Shell Feature Variables: Shell Features

The TCSH shell has several features that allow you to control how different shell operations work. The TCSH shell's features include those in the PDKSH shell as well as many of its own. For example, the TCSH shell has a **noclobber** option to prevent redirection from overwriting files. Some of the more commonly used features are **echo**, **noclobber**, **ignoreeof**, and **noglob**. (See Table 16-2.) The TCSH shell features are turned on and off by defining and undefining a variable associated with that feature. A variable is named for each feature, for example, the **noclobber** feature is turned on by defining the **noclobber** variable. You use the **set** command to define a variable and the **unset** command to undefine a variable. To turn on the **noclobber** feature you issue the command: **set noclobber**. To turn it off you use the command: **unset noclobber**.

```
$ set feature-variable
$ unset feature-variable
```

These variables are also sometimes referred to as toggles since they are used to turn features on and off.

echo

Setting echo enables a feature that displays a command before it is executed. The command **set echo** turns the echo feature on, and the command **unset echo** turns it off.

ignoreeof

Setting **ignoreeof** enables a feature that prevents users from logging out of the user shell with a CTRL-D. It is designed to prevent accidental logouts. With this feature turned off, you can log out by pressing CTRL-D. However, CTRL-D is also used to end user input entered directly into the standard input. It is used often for the mail program or for utilities such as **cat**. You could easily enter an extra CTRL-D in such circumstances and accidentally log yourself out. The **ignoreeof** feature prevents such accidental logouts. When it is set, you have to explicitly log out, using the **logout** command:

```
$ set ignoreeof
$ ctrl-d
Use logout to logout
$
```

noclobber

Setting **noclobber** enables a feature that safeguards existing files from redirected output. With the **noclobber** feature, if you redirect output to a file that already exists, the file will not be overwritten with the standard output. The original file will be preserved. There may be situations in which you use a name that you have already given to an existing file as the name for the file to hold the redirected output. The **noclobber** feature prevents you from accidentally overwriting your original file:

```
> set noclobber
> cat preface > myfile
myfile: file exists
$
```

There may be times when you want to overwrite a file with redirected output. In this case, you can place an exclamation point after the redirection operator. This will override the **noclobber** feature, replacing the contents of the file with the standard output:

```
> cat preface >! myfile
```

noglob

Setting **noglob** enables a feature that disables special characters in the user shell. The characters *****, **?**, **[]**, and **~** will no longer expand to matched file names. This feature is helpful if, for some reason, you have special characters as part of a file name. In the next example, the user needs to reference a file that ends with the **?** character, **answers?**. First the user turns off special characters, using the **noglob** option. Now the question mark on the command line is taken as part of the file name, not as a special character, and the user can reference the **answers?** file.

```
$ set noglob
$ ls answers?
answers?
```

TCSH Special Shell Variables for Configuring Your System

As in the BASH shell, you can use special shell variables in the TCSH shell to configure your system. Some are defined initially by your system, and you can later redefine them with a new value. There are others that you must initially define yourself. One of the more commonly used special variables is the **prompt** variable that allows you to create your own command line prompts. Another is the **history** variable with which you determine how many history events you want to keep track of.

In the TCSH shell, many special variables have names and functions similar to those in the BASH or PDKSH shells. Some are in uppercase, but most are written in lowercase. The **EXINIT** and **TERM** variables retain their uppercase form. However, **history** and **cdpath** are written in lowercase. Other special variables may perform similar functions, but have very different implementations. For example, the **mail** variable holds the same information as BASH **MAIL**, **MAILPATH**, and **MAILCHECK** variables together. See Table 16-3 for a list of these variables.

prompt, prompt2, prompt3

The **prompt**, **prompt2**, and **prompt3** variables hold the prompts for your command line. You can configure your prompt to be any symbol or string that you want. To have your command line display a different symbol as a prompt, you simply use the **set** command to assign that symbol to the **prompt** variable. In the next example, the user assigns a **+** sign to the **prompt** variable, making it the new prompt.

```
> set prompt = "+"
+
```

You can use a predefined set of codes to make configuring your prompt easier. With them, you can make the time, your user name, or your directory path name a part of your prompt. You can even have your prompt display the history event number of the current command you are about to enter. Each code is preceded by a **%** symbol, for example, **%/** represents the current working directory, **%t** the time, and **%n** your user name. **%!** will display the next history event number. In the next example, the user adds the current working directory to the prompt.

```
> set prompt = "%/ >"
/home/dylan >
```

The next example incorporates both the time and the history event number with a new prompt.

```
> set prompt = "%t %! $"
```

Here is a list of the codes:

Code	Function
%/	Current working directory
%h, %!, !	Current history number
%t	Time of day
%n	User name
%d	Day of the week
%w	Current month
%y	Current year

The **prompt2** variable is used in special cases when a command may take several lines to input. **prompt2** is displayed for the added lines needed for entering the command. **prompt3** is the prompt used if the spell check feature is activated.

cdpath

The **cdpath** variable holds the path names of directories to be searched for specified subdirectories referenced with the **cd** command. These path names form an array just like the array of path names assigned to the TCSH shell **path** variable. Notice the space between the path names.

```
> set cdpath=(/usr/chris/reports /usr/chris/letters)
```

history and savehist

As you learned earlier, the **history** variable can be used to determine the number of history events you want saved. You simply assign to it the maximum number of events that **history** will record. When the maximum is reached, the count starts over again from 1. The **savehist** variable, however, holds the number of events that will be saved in the file **.history** when you log out. When you log in again, these events will become the initial history list.

In the next example, up to 20 events will be recorded in your history list while you are logged in. However, only the last 5 will be saved in the **.history** file when you log out. Upon logging in again, your history list will consist of your last 5 commands from the previous session.

```
> set history=20
> set savehist=5
```

mail

In the TCSH shell, the **mail** variable combines the features of the **MAIL**, **MAILCHECK**, and **MAILPATH** variables in the BASH and PDKSH shells. The TCSH shell **mail** variable is assigned as its value an array whose elements contain both the time interval for checking for mail and the directory path names for mailbox files to be checked. To assign values to these elements, you assign an array of values to the **mail** variable. The array of new values is specified with a list of words separated by spaces and enclosed in parentheses. The first value is a number that sets the number of seconds to wait before checking for mail again. This value is comparable to that held by the BASH shell's **MAILCHECK** variable. The remaining values consist of the directory path names of mailbox files that are to be checked for your mail. Notice that these values combine the functions of the BASH and Korn shells' **MAIL** and **MAILPATH** variables.

In the next example, the **mail** variable is set to check for mail every 20 minutes (1200 seconds), and the mailbox file checked is in **usr/mail/chris**. The first value in the array assigned to mail is 1200, and the second value in the array is the path name of the mailbox file to be checked.

```
> set mail ( 1200 /usr/mail/chris )
```

You can, just as easily, add more mailbox file path names to the **mail** array. In the next example, two mailboxes are designated. Notice the spaces surrounding each element.

```
> set mail ( 1200 /usr/mail/chris /home/mail/chris )
```

TCSH Shell Initialization Files: .login, .tcshrc, .logout

The TCSH shell has three initialization files: **.login**, **.logout**, and **.tcshrc**. The files are named for the operation they execute. The **.login** file is a login initialization file that executes each time you log in. The **.logout** file executes each time you log out. The **.tcshrc** file is a shell initialization file that executes each time you enter the TCSH shell, either from logging in or by explicitly changing to the TCSH shell from another shell with the **tcsh** command.

.login

The TCSH shell has its own login initialization file called the **.login** file that contains shell commands and special variable definitions used to configure your shell. The **.login** file corresponds to the **.profile** file used in the BASH and PDKSH shells.

A **.login** file contains **setenv** commands that assign values to special environment variables, such as **TERM**. You can change these assigned values by editing the **.login** file with any of the standard editors. You can also add new values. Remember, however, that in the TCSH shell, the command for assigning a value to an environment variable is **setenv**. In the next example, the **EXINIT** variable is defined and assigned the Vi editor's line numbering and auto-indent options.

```
> setenv EXINIT 'set nu ai'
```

Be careful when editing your **.login** file. Inadvertent editing changes could cause variables to be set incorrectly or not at all. It is wise to make a backup of your **.login** file before editing it.

If you have made changes to your **.login** file and you want the changes to take effect during your current login session, you will need to reexecute the file. You do so using the **source** command. The **source** command will actually execute any initialization file, including the **.tcshrc** and **.logout** files. In the next example, the user reexecutes the **.login** file.

```
> source .login
```

If you are also planning to use the PDKSH shell on your Linux system, you need to define a variable called **ENV** within your **.login** file and assign it the name of the PDKSH shell's initialization file. If you should later decide to enter the PDKSH shell from your TCSH shell, the PDKSH shell's initialization file can be located and executed for you. In the example of the **.login** file shown next, you will see that the last command sets the PDKSH shell's initialization file to **.kshrc** to the **ENV** variable: `setenv ENV $HOME/.kshrc`.

.login

```
setenv term vt100
setenv EXINIT 'set nu ai'

setenv ENV $HOME/.kshrc
```

.tcshrc

The **.tcshrc** initialization file is executed each time you enter the TCSH shell or generate any subshells. If the TCSH shell is your login shell, then the **.tcshrc** file is executed along with your **.login** file when you log in. If you enter the TCSH shell from another shell, the **.tcshrc** file is automatically executed, and the variable and alias definitions it contains will be defined.

The **.tcshrc** shell initialization file is actually executed each time you generate a shell, such as when you run a shell script. In other words, each time a subshell is created, the **.tcshrc** file is executed. This allows you to define local variables in the **.tcshrc** initialization file and have them, in a sense, exported to any subshells. Even though such user-defined special variables such as **history** are local, they will be defined for each subshell generated. In this way, **history** is set for each subshell. However, each subshell has its own local **history** variable. You could even change the local **history** variable in one subshell without affecting any of those in other subshells. Defining special variables in the shell initialization file allows you to treat them like BASH shell exported variables. As discussed in Chapter 15, an exported variable in a BASH or PDKSH shell only passes a copy of itself to any subshell. Changing the copy does not affect the original definition.

The **.tcshrc** file also contains the definition of aliases and any feature variables used to turn on shell features. Aliases and feature variables are locally defined within the shell. But the **.tcshrc** file will define them in every shell. For this reason, **.tcshrc** usually holds such aliases as those defined for the **rm**, **cp**, and **mv** commands. The next example is a **.tcshrc** file with many of the standard definitions.

.tcshrc

```
set shell=/usr/bin/csh
set path= $PATH (/bin /usr/bin . )
set cdpath=( /home/chris/reports /home/chris/letters )

set prompt="! $cwd >"
set history=20

set ignoreeof
set noclobber

alias rm  'rm -i'
alias mv  'mv -i'
alias cp  'cp -i'
```

Local variables, unlike environment variables, are defined with the **set** command. Any local variables that you define in **.tcshrc** should use the **set** command. Any variables defined with **setenv** as environment variables, such as **TERM**, should be placed in the **.login** file. The next example shows the kinds of definitions found in the **.tcshrc** file. Notice that the **history** and **noclobber** variables are defined using the **set** command.

```
set history=20
set noclobber
```

You can edit any of the values assigned to these variables. However, when editing the path names assigned to **path** or **cdpath**, bear in mind that these path names are contained in an array. Each element in an array is separated by a space. If you add a new path name, you need to be sure that there is a space separating it from the other path names.

If you have made changes to **.tcshrc** and you want them to take effect during your current login session, remember to reexecute the **.tcshrc** file with the **source** command:

```
> source .tcshrc
```

.logout

The **.logout** file is also an initialization file, but it is executed when the user logs out. It is designed to perform any operations you want done whenever you log out. Instead of variable definitions, the **.logout** file usually contains shell commands that form a shutdown procedure. For example, one common logout command is the one to check for any active background jobs; another is to clear the screen and then issue a farewell message.

As with **.login**, you can add your own shell commands to the **.logout** file. Using the Vi editor, you could change the farewell message or add other operations. In the next example, the user has a **clear** and an **echo** command in the **.logout** file. When the user logs out, the **clear** command will clear the screen, and **echo** will display the message "Good-bye for now".

.logout

```
clear
echo "Good-bye for now"
```

TCSH Shell Programming

The TCSH shell, like the BASH and PDKSH shells, also has programming languagelike capabilities. You can define variables and assign values to them. You can place variable definitions and Linux commands in a script file and then execute that script. There are also loop and conditional control structures with which you can repeat Linux commands or make decisions on which commands you want to execute. You can also place traps in your program to handle interrupts.

The TCSH shell differs from other shells in that its control structures conform more to a programming language format. For example, the test condition for a TCSH shell's control structure is an expression that evaluates to true or false, not to a Linux command. A TCSH shell expression uses the same operators as those found in the C programming language. You can perform a variety of assignment, arithmetic, relational, and bitwise operations. The TCSH shell also allows you to declare numeric variables that can easily be used in such operations.

TCSH Shell Variables, Scripts, and Arguments

As you've already seen, the TCSH shell uses shell variables much the same way as the BASH and PDKSH shells do. You can define variables in a shell and assign values to them, as well as reference script arguments. You can also define environment variables that operate much like BASH shell exported variables. The TCSH shell differs in the way it defines variables and the type of variables you can define. The TCSH shell defines its variables using the TCSH shell commands **set**, **@**, and **setenv**. The TCSH shell also allows you to define numeric variables and arrays. The **@** command defines a numeric variable on which you perform arithmetic operations. Parentheses and brackets allow you to define and reference arrays.

Scripts also operate in much the same way, but with several crucial differences. A TCSH shell script must begin with a sharp (or pound) sign (**#**) in the first column of the first line. Also, though prompts can be output using the **echo** command, there is no **read** command to handle input. Instead, you need to redirect the standard input to a variable.

TCSH Shell Variables

In the TCSH shell, you need to first declare a variable before you can use it. You declare a variable with the **set** command followed by the variable's name. A variable name may be any set of alphabetic characters, including the underscore. The name may also include a number, but the number cannot be the first character in the name. A name may not have any other type of character, such as an exclamation point, ampersand, or even a space. Such symbols are reserved by the shell for its own use. A name may not include more than one word since the shell parses its command line on the space. The space is a delimiter between the different elements of the command line. The next example declares the variable **greeting**. You can later undefine the variable with the **unset** command.

```
> set greeting
```

You also use the **set** command to assign a value to a variable. You type in the keyword **set**, the variable name, the assignment operator, **=**, and then the value assigned. Any set of characters can be assigned to a variable. In the next example, the variable **greeting** is assigned the string "hello".

```
> set greeting="hello"
```

In the TCSH shell assignment operation, you either need to place spaces on both sides of the assignment operator or have no spaces at all. The assignment operation

```
> set greeting ="hello"
```

will fail because there is a space before the assignment operator, but not after.

You can obtain a list of all the defined variables by using the **set** command without any arguments. The next example uses **set** to display a list of all defined variables and their values.

```
> set
greeting hello
poet   Virgil
```

As in the BASH shell, the dollar sign, **$**, is a special operator that evaluates a shell variable. Evaluation retrieves a variable's value—usually a set of characters. This set of characters then replaces the variable name. In effect, wherever a **$** is placed before a variable name, the shell replaces the variable name with the value of the variable. In the next example, the shell variable **greeting** is evaluated and its contents, "hello", are then used as the argument for an **echo** command. The **echo** command prints a set of characters on the screen.

```
> echo $greeting
hello
```

TCSH Shell Scripts: Input and Output

You can easily define and use variables within a shell script. As in the example coming up, you can place Linux commands, such as the assignment operation and **echo**, in a file using a text editor. You can then make the file executable and invoke it on the command line as another command. Remember that to add the execute permission, you use the **chmod** command with a u+x permission or the 700 absolute permission. Within a script, you can use the **echo** command to output data. However, input is read into a variable by redirecting the standard input. There is no comparable version of the **read** command in the TCSH shell.

The TCSH shell examines the first character of a file to determine whether or not it is a TCSH shell script. Remember that all TCSH shell scripts must have as the first character on the first line, a **#** character. This identifies the file as a TCSH shell script. Notice the **#** character at the beginning of the **greet** script. The **#** character placed anywhere in the file other than the first character of the first line, operates as a common character.

greet

```
#
# Script to output hello greeting

set greeting="hello"
echo The value of greeting is $greeting
```

```
> chmod u+x greet
> greet
The value of greeting is hello
```

The **set** command combined with the redirection operation, **$<**, will read whatever the user enters into the standard input. The next example reads user input into the **greeting** variable.

```
> set greeting = $<
```

You can place the prompt on the same line as the input using the **echo** command. The TCSH shell uses a special option for **echo**, the **–n** option, which eliminates the new line character at the end of the output string. The cursor remains on the same line at the end of the output string:

```
> echo -n Please enter a greeting:
```

If you wish to include a space at the end of your prompt, you need to place the output string within double quotes, including the space:

```
> echo -n "Please enter a greeting: "
```

The **greetpt** script, shown next, contains a TCSH shell version of a prompt remaining on the same line as the input.

greetpt

```
#

echo -n "Please enter a greeting: "
set greeting = $<

echo "The greeting you entered was $greeting"
```

```
> greetpt
Please enter a greeting: hello
The greeting you entered was hello
>
```

Argument Array: argv

When a shell script is invoked, all the words on the command line are parsed and placed in elements of an array called **argv**. **argv[0]** will hold the command name. Beginning with **argv[1]** and on, each element will hold an argument entered on the command line. In the case of shell scripts, **argv[0]** will always contain the name of the shell script. Just as with any array element, you can access the contents of an argument array element by preceding it with a **$** operator. **$argv[1]** accesses the contents of the first element in the **argv** array—the first argument. If more than one argument is entered, they can be referenced with each corresponding element in the **argv** array. In the next example, the **myargs** script prints out four arguments. Four arguments are then entered on the command line

myargs

```
#

echo "The first argument is: $argv[1]"
echo "The second argument is: $argv[2]"
echo "The third argument is: $argv[3]"
echo "The fourth argument is: $argv[4]"
```

```
> myargs Hello Hi yo "How are you"
The first argument is: Hello
The second argument is: Hi
The third argument is: yo
The fourth argument is: How are you
>
```

An **argv** element can be abbreviated to the number of the element preceded by a **$** sign. **$argv[1]** can be written as **$1**. This makes for shell scripts whose argument references are very similar to BASH and PDKSH shell argument references. A special argument variable **argv[*]** references all the arguments in the command line. **$argv[*]** can be abbreviated as **$***. Notice that this is the same name used in the BASH shell to reference all arguments.

The **#argv** argument variable contains the number of arguments entered on the command line. This is useful for specifying a fixed number of arguments for a script. The number can be checked to see if the user has entered the correct amount.

The **arglist** script in the next example shows the use of both the **argv[*]** and **#argv** special argument variables. The user first displays the number of arguments, using **#argv**, and then uses **argv[*]** to display the list of arguments entered.

arglist

```
#

echo "The number of arguments entered is $#argv"
echo "The list of arguments is: $argv[*]"
```

```
> arglist Hello hi yo
The number of arguments entered is 3
The list of arguments is: Hello hi yo
```

Numeric Variables: @

In the TCSH shell, you can declare numeric variables using the **@** command instead of the **set** command. You can then perform arithmetic, relational, and bitwise operations on such variables. In this respect, the TCSH shell is similar to programming languages. Numeric and string variables are two very different types of objects managed in very different ways. You cannot use the **set** command on a numeric variable. The **@** command consists of the keyword **@**, the variable name, an assignment operator, and an expression. The next example declares the numeric variable **num** and assigns the value 10 to it.

```
> @ num = 10
```

Many different assignment operators are available for you to use, such as increments and arithmetic assignment operators. They are the same as those used in awk and in the C programming language. The expression can be any arithmetic, relational, or bitwise expression. You can create complex expressions using parentheses. The operands in an expression should be separated from the operator by spaces, for example, 10*5 is not a valid expression and should be written with spaces, 10 * 5. You can also use a numeric variable as an operand in an expression. In the next example, the variable **count** is declared as numeric and used in an arithmetic expression. Notice that count is evaluated with a **$** operator so that the value of count, 3, is used in the expression. See Table 16-4 for a list of numeric operators.

```
> @ count = 3
> @ num = 2 * ($count + 10)
> echo $num
26
```

Environment Variables: setenv

The TCSH shell has two types of variables: local variables and environment variables. A local variable is local to the shell it was declared in; an environment variable operates like a scoped global variable. It is known to any subshells, but not to any parent shells. An environment variable is defined with the **setenv** command. You assign a value to an environment variable using the **setenv** command, the variable name, and the value assigned. There is no assignment operator. In the next example, the greeting environment variable is assigned the value "hello".

```
> setenv greeting hello
```

Whenever a shell script is called, it generates its own shell. If a shell script is executed from another shell script, it will have its own shell separate from that of the first script. There are now two shells, the parent shell belonging to the first script and a subshell, which is the new shell generated when the second script was executed. When a script is executed from within another script, its shell is a subshell of the first script's shell. The original script's shell is a parent shell.

Each shell has its own set of variables. The subshell cannot reference local variables in the parent shell, but it can reference environment variables. Any environment variables declared in the parent shell can be referenced by any subshells.

Control Structures

As in other shells, the TCSH shell has a set of control structures that let you control the execution of commands in a script. There are loop and conditional control structures with which you can repeat Linux commands or make decisions on which commands you want to execute. The **while** and **if** control structures are more general purpose control structures, performing iterations and making decisions using a variety of different tests. The **switch** and **foreach** control structures are more specialized operations. The **switch** structure is a restricted form of the **if** condition that checks to see if a value is equal to one of a set of possible values. The **foreach** structure is a limited type of loop that runs through a list of values, assigning a new value to a variable with each iteration.

The TCSH shell differs from other shells in that its control structures conform more to a programming language format. The test condition for a TCSH shell control structure is an expression that evaluates to true or false, not a Linux command. One key difference between BASH shell and TCSH shell control structures is that TCSH shell structures cannot redirect or pipe their output. They are strictly control structures, controlling the execution of commands.

Test Expressions

The **if** and **while** control structures use an expression as their test. A true test is any expression that results in a non-zero value. A false test is any expression that results in a 0 value. In the TCSH shell, relational and equality expressions can be easily used as test expressions, because they result in 1 if true and 0 if false. There are many possible operators that you can use in an expression. The test expression can also be arithmetic or a string comparison, but strings can only be compared for equality or inequality.

Unlike the BASH and PDKSH shells, you must enclose the TCSH shell **if** and **while** test expressions within parentheses. The next example shows a simple test expression testing to see if two strings are equal.

```
if ( $greeting == "hi" ) then
    echo Informal Greeting
endif
```

The TCSH shell has a separate set of operators for testing strings against other strings or against regular expressions. The **==** and **!=** test for the equality and inequality of strings. The **=~** and **!~** operators test a string against a regular expression and test to see if a pattern match is successful or not. The regular expression can contain any of the shell special characters. In the next example, any value of greeting that begins with an upper- or lowercase *h* will match the regular expression, **[Hh]***.

```
if ( $greeting =~ [Hh]* ) then
    echo Informal Greeting
endif
```

Like the BASH shell, the TCSH shell also has several special operators that test the status of files. Many of these operators are the same. In the next example, the **if** command tests to see if the file **mydata** is readable. Table 16-5 lists these operators, and Table 16-6 lists TCSH shell commands and variables.

```
if ( -r mydata ) then
    echo Informal Greeting
endif
```

Shell Conditions: if-then, if-then-else, switch

The TCSH shell has a set of conditional control structures with which you make decisions about what Linux commands to execute. Many of these conditional control structures are similar to conditional control structures found in the BASH shell. There are, however, some key differences. The TCSH shell **if** structure ends with the keyword **endif**. The **switch** structure uses the keyword **case** differently. It ends with the keyword **endsw** and uses the keyword **breaksw** instead of two semicolons. Furthermore, there are two **if** control structures: a simple version that executes only one command,

and a more complex version that can execute several commands as well as alternative commands. The simple version of **if** consists of the keyword **if** followed by a test and a single Linux command. The complex version ends with the keyword **endif**. The TCSH shell's conditional control structures are listed in Table 16-7.

if-then   The **if-then** structure places a condition on several Linux commands. That condition is an expression. If the expression results in a value other than 0, then the expression is true, and the commands within the **if** structure are executed. If the expression results in a 0 value, then the expression is false, and the commands within the **if** structure are not executed.

The **if-then** structure begins with the keyword **if** and is followed by an expression enclosed in parentheses. The keyword **then** follows right after the expression. You can then specify any number of Linux commands on the following lines. The keyword **endif** ends the **if** command. Notice that, whereas in the BASH shell the **then** keyword is on a line of its own, in the TCSH shell, **then** is on the same line as the test expression. The syntax for the **if-then** structure is shown here:

```
if ( Expression ) then
        Commands
    endif
```

The **ifls** script shown next allows you to list files by size. If you enter an **s** at the prompt, each file in the current directory is listed, followed by the number of blocks it uses. If the user enters anything else, the **if** test fails and the script does nothing.

ifls

```
#
echo -n "Please enter option: "
set option = $<

if ($option == "s") then
        echo Listing files by size
        ls -s
    endif
```

```
> ifls
Please enter option: s
Listing files by size
total 2
    1 monday    2 today
>
```

if-then-else   Often, you need to choose between two alternatives based on whether or not an expression is true. The **else** keyword allows an **if** structure to choose between two alternatives. If the expression is true, then those commands immediately following the test expression are executed. If the expression is false, those commands following the **else** keyword are executed. The syntax for the **if-else** command is shown here:

```
if ( Expression ) then
        Commands
     else
        Commands
endif
```

The **elsels** script in the next example executes the **ls** command to list files with two different possible options, either by size or with all file information. If the user enters an **s**, files are listed by size; otherwise, all file information is listed. Notice how the syntax differs from the BASH shell version of the **elsels** script described in the previous chapter.

elsels

```
#
echo Enter s to list file sizes,
echo otherwise all file information is listed.
echo -n "Please enter option: "
set option = $<

if ($option == "s") then
    ls -s
    else
    ls -l
endif
echo Good-bye
```

```
> elsels
Enter s to list file sizes,
otherwise all file information is listed.
Please enter option: s
total 2
    1 monday      2 today
Good-bye
>
```

switch   The **switch** structure chooses among several possible alternatives. It is very similar to the BASH shell's **case** structure. A choice is made by comparing a string with several possible patterns. Each possible pattern is associated with a set of commands. If a match is found, the associated commands are performed. The **switch** structure begins with the keyword **switch** and a test string within parentheses. The string is often derived from a variable evaluation. A set of patterns then follows. Each pattern is preceded with the keyword **case** and terminated with a colon. Commands associated with this choice are listed after the colon. The commands are terminated with the keyword **breaksw**. After all the listed patterns, the keyword **endsw** ends the **switch** structure. The syntax for the **switch** structure is shown here:

```
switch (test-string)
    case pattern:
            commands
            breaksw
    case pattern:
            commands
            breaksw
    default:
            commands
            breaksw
    endsw
```

Each pattern will be matched against the test string until a match is found. If no match is found, the default option is executed. The default choice is represented with the keyword **default**. The **default** is optional. You do not have to put it in. However, it is helpful for notifying the user of test strings with no match.

A **switch** structure is often used to implement menus. In the program **lschoice**, in the next example, the user is asked to enter an option for listing files in different ways. Notice the **default** option that warns of invalid input.

lschoice

```
#
echo s. List Sizes
echo l. List All File Information
echo c. List C Files

echo -n "Please enter choice: "
set choice = $<
```

```
switch ($choice)
   case s:
      ls -s
      breaksw
   case l:
      ls -l
      breaksw
   case c:
      ls *.c
      breaksw
   default:
      echo Invalid Option
      breaksw
   endsw
```

```
> lschoice
s. List Sizes
l. List All File Information
c. List C Files
Please enter choice: c
io.c    lib.c    main.c
>
```

Loops: while and foreach

The TCSH shell has a set of loop control structures that allow you to repeat Linux commands: **while**, **foreach**, and **repeat**. The TCSH shell's loop control structures are listed in Table 16-7. The **while** structure operates like corresponding structures found in programming languages. Like the TCSH shell's **if** structure, the **while** structure tests the result of an expression. The TCSH shell's **foreach** structure, like the **for** and **for-in** structures in the BASH shell, does not perform any tests. It simply progresses through a list of values, assigning each value in turn to a specified variable. In this respect, the **foreach** structure is very different from corresponding structures found in programming languages.

while   The **while** loop repeats commands. A **while** loop begins with the keyword **while** and is followed by an expression enclosed in parentheses. The end of the loop is specified by the keyword **end**. The syntax for the **while** loop is shown here:

```
while ( expression )
      commands
   end
```

The **while** can easily be combined with a **switch** structure to drive a menu. In the next example, notice that the menu contains a **quit** option that will set the value of **again** to **no** and stop the loop.

lschoicew

```
#
set again=yes

while ($again == yes)
echo "1. List Sizes"
echo "2. List All File Information"
echo "3. List C Files"
echo "4. Quit"
echo -n "Please enter choice: "
set choice = $<

switch ($choice)
   case 1:
      ls -s
      breaksw
   case 2:
      ls -l
      breaksw
   case 3:
      ls *.c
      breaksw
   case 4:
      set again = no
      echo Good-bye
      breaksw
   default
      echo Invalid Option
   endsw

end
```

```
> lschoicew
1. List Sizes
2. List All File Information
3. List C Files
4. Quit
Please enter choice: 3
```

```
main.c    lib.c    file.c
1. List Sizes
2. List All File Information
3. List C Files
4. Quit
Please enter choice: 4
Good-bye
>
```

foreach   The **foreach** structure is designed to sequentially reference a list of values. It is very similar to the BASH shell's **for-in** structure. The **foreach** structure takes two operands—a variable and a list of values enclosed in parentheses. Each value in the list is assigned to the variable in the **foreach** structure. Like the **while** structure, the **foreach** structure is a loop. Each time through the loop, the next value in the list is assigned to the variable. When the end of the list is reached, the loop stops. Like the **while** loop, the body of a **foreach** loop ends with the keyword **end**. The syntax for the **foreach** loop is shown here:

```
foreach variable ( list of values )
     commands
end
```

In the **mylist** script, in the next example, the user simply outputs a list of each item with today's date. The list of items makes up the list of values read by the **foreach** loop. Each item is consecutively assigned to the variable grocery.

mylist

```
#
set tdate='date '+%D''

foreach grocery ( milk cookies apples cheese )
    echo "$grocery   $tdate"
end
```

```
$ mylist
milk        12/23/96
cookies     12/23/96
apples      12/23/96
cheese      12/23/96
$
```

The **foreach** loop is useful for managing files. In the **foreach** structure, you can use shell special characters in a pattern to generate a list of file names for use as your list of values. This generated list of file names then becomes the list referenced by the **foreach** structure. An asterisk by itself generates a list of all files and directories. ***.c** lists files with the **.c** extension. These are usually C source code files. The next example makes a backup of each file and places the backup in a directory called **sourcebak**. The pattern ***.c** generates a list of file names that the **foreach** structure can operate on.

cbackup

```
#

foreach backfile ( *.c )
    cp $backfile sourcebak/$backfile
    echo $backfile
end
```

```
> cbackup
io.c
lib.c
main.c
```

The **foreach** structure without a specified list of values takes as its list of values the command line arguments. The arguments specified on the command line when the shell file was invoked become a list of values referenced by the **foreach** structure. The variable used in the **foreach** structure is set automatically to each argument value in sequence. The first time through the loop, the variable is set to the value of the first argument. The second time, it is set to the value of the second argument, and so on.

In the **mylistarg** script in the next example, there is no list of values specified in the **foreach** loop. Instead, the **foreach** loop consecutively reads the values of command line arguments into the grocery variable. When all the arguments have been read, the loop ends.

mylistarg

```
#
set tdate='date '+%D''

foreach grocery ( $argv[*] )
    echo "$grocery    $tdate"
end
```

```
$ mylistarg milk cookies apples cheese
milk       12/23/96
cookies    12/23/96
apples     12/23/96
cheese     12/23/96
$
```

You can explicitly reference the command line argument by using the argv[*] special argument variable. In the next example, a list of C program files is entered on the command line when the shell file **cbackuparg** is invoked. In the **foreach** loop, argv[*] references all the arguments on the command line. Each argument will be consecutively assigned to the variable backfile in the **foreach** loop. The first time through the loop, $backfile is the same as $argv[1]. The second time through, it is the same as $argv[2]. The variable argnum is used to reference each argument. Both the argument and the value of backfile are displayed to show that they are the same.

cbackuparg

```
#

@ argnum = 1
foreach backfile ($argv[*])
    cp $backfile sourcebak/$backfile
    echo "$backfile $argv[$argnum]"
    @ argnum = $argnum + 1
end
```

```
> cbackuparg   main.c   lib.c   io.c
main.c main.c
lib.c lib.c
io.c io.c
```

Summary

You can use the TCSH shell's **history** utility to list and reference previous commands that you have executed. You can even edit those commands and execute the edited versions. With the TCSH shell's **alias** command, you can give another name to a command. The alias can reference a command or a command with its arguments.

The TCSH shell has a set of features that you can turn on and off. Some commonly used features are **ignoreeof**, **noclobber**, and **noglob**. The **ignoreeof** feature prevents accidental logouts, and **noclobber** prevents the redirection operation from overwriting existing files. The **noglob** feature treats special characters as merely ordinary characters.

Like the BASH and PDKSH shells, the TCSH shell also has a shell programming capability that operates like a programming language. You can define variables and assign values to them. You can use control structures to implement loops and conditions. You place variable definitions, shell commands, and control structures in a shell script and execute the script, just as you would do with a program.

Variables can be either strings or numeric variables. String variables are declared and assigned values with the **set** command. Numeric variables are declared and assigned values with the **@** command. The **@** command allows you to use complex arithmetic, relational, and bitwise expressions whose results can be assigned to a numeric variable. You can also declare environment variables. An environment variable is known to any subshells of the shell it was defined in. Environment variables are defined and assigned values with the **setenv** command. They are most often used for shell special variables.

The loop and condition structures correspond to similar structures in programming languages. The loop structures are the **while** and the **foreach** loops. The condition structures are the **if** and **switch** conditions. The **while** loop and **if** condition operate much as they do in programming languages. The loop continues until a test expression is false. The **if** condition executes its commands if its test expression is true. The test expression is a TCSH shell expression. The operators used in a TCSH shell expression are similar to those found in the C programming language. There is a wide range of assignment, arithmetic, relational, and bitwise operators, many of which are not available in the BASH or PDKSH shell. Like C program expressions, a TCSH shell expression is true if it results in a non-zero value; it is false if it results in a 0 value.

The **switch** structure works like a restricted version of the **if** structure. The **switch** structure compares a string with a set of possible patterns. If a match is found, then operations associated with that matched pattern are executed. **switch** is useful for implementing menus, from which a user makes a choice among several possible options.

The **foreach** structure runs through a list of values, assigning each value in turn to a specified variable. There is no test. The list of values can be generated by a pattern and shell special characters. For example, the asterisk, *****, will generate a list of your file names. A list of values can also be specified by a set of words. Each word is then a value assigned in turn to the **for** variable. The loop will always continue until all values have been assigned.

Event References	Function
!*event num*	References an event with event number
!*characters*	References an event with beginning characters
!?*pattern*?	References an event with a pattern in the event
!-*event num*	References an event with an offset from the first event
!*num*-*num*	References a range of events
Event Word References	
!*event num:word num*	References a particular word in an event
!*event num*:^	References first argument (second word) in an event
!*event num*:$	References last argument in an event
!*event num*:^-$	References all arguments in an event
!*event num*:*	References all arguments in an event
Event Editing Substitutions	
!*event num*:**s**/*pattern*/*newtext*/	Edits an event with a pattern substitution. References a particular word in an event.
!*event num*:**sg**/*pattern*/*newtext*/	Performs a global substitution on all instances of a pattern in the event
!*event num*:**s**/*pattern*/*newtext*/**p**	Suppresses execution of the edited event

Table 16-1. *TCSH Shell History Commands*

Shell Features	Function
set and **unset**	Shell features are turned on and off with the **set** and **unset** commands $ **set** *feature-variable* $ **set noclobber** *set noclobber on* $ **unset noclobber** *set noclobber off*
echo	Displays each command before executing it
ignoreeof	Disables CTRL-D logout
noclobber	Does not overwrite files through redirection
noglob	Disables special characters used for file name expansion: *****, **?**, **~**, and **[]**
notify	Notifies user immediately when background job is completed
verbose	Displays command after a history command reference

Table 16-2.   *TCSH Shell Features*

System Determined		Description
home	HOME	Path name for user's home directory
	LOGNAME	Login name
cwd		Path name of current working directory
Redefinable Special Variables		
shell	SHELL	Path name of program for login shell
path	PATH	List of path names for directories searched for executable commands
prompt		Primary shell prompt

Table 16-3.   *TCSH Shell Special Variables*

Redefinable Special Variables	Description
`mail`	Name of mail file checked by mail utility for received messages
User-Defined Special Variables	
`cdpath`	Path names for directories searched by **cd** command for subdirectories
`history`	Number of commands in your history list
`savehist`	Number of commands in your history list that you save for the next login session. Commands are saved in a file named **.history**
`EXINIT`	Initialization commands for Ex/Vi editor
`TERM`	Terminal name

Table 16-3. *TCSH Shell Special Variables (continued)*

Assignment Operators	Function/Description
`=`	Assignment
`+=`	Adds to expression and then assigns
`-=`	Subtracts from expression and then assigns
`*=`	Multiplies with expression and then assigns
`/=`	Divides into expression and then assigns
`%=`	Modulo operation with expression and then assigns
`++`	Increment variable
`--`	Decrement variable

Table 16-4. *Numeric Operators*

Arithmetic Operators	Function/Description
–	Minus unary operator
+	Addition
–	Subtraction
*	Multiplication
/	Division
%	Modulo
Relational Operators	
>	Greater-than
<	Less-than
>=	Greater-than-or-equal
<=	Less-than-or-equal
!=	Not-equal
==	Equal

Table 16-4. *Numeric Operators* (continued)

String Comparisons	Function/Description
==	Equal strings
!=	Not-equal strings
=~	Compares string to a pattern to test if equal. The pattern can be any regular expression
!~	Compares string to a pattern to test if not equal. The pattern can be any regular expression

Table 16-5. *Expression Operators*

Logical Operations	Function/Description
&&	Logical AND
||	Logical OR
!	Logical NOT
File Tests	
-e	File exists
-r	File is readable
-w	File can be written to, modified
-x	File is executable
-d	File name is a directory name
-f	File is an ordinary file
-o	File is owned by user
-z	File is empty

Table 16-5. *Expression Operators (continued)*

Shell Commands	Function
echo	Displays values **-n** eliminates output newline
eval	Executes the command line
exec	Executes command in place of current process. Does not generate a new subshell; uses the current one
exit	Exits from the current shell
setenv *var*	Makes variable available for reference by each new subshell (call-by-reference)

Table 16-6. *TCSH Shell Commands and Variables*

Shell Commands	Function
`printenv`	Displays values of environment variables
`set`	Assigns new values to variables. Used alone, lists all defined variables
`@`	Assigns numeric expressions
`shift`	Moves each command line argument to the left so the number used to reference it is one less than before—argument $3 would then be referenced by $2, and so on; $1 is lost
`unset`	Undefines a variable
`unsetenv`	Undefines an environment variable
Command Line Arguments	
`$argv[0]` `$0`	Name of Linux command
`$argv[n]` `$n`	The *n*th command line argument beginning from 1, **$1-$n** You can use **set** to change them
`$argv[*]` `$*`	All the command line arguments beginning from 1. You can use **set** to change them
`$#argv` `$#`	The count of the command line arguments

Table 16-6.   *TCSH Shell Commands and Variables* (continued)

Conditional Control Structures:
`if-then, else, switch`

`if`(*expression*) `then`
 commands
 `endif`
	If the expression is true, the following commands are executed. You can specify more than one Unix command

`if`(*expression*) `then`
 command
 `else`
 command
 `endif`
	If the expression is true, the command after **then** is executed. If the expression is false, the command following **else** is executed

Table 16-7.   *TCSH Shell Control Structures*

Conditional Control Structures:
`if-then, else, switch`

`switch`(*string*)
`case` **pattern**:
command
`breaksw`
`default:`
command
`endsw`
	Allows you to choose among several alternative commands

Loop Control Structures:
`while` **and** `foreach`

`while`(*expression*) *command* `end`	Executes commands as long as the expression is true
`foreach` *variable* **(arg-list)** *command* `end`	Iterates the loop for as many arguments as there are in the argument list. Each time through the loop, the variable is set to the next argument in the list; operates like **for-in** in the Bourne shell

Table 16-7. *TCSH Shell Control Structures* (continued)

PART FIVE

Editors and Utilities

Chapter Seventeen

The Vi Editor

Although many different kinds of editors may be available on any given Linux system, all systems have the two standard editors: Ed and Vi. Ed and Vi are standard applications that were originally developed for Unix systems along with the Ex editor. Vi, which stands for "visual," remains one of the most widely used editors in Linux. The line editor, Ed, is rarely used. As a line editor, it displays and edits only one line at a time, making it difficult to use. The Vi editor displays a whole screen of data at a time and allows you to edit any data shown on the screen.

When Unix was first developed, the Vi editor represented a significant advancement over other text editors of the time. Since then, more powerful and easy-to-use editors, such as WordPerfect, have become available on many Unix and Linux systems. Your particular Linux system may have a text editor or word processor that you are more familiar with. If so, you do not need to study the Vi editor. The Caldera Network Desktop contains the Crisplite editor, which is much easier to use than Vi. Still, it is helpful to know Vi, since it is standard on all Unix and Linux systems. If you ever have to work on another system with a different word processor than the one you use, you know that you can always use Vi. The Vi editor is the same on all systems and in all versions of Linux and Unix.

Because of its visual interface, Vi is easier than the Ed line editor for beginners to learn. However, Vi is also a very sophisticated editor with a variety of complex commands. It is easy to become confused and lost when first attempting to learn the features of this editor. There are often several ways to do the same operation with slightly different effects. This chapter will focus first on a central core of commands needed to perform basic editing operations. Once these core commands are mastered, you can consider the more complex operations described in sections that follow.

Vi Command, Input, and Line Editing Modes

Editors use a keyboard for two very different operations: to specify editing commands and to receive character input. As editing commands, certain keys will perform deletions, some will execute changes, and others will perform cursor movement. As character input, keys will represent characters that can be entered into the file that is being edited. In many common PC editors these two different functions are divided among different keys on the keyboard. Alphabetic keys are reserved for character input. Function keys and control keys specify editing commands such as deleting text or moving the cursor.

Such PC-style editors can rely on the existence of an extended keyboard that includes function and control keys. Unix, however, was designed to be independent of any specific type of keyboard. Any type of terminal or personal computer can be mapped into a Unix system. Editors in Unix were designed to assume a minimal keyboard with alphabetic characters, some control characters, as well as the ESC and ENTER keys. Instead of dividing the command and input functions among different keys, the Vi editor has two separate modes of operation for the keyboard: command mode and input mode. In command mode, all the keys on the keyboard become editing commands. In the input mode, the keys on the keyboard become input characters.

When you change modes, the functionality of the keyboard changes. When you invoke the Vi editor, you are placed in command mode. Each key now becomes an editing command. Pressing a key executes a certain command. For example, pressing the **x** key deletes a character from your text. Pressing the **1** key moves the cursor right one character. Some of these editing commands, such as **a** or **i**, enter the input mode. Upon pressing the **i** key, you leave the command mode and enter the input mode.

Once in the input mode, the keyboard again changes functionality. Each key now represents a character to be input to the text. The keyboard becomes like a typewriter. When you press a key, its corresponding character is added to the text. For example, pressing the **x** key simply adds an *x* to the text. Pressing the TAB key enters a tab character into the file. The one exception is ESC. Pressing ESC automatically returns you to the command mode, and the keys once again become editor commands. You can then easily re-enter the input mode with any of the input editing commands. As you edit text, you will find yourself constantly moving from the command mode to the input mode and back again.

Though the Vi command mode handles most editing operations, there are some, such as file saving and global substitutions, that it cannot perform. For such operations you need to execute line editing commands. You enter the line editing mode using the Vi colon command, **:**. The colon is a special command that allows you to perform one line editing operation. Upon pressing the colon, a line opens up at the bottom of the screen with the cursor placed at the beginning of the line. You are now in the line editing mode. In this mode, you enter an editing command on a line, press ENTER, and the command is executed. Entry into this mode is only temporary. Upon pressing ENTER, you are automatically returned to the Vi command mode, and the cursor returns to its previous position on the screen. Figures 17-1 and 17-2 illustrate the three different modes of operation in Vi.

The command and input operations constitute two very separate modes. Add to this the line editing mode, and you are faced with three very different modes of operation in Vi. The line editing mode operates on a line: you type in a command with its arguments and terminate the command by pressing ENTER. The Vi command mode, however, operates by single keys. Simply pressing a key or sequence of keys executes an editor command. The Vi input mode inputs characters into a text file. Any key is a valid character except for ESC. The ESC key returns you to the command mode.

Creating, Saving, and Quitting a File in Vi

With the Vi editor you can create, save, close, and quit files. The commands for each are not all that similar. Saving and quitting a file involves the use of special line editing commands, whereas closing a file is a Vi editing command. Creation of a file is usually specified on the same shell command line that invokes the Vi editor.

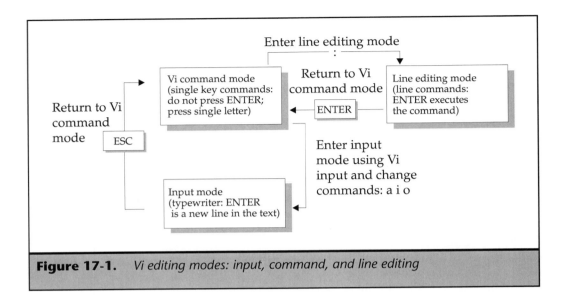

Figure 17-1.   *Vi editing modes: input, command, and line editing*

To edit a file, type **vi** and the name of a file on the shell command line. If a file by that name does not exist, the system will create it. In effect, giving the name of a file that does not yet exist instructs the Vi editor to create that file. The following command invokes the Vi editor, working on the file **booklist**. If **booklist** does not yet exist, the Vi editor will create it.

```
$ vi booklist
```

After executing the **vi** command, you enter Vi's command mode. Each key becomes a Vi editing command, and the screen becomes a window onto the text file. Text is displayed screen by screen. The first screen of text is displayed, and the cursor is positioned in the upper-left corner. With a newly created file, there is no text to display. This fact is indicated by a column of tildes at the left-hand side of the screen. The tildes represent that part of a screen that is not part of the file.

Remember that when you first enter the Vi editor you are in the command mode. To enter text, you need to enter the input mode. In the command mode, the **a** key is the editor command for appending text. Pressing this key places you in the input mode. Now, the keyboard operates like a typewriter and you can input text to the file. If you press ENTER, you will merely start a new line of text. After entering text, you can leave the input mode and return to the command mode by pressing ESC.

Once finished with the editing session, you exit Vi by typing two capital Z's, **ZZ**. You hold down the SHIFT key and press Z twice. This sequence first saves the file and then exits the Vi editor, returning you to the Linux shell.

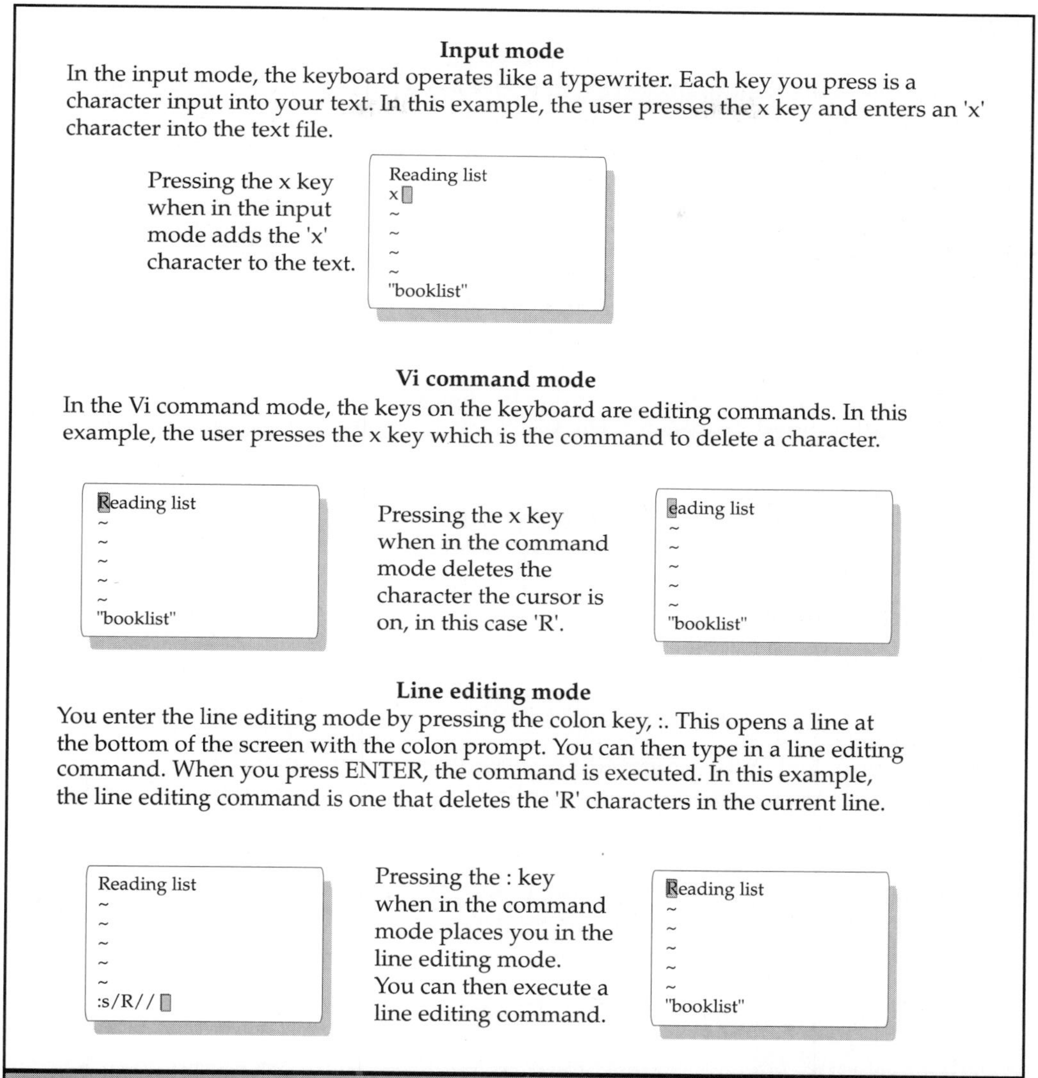

Input mode

In the input mode, the keyboard operates like a typewriter. Each key you press is a character input into your text. In this example, the user presses the x key and enters an 'x' character into the text file.

Pressing the x key when in the input mode adds the 'x' character to the text.

```
Reading list
x
~
~
~
~
"booklist"
```

Vi command mode

In the Vi command mode, the keys on the keyboard are editing commands. In this example, the user presses the x key which is the command to delete a character.

```
Reading list
~
~
~
~
~
"booklist"
```

Pressing the x key when in the command mode deletes the character the cursor is on, in this case 'R'.

```
eading list
~
~
~
~
~
"booklist"
```

Line editing mode

You enter the line editing mode by pressing the colon key, :. This opens a line at the bottom of the screen with the colon prompt. You can then type in a line editing command. When you press ENTER, the command is executed. In this example, the line editing command is one that deletes the 'R' characters in the current line.

```
Reading list
~
~
~
~
~
:s/R//
```

Pressing the : key when in the command mode places you in the line editing mode.
You can then execute a line editing command.

```
Reading list
~
~
~
~
~
"booklist"
```

Figure 17-2.   *Vi editing operations in input, command, and line editing modes*

When you edit a file, it is first read into a work buffer. Any changes or additions of text are made to the copy of the file in the work buffer. The original file remains on the disk. Only by executing a save command is the original file overwritten by the work buffer version. At the end of each session, the **zz** command will save the file before quitting, overwriting the original file with the work buffer version.

However, you may want to save a file several times throughout your editing session. Saving a file is performed by the line editing command **w**, which writes a file to the disk. It is equivalent to the Save command found in other word processors. To save a file in Vi, you first press the colon key to access the line editing mode, then type in a **w** and press ENTER. The file is saved, and you automatically return to the Vi command mode.

A mistake that beginners often make in attempting to save a file is to forget to press ESC first when in the input mode. The colon command is an editing command. It can only be executed within the command mode. If you are in the input mode and press the colon key, it will simply be taken as a colon character and input into the text. If you are in the input mode and you want to save your file, you must first press ESC to exit the input mode and enter the command mode. Then a **:w** command will save the file. Notice that the **:w** command with a file name also functions like the Save As operation in other word processors. The file currently being worked on is saved as another file.

You will find that you also need to use the **:w** command whenever you edit an unnamed file. When you invoke the Vi editor without a file name argument, you will automatically be editing an unnamed file. In the next example, the user invokes the Vi editor on the shell command line but does not specify any filename. In this case the user will edit an unnamed file.

```
$ vi
```

You can input text and perform editing operations on an unnamed file, but no actual file has yet been created. If you are editing an unnamed file, the Vi editor will not allow you to use **ZZ** to exit an editing session—you must first create the file. You do this using the **:w** save command followed by the new file's name. After you press the colon key, a line appears at the bottom of the screen. Next you enter the letter **w**, a space, the name of the file, and then press ENTER.

```
:w booklist
```

After pressing ENTER, you will return to the Vi command mode, and the cursor will return to its previous location on the screen. The new file name will be displayed at the bottom of the screen, and the **ZZ** command will now work. Note that if there already is a file with the name you selected, the save operation will fail. In this event, simply repeat the **:w** command with another file name.

You can quit the Vi editor using the **:q** command. Unlike the **ZZ** command, the **:q** command does not perform any save operation before it quits. In this respect, it has one major constraint. If there have been any modifications to your file since the last save operation, then the **:q** command will fail and you will not leave the editor. However, you can override this restriction by placing a **!** qualifier after the **:q** command. The command **:q!** will quit the Vi editor without saving any modifications made to the file in that session since the last save.

Many of the line editing commands correspond to Vi commands. A case in point is the **zz** Vi command. You can combine the commands **w** and **q** to perform the same operations as the **zz** Vi command. The command **:wq** will save a file and leave the Vi editor. **:wq** is equivalent to **zz**.

Managing Editing Modes in Vi

Saving, quitting, and adding text to a file involve all the editing modes available in Vi. Upon invoking Vi, you are placed into the command mode. The **a** command places you in the input mode so that you can add text. The ESC key returns you from the input mode to the command mode. To save or quit a file, you must enter the line editing mode with the colon command. The line editing commands **w** and **q** will save and quit the file. Pressing ENTER after entering the line editing command both executes the command and returns you to the Vi command mode.

Much of the difficulty in managing the Vi editor is keeping track of which mode you are in. During a Vi editing session, the keyboard is constantly changing state between the command and input modes. The two modes are exclusive. While in the input mode no editing commands may be executed, and while in the command mode nothing may be input. There is usually no alert telling you whether you are in the command or input mode. This can be devastating if you think you are in the input mode but actually are in the command mode. If, while in the command mode, you press keys thinking you are entering text, you are in fact executing a series of editing commands. Unintended editing operations could suddenly take place on the text.

If you lose track of which mode you are in, you can use ESC to indirectly determine the mode. Pressing ESC while in input mode returns you to command mode. However, pressing ESC while in command mode simply makes the computer beep. If you press ESC and hear a beep, you were already in command mode. If nothing happens, you were in input mode and have now returned to command mode.

A common error occurs if you attempt to end the editing session while in input mode. You can only end an editing session in command mode. Remember that entering **zz** while in input mode simply adds the characters to the text. Two Z's will appear on the screen, and Vi will remain in the input mode waiting for further input. To end an editing session when in input mode, you must first exit input mode by pressing ESC, and then type **zz**. Once in the command mode the keys become editing commands and two capital Z's, **zz**, are the command for ending the editing session and saving the text.

Vi Editing Commands:
Common Operations

This section presents a subset of Vi's many editing commands. Basic cursor movement, input, search, and editing operations are discussed. The Vi editor is designed to operate on many different text components, including lines, characters, words, sentences, and even paragraphs. This section will limit discussion to single characters and lines. Commands for operating on textual components such as words and sentences are discussed in the section on advanced commands later in the chapter. Figure 17-3 lists this basic set of Vi commands that you need to get started in Vi, and Table 17-1 lists the commands commonly used to move through the text.

Moving Through the Text in Vi

You can move through the text by moving the cursor, scrolling screen by screen, or moving to a specific line. Vi has the basic cursor movements for moving up and down, left and right, across the text displayed on the screen. You can also move forward and backward through the text a screen at a time. Sometimes you may need to move to a specific line in the text. You can do so in Vi using a line number.

Cursor Movement

While in command mode, you can move the cursor across the text by using the keys for movement commands. The **h**, **j**, **k**, and **l** commands perform the basic cursor movement operations. The **h** and **l** keys move the cursor horizontally across characters in a line. The **h** key moves the cursor one character to the left, and the **l** key moves it one character to the right. The **j** and **k** keys move the cursor up and down lines. The **j** key moves down one line and the **k** key moves up one line. Notice that if you hold a cursor command key down, the command will be repeated. Holding down the **l** key will move you to the end of a line.

Notice also, that to make moving the cursor easy, these keys are positioned near or under the fingertips of your right hand. When editing, you frequently need to move the cursor across characters in a line and from one line to another. Many keyboards also have a set of arrow keys that you can use instead of the **h**, **j**, **k**, and **l** keys. In addition, you can use ENTER in place of the **j** key to move the cursor down a line. The SPACEBAR can be used in place of the **l** key to move the cursor left one character.

Each text line begins at the left column of the screen and ends when you press ENTER. If the cursor is at the end of the line and you press the **l** key to move right, the computer will beep and the cursor will not move. The same is true if the cursor is on the first character of a line and you press the **h** key to move left. The beep indicates that the cursor has reached a text boundary.

The end of the line is not necessarily the right side of the screen; it is wherever you pressed ENTER. When moving to the right on a line with the **l** key, the cursor will stop where the text for that line ends. You can only move across text that actually exists in

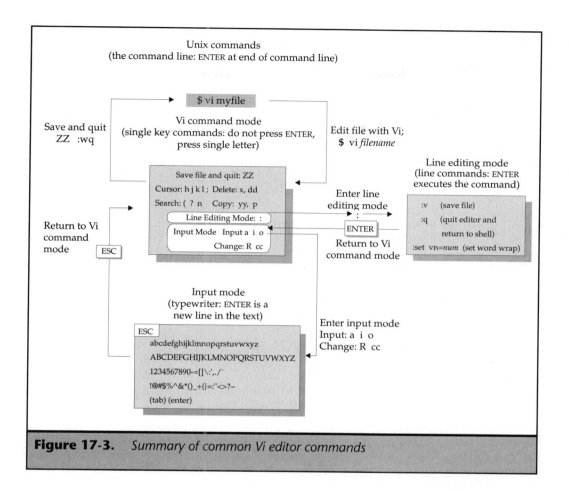

Figure 17-3. *Summary of common Vi editor commands*

the file. The space between the end of a line and the right side of the screen is dead space on the screen; it is not part of the text file. If the cursor is positioned at the end of a line and you then move the cursor to the next line, you will notice that the cursor moves to the end of the next line.

The screen operates like a window on your text file, showing only one screen of text at a time. You can move this window forward or backward across your text using various commands. If you position the cursor at the top or bottom line on the screen, the **j** and **k** keys will cause the screen to scroll vertically throughout the text file, line by line. The **j** key moves the cursor down the screen one line at a time. Once the cursor is on the last line of the screen, pressing the **j** key will move the screen down one line, losing one line off the top of the screen and including a new line at the bottom of the screen. Continually pressing the **j** key while the cursor is positioned at the last line

Cursor Movement	Effect	Delete	Effect
h	Left	x	Deletes character
l	Right	dd	Deletes a line
k	Up		
j	Down	**Change**	**Effect**
CTRL-F	Next screen	r	Replaces a character
CTRL-B	Previous screen	cc	Changes a line
g	Last line specific line	R	Overwrites
Input		**Move**	
a	Appends	p	Inserts deleted/copied text
i	Inserts	dd p	Moves a line
o	Opens a line		
Search		**Copy**	
/	Searches pattern	yy p	Copies a line
?	Searches pattern		
n	Repeats search		

Table 17-1. *Common Vi Editor Commands*

on the screen moves the screen down the text file, line by line. The reverse is true for the **k** key.

You also can move through the text a whole screen at a time using the CTRL-F and CTRL-B keys. The CTRL-F key moves forward one screen of text, and CTRL-B moves backward one screen of text. Once you have moved forward in your file, you may want to move back toward the beginning of your text. You can do so, screen by screen, by pressing CTRL-B.

Line Numbers: G

You can move to a particular line using the **G** command and a line number. Vi sequentially numbers each line of text. The **G** command (it must be uppercase *G*) moves the cursor to a particular line. You first enter the line number and then press the **G** key. The cursor then moves to that line. You can also use the **G** command to move quickly to the end of your file. If no line number is entered before you press the **G** key, then the cursor moves directly to the end of the file. The **G** key by itself is a quick way to locate the end of a very large file.

Modifying Text in Vi: Input, Deletions, and Changes

Editing your text usually involves modifying it in some way. You can add more text at different places in your file. You may decide to delete text that you have already entered. Or you may need to change part of your text. Vi has an extensive set of commands for inputting text in different ways as well as deleting or changing different text segments, such as characters, lines, sentences, words, and paragraphs. Vi also allows you to undo any changes you make to your file, even text that you have input. The undo command, **u**, will undo the previous Vi command. Be sure to keep this in mind as you make changes to your file. It is very easy, at times, to make unintentional changes to your file. You can easily undo such changes with the **u** command.

Input

You already know that when the Vi editor is invoked and a new file is created, you are placed in command mode. To enter text, you need to execute an input command, such as **a**, that will place you in the input mode. Once in the input mode, the keyboard becomes like a typewriter and any character you press is entered into the text.

Once in the input mode, you may enter as much text as you wish until you press ESC. You can also delete the most recently entered character by pressing BACKSPACE. Use of the BACKSPACE key is restricted to input mode and erases only characters to the left. By continually pressing BACKSPACE, you can erase all the characters keyed in since entering input mode.

Most PC-style word processors automatically wrap text for you when you reach the right margin, but Vi does not do so automatically. In Vi a new line is created in the text only when you press ENTER while in the input mode. Though Vi does not automatically insert new lines when the cursor reaches the end of the screen, it may appear that way on the screen display. Lines longer than the length of the screen are wrapped around to appear as two lines on the screen. However, the editor treats them as one. You can, if you wish, set a Vi option that will automatically insert new lines at a specified margin. This is the word-wrap margin, and you set it with the line editing command **:set wm**=*col*. In this case, *col* is the column for the right margin. The command **:set wm=70** will set the word-wrap margin to the 70th column. Whenever you reach the 70th column when entering text, a new line is automatically inserted.

There are several input commands, each of which enters the input mode at a different point in the text relative to the cursor. The most common input commands are **a** (append), **i** (insert), and **o** (open). The **a** key places the user into input after the character the cursor is on. The **i** key places the user into input before the character the cursor is on. The **o** key opens a new line below the line the cursor is on and places the user into input at the beginning of that new line. Because the **i** command inserts before the character the cursor is on, it is often used to insert text before a word. If the cursor is on the first character of a word, the **i** command will enter the insert mode before the word. The **a** command can be used to add text after a word. If the cursor is on the last character of a word, the **a** command will enter the input mode after the word.

The difference between the **i** and **a** commands becomes significant when you want to add text to either the beginning or end of a line. You use the **i** command to insert text at the beginning of a line, and the **a** command to add text to the end of a line. To insert text at the beginning of a line, you should place the cursor on the first character in the line. The **i** command will then insert text before that character. To add text at the end of a line, you should position the cursor on the last character in the line. The **a** command will then add text after that character. Be careful not to confuse the two commands. If the cursor is positioned on the last character in a line and you press the **i** key, the new text will be inserted before that last character. The same kind of error occurs if you use the **a** command to insert characters at the beginning of a line. When the cursor is positioned at the first character in a line and you press the **a** key, the new text is added after that first character, not at the beginning of the line.

Instead of just adding text on a given line, you may want to insert a whole new line. For this you use the **o** command. It can be thought of as inserting a line between two lines. You are not limited to input on that line. The new line is only a starting point for entering the input mode. Once in the input mode, pressing ENTER will add as many lines as you wish. In fact, the **o** command is equivalent to first placing the cursor at the end of a line, and pressing the **a** command and then ENTER. The **a** command places you into input and ENTER inserts a new line. The **o** command is often used to add text to the end of a file. The cursor is positioned on the last line of the file and the **o** command then opens up a new line below the end of the file. You then enter into the input mode and can add as much text as you want.

Deletions

The simplest deletion operations are those to delete single characters or whole lines of text. Pressing the **x** key deletes a single character. Whatever character the cursor is on will be deleted. The **dd** sequence of keys deletes the line that the cursor is on.

Changes

You can change any text by first deleting it with deletion commands and then entering the input mode to enter new text. To change a word, you could first repeatedly use the **x** command to delete the word and then use the **i** or **a** command to enter input and type in the new word. The Vi editor has a set of change commands that streamlines this process, automatically deleting words, lines, sentences, and paragraphs and placing you into the input mode. These are covered at length in the advanced section later in the chapter. Here, we will cover changing lines and characters, as those are the simplest operations.

The **cc** sequence of keys changes an entire line. First, **cc** deletes the text on the line, and then it enters input mode. You can then type in new text, until you press ESC to leave input mode. The **cc** command operates like a combination of the **dd** and **o** commands. **dd** deletes the line and **o** opens up a new line.

You use the **r** command to change a single character. The **r** command deletes whatever character the cursor is on and then waits for you to enter a replacement character. The character the cursor is on will be replaced by whatever character you enter. The **r** command, unlike other change commands, does not place you in the input mode. After typing in the replacement character, you remain in command mode.

The **R** key is a replacement command that overwrites text until you press ESC. You are placed in the input mode, but for every character you type in, a corresponding character is deleted from the text. This command may appear similar to an overwrite mode used in other types of word processors, but it is not. Like the **cc** command, you are actually placed in the input mode and must exit that mode with ESC before you can edit any further. Be careful not to confuse **r** and **R**. The command **r** will change only a single character. However, the command **R** will overwrite text until you press ESC. If you accidentally press **R** instead of **r**, you could unintentionally overwrite text. In this case, you need to press ESC and press the **u** command to undo the damage.

Undo

As you delete and change text, you may accidentally delete or change the wrong text and want to restore the text to its original condition. The undo command, **u**, lets you restore the text to its condition before the most recent editing command was executed. The **u** command will undo any modifications made by the input, deletion, and change commands. You may need to use this command a great deal as you learn Vi. It is easy to execute a command accidentally. If you accidentally delete a line, you can press the **u** key to restore the deleted text. If you change a line and decide you don't want the change, you can undo it with the **u** command.

Repeat Factor

You can delete or change more than one line at a time by typing in a number before the delete or change command. In those cases, the number does not represent a line number as it does with the **G** command. Instead, the number functions as a repeat factor. Any number entered before a command repeats that command (with the exception of the **G** command). For example, **3x** will delete three characters instead of one; **2dd** will delete the next two lines.

Again, be sure not to confuse the two uses for the numbers. For example, suppose you intend to use the **G** command to move to a line, then change your mind after entering a line number but before pressing **G**. Entering a line number such as 200 and then changing your mind and entering an **x** instead of a **G** will delete 200 characters. The repeat factor also applies to input and change commands. Let's say you enter the line number 50 and then execute an **i** command, instead of **G**, and input some text. Upon pressing ESC to end the input, the editor will insert 50 copies of the input into the file. Suddenly your file will contain 50 repetitions of the input just entered. If you do change your mind and decide to execute another editing command after entering a line number, you can erase the number by pressing ESC.

Should the mistake occur despite your best efforts, you can correct it with the undo command, **u**. A repeated editing command is taken as one editing operation and can be undone by pressing the **u** key. In the case of the 200 repeated **x** character deletions, all 200 deletions can be undone by pressing the **u** key immediately after the deletions occur.

Breaking and Joining Lines

The process of breaking or joining lines using Vi is more complex than that of PC-style editors. In a PC-style editor you simply press ENTER to break a line, or use BACKSPACE to join lines. In Vi, breaking a line requires the use of an input command to first enter the input mode in which you can then press ENTER. Joining a line requires a whole new Vi command, the uppercase **J** key. You cannot use BACKSPACE to join lines.

To break a line into two lines, place the cursor at the point in the line where you want it to be broken. Then enter the input command **i** or **a**. Remember that **i** inserts before the cursor and **a** appends after the cursor. Once in the input mode, press ENTER. Pressing ESC returns you to command mode. There are now two lines, the first terminated when you press ENTER. To join two lines, press **J**, and the line below the cursor is joined to the line that the cursor is on. It is as if you never pressed ENTER. However, in Vi, the new line character alone cannot be deleted by any of the deletion commands; the **dd** command deletes the new line character along with all the text on the line.

Copying, Moving, and Searching Text in Vi

You can copy and move text from one location to another in your file. Though it is possible to move and copy any text segment, such as words and sentences, this section discusses only the movement and copying of lines. You can also search your text for specific words or patterns. With the Vi editor, you can search forward or backward in your text as well as repeat searches.

Moving and Copying Lines: dd, yy, and p

To move text, you must first delete the text that you want to move. The **dd** command will delete a line. A number entered before the **dd** command will delete that many lines from and including the line that the cursor is on. These deleted lines are placed in the temporary buffer. Next, you move the cursor to the line where you want text inserted. Finally, press the **p** command, and the editor inserts the deleted lines after the line on which the cursor rests.

You can copy lines of text with the **yy** command. Preceding the **yy** command with a number will copy that many lines, including the line that the cursor is on. To copy lines of text, place the cursor on the first line to be copied. Enter the number of lines you want copied, followed immediately with the **yy** command. This command copies the lines to the temporary buffer. Then move the cursor to the line where the copied lines are to be inserted, and press the **p** command. The copied lines are inserted after the line the cursor is on. An uppercase **Y** is the same as the **yy** command and will also copy lines.

Searches

As you work on your text, you may need to search for and locate certain words or parts of words. The Vi editor has the ability to search forward and backward in a file for a given pattern. The slash key (**/**) is the Vi editing command for pattern searches. Pressing the slash key opens up a line at the bottom of the screen. A slash appears at the beginning of the line, and the cursor is positioned after the slash. You then enter the pattern you want to search for. When you press ENTER, the editor will search for the pattern, starting where the cursor was when the slash command was executed, and continuing toward the end of the file. The slash command is a forward search. If the pattern is found, the cursor is positioned at that instance of the pattern.

The question mark key (**?**) performs a pattern search, moving backward in a file. Pressing the question mark key also opens up a line at the bottom of the screen. After you type in a pattern, the search is conducted from the position of the cursor back toward the beginning of the file.

The **n** key is a command to repeat a search. A pattern is first entered and searched with the slash or question mark key. Pressing the **n** key initiates a search for the next instance of the pattern in the file. If the pattern was entered with a slash, the search will be carried out forward in the file. If the pattern was entered with a question mark, the search will be carried out backward toward the beginning of the file. If either the end or beginning of the file is reached, the search will wrap around. You can repeatedly press the **n** key to find more instances of the pattern throughout the file.

Advanced Vi Editing Commands

So far, only the basic Vi editing commands have been discussed, but there are, in fact, many more. Most lowercase editing commands have a corresponding uppercase command that performs the same action with some variation. For example, the lowercase **o**, which opens a line below the current line, has the counterpart **O**, which opens a line above the current line. This section examines different screen movement commands and then the different modifying commands, such as those that perform input, change, and delete operations.

You can also reference your text according to different text segments, such as a word, sentence, or paragraph. In the previous section, you only learned how to reference single characters or whole lines. For example, the **l** command moves the cursor left a character, and the **j** command moves the cursor down a line. However, you can also move across text segments using the **w**, **)**, and **}** commands. A **w** command moves left one word; the right parenthesis, **)**, moves one sentence; and the right brace, **}**, moves one paragraph. You can use these commands to qualify other Vi commands to operate on these text segments. For example, you can qualify the change command, **c**, with a word command, **w**, to change a word, **cw**. You can qualify a **d** command with a **)** command, **d)**, to delete a sentence. The qualifier is entered after the primary command.

Advanced Cursor Movement

Vi has many commands designed to let you move throughout your text any way you wish. You can move to different characters on a line and move across text segments such as words, sentences, and paragraphs. You can also move to different lines of text displayed on your screen: the top, bottom, or middle lines. You can even move to different lines using references such as line numbers, patterns, or marks. For example, you can mark a line with a special code letter and then later return to that line using just the code letter. Table 17-2 lists the Vi cursor movement commands.

Many of these movement commands can be thought of as positional references. For example, a line number or pattern can reference a particular line. A word or sentence command can reference a particular word or sentence. Such commands can be combined with modifying commands to change different text segments. You can combine a word reference with a change command to change a word. You can also combine a pattern with a delete command to delete text up to the line referenced by that pattern. You could combine the reference to the bottom line on the screen with the copy command to copy lines from the cursor to the bottom line. Keep the positional referencing aspect of these movement commands in mind as you examine them in this section. You can use them with commands in the next section to modify your text.

Movement to Referenced Lines: Line Numbers, Patterns, and Marks

Vi organizes text into lines that you can then reference using line numbers, patterns, or marks. As noted in the previous section, you can use the **G** command to locate a line with its number. The **G** command takes a preceding line number and positions the cursor at that line. If no line number is given, **G** goes to the end of the file by default. You can also use **G** with the change and delete commands. **dG** deletes the rest of the file from the current line. **cG** deletes the rest of the file and places the user into input mode.

A pattern search, indicated with a beginning slash, will locate the next line with that pattern and position the cursor on that line. The slash opens a line at the bottom of the screen and allows you to enter a pattern. Upon pressing ENTER, the next line with that pattern will be located and the cursor positioned on it. The question mark also performs a search for a pattern but toward the beginning of the file. The **?** searches backward, and the **/** searches forward.

The **n** command repeats the previous search, either forward or backward in the file. The uppercase **N** command also repeats the previous pattern search, but in the reverse direction. If a forward pattern search was effected using the **/** command, the **N** command will perform a backward search. If a backward search was performed using the **?** command, then **N** will perform a forward search.

The pattern search can be considered a text boundary. Delete and change commands can use patterns to reference lines. The delete command followed by a pattern search deletes all text between the current line and the line with the pattern. **d/hello/** deletes all lines from the current line to the line with "hello". **c/hello/** changes those lines.

Vi contains two special characters for designating the beginning and end of a word in a pattern. The beginning of a word is represented with a **\<**, and the end of a word is represented with a **\>**. The pattern **/\<make\>/** only searches for the line with the word "make." The pattern **/\<make/** searches for lines with a word beginning with "make," such as "makeup."

As a variation on the pattern command, the **%** command will locate a corresponding opening or closing parenthesis, bracket, or brace. If the cursor is positioned on an opening parenthesis, the **%** command will locate the next closing parenthesis no matter where that may be in the file. If the cursor is on a closing parenthesis, using **%** will search backwards for the next opening parenthesis. The same is true for braces and brackets. This command is especially helpful for programming language source code files that make extensive use of nested parentheses, brackets, and braces.

You can mark lines and use the marks as line references in other commands. The command **m** followed by a letter marks that line with the letter. A single quote placed before the letter references the line. You can use a mark in any command in place of a line number. **mb** marks a line with the letter *b*. The command **'bG** then goes to that line. The mark alone will also move to that line. **'b** moves to the line marked with a *b*. You can use a mark to reference lines to be deleted or changed. **'bd** deletes all lines from the current line to the line marked *b*.

The single quote is also used to reference your previous position in the text. You can move the cursor back to its previous location using two single quotes, **''**. In a sense, the second single quote is a mark that references the previous position to the cursor. Repeatedly pressing two single quotes moves you back and forth from your previous position to your current position.

Advanced Input, Change, Delete, Copy, and Undo Operations on Lines

As you saw in the previous section, Vi has several commands for inputting, changing, deleting, and copying lines of text. The basic commands for such operations are usually lowercase letters, such as **a**, **i**, and **o**. There are variations on these commands that use uppercase letters. The command for appending text is **a**, but the command for appending text at the end of a line is uppercase **A**. The uppercase **I** command inserts text at the beginning of a line. And you already know that lowercase o opens a line below the current line, and uppercase **O** opens a line above the current line. The uppercase

o command is useful for opening up a line at the top of the file, whereas the lowercase command is useful for opening up a line at the end of a file.

With the uppercase **C**, **S**, and **R** commands, you can change the remainder of a line, change an entire line, or overstrike a line. All these commands place you into the input mode. You remain in the input mode until you press ESC. All these commands can be thought of as different ways in which you enter input mode. The **C** command changes the remainder of the line. From the character the cursor is on to the end of the line is deleted, and then you enter input mode. Whatever you input replaces the deleted remainder of the line. The **S** command changes a whole line. It is the same as the **cc** command. The line is deleted and the user is placed into the input mode. The **R** command is similar to overstrike mode in which you continually replace characters until you press ESC.

The **X** command deletes the character before the cursor. It functions like a BACKSPACE key on most word processors. It differs from the lowercase **x** command, which deletes the character the cursor is on. The **D** command deletes all text from the character the cursor is on to the end of the line.

The **Y** command copies the current line. A number entered before the **Y** command copies that many lines beginning with the current line. **Y** is the same as **yy**.

The **P** command puts copied or deleted text before the text the cursor is on. If lines were deleted or copied, then **P** inserts them before the line the cursor is on. This is the complement of the lowercase **p** command, which places lines after the line the cursor is on. If words or letters were copied or deleted, the **P** command inserts text on the same line, but before the character the cursor is on. The lowercase **p** command will insert text after the cursor. Think of **P** as before and **p** as after.

The uppercase **U** is an undo command that undoes all changes to a line. The lowercase **u** only undoes the most recent change.

Change, Delete, Copy, and Put Operations on Text Segments

You can copy, delete, or move words, sentences, or paragraphs by using the **c**, **d**, or **y** command with the appropriate text reference. A **c** command followed by a **w** will change a word, **cw**. A **c** command followed by a parenthesis will change a sentence, **c)**, and a **c** command followed by a brace will change a paragraph, **c}**. A **d** command followed by a **w** will delete the word the cursor is on, **dw**, and a **db** command deletes the previous word. A **d** command followed by a parenthesis will delete a sentence, **d)**, and a **d** command followed by a brace will delete a paragraph, **d}**.

To delete the whole word, be sure that the cursor is positioned at the beginning of the word. The **dw** command actually deletes from the character that the cursor is positioned on, up to the end of the word. If the cursor is on, say, the fourth character, then only the word from the fourth character on will be deleted. For example, if the cursor is on the *a* in "create" and you press **dw**, the, "ate" will be deleted, leaving "cre". This is true of all other delete operations on text segments. If the cursor is in the middle of a sentence, and you use the delete command, **d)**, to delete the sentence, only the text from the middle to the end of the sentence will be deleted. To delete the whole sentence, position the cursor at the beginning of the sentence. An open parenthesis command will do this for you, **(d)**.

Repeat factors can also be used with any of the delete or change commands that reference text segments. For example, **4dw** will delete four words instead of one. Pressing **3cw** will change three words instead of one. You can also change or delete several sentences at a time by entering a number before the sentence change or delete commands. The same applies to paragraphs.

Just as you can change or delete text segments, you can also copy or move them. The **y** command with the **w** or **b** command will copy words, **yw** or **yb**. The **y)** and **y}** commands will copy a sentence or a paragraph. You could use the **y}** command to copy a paragraph and then use the **p** or **P** commands to insert a copy of the paragraph elsewhere in the text.

The **d** command combined with the **p** or **P** command will move text from one place to another in your file. To move a sentence, you could first delete it with the **d)** command and then insert it elsewhere using the **p** command. To move a paragraph from one place to another, you first delete it with the **d}** command, move the cursor to the paragraph you want to insert it before, and then press the **p** command to insert the paragraph.

Named and Numbered Buffers

Vi has nine numbered buffers. As text is deleted or copied it is moved into these buffers. The number of the buffer corresponds to the recency of deleted or copied text. The fifth last deletion or copy is held in the fifth buffer. The text deleted or copied before the last deletion or copy is held in the second buffer. You can access this previously deleted or copied text by entering a double quote before the number of the buffer, followed by a **p** or **P** command. **"5p** inserts the fifth recently deleted or copied text; **"2p** inserts the second recently deleted or copied text.

In Figure 17-4, the user deletes and copies data into the numbered buffers. The first deletion places the line "tomato paste" into the first buffer. Then, upon executing a copy command, the contents of the first buffer are moved down to the second buffer, and the copied word is placed in the first buffer. The user then references the second buffer and inserts its contents at the end of the file using the command **"2p**. On the tenth deletion or copy, the first data placed in a buffer will be lost, in this case "tomato paste".

In addition to the numbered buffers, Vi has 26 named buffers, one for each lowercase letter of the alphabet. You reference a named buffer using a double quote and the buffer's letter name. **"a** references buffer *a*. You can reference a named buffer to place deleted or copied text into it, and later insert this text into your file using the **p** command.

The double quote placed before a letter and then followed by a deletion or copy command will place the deleted or copied text into a buffer named with that letter.

chocolate milk and lowfat milk skim milk tomato paste vegetable soup canned milk	Delete line d d	Deleted line is placed in most recent buffer 1 tomato paste
chocolate milk and lowfat milk skim milk vegetable soup canned milk	Copy a word y w	Copied word is placed in first buffer and contents of first buffer bumped to second 1 vegetable 2 tomato paste
tomato paste chocolate milk and lowfat milk skim milk vegetable soup canned milk		Reference the second buffer and insert its contents with the P command " 2 P

Figure 17-4. *Referencing Vi numbered buffers*

"bdw deletes a word and places it in buffer *b*. The text of the named buffer can be inserted later by referencing the named buffer with the double quote and the letter name and using this reference with the **p** or **P** command. **"bp** inserts the contents of buffer *b*, the deleted word.

In Figure 17-5, the command **"bdd** deletes the first line, which is then placed in buffer *b*. The user references the buffer with a double quote and the buffer name, **"b**, and inserts its contents at the end of the file using the **p** command.

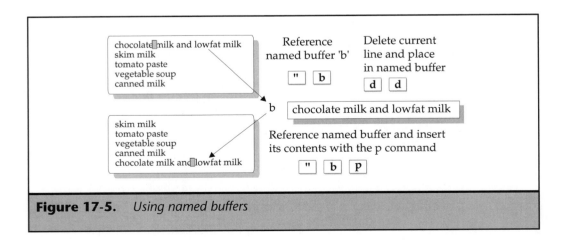

Figure 17-5. *Using named buffers*

Line Editing Commands

The Vi line editing commands include the same commands as those listed for the Sed editor, as described in Chapter 14. Most editing tasks are more easily executed with Vi commands. However, if you want to reference text using their line numbers, you will need to use the line editing commands. For example, suppose you want to delete lines 9 through 17. With Vi screen commands you can locate line 9 and then figure out that you need to delete the next 8 lines. With the line editing commands, you simply reference the range of lines 9,17 in a delete command, **d: 9,17 d**. The line referencing capability of the line editing commands is especially helpful when you want to make global operations. You can reference the entire text with the range **1,$**. The **$** is a special character that references the last line in a file.

As previously noted, the colon, **:**, is a Vi editing command that opens up a line at the bottom of the screen and allows you to enter a line editing command. After entering the line editing command, the cursor returns to its Vi position on the screen, and you continue working in the Vi editing mode. The line editing mode in Vi is most often used for global operations. These are usually entered within Vi as one line editing command using the colon.

You perform a global substitution by referencing all lines in the file and executing a substitution command on each one. The **$** references the last line in the file, and the range **1,$** references all lines in the file. A substitution command will substitute a matched pattern with a replacement pattern, and, when modified with a **g**, will replace text throughout the entire line. All instances of the pattern on the line will be replaced. The global line reference combined with the substitution command will perform a global substitution. Here is the format for such a command:

```
: 1,$ s/pattern/text/g
```

The next command replaces all instances of the pattern "milk" with the pattern "yogurt".

```
: 1,$ s/milk/yogurt/g
```

As with Sed, all special characters are operative in Vi line editing operations. In the next example, the first word in each line is replaced by a minus sign. The circumflex, **^**, when used in a pattern, is a special character indicating the beginning of a line. The brackets indicate a range of possible characters. **[a-z]** matches on any lowercase characters. The ***** is a special character that matches on repeated instances of the preceding character. **[a-z]*** will match on any sequence of alphabetic characters. A space follows. The pattern searches for any set of alphabetic characters at the beginning of a line and ending with a space. The replacement text of the substitution command consists only of a minus sign and a space.

```
: 1,$ s/^[a-z]* /- /
```

Options in Vi: set and .exrc

Vi has a set of options with which to configure your editor. You set an option with the **set** line editing command. You can set options within Vi using the Vi line editing mode. The **set** command followed by the option name sets the option on. If the characters "no" are attached to the beginning of the option name, then the option is set off. For example, the command **set number** sets the number option, which numbers your lines; whereas the command **set nonumber** turns off the number option. The command **set** by itself provides a list of all options the user has set. If an option is already set, the command **set** followed by that option's name will display the value of the option. The command **set all** will display the settings of all the options.

The Vi Initialization File: .exrc

You may want to set certain options for every file you edit. Instead of setting these options manually for each file each time you edit them, you can place these options in your **EXINIT** shell variable, or in editor initialization files, and have them automatically set for you. To use the **EXINIT** variable to set your options automatically, you need to assign the **EXINIT** variable a quoted **set** command specifying what options you want set. Whenever you invoke Vi, the **set** command stored in **EXINIT** is automatically executed. In the next example, the user assigns to the **EXINIT** variable, the quoted **set** command to set both the **nu** option for numbering lines and the **ic** option for ignoring case in searches.

```
$ EXINIT='set nu ic'
```

Though you can assign the **set** command to the **EXINIT** variable in your shell, you would normally assign it in your login or shell initialization files. Then, whenever you log in, the **EXINIT** variable is automatically assigned its **set** command. In the next example, the quoted **set** command is assigned to **EXINIT** in the user's **.bash_profile** initialization file.

.bash_profile

```
EXINIT='set nu ic'
```

Options set in this way will be set for every file you edit. However, there are options that you may need for only a selected set of files. For example, you may want to number lines in only your C source code files, and word-wrap your lines only in your document files. You can tailor your options for a selected set of files by using an editor initialization file called **.exrc**. The **.exrc** file contains commands to configure your editor. When Vi is invoked, the shell first searches for an **.exrc** file in the current working directory. If there is one, the shell runs it, executing the commands. These are usually **set** commands setting the options for the editor. In the next example, the **.exrc** file contains the **set** commands to set the number and ignore case options.

.exrc

```
set nu
set ic
```

If there is no **.exrc** file in your working directory, the shell searches your home directory for an **.exrc** file. You can have a separate **.exrc** file in as many directories as you wish. This allows you to customize the editor according to the files you have in a given directory. For example, a directory with your source code files may require that line numbers be displayed. The **.exrc** file in this directory would have a **set** command that sets the **number** option. When you invoke the editor in this directory, the **.exrc** file in this directory will be read and its commands executed, automatically setting the **number** option. In yet another directory, you may need to have your lines word wrapped. The **.exrc** file in that directory would have the **set** command for setting the **wordwrap** option. When you invoke the editor in that directory, your lines will be automatically wrapped.

There are options that you can set that control aspects of the search operation. You can ignore case, quote special characters, or wrap the search around the end or beginning of the file. If you set the **ignorecase** option, then searches will ignore upper- or lowercase characters in making matches. A search for **/There** will retrieve both "there" and "There." You can abbreviate the **ignorecase** option with **ic**. The commands **set ignorecase** and **set ic** turn the option on, whereas **set noignorecase** and **set noic** turn it off. The **wrapscan** option allows a search to wrap around the file. A forward search, once the search has reached the end of the file, will wrap around to the beginning and continue searching until the current cursor position. A backward search, once the beginning of the file has been reached, will wrap around to the end and continue.

There are several options that you can set to control how your text is displayed. You can display text with line numbers, display nonprinting characters, limit the number of lines displayed on the screen, or affect tab positions in the text. You have already seen the command **set number**, which sets the line numbering option. It can be abbreviated to **set nu**. You can use the **nonumber** option to turn the line numbering option off: **set nonumber**.

You set the amount of spaces displayed for tabs with the **tabstop** option. The command **set tabstop=5** sets the number of spaces between tabs to 5. The **tabstop** option can be abbreviated to **ts**. **set ts=3** sets the tab stops to 3 spaces.

The **tabstop** option is only a display option. It does not affect the tab spacing in the actual text file. Though the tab stops may be set to 5 in the editor, the tabs may still print out on a printer at the standard 8 spaces.

There are several options that affect the way you input text. These options take effect when you are in the Vi input mode and are typing in text. While in the input mode, you can automatically start a new line at a specified margin, you can automatically indent a new line, you can check for an opening parenthesis when entering a closing parenthesis, and you can determine the number of spaces you can backtab when in input.

The **wrapmargin** option, which can be abbreviated to **wm**, determines the position of the right margin of the text. When inputting text with **wrapmargin** on, a line is wrapped at the margin to the next line by automatically inserting a new line character. The command **set wrapmargin=30** will create an input margin of 30 characters. When you type in the 30th character of a line, a new line will automatically be inserted, and you begin at that new line. You can cancel the right margin by setting the **wrapmargin** option to 0: **set wm=0**. If the **wrapmargin** option is off, a new line will not be automatically inserted; you must press ENTER or you will continue on the same line.

The **autoindent** option, abbreviated **ai**, implements automatic indenting. The **autoindent** option works in the input mode while you are entering text. When you enter tabs to indent with the autoindent on, the next line will automatically be indented by the same amount of tabs. If the current line is further indented, the next line will also be indented to the same extent. Though the **autoindent** option allows you to increase the indent, you may also need to lessen the extent of the indentation at some point. You might want the next line to start farther to the left. Each tab in an autoindent can be canceled on an input line, one by one, with CTRL-D. The first CTRL-D shifts the cursor back by one tab; the second CTRL-D shifts the cursor back by another tab. You can always turn off the autoindent with the **set noai** command.

Summary: the Vi Editor

The Vi editor is a text editor used to create text files. Vi has three modes: command mode, input mode, and line editing mode. In each mode, the nature of the keyboard changes. In command mode, each key is an editor command. In the input mode, the keyboard becomes a typewriter, with each key inputting a character into the text file.

In line editing mode, a line opens up at the bottom of the screen and allows you to enter a line editing command.

You edit a file by specifying its name on the shell command line that invokes the Vi editor. You save and quit a file with the commands **w** and **q!**. These are entered in line editing mode. The colon is the command to enter line editing mode. The **ZZ** command will end the session, saving the file and quitting Vi.

When using the Vi editor, you are constantly changing between input and command modes. Input commands such as **a** and **i** will place you directly into the input mode. The change commands such as **cc** will first delete text and then place you in the input mode. Though there are many ways to enter the input mode, there is only one way to leave it—with ESC. Once in the input mode, pressing ESC will return you to the command mode.

Vi is a sophisticated editor with an extensive number of commands for full screen text manipulation. You can move across words, sentences, and paragraphs. Most lowercase commands have an uppercase counterpart. A lowercase **i** for input has an uppercase **I** for input at the beginning of a line. The first section of this chapter focuses on a core set of commands needed to perform basic editing operations. The later sections focus on the advanced features of Vi.

Editing commands in the Vi editor deal with text as characters, lines, words, sentences, and paragraphs. There are change, copy, and deletion operations that operate on all of these text segments. (See Figure 17-6 and Tables 17-2 through 17-5.) You can move and copy text, undo text, and search forward and backward through the text for patterns. Often these commands contain similar components with some differences. The deletion command for deleting a character is **x** whereas the deletion command for deleting a line is **dd**. Sometimes you may accidentally delete or change text. The **u** command undoes the previous editing operation. If you unintentionally delete or change text, you can undo the operation by pressing the **u** key.

The Vi editor also has an extensive set of options that are set with the **set** command. These options can set such features as line numbering and word wrap. You can set options manually within the editor or you can assign a quoted **set** command to the **EXINIT** variable in your login or shell initialization files. The options specified in that **set** command will be automatically set when you invoke the editor. You can also create an editor initialization file, **.exrc**, and place **set** commands in it. Whenever you invoke the Vi editor, the commands in the **.exrc** file in the current directory are executed.

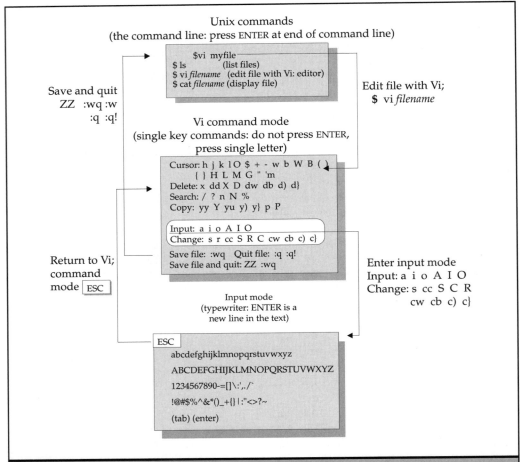

Unix commands
(the command line: press ENTER at end of command line)

```
$vi myfile
$ ls          (list files)
$ vi filename (edit file with Vi: editor)
$ cat filename (display file)
```

Save and quit
ZZ :wq :w
   :q :q!

Edit file with Vi;
$ vi filename

Vi command mode
(single key commands: do not press ENTER,
press single letter)

```
Cursor: h j k l O $ + - w b W B ( )
        { } H L M G " 'm
Delete: x dd X D dw db d) d}
Search: / ? n N %
Copy: yy Y yu y) y} p P
Input: a i o A I O
Change: s r cc S R C cw cb c) c}
Save file: :wq   Quit file: :q :q!
Save file and quit: ZZ :wq
```

Return to Vi;
command
mode ESC

Enter input mode
Input: a i o A I O
Change: s cc S C R
         cw cb c) c}

Input mode
(typewriter: ENTER is a
new line in the text)

```
ESC
abcdefghijklmnopqrstuvwxyz
ABCDEFGHIJKLMNOPQRSTUVWXYZ
1234567890-=[]\:',./`
!@#$%^&*()_+{}|:"<>?~
(tab) (enter)
```

Figure 17-6. *VI editor commands and keyboard modes*

Cursor Movement	Effect	Cursor Movement	Effect
h	Moves left	(	Moves to previous sentence
l	Moves right	)	Moves to end of sentence, then next

Table 17-2. *Summary of Vi Editor Commands*

Cursor Movement	Effect	Cursor Movement	Effect
k	Moves up	{	Moves to start of paragraph
j	Moves down	}	Moves to next paragraph
w	Moves forward a word	CTRL-F	Moves to next screen
b	Moves backward a word	CTRL-B	Moves to previous screen
W	Moves forward space delimited word	CTRL-D	Scrolls forward one-half screen
B	Moves backward space delimited word	CTRL-U	Scrolls backward one-half screen
e	Moves forward to end of next word	H	Moves to top of screen
E	Moves forward to end of next space delimited word	L	Moves to bottom of screen
0	Moves to start of line	M	Moves to middle of screen
$	Moves to end of line	G	Moves to last line or specific line
–	Moves to start of prior line	' '	Moves to previous cursor position
+	Moves to start of next line	'm	Moves to line with mark
Input		**Input**	
a	Appends after cursor	I	Inserts at beginning of line
A	Appends at end of line	o	Opens a line below current line
i	Inserts before cursor	O	Opens a line above current line

Table 17-2.   *Summary of Vi Editor Commands* (continued)

Delete	Effect	Delete	Effect
x	Deletes character cursor is on	dG	Deletes rest of the file
X	Deletes character before cursor	dw	Deletes a word
dd	Deletes a line	d)	Deletes a sentence
D	Deletes rest of the line	d}	Deletes a paragraph
Move		**Move**	
p	Inserts deleted/copied text	d) p	Moves a sentence
dw p	Moves a word	d} p	Moves a paragraph
dd p	Moves a line	x p	Moves a character
Change		**Change**	
s	Changes the character cursor is on	cG	Changes rest of the file
r	Replaces the character cursor is on	cw	Changes a word
cc	Changes a line	c)	Changes a sentence
S	Changes a line	c}	Changes a paragraph
C	Changes rest of the line	R	Overwrites
Copy		**Copy**	
yw	Copies a word	yG	Copies rest of the file
yW	Copies space delimited word	yw	Copies a word
Y	Copies a line	y)	Copies a sentence
yy	Copies a line	y}	Copies a paragraph
Search		**Search**	
/	Searches pattern forward	n	Repeats search
?	Searches pattern backward	N	Repeats search in opposite direction

Table 17-2.   *Summary of Vi Editor Commands* (continued)

Key	Cursor Movement
h	Moves cursor left one character
l	Moves cursor right one character
k	Moves cursor up one line
j	Moves cursor down one line
w	Moves cursor forward one word
W	Moves cursor forward one space delimited word
b	Moves cursor back one word
B	Moves cursor back one space delimited word
e	Moves cursor to the end of the next word
E	Moves cursor to the end of the next space delimited word
0	Moves cursor to the beginning of the line
$	Moves cursor to the end of the line
ENTER	Moves cursor to beginning of next line
–	Moves cursor to beginning of previous line
(	Moves cursor to beginning of sentence
)	Moves cursor to end of sentence; successive command moves to beginning of next sentence
{	Moves cursor to beginning of paragraph
}	Moves cursor to end of paragraph
CTRL-F	Moves forward by a screen of text; the next screen of text is displayed
CTRL-B	Moves backward by a screen of text; the previous screen of text is displayed
CTRL-D	Moves forward by one-half screen of text
CTRL-U	Moves backward by one-half screen of text
G	Moves cursor to last line in the text

Table 17-3.   *Vi Editor Commands*

Key	Cursor Movement
*num*G	Moves cursor to specific line number **45G** will place the cursor on line 45
H	Moves cursor to line displayed on screen
M	Moves cursor to middle line displayed on screen
L	Moves cursor to bottom line displayed on screen
' '	Moves the cursor to its previous location in the text
m*mark*	Places a mark on a line of text; the mark can be any alphabetic character
' *mark*	Moves the cursor to the line with the mark
Input	All input commands place the user in input; the user leaves input with ESC
a	Enters input after the cursor
A	Enters input at the end of a line
i	Enters input before the cursor
I	Enters input at the beginning of a line
o	Enters input below the line the cursor is on; inserts a new empty line below the one the cursor is currently on
O	Enters input above the line the cursor is on; inserts a new empty line above the one the cursor is currently on
Delete	
x	Deletes the character the cursor is on
X	Deletes the character before the character the cursor is on
dw	Deletes the word the cursor is on
db	Deletes to beginning of a word
dW	Deletes space delimited word
dB	Deletes to beginning of a space delimited word
dd	Deletes the line the cursor is on

Table 17-3. *Vi Editor Commands* (continued)

Delete

D	Deletes the rest of the line the cursor is on
d0	Deletes text from cursor to beginning of line
d	Deletes following text specified
d)	Deletes the rest of a sentence
d}	Deletes the rest of a paragraph
dG	Deletes the rest of the file
dm	Followed by a mark, deletes everything to mark
dL	Deletes the rest of the screen
dH	Deletes to the top of the screen
J	Joins the line below the cursor to the end of the current line; in effect, deleting the new line character of the line the cursor is on

Change — Except for the replace command, **r**, all change commands place the user into input after deleting text

s	Deletes the character the cursor is on and places the user into the input mode
cw	Deletes the word the cursor is on and places the user into the input mode
cb	Changes to beginning of a word
cW	Changes space delimited word
cB	Changes to beginning of a space delimited word
cc	Deletes the line the cursor is on and places the user into input
C	Deletes the rest of the line the cursor is on and places the user into input
c0	Changes text from cursor to beginning of line
c	Changes following text specified
c)	Changes the rest of a sentence
c}	Changes the rest of a paragraph

Table 17-3. *Vi Editor Commands (continued)*

Change

cG	Changes the rest of the file
cm	Followed by a mark, changes everything to mark
cL	Changes the rest of the screen
cH	Changes to the top of the screen
r	Replaces the character the cursor is on; after pressing **r** the user enters the replacement character; the change is made without entering input; the user remains in the Vi command mode
R	First places into the input mode, then overwrites character by character; appears as an overwrite mode on the screen but actually is in input mode
Move	Moves text by first deleting it, moving the cursor to desired place of insertion, and then pressing the **p** command. (When text is deleted, it is automatically held in a special buffer.)
p	Inserts deleted or copied text after the character or line the cursor is on
P	Inserts deleted or copied text before the character or line the cursor is on
dw p	Deletes a word, then moves it to the place you indicate with the cursor (press **p** to insert the word *after* the word the cursor is on)
dw P	Deletes a word, then moves it to the place you indicate with the cursor (press **P** to insert the word *before* the word the cursor is on)
dd p	Deletes a line, then moves it to the place you indicate with the cursor (press **p** to insert the word *after* the line the cursor is on)
d p	Deletes following text specified, then moves it to the place you indicate with the cursor (press **p** or **P**)
d) p	Moves the rest of a sentence
d} p	Moves the rest of a paragraph
dG p	Moves the rest of the file
dm p	Followed by a mark, moves everything to mark
dL p	Moves the rest of the screen

Table 17-3.   *Vi Editor Commands* (continued)

Move	
dH p	Moves to the top of the screen
Copy	Copy commands are meant to be used in conjunction with the **p** command. Upon copying text, the user moves the cursor to the place where the copy is to be inserted; the **p** command then inserts the text after the character or line the cursor is on
yw	Copies the word the cursor is on, then moves the word to the place you indicate with the cursor (press **p** to insert after the word the cursor is on)
yb	Copies to beginning of a word
yW	Copies space delimited word
yB	Copies to beginning of a space delimited word
yy or **Y**	Copies the line the cursor is on, then moves the line to the place you indicate with the cursor (press **p** to insert after the line the cursor is on)
y	Copies following text specified
y)	Copies the rest of a sentence
y}	Copies the rest of a paragraph
yG	Copies the rest of the file
ym	Followed by a mark, copies everything to mark
yL	Copies the rest of the screen
yH	Copies to the top of the screen
Search	The two search commands open up a line at the bottom of the screen and allow the user to enter a pattern to be searched for; press ENTER after typing in the pattern
/*pattern*	Searches forward in the text for a pattern
?*pattern*	Searches backward in the text for a pattern
n	Repeats the previous search, whether it was forward or backward
N	Repeats the previous search in opposite direction

Table 17-3. *Vi Editor Commands (continued)*

Search	
/	Repeats the previous search in forward direction
?	Repeats the previous search in backward direction
Buffers	There are 9 numbered buffers and 26 named buffers; named buffers are named with each lowercase letter in the alphabet, *a-z*. You use the double quote to reference a specific buffer
"*buf-letter*	Named buffer—references a specific named buffer, **a**, **b**, etc.
"*num*	Numbered buffer—references a numbered buffer with a number *1-9*

Table 17-3. *Vi Editor Commands* (continued)

File Operation		Effect
w	Write	Saves file
r *filename*	Read	Inserts file text
q	Quit	Quits editor
Delete, Move, and Copy		
d	Delete	Deletes a line or set of lines
m*Num*	Move	Moves a line or set of lines by deleting them and then inserting them after line *Num*
co*Num*	Copy	Copies a line or set of lines by copying them and then inserting the copied text after line *Num*
Line Reference		**Description**
Num	Line number	A number references that line number
*Num***,** *Num*	Set of lines	Two numbers separated by a comma references a set of lines

Table 17-4. *Vi Line Editing Commands*

Line Reference		Description
Num–Num	Range of lines	Two numbers separated by a dash references a range of lines
–Num	Offset reference	The minus sign preceding a number offsets to a line before the current line
+Num	Offset reference	The plus sign preceding a number offsets to a line after the current line
$	Last line in file	The dollar sign symbol references the last line in the file
/*Pattern*/	Pattern ref	A line can be located and referenced by a pattern; the slash searches forward
?*Pattern*?	Pattern ref	A line can be located and referenced by a pattern; the question mark searches backward
g/*Pattern*/	Global pattern	A set of lines can be located and referenced by a repeated pattern reference; all lines with a pattern in it are referenced
Special Character		
.	Any character	Matches on any one possible character in a pattern
*	Repeated chars	Matches on repeated characters in a pattern
[]	Classes	Matches on classes of characters, a set of characters, in the pattern
^	Start of a line	References the beginning of a line
$	End of a line	References the end of a line
/<	Start of a word	References the start of a word
>/	End of a word	References the end of a word

Table 17-4. *Vi Line Editing Commands (continued)*

Substitution Command		Description
s/*pattern*/*replacement*/	Substitution	Locates pattern on a line and substitutes pattern with replacement pattern
s/*pattern*/*replacement*/**g**	Global substitution on a line	Substitutes all instances of a pattern on a line with the replacement pattern
Num–Num **s**/*pattern*/*replacement*/	Substitution	Performs substitutions on the range of lines specified
1,$ s/*pattern*/*replacement*/**g**	Global substitution on the file	Substitutes all instances of a pattern in the file with the replacement pattern

Table 17-4. *Vi Line Editing Commands* (continued)

Search Option	Abbreviation	Default	Description
ignorecase	ic	**noic**	Ignores upper- and lowercase in searches
magic		magic	Makes special characters effective
wrapscan	ws	**nows**	Wraps search around to beginning of file
Display Option			
number	nu	**nonm**	Displays line numbers
list		nolist	Tabs, and displays new line with **^I** and **$**
window		window=23	Sets number of lines displayed on screen
tabstop	ts	**ts=8**	Sets tab spacing for editor display only

Table 17-5. *Vi Search, Display, and Input Options*

Input Option	Abbreviation	Default	Description
wrapmargin	wm	wm=0	Inserts new line at right margin while inputting
autoindent	ai	noai	Automatically indents; CTRL-D back indents
shiftwidth	sw	sw=8	Backtab and line shift spacing
showmatch	sm	nosm	Shows opening (, {, [shows closing), },]
beautify	bf	nobt	Prevents input of control characters

Table 17-5. *Vi Search, Display, and Input Options* (continued)

Chapter Eighteen

The Emacs Editor

The Emacs editor operates much like a standard word processor. The keys on your keyboard are input characters. Commands are implemented with special keys such as control (CTRL) keys and alternate (ALT) keys. There is no special input mode, as there is in Vi or Ed. You type in your text, and if you need to execute an editing command, such as moving the cursor or saving text, you use a CTRL key.

Such an organization makes the Emacs editor easy to use. However, Emacs is anything but simple—it is a sophisticated and flexible editor with several hundred commands. Emacs also has special features, such as multiple windows. You can display two windows for text at the same time. You can also open and work on more than one file at a time, and display each on the screen in its own window.

A GNU version of Linux was developed by Richard Stallman and is available on your Caldera CD-ROM. It is a standard feature on most Linux systems. The Emacs editor, however, is not installed as part of your Express Install. To use Emacs, you will first have to use glint to install the Emacs software package. Be sure to log in as the root user and mount your Caldera CD-ROM first.

Emacs derives much of its power and flexibility from its ability to manipulate buffers. Emacs can be described as a buffer-oriented editor. Whenever you edit a file in any editor, the file is copied into a work buffer, and editing operations are made on the work buffer. In many editors, there is only one work buffer, allowing you to open only one file. Emacs can manage many work buffers at once, allowing you to edit several files at the same time. You can edit buffers that hold deleted or copied text. You can even create buffers of your own, fill them with text, and later save them to a file.

Creating a File Using Emacs

You invoke the Emacs editor with the command **emacs**. You can enter the name of the file you want to edit, or if the file does not exist, it will be created. In the next example, the user prepares to edit the file **mydata** with Emacs.

```
$ emacs mydata
```

Like Vi, Emacs is a full screen editor. In the case of a newly created file, the screen will be empty except for the bottom two lines. The cursor will be positioned in the upper-left corner. The bottom line is called the echo area, and it functions as a kind of Emacs command line. It is also used to display Emacs messages. The line above it is called the mode line and is used to display status information about the text being edited. The mode line will be highlighted in reverse video. The different features displayed on an Emacs screen are illustrated in Figure 18-1.

To enter text, you simply start typing—you are always in the input mode. Editing commands, such as movement commands, are implemented with CTRL keys. For example, to move the cursor right, use CTRL-**f**, and to move the cursor left, use CTRL-**b**. To move up one line, use CTRL-**p**, and to move down one line, use CTRL-**n**.

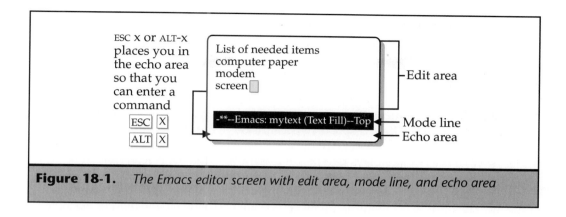

Figure 18-1. *The Emacs editor screen with edit area, mode line, and echo area*

You can save your text at any time with the CTRL-**x** CTRL-**s** command sequence. Many Emacs commands are made up of CTRL key combinations. The command sequence to quit the editor is CTRL-**x** CTRL-**c**. When you have finished editing the file, you should first save the file with CTRL-**x** CTRL-**s** before quitting the editor with CTRL-**x** CTRL-**c**.

Meta-Keys, Line Commands, and Modes

The Emacs editor operates much like any normal word processor. There is only one mode, the input mode. If you hit any character key you are entering data into the file. All character keys are input characters, not commands. A character key can be thought of as any key you type in directly, as opposed to CTRL keys or ALT keys. Character keys are any keys you could type in at a typewriter.

Commands are assigned to CTRL keys as well as meta-keys. In this version of Emacs, a meta-key may be either an ALT key sequence or escape (ESC) key sequence. On other systems, they may be one or the other. ALT key sequences operate like CTRL keys. While you hold down ALT, you press another key, and then let up on both. The ESC key sequence is slightly different. First, you press ESC and let up on it. Then you press another key. ESC key sequences have been in use far longer than ALT keys because many older keyboards do not have ALT keys. For this reason, this chapter will describe meta-keys as ESC key sequences, bearing in mind that meta-keys could also be implemented as ALT keys on your terminal.

CTRL keys and meta-keys constitute only a part of the many commands available in Emacs. All commands can be entered using command words typed in the echo area. (Think of the echo area as the Vi line editing mode.) The meta-key commands ALT-**x** or ESC **x** will place you in the echo area. Once in the echo area, you execute a command by typing in the command and any of its arguments and pressing ENTER. Table 18-1 lists the Emacs editing commands.

The mode line displays status information about the text being edited. The mode line is made up of several components, with the following form:

```
-ST-Emacs: BufferName  (major minor)------Place--
```

The first field, ST, indicates whether the file has been saved or not since the last change to the text. If the field displays two asterisks, **, the text has been changed, but not yet saved. If the field displays two dashes, --, the text has not been changed since the last save. If the field displays two percent signs, %%, the file is read-only and cannot be modified.

The NAME field is the name of the buffer. In the case of files, this will be the name of the file. The PLACE field indicates how far you are positioned in the file. For example, if the PLACE field is 40%, the text being displayed is 40 percent of the way through the file. In the next example, the mode line indicates that the file has not been saved since the last change, the name of the buffer is **mytext**, and the cursor is positioned at the top of the file.

```
-**-Emacs: mytext      (text fill)----  --Top--
```

The MAJOR/MINOR field indicates the major and minor modes for editing the file. Emacs recognizes several major modes, the most common of which is the text mode. Different types of files require special editing configurations. A C program file, for example, may need special indentation features. For this reason, there is a special editing mode for C programs. Emacs recognizes other standard modes, such as nroff and Lisp. Emacs determines the mode by examining the extension used in the file name. A .c extension indicates a C program file. In that case, Emacs will use the C mode. If there is no extension, Emacs will use the text mode. If, for some reason, Emacs cannot determine the mode for the file, it will use the fundamental mode, which offers no special features.

Emacs has three minor modes: fill, overwrite, and abbrev. The fill mode is usually the default. It automatically wraps long lines in the file. The overwrite mode allows you to overwrite text, and the abbrev mode allows you to use abbreviations when entering text.

Emacs Editing Commands

The Emacs editing commands perform many of the same operations found in other editors. All the commands are implemented with CTRL keys, ALT keys, or an ESC key sequence. Many also have a command name that you can enter in the echo area. This section describes many of the most useful commands.

Movement Commands

As in Vi, Emacs has a set of basic cursor movement commands. CTRL-**f** moves the cursor forward one character, and CTRL-**b** moves the cursor back one character. The CTRL-**f** and CTRL-**b** commands can be thought of as right and left cursor movement on a line. However, whereas in Vi, right and left cursor movement is limited to a line, the back and forward cursor movement of Emacs is not. Emacs views the file as a stream of characters, not a set of lines. A backward cursor movement moves back across characters in the file and may continue back across lines. The same is true for the forward movement.

There are also commands that move you forward and backward in the text by lines and by screens. The CTRL-**n** and CTRL-**p** commands move the cursor up and down lines. CTRL-**n** moves the cursor down to the next line. If the line is the last line on the screen, the screen will scroll to display the next line. CTRL-**p** moves the cursor up to the previous line. If the cursor is on the top line, the screen will scroll to display the previous line. The CTRL-**v** and CTRL-**z** commands move you through the text, screen by screen. CTRL-**v** moves you forward to the next screen of text. CTRL-**z** moves you backward to the previous screen of text.

You can also move according to text segments, such as words and paragraphs. The meta-key commands ESC **f** and ESC **b** move the cursor forward and backward by a whole word. ESC **]** moves you to the beginning of the next paragraph. ESC **[** moves you to the previous paragraph. Any of these commands let you quickly move through the text in either direction. There are also movement commands that position you in particular places in the text. The CTRL-**a** command positions you at the beginning of a line. The CTRL-**e** command positions you at the end of a line. CTRL-**l** moves you to the center of the screen. ESC **<** moves you to the beginning of the file, and ESC **>** moves you to the end of the file.

You can repeat a command by preceding it with the Emacs repeat command, ESC *num*, where *num* is the number of times the next command you enter will be repeated. For example, to move the cursor five characters to the right, first enter the repeat command with the number 5 followed by the CTRL-**f** command:

```
Esc 5 Ctrl-f
```

You can use the repeat command in the same way for input. The ESC key and a number followed by any character inputs the character that number of times into the text. ESC **3 T** enters three *T*'s into the text.

Deletions

Deleting text permanently removes the text from the file. There are two basic deletion operations: one to delete the character before the cursor and one to delete the character after the cursor. CTRL-**d** deletes the character after the cursor. The DEL key deletes the character before the cursor. They are comparable to pressing BACKSPACE.

Kill Buffers and Moving Text

Emacs makes a distinction between deleting and killing text. Deleting text permanently removes the text from the file. Killing text removes the text from the file buffer, but copies it into what is called a kill buffer from which it can later be retrieved. Killing text works much like the deletion process in Vi. Killed text is placed in one of a set of kill buffers set up by the editor. As you kill text, each kill buffer is filled in turn. The kill buffers are circularly linked. When all are filled, the first one used is overwritten with the next text that is killed.

At any time, you can insert the contents of any kill buffer back into the text. In this sense, the kill commands are meant to be one part of a text movement operation. You kill and thereby remove text from one place in your file. Then you can move to a different location and insert the removed text.

You can remove (kill) different segments of text, such as words or lines. The ESC DEL command removes the word before the cursor, and the ESC **d** command removes a word after the cursor. You can precede these kill commands with the repeat command, ESC *num*, to delete several words. For example, ESC **3** ESC **d** will delete three words.

The CTRL-**k** command removes the remainder of a line. To remove a whole line, first place the cursor at the beginning of the line with the CTRL-**a** command, and then issue a CTRL-**k** command. However, a CTRL-**k** does not remove the new line character at the end of the line. The line is still there, it is merely empty. To remove the new line character as well, enter another kill command: CTRL-**k** CTRL-**k**. The second CTRL-**k** deletes the new line character. To remove an empty line, you only need to enter one CTRL-**k**, since there is no text, just the new line character. As in the case of removing words, you can precede the CTRL-**k** command with the repeat command in order to remove several lines. For example, ESC **10** CTRL-**k** CTRL-**k** will delete ten lines.

Once you have removed text to a kill buffer, you can reinsert it in the file with the CTRL-**y** command. CTRL-**y** is often referred to as the yank command. Whatever text has been placed in the kill buffer will be inserted into the text. If the kill buffer contains words, CTRL-**y** will insert words. If the kill buffer contains lines, CTRL-**y** will insert lines.

Moving text involves first removing text to a kill buffer with a kill command and then inserting the text with the yank command, CTRL-**y**. In Figure 18-2 the user removes a line and moves it to another place in the file. In the next example, the command sequence moves the current line of text up five lines. Notice the use of the repeat command before the cursor movement command.

```
Ctrl-k Ctrl-k
Esc 5 Ctrl-p
Ctrl-y
```

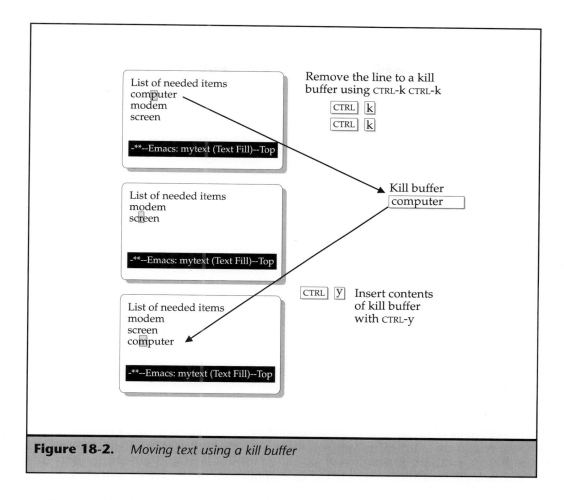

Figure 18-2.   *Moving text using a kill buffer*

If you accidentally remove too many lines or insert text in the wrong place, you can undo it with CTRL-**x u**. Emacs even allows you to undo all changes to the text since the editing session began with the ESC **x** command.

Regions: Point and Mark

You can select a block of text by creating a region relative to the cursor. A region is any text between the character the cursor is on and any previously marked text. You mark a place in the text with the CTRL-**@** command. That marked place is the end of your region. Then move the cursor to any other point in the file. The text between the marked character and the cursor is your region. Technically, the cursor position is referred to as the point and the marked character is referred to as the mark.

There are commands that perform operations on regions. For example, you can copy or remove regions. CTRL-**w** kills a region, removing it to a kill buffer. The ESC **w** command copies a region to a kill buffer. You could remove a region with CTRL-**w**, and then use CTRL-**y** to reinsert the region in the file—in effect, moving the region.

Emacs does not display a mark in the file. If you forget where you placed the mark, you can use the CTRL-**x** CTRL-**x** command sequence to locate the mark. The CTRL-**x** CTRL-**x** command interchanges the point and the mark, moving the cursor to the position where you placed the mark. You can move the cursor back to its original position with another CTRL-**x** CTRL-**x** sequence.

You can also define different text segments as regions. The mark-paragraph command, ESC **h**, selects a paragraph the cursor is on as a region. The point is the beginning of the paragraph and the mark is placed at the end of the paragraph. CTRL-**x** CTRL-**p** selects the page the cursor is on, making the page a region. The mark-whole-buffer command, CTRL-**x h**, selects the entire buffer, making the whole text a region. Here are examples of these region commands:

```
Esc h   Ctrl-w            Delete a paragraph
Esc h   Esc w             Copy a paragraph
Ctrl-x Ctrl-p   Esc w     Copy a page
Ctrl-x h   Esc g          Justify entire text
```

Incremental Searches

You enter searches with the CTRL-**s** command. The CTRL-**s** command places you in the echo area where you type in the pattern to be searched for. The CTRL-**s** command performs an incremental search. Emacs begins the search as soon as you enter the first character. As you enter more characters in the pattern, Emacs locates text that matches the growing pattern. For example, if you are typing in the word "preface," upon typing **p**, the cursor moves to the next *p* in the text. Upon typing **r**, the cursor moves to "pr". You end the input by pressing ESC. Here is the basic form to search forward in a file for a pattern:

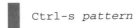

```
Ctrl-s pattern
```

The CTRL-**r** command searches backward in a file. Neither command will wrap around. The CTRL-**s** command stops at the end of the file, and the CTRL-**r** command stops at the beginning of the file. Emacs remembers the last pattern searched. A CTRL-**s** or CTRL-**r** command entered without a pattern will search for the previous pattern.

Regular Expression Searches

The Emacs editor allows you to use any of the regular expression special characters used in the Vi, Ex, and Ed editors. To use a regular expression in a search, you precede

CTRL-**s** or CTRL-**r** search commands with ESC. Thus, ESC CTRL-**s** or ESC CTRL-**r** allow you to use regular expressions in your search string.

Substitutions: Replace and Query-Replace

You perform substitutions in Emacs using either a replace or query-replace operation. The replace operation performs global substitutions. For this reason it is rarely used. The query-replace operation allows you to perform single substitutions. In fact, it will search for an instance of a pattern and then query you as to whether you want to replace it, skip it, or quit the query-replace operation. This gives you more control over the substitutions. Both operations have special commands for searching regular expressions.

Global Substitutions: Replace

You perform straightforward global substitutions using the **replace-string** command. You enter this command in the echo area. It is not bound to any key. You access the echo area with ESC **x**, and then type in the command **replace-string**. You are then prompted for a pattern and its replacement text. This command has the same effect as the global substitution operations in Ex. The **replace-string** command cannot operate on any regular expressions. If you want to use regular expressions in a replace operation, you need to use the **replace-regexp** command.

Query-Replace

The ESC **%** command is the **query-replace** command. It searches for and then replaces text. It operates somewhat like the substitution command in the Ex editor. First you enter ESC **%** followed by the pattern to be replaced, and then press ENTER. On the same line, enter the replacement text and again press ENTER. The first instance of the pattern is located. You then have several possible options, each represented by a key. If you enter **y**, for example, you will replace the text and move on to the next instance. An **n** will skip replacement of this instance and move on to the next.

```
Esc % pattern  Enter replacement-text  Enter
query-replace option
```

The options for the **query-replace** command are listed in the following table:

y or SPACEBAR	Changes and advances to next instance of pattern
n or DEL	Skips the change and advances
^	Goes back to previous instance of pattern
!	Replaces all remaining instances

	Replaces and exits
ESC	Exits **query-replace**

The following sequence replaces the next instance of the pattern "milk" with "yogurt" and then advances to the next instance. The user would exit the query-replace operation by pressing ESC.

```
Esc % milk
yogurt

y
```

Like the search commands, the **query-replace** command does not allow special characters in the search pattern. If want to use special characters, you need to use the command **query-replace-regexp**. You enter this command in the echo area by first pressing ESC **x**.

Using Windows in Emacs

Windows allow you to view different parts of the same file, or to view different files at the same time. A window command is usually a CTRL-**x** followed by a specified number. For example, CTRL-**x 2** opens up a new window on the text. CTRL-**x 0** closes the current window. The Emacs window commands are listed in Table 18-2.

When you have more than one window open, the one with the cursor is known as the current window. This is the one that is active. Any editing commands will operate on the text displayed in this window. You can move to another window with the CTRL-**x o** and CTRL-**x p** commands. CTRL-**x o** will move from one window to the next, sequentially, in the order they were opened. CTRL-**x p** moves to the previous window. You can close a window with CTRL-**x 0** and close all but the current window with CTRL-**x 1**.

When you open a new window, you can display it either next to or below the current window. The CTRL-**x 5** command splits the screen horizontally into two windows displayed side by side. The CTRL-**x 2** command splits the screen vertically, with one window above the other.

Once you have opened your window, you can change its size with the CTRL-**x ^** and CTRL-**x }** commands. CTRL-**x ^** extends the current window vertically, increasing its height. CTRL-**x }** extends the current window horizontally, increasing its width.

Windows are very helpful for moving text in your file. When you first open a new window on the same text, the new window shows the same text as the old one. In the new window, you can then move to other parts of the text. You can remove text in one window to a kill buffer, change to another window, and then insert the removed text using the other window.

Windows are also helpful for displaying what you have already written. You can easily check what you have written in another part of your document by displaying it in another window as you write.

Buffers and Files

As mentioned earlier, when you edit a file with any editor, the file's contents are read from the disk into a buffer in memory. A buffer is a segment of memory used to hold characters. You can think of it as an array of characters. You then perform editing operations on the buffer. When you have finished editing the buffer, you save the contents of the buffer to the file.

Emacs focuses on the fact that editors actually operate on buffers. You can edit buffers used for files or buffers used for other purposes. You can even create your own buffers, enter text into them; and, if you want, you can later save the contents to a file. The Vi editor, by contrast, allows you to edit only one file buffer.

File Buffers

Buffers used for files are created when you open a file. You can also simply open a buffer and then later save it to a file. In either case, the buffer becomes tied to that file. Such buffers are called file buffers. The command sequence CTRL-**x** CTRL-**f** *filename* opens a file with its own buffer. The command sequence CTRL-**x** CTRL-**s** saves the contents of the buffer to the file, and the command sequence CTRL-**x** CTRL-**c** quits the file. The different file buffer commands are listed in Table 18-3.

You can have more than one file open at the same time, each with its own buffer. To display two file buffers at the same time on the screen, you need to use the window commands discussed in the previous section. CTRL-**x** **2** first creates a new window. Then CTRL-**x** CTRL-**f** *filename* displays that file buffer in the new window. The command CTRL-**x** **4 f** *filename* performs both operations, creating a new window and displaying another file buffer in it.

Emacs has a special utility called dired that interfaces with your directory and allows you to select files in your directory for editing, saving, and even deletion. You enter the dired utility with the command CTRL-**x d**. A list of files in your directory is then displayed. The list is more like a menu. Each file name is really an item on the menu. You move from one item to the next and perform operations on it.

The dired utility has its own set of commands for moving from one item to the next and for selecting items. The **n** command moves to the next file name. The **p** command moves to the previous file name. The **e** command opens the file for editing. If the name selected is a directory, then dired changes directories and displays the file names in the new directory. The name .. is the directory name for the parent directory. Selecting it moves you up the directory tree to the parent directory, displaying its file names.

You can also save and delete files. Moving to a file and pressing **s** marks the file for saving. Moving to a file and pressing **d** marks the file for deletion. The file is not actually deleted until you leave the dired utility. Should you change your mind, the **u** command will remove any marks for saving or deletion. You leave the dired utility by changing back to your previous buffer with the CTRL-**x b** command.

Unattached Buffers

With the command CTRL-**x b**, you can create buffers not associated with any files. When you press CTRL-**x b**, Emacs prompts you for the name of the buffer. If the buffer does not already exist, a new one will be created. You can also use CTRL-**x b** to change to a specific buffer. After the CTRL-**x b**, simply enter the name of the buffer at the prompt. The buffer that you select will be displayed in the current window. In this way, you can use CTRL-**x b** to change from one buffer to another. CTRL-**x** CTRL-**b** displays a list of all buffers.

If you want to open up a new buffer in its own new window, you must first open the new window, change to the new window, and then open the new buffer with the CTRL-**x b** command. You can open a new window and a new buffer at the same time with the CTRL-**x 4b** command. Upon entering the command, a new window will be opened up, and you will be prompted for the name of the buffer.

Figure 18-3 shows three windows, each used to edit a buffer. Of the three buffers, one is a file buffer, **mytext**, and the two others are unattached buffers: **topics** and **preface**. As the user works in **mytext**, he or she can switch to the other windows, adding new topics in the **topics** buffer, or composing more text for the **preface**. When the user quits Emacs, the contents of the unattached buffers are lost. However, the user could copy the contents of an unattached buffer into a file buffer, or simply save the unattached buffer directly to a file of its own.

You do not necessarily need to have a separate window for each buffer. The CTRL-**x b** command will actually switch your window from editing one buffer to another buffer. In Figure 18-4, the user is first working on the **mytext** buffer and then switches to working on the **topics** buffer using the same window. CTRL-**x b topics** switches the user to the **topics** buffer. Buffers are sequentially ordered according to when you created them. CTRL-**x b** by itself switches to the next buffer in that order.

Like dired, there is a special utility for managing buffers. The command **buffer-menu** places you into an interactive utility that displays all buffer names. Using the same commands as in dired, you can change to buffers, delete buffers, or save buffers. You enter the **buffer-menu** command in the echo area, which you access with ESC **x**.

Help

Emacs provides several help utilities, such as an online manual and a tutorial. You access the help utilities through a CTRL-**h** sequence. CTRL-**h** followed by another CTRL-**h**

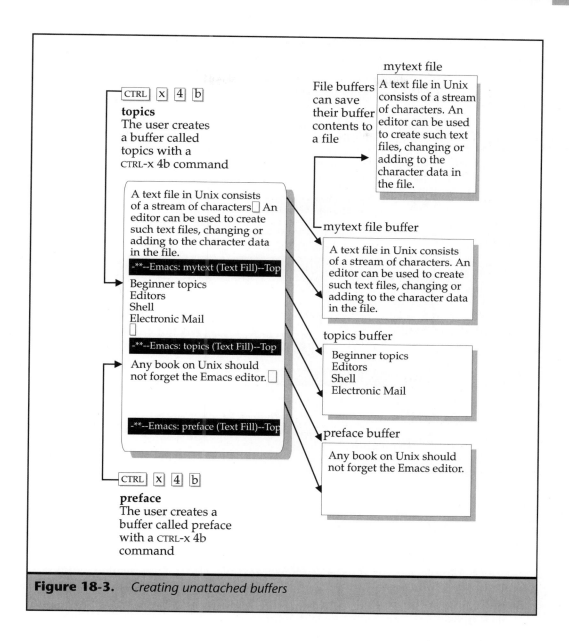

Figure 18-3. *Creating unattached buffers*

lists the many possible options. An option of special note is the tutorial. CTRL-**h t** places you into an online tutorial that provides you with special lessons on Emacs. Table 18-4 lists the Emacs help commands.

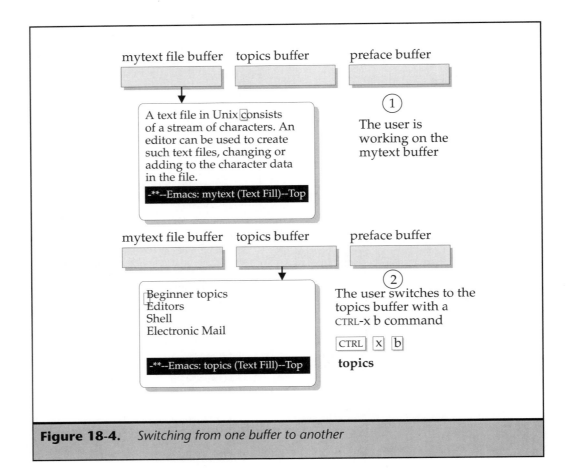

Figure 18-4. *Switching from one buffer to another*

Summary: Emacs

Emacs is a buffer-oriented text editor that you can use like a word processor. All keys are input keys. Commands are bound to CTRL keys and meta-keys. A meta-key may be either an ESC sequence or an ALT key. An Emacs text file is character oriented, not line oriented. You can move character by character, word by word, or paragraph by paragraph throughout the file.

Emacs makes a distinction between deleting text and removing text. Deletions are permanent, whereas removing text places the text in a buffer that you can later access. These buffers are called kill buffers, and the commands that remove text are called kill commands. Emacs terminology often refers to killing a word or killing a line. This means that a word or line has been removed from the text and placed in a kill buffer.

You can insert the contents of a kill buffer at a later point in the file. You move text by first removing text to a kill buffer and then inserting it at another point in the file.

Emacs allows you to open several windows on the screen in which you can display either the same file or different files. You can split the screen into windows horizontally or vertically. The windows can display different parts of the same file. You can move text by removing it in one window and then inserting it in the text displayed in another window.

You can open several files at once, each with its own buffer. You can also create your own buffers that are unattached to any file. You can then easily change from one buffer to another, editing each in turn. You can even access the kill buffers and edit them. The buffer-menu utility provides a menu interface for all your buffers, making it easier to select the one you want.

You can display several buffers at the same time, each in its own window. A buffer used for a file is a file buffer. When you display more than one file buffer on the screen, you are displaying the contents of two files on the screen at the same time. The dired utility provides a menu interface for all files in your directory, allowing you to open, save, or delete specific ones.

Cursor Movement	Effect
CTRL-**b**	Moves left one character (backward to the previous character)
CTRL-**f**	Moves right one character (forward to the next character)
CTRL-**n**	Moves down one line (the next line)
CTRL-**p**	Moves up one line (the previous line)
CTRL-**v**	Moves forward one screen
CTRL-**z**	Moves backward one screen
CTRL-**l**	Moves to center of screen
ESC **f**	Moves forward one word
ESC **b**	Moves backward one word
ESC **]**	Moves to next paragraph
ESC **[**	Moves back to previous paragraph

Table 18-1. *Emacs Editor Commands*

Cursor Movement	Effect
CTRL-**a**	Moves to beginning of a line
CTRL-**e**	Moves to end of a line
ESC **<**	Moves to beginning of buffer, usually beginning of file
ESC **>**	Moves to end of buffer, usually end of file
ESC *num*	Repeats the following command *num* number of times
ESC **x**	Moves to echo area to enter a command
Deletions	
DEL	Deletes the character before the cursor
CTRL-**d**	Deletes the character after the cursor
Kills and Yanks	
CTRL-**k**	Removes the remainder of a line (kills the rest of the line)
CTRL-**k** CTRL-**k**	Removes the remainder of a line and the new line character at the end
ESC **d**	Removes a word after the cursor
ESC DEL	Removes the word before the cursor
ESC **k**	Removes the remainder of a sentence
CTRL-**w**	Removes a region (deletes a block)
CTRL-**y**	Inserts (yanks) the contents of a kill buffer into the text
CTRL-**x** **u**	Undoes the previous command
Search and Replace	
CTRL-**s**	Searches for a pattern forward in the text
CTRL-**r**	Searches for a pattern backward in the text (reverse)
ESC CTRL-**s**	Searches for a regular expression forward in the text

Table 18-1. *Emacs Editor Commands* (continued)

Search and Replace	Effect
ESC CTRL-**r**	Searches for a regular expression backward in the text
replace string	Performs a global substitution
replace regexp	Performs a global substitution using regular expression
query-replace-regexp	Searches for a regular expression in query and replace operation
ESC **%** *pattern* ENTER *replacement* ENTER	Queries and replaces a pattern

Key	
SPACEBAR	Replaces and moves to next instance
DEL	Does not replace and moves to next instance
ESC	Quits search-replace operation
.	Replaces and exits
!	Replaces all remaining instances
^	Moves back to previous replacement

Regions

CTRL-**@** or CTRL-SPACEBAR	Marks a region (block)
CTRL-**x** CTRL-**x**	Exchanges cursor (point) and marks
ESC **H**	Marks a paragraph as a region
CTRL-**x** CTRL-**p**	Marks a page as a region
CTRL-**x h**	Marks the entire text in buffer as a region

Text Format

auto-fill-mode	Sets fill mode option
ESC *num* CTRL-**x f**	Sets position of right margin
ESC **q**	Justifies a paragraph
ESC **q**	Justifies a region

Table 18-1. *Emacs Editor Commands (continued)*

Command	Effect
CTRL-**x** 2	Splits to new window vertically
CTRL-**x** 5	Splits to new window horizontally
CTRL-**x** o	Selects other window
CTRL-**x** p	Selects previous window
ESC CTRL-**v**	Scrolls the other window
CTRL-**x** 0	Closes current window
CTRL-**x** 1	Closes all but the current window
CTRL-**x** ^	Extends the current window vertically
CTRL-**x** }	Extends the current window horizontally

Table 18-2.   *Emacs Window Commands*

File Buffer Command	**Effect**
CTRL-**x** CTRL-**f**	Opens and reads a file into a buffer
CTRL-**x** CTRL-**s**	Saves the contents of a buffer to a file
CTRL-**x** CTRL-**c**	Quits editor
CTRL-**x** CTRL-**v**	Closes the current file and opens a new one (visiting a new file)
CTRL-**x** **i**	Inserts contents of a file to a buffer
CTRL-**x** CTRL-**q**	Opens a file as read-only; you cannot change it
CTRL-**x** **d**	Enters the dired buffer that has a listing of your current directories; moves to different file and directory names; displays other directories; selects and opens files n Moves to next file or directory name p Moves to previous file or directory name e If the cursor is on a directory, enters that directory; if the cursor is on a file, opens that file s Marks a file for saving d Marks a file for deletion u Unmarks a file for deletion x Executes marked files
Buffer Command	
CTRL-**x** **b**	Changes to another buffer; you are prompted for the name of the buffer to change to (to create a new buffer, enter a new name)
CTRL-**x** **k**	Deletes (kills) a buffer
CTRL-**x** CTRL-**b**	Displays a list of all buffers
ESC **x buffer-menu**	Selects different buffers from a list of buffers d or k Marks a buffer for deletion u Unmarks a buffer s Marks a buffer for saving x Executes marked buffers

Table 18-3.   *Emacs File Buffer and Buffer Commands*

Help Command	Effect
CTRL-**h** CTRL-**h**	Lists possible help options
CTRL-**h** **i**	Accesses the Emacs manual
CTRL-**h** **t**	Runs the Emacs tutorial
CTRL-**h** **b**	Displays keys and the commands they represent

Table 18-4.   *Emacs Help Commands*

PART SIX

System Administration

Chapter Nineteen

Device Configuration

A s a version of Unix, Linux is designed to serve many users at the same time. As an operating system, Linux provides an interface between the users and the computer with its storage media, such as hard disks and tapes. Users have their own shells through which they interact with the operating system. However, you may need to configure the operating system itself in different ways. You may need to add new users, printers, or terminals. You have already seen in Chapter 7 how to add new file systems. Such operations come under the heading of system administration. The person who performs such actions is referred to as either a system administrator or a superuser. In this sense there are two types of interaction with Linux: regular users' interaction and the superuser, performing system administration tasks. This chapter will cover only the basic operations in system administration. You will learn about system states, managing users, and configuring printers and terminals. The chapter is meant to be an introduction to the complex tasks of system administration. Tables 19-1 through 19-7 are found at the end of the chapter for your reference.

System Management: Superuser

To perform system administration operations you must first have the correct password that allows you to log in as the root user, or superuser. Since a superuser has the power to change almost anything on the system, such a password is usually a carefully guarded secret given only to those whose job it is to manage the system. With the correct password you can log into the system as a system administrator and configure the system in different ways. You can start up and shut down the system as well as change to a different operating mode, such as a single-user mode. You can also add or remove users, add or remove whole file systems, back up and restore files, and even designate the system's name. The different commands that you use in system management are listed in Table 19-1.

When you log into the system as a superuser you are placed in a shell from which you can issue administrative Linux commands. The prompt for this shell is a sharp sign, **#**. In the next example, the user logs into the system as a superuser. The password is, of course, not displayed.

```
login: root
password:
#
```

As the root user you can use the **passwd** command to change the password for the root login as well as for any other user on the system.

```
# passwd root
New password:
Re-enter new password:
#
```

While logged into a regular user account, it may be necessary for you to log into the root and become a superuser. Ordinarily you would have to log out of your user account first and then log into the root. Instead, you can use the **su** command to log in directly to the root while remaining logged into your user account. A CTRL-**d** will return you to your own login. In the next example, the user is already logged in. The **su** command then logs the user into the root, making the user a superuser.

```
$ pwd
/home/chris
$su
login: root
password:
# pwd
/
# ^D
$
```

The Root User Desktop

Your Caldera Network Desktop provides you with several Redhat system configuration tools that simplify many system administration tasks. These tools are only available on your root user desktop. You first have to log in as the **root** user and provide the password. Once logged in, you can issue the **startx** command to start your root user desktop. Unlike a regular user's desktop, the root user desktop displays numerous icons for system configuration tools. Table 19-1 lists these tools, and Figure 19-1 shows the root user desktop icons.

The usercfg utility allows you to manage users and groups—adding, modifying, or deleting user accounts (discussed later in this chapter). The netcfg utility allows you to configure your network interfaces (see Chapter 20). With the fstool utility you can configure your file systems—mounting, unmounting, and formatting them (see Chapter 7). With timetool you can set the system time and date (discussed in this chapter). Using printtool, you can configure new printers, interfacing them with your system (discussed in this chapter). Finally, you use the glint utility to install software packages from your Caldera CD-ROM (see Chapter 3). You can also use glint to uninstall them.

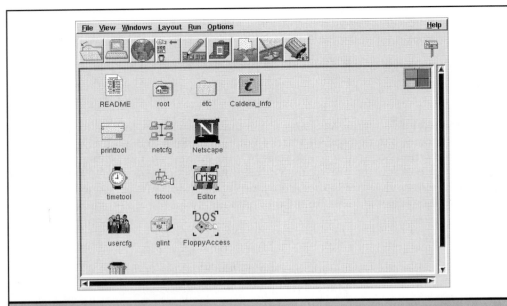

Figure 19-1. *The root user desktop: usercfg, netcfg, timetool, printtool, fstool, glint*

System Time and Date

You can easily set the system time and date using the time configuration utility on your root user desktop. This is represented on the desktop by the icon labeled "timetool." Recall that you set the time and date when you first installed your system. You should not need to do so again. However, if you entered the time incorrectly or moved to a different time zone, you could use this utility to change your time without having to reinstall your system.

Double-click on the timetool icon to open the Time Configuration window. You can make changes to any part of the time you wish (see Figure 19-2). Move your mouse pointer to the hour, for example, and then click. The hour will be highlighted. You use the two triangles below the time and date display to increase or decrease the time or date entry. If you select the hour, then clicking on the upper triangle will set the time forward to the next hour. The bottom inverted triangle will move the hour backward. The same is true for the date.

Once you have set the new time and date, click on the Set System Clock button at the bottom of the window. Then click on the Exit Time Machine button to exit the Time Configuration window.

You can also use the **date** command on your root user command line to set the date and time for the system. As an argument to **date**, you list (with no delimiters)

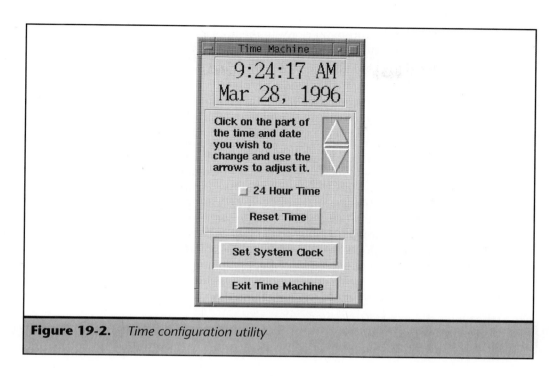

Figure 19-2. *Time configuration utility*

the month, day, time, and year. In the next example the date is set to September 18 at 2:30 p.m., 1996 (09 for September, 18 for the day, 1430 for the time, and 96 for the year):

```
# date 0918143096
Sat Sept 18 14:30:00 EDT 1996
```

Scheduling Tasks: crontab

Though not a system file, you will find a crontab file very helpful in maintaining your system. A crontab file lists actions to take at a certain time. The cron daemon constantly checks the user's crontab file to see if it is time to take these actions. Any user can set up a crontab file of his or her own. The root user can set up a crontab file to take system administrative actions, such as backing up files at a certain time each week or month.

A crontab entry has six fields: the first five are used to specify the time for an action and the last field is the action itself. The first field specifies minutes (0-59), the second field the hour (0-23), the third field is the day of the month (1-31), the fourth field is the month of the year (1-12), and the fifth field is the day of the week (0-6), starting with 0 as Sunday. In each of the time fields you can specify a range, a set of values, or use the asterisk to indicate all values. For example, 1-5 for the day-of-week field would specify Monday through Friday. In the hour field, 8, 12, 17 would specify 8 a.m., 12 noon, and 5 p.m. An * in the month-of-year field would indicate every month. The following example backs up the **projects** directory at 2:00 a.m. every weekday.

```
0 2 1-5 * * tar cf  /home/chris/backp   /home/chris/projects
```

You use the **crontab** command to install your entries into a crontab file. To do this you first create a text file and type your crontab entries. Save this file with any name you wish, such as **mycronfile**. Then to install these entries, enter **crontab** and the name of the text file. The **crontab** command takes the contents of the text file and creates a crontab file in the **/usr/spool/cron** directory, adding the name of the user that issued the command. In the next example, the root user installs the contents of the **mycronfile** as the root's crontab file. This will create a file called **/usr/spool/cron/root**. If a user named justin installed a crontab file, it would create a file called **/usr/spool /cron/justin**. You can control use of the **crontab** command by regular users with the **/etc/cron.allow** file. Only users with their names in this file can create crontab files of their own.

```
# crontab mycronfile
```

You should never try to edit your crontab file directly. Instead, use the **crontab** command with the **-e** option. This will open your crontab file in the **/usr/spool/cron** directory with the standard text editor, such as Vi. **crontab** with the **-l** option will display the contents of your crontab file, and the **-r** option will delete the entire file. Invoking **crontab** with another text file of crontab entries will overwrite your current crontab file, replacing it with the contents of the text file.

System States: init and shutdown

Your Linux system has several states, numbered from 0 to 6, and a single-user state represented by the letters **s** and **S**. When you power up your system, you enter the default state. You can then change to other states with the **init** command. For example, state 0 is the power down state. The command **init 0** will shut down your system. State 6 stops the system and reboots. Other states reflect how you want the system to be used. State 1 is the administrative state, allowing access only to the superuser. This allows you as administrator to perform administrative actions without interference from others. State **s** is a single-user state that allows use of the system by only one user. State 2 is a partial multiuser state, allowing access by many users, but with no remote file sharing. State 3, the default state, is the multiuser state that implements full remote file sharing. You can change the default state by editing the **/etc/inittab** file and changing the **init** default entry. The states are listed in Table 19-3.

No matter what state you start in, you can change from one state to another with the **init** command. If your default state is 2, you will power up in state 2, but you can change to, say, state 3 with **init 3**. In the next example, the **init** command changes to state **s**, the single-user state.

```
# init s
```

Though you can power down the system with the **init** command and the 0 state, you can also use the **shutdown** command. This command has a time argument that gives users on the system a warning before you power down. You can specify an exact time to shut down or a period of minutes from the current time. The exact time is specified by *hh:mm* for the hour and minutes. The period of time is indicated by a + and the number of minutes. The **shutdown** command takes several options with which you can specify how you want your system shut down. The **–h** option simply shuts down the system, whereas the **–r** option shuts down the system and then reboots it. In the next example, the system is shut down after ten minutes. The shutdown options are listed in Table 19-4.

```
# shutdown -h +10
```

To shut down the system immediately, you can use **+0** or the word **now**. The following example has the same effect as the CTRL-ALT-DEL method of shutting down your system, as described in Chapter 3. It shuts down the system immediately and then reboots.

```
# shutdown -r now
```

With the **shutdown** command you can include a warning message to be sent to all users currently logged in, giving them time to finish what they are doing before you shut them down.

```
# shutdown -h +5  "System needs a rest"
```

If you do not specify either the **–h** or the **–r** options, the **shutdown** command will shut down the multiuser mode and shift you to an administrative single-user mode. In effect, your system state changes from 3 (multiuser state) to 1 (administrative single-user state). Only the root user is active, allowing the root user to perform any necessary system administrative operations that other users might interfere with.

You use the **runlevel** command to see what state you are currently running in. In the next example the system is running in state 3. The word "runlevel" is another term for state.

```
# runlevel
N 3
```

System Initialization Files: /etc/rc.d

Each time you start your system, it reads a series of startup commands from system initialization files located in your **/etc/rc.d** directory. These initialization files are organized according to different tasks. Some are located in the **/etc/rc.d** directory itself and others are located in a subdirectory called **init.d**. You should not have to change any of these files. Configuration tools such as netcfg and fstool will make changes for you. The organization of system initialization files varies among Linux distributions. The Redhat organization is described here. Some of the files you will find in **/etc/rc.d** are listed in Table 19-2.

The **/etc/rc.d/rc.sysinit** file holds the commands for initializing your system, including the mounting of your file systems. The **/etc/rc.d/rc.local** file is the last initialization file executed. Here you can place commands of your own. If you look at this file, you will see the message that is displayed for you every time you start the system. You can change that message if you wish.

The **/etc/rc.d/init.d** directory is designed primarily to hold files that both start up and shut down different specialized daemons. It is here that network and printer daemons are started up. You will also find files to start font servers and Web site daemons. These files perform double duty, starting up a daemon when the system starts up and shutting down the daemon when the system shuts down. The type of files in **init.d** are designed in a way to make it easy to write scripts for starting up and shutting down specialized applications. The **skeleton** file is a sample file for how to write scripts for this directory. It uses functions defined in the **functions** file, as do many of the other **init.d** files. Many of these files are set up for you automatically. You will not need to change them. If you do, be sure to do your homework on how they work first.

When you shut down your system, the **halt** file, which contains the commands to do this, is called. The files in **init.d** will be called to shut down daemons, and the file systems will be unmounted. In the current distribution of Redhat, **halt** is located in the **init.d** directory. For other distributions, it may be called **rc.halt** and located in the **/etc/rc.d** directory.

Managing Users

As a superuser you can manage user logins on your system. You can add or remove users as well as add and remove groups. You also have access to system initialization files that you can use to configure all user shells. And you have control over the default initialization files that are copied into an account when it is first created. With them, you can decide how accounts are to be initially configured.

You can obtain information about users on your system with the **who** command. Add the **-u** option to display a list of those users currently on the system. The command displays the login name, the login port, the date and time of login, the length of inactivity (if still active), and the process ID for the login shell. For example:

```
# who -u
root        console      Oct 12 10:34      .       1219
valerie     tty1         Oct 12 22:18      10      1492
```

Adding and Removing Users with usercfg

You can add as many new user accounts as you wish, or remove existing ones. You add a new user account with the user configuration utility. This is represented on the desktop by the icon labeled "usercfg."

Double-clicking on the icon starts the utility, which opens the main User Configuration window. This window, labeled "UserCfg," lists all current user accounts on your system. Notice that your own personal user account is listed (see Figure 19-3).

To add a user, click on the Add button on the bottom left of the UserCfg window. This will open a new window with fields for user account information (see Figure 19-4). In the Name field, enter the login name you want to give for this account. "Name" is not a person's name, it is the name for the account, such as root or richlp. This login name must be eight characters or less and cannot have any spaces or punctuation.

Upon entering the login name, the other fields will be filled with default values, except for the Full Name field. Move to this field and type in the user's real name, first and last. You can then enter a password for this account. The user can change it later from within this account using the **passwd** command. The system will generate a default password for you. However, you can change it at this point. Notice that before the Password field, there is a small inverted triangle indicating a drop-down menu. Click and hold on this to open a menu with password options. One of these options is to edit the password. Upon selecting this, you can type in a password of your own choosing. Click OK to enter the password. The password will appear in the Password

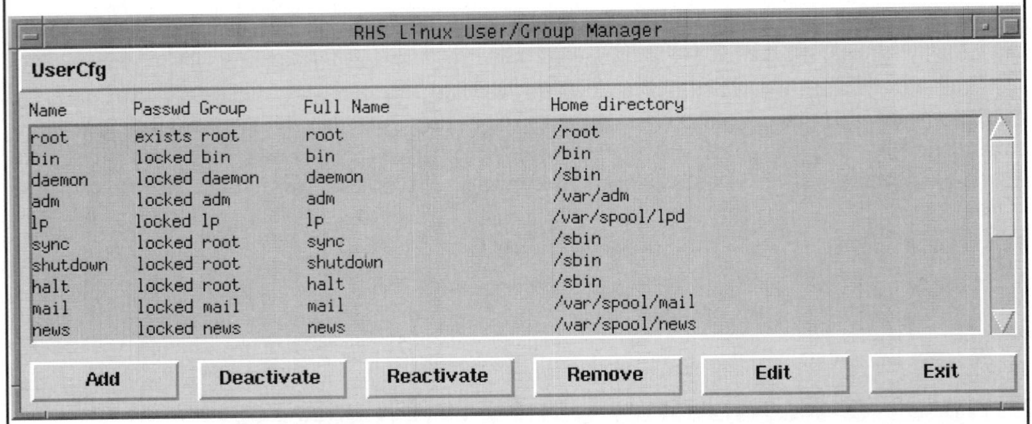

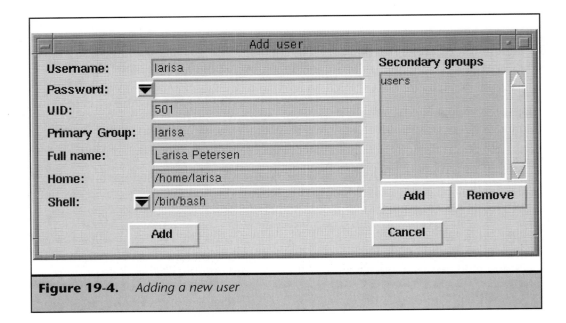

Figure 19-3.   *User configuration utility*

field. Other options are to have no password (none) or to lock the account until you choose a password at a later date (locked).

Other fields allow you to select the login shell, the user's home directory, or the user groups. You will not need to change any of these. When you are finished with all

Figure 19-4.   *Adding a new user*

the fields, click on the Add button at the bottom of this window. You will then be asked if you want to set up a home directory for this user. Choose OK. The new user will be displayed on the UserCfg window.

To remove a particular user, first click on that user's name in the UserCfg window. Then click on the Remove button. You will be asked to confirm that you want to remove the user. Choose YES. Now you will be asked if you want to remove the user's home directory and email information. Again choose YES. You are then asked if you want to modify the owner of orphaned files. Removing the user does not automatically erase that user's files. Such files are known as orphaned files. By modifying ownership, you can access and remove them. The owner of such files will be designated by the term "nobody."

You may at times want to lock an account, denying all access to it and its files. You can do this by deactivating the account—in effect, turning it off. The files for this account remain intact, and when you decide to reactivate the account, the files can then be accessed.

To deactivate an account, click on that account's name in the UserCfg window. Then click on the Deactivate button. You are given the option to compress the account's files, which will save disk space. (You are actually asked if you want to compress the user's home directory.) Choose YES to compress the user's files.

To reactivate the account, just click on the user's name in the UserCfg window, and then click on the Reactivate button. If the files were compressed on deactivation, they will now be decompressed.

Any utility to add a user, such as usercfg, makes use of certain default files and directories to set up the new account. There are a set of path names that usercfg uses to locate these default files or to know where to create certain user directories. For example, **/etc/skel** holds initialization files for a new user. A new user's home directory is placed in the **/home** directory. You can change these path names, if you wish, by selecting the **set paths** item in the UserCfg menu located in the upper-left corner of this window. A window will open, listing entries for all the path names. You can then change the ones you want. A list of the path names follows:

/home	Location of the user's own home directory
/mail	Location of the user's mail directory
/etc/skel	Holds the default initialization files for the login shell, such as **.bash_profile** and **.cshrc**
/etc/shell	Holds the login shells, such as BASH or TCSH

The /etc/passwd File

When you add a user, an entry for that user is made in the **/etc/passwd** file, commonly known as the password file. Each entry takes up one line that has several fields separated by colons. The fields are

username	Login name of the user
password	Encrypted password for the user's account
user id	Unique number assigned by the system
group id	Number used to identify the group the user belongs to
comment	Any user information, such as the user's full name
home directory	The user's home directory
login shell	Shell to run when the user logs in; this is the default shell, usually **/bin/bash**

The following is an example of a **/etc/passwd** entry. The entry for Mark has a * in its password field, indicating that a password has not yet been created for this user. For such entries you have to use **passwd** to create a password. Notice also that user IDs, in this particular system, start at 500 and increment by one.

```
richp:YOTPd3Pyy9hAc:500:500:Caldera Desktop
    User:/home/richp:/bin/bash
mark:*:501:501:Caldera Desktop User:/home/mark:/bin/bash
```

The **/etc/passwd** file is a text file that you can edit using a text editor. You can change fields in entries and even add new entries. The only field you cannot effectively change is the password. This has to be encrypted. To change the password field, you should always use the **passwd** command.

Though you can make entries directly to the **/etc/passwd** file, it is easier and safer to use usercfg or the adduser and useradd utilities. These programs will not only make entries in the **/etc/passwd** file, but also create the home and mail directories for the user as well as install initialization files in the user's home directory.

Managing User Environments: /etc/skel

Each time a user logs in, two profile scripts are executed. There is a system profile script that is the same for every user, and there is the **.bash_profile** script that each user has in his or her home directory. The system profile script is located in the **/etc** directory and named **profile** with no preceding period. As superuser, you can edit the profile script and put in any commands that you want executed for each user when he or she logs in. For example, you may want to define a default path for commands in case the user has not done so. Or you may wish to notify the user of recent system news or account charges.

When you first add a user to the system, you must provide the user with a skeleton **.bash_profile** file. The **useradd** command will do this automatically by searching for a **.bash_profile** file in the directory **/etc/skel** and copying it to the user's new home directory. The **/etc/skel** directory contains a skeleton initialization file for **.bash_profile** files or, if you are using the C-shell as your login shell, **.login** and **.logout** files. It also provides initialization files for BASH and C-shell: **.bshrc** and **.cshrc**.

As superuser, you can configure the **.profile** file in the **/etc/skel** any way you wish. Usually, basic system variable assignments are included that define path names for commands, system prompts, mail path names, and terminal default definitions. In short, the **PATH**, **TERM**, **MAIL**, and **PS1** variables are defined. Once users have their own **.bash_profile** files, they can redefine variables or add new commands as they wish.

Adding Users with adduser

You can also add a new user to the system with the **adduser** command. This command is entered on your command line and is very easy to use. There are different versions of adduser. The one on Redhat Linux comes from the Debian Linux distribution. It operates somewhat differently from other distributions, such as Slackware. This version of adduser takes as its argument the user name for the account you are creating. Upon pressing ENTER, it then creates the new account using default values. You can use **passwd** to create a password for the new account. This adduser program is a shell script located in the **/usr/sbin** directory. If you are familiar with shell programming, you can edit this script to change its default values.

```
# adduser robert
Looking for first available UID... 503
Looking for first available GID... 503
Adding login: robert...done.
Creating home directory: /home/robert...done.
Creating mailbox: /var/spool/mail/robert...done.
Don't forget to set the password.
 # passwd robert
Changing password for robert
Enter an empty password to quit.
New password (? for help):
New password (again):
Password changed for robert
#
```

With different versions of adduser found on other Linux distributions, you simply enter the word **adduser** without any arguments. You are then prompted for each piece of information needed to set up a new user. At the end of each prompt, within brackets, adduser will display a default value. To accept this default value as your entry, just press ENTER. After you have typed all your entries, adduser will create the new account. Once you have added a new user login, you need to give the new login a password. The login is inaccessible until you do.

Adding and Removing Users with useradd, usermod, and userdel

Other distributions of Linux may use useradd, usermod, and userdel to manage user accounts. All these commands take in all their information as options on the command line. If an option is not specified, they use predetermined default values. With the **useradd** command you enter values as options on the command line, such as the name of a user to create a user account. It will then create a new login and directory of that name using all the default features for a new account.

```
# useradd chris
```

The useradd utility has a set of predefined default values for creating a new account. The default values are the group name, the user ID, the home directory, the **skel** directory, and the login shell. The group name is the name of the group the new account is placed in. By default, this is "other," which means that the new account belongs to no group. The user ID is a number identifying the user account. This starts at 1 with the first account and increments automatically for each new account. The **skel** directory is the system directory that holds copies of initialization files. These initialization files are copied into the user's new home directory when it is created. The login shell is the path name for the particular shell the user will use. You can display these defaults using the **useradd** command with the **-D** option. The **useradd** command has options that correspond to each default value. Table 19-5 holds a list of all the options that you can use with **useradd**. You can use specific values in place of any of these defaults when creating a particular account. Once you have added a new user login, you need to give the new login a password. The login is inaccessible until you do. In the next example, the group name for the chris account is set to intro1 and the user ID is set to 578.

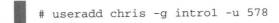

```
# useradd chris -g intro1 -u 578
```

The **usermod** command allows you to change the values for any of these features. You can change the home directory or user ID. You can even change the user name for the account.

When you want to remove a user from the system, you can use the **userdel** command to delete the user's login. In the next example the user chris is removed from the system.

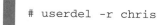

```
# userdel -r chris
```

Adding and Deleting Groups

Redhat distributions of Linux use the usercfg utility to manage groups. On other Linux distributions you can manage groups with the **groupadd**, **groupmod**, and **groupdel** commands. Groups are listed in the **/etc/group** file with one entry per file and several fields separated with colons. The fields for the group entries are as follows:

group name	Name of the group; must be unique
password	Usually an asterisk to allow anyone to join the group; a password can be added to control access
group id	Number assigned by the system to identify this group
users	List of users that belong to the group

Here is an example of an entry in an **/etc/group** file. The group is called engines, there is no password, the group ID is 100, and the users that are part of this group are chris, robert, valerie, and aleina.

```
engines::100:chris,robert,valerie,aleina
```

As in the case of the **/etc/passwd** file, you can edit the **/etc/group** file directly using a text editor. Instead of using either usercfg or groupdel, you could just delete the entry for that group in the **/etc/group** file. However, this can be risky should you make accidental changes.

Managing Groups Using usercfg

You can add, remove, and modify any groups easily with the usercfg utility on your root user desktop. To manage groups using usercfg, first open the UserCfg menu in the upper-left corner of the UserCfg window. This menu lists several options, one of which is Edit Groups. Another is Edit Users. To work on groups choose the Edit Groups item. When you are finished working on groups and want to return to working on users, choose the Edit Users item on this menu.

A Group window will be displayed, listing all your groups (see Figure 19-5). Each entry will have three fields: the group name, the group ID, and the number of users that are part of this group. You can use the scroll bar on the side to move through the list of groups. At the bottom of the window are three buttons: to add a group, just click on the Add button; to delete or change a group, first click on a group entry in the list

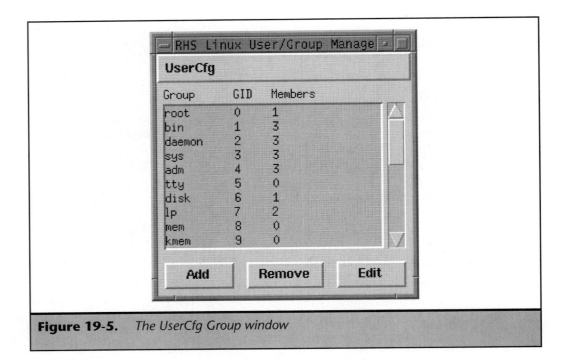

Figure 19-5. *The UserCfg Group window*

to select it, and then click on the Remove button to remove a group or the Edit button to modify a group.

Upon choosing the Add button, another window opens that prompts you for the various fields making up a group entry (see Figure 19-6). In the box labeled Name you enter the name of the group. A group ID will already be entered for you in the GID box, but you can enter one of your own if you wish. The lower half of the window contains a list of users that belong to this group. You can scroll through the list using the scroll bar. Initially this list will be empty. To add users to this list, you click on the Add button to the left of the list. This opens yet another window where you can select the users you want in your group. This window displays a list of all users, again with a scroll bar that you can use to see all the names. To add a user to the group, first click on the user in the list and then click on the Add button located at the bottom left of this window. You can add as many users as you want. Once you have added all the users you want to a group, click on the Done button located in the lower-right corner of the window. This returns you to the Group window where the list of users for the group now includes all the users you just added. You can also use this window to remove users from a group. Below the Add button is a Remove button. From the list, select the user you want to remove, and then click on the Remove button.

Once you have finished making all your entries, you click on another button labeled Add located in the lower-left corner of the window. This window will close,

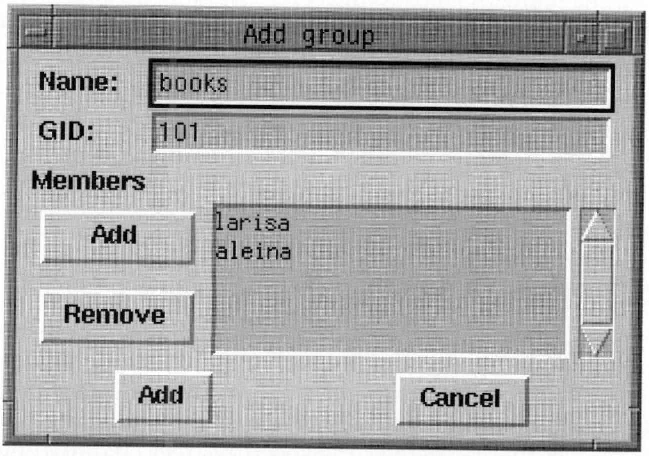

Figure 19-6. *New Group window*

and you will return to the Group window. You will see the new group added to the list of groups.

The Edit operation works much the same way as the Add operation. You are presented with a window listing the Name and GID entries as well as the list of users for the group. You can then change the name or group ID, and remove users from the group or add new ones.

Managing Groups Using groupadd, groupmod, and groupdel

With the **groupadd** command you can create new groups. When you add a group to the system, the system will place the group's name in the **/etc/group** file and give it a group ID number. **groupadd** only creates the group category. Users are individually added to the group. In the next example, the **groupadd** command creates the engines group.

```
# groupadd engines
```

You can delete a group with the **groupdel** command. In the next example, the **engines** group is deleted.

```
# groupdel engines
```

You can change the name of a group or its ID using the **groupmod** command. Just enter **groupmod -g** with the new ID number and the group name. To change the name of a group, you use the **-n** option. Enter **groupmod -n** with the new name of the group followed by the current name. In the next example, the engines group has its name changed to caboose.

```
# groupmod -n caboose engines
```

Installing and Managing Devices

All the peripherals, such as printers, terminals, and modems, are connected to your Linux operating system through special files called device drivers. Such a file contains all the information your operating system needs to control the specified device. This design introduces great flexibility. The operating system is independent of the specific details for managing a particular device; the specifics are all handled by the device file. The operating system simply informs the device what task it is to perform, and the device file tells it how. If you change devices, you only have to change the device file, not the whole system.

The name of a device file is designed to reflect the task of the device. Printer device files begin with **lp** for "line print." Since you could have more than one printer connected to your system, the particular printer device files are distinguished by two or more numbers or letters following the prefix **lp**, such as **lp0**, **lp1**, **lp2**. The same is true for terminal device files. They begin with the prefix **tty**, for "teletype," and are further distinguished by numbers or letters such as **tty0**, **tty1**, **ttyS0**, and so on.

In Linux there are two types of devices: block and character. A block device, such as a hard disk, transmits data a block at a time. A character device, such as a printer or modem, transmits data one character at a time, or rather as a continuous stream of data, not as separate blocks. Device driver files for character devices will have a **c** as the first character in the permissions segment displayed by the **ls** command. Device driver files for block devices will have a **b**. In the next example, **lp0** (the printer) is a character device and **hda1** (the hard disk) is a block device.

```
# ls -l hda1 lp0
brw-rw----   1 root     disk       3,   1 Sep  7  1994 hda1
crw-r-----   1 root     daemon     6,   0 Dec 31  1979 lp0
```

Installing and maintaining new devices such as printers and terminals is a task for system administration. To install a new printer, you have to be logged into the system as the root user, the superuser. You can then modify files in key directories such as those for devices in the **/dev** directory.

The numbers that follow a device file prefix are unique identifiers for the device. As such, they can only be created by the operating system. You cannot create them yourself.

Creating Device Files: mknod

You use the **mknod** command to create a device file, either a character or block type. The **mknod** command has the following syntax:

mknod *options device device-type major-num minor-num*

The device type can be either **b**, **c**, **p**, or **u**. As already mentioned, the **b** indicates a block device, and **c** is for a character device. The **u** is for an unbuffered character device, and **p** is for a FIFO device. Devices of the same type often have the same name, for example, Ethernet cards will all have the name **eth**. Devices of the same type are then uniquely identified by a number that is attached to the name. This number has two components, the major number and the minor number. Devices may further have the same major number, but if so, the minor number will always be different. This major and minor structure is designed to deal with situations in which several devices may be dependent on one larger device, such as several modems connected to the same I/O card. They would all have the same major number that would reference the card, but each modem would have a unique minor number. Both the minor and major numbers are required for block and character devices (**b**, **c**, and **u**). However, they are not used for FIFO devices.

Installing and Managing Printers

Your Linux system can easily access printers connected to your PC. Setting up a printer interface is fairly simple. It is a matter of determining a device file to use and placing printer configuration entries in your **printcap** file. You may also have to set up printing filters. The PrintTool utility on your root user desktop can provide a very easy interface for setting up and managing your printers (its icon is shown here).

printtool

Using just PrintTool, you can easily install a printer on your Linux system. Follow these steps:

1. In the PrintTool window, select the Add button. This opens up an Edit window that displays several fields in which you enter printer configuration information.

2. In the Names field, you enter in the names you want to use for the printer. Each name is separated by a |. You should include **lp** as one of your names. **lpr** used without a specified printer name will use the printer named **lp**.

3. In the Spool directory fields, the default spool directory will already be entered for you. You can change it to another directory if you wish.

4. For the Device field, it's customary to enter **/dev/lp1**. This is the parallel printer device for computers that use an AT bus which most computers today use. If you have a serial device you will have to use a different device name.

5. For the Input Filter you can click on the Select button to display a window with three fields. Each field has a Select button by it that will display a set of currently available options. The Select button for the PrinterType field opens a menu of printers that you can choose from. The Select button for the Resolution field lists several possible resolutions. The Select button for the PaperSize field lists paper sizes such as letter and legal.

6. When you are finished, click on the OK button to close the window and do the same for the Edit window. You will see your printer listed in the PrintTool window, as shown in Figure 19-7.

7. Choose the Quit item from the PrintTool menu to quit PrintTool. You are now ready to print.

For a detailed explanation of printer installation, see the **Printing-HOWTO** file in **/usr/doc/HOWTO**.

The Redhat distribution of Linux creates three device names for parallel printers automatically during installation. They are **lp0**, **lp1**, and **lp2**. (Most systems these days use **lp1**.) The number used in these names corresponds to a parallel port on your PC. **lp0** references the LPT1 parallel port usually located at address 0x03bc. **lp1** references the LPT2 parallel port located at 0x0378, and **lp2** references LPT3 at address 0x0278. If you are not sure at what address your parallel port is located, you can use the **msd.exe** command on your DOS system to find out. **lp0** connects to an XT bus and **lp1** connects to an AT bus.

You use **mknod** to make a printer device. Printer devices are character devices and must be owned by the root and daemon. The permissions for printer devices are write and execute for the owner and read for the group, 620 (see Chapter 7 for a discussion of file permissions). The major device number is set to 6, and the minor device number is set to the port number of the printer, such as 0 for LPT1 and 1 for LPT2. Once the device is created, you use **chown** to change its ownership to **root.daemon**. In the next example, a parallel printer device is made on the first parallel port, **/dev/lp0**. The **−m** option specifies the permissions, in this case, 620. The device is a character device, as indicated by the **c** argument following the device name. The major number is 6, and

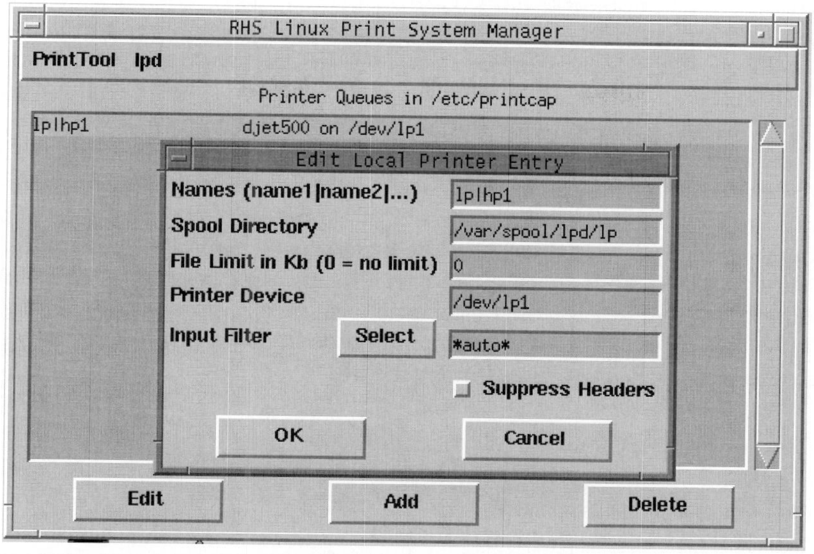

Figure 19-7.   *Using Printtool to install a new printer*

the minor number is 0. If you were making a device at **/dev/lp2**, the major number would still be 6 but the minor number would be 2. Once made, the **chown** command then changes the ownership of the parallel printer device to **root.daemon**.

```
# mknod -m 620 /dev/lp0 c 6 0
# chown root.daemon /dev/lp0
```

Be sure to check that a spool directory has been created for your device. If not, you will have to make one.

When your system prints a file, it makes use of special directories called spool directories. A print job is a file to be printed. When you print a file to a printer, a copy of it is made and placed in a spool directory set up for that printer. The location of the spool directory is obtained from the printer's entry in the **/etc/printcap** file. In the spool directory two files are made for each print job. One begins with **df** and is the data file containing the copy of the file to be printed. The other begins with **cf** and is the control file for the print job. It contains information about the print job, such as the user it belongs to.

The **/etc/printcap** file holds entries for each printer connected to your system. A printcap entry holds information such as the path name for a printer's spool directory and the device name of the printer port that the printer uses. The first field in a printcap entry is a list of possible names for the printer. These are names you can make up yourself, and you can add others if you wish. Each name is separated by a |. You use these names to identify the printer when entering various printer commands or options, such as the **-P** option. They are also used for special shell variables, such as the **PRINTER** variable, used in many initialization scripts.

The fields following the list of names set different fields for your printer. The fields have two letter names and are usually assigned a value using the **=**. These assignments are separated by colons. Three of the more important fields are **lp**, **sd**, and **of**. **lp** is set to the device name that the printer uses. **sd** is set to the path name of the spool directory, and **of** is set to the particular filter used for this printer. Some have Boolean values and will just list the field name with no assignment for a true value. You can find a complete listing of the printcap fields in the printcap man pages: **man 8 printcap**. An example of a printcap entry follows.

```
##PRINTTOOL## LOCAL djet500c 600x600 letter {}
hp1|lp:\
    :sd=/var/spool/lpd/lp:\
    :mx#0:\
    :lp=/dev/lp1:\
    :if=/var/spool/lpd/lp/filter:
```

Instead of making your own entries in the **/etc/printcap** file, you can use the Redhat printtool utility, located on your root user desktop, to make them for you automatically.

Printing on your system is handled by a print daemon called **lpd**. **lpd** is constantly running, waiting for print jobs and then managing their printing procedures. **lpd** takes its print jobs from a print queue that you can list using the **lpq** command. The **lpr** command will place a job on the print queue, and **lpd** will then take it in turn and print it. As noted in Chapter 5, **lpr** takes as its argument the name of a file. You can also feed data to **lpr** through the standard input, piping in the data to be printed from another operation. The **-P** option allows you to specify a particular printer. In the next example, the user first prints the file **preface**. Then she uses the **cat** command to generate combined output of the files **intro** and **digest**. This is piped to the **lpr** command, which will then print it. Finally, the user prints the file **report** to the printer with the name **hp1**.

```
$ lpr preface
$ cat intro digest | lpr
$ lpr -Php1 report
```

You can also print directly to the printer by simply redirecting output to the printer's device file. This does not place anything on the print queue. The print operation becomes a command to be immediately executed. However, your system is occupied until the file completes printing. The following example uses this technique to print the **report** file to a printer connected to device **lp1**.

```
$ cat report > /dev/lp1
```

To manage the printing jobs on your printer or printers, enter the command **lpc** and press ENTER. You are then given an LPC> prompt at which you can enter **lpc** commands to manage your printers and their jobs. The **status** command with the name of the printer displays whether the printer is ready, how many print jobs it has, and so on. The **stop** and **start** commands can stop a printer and start it back up. See Table 19-6 for a listing of **lpc** commands.

```
# lpc
lpc> status hp1
hp1|lp1:
    queuing is enabled
    printing is enabled
    1 entry in spool area
```

You can manage the print queue using the **lpq** and **lprm** commands. **lpq** lists the printing jobs currently on the print queue. With the **-P** option and the printer name you can list the jobs for a particular printer. If you specify a user name, you can list the print jobs for that user. With the **-l** option, **lpq** displays detailed information about each job. If you want information on a specific job, you can just use that job's ID number with **lpq**.

With the **lprm** command you can remove a printing job from the queue, erasing it before it can be printed. **lprm** takes many of the same options as **lpq**. To remove a specific job, just use **lprm** with the job number. To remove all printing jobs for a particular user, enter **lprm** with the user name. To remove all printing jobs for a particular printer, you use the **-P** option with the printer name.

lprm has a special argument indicated by a dash, **-**, that references all print jobs for the user who issues the command. For example, to remove all your own print jobs, you can just enter **lprm -**. If you logged in as the root user, then **lprm -** will remove all print jobs for all printers and users from the print queue, emptying it completely.

You should not use **lprm** to kill a printing job that has already started printing. Instead, you may have to use the **kill** command on the print job process. You can display processes using the **ps -ax command**, then use **kill** and the number of the process to end it. For a job that is already printing, you will see a process for its filter. This is the process to kill.

Installing and Managing Terminals and Modems

With a multiuser system such as Linux, you will probably have several users logged in at the same time. Each user, would, of course, need his or her own terminal through which to access the Linux system. The monitor on your PC acts as a special terminal called the console, but you can add other terminals through either the serial ports on your PC or through a special multiport card installed on your PC. The other terminals can be stand-alone terminals or PCs using terminal emulation programs. For a detailed explanation of terminal installation, see the **Term-HOWTO** file in **/usr/doc/HOWTO**. A brief explanation is provided here.

For each terminal you add, you must create a character device on your Linux system. As with printers, you use the **mknod** command to create terminal devices. The permissions for a terminal device are 660. Terminal devices are character devices with a major number of 4 and minor numbers usually beginning at 64. The serial ports on your PC are referred to as COM1, on up to COM4. They correspond to the terminal devices **/dev/ttyS0** through **/dev/ttyS3**. Note that several of these serial devices may already be used for other input devices such as your mouse and for communications devices such as your modem. If you have a serial printer, then one will already be used for that. Before you create a terminal device, first determine the serial port it is connected to. If you've installed a multiport card, you will have many more ports to choose from. Once you have created the terminal device you then change its ownership to that of **root.tty**. In the next example, the user creates a terminal device for the COM3 port, **/dev/ttyS2**.

```
#   mknod   -m 660 /dev/ttyS2   c 4 66
#   chown root.tty   /dev/ttyS2
```

Terminal devices are managed by your system using the **getty** program and a set of configuration files. When your system starts, it reads a list of connected terminals in the **inittab** file and then executes a **/etc/getty** program for each one. The **getty** program sets up the communication between your Linux system and a specified terminal. It obtains from the **/etc/gettydefs** file certain parameters such as speed and the login prompt as well as any special instructions.

```
# Format: <speed># <init flags> # <final flags> #<login
    string>#<next-speed>
# 38400 fixed baud Dumb Terminal entry
DT38400# B38400 CS8 CLOCAL # B38400 SANE -ISTRIP CLOCAL #@S login:
    #DT38400
```

The **/etc/inittab** file holds instructions for your system on how to manage terminal devices. A line in the **/etc/inittab** file has four basic components: an ID, runlevel, action, and process. Terminal devices are identified by ID numbers, beginning with 1 for the first device. The runlevel at which the terminal operates is usually 1. The action is usually "respawn," which says to continually run the process. The process is a call to **/etc/getty** with the baud rate and terminal device name.

The /etc/ttys file associates the type of terminal used with a certain device. It consists of two columns, the first for the type of terminal and the second for the terminal device names. A terminal type is a special term as defined in the **termcap** file. For example, **vt100** refers to a VT100 terminal, and **tvi920c** refers to a TeleVideo 920c. **console** refers to the monitor on your system. The terminal type is assigned to a user's **TERM** shell variable when logging in through the corresponding device.

/etc/termcap holds the specifications for different terminal types. These are the different types of terminals users could use to log into your system. Your /etc/termcap file is already filled with specifications for most of the terminals currently produced. An entry in the /etc/termcap file consists of various names that can be used for a terminal separated by a | and then a series of parameter specifications, each ending in a colon. It is here that you find the name used for a specific terminal type. You can use **more** to display your /etc/termcap file and then use a search, **/**, to locate your terminal type.

```
tvi925|925|televideo model 925:\
    :hs:xn:am:bs:co#80:li#24:cm=\E=%+ %+
        :cl=\E*:cd=\Ey:ce=\Et:is=\El\E":\
    :al=\EE:dl=\ER:im=:ei=:ic=\EQ:dc=\EW:if=/usr/lib/tabset
        /stdcrt:\
    :ho=^^:nd=^L:bt=\EI:pt:so=\EG4:se=\EG0:sg#1:us=\EG8:ue=
        \EG0:ug#1:\
    :up=^K:do=^V:kb=^H:ku=^K:kd=^V:kl=^H:kr=^L:kh=^^:ma=^V^J^L :\
    :k1=^A@\r:k2=^AA\r:k3=^AB\r:k4=^AC\r:k5=^AD\r:k6=^AE\r:k7=^AF
        \r:\
    :k8=^AG\r:k9=^AH\r:k0=^AI\r:ko=ic,dc,al,dl,cl,ce,cd,bt:\
    :ts=\Ef:fs=^M\Eg:ds=\Eh:sr=\Ej:
```

There are many options that you can set for a terminal device. To change these options you can use the **stty** command instead of changing configuration files directly. **stty** with no arguments lists the current setting of the terminal.

When a user logs in, it is helpful to have the terminal device initialized using the **tset** command. Usually the **tset** command is placed in the user's **.bash_profile** file and is automatically executed whenever he or she logs into the system. You use the **tset** command to set the terminal type and any other options the terminal device requires. A common entry of **tset** for a **.bash_profile** file follows. The **-m dialup:** option prompts the user to enter a terminal type. The type specified here is a default type that will be displayed in parentheses. The user just presses ENTER to choose the default. The prompt will look like this: **TERM=(vt100)?**

```
eval `tset -s -Q -m dialup:?vt00`
```

LILO

You can configure your Linux Loader (LILO) using the **/etc/lilo.conf** file and the command **lilo**. If you examine your **/etc/lilo.conf** file, you will find it organized into different segments called stanzas, one for each operating system that LILO is to start up. If your Linux system shares your computer with a DOS system, you should see two stanzas listed in your **/etc/lilo.conf** file, one for Linux and one for DOS. Each stanza will indicate the hard disk partition that the respective operating system is located on. It will also include an entry for the label. This is the name you enter at the LILO prompt to start that operating system.

You can, if you wish, make changes directly to the **/etc/lilo.conf** file using a text editor. Whenever you make a change, you have to execute the **lilo** command to have it take effect. Type **lilo** and press ENTER.

/etc/lilo.conf

```
# general section
boot = /dev/hda
install = /boot/boot.b
message = /boot/message
prompt
# wait 20 seconds (200 10ths) for user to select the entry to load
timeout = 200
# default entry
default = dos
image = /vmlinuz.gen
     label = linux
     root = /dev/hda3
     read-only
other = /dev/hda1
     label = dos
     table = /dev/hda
     loader = /boot/chain.b
```

Unless specified by the default entry, the default operating system that LILO boots is the one whose segment is the first listed in the **lilo.conf** file. Because the Linux stanza is the first listed, this is the one that LILO will boot if you do not enter anything at the LILO prompt. If you would like to have your DOS system be the default, you can use **lilo** with the **-D** option to reset the default, or edit the **lilo.conf** file to assign a value to **default**. You could also use a text editor to place the DOS stanza first, before the Linux stanza. Be sure to execute **lilo** to have the change take effect. The next time you start your system, you could just press ENTER at the LILO prompt to have DOS loaded, instead of typing **dos**.

```
# lilo -D dos
```

There are a number of LILO options that you can set using either command line options or by setting options in the **lilo.conf** file. These are listed in Table 19-7.

Summary: System Administration

You may need to perform basic system administration operations such as adding or deleting users, adding file systems to your file structure, and configuring different devices such as printers and terminals. To have the permission to perform such tasks you need to log into the system as a superuser. To become the superuser you have to log in as the root user. The root login gives you total control, allowing you to change any feature of the system.

You can determine in what mode the system will run. There is a single-user mode, a multiuser mode, an administrative mode, as well as a shutdown mode. The multiuser mode is usually the default. You use the shutdown mode to turn the system off or to change to another mode.

As a superuser, you can manage other users on the system, adding user logins and passwords as well as deleting user logins. You can create groups or delete groups and add or remove users from groups. You can also add devices such as printers, modems, and terminals. To add a device, you use the **mknod** command to create a device file for it. You may also have to make entries in various configuration files, depending on the type of device you are adding.

Your root user desktop holds many useful utilities for managing the various system administration tasks. The usercfg program lets you easily add, remove, and modify both users and groups. The timetool utility lets you set the system date and time. The printtool utility will automatically configure your printer for you, placing the appropriate entry in your **/etc/printcap** file. The netcfg program lets you configure network interfaces (as discussed in Chapter 20), and the fstool program lets you manage your file systems, mounting and unmounting them as you wish (see Chapter 7).

Root User Desktop Utility	Description
usercfg	Manages your users and groups, allowing you to add, remove, or modify users as well as add, remove, and modify groups
timetool	Sets the system date and time
printtool	Configures a printer, creating a printer device and printcap entry for the printer
netcfg	Configures your network interfaces (see Chapter 20)
fstool	Configures your file systems, allowing you to mount, unmount, add, remove, or format file systems using your **/etc/fstab** file (see Chapter 7)
Basic System Adminstration	
su root	Logs a superuser into the root from a user login; the superuser returns to the original login with a CTRL-**d**
passwd *login-name*	Sets a new password for the login name
crontab *options file-name*	With *file-name* as an argument, installs **crontab** entries in the file to a crontab file; these entries are operations executed at specified times **-e** Edits the crontab file **-l** Lists the contents of the crontab file **-r** Deletes the crontab file
init *state*	Changes the system state (see Table 19-3)
lilo *options Config-file*	Reconfigure the Linux Loader (LILO)
shutdown *options time*	Shuts down the system; similar to CTRL-ALT-DEL
date	Sets the date and time for the system
mknod	Creates a device such as a printer or terminal device

Table 19-1. *System Administration Commands*

Basic System Administration	Description
adduser *username*	Adds a new user, creating a password file entry and home and mail directories with initialization files; uses **passwd** command to create a password for the user
Printer Management	
lpr *options file-list*	Prints a file; copies the file to the printer's spool directory and places it on the print queue to be printed in turn **-P***printer* Prints the file on the specified printer
lpq *options*	Displays the print jobs in the print queue **-P***printer* Prints queue for the specified printer **-l** Prints a detailed listing
lprm *options Printjob-id* or *User-id*	Removes a print job from the print queue; you identify a particular print job by its number as listed by **lpq**; if you use *User-id*, it will remove all print jobs for that user **-** Refers to all print jobs for the logged-in user; if the logged-in user is the root, it refers to all print jobs **-P***printer* Removes all print jobs for the specified printer
lpc	Manages your printers; at the LPC> prompt you can enter commands to check the status of your printers and take other actions (see Table 19-6 for a list of **lpc** commands)
Terminal Management	
stty	Allows you to set different options for a terminal device
tset *options*	Initializes your terminal device with a specific terminal type

Table 19-1.   *System Administration Commands (continued)*

File	Description
/etc/inittab	Sets the default state as well as terminal connections
/etc/passwd	Contains user password and login configurations
/etc/group	Contains a list of groups with configurations for each
/etc/fstab	Automatically mounts file systems when you start your system
/etc/lilo.conf	The LILO configuration file for your system
/etc/printcap	Contains a list of each printer and its specifications
/etc/termcap	Contains a list of terminal type specifications for terminals that could be connected to the system
/etc/gettydefs	Contains configuration information on terminals connected to the system
/etc/skel	Directory that holds the versions of initialization files such as **.bash_profile** that are copied to new users' home directories
/etc/ttys	List of terminal types and the terminal devices with which they correspond
System Initialization Files	
/etc/rc.d	Directory that holds system startup and shut down files
/etc/rc.d/rc.sysinit	Initialization file for your system
/etc/rc.d/rc.local	Initialization file for your own commands; you can freely edit this file to add your own startup commands; it is the last startup file executed
/etc/rc.d/init.d	Directory that holds many of the initialization files to start up and shut down various daemons

Table 19-2. *System Administration Configuration Files*

System Initialization Files	Description
/etc/rc.d/init.d/halt	Operations performed each time you shut down the system, such as unmounting file systems; called **rc.halt** in other distributions
/etc/rc.d/init.d/lpd.init	Start up and shut down the **lpd** daemon
/etc/rc.d/init.d/inet	Operations to set up network interfaces and the **inet** daemon; calls the **networks** file
/etc/rc.d/init.d/httpd.init	Operations to start up and shut down your Web server daemon, **httpd**
/etc/rc.d/init.d/cfs.init	Operations to start up and shut down your Caldera font server
/etc/rc.d/init.d/ipx	Operations to start up and shut down your NetWare IPX daemon

Table 19-2.   *System Administration Configuration Files* (continued)

State	Description
init *state*	Changes the system state; you can use it to power up or power down a system, allow multiuser or single-user access; the **init** command takes as its argument a number representing a system state
System States	
0	Halt (do *not* set the default to this); shuts down system completely
1	Administrative single-user mode; denies other users access to the system but allows root access to entire multiuser file system
2	Multiuser, without NFS (the same as 3, if you do not have networking)

Table 19-3.   *Redhat's Runlevel States for System*

System States	Description
s or S	Single user; only one user has access to system; used when you want all other users off the system or you have a single-user personal system
3	Full multiuser mode; allows remote file sharing with other systems on your network
4	Unused
5	X11 only
6	Reboots; shuts down and restarts the system (do *not* set the default to this)

Table 19-3. *Redhat's Runlevel States for System* (continued)

Option	Description
shutdown **[-rkhncft]** *time* [*warning-message*]	Shuts the system down after the specified time period, issuing warnings to users; you can specify a warning message of your own after the time argument; if neither **-h** or **-r** are specified to shut down the system, the system sets to the administrative mode, runlevel state 1
Argument	
time	Has two possible formats—it can be an absolute time in the format *hh:mm*, with *hh* the hour (one or two digits) and *mm* the minute (in two digits); it can also be in the format +*m*, with *m* the number of minutes to wait; the word **now** is an alias for **+0**
Option	
-t *sec*	Tells **init** to wait *sec* seconds between sending processes the warning and the kill signal, before changing to another runlevel

Table 19-4. *System Shutdown Options*

Option	Description
-k	Doesn't really shut down; only sends the warning messages to everybody
-r	Reboots after shutdown, runlevel state 6
-h	Halts after shutdown, runlevel state 0
-n	Doesn't call **init** to do the shutdown—you do it yourself
-f	Does a *fast* reboot
-c	Cancels an already running shutdown; no time argument

Table 19-4.   *System Shutdown Options* (continued)

Command	Description
useradd *username options*	Adds new users to the system
usermod *username options*	Modifies a user's features
userdel –r *username*	Removes a user from the system
useradd, usermod Options	
-u *userid*	Sets the user ID of the new user; the default is the increment of the highest number used so far
-g *group*	Sets a group or name
-d *dir*	Sets the home directory of the new user
-s *shell*	Sets the login shell directory of the new user
-c *str*	Adds a comment to the user's entry in the system password file: **/etc/passwd**
-k *skl-dir*	Sets the skeleton directory that holds skeleton files, such as **.profile** files, that are copied to the user's home directory automatically when it is created; the default is **/etc/skel**

Table 19-5.   *User and Group Management Commands (for Redhat use* **usercfg** *or* **adduser** *instead)*

useradd, usermod Options	Description
-D	Displays defaults for all settings
Group Management Commands	
groupadd	Creates a new group
groupdel	Removes a group
groupmod *option*	Modifies a group -g Changes a group ID -n Changes a group name

Table 19-5.   *User and Group Management Commands (for Redhat use* usercfg *or* adduser *instead)* (continued)

Command	Operation
help [*command* ...]	Prints a short description of each command
abort *printers*	Terminates an active spooling daemon on the local host immediately and then disables printing for the specified printers; use **all** to indicate all printers
clean *printers*	Removes any temporary files, data files, and control files that cannot be printed
disable *printers*	Turns the specified printer queues off; new jobs will not be accepted
down *printers message*	Turns the specified printer queue off, disables printing and puts message in the printer status file
enable *printers*	Enables spooling for the listed printers; allows new jobs into the spool queue
quit or exit	Exits from lpc

Table 19-6.   lpc *Commands*

Command	Operation
restart *printers*	Starts a new printer daemon; used if the printer daemon, **lpd**, dies, leaving jobs yet to be printed
start *printers*	Enables printing and starts a spooling daemon for the listed printers
status *printers*	Displays the status of daemons and queues on the local machine
stop *printers*	Stops a spooling daemon after the current job completes and disables printing
topq *printer* [*jobnum* ...] [*user* ...]	Places the jobs in the order listed at the top of the printer queue
up *printers*	Enables everything and starts a new printer daemon; undoes the effects of **down**

Table 19-6.   **lpc** *Commands* (continued)

Command Line Option	lilo.conf option	Description
-b *bootdev*	**boot=***bootdev*	Boot device
-c	**compact**	Enables map compaction; speeds up booting
-d *dsec*	**delay=***dsec*	Timeout delay to wait for you to enter the label of an operating system at the LILO prompt when you boot up
-D *label*	**default=***label*	Uses the kernel with the specified label, instead of the first one in the list, as the default kernel to boot
-i *bootsector*	**install=***bootsector*	File to be used as the new boot sector

Table 19-7.   *LILO Options for Command Line and **lilo.conf***

Command Line Option	lilo.conf option	Description
-f *file*	**disktab=***file*	Disk geometry parameter file
-l	**linear**	Generates linear sector addresses instead of sector/head/cylinder addresses
-m *mapfile*	**map=***mapfile*	Uses specified map file instead of the default
-P fix	**fix-table**	Fixes corrupt partition tables
-P ignore	**ignore-table**	Ignores corrupt partition tables
-s *file*	**backup=***file*	Alternates save file for the boot sector
-S *file*	**force-backup=***file*	Allows overwriting of existing save file
-v	**verbose=***level*	Increases verbosity
-u		Uninstalls LILO by copying the saved boot sector back
-V		Prints version number
-t		Test only; does not really write a new boot sector or map file; uses together with **-v** to find out what LILO is about to do
-I		Displays label and path name of running kernel; label is held in BOOT_IMAGE shell variable

Table 19-7. *LILO Options for Command Line and **lilo.conf** (continued)*

Chapter Twenty

Network Administration

L inux systems are configured to connect into networks that use the TCP/IP protocols. These are the same protocols that the Internet, as well as many local networks, use. In Chapter 10 you were introduced to TCP/IP, a robust set of protocols that are designed to provide communications between systems with different operating systems and hardware. The protocols were developed in the 1970s as a special DARPA project to enhance communications between universities and research centers. The protocols were originally developed on Unix systems with much of the research carried out at the University of California, Berkeley. Linux, as a version of Unix, benefits from much of this original focus on Unix.

The TCP/IP protocols actually consist of different protocols, each designed for a specific task in a TCP/IP network. The two basic protocols are the Transmission Control Protocol (TCP), which handles receiving and sending communications, and the Internet Protocol (IP), which handles transmitting communications. Other protocols provide various network services. The Domain Name Service (DNS) provides address resolution. The File Transmission Protocol (ftp) provides file transmission, and Network File Systems (NFS) provides access to remote file systems. Table 20-1 lists the different TCP/IP protocols.

Administering and configuring a TCP/IP network on your Linux system is not particularly complicated. There are a set of configuration files that your system uses to set up and maintain your network. Table 20-2 has a complete listing. Many of these can be managed using administrative programs such as netcfg on your root user desktop. You can also use the more specialized programs, such as netstat, ifconfig, and route. Some configuration files are easy to modify yourself using a text editor. Table 20-3 lists the commonly used network administration programs.

If, during your installation, you entered the configuration information for your network, your system is ready to go. If your Linux system is already connected to a network, say an Ethernet network, then you do not need anything from this chapter, unless you want to understand how Linux is setting up your network connections. If you dial into a network through a modem, say to an Internet Service Provider (ISP), you will find the SLIP and PPP sections of this chapter useful. These tell you how to have your Linux system dial up an ISP and make the correct network connection. If you are having difficulty connecting to a network, or you are setting one up yourself, then all the information in this chapter will be helpful.

TCP/IP Network Addresses

As explained in Chapter 10, a TCP/IP address is organized into four segments consisting of numbers separated by periods. This is called the IP address. Part of this address is used for the network address, and the other part is used to identify a particular host in that network. The network address identifies the network that a particular host is a part of. Usually the network part of the address takes up the first three segments and the host takes the last segment. Altogether, this forms a unique address with which to identify any computer on a TCP/IP network. For example, in the IP address 199.35.209.72, the network part is 199.35.209 and the host part is 72. The host is a part of a network whose own address is 199.35.209.0.

The IP address of the host, or host address, is only one of several addresses you will need in order to connect the host to a network. In addition, you will need the network address, broadcast address, gateway address (if there is one), nameserver address, and a network mask, or netmask. All of these are asked for during installation. If you provided them at that time, they will all be automatically entered into the appropriate configuration files. Also, any entries that you make through the netcfg utility on your root user desktop will be entered. (Table 20-2 lists these network configuration addresses.)

Network Address

You can easily figure out the network address using your host address. It is the network part of your host address, with the host part set to 0. So the network address for the host address 199.35.209.72 is 199.35.209.0.

Systems derive the network address from the host address using the netmask. For those familiar with computer programming, a bitwise AND operation on the netmask and the host address results in zeroing the host part, leaving you with the network part of the host address.

Broadcast Address

The broadcast address allows a system to send the same message to all systems on your network at once. As with the network address, you can easily figure it out using your host address; it has the host part of your address set to 255. The network part remains untouched. So the broadcast address for the host address 199.35.209.72 is 199.35.209.255 (you combine the network part with 255 in the host part).

Gateway Address

Some networks will have a computer designated as the gateway to other networks. Every connection to and from the network to other networks passes through this gateway computer. If you are on this type of network, you will have to provide the gateway address. If your network does not have a gateway, or you use a stand-alone system or dial into an Internet Service Provider, you do not need a gateway address.

Usually a gateway address has the same network part of a hostname, with the host part set to 1. The gateway address for the host address 199.35.209.72 may be 199.35.209.1. However, this is just a convention. To be sure of your gateway address, ask your network administrator for it.

Nameserver Addresses

Many networks, including the Internet, have computers that operate as domain nameservers to translate the domain names of networks and hosts into IP addresses.

This makes your computer identifiable on a network, using just your domain name rather than your IP address. You can also use the domain names of other systems to reference them, so you don't have to know their IP addresses. You do, however, have to know the IP addresses of any domain nameservers for your network. You can obtain the addresses from your system administrator (there is often more than one). Even if you are using an Internet Service Provider, you will have to know the address of the domain nameservers that your ISP operates for the Internet.

Netmask

The netmask is used to derive the address of the network you are connected to. The netmask is determined using your host address as a template. All the numbers in the network part of your host address are set to 255, and the host part is set to 0. This then is your netmask. So the netmask for the host address 199.35.209.72 is 255.255.255.0. The network part, 199.35.209, has been set to 255.255.255, and the host part, .72, has been set to 0. Systems can then use your netmask to derive your network address from your host address. They can determine what part of your host address makes up your network address and what those numbers are.

TCP/IP Configuration Files

A set of configuration files in the **/etc** directory, shown in the following table, are used to set up and manage your TCP/IP network. They specify such network information as host and domain names, IP addresses, and interface options. It is in these files that the IP addresses and domain names of other Internet hosts that you want to access are entered. If you configured your network during installation, you will already find that information in these files. The netcfg program on your desktop and the netconfig program on your command line both provide an easy interface for entering the configuration data for these files.

File	Function
/etc/hosts	Associates hostnames with IP addresses
/etc/networks	Associates domain names with network addresses
/etc/rc.d/init.d/inet	Contains commands to configure your network interface when you boot up
/etc/hostname	Holds the hostname of your system

Identifying Hostnames: /etc/hosts

Without the unique IP address that the TCP/IP network uses to identify computers, a particular computer could not be located. Since IP addresses are difficult to use or remember, domain names are used instead. For each IP address there is a domain name. When you use a domain name to reference a computer on the network, your system translates it into its associated IP address. This address can then be used by your network to locate that computer.

Originally, it was the responsibility of every computer on the network to maintain a list of the hostnames and their IP addresses. This list is still kept in the /etc/hosts file. When you use a domain name, your system looks up its IP address in the **hosts** file. It is the responsibility of the systems administrator to maintain this list. Because of the explosive growth of the Internet and the development of more and more very large networks, the responsibility for associating domain names and IP addresses has been taken over by domain nameservers. However, the **hosts** file is still used to hold the domain names and IP addresses of frequently accessed hosts. Your system will always check your **hosts** file for the IP address of a domain name before taking the added step of accessing a nameserver.

The format of a domain name entry in the **hosts** file is the IP address followed by the domain name, separated by a space. You can then add aliases for the hostname. After the entry, on the same line, you can enter a comment. A comment is always preceded by a **#** symbol. You will already find an entry in your **hosts** file for "localhost" with the IP address 127.0.0.1. Localhost is a special identification used by your computer to enable users on your system to communicate locally with each other. The IP address 127.0.0.1 is a special reserved address used by every computer for this purpose. It identifies what is technically referred to as a loopback device.

/etc/hosts

```
127.0.0.1        richlp.ix.com          localhost
199.35.209.72    richlp.ix.com
204.32.168.56    pango1.train.com
202.211.234.1    rose.berkeley.edu
```

Network Name: /etc/networks

The /etc/networks file holds the domain names and IP addresses of networks that you are connected to, not the domain names of particular computers. Networks have shortened IP addresses. Depending on the type of network, they will use one, two, or three numbers for their IP addresses. You will also have your localhost network IP address 127.0.0.0. This is the network address used for the loopback device.

The IP addresses are entered, followed by the network domain names. Recall that an IP address consists of a network part and a host part. The network part is the network address you will find in the **networks** file. You will always have an entry in this file for the network portion of your computer's IP address. This is the network address of the network your computer is connected to.

/etc/networks

```
loopback 127.0.0.0
ix.com 199.35.209.0
```

Network Initialization: /etc/rc.d/init.d/inet

The **/etc/rc.d/init.d/inet** file holds the startup commands for configuring your network. Many of the entries are automatically made for you when you use netcfg or configure your network during installation. You will find the `ifconfig` and `route` commands, for example, as described in the next section. You will also find your hostname, network address, and the other required addresses. You should never attempt to modify this file directly unless you are sure of what you are doing and know something about Linux shell programming. If you are using another Linux distribution such as Slackware, the initialization file may be called **/etc/rec.d/rc.inet1** or simply **/etc/rc.inet1**.

/etc/hostname

The **/etc/hostname** file holds your system's hostname. To change your hostname, you change this entry. The netcfg program allows you to change your hostname and will place the new name in **/etc/hostname**. Instead of displaying this file to find your hostname, you can use the `hostname` command.

```
$ hostname
richlp
```

Network Interfaces and Routes: ifconfig and route

Your connection to a network is made by your system through a particular hardware interface such as an Ethernet card or a modem. Data passing through this interface is then routed to your network. The `ifconfig` command configures your network interfaces, and the `route` command will route them accordingly. The NetCfg window on your Caldera Network Desktop performs the same configuration of network interfaces as `ifconfig` and `route`. If you configure an interface with netcfg, you do not have to use `ifconfig` or `route`. If you are using another Linux system, the netconfig utility also performs the same configuration as netcfg. However, you can directly configure interfaces using `ifconfig` and `route`, if you wish.

Every time you start your system, the network interfaces and their routes have to be established. You can have this done automatically for you when you boot up by placing the **ifconfig** and **route** commands for each interface in the **/etc/rc.d/init.d/inet** initialization file, which is executed whenever you start your system. If you use netcfg on your Caldera Network Desktop to configure your network interfaces, then the appropriate **ifconfig** and **route** commands are automatically added to the **/etc/rc.d/init.d/inet** file. You do not have to add them. If you did not use the **netcfg** command, you have to enter them yourself.

netcfg

The easiest way to create a network interface is to use the netcfg program on your root user desktop. Just log into the root account and use **startx** to start the desktop. You will see an icon labeled "netcfg." Double-click on it, and it will display a window showing all your network interfaces. As shown in Figure 20-1, with netcfg you can change and add to your network configuration.

The NetCfg window displays interfaces, nameservers, and hosts. Each is displayed and managed in its own window, with its own buttons. The Interface window lists your current interfaces. You can use the buttons at the bottom of this window to add, configure, activate, or deactivate an interface. When adding a new interface, another window will open up, listing entry boxes for required information. Here, you enter such information as the interface's name and IP address. Upon closing this window, you will see an entry for this interface appear in the Interface window.

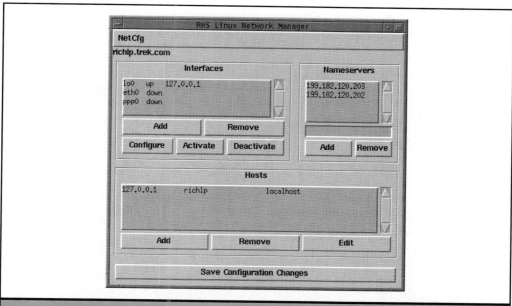

Figure 20-1. *The netcfg utility*

The Nameserver window to the right lists all current nameservers. You can use its buttons to add or remove nameservers. Any entries you make here are automatically entered into the **/etc/resolv.conf** file. The bottom window lists the hosts with their IP numbers and hostnames. These are other computers that you are connected to. With the window's buttons you can add or remove hosts or edit the current hosts. Changes and new entries will be saved to your **/etc/hosts** file.

You can also change your hostname. Select the hostname item on the NetCfg menu in the upper-left corner. You will then be prompted for a new hostname. Your entry will be placed in the **/etc/hostname** file, replacing the previous one.

Once you have made all your changes, click on the Save Configuration button to make them permanent. The new information you entered will be added to the appropriate network configuration files.

ifconfig

The **ifconfig** command takes as its arguments the name of an interface and an IP address, as well as options. **ifconfig** then assigns the IP address to the interface. Your system now knows that there is such an interface and that it references a particular IP address. In addition, you can specify whether the IP address is a host or network address. You can use a domain name for the IP address, provided the domain name is listed along with its IP address in the **/etc/hosts** file. The syntax for the **ifconfig** command follows:

```
# ifconfig  interface  -host_net_flag  address  options
```

The *host_net_flag* can be either **-host** or **-net** to indicate a host or network IP address. The **-host** flag is the default. The **ifconfig** command can have several options, which set different features of the interface, such as the maximum number of bytes it can transfer (**mtu**) or the broadcast address. The **up** and **down** options activate and deactivate the interface. In the next example, the **ifconfig** command configures an Ethernet interface.

```
# ifconfig eth0  204.32.168.56
```

For a simple configuration such as this, **ifconfig** automatically generates a standard broadcast address and netmask. The standard broadcast address is the network address with the number 255 for the host address. Remember that the standard netmask is 255.255.255.0. However, if you are connected to a network with a particular netmask and broadcast address, you will have to specify them when you use **ifconfig**. The option for specifying the broadcast address is **broadcast**; for the network mask it is **netmask**. Table 20-4 lists the different **ifconfig** options. In the next example, **ifconfig** includes the netmask and broadcast address.

```
# ifconfig eth0 204.32.168.56    broadcast 204.128.244.127
netmask 255.255.255.0
```

Point-to-point interfaces such as Parallel IP (PLIP), Serial Line IP (SLIP), and Point-to-Point Protocol (PPP) require that you include the **pointopoint** option. A PLIP interface name is identified with the name plip with an attached number, for example, **plip0** is the first PLIP interface. SLIP interfaces use **slip0**, and PPP interfaces start with **ppp0**. Point-to-point interfaces are those that usually operate between only two hosts, such as two computers connected over a modem. When you specify the **pointopoint** option, you need to include the IP address of the host. Later in the chapter you will see how you can use SLIP and PPP interfaces to dial up and connect your system to an Internet Service Provider.

In the next example, a PLIP interface is configured that connects the computer at IP address 199.35.209.72 with one at 204.166.254.14. If there were domain addresses listed for these systems in **/etc/hosts**, those domain names could be used in place of the IP addresses.

```
# ifconfig  plip0  199.35.209.72  pointopoint 204.166.254.14
```

Should you need to, you can also use **ifconfig** to configure your loopback device. The name of the loopback device is **lo**, and its IP address is the special address 127.0.0.1. The following example shows the configuration.

```
# ifconfig lo 127.0.0.1
```

The **ifconfig** command is very useful for checking on the status of an interface. If you enter the **ifconfig** command alone with the name of the interface, information about that interface is displayed.

```
# ifconfig eth0
```

To see if your loopback interface is configured, you can use **ifconfig** with the loopback interface name, **lo**.

```
# ifconfig lo
lo          Link encap:Local Loopback
```

```
        inet addr:127.0.0.1  Bcast:127.255.255.255
Mask:255.0.0.0
        UP BROADCAST LOOPBACK RUNNING  MTU:2000  Metric:1
        RX packets:0 errors:0 dropped:0 overruns:0
        TX packets:12 errors:0 dropped:0 overruns:0
```

Routing

A packet that is part of a transmission takes a certain *route* to reach its destination. On a large network, packets are transmitted from one computer to another until the destination computer is reached. The route determines where the process starts and what computer your system needs to send the packet to in order for it to reach its destination. On small networks, routing may be static; that is, the route from one system to another is fixed. One system knows how to reach another, moving through fixed paths. However, on larger networks and on the Internet, routing is dynamic. Your system knows the first computer to send its packet off to, and then that computer takes it from there, passing it on to another that then determines where to pass it on to. For dynamic routing, your system needs to know very little. Static routing, however, can become very complex, since you have to keep track of all the network connections.

Your routes are listed in your routing table in the **/proc/net/route** file. To display the routing table, enter **route** with no arguments.

```
# route
Kernel routing table
Destination      Gateway      Genmask       Flags MSS    Window Use Iface
loopback           *          255.0.0.       U    1936     0     12  lo
pango1.train.com   *          255.255.255.0  U    1936     0      0  eth0
```

Each entry in the routing table has several fields, providing information such as the route destination and the type of interface used. The different fields are listed in the following table.

Field	Description
Destination	Destination IP address of the route
Gateway	IP address or hostname of the gateway the route uses; * indicates no gateway is used
Genmask	The netmask for the route

Field	Description
Flags	Type of route: U=up, H=host, G=gateway, D=dynamic, M=modified
MSS	TCP MSS for route
Metric	Metric cost of route
Ref	Number of routes that depend on this one
Window	TCP window for AX.25 networks
Use	Number of times used
Iface	Type of interface this route uses

You should have at least one entry in the routing table for the loopback interface. If not, you will have to route the loopback interface using the **route** command. The IP address for an interface has to be added to the routing table before you can use that interface. You add an address with the **route** command and the **add** option.

```
route  add  address
```

The next example adds the IP address for the loopback interface to the routing table.

```
route add 127.0.0.1
```

The **add** argument has several options, as specified in the man pages for **route**. If you are adding a specific static route, you will need to use these options to specify such features as the netmask, gateway, interface device, or destination address. However, if an interface has already been brought up by **ifconfig**, then **ifconfig** can draw much of its information from the interface configuration. For example, to set a route for an Ethernet connection that has already been configured by **ifconfig**, you only need to enter the **-net** option and the IP address of the destination. **ifconfig** uses the IP address to locate the interface configured for it and then uses that information to establish the route. The following example is the routing of an Ethernet interface.

```
# route add -net  204.32.168.0
```

If your system is connected to a network, there should be at least one entry in your routing table that specifies the default route. This is the route taken by a message packet when no other route entry leads to its destination. The destination for a default route is the keyword **default**.

You can delete any route you've established by invoking **ifconfig** with the **del** argument and the IP address of that route, as in this example:

```
# route del -net    204.32.168.0
```

Monitoring Your Network: ping and netstat

With the ping program you can check to see if you can actually access another host on your network. Ping will send a request to the host for a reply. The host then sends a reply back, and it is displayed on your screen. Ping will continually send such a request until you stop it with a break command, a CTRL-C. You will see one reply after another scroll by on your screen until you stop the program. If ping cannot access a host, it will issue a message saying that the host is unreachable. If ping fails, it is an indication that your network connection is not working. It may just be the particular interface, or a basic configuration problem, or a bad physical connection. To use ping, enter **ping** and the name of the host.

```
$ ping rose
```

The netstat program provides real-time information on the status of your network connections, as well as network statistics and the routing table. Netstat has several options you can use to bring up different information about your network.

```
# netstat
Active Internet connections
Proto Recv-Q Send-Q Local Address  Foreign Address        (State)      User
tcp   0      0  richlp.ic.com:01  pango1.train.com.:ftp  ESTABLISHED  dylan
Active UNIX domain sockets
Proto RefCnt Flags      Type         State       Path
unix  1      [ ACC ]    SOCK_STREAM  LISTENING   /dev/printer
unix  2      [ ]        SOCK_STREAM  CONNECTED   /dev/log
unix  1      [ ACC ]    SOCK_STREAM  LISTENING   /dev/nwapi
unix  2      [ ]        SOCK_STREAM  CONNECTED   /dev/log
unix  2      [ ]        SOCK_STREAM  CONNECTED
unix  1      [ ACC ]    SOCK_STREAM  LISTENING   /dev/log
```

The **netstat** command with no options will list the network connections on your system. (See Table 20-5 at the end of the chapter for **netstat** options.) First, active

TCP connections are listed and then the active domain sockets. The domain sockets contain processes used to set up communications between your system and other systems. The various fields are described in the following table.

Field	Description
Proto	Protocol used for the connection: TCP, UDP
Recv-Q	Bytes received but not yet used by the system
Send-Q	Bytes sent to remote system, but not yet confirmed as received
Local Address	Local hostname and port number
Foreign Address	Remote hostname and port number assigned to a connection; port number can be connection type, such as telnet or ftp
(State)	State of connection to remote host ESTABLISHD, connection established SYN_SENT, trying to make connection SYN_REC, connection being created FIN_WAIT1, connection shutting down CLOSED, connection closed LISTEN, listening for remote connection UNKNOWN, unknown state

Domain Socket

Proto	Protocol for socket, usually **unix**
RefCnt	Number of processes currently in socket

Flag

Type	Mode socket is accessed
State	State of the socket FREE, socket is not used LISTENING, waiting for connection UNCONNECTED, no current connection CONNECTING, trying to make connection CONNECTED, currently connected DISCONNECTING, closing a connection
Path	Path name used by processes to access socket

You can use **netstat** with the **-r** option to display the routing table, and **netstat** with the **-i** option displays the usage for the different network interfaces. The following table explains the coded information.

```
# netstat -i
Kernel Interface table
Iface    MTU Met  RX-OK RX-ERR RX-DRP RX-OVR   TX-OK TX-ERR TX-DRP TX-OVR Flags
lo      2000   0      0      0      0      0      58      0      0      0 BLRU
```

MTU	Maximum number of bytes for one packet
RX-OK	Packets received with no errors
RX-ERR	Packets received with errors
RX-DRP	Packets dropped
RX-OVR	Packet overrun errors
TX-OK	Packets sent with no errors
TX-ERR	Packets sent with errors
TX-DRP	Packets dropped in transmission
TX-OVR	Packets dropped in transmission with overrun errors
Flags	Interface characteristics: A, receives packets for Multicast addresses B, receives broadcasts D, debugging is on L, loopback interface M, promiscuous mode N, no trailers processed on packets O, address resolution protocol is off P, point-to-point interface R, interface is running U, interface is activated, up

Domain Name Service (DNS)

Each computer connected to a TCP/IP network such as the Internet is identified by its own IP address. An IP address is a set of four numbers specifying the location of a network and of a host (a computer) within that network. IP addresses are difficult to remember, so a domain name version of each IP address is also used to identify a host. As described in Chapter 10, a domain name consists of two parts, the hostname and the domain. The hostname is the computer's specific name, and the domain identifies the network that the computer is a part of. The domains used for the United States usually have extensions that identify the type of host. For example, **.edu** is used for educational institutions and **.com** is used for businesses. International domains usually have extensions that indicate the country they are located in, such as **.du** for Germany or **.au** for Australia. The combination of a hostname, domain, and extension forms a unique name by which a computer can be referenced. The domain can, in turn, be split into further subdomains.

As you know, a computer on a network can still only be identified by its IP address, even if it has a domain name. You can use a domain name to reference a computer on a network, but this involves using the domain name to look up the corresponding IP address in a database. The network then uses the IP address, not the domain name, to access the computer. Before the advent of very large TCP/IP networks such as the Internet, it was feasible for each computer on a network to maintain a file with a list of all the domain names and IP addresses of the computers connected on its network. Whenever a domain name was used, it was looked up in this file and the corresponding IP address located. You can still do this on your own system for remote systems that you access frequently.

As networks became larger, it became impractical and, in the case of the Internet, impossible for each computer to maintain its own list of all the domain names and IP addresses. To provide the service of translating domain addresses to IP addresses, databases of domain names were developed and placed on their own servers. To find the IP address of a domain name, a query is sent to a nameserver that then looks up the IP address for you and sends it back. In a large network, there can be several nameservers covering different parts of the network. If a nameserver cannot find a particular IP address, it will send the query on to another nameserver that is more likely to have it. Nameservers can also provide information such as the company name and street address of a computer, or even the person maintaining it.

Nameservers are queried by resolvers. These are programs specially designed to obtain addresses from nameservers. To use domain names on your system, you will have to configure your own resolver. Your local resolver is configured by your **/etc/host.conf** and **/etc/resolv.conf** files.

host.conf

Your **host.conf** file lists resolver options (shown in the following table). Each option can have several fields, separated by spaces or tabs. You can use a **#** at the beginning of a line to enter a comment. The options tell the resolver what services to use. The order of the list is important. The resolver will begin with the first option listed and move on to the next ones in turn. You will find the **host.conf** file in your **/etc** directory along with other configuration files.

order	Specifies sequence of name resolution methods
	hosts Checks for name in the local **/etc/host** file
	bind Queries a DNS nameserver for address
	nis Uses Network Information Service protocol to obtain address
alert	Checks addresses of remote sites attempting to access your system; you turn it on or off with the **on** and **off** options
nospoof	Confirms addresses of remote sites attempting to access your system
trim	For checking your local hosts file, removes the domain name and checks only for the hostname; allows you to use just a hostname in your host file for an IP address instead of the complete **host.domain.ext** name
multi	For checking your local hosts file, allows a host to have several IP addresses; you turn it on or off with the **on** and **off** options

In the next example of a **host.conf** file, the **order** option instructs your resolver to first look up names in your local **/etc/hosts** file and then, if that fails, to query domain nameservers. The system does not have multiple addresses.

/etc/host.conf

```
# host.conf file
# Lookup names in host file and then check DNS
order bind host
# There are no multiple addresses
multi off
```

/etc/resolv.conf

For the resolver to do its job, it must have access to domain nameservers. In the **resolv.conf** file you provide the resolver with the addresses of the domain nameservers that your system has access to. There are three different types of entries that you can make in your **resolv.conf** file, each preceded by one of three keywords; domain, nameserver, and search. For the domain entry you list the domain name of your system. You can, if you wish, add search entries. A search entry provides a list of domains to try if only a hostname is given. If there is a system that you access frequently, you could enter its domain name in a search entry and then just use its hostname as the address. Your resolver will then try to find the hostname using the domain name listed in the search entry.

Following the search entries, if there are any, you place your nameserver entries. For each nameserver your system has access to you enter **nameserver** and the nameserver's IP address. There may be several nameservers that you can access. The order is important. Often networks will have a primary nameserver followed by several secondary ones. The primary one is expected to be queried first. To do this you must have its IP address entered in the first nameserver entry.

The following is an example of a **resolv.conf** file. The domain of the host computer is **berkeley.edu**. The IP addresses of the nameservers for this domain are listed in the nameserver entries. The search entry will allow just the hostname for a computer in the **unc.edu** domain to be used as an address. For example, to access **sunsite.unc.edu**, a user would only have to enter the hostname as an address, **sunsite**.

/etc/resolv.conf

```
#  resolv.conf file
domain berkeley.edu
search unc.edu
nameserver  204.199.87.2
nameserver  204.199.77.2
```

Setting Up Your Own Nameserver: named

If you are administering a network and you need to set up a nameserver for it, you can configure a Linux system to operate as a nameserver. To do so you have to start up the **named** daemon. **named** is designed to start with the system and then wait for domain name queries. It makes use of several configuration files that enable it to answer requests. The **named.boot** file specifies the domain that the server supports as well as the directory for its working files. The **named.hosts** file holds information about that domain. It consists of resource records that list information about the different hosts in the domain. The records use a very specific format with codes placed in appropriate fields. The **named.rev** file maps IP addresses to hostnames. The **named.ca** file sets up caching for the nameserver. The process of setting up your own nameserver can be complicated. Refer to HOW-TO documentation, the man entry for **named**, and to Linux texts specializing in network administration.

SLIP and PPP

As an alternative to hardwired network connections such as Ethernet, you can use a modem with telephone lines. There are two protocols that can transmit IP communications across the telephone lines. These are the Serial Line Internet Protocol (SLIP) and the Point-to-Point Protocol (PPP). SLIP is an older protocol, whereas PPP is more recent, though very stable. Many high-speed connections used by current Internet Service Providers (ISP) use PPP. The SLIP and PPP protocols are especially designed for users who connect their systems to the Internet over a modem and telephone line. Usually a connection is made to an ISP that then connects the system to the Internet through its own systems.

An Internet Service Provider will support either SLIP or PPP on a given line. Find out which protocol your ISP supports. You need to use one or the other. For example, Netcruiser accounts provided by Netcom use the PPP protocol, whereas many of their Shell accounts use SLIP protocols.

Setting up a SLIP or PPP connection can be a complicated process. For more detailed explanations, see the PPP-HOW-TO and the Net-2-HOW-TO documents in **/usr/doc/HOW-TO**. There are also Web page instructions in **/usr/doc/HTML**.

Preparations for Connecting to SLIP or PPP

To make a SLIP or PPP connection you must have TCP/IP networking enabled and a loopback interface configured. The Caldera Network Desktop does this automatically. Internet Service Providers usually maintain domain nameservers that you can use. You have to find the IP address of these nameservers and enter them into your **/etc/resolv** file. You can also use netcfg on the desktop to enter the address, and netcfg will place them in the **/etc/resolv** file for you. In any event, use **more** or **cat** to display the contents of **/etc/resolv** to make sure the domain name addresses are there. Without them, none of the addresses you enter will be recognized.

SLIP and CSLIP: dip

There are two types of SLIP connections, the standard one referred to as just SLIP, and the newer Compress SLIP, referred to as CSLIP. Be sure you know which type of connection your Internet Service Provider is giving you. You will have to specify one or the other as your protocol mode when you connect. Except for specifying the mode, the connection procedure is the same for both. References to SLIP will apply to both SLIP and CSLIP unless specifically noted.

You use the **dip** program to manage and set up your SLIP connection. Given the appropriate information, **dip** will make a connection for you to your ISP. You can then use all the Internet applications on your system, such as Netscape or ftp.

The **dip** program operates like an interpreter. In a file called a **dip** script you specify certain commands needed to log into the ISP and make the connection. The **dip** program then reads the commands in this file, executing them one by one. For example, the command **dial** will use your modem to dial up your ISP. A **dip** script has an extension .dip. Once your **dip** script is ready, you can then invoke **dip** with the name of the script. You may also want to add the **-v** option to display each command as it executes to see if any problems arise. The following shows the basic syntax for invoking **dip**.

```
$ dip -v  scriptfile.dip
```

Table 20-6 lists the different commands for a **dip** script. Several of the key commands are **port**, **speed**, **dial**, **get**, **modem**, **mode**, and **default**. **dip** also uses several special variables that hold connection information, such as $rmtip that holds the IP address of the remote system.

Scripts will vary slightly depending on the different login procedures of Internet Service Providers. The login prompt, phone number, and connect string vary from one ISP to another. However, there are two significantly different formats, depending on whether your ISP provides you with a static or dynamic IP address. To set up a SLIP connection, determine what type of IP address your ISP is giving you.

If you have difficulty connecting to your system with a **dip** script, you might want to run **dip** in the interactive mode, **-t**. In this mode, **dip** generates its own shell with the prompt DIP>. You can then enter **dip** commands one at a time at the prompt. If you also use the **-v** option, **dip** will display a detailed description of all the actions it takes. For the login process you could also use the **term** command at the **dip** prompt. This places you in a terminal mode in which you will be prompted directly by your ISP system for your user ID and password. Once connected, a CTRL-] returns you to the **dip** shell prompt. You can then continue, setting the route and mode. **term** is a way for you to see exactly what login and password prompts the remote ISP system is sending you. Once you have worked out the connection procedure, it is, of course, much easier to use a **dip** script.

```
#  dip -t -v
 DIP>
```

If you need to cut a **dip** connection, you use the **dip** command with the **-k** option. You can also add the **-l** option and a line to cut a specific connection. The **dip** command with just **-k** will cut the most recent connection. The **-k** option is helpful if you succeed in making a connection but for some reason are unable to log in or establish your line mode. The connection will remain active until you specifically cut it by entering **dip** with the **-k** option.

```
$ dip -k
```

Static IP Addresses in dip Scripts

A static IP address is an address that your ISP gives you to keep. Your computer is always identified by this address. When you initiate a SLIP connection to the ISP's remote host, you use your static IP address to identify your system. For connections using a static IP address, you assign your static IP address to the variable **$local** and the ISP remote host's address to the variable **$remote**. You use the **get** command to assign a value to a variable. These assignments take place at the very beginning of your **dip** script. **dip** will look for the respective IP addresses in these variables. Once the IP addresses are set, you can continue with the commands for the login procedure. A listing of the different **dip** variables is provided in Table 20-7.

```
get $local   static-IP-address
get $remote  remote-IP-address
```

The dip Script

The following is an example of a **dip** script using a static address. An example of this script can be found in the man page for **dip**. The script begins with a series of commands to set up the modem. First the device the modem is on is determined. The com1, com2, com3, and com4 ports correspond to **/dev/cua0**, **/dev/cua1**, **/dev/cua2**, and **/dev/cua3**. Notice that the device counts from 0, so that com4 corresponds to **cua3**. The speed is then set to 38400, the standard setting for a v.28 modem. The **init** command specifies the initialization string for the modem. Here you enter any special codes for your particular modem. The **reset** command takes that string and uses it to initialize the modem.

mystatic.dip

```
# For a static IP address assign your system's IP address to the variable $local
get $local 199.35.209.72
# For a static IP address assign the remote system's IP address to the variable
$remote
get $remote 163.179.4.22
# Set the netmask to 255.255.255.0
netmask 255.255.255.0
# Set port and speed.
port modum
reset
speed 38400
wait OK 2
init AT&FE1Q0V1X1&K3L0
```

```
# The Standard errlvl values:
#   0 - OK
#   1 - CONNECT
#   2 - ERROR
#   3 - BUSY
#   4 - NO CARRIER
#   5 - NO DIALTONE
if $errlvl != 0 goto modem_trouble
dial 777-8888
if $errlvl != 1 goto modem_trouble
# Connection made, now login to the system.
wait CONNECT 15
if $errlvl != 0 goto error
wait ogin: 20
if $errlvl != 0 goto error
send richlp\n
wait word: 20
if $errlvl != 0 goto error
send richlp843\n
# We are now logged in.
# Set up the SLIP operating parameters.
get $mtu 1500
# Sets up SLIP connection as default route for mode use PPP or CSLIP.
default
mode CSLIP
print You are now connected to $locip as  $rmtip
goto exit
modem_trouble:
print Trouble occurred with the modem...
error:
print CONNECT FAILED to $remote
quit 1
exit:
exit
```

Next the static and remote IP addresses are assigned to the **$local** and **$remote** variables. The actual login can now proceed. The **dial** command dials the indicated number. If the dial-in fails to make a connection, it will return an error value to the **$errlvl** variable. This value is checked right after the **dial** command to see if there was a problem and to skip the rest of the script, printing out an error message, if there was. The **wait** command then waits for a connect string. This may vary by ISP. For some it may be the word CONNECT, for others it may be the baud rate, such as 38400. **wait** will continually look for the connect string in transmissions that the remote host is sending you. The number after the connect string is the number of seconds to wait for it to come through. After this period, **wait** will time out instead of just waiting indefinitely. Again **$errlvl** is checked to see if this failed. Be sure you know what the connect string is. If you don't, check with your ISP or try using the terminal mode to interactively log in and see what the remote system is sending you. In response to the connect string, you can then send a return. The symbol for a return is **\n**. For some remote hosts you may have to use the DOS version of a return, which is represented by two symbols, **\r\n**.

The next **wait** command waits for the remote host to send you the login prompt. You only need the last part of the prompt, not the whole word. Usually the prompt is **login:**, and you only have to specify **ogin:**. If this does not work, check with your ISP to find out what your login prompt is. After the login prompt is received, the **send** command sends the user's login name. You will have to enter a return at the end of the login name, as in: **richlp\n**. Some ISPs require that you qualify your login name. For example, Netcom requires that you enter a $ before the login name for CSLIP, and a **#** before the login name, as in **#richlp\n**. The next **wait** command waits for the password prompts to be sent. This is usually "password:" and you only need the last few characters, **word:**. Then you use the **send** command to send your password. You will have to include the return, **\n**.

A **print** command then tells you that you were able to connect and displays the remote host's address. You now have to configure the connection, setting the route and the type. The **default** command makes this connection your default route. The **mode** command determines the type of connection. This depends on the type of connection your ISP is giving you. You can have a standard SLIP connection, as indicated by SLIP, or you could have a compressed SLIP connection, as indicated by CSLIP. Use the appropriate one with the **mode** command to establish your TCP/IP connection.

Dynamic IP Addresses with dip

A dynamic IP address is an address that your ISP gives you when you connect to the system. Your ISP keeps a pool of IP addresses that it hands out to users as they connect. This means that your IP address may be different each time you connect—you will not know ahead of time what your IP address will be. As part of the connect procedure, your ISP will send your system the IP address it has assigned you for this session. You then need to detect this address and use it as your system's IP address on the Internet.

Your ISP will send your system the IP address after you connect and log in. You then have to grab this address and assign it to the **$local** variable. The **get** command with the option **remote** will assign a value that is received from the remote host, in this case, the ISP's remote system you are connecting to. After you send your password, but before you set the default route and the mode, you enter the following **get** commands. You first receive the remote system's IP address and then the local IP address for your system. There is no earlier assignment of a value to either the **$local** or **$remote** variable.

```
get $remote remote
get $local remote
```

You can add a timeout number at the end of these commands in case the remote system fails to send them.

mydynamic.dip

```
# Set the netmask to 255.255.255.0
netmask 255.255.255.0
# Set port and speed.
port modum
speed 38400
reset
wait OK 2
init AT&FE1Q0V1X1&K3L0
if $errlvl != 0 goto modem_trouble
dial 777-8888
if $errlvl != 1 goto modem_trouble
wait CONNECT 15
# Connection made, now login to the system.
wait ogin: 20
if $errlvl != 0 goto error
send richlp\n
wait word: 20
if $errlvl != 0 goto error
send richlp843\n
# We are now logged in.
# get the dynamically provided IP address for the remote system
get $remote remote
# get the dynamically provided IP address assigned for the local system, your
system
get $local remote
# Set up the SLIP operating parameters.
```

```
get $mtu 1500
# Sets up SLIP connection as default route for mode use PPP or CSLIP.
default
mode CSLIP
print You are now connected to $locip as  $rmtip
goto exit
modem_trouble:
print Trouble occurred with the modem...
error:
print CONNECT FAILED to $remote
quit 1
exit:
exit
```

With Redhat's ntchg program on the root user's Caldera Network Desktop, you can more easily configure your **dip** scripts. The upper-left box of the NetCfg window displays your different network interfaces. For a SLIP connection you can choose to add a new interface and then select the SLIP type. You are offered three different options: Ethernet, SLIP, and PPP. You are also asked to name the interface. A SLIP interface name consists of **sl** followed by a number, beginning with 0, as in **sl0**. It is possible to use **dip** to configure a PPP connection, but it is far more reliable to use the **pppd** program described a little later in the chapter.

Having named your interface, you are then presented with a window listing the different values used by a **dip** script, including your phone number, IP address, password, and login name. Enter the values in the appropriate fields. Then click OK. These values are used in a specially designed **dip** script called **/etc/dip-script**. When you activate this SLIP interface, this script executes and the **dip** values you entered are inserted in the appropriate places. You can edit the **/etc/dip-script** file if you need to. You can also copy it, make changes to the copy, and use that instead of **/etc/dip-script**. There is a place in your SLIP interface configuration for entering either your own **dip** script or the default

/etc/dip-script

```
# dip-script-- used with RHS netcfg for SLIP, CSLIP, and PPP
# Version:     0.1
# Author:      Fred N. van Kempen
# Modified:    Marc Ewing for Red Hat Software
main:
# Lines to be deleted for dynamic addressing
  get $local @@@local-ip@@@
  get $remote @@@remote-ip@@@
  port modem
```

```
   speed @@@modem-speed@@@
   reset
 # You may need to send some modem set-up string here
   init AT&FE1Q0V1X1&K3L0
   send ATDT@@@phone-number@@@\r
   wait CONNECT 45
   if $errlvl != 0 goto error
 # You may need to change \n to \r\n
login:
 # You may not need this sleep
   sleep 3
 # You'll need to set this "ogin:" to match the login
 # string of the host you are dialing
   wait ogin: 10
   if $errlvl != 0 goto error
   send @@@login-id@@@\n
   if $errlvl != 0 goto error
 # Same here, for the password
   wait word: 10
   if $errlvl != 0 goto error
   send @@@password@@@\n
   wait @@@connect-string@@@ 30
   if $errlvl != 0 goto error
loggedin:
 # Lines to be added for dynamic addressing, currently commented out
 # get $remote  remote
 # get  $local  remote
get $mtu @@@mtu@@@
   default
done:
   print CONNECTED to $remote with address $rmtip
   mode @@@connection-type@@@
   exit
error:
   print @@@connection-type@@@ to $remote failed.
```

The **/etc/dip-script** file as provided is designed for static IP addresses. If your ISP provides dynamic IP addresses, you will have to change the **/etc/dip-script** file or make a copy and change that, designating the copy as your **dip** script in the netcfg interface configuration. You will have to delete the two **get local** and **get remote** entries at the top of the file and enter the **get $remote remote** and get **$local remote** entries right before the **default** command.

Providing Incoming SLIP Connections from Other Systems: diplogin

With Linux, not only can you make a SLIP connection to a remote system, but other systems can make their own SLIP connections to your system. Another system can dial into your system and make a SLIP connection. If you have provided an account for a user on that remote system, then the user could dial in a SLIP connection and log into that account. Such remote dial-up SLIP connections are managed by **dip** with the **-i** option. This places **dip** in a dial-in mode to receive incoming connections. This invocation of **dip** can also be made by **diplogin**, which is a symbolic link to **dip**. In the dial-in mode, **dip** will prompt a remote user for a user ID and a password, and then make the SLIP connection.

You first have to create an account for the remote user on your system. You can use **usercfg** or **adduser** to create the account. If you are concerned with security, you might want to place the user's home directory in a special directory that you can more easily control, such as **/tmp**. Creating a user account places an entry for that user in the **/etc/passwd** file. In the following entry the user's name is **robert**, the password is **starq**, and the home directory is **/tmp**.

```
robert:starq:204:12:UUNET:/tmp:/usr/sbin/diplogin
```

The last field in the password entry specifies the type of login shell the user will have. Here the login shell is **diplogin**, which is a symbolic link to the **dip** program. **dip** will search for the user name in the **/etc/diphosts** file to obtain login and configuration information.

Once you have created the account, you have to configure its SLIP connection. These configurations are placed in the **/etc/diphosts** file. There are seven fields to each entry, separated by colons. The first is the user ID, followed by a secondary password. The third field is the hostname or IP address of the remote system, followed by the hostname or IP address of your local system. The fifth field is the network mask followed by an informational field for comments. The last field specifies the connection parameters for the account, such as the protocol (CSLIP or SLIP) and the MTU value.

If you specified a secondary password, **diplogin** will prompt for this password before the standard user login procedure.

/etc/diphosts

```
# user : password : remote host : local host : netmask : comments :
protocol,MTU
robert:starq:rose.berkeley.edu:richlp.ix.com:255.255.255.0::SLIP,1500
valerie::pango1.train.com: richlp.ix.com:255.255.255.0::CSLIP,296
```

PPP

The Point-to-Point Protocol (PPP) is a more recent and more versatile protocol that is quickly becoming popular. It provides a much more stable connection and can support a variety of network protocols, not just the Internet Protocols. PPP performs much of its work automatically. It does not need a set of commands for each specific step as SLIP does. PPP will automatically determine remote IP addresses, static or dynamic.

A PPP connection is set up using the **pppd** program. **pppd** will configure your connection, setting MTU limits and obtaining IP addresses. However, unlike **dip**, **pppd** does not make the initial connection. It does not dial up through your modem and provide login and password information. To use **pppd** you first have to establish the connection to the remote host. You can make such a connection using the chat program, which has its own options and format. The chat program first makes the connection, and then **pppd** configures it. However, you do not have to call chat first and then **pppd**. **pppd** is designed to take as its argument a program that will make the connection, in this case **chat**. You simply specify chat along with its options on the command line with **pppd**. In fact, the entire **pppd** operation takes place on one command line, unlike the **dip** script.

Static and dynamic IP addresses are distinguished by **pppd** by whether you include a set of IP addresses as an argument on the command line and the use of the **noipdefault** option. If you do include the IP addresses, then **pppd** assumes you have a static connection and these are the remote and local addresses to use to establish that connection. If you do not specify any addresses as arguments, then **pppd** assumes a default remote and local address. The default local address is the IP address of your systems as specified in your **/etc/hostname** file. A default remote address will try to be determined from remote addresses in your **/etc/hosts** file. This assumes you use dynamic addresses and will look for them when a connection is made. To have **pppd** assume dynamic addresses, you use the **noipdefault** option, and make sure not to specify any addresses. **noipdefault** instructs **pppd** not to use default addresses. With no addresses specified, **pppd** then assumes that dynamic addresses will be received from the remote host.

The local and remote static addresses are entered next to each other, separated by a colon. The local address is entered first. The following example specifies a local address of 199.35.209.72 and a remote address of 163.179.4.22.

```
199.35.209.72:163.179.4.22
```

Should you use a dynamic remote address, you can specify just your local address followed by the colon. **pppd** will then use your local address and dynamically receive your remote address.

```
199.35.209.72:
```

Since your local address as specified in your **/etc/hostname** file is your default local address, you do not even have to enter it on the command line. You could just enter the **pppd** command with no addresses. **pppd** will use your hostname address as your local address and receive a remote address from the remote host.

Most Internet Service Providers that use dynamic addresses will provide you with both the local and remote address. In this case you do not enter any addresses at all, and you have to specify the **noipdefault** option. **noipdefault** will prevent the use of the **hostname** address as the default local address. Lacking any addresses, **pppd** will obtain both from the remote host.

Chat Scripts

The best way to use chat is to invoke a chat script. To make a connection, chat has to specify all the connection information: the telephone number, login prompt and user ID, password prompt and password, and any connect strings. You could enter this as a string after the **chat** command on the command line, but this makes for a very long and complex command line. Instead, you can create a file with the chat information in it and then use the **-f** option and the file name with the **chat** command. Such files are called chat scripts.

A chat script consists of one line organized into different segments for the parts of the connection procedure. Each segment consists of an expect-reply pair of strings. The first string is what you expect to receive and the second string is what you are sending. If you expect to receive nothing, then you use a null string, **""**. The first segment may be an initialization of a modem. You expect nothing at first, so it begins with the null string. Then you specify the codes for your modem initialization. When entering the codes for your initialization string, you will have to escape any code beginning with **&**. For chat the **&** is a break and will stop the process. As shown here, both **&FE1** and **&K3** are preceded by a backslash to quote their **&**.

```
""   AT\&FE1Q0V1X1\&K3L0
```

The next segment first expects a response from your modem of "OK," indicating that there was no problem initializing your modem. Then, in response, you are ready to dial the telephone number.

```
OK   ATDT8888888
```

You will usually receive a connect string indicating that you have connected to the remote system. This can vary from system to system. There may not even be a connect string at all. On many systems the connect string is the word CONNECT, on others it is the baud rate, or speed. In this example, the user receives the speed as the connect string. The response to a connect string is usually nothing, though it can also be a newline. Recall that you represent no response with an empty string—two double quotes, **" "**. The newline is represented in a chat script with a **\n**. (Some remote systems expect an MS-DOS newline, which is actually a carriage return character, **\r**, followed by a newline character, **\n**.) See Table 20-8 for a listing of chat script special characters. In the next example, a newline is sent in response.

```
38400   \n
```

After the connect string, the remote system usually sends the login prompt. This is often the word "login" with a colon. You only need the last few characters, **ogin:**. Don't forget the colon. In reply, you send your user ID. Depending on your ISP, you may have to add **\n** to the user ID to enter a newline, as in **richlp\n**. ISPs may require you to include other characters, such as a preceding **#** for Netcom Netcruiser accounts.

```
ogin:   richlp
```

After the login you can expect the password prompt. Again, you only need the last few characters, **word:**. In response, you send your password. If needed, be sure to add the **\n** to enter the newline.

```
word:   mypass
```

All this fits together on just one line. You have a sequence of words indicating alternating received and sent text.

```
""   AT\&FE1Q0V1X1\&K3L0 OK   ATDT8888888 38400   \n   ogin:   richlp
word:   mypass
```

In a chat script, you can break the receive and send pairs into separate lines, one pair to a line, with the strings for each pair separated by a space or tab. You could also put it all on the very first line if you wish. The file name for the script has the extension **.chat**. The next example shows the **mycon.chat** script with pairs entered on separate lines.

mycon.chat

```
""AT\&FE1Q0V1X1\&K3L0
OK  ATDT4448888
38400  \n
ogin:  richlp
word:  mypass
```

You can then call the chat script with the **chat** command and the **-f** option, as shown here. The chat program will use the information in the chat script to initialize your modem, dial up your remote host, and then log in with your user ID and password.

```
chat -f  mycon.chat
```

Many remote systems and modes will send error messages if something should go wrong in the connection process. You can use the special expect string, **abort** followed by a key term, to detect such an error message. If such a term is received, chat cancels the connection procedure. If you are using a command line only, you can enter abort strings either where you would expect them to occur in the connection process or at the very beginning. Within a chat script, as shown here, the abort strings are placed at the beginning. The next example would expect a NO CARRIER or a BUSY response before the login prompt. In either case an initial connection failed, and chat will cancel the remaining steps. Notice the quotes around NO CARRIER. If a string has a space in it, you have to quote it.

mycon.chat

```
abort 'NO CARRIER'
abort BUSY
"" AT\&FE1Q0V1X1\&K3L0
OK  ATDT4448888
38400  \n
ogin:  richlp
word:  mypass
```

Instead of a separate call to chat you can incorporate it into your invocation of the **pppd** command; chat will make the connection and then **pppd** will configure it.

The Point-to-Point Protocol daemon (**pppd**) is invoked with several possible options. Its standard syntax is

```
pppd  options  serial-device-name  speed  local:remote-addresses
ppp-options
```

The *serial-device-name* is the device name for your modem. This is likely to be **/dev/cua** with a number attached, usually from 0 to 3, depending on the port you are using for your modem. Port 1 is **cua0**, port 2 is **cua1**, and so on. The *speed* is the baud rate. For a 14.4 modem this is 14400. For a v.28 modem this is 38400, or even 56700. Check with your ISP provider and your modem documentation for the highest speed you can support.

The options specify configuration features such as your MTU size and whether you are receiving a dynamic IP address. The **connect** option instructs **pppd** to make a connection. It takes as its argument a Linux command that will actually make the connection—usually the **chat** command. You enter **pppd** followed by the **connect** option and the **chat** command with its **-f** option and chat script file name. The **chat** command and its **-f** option with the chat file name are all enclosed in quotes to distinguish them from other **pppd** options. In the next example, the user invokes **pppd** with the **chat** command using the **mycon.chat** chat script. The modem is connected to port 4, **/dev/cua3**, and the speed is 38400 baud.

```
# pppd -connect  'chat -f  mycon.chat'  /dev/cua3   38400
```

PPP Options

pppd has a great many options. The more commonly used ones are listed in Table 20-9. See the **pppd** man pages for a complete list. For example, the **mru** option sets the "maximum receive unit" size. **pppd** instructs the remote system to send packets no larger than this size. The default is 1500; 296 or 542 is recommeded for slower modems. The **defaultroute** option instructs **pppd** to set up the PPP connection as the default route. The lack of any addresses comibined with the **noipdefault** option instructs **pppd** to detect and use a dynamic IP address from the ISP remote system. You have to specify this option if you have an ISP that supplies dynamic IP addresses. The **crtscts** option uses hardware flow control, and the **modem** option uses the modem control lines. You can list the options after the speed on the command line, as shown here:

```
# pppd -connect  'chat -f  mycon.chat'  /dev/cua3   38400   mru
1500
defaultroute noipdefault crtscts modem asynchap 0
```

In the following command, the presence of addresses instructs **pppd** to use these addresses to establish a static connection. The local address is 199.35.209.72 and the remote address is 163.179.4.22.

```
# pppd -connect 'chat -f  mycon.chat'  /dev/cua3   38400
199.35.209.72:163.179.4.22 mru 1500 defaultroute crtscts modem
```

This can make for a very lengthy and complex command line, depending on how many options you need. As an alternative, **pppd** allows you to enter options in the file **/etc/ppp/options** as well as in a **.ppprc** file. **pppd** will automatically read and use the options specified in these files each time it is invoked. You can specify as many options as you wish, entering each on a separate line. With the **#** symbol you can also enter comments, explaining the options and their settings. The **/etc/ppp/options** file contains system default options for **pppd**. You create this file as the root user, and it is the first options file called when **pppd** is invoked. Each user can have a **.ppprc** file in his or her own home directory. These options are specified by a particular user and are read after the system's **/etc/ppp/options** file. A brief example of an options file is shown here.

/etc/ppp/options

```
# /etc/ppp/options -*- sh -*- general options for pppd
crtscts
defaultroute
modem
mru 542
asyncmap 0
netmask 255.255.255.0
noipdefault
```

To make this process easier, the Redhat implementation of Linux includes a file in the **/etc/ppp** directory called **options.tpl**, an options template. This already lists all the options with default values and includes extensive explanations of each option. However, all the options are commented out with a preceding **#** at the beginning of each line. Instead of creating your own options file from scratch, you could copy the **options.tpl** to **options**, making it the options file. Then, with an editor such as Vi, you could remove the **#** symbol from the beginning of the line for the options you want to use. For example, to enable **noipdefault**, use your editor to locate that line and delete the preceding **#**. To turn an option back off, use your editor to reinsert a **#** at the beginning of that option's line. With this approach you can quickly specify all the options you need. Now when you invoke **pppd** you do not have to enter any of these options on the command line.

With your options specified in the **/etc/ppp/options** file, you then only need to enter the **pppd** command with the chat invocation, the device name for your modem, and the modem speed.

```
$ pppd -connect  'chat -f  mycon.chat'  /dev/cua3   38400
```

You can reduce your entry even further by placing the **pppd** invocation in a shell script and then just executing the shell script. Recall that a shell script is a text file that you create with any text editor. You type the command invocation with all its arguments as you would on the command line. Be sure to precede the **pppd** command with an **exec** command. **exec** runs **pppd** from your command-line shell, not the script's shell. Be sure to include a full path name for the **chat** script (/etc/ppp /mycon.chat). You then make the script executable with the command **chmod 755** *script-name*. Then place it in the **/usr/local/bin** directory. Now to execute your **pppd** operation, just enter the script name on the command line and press ENTER. In the next example, the **pppd** connect operation is placed in a shell script called **pppcon**, and the user simply enters **pppcon** to invoke **pppd**.

pppcon

```
exec pppd  -connect  'chat -f  /etc/ppp/mycon.chat'  /dev/cua3  38400
```

```
$ pppcon
```

You are now ready to try **pppd** to connect to your remote system. Any number of things may go wrong. You may not have the right connect string or the modem may be initializing wrong. **pppd** will log descriptions of all the steps it is taking in the **/var/log/messages** file. You can use **more**, **tail**, or **cat** to list these descriptions even as **pppd** is operating. For a successful connection you will see the IP addresses listed as shown here.

```
$ tail /var/log/messages
```

The following command will give you an ongoing display of messages as they are entered in the **/var/log/messages** file. Use a CTRL-C to end the process.

```
$ tail -f /var/log/messages
Mar 23 20:01:03 richlp pppd[208]: Connected...
Mar 23 20:01:04 richlp pppd[208]: Using interface ppp0
Mar 23 20:01:04 richlp kernel: ppp: channel ppp0 mtu = 1500, mru =
1500
Mar 23 20:01:04 richlp kernel: ppp: channel ppp0 open
Mar 23 20:01:04 richlp pppd[208]: Connect: ppp0 -- /dev/cua3
Mar 23 20:01:09 richlp pppd[208]: local  IP address 204.32.168.68
Mar 23 20:01:09 richlp pppd[208]: remote IP address 163.179.4.23
```

The Redhat distribution of Linux provides you with a sample login PPP script called **ppp-on** in the **/usr/sbin** directory. You can use a text editor to set the correct values to certain variables such as Phone and Password. You also must be careful to set the correct arguments and options for both the **chat** and the **pppd** commands. If you have already set options in the **/etc/ppp/options** file, you can remove most of the options that you would normally specify on the command line. Also be sure to set the correct speed and device name for the modem. Once working, all you then have to enter is **ppp-on** to establish your PPP connection.

It is also possible to use **dip** to invoke **pppd** and set up a PPP connection. When you set the mode to PPP in a **dip** script, you are in fact executing the **pppd** program. In this case you would not need a **chat** script to make the connection, since **dip** has already done this. However, there are several options that **pppd** needs to have set when it is invoked. These options cannot be specified in the **dip** script. Instead you have to set them up in the **/etc/ppp/options** file that **pppd** automatically reads whenever it is executed.

To disconnect your PPP connection, you invoke **pppd** with the **disconnect** option. You must use chat to instruct your modem to hang up. For this you may have to send a modem command such as H0. You will probably find it more convenient to place the **chat** commands in a chat file, as shown here. To make the disconnect process easier, you can place the **pppd** commands within a shell script, just as can be done for the connect process.

turnoff.chat

```
-- \d+++\d\c  OK
ATH0 OK
```

```
# pppd disconnect  'chat  -f   turnoff.chat'
# ppp-off
```

If you have trouble disconnecting, try the **ppp-off** command. This is a shell script located in **/usr/sbin** that kills the PPP process directly.

Providing Incoming PPP Connections from Other Systems

As with SLIP, you can also configure your system to be a PPP server, allowing remote systems to dial into yours and make PPP connections. You only need to create one special account and a script to invoke **pppd** with the **-detach** and **silent** options. The script is usually called **ppplogin**—here is an example:

/etc/ppp/ppplogin

```
exec pppd -detach silent modem crtscts
```

With the **-detach** option, **pppd** won't detach itself from the line it is on. The **silent** option makes **pppd** wait for a remote system to make a link to your system. The **modem** option monitors the modem lines, and **crtscts** uses hardware flow control.

The special account has the name **ppp**. The **/etc/passwd** entry for the **ppp** account would appear as follows.

```
ppp:*:501:300:PPP Account:/tmp:etc/ppp/ppplogin
```

PPP Security: CHAP

To ensure security for PPP connections you have to use additional protocols. Two have been developed for PPP, the Password Authentication Protocol (PAP) and the Challenge Handshake Authentication Protocol (CHAP). CHAP is considered a more secure protocol. It uses an encrypted challenge system that requires the two connected systems to continually authenticate each other. The keys for the encryption are kept in the **/etc/ppp/chap-secrets** file. To use CHAP in your PPP connections, you include the **auth** option when you invoke **pppd**. Also, you must enter the required information for the remote host into the **/etc/ppp/chap-secrets** file. The following is an example of a **/etc/ppp/chap-secrets** entry. Entries for the PAP protocol in **/etc/ppp/pap-secrets** have the same format.

etc/ppp/chap-secrets

```
pango1.train.com   richlp.ix.com       "my new hat"
     *             richlp.ix.com       "confirmed tickets"
richlp.ix.com      pango1.train.com    "trek on again"
```

A CHAP secrets entry has up to four fields: the client's hostname, the server's hostname, a secret key, and a list of IP possible addresses. For a particular computer trying to make a connection to your system, you can specify that it supply the indicated secret key. Instead of specifying a particular computer, you can use an * to indicate any computer. Any system that knows the designated secret key can connect to your system. In the first entry in the following example, the server is the user's own system, **richlp.ix.com**, and it allows **pango1.train.com** to connect to it if it provides the secret key specified. In the next entry any remote system can connect to **richlp.ix.com** if they know the secret key "confirmed tickets."

```
pango1.train.com    richlp.ix.com    "my new hat"
    *               richlp.ix.com    "confirmed tickets"
```

You also have to make entries for remote systems that you want to access. In that case the remote system is the PPP server and you are the client. In the next example, **richlp** can connect to pango1 with the secret key "trek on again."

```
richlp.ix.com    pango1.train.com     "trek on again"
```

Summary: Network Administration

TCP/IP networks are configured and managed with a set of utilities such as **netcfg**, **ifconfig**, **route**, and **netstat**. **ifconfig** operates from your root user desktop and allows you to fully configure your network interfaces, adding new ones and modifying others. Entries are made automatically to the respective configuration files. Your system uses a variety of network configuration files as shown in Table 20-2. **ifconfig** and **route** are lower level programs that require more specific knowledge of your network to use effectively. **netstat** provides you with information about the status of your network connections.

If your system does not have a direct hardware connection to a network, such as an Ethernet connection, and you dial into a network through a modem, you will probably have to set up a SLIP or PPP connection. If you are using an Internet Service Provider, you have to set up such a connection. SLIP connections are easily set up using the dip program with dip scripts. PPP connections use chat scripts and an options file. PPP is a new protocol that is becoming much more widely used.

Protocol	Description
Transport	
TCP	Transmission Control Protocol; places systems in direct communication
UDP	User Datagram Protocol
Routing	
IP	Internet Protocol; transmits data
ICMP	Internet Control Message Protocol; status messages for IP
RIP	Routing Information Protocol; determines routing
OSPF	Open Shortest Path First; determines routing
Network Addresses	
ARP	Address Resolution Protocol; determines unique IP address of systems
DNS	Domain Name Service; translates hostnames into IP addresses
RARP	Reverse Address Resolution Protocol; determines addresses of systems
User Services	
FTP	File Transfer Protocol; transmits files from one system to another using TCP
TFTP	Trivial File Transfer Protocol; transfers files using UDP
TELNET	Remote login to another system on the network
SMTP	Simple Mail Transfer Protocol; transfers email between systems
Gateway	
EGP	Exterior Gateway Protocol; provides routing for external networks

Table 20-1. *TCP/IP Protocols*

Protocol	Description
Gateway	
GGP	Gateway-to-Gateway Protocol; provides routing between Internet gateways
IGP	Interior Gateway Protocol; provides routing for internal networks
Network Services	
NFS	Network File Systems; allows mounting of file systems on remote machines
NIS	Network Information Service; maintains user accounts across a network
RPC	Remote Procedure Call; allows programs on remote systems to communicate
BOOTP	Boot Protocol; starts system using boot information on server for network
SNMP	Single Network Management Protocol; provides status messages on TCP/IP configuration

Table 20-1. *TCP/IP Protocols* (continued)

Address	Description
Host address	IP address of your system; it has a network part to identify the network you are on and a host part to identify your own system
Network address	IP address of your network (network part of your host IP address with host part set to 0)
Broadcast address	IP address for sending messages to all hosts on your network at once (network part of your host IP address with host part set to 255)
Gateway address	IP address of your gateway system if you have one (usually the network part of your host IP address with host part set to 1)
Domain nameserver addresses	IP addresses of domain nameservers that your network uses
Netmask	Network part of your host IP address set to 255 with host part set to 0 (255.255.255.0)
Files	
/etc/hosts	Associates hostnames with IP addresses
/etc/networks	Associates domain names with network addresses
/etc/rc.d/init.d/inet	Script to configure your Ethernet interface when you boot up
/etc/host.conf	Lists resolver options
/etc/hosts	Lists domain names for remote hosts with their IP addresses
/etc/resolv.conf	Lists domain nameserver names, IP addresses (Nameserver), and domain names where remote hosts may be located (Search)
/etc/protocols	Lists protocols available on your system
/etc/services	Lists available network services such as ftp and telnet
/etc/hostname	Holds the name of your system

Table 20-2. *TCP/IP Configuration Addresses and Files*

Program	Description
netcfg	The root user desktop program for configuring and managing your network interfaces
ifconfig *-hostflag IP-address options*	Configuration of a network interface
route *action IP-address*	Routes a network interface; **route** by itself lists the routing table
ping *hostname*	Checks to see if a remote host is reachable; use CTRL-C to stop
netstat	Issues reports on state of network connections
hostname	Displays your current hostname
dip *options dip-script*	For modem connections, creates a SLIP connection
pppd *chat-script dev speed options*	For modem connections, creates a PPP connection

Table 20-3.   *Network Administration Programs*

Option	Description
`interface`	Name of the network interface; these are usually located in the **/dev** directory—for example, /dev/eth0
`aftype`	Address family for decoding protocol addresses; default is **inet**, currently used by Linux
`up`	Activates an interface
`down`	Deactivates an interface
`-arp`	Turns ARP on or off; preceding – turns it off
`-trailers`	Turns on or off trailers in Ethernet frames; preceding – turns it off
`-allmulti`	Turns on or off the promiscuous mode; preceding – turns it off; this allows network monitoring.
`metric` *n*	Cost for interface routing (not currently supported)
`mtu` *n*	Maximum number of bytes that can be sent on this interface per transmission
`dstaddr` *address*	Destination IP address on a point-to-point connection
`netmask` *address*	IP network mask; preceding – turns it off
`broadcast` *address*	Broadcast address; preceding – turns it off
`point-to-point` *address*	Point-to-point mode for interface; if address is included, it is assigned to remote system
`hw`	Sets hardware address of interface
address	Hostname or IP address assigned to interface

Table 20-4. `ifconfig` *Options*

Option	Description
-a	Displays information about all internet sockets, including those sockets that are just listening
-i	Displays statistics for all network devices
-c	Continually displays network status every second until the program is interrupted
-n	Displays remote and local address as IP addresses
-o	Displays timer states, expiration times, and backoff state for network connections
-r	Displays the kernel routing table
-t	Displays information about TCP sockets only, including those that are listening
-u	Displays information about UDP sockets only
-v	Displays version information
-w	Displays information about raw sockets only
-x	Displays information about Unix domain sockets

Table 20-5. `netstat` *Options*

Option	Description
-v	Verbose mode; displays descriptions of all actions taken
-t	Test mode; places you in an interactive shell with the prompt DIP>
-p *mode*	Sets mode, line protocol, to either CSLIP or SLIP
-a	Prompts for user name and password
-i	Acts as a dial-in server
-k	Kills the **dip** process that runs (has locked) the specified tty device (see **-l** option), or else the most recent invocation of **dip** (a process started by somebody else is not killed)
-l *tty_line*	Indicates the line to be killed (requires **-k** option)
-m *mtu*	Sets the maximum transfer unit (MTU) (default is 296)
Command	
chatkey *keyword code*	Adds a keyword and error-level code to error codes returned by dial
config *args*	Directly configures SLIP interface
databits *bits*	Number of bits in connection (default is 8)
default	Sets default route
dial *telephone-number*	Dials the telephone number
echo *on* / *off*	The arguments **on** or **off** turn echo on or off. With echo on, **dip** will display what it sends and receives from the modem
flush	Eliminates unread responses from the modem
get *$var value*	Sets the variable *$var* to the value
get *$var*	Sets the variable *$var* to the next value received across the line connection
get *$var* **ask**	Prompts the user to enter a value for the variable
goto *label*	Jumps to *label* in **dip** script

Table 20-6. **dip** *Options and Commands*

Command	Description
help	Lists **dip** commands
if $var operator number	Tests the value of a variable; the number must be an integer
init string	Initialization string for modem; default string is ATE0 Q0 V1 X1
mode SLIP/CSLIP	Sets the protocol mode for the connection and places **dip** in daemon mode
modem type	Sets the modem type: HAYES
netmask	Sets the netmask for the route **dip** takes
parity E/O/N	Sets the parity to even, odd, or none
password	Prompts the user to enter a password
print	Displays text to your screen
port dev	Sets the port that **dip** will use
quit	Exits **dip**
reset	Sends the **init** string to the modem
send text	Sends text to remote host
sleep number	Delays processing for number of seconds
speed number	Sets the baud rate for the connection: 2400, 9600, 38400, 56700
stopbits bits	Sets the number of stop bits
timeout number	Default timeout set to number of seconds
term	Places **dip** in terminal emulation mode so it operates like a terminal; you can then interact with the remote system directly for login and password prompts (press CTRL-] to return to **dip**)
wait word number	**dip** waits for the specified word to be received for the number of seconds

Table 20-6. **dip** *Options and Commands* (continued)

Variable	Description
$local	Hostname of the local system; your hostname
$locip	IP address for the local system; your own IP address
$remote	Hostname of remote system that you are connected to
$rmtip	IP address of remote system
$mtu	Maximum transfer unit; the maximum number of bytes transferred at one time
$modem	Type of modem used (read only)
$port	Name of the serial device **dip** uses (read only)
$speed	Speed for the serial device (read only)
$errlvl	Holds the result code returned by the last command executed; you can use it to test for errors; 0 indicates success (read only)

Table 20-7.   **dip** *Variables*

Option	Description
-f *filename*	Executes **chat** commands in the **chat** script with name *filename*
-l *lockfile*	Makes UUCP style like file using *lockfile*
-t *num*	Timeout set to *num* seconds
-v	A description of all **chat** actions are output to the /log/messages file; use **tail**, **cat**, or **more** on this file to display the descriptions **tail /log/messages**

Special Character

BREAK	Sends break to modem
''	Sends null string with single newline character

Table 20-8.   **chat** *Options and Special Characters*

Special Character	Description
\b	BACKSPACE
\c	Suppresses newline sent after reply string
\d	Makes **chat** wait for one second
\K	Sends break when specifying string for modem initialization, and codes beginning with K may have to be escaped
\n	Sends newline characters
\N	Sends null character
\p	Pauses for 1/10 of a second
\q	String does not appear in **syslog** file
\r	Sends or expects a new line
\s	Sends or expects a space
\t	Sends or expects a tab
\\	Sends or expects a backslash
\\nnn	Specifies a character in octal
^C	Specifies a control character

Table 20-8.   **chat** *Options and Special Characters* (continued)

Option	Description
device-name	Uses the specified device; if the device name does not have **/dev** preceding it, **pppd** will add it for you
speed *num*	Sets the modem speed (baud rate)
asyncmap *map*	Sets the async character map that specifies what control characters cannot be sent and should be escaped
auth	Requires the remote host to authenticate itself
connect *Linux-command*	Uses the Linux command to set up the connection; the Linux command here is usually **chat**, which makes the actual connection
crtscts	Uses hardware flow control
xonxoff	Uses software flow control
defaultroute	pppd sets a default route to the remote host
disconnect *Linux-command*	Runs the specified command after **pppd** cuts its connection; this is usually a **chat** operation
escape *c,c,...*	Causes the specified characters to be escaped when transmitted
file *filename*	Reads **pppd** options from the specified file
lock	Uses UUCP style locking on the serial device
mru *num*	Sets the maximum receive units to *num*
netmask *mask*	Sets the PPP network interface mask
noipdefault	For dynamic IP addresses provided by ISP; searches the incoming data stream from the remote host for both the local and remote IP addresses assigned to your system for that Internet session; you must have this option to connect with a dynamic IP address
passive	Makes **pppd** wait for a valid connection instead of failing when it can't make the connection immediately

Table 20-9.   **pppd** *Options*

Option	Description
silent	**pppd** waits for a connection to be made by a remote host

Table 20-9. **pppd** *Options* (continued)

Appendix A

Hardware Boot Parameters

The auto-detection feature of the Installation program should determine exactly what hardware you have and allow the installation of the Caldera Network Desktop to proceed without problems.

Occasionally, however, the auto-detection feature needs some "help" to correctly locate and use your hardware. If necessary, you provide this help by entering boot parameters when you start the installation process.

Each boot parameter indicates a type of hardware (or other option) and one or more values that identify that hardware or option so that it can be correctly used. Boot parameters are entered at the boot manager prompt, before the Caldera Network Desktop (or installation) actually starts. For example, at the boot manager prompt, you might normally enter **linux** (or press ENTER if linux is the default).

```
LILO: linux
```

If you determine during installation that boot parameters are needed, you might enter something like this instead:

```
LILO: linux cdu31a=0x340,13 eth0=11,0x260,0,0,eth0
```

This example indicates the addressing information for a Sony CD-ROM drive and an Ethernet card. The equal sign (=) separates the parameter from the value you provide. Spaces separate multiple boot parameters.

You can also use boot parameters to turn off the auto-detection feature if needed. For example, if the auto-detection feature checks for some types of CD-ROM drives, it may interfere with the configuration of some network cards as a side effect. You can overcome this by providing information about your CD-ROM drive and turning off the auto-detection, thus maintaining your network card configuration.

Recommended Boot Parameters

Below are some recommended boot parameters to help you access and configure hardware that may not respond well to the auto-detection. To use boot parameters, you may need to know information such as the IRQ interrupt and memory address used by your hardware. Consult your hardware documentation or call your manufacturer. If you have MS-DOS already configured on your computer, you may be able to discover some relevant hardware information by reviewing the **config.sys** file in MS-DOS.

Items enclosed in square brackets in the syntax diagrams are optional when you enter your parameters. Items in the syntax descriptions that are in italics are variables for which you must supply a value.

After entering one of these parameters at the boot manager prompt, watch the kernel messages to see if the device was recognized correctly. Messages will generally either display "failed" or the name of the device with the correct port, IRQ, and other information.

After the device-specific listings are several additional settings that you can use to control the action of the kernel and device modules during startup.

IDE Hard Disk Controller

These parameters are rarely needed. hda is the first IDE hard disk, hdb is the second, and so on. The syntax for the boot parameter to recognize the hard disk is

```
hdx=cylinders,heads,sectors[,wpcom,IRQ]
```

Here are two examples:

```
hda=989,17,35
hdb=989,17,35,989,14
```

XT Hard Disk Controller

The syntax is

```
xd=type,IRQ,port,DMA
```

Here is an example:

```
xd=0,5,0x320,3
```

Ethernet Network Card

This should work for all Ethernet cards. This parameter is required for NE2000 cards. The syntax is

```
ether=IRQ,port,starting address,ending address,device
```

Here is an example:

```
ether=14,0x340,0,0,eth0
```

CD-ROM Drives

For the Sony CDU31a or CDU33a CD-ROM, the syntax is

```
cdu31a=port,IRQ[,PAS]
```

In the previous two parameters, the PAS option refers to the Pro-Audio Spectrum card, a dual sound and CD-ROM card shipped with some multimedia systems.

For the Sony CDU535/531 CD-ROM, the default port and IRQ (if no parameter is supplied) are 0x340, 0, respectively, with the 0 value indicating no interrupt:

```
sonycd535=port,IRQ
```

For the Philips/LMS, CM205, CM206 CD-ROM drive, the default port and IRQ (if no parameter is supplied) are 0x340, 5, respectively:

```
cm205cd=port,IRQ
cm206cd=port,IRQ
```

The ATAPI CD-ROM syntax, using any IDE controller (hda, hdb, hdc, hdd), is

```
hdx=cdrom
```

For the Aztech CD-ROM (also used for Orchid and Wearnes), the default port if no parameter is supplied is 0x320:

```
aztcd=port
```

The Goldstar R420 CD-ROM drive syntax is

```
gscd=port
```

For the Mitsumi FX001S/D, the default port and IRQ if no parameter is supplied are 0x320, 10, respectively:

```
mcd=port,IRQ[,mcdwait]
```

For the SoundBlaster Pro Multi-CD, specify the type as 1 for SB, 2 for Lasermate, or 3 for SPEA:

```
sbpcd=port,type
```

or

```
sbpcd=type,port
```

SCSI Controllers

For the Segate ST01/02, the default port and IRQ if no parameter is supplied are 0xc800, 5, respectively:

```
st01=port,IRQ
st02=port,IRQ
```

The syntax for the Future Domain TMC 8xx/950 is

```
tmc8xx=port,IRQ
```

For the Trantor T128/128F/228, the default port and IRQ if no parameter is supplied are 0xcc000, 15, respectively:

```
t128=port,IRQ
```

The syntax for the NCR 5380 family is

```
generic_NCR5380=port,IRQ,DMA Channel
```

For the NCR 53c406a, the default values if no parameter is supplied are 0xd8000, 0x330, 11, and 5, respectively:

```
ncr53c406a=MEM,port,IRQ,DMA Channel
```

For the Adaptec 1520/1522, the default values if no parameter is supplied are 0x330, 9, and 7 for the first three items. The Reconnect value is 0 or 1:

```
aha152x=port,IRQ,SCSI_ID,Reconnect
```

For the Adaptec 1542, the default port value if no parameter is supplied is 0x330:

```
aha1542=port[,buson,busoff[,dmaspeed]]
```

For the Adaptec 274x/284x/294x, one of the following two options may be used:

```
aic7xxx=extended
aic7xxx=no_reset
```

For the Buslogic family, the default port value if no parameter is supplied is 0x330. The no_probe value can be used in place of the port address:

```
buslogic=port
buslogic=no_probe
```

For the Pro Audio Spectrum 16, the default values if no parameter is supplied are 0x388, 255; the 255 signifying no interrupt:

```
pas16=port,IRQ
```

For the Max Anzahl SCSI, the value *N* is the device number between 1 and 8:

```
max_scsi_luns=N
```

Mouse Devices

The syntax for the Logitech busmouse is

```
bmouse=IRQ
```

Additional Parameters

To specify where the kernel should look for the root of the Linux file system, indicate the device, including partition number. The first example indicates the first partition of the first IDE hard disk. The second example indicates the second partition of the third SCSI hard disk:

```
root=/dev/hda1
root=/dev/sdc2
```

To reserve a memory port with a certain number of bytes, for I/O or devices, use the following (with both numbers in hexadecimal):

```
reserve=port,bytes
```

For example, to reserve 16 bytes at address 0x340:

```
reserve=0x340,10
```

To indicate that no math coprocessor is installed, use the following, with a space on each side:

```
no387
```

Appendix B

Configuring the X-Windows System

X-Windows is designed for flexibility—there are various ways you can configure it. You can run it on most of the different video cards available, even accelerated graphics cards. X-Windows is not tied to any specific window manager or file manager. There are a variety of different window managers for you to choose from. Each user on your system could run a different window manger, each using the underlying X-Windows interface. You can even run X-Windows programs without any window or file managers.

You can configure your own X-Windows interface using the **.Xclients** configuration file where window mangers, file managers, and initial X-Windows applications can be selected and started up. There is also a set of specialized X-Windows commands that you can use to configure your root window, load fonts, or configure X-Windows resources such as setting the color of window borders. You can also download X-Windows utilities from online sources like sunsite in the **/pub/Linux/X11** directory. If you have to compile an X-Windows application, there are special procedures you may have to use as well as support packages that should be installed.

XFree86 Servers

The XFree86 servers provide a wide range of hardware support but can be challenging to configure. If you have installed the correct XFree86 server (see Table B-1), you can configure it by running either **xf86config** or **Xconfigurator**. These utilities ask you questions about your hardware and create an **/etc/XF86Config** file.

XFree86 servers support the hardware listed in Table B-1. For specific model information, you can consult the Caldera Web page or the XFree86 documentation in the **/usr/docs/XFree86-HOWTO** file and in the **/usr/docs/XFree86-3.1.1-1** directory. There you will find files for the specific servers available. The **AccelCards** file lists all the hardware currently supported, including chipsets, and the **Monitors** file lists monitor configurations.

XFree86 servers are not installed by default but are located on the Caldera CD-ROM in the directory **/packages/RPMS**. Each package that contains an XFree server starts with XFree86. The name of a particular server usually includes the type of card it supports. For example, if you have an S3 chipset on your graphics video card, you first have to install the XFree86_S3 package. You have to install the package appropriate for your graphics card. If you are using a simple Monochrome or VGA card, you install just the XF86_Monochrome or XF86_VGA generic server. However, if you have an accelerated graphics card, you first have to find out what chipset is used on it. Consult the manual or documentation that comes with the card. You can also use a utility called Superprobe that will analyze your card to determine its chipset. First read the man pages for Superprobe to determine the correct arguments to use when invoking it. If you are not sure what server to use, just install all of them. There are different cards that can use the same server.

```
rpm -i XFree86_S3-3.1.1-1.rpm
```

Server	Type
XF86_SVGA	Color SVGA accelerated server
XF86_VGA16	16-color SVGA and VGA accelerated server
XF86_Mono	Monochrome accelerated server
XF86_S3	S3 accelerated server
XF86_8514	8514/A accelerated server
XF86_Mach8	ATI Mach8 accelerated server
XF86_Mach32	ATI Mach32 chipset accelerated server
XF86_P9000	Weitek accelerated server
XF86_Video7	Video7/Headland Technologies accelerated driver
XF86_W32	ET 4000/W32 accelerated server
XF86_WstDig	Western Digital accelerated driver
XF86_agx	IIT AGX accelerated server
XF86_ark	ARK Logic Graphics accelerated driver
XF86_ati	ATI accelerated driver (not those using Mach8, Mach32, or Mach64 chipsets)
XF86_cirrus	CirrusLogic accelerated driver
XF86_Trident	Trident accelerated driver
XF86_tseng	Tseng accelerated driver
XF86_Oak	Oak Technologies accelerated driver
XF86_Mach64	ATI Mach64 chipset accelerated server

Table B-1. *XFree86 Servers and Drivers*

If you do not find the server package you need on the CD-ROM, you can locate it at sunsite or mirror sites in the Redhat distributions directory, **/pub/Linux/distributions /redhat/redhat-3.0.3/i386/RedHat/RPMS**. Download and install it.

Once you have installed your XFree86 server, you then configure your X-Windows interface. This involves creating a configuration file called **Xconfig**, located in the **/etc/X11** directory, that contains all the specifications for your graphics card, monitor, keyboard, and mouse. Although you could create the file directly, it is better to use a configuration utility such as **Xconfigurator** or **xf86config**. With these you just answer questions about your hardware and the program will generate the appropriate **Xconfig** file.

You will need specific information on hand about your hardware. For your monitor, you will have to know the horizontal and vertical sync frequency ranges and bandwidth. For your graphics card, you have to know the chipset and you may need to know the clocks. For your mouse, you should know whether it is a Microsoft compatible mouse or some other brand such as Logitech. Also, know the port that your mouse is connected to.

Xconfigurator provides you with a full-screen interface where you can use arrow keys to move through lists of possible selections. However, if you should have problems configuring with **Xconfigurator**, you should use **xf86config**, which presents you with line mode prompts where you type in responses or enter a menu selection. In addition, it provides more explanation of each step and has some graphic card configurations on hand not available in **Xconfigurator**. For your monitor, you will be presented with a set of preconfigured monitors. If your monitor is not listed, choose the Generic or Generic MultiSync selection.

If you purchase the full Caldera Network Desktop, you will use a proprietary configuration tool called Accelerated X. Accelerated X is much easier to use, automatically installing its own servers for various graphics cards. Details on Accelerated X are provided in the Caldera manual that comes with the full version for the Desktop and are also available online on the Caldera Web site.

X-Windows and Window Managers

As noted in Chapter 3, instead of the command line interface, you can use an X-Windows window manager and file manager, allowing you to interact with your Linux system using windows, icons, and menus. Window managers provide basic window management operations such as the opening, closing, and resizing of windows, and file managers allow you to manage and run programs using icons and menus. In addition, a file manager allows you to copy, move, or erase files, as well as open up windows for different directories.

There are several window managers available for Linux. Two of the more popular Linux window managers are the Free Virtual window manager (**fvwm**) and Xview (**olwm**), the Linux version of the Unix Open-Look interface. The Caldera Desktop currently uses **fvwm**. With a window manager, you can think of a window as taking the place of a command line. Operations you perform through the window are interpreted and sent to the Linux system for execution. Window managers operate off of an underlying graphics utility called X-Windows, which actually provides the basic window operations that allow you to open, move, and close windows as well as display menus and select icons. **fvwm** and Xview manage these operations, each in their own way, providing their own unique interfaces. The advantage of such a design is that you can have different window managers that can operate on the same Linux system, but remember that all window managers, no matter how different they may appear, use X-Windows tools. In this sense, Linux is not tied to one type of Graphical User Interface (GUI). On the same Linux system one user may be using the **fvwm** window manager, while at the same time, another may be using the Xview window manager, and still another may use the Caldera Desktop.

Your Caldera Network Desktop uses the **fvwm** window manager which provides its own proprietary file and program manager, simply referred to as the Desktop. The name of the Caldera Desktop program is **lg**. With Caldera Lite, you are granted three free months' use of the Caldera Desktop, after which it will become inoperable. At that time you can purchase the full Caldera Network Desktop, or you can continue to use the **fvwm** file manager without any of the file management features provided by the Caldera Desktop.

There are GNU file managers available that you can download and install. With such a file manager, you will be able to use icons and menus, instead of just the windows provided by **fvwm**. You can download file managers from Linux ftp sites such as **sunsite.unc.edu** and its mirror sites, and these file managers are located in the **/pub/Linux/X11/xutils/managers** directory. Two popular ones are **xfm-1.3.2.tar.gz** and **pfm-1.0.tgz**. The **xfm** file manager is also available as a Redhat software package ready to be installed, and is located in the Redhat directory at sunsite, **/pub/Linux/distributions/redhat/redhat-3.0.3/i386/RedHat/RPMS**, and is named **xfm-1.3.2-2.i386.rpm**. There are also other window managers available for your use such as **twm** or **olvwm**. **olvwm** is a virtual window manager for Xview. You can also download these window managers from the same Linux ftp sites mentioned earlier, and they are located in the **/pub/Linux/X11/window-managers** directory.

fvwm is a GNU public licensed software—it is yours free of cost, and if you use **fvwm** by itself, you can still run any X-Windows program. **fvwm** will start up with a terminal window where you can type Linux commands. You will not have any icons or any file manager windows. However, you can type the name of an X-Windows application and upon pressing ENTER, the X-Windows application will start up with its own window. It is best to invoke an X-Windows application as a background process by adding an ampersand after the command. A separate window will open up for the X-Windows application that you can work in. In Figure B-1, an Xterm window is open and the Netscape Browser has been started using this command: **netscape &**. You can see the Netscape application behind the Xterm window. Just click on the Netscape window to move it to the front and work with it. You can run any of the X-windows software included on your Caldera CD-ROM this way. Often the name of an X-Windows application begins with an X, although there are exceptions such as Netscape and Mosaic. You can also download a wide variety of X-Windows software from Linux ftp sites. They are usually in a directory named **/X11** such as **/pub/Linux/X11** in **sunsite.unc.edu**.

Very rarely is an X-Windows application tied to a particular window manager. You can run an X application such as Netscape with just **fvwm**, Xview, or the Caldera

Desktop. It is even possible to run X-Windows applications without any window managers at all. You can still open a very simple Xterm window and start up X applications from there. An X application really only needs X-Windows to operate.

Behind the **fvwm** window the screen is covered by a gray-shaded area. If you click anywhere on this area, anywhere that's not a window, a pop-up menu will appear with options for the screen saver and for quitting **fvwm**. Use this menu, also shown in Figure B-1, to exit and return to the command line.

If you start up **fvwm** as the **root** user, then a control panel window will automatically be displayed. The control panel has menus and simple fixed graphic icons for accessing all the configuration utilities such as printtool, usercfg, and netcfg. All the configuration utilities remain available to you—they are all part of the Redhat distribution of Linux which remains yours to keep. If you look at the **.Xclients.bak** file you will see a call to the control panel program. Once in **fvwm**, you can close the control panel, and later reopen it by entering **control-panel &** at the prompt in an Xterm window.

As an alternative to **fvwm** and a file manager, you can use other window managers such as Xview or Motif. Xview and Motif are more than just window managers. They provide full desktop interface with a file manager and utilities such as a windows-based editor. As noted previously, Xview is the version of Sun System's Open-Look interface. Those familiar with Open-Look will find that the Linux version runs much the same

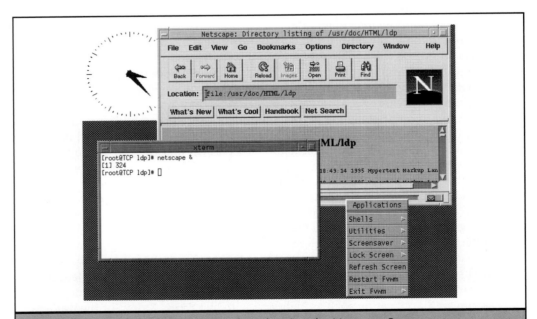

Figure B-1. *An opened Xterm window showing the Netscape Browser*

way. You can download Xview free of cost from most Linux ftp sites. Xview is available as a Redhat software package ready to be installed. It is located in the Redhat directory at sunsite, **/pub/Linux/distributions/redhat/redhat-3.0.3/i386/RedHat/RPMS**, and called **xview-3.2pl-2.i386.rpm**. Motif is proprietary software that you have to purchase from a vendor for about $150. However, there are Motif-like file manager packages available under the GNU public license such as **mfm-1.3.tar.gz** that you can obtain from sunsite in the **/pub/Linux/X11/xutils/managers** directory. Both Motif and Xview are the two major competing window interfaces provided for Unix, representing two different window standards. These two standards have been recently integrated into a new GUI standard for Unix called the Common Desktop Environment, CDE. Linux versions of CDE desktop interfaces are currently under development.

You can now see that a desktop is composed of several components, X-Windows, a window manager, and a file manager, as well as other utilities such as a program manager. A significant advantage of the Caldera Desktop is that it integrates all of these features into one package. You do not have to install and manage all of these separate components.

.Xclients

The commands to run your window manager and desktop are found in your **.Xclients** script. Each user has an **.Xclients** script in their own home directory (notice that the **.Xclients** name begins with a period). When you enter the **startx** command, the **.Xclients** script in your home directory is run, executing the command in it to start up your window manager and desktop.

The **.Xclients** file is currently set to start up the **fvwm** window manager and the Caldera Desktop. You will find the **fvwm** command and the command for the Caldera Desktop, **xclientlg**, in this script, as shown here. This **.Xclients** script first checks to see if **fvwm** is installed. Then, if the Caldera Desktop (**lg**) is installed, the Caldera Desktop (**xclientlg**) is started up, followed by the **fvwm** window manager. If the Caldera Desktop is not available, then an X-Windows terminal window is opened using the command **xterm &**, followed by **fvwm**.

.Xclients

```
#!/bin/bash
# Caldera Network Desktop - .Xclients - root
xsetroot -solid steelblue
# Caldera Font Server
# Some users report "xset fp+ tcp/localhost:7001" works better for them.
if [ -f /usr/cfs/fs/cfs ]; then
    xset fp+ tcp/'hostname -s':7001
fi
```

```
# FVWM and the Desktop
if [ ! -z $(type -path fvwm) ]; then
        if [ ! -z $(type -path lg) ]; then
                # We do cubesize to leave more colors free.
                # Default is colorcubesize 5 for LG.
                xclientlg $$ -colorcubesize 4 &
                exec fvwm
        else
                xterm &
                exec fvwm
        fi
else
        xterm &
        exec twm
fi
```

If you want to run just **fvwm** without the Caldera Desktop, or run a different window manager or desktop such as Xview, it is best to use an alternative version of **.Xclients** called **.Xclients.bak**. All users on your system have their own **.Xclients.bak** script, which is already set up to run **fvwm**. Should you want to run Xview, you can edit **.Xclients.bak** and replace the **fvwm** command with **olwm**. Make a copy of your current **.Xclients** script and then copy **.Xclients.bak** to **.Xclients**, overwriting the original. Then, when you enter **startx**, the Xview desktop will start up, including its file manger (you must have first downloaded and installed Xview on your system, of course). The **.Xclients.bak** script is shown here. This script first starts up **xterm &** and then the **xclock** application. If you don't want **xclock** started up, you can comment out its commands by entering a preceding **#**. Then **fvwm** is started. If **fvwm** is not installed, then **twm**, another GNU window manager, is started up. Another version of the original **.Xclients** script that uses the Caldera desktop is named **.xsessions** and resides on each user's home directory. Should you want to switch back to the Caldera Desktop, you can copy **.xsessions** to **.Xclients**.

.Xclients.bak

```
#!/bin/bash

xterm &

if [ ! -z $(type -path oclock) ]; then
     oclock -geometry +0+0 &
else
```

```
        xclock -geometry +0+0 &
fi

if [ ! -z $(type -path fvwm) ]; then
        exec fvwm
else
        exec twm
fi
```

If you want to also have the use of icons and file management windows, you must use a file manager. First, download and install a file manager in your system. Then, in the **fvwm** version of the **.Xclients** script, place the file manager command after the **fvwm** command. Be sure to place an ampersand after it. For example, to use the **xfm** file manager, you place the **xfm** command before **fvwm**.

```
xfm &
exec fvwm
```

X-Windows Command Line Arguments

You can start up any X-Windows either within an **.Xclients** script or on the command line in an Xterm window. Most X-Windows applications take a set of standard X-Windows arguments used to configure the window and the display that the application will use. You can set the color of the window bars, give the window a specific title, specify the color and font for text, as well as position the window at a specific location on the screen. Table B-2 lists these X-Windows arguments. They are discussed in detail in the X man pages, **man X**.

One commonly used argument is **-geometry**. This takes an additional argument that specifies the location on the screen where you want an application's window displayed. You will notice that in the **.Xclients.bak** file, the **xclock** X-Windows application is called with a geometry argument. A set of up to four numbers specifies the position. **+0+0** references the upper left-hand corner. There you will see the clock displayed when you start up X-Windows. **-0-0** references the upper right-hand corner.

```
& xclock -geometry +0+0 &
```

With the **-title** option, you can set the title displayed on the application window. Notice the use of quotes for titles with more than one word. You set the font with the **-fn** argument and the text and graphics color with the **-fg** argument.

-bg sets the background color. The following example starts up an Xterm window with the title "My New Window" in the title bar. The text and graphics color is green and the background color is gray. The font is Helvetica.

```
$ xterm -title "My New Window"  -fg green -bg gray  -fn
/usr/fonts/helvetica  &
```

X-Windows Commands and Configuration Files

The X-Windows system uses several configuration files as well as X-Windows commands to configure your X-Windows system. Some of the configuration files belong to the system and should not be modified. However, each user has his or her own set of configuration files such as **.Xclients** and **.Xresources** that can be used to configure their own X-Windows interface. Many of the configuration files are actually shell scripts automatically executed when X-Windows is started up with the **startx** command. Within these configuration scripts or on an Xterm window command line, you can execute X-Windows commands used to configure your system. With commands such as **xset** and **setroot**, you can add fonts or control the display of your root window. Table B-2 provides a list of X-Windows configuration files and commands. You can obtain a complete description of your current X-Windows configuration using **xdypinfo**. The X man pages provide a detailed introduction to the X-Windows commands and configuration files.

```
$ man X
```

X-Windows Configuration Files

X-Windows is already started up using the **xinit** command. However, you do not invoke this command directly. It is invoked by the **startx** command that you always use to start X-Windows. Both of these commands are found in the **/usr/X11R6/bin** directory along with many other X-Windows-based programs. Here you will also find the **startx** command that you use to start up X-Windows. The **startx** command is a shell script that executes the **xinit** command. The **xinit** command, in turn, runs an X-Windows initialization script called **.xinitrc**, found in the **/usr/X11R6/lib/X11/xinit** directory. This **.xinitrc** script, in turn, runs the **.Xclients** script in a user's home directory. **.Xclients** then starts up the window and file managers. If there is no **.Xclients** script in the home directory, then **.xinitrc** will just start up **fvwm** and an Xterm window.

xinit will also look for an **.xinitrc** script to run in the user's home directory. This is not set up in the Redhat distribution of Linux. Instead of an **.xinitrc** script, the **.Xclients** script is used which is run by the system's **xinitrc** script. However, you can create an **.xinitrc** script if you want, and other distributions of Linux may use it instead of **.Xclients**. You can consult the man pages on **xinit** and **startx** for more information.

In addition to **xinit**, there are also commands to configure your X-Windows interface. Currently, these configurations are handled by your Caldera Desktop. However, without the Desktop, you will have to set up these configurations yourself. X-Windows configurations are listed in a resource file in the user's home directory named **.Xresources** (on other distributions this may be **.Xdefaults**). A copy of **.Xresources** called **.Xdefaults.bak** currently resides on each user's home directory; there is no **.Xresources** file. To create an **.Xresources** file, just copy **.Xdefaults.bak** to **.Xresources**. You can edit any of the entries. The configuration is carried out by the **xrdb** command which reads the **.Xresources** file. **xrdb** is executed automatically in the **.xinitrc** script. See the man pages on **xrdb** for more details on resources. Also, you can find a more detailed discussion of X resources as well as other X-Windows commands in the X man pages.

The **.Xmodmap** file holds configurations for your input devices such as your mouse and keyboard (for example, you can bind keys such as backspace or reverse the click operations of your right and left mouse buttons). The **.Xmodmap** file is read by the **xmodmap** command, also executed in **.xinitrc**. Currently, there is an **.Xmodmap** file in user home directories that maps the backspace. See the man pages on **xmodmap** for more details.

X-Windows Commands

The **xset** command sets different options such as turning on the screen saver or setting the volume for the bell and speaker. You can also use **xset** to load fonts. See the **xset** man pages for specific details. With the **b** option and the **on** or **off** argument, **xset** will turn your speaker on or off. The following example turns the speaker off.

```
xset b on
```

You also use the **b** option to set the volume and duration of the bell. The **b** option takes three numbers, the first to specify the volume from a range of 0 to 100, the second for the frequency, and the third specifies the number of milliseconds the bell will sound (volume, frequency, milliseconds). The next example reduces the volume by half, sets the frequency at 7000, and a duration of 120 milliseconds.

```
xset b 50  7000  120
```

You use **xset** with the **-s** option to set the screen saver. Two numbers entered as arguments will specify the length and period in seconds, respectively. The length is the number of seconds the screen saver waits before activating. The period is how long it waits before regenerating the pattern.

The **xsetroot** command lets you set the features of your root window (setting the color or displaying a bitmap pattern—you can even use a cursor of your own design). Table B-2 lists the different **xsetroot** options. See the man pages for **xsetroot** for options and details. The following **xsetroot** command uses the **-solid** option to set the background color of the root window to blue.

```
xsetroot -solid blue
```

Fonts

Your X-Windows fonts are located in a directory called **/usr/X11R6/lib/X11/fonts**. X-Windows fonts are loaded using the **xfs** command. **xfs** reads the **/etc/X11/fs/config** configuration file that lists the font directories in an entry for the term "catalogue." The X man pages provides a detailed discussion on fonts. To install a set of fonts, you place them in a directory whose path you can add to the catalogue entry to have them automatically installed. You can also separately install a particular font with the **xset** command and its **+fp** option. Fonts for your system are specified in a font path which is a set of file names, each holding a font (the file names include their complete path). An example of the catalogue entry in the **/etc/X11/config** file follows. This is a comma-delimited list of directories where X-Windows will first look for fonts.

```
catalogue =
/usr/X11R6/lib/X11/fonts/misc/,/usr/X11R6/lib/X11/fonts/Speedo/
,/usr/X11R6/lib/X11/fonts/Type1/,/usr/X11R6/lib/X11/fonts/75dpi/
,/usr/X11R6/lib/X11/fonts/100dpi/
```

Before you can access newly installed fonts, you first have to index them with the **mkfontdir** command, which you enter from within the directory containing the new fonts. You can also use the directory path as an argument to **mkfontdir**. After indexing the fonts, you can then use the **xset** command with the **fp rehash** option to load the fonts. To have the fonts automatically loaded, add the directory with full path name to the catalogue entry in the **xfs** configuration file. The following shows how to install a new font and load it.

```
cp newfont.pcf  ~/myfonts
mkfontdir ~/myfonts
xset fp rehash
```

Within a font directory, there are several special files that hold information about the fonts. The **fonts.dir** file lists all the fonts in that directory. In addition, you can set up a **fonts.alias** file to give other names to a font. Font names tend to be very long and complex. A **fonts.scale** file holds the names of scalable fonts. See the man pages for more details on **xfs** and **mkfontdir**.

With the **xset +fp** and **-fp** options, you can specifically add or remove particular fonts. **fn** with the **rehash** argument will then load the fonts. With the default argument, the default set of fonts are restored. The **+fp** adds a font to this font path. For your own fonts, you can place them in any directory and specify their file name including their complete path. The next example adds the **myfont** font from the **/usr/local/fonts** directory to the font path. The **fp** option with the **rehash** argument then loads the font.

```
xset +fp  /usr/local/fonts/myfont
xset fp rehash
```

To remove this font, you would use **xset -fp /usr/home/myfont** and follow it with the **xset fp rehash** command. Should you want to just reset your system to the set of default fonts, you enter the following:

```
xset fp default
xset fp rehash
```

With **xlsfonts** you can list the fonts currently installed on your system. To display an installed font in order to see what it looks like, you use **xselfonts**. You can browse through your fonts, selecting the ones you like.

Compiling X-Windows Applications

To compile X-Windows applications, you should first make sure that the XFree86 development package is installed. This contains header files and libraries used by X-Windows programs. The name of the package is **XFree86-devel-3.1.2-2.i386.rpm**.

Many X-Windows applications require that a Makefile be generated that is configured to your system. This is done using an Imakefile provided with the application source code. The **xmkmf** command installed on your system can take an

Imakefile and generate the appropriate Makefile. Once you have the Makefile, you can use the **make** command to compile the application. The **xmkmf** command actually uses a program called **imake** to generate the Makefile from the Imakefile; however, you should never use **imake** directly. Consult the man pages for **xmkmf** and **make** for more details.

X-Windows Commands	Explanation
xterm	Opens up a new terminal window
xset	Sets X-Windows options; see man pages for complete listing
	-b Configures bell
	-c Configures key click
	+fp *fontlist* Adds fonts
	-fp *fontlist* Removes fonts
	led Turns on or off keyboard LEDs
	m Configures mouse
	p Sets pixel color values
	s Sets the screen saver
	q Lists current settings
xsetroot	Configures the root window
	-cursor *cursorfile maskfile* Sets pointer to bitmap pictures when pointer is outside any window
	-bitmap *filename* Sets root window pattern to bitmap
	-gray Sets background to gray
	-fg *color* Sets color of foreground bitmap
	-bg *color* Sets color of background bitmap
	-solid *color* Sets background color
	-name *string* Sets name of root window to string
xmodmap	Configures input devices; reads the **.Xmodmap** file
	-pk Displays current keymap
	-e *expression* Sets key binding
	keycode NUMBER = KEYSYMNAME Sets key to specified key symbol
	keysym KEYSYMNAME = KEYSYMNAME Sets key to operate the same as specified key
	pointer = NUMBER Sets mouse button codes

Table B-2.   *X-Windows Commands, Configuration Files, and Arguments*

X-Windows Commands	Explanation
xrdb	Configures X-Windows resources; reads the **.Xresources** file
xdm	X-Windows Display Manager; runs the XFree86 server for your system; usually called by **.xinitrc**
startx	Starts up X-Windows by executing **xinit** and instructing it to read the **.Xclients** file
xfs *config-file*	The X-Windows font server
mkfontdir *font-directory*	Indexes new fonts, making them accessible by the font server
xlsfonts	Lists fonts on your system
xfontsel	Displays installed fonts
xdpyinfo	Lists detailed information about your X-Windows configuration
xinit	Starts up X-Windows, first reading the system's **.xinitrc** file; when invoked from **startx** it also reads the user's **.Xclients** file; **xinit** is not called directly, but through **startx**
xmkmf	Creates a Makefile for an X-Windows application using the application's Imakefile; invokes **imake** to generate the Makefile (never invoke **imake** directly)

Configuration Files

.Xclients	User's X-Windows initialization file
.Xresources	User's X-Windows resource configuration file; does not initially exist; make a copy from **.Xdefaults.bak**; use only if not using the Caldera Desktop
.Xclients.bak	Version of **.Xclients** that invokes only **fvwm**, without the Caldera Desktop
.Xdefaults.bak	Copy of default settings for **.Xresources** file
/usr/X11R6/lib/X11 /xinit/xinitrc	System X-Windows initialization file; automatically read by **xinit**

Table B-2.   *X-Windows Commands, Configuration Files, and Arguments* (continued)

Configuration Files	Explanation
.xinitrc	Another X-Windows configuration file read automatically by **xinit**, if it exists (currently there is no **.xinitrc** file; **.Xclients** is used instead)
/usr/lib/X11/rgb.txt	X-Windows colors; each entry has four fields; the first three fields are numbers for red, green, and blue; the last field is the name given to the color
X-Windows Application Configuration Arguments	See X man pages for detailed explanations
–bw *num*	Borderwidth of pixels in frame
–bd *color*	Border color
–fg *color*	Foreground color (for text or graphics)
–bg *color*	Background color
–display *display-name*	Displays client to run on; displays name consisting of hostname, display number, and screen number (see the X man pages)
–fn *font*	Font to use for text display
–geometry *offsets*	Location on screen where X-Windows application window is placed; offsets are measured relative to screen display
–iconic	Starts application with icon, not with open window
–rv	Switches background and foreground colors
–title *string*	Title for the window's title bar
–name *string*	Name for the application
xrm *resource-string*	Specifies resource value

Table B-2.   *X-Windows Commands, Configuration Files, and Arguments* (continued)

X-Windows Commands	Explanation
Desktops, Window and File Managers	
`xclient1g`	The Caldera Desktop
`fvwm`	The **fvwm** window manager
`olwm`	The Xview window manger
`mwm`	The Motif window manager
`xfm`	The XFM file manager
`mfm`	A Motif-like file manager

Table B-2.   *X-Windows Commands, Configuration Files, and Arguments* (continued)

Appendix C

Software Packages Included on the Caldera CD-ROM

The Caldera Network Desktop CD-ROM contains over 400 MB of compressed software. The software is divided into packages based on its function. For example, one software package contains the Desktop interface and related components, another package contains the World Wide Web server, and another contains the NetWare client.

You determined what packages are on your system by the Installation option you selected while installing the Network Desktop.

You can install additional packages from the CD-ROM or from another location, such as a hard disk archive of the CD-ROM, or the Caldera ftp site. This appendix lists the packages that are available, shows you which packages were installed by the Installation option you selected, and lists which packages are Caldera Proprietary and which are freely distributable.

The packages on the Caldera CD-ROM were created using the Redhat Package Management system, from Redhat software. This system allows you to install a package with a single command. You can also uninstall a package with a single command, cleaning all files and configuration information from your system for the removed package.

If you need to locate a specific file or software package, you can also refer to the online index of files.

Recommended Installation: Packages Included

Table C-1 lists the package names for all packages that were installed if you selected the Recommended Installation option to install the Caldera Network Desktop.

To understand these package names, refer to Table C-4, which describes all packages, found later in this appendix. All package names are case sensitive. Packages beginning with a capital letter are listed before other packages beginning with the same letter.

aout-libs	adduser	anonftp	apache
at	bash	bc	bdflush
bin86	bind-utils	binutils	byacc
CND-bindery-utils	CND-kernel-source	CND-nds-utils	CND-queue-mgmt

Table C-1.   *Packages Included in the Recommended Installation*

CRiSPlite	calderadoc	calderize	color-ls
control-panel	cpio	crontabs	dev
dialog	diffutils	dip	dosemu
dthelp	e2fsprogs	ed	elm
etcskel	faq	file	fileutils
findutils	flex	flying	fontis
fstool	fvwm	fwhois	gawk
gcc	gcc-c++	getty_ps	ghostscript
ghostscript-fonts	ghostview	glint	gpm
grep	groff	gzip	hdparm
helptool	howto	howto-html	initscripts
iBCS	ipx	ispell	kbd
ldp	ld.so	less	lg
lga	libc	libc-devel	libc-include
libg++	libgr	lilo	liloconfig
lrzsz	lynx	MAKEDEV	m4
mailx	make	man	mancala
man-pages	metamail	minicom	modemtool
modules	mpage	mtools	NetKit-A
NetKit-B	NetKit-B-lpr	ncftp	ncompress
ncurses	nenscript	net-tools	netcfg
netscape	nfs-server	npasswd	nwclient
patch	pcmcia-cs	perl	popclient
ppp	printtool	procinfo	procmail
procps	psmisc	python	pythonlib
readline	rpm	rootfiles	rxvt

Table C-1.   *Packages Included in the Recommended Installation* (continued)

SysVinit	sed	send-pr	sendmail
setup	seyon	sh-utils	slang
slsc	stat	strace	svgalib
sysklogd	tar	tcltk-tcl	tcltk-tk
tcp_wrapper	tcsh	termcap	texinfo-info
textutils	time	timetool	tksysv
transfig	tset-jv	tunelp	usercfg
util-linux	vim	vixie-cron	which
wu-ftpd	XFree86	XFree86-fonts	Xaccel
Xaw3d	Xconfigurator	xfig	xforms
xgammon	xlockmore	xmplay	xpaint
xpm	xtetris	xv	yp-clients
zgv	zoneinfo		

Table C-1. *Packages Included in the Recommended Installation* (continued)

Minimal Installation: Packages Included

Table C-2 lists the package names for all packages that were installed if you selected the Minimal Installation option.

To understand these package names, refer to Table C-4, which describes all packages, found at the end of this appendix. All package names are case sensitive. Packages beginning with a capital letter are listed before other packages beginning with the same letter.

Caldera-Proprietary Packages

While much of the Caldera Network Desktop is based on Linux and other freely-distributable software components, the software packages listed in Table C-3 have been created or licensed by Caldera. They are not included with your Caldera Lite CD-ROM, except for a 90-day free trial of the Desktop interface and the CRiSPlite editor. However, all are included in the Complete Network Desktop 1.0, which you can purchase at a discount.

adduser	aout-libs	at	bash
bdflush	calderize	cpio	crontabs
dev	dialog	diffutils	dip
e2fsprogs	etcskel	file	fileutils
findutils	gawk	getty_ps	gpm
grep	groff	gzip	hdparm
initscripts	ipx	kbd	ld.so
less	libc	lilo	MAKEDEV
m4	mailx	man	man-pages
modules	mtools	NetKit-A	NetKit-B
ncompress	ncurses	net-tools	nfs-server
npasswd	nwclient	patch	pcmcia-cs
perl	ppp	procinfo	procps
readline	rootfiles	rpm	SysVinit
sed	send-pr	sendmail	setup
sh-utils	strace	sysklogd	tar
tcp_wrapper	tcsh	termcap	textutils
time	tset-jv	tunelp	util-linux
vim	vixie-cron	wu-ftpd	yp-clients
zoneinfo			

Table C-2.   *Packages Included in the Minimal Installation*

Description of Available Packages

Table C-4 lists all packages included on the Caldera CD-ROM, with a brief description and size requirement for each. Some software that you may want to install is listed in this table under the package name, not under the name of the utility that you wish to

Package Name	Description
CND-bindery-utils	NetWare Client bindery server administration tools
CND-nds-utils	NetWare Client NDS server administration tools
CND-queue-mgmt	NetWare Client Print Queue administration tools
CRiSPlite	CRiSPlite editor from Vital Corp (90-day trial with Caldera Lite)
XBasic	XBASIC program development tool
Xaccel	Accelerated X server from X-Inside
caldera-doc	Documentation for Caldera components
dthelp	Online help for the Desktop
fontis	Caldera Font Server
lg	Desktop Interface from Visix Software, Inc. (90-day trial with Caldera Lite)
lga	Runtime libraries for various Desktop utilities
netscape	Netscape Navigator 2.0, from Netscape Communications
nwclient	Caldera NetWare Client, based on technology from Novell, Inc.
cbu	Caldera BACKUP.UNET backup utility from MTI

Table C-3. *Caldera-Proprietary Packages Provided in the Caldera Network Desktop (**not** included in Caldera Lite and may **not** be redistributed)*

use. For example, the World Wide Web server is listed under the package name apache, the name of the HTTP server software. For more information on a particular utility, consult the Caldera online file index.

If you selected the Complete Install option during installation, most of these packages were installed. Some redundant, hardware-related, or specialized packages are included on this list, but they may not have been installed by the Complete Install option.

 NOTE: In the size field, the letter K indicates kilobytes and MB indicates megabytes. All package names are case sensitive when used with the rpm utility. Unfortunately, the following list is not strictly in alphabetical order, and the descriptions are sometimes less than adequate.

Package Name	Size	Brief Description
grep	188 K	GNU grep Utilities
ld.so	279 K	Linux dynamic loader
libc	869 K	libc and related libraries
aout-libs	4 MB	Compatability libraries for old a.out applications
sed	58 K	GNU Stream Editor
fileutils	290 K	GNU File Utilities
util-linux	698 K	Rik Faith's utility collection for Linux
bash	487 K	GNU Bourne Again Shell (bash)
bdflush	10 K	System Cache flusher
rootfiles	3 K	root dot files
dev	N/A	Device entries in /dev
MAKEDEV	24 K	Script to make and update /dev entries
etcskel	3 K	skeleton user dot files
initscripts	24 K	inittab and /etc/rc.d scripts
SysVinit	108 K	Sys V init
kbd	1 MB	Linux keymap utilities
lilo	46 K	Boot loader for Linux and other operating systems
termcap	185 K	termcap file
setup	10 K	Simple setup files
e2fsprogs	660 K	Tools for second extended (ext2) filesystem
modules	99 K	Module utilities
sh-utils	307 K	GNU sh Utilities
syslogd	44 K	Linux system and kernel logger
gawk	365 K	GNU gawk text processor

Table C-4. *Name, Size, and Description for all Caldera Packages*

Package Name	Size	Brief Description
gzip	232 K	GNU gzip file compression
cpio	57 K	GNU cpio archiving program (used by rpm)
rpm	210 K	Redhat's Packaging System
tar	192 K	GNU Tape Archiver (tar)
NetKit-A	197 K	Various network programs (part 1)
NetKit-B	787 K	Various network programs (part 2)
file	99 K	file(1) command
findutils	130 K	GNU Find Utilities (find, xargs, and locate)
procps	115 K	Process monitoring utilities
CND-bindery-utils	2.2 MB	Caldera NetWare Bindery Administration Utilities
CND-kernel-source	10 MB	Linux kernel sources
CND-nds-utils	1.4 MB	Caldera NetWare Directory Services Administration Utilities
CND-queue-mgmt	28 K	Caldera NetWare Queue Management Utilities
CRiSPlite	3 MB	CRiSPlite Editor
ElectricFence	27 K	Electric Fence C memory debugging library
ImageMagick	1.3 MB	Image display, conversion, and manipulation under X
ImageMagick-devel	694 K	static libraries and header files for ImageMagick development
NetKit-B-lpr	146 K	Printing support (lpr, lpd, etc.)
XBasic	12.7 MB	XBasic Program Development Environment
XFree86	12 MB	XFree86 Window System
XFree86-8514	2 MB	XFree86 8514 server
XFree86-AGX	2.3 MB	XFree86 AGX server

Table C-4.   *Name, Size, and Description for all Caldera Packages (continued)*

Package Name	Size	Brief Description
XFree86-Mach32	2.2 MB	XFree86 Mach32 server
XFree86-Mach64	2.3 MB	XFree86 Mach64 server
XFree86-Mach8	2 MB	XFree86 Mach8 server
XFree86-Mono	1.4 MB	XFree86 Mono server
XFree86-P9000	2.3 MB	XFree86 P9000 server
XFree86-S3	2.5 MB	XFree86 S3 server
XFree86-SVGA	2.6 MB	XFree86 SVGA server
XFree86-VGA16	1.3 MB	XFree86 VGA16 server
XFree86-W32	2.1 MB	XFree86 W32 server
XFree86-Xvfb	2.1 MB	XFree86 Xvfb server
XFree86-devel	6.4 MB	X11R6 static libraries, headers, and programming man pages
XFree86-fonts	4.8 MB	X11R6 fonts (only needed on server side)
Xaccel	5 MB	X Inside's Accelerated-X X11 Display Server
Xaw3d	972 K	X athena widgets in 3d
Xconfigurator	65 K	X configuration utility
abuse	6.3 MB	Abuse—an X/SVGA game
acm	3.5 MB	X based flight combat
adduser	4 K	User creation program
amd	213 K	NFS automount daemon
anonftp	974 K	enables anonymous ftp access
apache	288 K	HTTP server daemon (WWW server)
arena	387 K	A WWW HTML-3 browser
ash	98 K	Small Bourne shell from Berkeley
at	35 K	at job spooler
autoconf	258 K	GNU autoconf—source configuration tools

Table C-4. *Name, Size, and Description for all Caldera Packages (continued)*

Package Name	Size	Brief Description
bc	127 K	GNU bc
bin86	73 K	Real mode 80 x 86 compiler and linker
bind	251 K	BIND—DNS nameserver
bind-lib	94 K	DNS resolver library and headers
bind-utils	267 K	DNS utils—host, dig, dnsquery, nslookup
binutils	1 MB	GNU Binary Utility Development Utilities
bison	155 K	GNU parser generator
bm2font	538 K	Converts bitmaps to LaTeX fonts
byacc	59 K	Public domain yacc parser generator
calderadoc	2.6 MB	Caldera Documentation
cmm	614 K	C Minus Minus Scripting Language
cmu-snmp	649 K	CMU SNMP agent
cmu-snmp-utils	542 K	CMU SNMP utilities
color-ls	61 K	color ls—patched from GNU fileutils
colour-yahtzee	19 K	color tty yahtzee
control-panel	179 K	Redhat Control Panel
crontabs	2 K	root crontab file
csh	172 K	BSD C-shell
cvs	436 K	Concurrent Versioning System
cxhextris	32 K	Color X11 version of hextris
dialog	52 K	tty dialog boxes
diffutils	152 K	GNU diff utilities
dip	68 K	dip modem dialer
doom	4.9 MB	DOOM for Linux Consoles and X-Windows
dosemu	948 K	DOS emulator

Table C-4.   *Name, Size, and Description for all Caldera Packages* (continued)

Package Name	Size	Brief Description
dthelp	568 K	Caldera Desktop Help
dump	148 K	dump/restore backup system
e2fsprogs-devel	152 K	e2fs static libs and headers
ed	106 K	GNU Line Editor
efax	151 K	Sends and receives faxes over class 1 or class 2 modems
eject	10 K	Ejects ejectable media and controls auto ejection
elm	5.4 MB	ELM mail user agent
emacs	12.6 MB	GNU Emacs
emacs-el	9.9 MB	.el source files—not necessary to run Emacs
emacs-nox	1.4 MB	emacs-nox—no X libraries required
exmh	1.2 MB	EXMH mail program
ext2ed	302 K	ext2 filesystem editor for hackers *only*
f2c	216 K	Fortran to C conversion
faces	141 K	Face saver database tools
faces-xface	20 K	Utilities to handle X-Face headers
faq	1.2 MB	Linux FAQ Package
flex	258 K	GNU fast lexical analyzer generator
flying	252 K	Pool, snooker, air hockey, and other table games
fontis	6.5 MB	Caldera Font Server and Installer
fort77	7 K	Driver for f2c
fortune-mod	2.1 MB	Fortune cookie program with bug fixes
fstool	37 K	File System Configuration Tool
fvwm	611 K	Feeble (Fine?) Virtual Window Manager

Table C-4. *Name, Size, and Description for all Caldera Packages (continued)*

Package Name	Size	Brief Description
fwhois	8 K	finger-style whois
gcal	838 K	Extended calendar with highlighting, holidays, etc
gcc	2.2 MB	GNU C Compiler
gcc-c++	1.5 MB	C++ support for gcc
gcc-objc	1.4 MB	Objective C support for gcc
gdb	1 MB	Symbolic debugger for C and other languages
getty_ps	89 K	getty and uugetty
ghostscript	1.3 MB	PostScript interpreter and renderer
ghostscript-fonts	3.3 MB	Fonts for GhostScript
ghostview	156 K	X11 PostScript viewer (needs ghostscript)
giftrans	20 K	Converts and manipulates GIFs
git	495 K	GIT—GNU Interactive Tools
glint	186 K	Graphical Linux Installation Tool
gn	167 K	gopher server
gnuchess	1.4 MB	Computer chess program
gnuplot	497 K	Plotting package
gpm	184 K	General purpose mouse support for Linux
groff	2.6 MB	GNU groff text formatting package
hdparm	27 K	Utility for setting (E)IDE performance parameters
helptool	10 K	Simple Help File Searching Tool
howto	1.4 MB	Various HOWTOs from the Linux Documentation Project
howto-dvi	1.1 MB	dvi versions of the HOWTOs
howto-html	829 K	html versions of the HOWTOs

Table C-4. *Name, Size, and Description for all Caldera Packages (continued)*

Package Name	Size	Brief Description
howto-ps	2.2 MB	Postscript versions of the HOWTOs
howto-sgml	2.2 MB	sgml source versions of the HOWTOs
iBCS	187 K	iBCS module
imap	658 K	Provides support for IMAP and POP network mail protocols
indent	83 K	GNU C indenting program
intimed	4 K	Time server for clock synchronization
ipx	26 K	Internet Packet eXchange Utilities
ircii	1.6 MB	Popular Unix Irc client
ircii-help	292 K	Help Files and Documentation for ircii
ispell	2.6 MB	GNU ispell—interactive spelling checker
jed	743 K	Editor with multiple, keybindings, a C-like extension language, colors, and many other features
jed-xjed	136 K	X binary of JED
joe	976 K	Easy-to-use editor
koules	262 K	Well-done SVGA lib game
kterm	175 K	Kterm (Kanji Terminal Emulator)
ldp	4.3 MB	LDP and HOWTO Package
less	121 K	Text file browser—less is more
lg	7 MB	CND Desktop Metaphor
lga	7 MB	LG Advantage run-time system
lha	52 K	Creates and expands lharc format archives
libc-debug	4.2 MB	libc with debugging information
libc-devel	32 K	Additional libraries required to compile
libc-include	770 K	Include files for libc and related libraries

Table C-4. *Name, Size, and Description for all Caldera Packages* (continued)

Package Name	Size	Brief Description
libc-profile	1.2 MB	libc with profiling support
libc-static	1.4 MB	Libraries for static linking
libf2c	108 K	Shared libraries for f2c programs
libf2c-static	212 K	Static libraries for f2c programs
libg++	5.6 MB	GNU g++ library
libgr	640 K	Graphics libs, fbm, jpeg, pbm, pgm, png, pnm, ppm, rle, tiff, zlib
libgr-devel	955 K	Headers and static libraries for building with the libraries
libgr-progs	99 K	Utility programs
liloconfig	19 K	Text based LILO configuration tools
lout	3.4 MB	Lout text formatting system
lout-doc	4 MB	Full lout documentation
lrzsz	72 K	lrzz—sz, rz, and friends
lynx	575 K	tty WWW browser
m4	120 K	GNU Macro Processor
macutils	230 K	Utilities for manipulating Macintosh file formats
mailx	91 K	/bin/mail
make	237 K	GNU Make
man	84 K	Manual page reader
mancala	22 K	Mancala game
xforms	1.2 MB	X Forms library
man-pages	1.2 MB	System manual pages from the Linux Documentation Project
maplay	95 K	Plays MPEG 2 audio files in 16-bit stereo
mb	353 K	MetalBase relational database

Table C-4. *Name, Size, and Description for all Caldera Packages (continued)*

Package Name	Size	Brief Description
mc	629 K	Midnight Commander visual shell
metamail	309 K	Collection of MIME handling utilities
mh	3.5 MB	MH mail handling system (with POP support)
minicom	163 K	TTY mode communications package à la Telix
mirror	37 K	Mirror, a perl script for mirroring an ftp site
mkdosfs-ygg	22 K	Creates a DOS FAT filesystem on a device
mkisofs	46 K	Creates a ISO9660 filesystem image
modemtool	4 K	Configuration tool for /dev/modem
moonclock	29 K	Traditional clock with moon phase hacks
mpage	49 K	Places multiple pages of text onto a single Postscript page
mt-st	12 K	Tape controller (mt)
mtools	569 K	Programs to access DOS disks w/o mounting them
multimedia	181 K	A CD player and audio mixer for X11
ncftp	114 K	ftp client with a nice interface
ncompress	21 K	A fast compress utility
ncurses	2.2 MB	curses terminal control library
ncurses-devel	1.4 MB	Development libraries for ncurses
nenscript	25 K	Converts plain ASCII to PostScript
net-tools	155 K	Basic Network Tools
netcfg	44 K	Network Configuration Tool
netscape	4.9 MB	Netscape Navigator 2.0
netpbm	1.1 MB	Loads of image conversion and manipulation tools (hpcd support is missing due to a very restrictive redistribution clause)

Table C-4.   *Name, Size, and Description for all Caldera Packages* (continued)

Package Name	Size	Brief Description
nfs-server	142 K	NFS server daemons
npasswd	30 K	npasswd—passwd and friends
npasswd-dicts	2 MB	Auxiliary npasswd dictionaries
nvi	1.9 MB	New Berkeley Vi Editor (Experimental)
nwclient	3.2 MB	NetWare Client
open	11 K	Tools for creating and switching between virtual consoles
p2c	534 K	Pascal to C converter and libraries
patch	59 K	GNU patch Utilities
pcmcia-cs	381 K	PCMCIA card services
pdksh	359 K	Public Domain Korn Shell
perl	5.6 MB	Practical Extraction and Report Language
perl4	1.2 MB	Practical Extraction and Report Language (old version)
pidentd	102 K	Internet Daemon: Authorization, User Identification
pine	1.4 MB	MIME compliant mail reader with news support as well
pmake	136 K	Berkeley's Parallel Make
popclient	28 K	POP—retrieve mail from a mailserver using Post Office Protocol
ppp	206 K	ppp daemon package for Linux
printtool	25 K	Printer Configuration Tool
procinfo	22 K	/proc filesystem information
procmail	184 K	procmail mail delivery agent
psmisc	35 K	More ps type tools for /proc filesystem
python	2.6 MB	Very high level scripting language with X interface

Table C-4. *Name, Size, and Description for all Caldera Packages (continued)*

Package Name	Size	Brief Description
pythonlib	27 K	Library of python code used by various Redhat programs
rcs	551 K	RCS—version control system
rdate	5 K	Remote clock reader (and local setter)
rdist	127 K	File distributor—maintain files on multiple machines
readline	373 K	Library for reading lines from a terminal
rxvt	63 K	rxvt—terminal emulator in an X window
send-pr	111 K	Problem Report Mailer
sendmail	826 K	sendmail mail transport agent
seyon	230 K	X communications program for modems
sharutils	71 K	GNU shar utils—shar, unshar, uuencode, uudecode
slang	155 K	Shared library for C-like extension language
slang-devel	426 K	Static library and header files for slang C-like language
slrn	170 K	Small NNTP newsreader
slsc	103 K	Spreadsheet based on sc, but with many enhancements
spice	448 K	SPICE circuit simulator
stat	7 K	File information reporter
statserial	9 K	Displays status of the serial lines in a terminal
strace	100 K	Prints system call strace of a running process
svgalib	535 K	Library for full screen [S]VGA graphics
svgalib-devel		Development libraries and includes files for [S]VGA graphics
swatch	27 K	System log watcher and alarm

Table C-4.   *Name, Size, and Description for all Caldera Packages* (continued)

Package Name	Size	Brief Description
symlinks	9 K	Symbolic link sanity checker
taper	248 K	Backup system
tcltk-Tix	1.7 MB	The Tix library version 4.0b5
tcltk-blt	1 MB	The BLT library version 1.8
tcltk-expect	1.1 MB	Expect version 5.18
tcltk-expect-demos	134 K	A set of demo programs from the Expect
tcltk-tcl	1.2 MB	Tool Command Language version 7.4, with shared libraries
tcltk-tclX	2.8 MB	Extended Tcl (TclX) version 7.4a-p1, and TkX version 4.0a-p1
tcltk-tk	3.2 MB	Tk toolkit for Tcl, version 4.0, with shared libraries
tcp_wrapper	135 K	Security wrapper for tcp daemons
tcpdump	204 K	Dumps packets that are sent or received over a network interface
tcsh	443 K	Enhanced C-shell
tetex	17 MB	TeX typesetting system and MetaFont font formatter
tetex-afm	326 K	afm (Adobe Font Metrics) fonts and utilities
tetex-dvilj	285 K	dvi to laserjet converter
tetex-dvips	538 K	dvi to postscript converter
tetex-latex	6.5 MB	LaTeX macro package
tetex-xdvi	146 K	X11 previewer
tetex-xtexsh	1.3 MB	X11 shell for TeX work
texinfo	426 K	texinfo formatter and info reader
texinfo-info	122 K	Text-based standalone info reader
textutils	431 K	GNU Text Utilities

Table C-4. *Name, Size, and Description for all Caldera Packages (continued)*

Package Name	Size	Brief Description
time	16 K	GNU time Utilities
timetool	11 K	Time and Date Configuration Tool
tin	548 K	tin News Reader
tksysv	29 K	X/Tk based SYSV Runlevel Editor
transfig	190 K	Converts .fig files (such as those from xfig) to other formats
trn	446 K	Threaded News Reader
trojka	18 K	Falling blocks game similar to xjewels or tetris for curses
tset-jv	27 K	Change terminal settings
tunelp	10 K	Configures kernel parallel port driver
typhoon	257 K	Library and utilities for relational databases
umb-scheme	150 K	Scheme interpreter from U. of Massachusetts at Boston
unarj	15 K	Decompressor for .arj format archives
unzip	257 K	Unpacks .zip files such as those made by pkzip under DOS
usercfg	84 K	User and Group Configuration Tool
uucp	1 MB	GNU uucp
vga_cardgames	111 K	Klondike, oh hell, solitaire, and spider for Linux console
vga_gamespack	55 K	Othello, minesweeper, and connect-4 for the Linux console
vga_tetris	123 K	svgalib based tetris games
vim	465 K	VIsual editor iMproved
vixie-cron	55 K	Vixie cron daemon
vlock	10 K	Locks one or more virtual consoles

Table C-4. *Name, Size, and Description for all Caldera Packages* (continued)

Package Name	Size	Brief Description
which	4 K	Finds which executable would be run based on your PATH
words	424 K	English dictionary for /usr/dict
wu-ftpd	142 K	Washington University ftp daemon
x3270	445 K	X based 3270 emulator
xanim	416 K	Viewer for various animated graphic formats, include quicktime and flic
xbill	183 K	Kill the bill—this one's very popular at Redhat
xboard	340 K	X11 interface for gnuchess
xchomp	38 K	PacMan type game for X
xdaliclock	74 K	Graphical digital clock
xdemineur	27 K	Minesweeper game
xearth	199 K	Displays a lit globe
xevil	871 K	A fast-action explicitly violent game for X
xfig	658 K	X11 drawing tool
xfishtank	397 K	Turns your X root into an aquarium
xfm	762 K	X File Manager
xgammon	3.4 MB	One or two player backgammon game
xgopher	297 K	X based gopher client
xjewel	50 K	Game like Sega's columns
xlander	24 K	Moon landing simulation
xliststat	2.6 MB	xlist by David Betz with statistics extensions
xloadimage	239 K	X based image viewer
xlockmore	323 K	X terminal locking program with many screensavers
xmailbox	35 K	X based Mail notification tool

Table C-4. *Name, Size, and Description for all Caldera Packages* (continued)

Package Name	Size	Brief Description
xmorph	83 K	Morphing program with an X interface
xmplay	205 K	X MPEG viewer
xpaint	494 K	Paint program for X
xpat2	466 K	X Patience—various solitaire card games
xpilot	1.2 MB	Arcade-style flying game
xpm	160 K	X11 Pixmap Library
xpuzzles	363 K	Various geometry puzzles including Rubik's Cube
xscreensaver	550 K	X screen savers
xsnow	28 K	For those who want Christmas 12 months a year
xsysinfo	19 K	Display bar graphs of system load
xterm-color	207 K	Ansi Color xterm
xtetris	42 K	X11 version of tetris
xtrojka	71 K	Falling blocks game similar to xjewels or tetris
xv	4.7 MB	Top X-based image viewer
xwpe	1.6 MB	X Windows Programming Environment
xwpick	46 K	Efficient X screen grabber
xxgdb	94 K	X interface to the gdb debugger
yp-clients	53 K	NIS (YP) clients
ypserv	82 K	NIS/YP server
zapem	162 K	Space invaders-like game
zgv	132 K	Console viewer for many graphics formats
zip	141 K	Creates .zip files
zoneinfo	342 K	Time zone utilities and data

Table C-4.   *Name, Size, and Description for all Caldera Packages* (continued)

Package Name	Size	Brief Description
zsh	508 K	Enhanced Bourne shell
calderize	70 K	Caldera Changes to Redhat Linux
cbu	10 MB	Caldera BACKUP.UNET Distributed Network Backup System
ical	1 MB	Calender application made with Tcl7.4/Tk4.0
indexhtml	5 K	Redhat html index page
inn	1.3 MB	InterNetNews news transport system
kernel-modules	684 K	Loadable kernel modules
kernel-source	9.4 MB	Linux kernel sources
samba	882 K	SMB client and server
screen	363 K	Screen—Manages multiple sessions on one tty
sdlN2x	142 K	SDL Communications Linux N2x drivers
stallion	837 K	Stallion Multiport Serial Driver for Linux

Table C-4. *Name, Size, and Description for all Caldera Packages* (continued)

Appendix D

Creating Nonstandard Install Diskettes

Because some of the auto-detection features of the Caldera Installation process can interfere with the operation of some hardware, you may need to create a new Install diskette that does not include the auto-detection features.

For example, an NE2000 Ethernet card may stop responding to the system after a CD-ROM drive auto-detection probe. When this happens, you can neither use the Ethernet card, nor access your CD-ROM drive. The system may even hang during installation. The solution is to create an Install diskette that only includes drivers for your particular CD-ROM and network card, and provide hardware boot parameters to direct the use of these devices (see Chapter 2 and Appendix A). By doing this, the probing for various devices (which the included Install diskette does) is not allowed to interfere with the operation of your system, and the installation can proceed.

To create a new Install diskette, you use the **rawrite** command in DOS, or the **dd** command in Linux to copy a new Install diskette image from the Caldera CD-ROM to a blank 3 1/2-inch diskette. A more recent image may also be available on the Caldera ftp site.

The **rawrite** command is included on the Caldera CD-ROM in the **\dosutils** directory. Simply enter this command and you will be prompted for the image name and destination floppy disk drive.

```
D:\DOSUTILS\RAWRITE
```

To create a new diskette in Linux, use the **dd** command as shown next, substituting the correct image file name from the spanning diagrams, and the correct floppy device if yours is nonstandard.

```
dd if=inst0009.img of=/dev/fd0
```

Use the tables on the following pages to locate your hardware devices. Then use the spanning tree diagrams, shown in Figures D-1 and D-2 at the end of this appendix to choose the correct Install diskette image to create. Once this diskette is created, you can use it just like the Install diskette that Caldera provided, whenever it is mentioned in the Installation instructions. The images from the spanning tree are located on the Caldera CD-ROM in the directory **/images.cnd/1213**.

Selecting an Install Diskette Image

Use Tables D-1, D-2, and D-3 to select values that correspond to the spanning tree, shown in Figures D-1 and D-2.

CD-ROM Drives

The following CD-ROM drives are supported via loadable modules:

- Goldstar R420
- Mitsumi
- Matsushita/Panasonic
- SoundBlaster Pro
- Aztech/Orchid/Okano/Wearnes
- Sony CD535/531
- Laser Magnetic Storage CM 206

Ethernet card value	Ethernet card on your computer
Ether-1	None
Ether-2	SMC Ultra or Elite
Ether-3	Western Digital 80 x 3
Ether-4	3Com 3c501, 3c503, 3c509, or 3c579
Ether-5	NE2100 and compatible, AMD LANCE, PCnet, AT1500
Ether-6	NE2000, NE1000, Cabletron E21xx, DEPCA, EtherWorks 3, HP PCLAN+ (27247B and 27252A), HP PCLAN (27245 and other 27xxx series), SK-G16

Table D-1.   *Ethernet Cards*

SCSI value	SCSI peripherals on your computer
SCSI-1	None
SCSI-2	Adaptec or Buslogic
SCSI-3	EATA-DMA; UltraStor 14F, 24F, 34F; Future Domain 16xx; NCR5380, NCR53c7, 8xx; or Always IN2000
SCSI-4	Other brands and models not listed here

Table D-2.   *SCSI Cards*

Use the values that you selected from Tables D-1, D-2, and D-3 to select an Install diskette image from the spanning trees on the following pages. The numbered images are located on the CD-ROM in the directory **/images.cnd/1213**.

CD-ROM drive value	CD-ROM drive on your computer
CDROM-1	Any of the drives in the previous list, supported by loadable modules
CDROM-2	Sony CDU31A or Sony CDU33A
CDROM-3	Laser Magnetic Storage CM205

Table D-3.   *CD-ROM Drive Values*

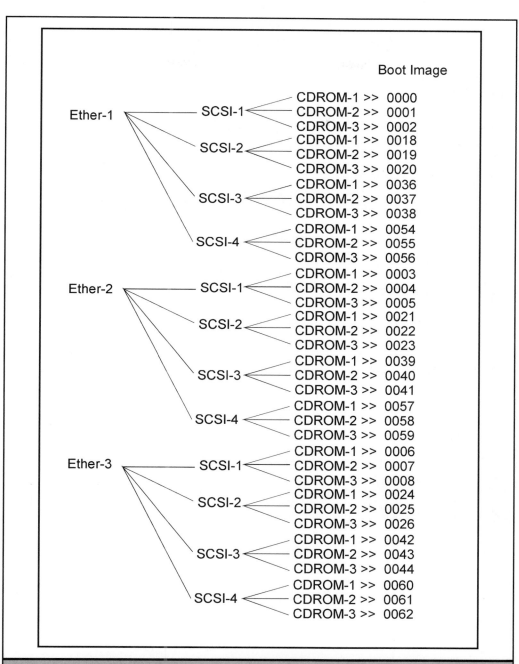

Figure D-1. *Spanning tree*

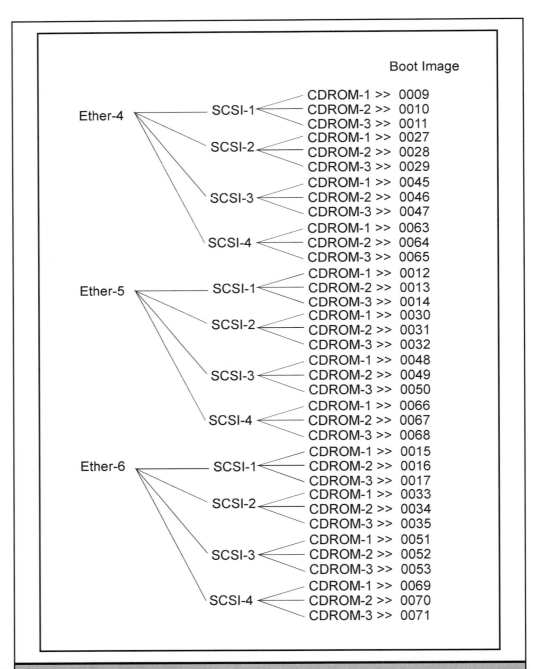

Figure D-2. *Spanning tree*

Index

M